John Locke's Political Philosophy and the Hebrew Bible

John Locke's treatises on government make frequent reference to the Hebrew Bible, while references to the New Testament are almost completely absent. To date, scholarship has not addressed this surprising characteristic of the treatises. In this book, Yechiel Leiter offers a Hebraic reading of Locke's fundamental political texts. In doing so, he formulates a new school of thought in Lockean political interpretation and challenges existing ones. He shows how a grasp of the Hebraic underpinnings of Locke's political theory resolves many of the problems, as well as scholarly debates, that are inherent in reading Locke. More than a book about the political theory of John Locke, this volume is about the foundational ideas of Western civilization. While focused on Locke's Hebraism, it demonstrates the persistent relevance of the Biblical political narrative to modernity. It will generate interest among students of Locke and political theory, philosophy and early modern history, and within Bible study communities.

Yechiel J. M. Leiter is President of the Veresta Group and Senior Fellow at the Herzl Institute and the Kohelet Policy Forum in Jerusalem.

John Locke's Political Philosophy and the Hebrew Bible

YECHIEL J. M. LEITER

Herzl Institute

Kohelet Policy Forum

CAMBRIDGE
UNIVERSITY PRESS

CAMBRIDGE
UNIVERSITY PRESS

University Printing House, Cambridge CB2 8BS, United Kingdom

One Liberty Plaza, 20th Floor, New York, NY 10006, USA

477 Williamstown Road, Port Melbourne, VIC 3207, Australia

314–321, 3rd Floor, Plot 3, Splendor Forum, Jasola District Centre, New Delhi – 110025, India

79 Anson Road, #06–04/06, Singapore 079906

Cambridge University Press is part of the University of Cambridge.

It furthers the University's mission by disseminating knowledge in the pursuit of education, learning, and research at the highest international levels of excellence.

www.cambridge.org
Information on this title: www.cambridge.org/9781108428187
DOI: 10.1017/9781108552370

© Yechiel J. M. Leiter 2018

First published 2018

Printed in the United States of America by Sheridan Books, Inc.

A catalogue record for this publication is available from the British Library.

Library of Congress Cataloging-in-Publication Data
NAMES: Leiter, Yechiel M., author.
TITLE: John Locke's political philosophy and the Hebrew Bible / Yechiel J.M. Leiter, Herzl Institute.
DESCRIPTION: New York : Cambridge University Press, 2018. |
Includes bibliographical references and index.
IDENTIFIERS: LCCN 2017055353 | ISBN 9781108428187 (hardback : alk. paper)
SUBJECTS: LCSH: Politics in the Bible. | Bible. Old Testament–Criticism, interpretation, etc. |
Locke, John, 1632–1704. | Political science–Philosophy.
CLASSIFICATION: LCC BS1199.P6 L45 2018 | DDC 320.01–dc23
LC record available at https://lccn.loc.gov/2017055353

ISBN 978-1-108-42818-7 Hardback

Contents

Preface

When I try to trace the mental processes that led to this book, my mind drifts back to my elementary school years. It was a religious education, the day divided between rigorous religious study in the morning and "secular" study in the afternoon. They shared the same day, but the religious and the secular could not have been farther apart. History, for example, belonged to the secular, including the histories of ancient Mesopotamia, Egypt, Greece, and Rome, and yet no one – religious or secular – pointed out that the Bible, Mishnah, and Talmud, taught that very day, every day, coincided on the time line with those histories. The realization of that fact came to me as a kind of epiphany in the fifth or sixth grade (a benefit of daydreaming perhaps), and it included a youthful hunch that the beginnings of recorded civilization in Mesopotamia (PM) and the Bible (AM) might also be substantively interrelated, as might the wisdom of the Talmud (AM) and the glory of Rome (PM).

As time progressed, my quest for parallel historical narratives that somehow connect grew into a search for the theological nature of the universalistic and particularistic elements ensconced within Hebraic teachings, accompanied by the realization that they were not quite as bifurcated as they had been presented. The rebirth of Israel, heralded in its political and legal letters of incorporation as both a *Jewish* and *democratic* state, had much to do with this intellectual awakening within me; for here was an ancient civilization to which I belonged, claiming, Bible and history in hand, sovereign entitlement as a nation-state, while pursuing its place among the nations of the world based on recognized and shared universal values.

This quest was accompanied by a search for a structured understanding of the nature of government and philosophy of politics, brought on by the tumultuous 1990s. The functional disintegration of the Soviet empire that prima facie spelled out the theoretical defeat of communism was a watershed event, but I wondered about Francis Fukuyama's assertion that democracy's victory meant that humankind was left with nowhere to progress. An end of history was after all a theological concept; but was this what the Bible had in mind when it spoke of an "end of days"? Was consensual government the Messiah? Was this what the architects of government by the people really had in mind?

Along with a restudying of Biblical narrative, I returned to the seventeenth-century greats of political theory who helped usher us into the modern age. Some texts I had already studied and others I read for the first time, but what was now salient in my mind – something I simply had not taken note of previously – was the frequency with which theorists such as Grotius, Hobbes, Harrington, and Locke used the Hebrew Bible to establish their arguments. When the work of Jerusalem's Shalom Institute led by my friends Yoram Hazony and Dan Polisar, as well as articles by Fania Oz-Salzberger, came to my attention (hitherto preoccupied more with politics rather than with political theory), my previously unidentified and unnamed intellectual fascination took on the clearly defined discipline of *political Hebraism*.

I found no text more Hebraic than John Locke's *Two Treatises of Government*, that because it is exclusively so. His predecessors and contemporaries who used Hebraic texts as proof-texts quoted with no less frequency from Greek and Roman, as well as New Testament sources. Indeed, it is hard to escape the Christological orientation of their writings, but in the *Two Treatises*, copiously filled with Hebraic sources, it is difficult to find traces of Christology, if at all. What I found even more perplexing was the fact that Lockean scholarship, though robust and contentious, makes next to nothing of this fact, and where the unusual Hebraic nature of his resourcing is recognized, there remains no attribution of political Hebraism to his writing. That left me what I thought was ample room for academic contribution, for a thesis arguing for a Hebraic reading of the *Two Treatises*. My Master's thesis concentrated entirely on the *First Treatise* and my PhD thesis focused primarily on the Hebraism of the *Second Treatise*. This book is the outgrowth of both.

I believe that the cumulative effect of this analysis will offer ample proof that Locke anchored his political theory of civil government in the Hebrew Bible, and that he did so not for stylistic or ornamental reasons, but rather because he saw it as an authoritative text that could legitimate the moral nature of consensual government that he came to advocate.

If Locke's personal religious beliefs did not prevent him from being a political Hebraist, the defining of Locke in this manner has the potential of opening an entirely new vista of appreciation for Locke's political theories. And while a Hebraic reading of Locke will undoubtedly raise certain questions that will necessitate further historical and theoretical research, it may provide additional answers to difficult questions that have as yet not found satisfactory explanations.

In addition, it would be hard to imagine the resurgent interest in political Hebraism, of which this book is but a small part, manifesting itself without the reemergence of Jewish sovereignty in the Land of Israel. The phenomenon of modern Israel, though, has neither been easily understood nor taken for granted. While Israel struggles to identify its national character and reconcile its own place within the Middle East as well as on the international stage, a keener understanding of its own Hebraic legacy might prove vital to all involved. Domestically, such an augmented appreciation for Israel's historical Hebraic contributions may encourage a constructive outward and inclusive attitude among those with a more isolationist and exclusivist inclination. Within the international community, a deeper understanding of the Hebraic roots of political theory might also engender a greater appreciation for Israel's contemporary role. Without any intention of theoretical overreach, I will add my hope that this book will contribute to that very practical field of international politics as well.

The stakes then are quite high. If my thesis is correct, it would mean that most discussions of Lockean political thought miss the main point, that they use the wrong scaffold to assemble the theoretical construct that Locke intended. It also means that the seventeenth century's break with the past was far less complete than generally assumed, at least to the degree that Locke's political writing helped create that fissure. And finally, it means that a fundamental dimension of the American founding, the Lockean dimension, has not been properly understood and appreciated.

The significance of this is something Yoram Hazony, one of Israel's most original and consequential thinkers, is keenly aware of, and it is thanks to him and his colleagues at the helm of Jerusalem's Herzl Institute, Ofir Haivri and Meirav Jones, that I have had the time, impetus, and intellectual setting to turn my postdoctoral research into a book. To them I am grateful beyond words for the opportunity to participate as a resident Fellow in the Institute's activities, as I believe it is enriching that special sanctum where philosophy, bible studies, political theory, and intellectual history meet, while moving the goalpost of interdisciplinary relevance to a higher and better place.

As much of the research for this book was done in the context of my PhD, I owe a tremendous debt of gratitude to my mentor, Professor Fania Oz-Salzberger, who guided both of my dissertations from start to finish. Without her persistent and patient counsel this book would not have been possible. There were frustrating moments to be sure, especially when my anxious midlife foray into academic research assumed a greater countenancing of the expeditious and the streamlined, but her consistently unyielding demands for further research, precision of presentation, and linguistic excellence proved to be as inspiring as they were imperative. Through her rare ability to fuse the excitement of originality with the requisite caution of academic exactitude I have learned much, with a personal significance that stretches beyond the boundaries of this work. It has been a distinct honor and privilege to study under Fania's tutelage.

I am most fortunate as well to have had Professor Michael Heyd of the Hebrew University and Professor Menachem Lorberbaum of Tel Aviv University join with Professor Oz-Salzberger to form my dissertation committee. Their sagacious critiques and invaluable recommendations helped ensure greater focus and precision, making my PhD thesis a better and more accurate work. I am particularly grateful to Professor Heyd for going well beyond the call of duty by taking the time to share with me some of his yet unpublished theories on the development of seventeenth-century secularism and Christian theology.

I am also indebted to Professor Aharon ben Ze'ev, the former president of Haifa University, who encouraged me to study at Haifa after I left my position at Israel's Ministry of Finance, and initially introduced me to Professor Oz-Salzberger.

Some of my research was conducted at the same time that I served as a senior policy analyst at the Jerusalem Center for Public Affairs. My thanks go to Ambassador Dr. Dore Gold and Mrs. Chaya Hershkovitz, respectively the president and director of the Center, for affording me an atmosphere conducive to pursuing my academic research.

The advice of good friends is indispensable for the success of any composition. Dr. Asael Abelman has read parts of the research and made critical substantive recommendations without which my original academic text would have been sorely deficient.

I did not trouble my dear friend Henry Schwartz to read the manuscript as it was being written out of respect for his superhuman workload.

But Henry, who has supported my work as far back as my memory serves, was with me every step of the way, and I would not have made it to the end zone without his encouragement and assistance. He has been my older brother and confidant, and through our friendship I have been graced with the privilege of sharing, if but in a small way, in his unstinting efforts to make the world a safer and better place.

My wife, Chani, and our children, Moshe (and Tzippi), Neriyah (and Liat), Sarah, David, Sophia (and Yair), Shmuel, Noam, and Amikam, have always endured my ever-changing schedule, and adding regimented hours of academic research to it did not make matters easier for them. Juggling a full professional workload with writing a book sometimes meant long hours for me away from home and at other times long hours for them wishing that I was away from home. They are an integral part of this composition, and I thank them. Our grandchildren, Carmi, Maayan, Harel, Tzur, Hadar, Kerem, and Dror, have added perspective and patience to the labor of putting the finishing touches on the work, for which I am richer and grateful. Who knows, maybe by the time they get around to studying political theory, the Hebraism of Locke's *Two Treatises* will have become accepted academic currency. I hope, at least, that on the way they merit an elementary school education less schismatic than the one their grandfather endured.

I am dedicating this book to my parents, Dr. N. Z. and Hannah Leiter. My father read an initial draft copy, made critical substantive comments, and offered stylistic and linguistic advice, while my mother, with her encouraging interest and enthusiasm throughout the entire process, inspired me to plod on whenever intellectual fatigue began to set in. I am indebted to them for that and for everything they stand for: devotion to truth; passion for knowledge; reverence for tradition and respect for innovation; commitment to family, country, and nation; and so much more. May this serve as but a small token of gratitude, and of the esteem in which I hold them.

Acknowledgments

I want to thank the folks at Cambridge University Press who accepted my manuscript for publication and saw the laborious process through with patience and professionalism: My publisher, Dr. Beatrice Rehl, who was kind enough to walk me through all the steps that never seemed to end; the editorial assistant, Edgar Mendez; the content manager, Katherine Tengco Barbaro; the copyeditor, Ron Jost; and project manager of SPI Global, Divya Arjunan, all a pleasure to work with. A special word of thanks to Fern Seckbach as well for her indispensable assistance with the index editing.

Introduction

The High Stakes of a Hebraic Rereading of Locke

The influence of English philosopher John Locke (1632–1704) on Western political theory in general and the American founding in particular was dramatic, and one need not look further than the Declaration of Independence for proof. The wording of the Declaration is so similar to Locke's wording in his *Two Treatises of Government* that historians who claim that Thomas Jefferson copied Locke, and dubbed Locke the "American philosopher" and his *Two Treatises* the "gospel" of the American Revolution, appear more than convincing.[1] This means that a

---

[1] Historical research conducted between the 1920s and 1950s, such as the works of Carl Becker and Louis Hartz, granted Locke the status of an "American philosopher," and credited him as the source of ideas that Thomas Jefferson incorporated into the Declaration of Independence. Both of their assessments are sweeping and determinate. Becker concludes that Locke was "political gospel" for the founding fathers and that in penning the Declaration of Independence, "Jefferson copied Locke." Carl Becker, *The Declaration of Independence: A Study in the History of Political Ideas* (New York: Harcourt, 1922), pp. 27–28, and 79. The influential Hartz is no less emphatic when he writes that, "Locke dominates American political thought, as no thinker anywhere dominates the political thought of a nation." Louis Hartz, *The Liberal Tradition in America: An Interpretation of American Political Thought Since the Revolution* (New York: Harcourt, 1955), pp. 11–13.

Locke's influence, though, went through a profound reassessment in the writing of J. G. A. Pocock. For Pocock it was not the notions of natural rights and individual liberty inherent in Lockean thought that won the day for enlightenment, but rather the *republican* ideas of civic responsibility and virtuous character of citizenship central to the writings of Niccolo Machiavelli and James Harrington and drawn from the wisdom of classical Roman greats such as Cicero, Livy, Plutarch, and Tacitus. Pocock's approach is not a syncretic one as he understands republicanism and liberalism to be mutually exclusive strands of thought, and the moment he put the focus on Rome, Machiavelli, and republicanism, Locke and his liberalism fell by the wayside. Indeed, central to Pocock's

I

full and robust understanding of the American founding necessitates a proper reading of Locke's *Two Treatises*.

It has become a commonplace that the *Two Treatises* belongs to the genre of early modern political writings that shifted the focus of political power from the assumption of divine will to human agency. It is in this vein that staple ideas of the American founding as ensconced in its letters of incorporation are generally associated with the Enlightenment and its

"republican revisionism" is the attribution of a relatively minor historical role to Locke. "Among the revolutionary effects of the reevaluation of his historical role," he writes, "... has been a shattering demolition of his myth: not that he was other than a great and authoritative thinker, but that his greatness and authority have been wildly distorted by a habit of taking them unhistorically for granted." J. G. A. Pocock, *The Machiavellian Moment* (Princeton, NJ: Princeton University Press, 2003), p. 424. See also Bernard Bailyn, *The Origins of American Politics* (New York: Vintage Books, 1968), p. 41; Gordon S. Wood, *Creation of the American Republic: 1776–1787* (New York: W.W. Norton and Company, 1972); Caroline Robbins, *The Eighteenth-Century Commonwealthman: Studies in the Transmission, Development and Circumstance of English Liberal Thought from the Restoration of Charles II Until the War with the Thirteen Colonies* (Indianapolis, IN: Liberty Fund, 2004); and Mark Goldie (ed.), *The Reception of Locke's Politics: From the 1690s to the 1830s*, vol. 1 (London: Pickering & Chatto, 1999), p. liii.

A convincing counterargument to Pocock's *republican revisionism* has been made by Steven M. Dworetz. While dubbing Pocock's arguments "mystifying," he uses a plethora of primary textual sources, such as political pamphlets, state papers, newspapers, and correspondence, to prove that even though the first American edition of the *Second Treatise* was only printed in Boston in 1773, on crucial political matters Locke's ideas on government were the most frequently cited non-Biblical sources by the American Revolutionists both before and after the initial American printing. Steven M. Dworetz, *The Unvarnished Doctrine: Locke, Liberalism, and the American Revolution* (Durham, NC: Duke University Press, 1990), p. 35. Dworetz considers "the fall of liberalism and the rise of republicanism in the historiography of the American Revolution" to be "the most stunning reversal in the history of political thought." Ibid, p. 140. Dworetz was followed by Jerome Huyler who argues in his *Locke in America* that the fundamental error of the *republican revisionists* was to see republicanism and liberalism as contradictory concepts, whereas understanding their inherent complementarity would have allowed for the granting of an important place for Locke's *Second Treatise* in the American Revolution. Jerome Huyler, *Locke in America* (Lawrence, KS: University Press of Kansas, 1995). See also W. M. Spellman, who shares this opinion. Spellman states that Locke was the "party line" during the era of the American Revolution and supportively quotes Louis Hartz's assertion that "Lockean liberalism had defined not only revolutionary debate but all subsequent American thought and behavior." W. M. Spellman, *John Locke* (New York: Macmillan Press, 1997), pp. 135–139. For Locke's definitive influence see also Amanda Porterfield, *The Protestant Experience in America* (London: Greenwood Publishing, 2006), p. 208; Michael Foley, *American Credo: The Place of Ideas in US Politics* (Oxford: Oxford University Press, 2007), pp. 38–39; and Yuhtaro Ohmori, *'The Artillery of Mr. Locke': The Use of Locke's 'Second Treatise' in Pre-Revolutionary America, 1764–1776* (Ann Arbor, MI: UMI Dissertation Services, 1988), pp. 18–19.

replacement of revelation with reason. It is sure to come as a surprise then that Locke himself did not absent scriptural revelation from his modernizing concepts such as inalienable rights of individuals based on natural law, government through popular consent, the right to revolution, the right to private property, individual freedoms, natural equality, and the limitation of governmental powers. Actually, the very opposite is true.

Careful study of Locke's wording in the *Two Treatises* reveals a political theory wholly dependent on divine will as the yardstick of its moral legitimacy. It is in fact a text heavily laden with Biblical references, and while this has not been lost on some of the vast scholarship on Locke, the fact that these Biblical quotes are specifically and almost exclusively taken from the Hebrew Bible has indeed been ignored. This is shocking. *Why would the godfather of the American founding use the Hebrew Bible so copiously to establish his political theory while hardly referencing the New Testament at all? And why would Locke scholarship avoid any attempt to wrestle with this question?*

Indeed, of the more than five hundred scholarly works on Locke's political theory there is but one that asks the question, struggles to find a solution, yet leaves it unanswered. In his important book *God, Locke, and Equality: Christian Foundations of Locke's Political Thought*, preeminent scholar Jeremy Waldron tries to unravel Locke's intentions in quoting the Old Testament so copiously, but admits that "we have circled several times around the question of the absence of New Testament material from the *Two Treatises of Government* without really answering it."[2]

This book tries to resolve the question by arguing, for the first time, in favor of a Hebraic reading of Locke's classical political text. In doing so it formulates a new school of thought in Lockean political interpretation and challenges existing ones. But rather than merely add yet another dimension of theoretical wrangling over Lockean political theory, the book shows how appreciation of the Hebraic underpinnings of Locke's political theory actually solves many of the problems inherent in reading Locke and beats many of the crossed swords of academic debate over his intentions into ploughshares.

Because Locke was one of the most important forbearers of Western freedom, a more correct understanding of his political thinking is of critical import, particularly at this time in history when the need to

---

[2] Jeremy Waldron, *God, Locke, and Equality: Christian Foundations in Locke's Political Thought* (Cambridge: Cambridge University Press, 2002), p. 214.

mediate a balance between modern secularism and resurgent religious identities is so palpable. Such a reading can perhaps serve to foster a more vigorous comprehension of freedom's contemporary relevance.

To be fair, Locke is a historical figure not easy to categorize or classify. Few major intellectual figures have been as enigmatic as Locke has been for students of political theory, and he continues to be the focus of intensive academic research and debate. His political theories have been interpreted as both radical and moderate, both capitalist and anti-capitalist, and both atheist and devoutly Christian. Some scholars have attributed to Locke a major role in the evolution of liberalism while others have cast his influence in a minor light. Similar debates rage over the degree of his influence on the English, French, and American revolutions. In fact, one would be hard-pressed to find anything that is universally agreed upon in Lockean scholarship with regard to his political theory. Well, almost. Barring some recent pathbreaking scholarship,[3] there is general widespread agreement, at least by default, that Locke was *not* a political Hebraist.

My reading of Locke's political theories as specifically Hebraic belongs to the broader study of *political Hebraism*, a nascent academic endeavor that is chartering a new theoretical course for understanding classical political ideas, or is at least renewing intellectual appreciation for the Hebraic underpinnings of modern political theory that have often been overlooked or underrated.

The political, economic, judicial, social, and cultural ideas ensconced in the Hebrew Bible, as well as in the Talmud, and in later rabbinical literature through Maimonides and beyond, played a significant role in

---

[3] Initial steps toward the examination of Locke's works through Hebraic lenses can be found in Fania Oz-Salzberger, "The Political Thought of John Locke and the Significance of Political Hebraism," *Hebraic Political Studies* 1, 5 (2006), pp. 568–592, a work that helped inspire this book. There are also a few articles dedicated to this subject that appear in *Jewish Political Studies Review* 9, 3–4, in a volume entitled "John Locke and the Bible, Leo Strauss as Jew and Philosopher" (1997), including: George Gross, "Notes for Reading the Bible with John Locke" and Richard Sherlock, "The Theology of Toleration: A Reading of Locke's The Reasonableness of Christianity." These articles have served to open the door to further more in-depth study of Locke's political Hebraism, the purpose of which this book comes to serve. Mention must also be made of Kim Ian Parker's *The Biblical Politics of John Locke* (Waterloo, ON: Wilfred Laurier University Press, 2004). This is an especially important work that convincingly makes the case for a requisite grounding of Locke's *Two Treatises* in the Hebrew Bible. Yet the author, to my understanding, places his reading of Locke not in a Hebraic context, but in a Christological one, while glossing over the curious absence of New Testamentism in Locke's work.

shaping ways of thinking for many European theologians, philosophers, and statesmen, most of whom were not Jewish.[4] Their reading of the original Biblical text as belonging to the historical and political experience of the Jewish people, while maintaining relevancy for all humankind, makes it more accurate to refer to the ancient Hebrew text as the Hebrew Bible, rather than as the Old Testament or as the old part of the Christian Bible, hence *Hebraism.* Connate to this new reading is an appreciation of the independent nature of the Hebrew teachings, which were outside the realm of Christological contextualization and, at times, markedly different or even in stark opposition to it.

The emergence of this field of study, or in essence, rediscovery of it, makes it possible to pursue new interpretive perspectives of historical and philosophical issues as well as the possible solutions to the intellectual quagmires they have presented. The Greek, Roman, and Christian contributions to modern Western politics are broadly established in historical research thanks to the works of numerous scholars, notably J. G. A. Pocock, Richard Tuck, and Quentin Skinner.[5] But as for the question of the specifically Hebraic contribution to the evolution of political ideas and systems, historical research is still in relative infancy. Infancy perhaps, but the first words have been spoken, and with the publication of Eric Nelson's book *The Hebrew Republic: Jewish Sources and the Transformation of European Political Thought,*[6] they are fast becoming whole and convincing sentences.

---

[4] Pathbreaking works leading this new field of research include Daniel J. Elazar, *Covenant Tradition and Politics,* 4 volumes (New Brunswick, NJ: Transaction Publishers, 1996); the scholarly quarterly *Hebraic Political Studies,* published by the Shalem Center in Jerusalem; and the compendium *Political Hebraism: Judaic Sources in Early Modern Political Thought.* See in particular Yoram Hazony, "Does the Bible Have a Political Teaching?" in *Hebraic Political Studies* 1, 2 (Winter 2006), pp. 137–161. And most importantly Hazony's opus, *The Philosophy of the Hebrew Scriptures* (Cambridge: Cambridge University Press, 2012), and Joshua Berman, *Created Equal* (Oxford: Oxford University Press, 2008).

Other important works that deal with Christian Hebraism in a more general sense include: Frank Manuel, *The Broken Staff* (Cambridge, MA: Harvard University Press, 1992), and Aaron L. Katchen, *Christian Hebraists and Dutch Rabbis* (Cambridge, MA: Harvard University Press, 1984).

[5] Pocock, *The Machiavellian Moment.* Richard Tuck, *Natural Rights Theories: Their Origin and Development* (Cambridge: Cambridge University Press, 1979). Quentin Skinner, *Liberty before Liberalism* (Cambridge: Cambridge University Press, 1998).

[6] Eric Nelson, *The Hebrew Republic: Jewish Sources and the Transformation of European Political Thought* (Cambridge, MA: Harvard University Press, 2010).

Political Hebraism, Nelson argues, must not just take its hitherto ignored place among the other influences of modern political thought, but, in pointed contradistinction to what has been staple to the history of political philosophy, must in fact replace them, as the emergence of modern political theory was decidedly not secular (Greco-Roman) but religious in nature and predicated on the Hebrew Bible. Nelson's thesis is revolutionary but the evidence he provides is incontrovertible. It provides us not only with a new way with which to understand the great political thinkers of the seventeenth century, but with a contemporary way of understanding the basis of modern political thought that significantly differs from what has commonly been assumed.

Nelson shows that while a special focus on the Hebrew Bible existed throughout the ages, even during medieval times, the Reformation unleashed a Hebraic revival that included widespread study of the Hebrew Bible in its original language without the commentary and catechism of the Roman Catholic Church.[7] The devaluation of the Christological interpretation along with a Hebraic resurgence is decidedly not what Luther had in mind, but as Diana Muir Appelbaum has

---

[7] "Luther's conviction that the way of a true Christian was to seek salvation through the Bible – and only through the Bible – had, for the very first time, placed the study of the original Biblical languages at the heart of the Christian ministry. If one could no longer rely on commentaries, translations, or the authority of the institutional Church for guidance in the life of the spirit, then it became a matter of the utmost urgency to understand the Biblical text correctly, to read the Hebrew Bible in its original language." Nelson, *The Hebrew Republic*, pp. 7–8. Nelson goes on to explain that while there were "Catholic Hebraists of great distinction" both prior and subsequent to the Reformation, "Yet it is undeniable that, after the rupture of 1517, the story of Christian Hebraism becomes a disproportionately Protestant story, unfolding for the most part in the great centers of learning in the United Provinces, Northern Germany, and England." Ibid, pp. 12–13.
In his excellent study on Reformed political theology, Glenn Moots strikes a similar chord with regard to Jean Calvin and his colleagues. "The study of Reformed political theology must begin with its Hebraic roots. While Reformed theologians pursued reforms of Roman Catholicism on points common to all Protestant traditions, the Reformed variant of Protestantism is marked by three important emphases. The first was an emphasis on Biblical languages, consistent with the humanist training of the founders of Reformed Protestantism. Reemphasizing Hebrew, sometimes even rabbinic sources, encouraged a new and independently minded study of the Hebrew Scriptures (the 'Old Testament'). This then led to a second innovation, Biblical covenants as a leitmotif of theology and Biblical interpretation. The third innovation was the construction of a theological garment that attempted to seamlessly integrate Hebrew Scriptures and the Christian Scriptures—the 'Old' and 'New' Testaments." Glenn Moots, *Politics Reformed: The Anglo-American Legacy of Covenant Theology* (Columbia, MO: University of Missouri Press, 2010), p. 33.

demonstrated, it was the inevitable result of his popularization and direct reading of the Hebrew Bible.[8]

This attitudinal sea change toward the Bible and its study resulted in a multi-denominational flowering of Hebraic Christian scholarship across Europe,[9] reaching its zenith in the seventeenth-century writings of the great political philosophers of the age, and then waning in the eighteenth century when, as Fania Oz-Salzberger comments, "the Enlightenment threw out the political baby along with the theological bathwater."[10]

In the context of his assault on Christian morality and the enervating of political traditions affected by it, Nicollo Machiavelli (1469–1527), who Oz-Salzberger calls the "significant predecessor" of seventeenth-century Hebraism, turned to figures and events of the Hebrew Bible to support his political theory in both his major and minor works. In his search for contemporary political guidance Machiavelli placed great importance on ancient history, and the Hebrew Bible, even if it was not for him of divine origin, was one of those histories. As a secular political document it also projected an advocacy of the human strength (as opposed to Christian

---

[8] In her important work on Biblical Nationalism and the emergence of sixteenth-century states, Diana Muir Appelbaum writes, "Luther himself continued to understand the Old Testament as Christological Narrative ... But when Luther told Christians to read the Bible for themselves, they did." Earlier she strikes the same theme as Nelson, "the key to understanding the emergence of Biblical nationalism in the sixteenth-century Europe was the rediscovery of the Bible by a Latin Christian culture in which, prior to 1517, almost no one read the Bible. Before Luther, Roman Catholics rarely read complete Bibles; they preferred Bible substitutes: paraphrases, epitomes, and commentaries edited to emphasize Christological interpretations of the Hebrew Bible. The discourse of Biblical nationhood visible in the suddenly popular full-text Bibles therefore came as new revelation to a Western European public who had not encountered it before." Diana Muir Appelbaum, "Biblical Nationalism and the Sixteenth-Century States," *National Identities* 15, 4 (2013), pp. 317–332, DOI: 10.1080/14608944.2013.814624.

[9] In 1694, a book printed in Rome by one Carlo Giuseppe Imbonati documents just how extensive Hebrew scholarship became in the Christian world. The book, entitled *Bibliotheca Latino-Hebraica* (Rome: 1694), lists no fewer than 1,300 works by Christian Hebraists of that period. See Nelson, *The Hebrew Republic*, p. 14.

[10] "Political Hebraism flourished in European thought for about a century and a half, roughly between Bodin and Locke, with Machiavelli as a significant predecessor. The great tide of political and legal-minded Hebraism emerged in mid-seventeenth century England, when jurist John Selden built his excellent scholarly reputation upon it, and republican theorists John Milton and James Harrington endowed it with hands-on political significance. Its ebb began in the early eighteenth century, when the Enlightenment threw out the political baby along with the theological bathwater." Oz-Salzberger, "The Political Thought of John Locke," p. 232.

weakness) and the management of human passions that he was seeking, and that was not necessarily provided by other histories.[11]

Jean Bodin (1530–1596) was a French Catholic who was fluent in Hebrew and insisted on the importance of the history of the ancient Hebrews. His Hebraism comes to the fore especially in his *Colloquium Heptaplomeres*,[12] and in his pursuit of the ultimate political design in his classic works *Methodus* and *Les Six livres de la Republique*, he saw the *Respublica Hebraeorum* as an exemplary model to be followed. Bodin's reading of the Hebrew texts led him to the conclusion that a statist centralized polity in which all powers belonged to a divinely ordained king at the top of the power pyramid was optimum, because it ensured indivisible state sovereignty.[13]

The same Hebrew texts led Bodin's philosophical nemesis Johannes Althusius (1563–1638), a Calvinist from Westphalia, to very different conclusions regarding the ideal polity. In his classic work *Politica Methodice Digesta*, Althusius wrote the first political philosophy that presented a comprehensive theory of federal republicanism, which derived from the Bible but was not dependent on a theological system. Where Bodin saw Biblical justification of absolute monarchy by divine right, Althusius saw a Biblically inspired covenantal view of human society predicated on consent rather than imposition.[14]

---

[11] Christopher Lynch makes the suggestion that the Old Testament might have been more important than other ancient histories for Machiavelli because of its emphasis on human strength and excellence. See Christopher Lynch, "Machiavelli on Reading the Bible," *Hebraic Political Studies* 1, 2 (2006), pp. 162–185. Lynch provides a concise overview of how Machiavelli used the Old Testament in his writing.

[12] This book, a dialogue between seven different kinds of believers, circulated clandestinely in high intellectual circles in the second half of the seventeenth century. Richard Popkin writes: "The Jew in the story is a most benign, reasonable character, who beats down all of the Christians claims. The work ends with a strong plea for universal toleration of all faiths. Bodin's picture of the Jew is of very moral, learned and reasonable person, more so than anyone else." Richard Popkin, "The Image of Judaism in Seventeenth Century Europe," in R. Crocker (ed.), *Religion, Reason and Nature in Early Modern Europe* (Dordrecht: Kluwer Academic Publishers, 2001), p. 184. See also Anna Maria Lazzarino Del Grosso, "The Respublica Hebraeorum as a Scientific Political Model in Jean Bodin's 'Methodus'," *Hebraic Political Studies* 1, 5 (2006), pp. 550–567.

[13] For an analysis of Bodin's use of the *Respublica Hebraeorum* see Del Grosso, "The Respublica Hebraeorum as a Scientific Political Model," pp. 549–556.

[14] Alan Mittleman, "Some Thoughts on the Covenantal Politics of Johannes Althusius," in *Political Hebraism: Judaic Sources in Early Modern Political Thought*, pp. 72–89. Daniel J. Elazar, "Althusius and Federalism as Grand Design," www.jcpa.org/dje/articles2/althus-fed.htm, and *Covenant & Commonwealth: The Covenant Tradition in Politics*, vol. II (New Brunswick, NJ: Transaction Publishers, 1996), esp. pp. 311–333.

Political crises in the early-seventeenth-century Dutch Republic coincided with heightened scholarly interest in Hebraic learning at Leiden University and an influx of Jews into the United Provinces. Two good friends, Petrus Cunaeus (1586–1638) and Hugo Grotius (1583–1645), both sought historical precedent that could be manifestly applied in order to prevent civil strife from tearing the fledgling Republic apart. Cunaeus was the foremost professor of political science at Leiden, a stronghold of Calvinist orthodoxy with an abundance of scholars of the Hebrew language and Hebraic texts. In his seminal political work *De Republica Hebraeorum (On the Republic of the Hebrews*[15]*)*, he argued that the most salient point to be learned from the Hebrew Bible was that unity kept the Hebrew Republic ("the best and holiest of all Republics") together, and it was disunity that spelled its doom.[16] Cunaeus's work is replete with quotes from Maimonides with which he intended to show how republican unity could be maintained. In one of his earliest works, *De Republica Emendanda (On How to Amend the Dutch Polity)*, Grotius had also attempted a comparison between the Dutch and Hebrew constitutions, but it did not successfully garner public attention. Cunaeus's opus, on the other hand, captured the limelight because it was printed at a time when Dutch civil tensions had peaked.

Grotius was an Arminian, a recognized scholar of the Hebrew language and Hebrew literature who advocated the granting of rights to the Jews in Holland comparable to those rights granted to Catholics. He corresponded with rabbinic scholar/activist Menasseh ben Israel,

---

[15] The Italian humanist Carlo Sigonio (1524–1584) had already written a book with the same title in the context of his histories on ancient republics. For an analysis of Sigonio's work, see Guido Bartolucci, "Carlo Sigonio and the 'Respublica Hebraeorum': A Re-evaluation," *Hebraic Political Studies* 3, 1 (Winter 2008), pp. 19–59. See also Guido Bartolucci, "The Influence of Carlo Sigonio's 'De Republica Hebraeorum' on Hugo Grotius' 'De Republica Emendanda'," *Hebraic Political Studies* 2, 2 (Spring 2007), pp. 193–210. Three important additional works of the era that deal paradigmatically with the Biblical Hebrew polity include: Cornelius Bonaventure Bertram's *De politia judaica tam civili quam ecclesiastica* (Geneva: 1574), Wilhelm Zepper's *Legum Mosicarum forensium explanation* (Herborn: 1604), and William Schikard's *Mishpat Ha-Melek, Jus Regium Habraeorum, e Tenebris Rabbinicus erustum & luci donatum* (Leipzig: 1674). For a thorough assessment of these works see Kalman Neuman, *The Literature of the Respublica Judaica: Descriptions of the Ancient Israelite Polity in the Antiquarian Writing for the Sixteenth and Seventeenth Centuries*, PhD Thesis, Hebrew University, 2002.

[16] In his discussion of "Seventeenth-Century Uses of Historical Judaism," Frank Manuel writes that Cunaeus's theme was commonly shared. "If there is one theme that runs through much of Christian historiography of the ancient Hebrew commonwealth, it is the proposition that discord brought about its downfall." Manuel, *The Broken Staff*, p. 121.

and was an admitted great admirer of Maimonides, whom he quotes with frequency in his classic opus *De Jure Belli ac Pacis* (*The Rights of War and Peace*) as well as in his other works. In his *Mare Liberum* (1609) Grotius presents a legal argument for the notion of an open sea that intended to defend Dutch maritime superiority. Grotius taps Talmudic references to bolster his argument in favor of a borderless sea, as does the work of his nemesis English Hebraist John Selden (a figure to be discussed momentarily), *Mare Clausum* (1635), which argues for a closed sea. It was Cunaeus who was later drafted by the States of Holland to respond to Selden and defend the Grotian position. Though a Hebraist of the first order, Grotius did not usually quote Hebraic sources in the original, relying instead on Latin translations, which led to mistaken understandings of important texts.[17]

Across the English Channel political Hebraism was represented by some of the century's greatest thinkers, all of Protestant background, including: John Selden (1584–1654), Robert Filmer (1590–1653), Thomas Hobbes (1588–1679), John Milton (1608–1674), James Harrington (1611–1677), Algernon Sidney (1623–1683), and John Locke.

Selden, a parliamentarian and civil servant, was dubbed "Rabbi and Revered Teacher" by a contemporary as the depth and breadth of his knowledge of Hebraic texts, both Biblical and rabbinic, was as well-known as it was unsurpassed.[18] He mastered Hebrew and Aramaic texts

---

[17] Regarding Grotius's secondhand reading of Hebraic sources, see Phyllis S. Lachs, "Hugo Grotius' Use of Jewish Sources in On the Law of War and Peace," *Renaissance Quarterly* 30, 2 (Summer 1977), pp. 181–200. For a more updated assessment see Neuman, *The Literature of the Respublica Judaica*, pp. 138–142, especially *ft.* 13. For an overview of Grotian Hebraism see Arthur Eyffinger, "How Wondrously Moses Goes Along with the House of Orange! Hugo Grotius' 'De Republica Emendanda' in the Context of the Dutch Revolt," in *Political Hebraism: Judaic Sources in Early Modern Political Thought*, pp. 107–147. As for the Hebraism of Petrus Cunaeus, see Arthur Eyffinger, "Introduction," in *Petrus Cunaeus: The Hebrew Republic* (Jerusalem: Shalem Press, 2006), pp. ix–lxx. For Grotius's influence on John Milton, see Fania Oz-Salzberger, "Social Justice and the Right of the People: The Seventeenth Century Reads the Hebrew Bible," paper presented at the Princeton Conference on Political Hebraism, September 7–9, 2008, p. 9.

[18] Jason P. Rosenblatt, *Renaissance England's Chief Rabbi: John Selden* (Oxford: Oxford University Press, 2006), p. 4. For a more concise assessment of Selden's Hebraism, see Jason P. Rosenblatt, "Rabbinic Ideas in the Political Thought of John Selden," in *Political Hebraism: Judaic Sources in Early Modern Political Thought*, pp. 191–206. For the latest, most exhaustive study of Selden, see Ofir Haivry, *John Selden and the Western Political Tradition* (Cambridge: Cambridge University Press, 2017). I am indebted to Dr. Haivry for privileging me with review of one of his early drafts.

in the original and wrote copiously of their universal validity. Maimonides, whom he quotes regularly, remained his favorite authority throughout his life.[19] His commentaries on Hebraic legal texts and concepts intended not to create a holistic political philosophy but rather to formulate a civil legal structure that would obligate social morality and ethical personal behavior. The titles and topics of Selden's works speak best of his Hebraic erudition. They include: *De Diis Syris*, which elaborates on the foreign Gods condemned by the Hebrew Bible; *De Successionibus ad Leges Ebraeorum in Bona Defunctorum*, which covers in full the Jewish law of inheritance; *De Successione in Pontificatum Ebraeorum*, which discusses succession in the Hebrew priesthood; *De Jure Naturali et Gentium juxta Disciplinam Ebraeorum*, which identifies the imperatives of natural law as the rabbinic Noachide laws; *De Anno Civili*, which presents an account of the Jewish calendar; *Uxor Ebraica seu De Nuptiis et Divortiis Veterum Ebaeorum*, on the Jewish law of marriage and divorce; and the massive *De Syndriis*, a study of the supreme Jewish legal authority, the Sanhedrin. When Selden's frank parliamentary criticism of Charles I landed him in prison (1629), his request was that a complete Babylonian Talmud be brought to his jail cell.[20]

For Robert Filmer, Scripture was an inviolable political authority, and as such a necessary ingredient in the formulation of political theory. In his famous work *Patriarcha*, Filmer frequently quotes the Hebrew Bible in his defense of monarchical absolutism. For Filmer, the most important political facts contained in Scripture occur in the opening pages of the Book of Genesis where God gave the world to the first man. This divine gift made Adam lord over the earth, and ever since, sovereign authority has been attained through divinely granted fatherly authority. This was an immutable religious and political concept for Filmer, which was to be forcefully contested by both Algernon Sidney and John Locke.

In his classic work *Leviathan*, Thomas Hobbes presents a detailed account of the politics of the Hebrew Bible. His quotations, though, are from translations such as the Septuagint and Vulgate versions, indicating that he was not a master of the Hebrew language,[21] and in further contrast to Selden did not use an abundance of Talmudic or rabbinic

[19] Ibid, p. 67.
[20] Rosenblatt, *Renaissance England's Chief Rabbi*, p. 2. Steven Grosby, "Reading the Talmud in the Tower of London" (Library of Law and Liberty, July 31, 2013, www.libertylawsite.org/2013/07/31/reading-the-talmud-in-the-tower-of-london/).
[21] See Menachem Lorberbaum, "Making Space for Leviathan: On Hobbes' Political Theory," *Hebraic Political Studies* 2, 1 (Winter 2007), p. 80.

texts. Opinions vary as to what motivated Hobbes to expound on Biblical politics, with an important school of thought arguing that it was for purely polemical purposes.[22] But even if Biblical quotation was for Hobbes a partial ruse for his personal atheism, it is clear that he found important precedent in the political account of the Hebrew Bible for notions of covenant (social contract) and sovereignty (kingly authority in all areas of social life), two concepts vital to his political theory.[23]

John Milton knew Biblical Hebrew as well as the Aramaic of the Talmud. He revered Selden and followed his lead on the definition of many rabbinic texts.[24] Milton understood the Mosaic polity to be the most perfect, and the republicanism he advocated was intended to emulate it. Like Hobbes, Milton cited Biblical precedent for his covenantal ideas, but unlike Hobbes, his notion of the social contract was religiously

---

[22] See Leo Strauss, *The Political Philosophy of Hobbes: Its Basis and Genesis*, Elsa Sinclair (trans.) (Chicago, IL: University of Chicago Press, 1957). J. G. A. Pocock, "Time, History, and Eschatology in the Thought of Thomas Hobbes," in *Politics, Language and Time: Essays on Political Thought and History*, Pocock (ed.) (New York: Antheneum, 1971), pp. 148–201. See also Paul D. Cooke, *Hobbes and Christianity: Reassessing the Bible in Leviathan* (Lanham, MD: Rowman & Littlefield, 1996), who agrees with Strauss that Hobbes used the Bible subversively; and see Paul Dumouchel, who disagrees: "The Political Problem of Religion: Hobbes' Reading of the Bible," in *English Philosophy in the Age of Locke*, M. A. Stewart (ed.) (Oxford: Clarendon Press, 2000), pp. 1–27. See also Roy Harrison, *Hobbes, Locke and Confusion's Masterpiece: An Examination of Seventeenth-Century Political Philosophy* (Cambridge: Cambridge University Press, 2003), p. 59. A. P. Martinich is also of the opinion that Hobbes did not intend his Biblical quotation subversively. "Although Hobbes was not in every way strictly either a Lutheran or a Calvinist, he did represent himself as in large agreement with them and as being within the Protestant tradition of his time." A. P. Martinich, "The Bible and Protestantism in *Leviathan*," in *The Cambridge Companion to Hobbes's Leviathan*, Patricia Springborg (ed.) (Cambridge: Cambridge University Press, 2007), p. 389.

[23] Lorberbaum, "Making Space for Leviathan," p. 80. Lorberbaum writes, "In its theory of sovereign supremacy, Hobbes' political philosophy marks a turning point in the shift to secularization within European cultural and political history." Ibid, p. 83. See also Quentin Skinner, *Reason and Rhetoric in the Philosophy of Hobbes* (Cambridge: Cambridge University Press, 1996), and Warren Zev Harvey, "The Israelite Kingdom of God in Hobbes," *Hebraic Political Studies* 1, 3 (2006), pp. 310–327. For more about Hobbes's use of Scripture, see Ernst Graf Reventlow, *The Authority of the Bible and the Rise of the Modern World* (London: SCM Press, 1984), pp. 208–222.

[24] Rosenblatt, *Renaissance England's Chief Rabbi*, p. 3. Elsewhere, Rosenblatt writes, "John Selden, the most learned person in England in the seventeenth century and the author of a half dozen immense rabbinical works, is the principal source of Milton's Jewish learning." Jason P. Rosenblatt, *Torah and Law in Paradise Lost* (Princeton, NJ: Princeton University Press, 1994), p. 85. Similarly, Frank Manuel writes that, "If Milton had a 'rabbi,' it was his countryman John Selden, a Talmudist, a scholar of rabbinics, but surely not a mystical cabbalist." Manuel, *The Broken Staff*, p. 146.

grounded, the purpose of which was to guarantee political liberty, not monarchical absolutism. It was through the Hebrew Bible that Milton justified the execution of Charles I in his *The Tenure of Kings and Magistrates*, and it was upon the same source that Milton relied to defend the parliamentary revolution and the Cromwellian commonwealth in his *A Defence of the People of England*. Milton's more famous literary works written after the Restoration, *Paradise Lost, Paradise Regained*, and *Samson Agonistes*, are based on Biblical imagery, concepts, and figures.[25]

James Harrington was strongly influenced by both Machiavelli and Hobbes but forged his own independent political theory. In his *The Commonwealth of Oceana* he presents a blueprint for the ideal republic, which is based on an assessment of the commonwealth of Israel. Israel's ancient republic as described in the Hebrew Bible was an exemplary one because its structure and dictates were God-given and hence, as Milton argues, infallible. The ultimate unwinding of the Hebrew Republic was due, argues Harrington, not to the imperfection of the polity's divine format but to the failure of the Jewish people to live up to its dictates. Harrington, like Milton, held John Selden in the highest esteem, calling him "the ablest Talmudist of our age or of any,"[26] and in his *The Prerogatives of Popular Government*, Harrington follows Selden's *De Synedriis* in holding up the Sanhedrin as the model for Parliament.[27]

Algernon Sidney was beheaded by Charles II for his anti-monarchical revolutionary republican activity. In his *Court Maxims*, Sidney argues that humans are required to use their own reason when attempting to follow the laws of God. This was his philosophical understanding of the Biblical text that had a political lesson: the Hebrew Bible that told the story of the Hebrew Republic contained general directives of proper governance for all humankind. It was both the law of reason and the law of God that obligated total objection to tyrannical forms of government. It was from the Hebrew Bible that Sidney also learned that the ancient Hebrews never allowed their kings to enjoy a divine status. And it was this Hebraic anti-monarchical notion that he used to refute Filmer's

[25] See ibid, particularly Chapters 3 and 4, for a detailed analysis of Milton's use of the Hebrew Bible in these texts. See also Nelson, *The Hebrew Republic*, pp. 37–56, for a riveting discussion on how Milton chose to interpret the Biblical law of kingship.

[26] James Harrington, *The Prerogatives of Popular Government*, bk. II, in *The Political Works of James Harrington*, J. G. A. Pocock (ed.) (Cambridge: Cambridge University Press, 1977), p. 531.

[27] Rosenblatt, *Renaissance England's Chief Rabbi*, p. 6.

Patriarcha[28] when he wrote his *Discourses Concerning Government* (published fifteen years after his death).[29]

Like Sidney, John Locke responded to Filmer's Biblically based advocacy of patriarchal absolutism. In his *First Treatise of Government* he puts forth a step-by-step refutation of Filmer's arguments, not by deprecating the importance of Biblical teachings but rather by demonstrating that Filmer misunderstood the Biblical message. He quotes the Hebrew Bible extensively, more than eighty times in fact, quantitatively far more than Filmer himself, and the context of his arguments clearly indicates the definitive authority he attributed to the Biblical text. In his *Second Treatise of Government* Locke lays out his own theory of consensual government, and though it is not a refutation, neither of Filmer's nor of anyone else's absolutism, Locke nevertheless turns to copious references from the Hebrew Bible, here some twenty-five times, in order to buttress his arguments.

This fact alone is not unusual and would comfortably place Locke in the pantheon of seventeenth-century Hebraists. What is fascinating about Locke's *Two Treatises of Government*, though, the reason it stands apart, is not because it is replete with Hebraic sources, but because they are practically the *only* sources he offers.[30] "Both treatises are," Kim Ian Parker has argued, "grounded on the same biblical bedrock,"[31] but the bedrock is unignorably and uniquely Hebraic. The theorists mentioned

---

[28] Filmer wrote *Patriarcha* sometime close to his death in 1653, but the work was not published until 1680.

[29] I have not included Benedict Spinoza in this overview of important seventeenth-century Hebraists for the following reason. While considerable differences exist between the theorists I have mentioned in terms of how and what they gleaned from the Biblical text, notions of universal and contemporary relevancy, to one degree or another, run like a strand through their theories. Spinoza, on the other hand, makes the case for a new political science in his *Theological Political Tractate* that severely limits the scope of Hebraism by arguing that Biblical political theory applied only to the Jewish people, and that only as long as they enjoyed sovereignty. Yirmiyahu Yovel writes, for example, that, "For Spinoza, the historical religions (above all, Judaism and Christianity) are the greatest obstacles to clear philosophical knowledge." Yirmiyahu Yovel, *Spinoza and Other Heretics: The Marrano of Reason* (Princeton, NJ: Princeton University Press, 1989), p. 3. That is not something that one could find in the writings of the Hebraists mentioned here. See also Menachem Lorberbaum, "Spinoza's Theological-Political Problem," *Hebraic Political Studies* 1, 2 (2006), p. 204.

[30] Some of the other sources Locke does mention include: English ecclesiastic Richard Hooker (II: 5, 15); Peruvian historian Garcilasso de la Vega (II: 14); Spanish scientist Josephus Acosta (II: 102); early Christian apologist Justin Martyr (II: 103); and the classical Roman poet Juvenal (II: 235).

[31] Parker, *The Biblical Politics of John Locke*, p. 144.

earlier quoted the Hebraic sources, as well as Talmudic and later rabbinic texts, but they did not focus exclusively on the Hebrew Bible, as they culled their source material from the New Testament as well, along with plentiful quotations from the Greek and Roman classics. (Selden is perhaps the one exception, but his stated objective was the exegesis of Hebraic texts, not the presentation of an all-encompassing political theory.) Even Filmer, whom Locke is coming to refute in the *First Treatise*, quotes conspicuously and meaningfully from the New Testament. He indeed uses six pages of Old Testament quotations as proof-texts, but he also makes no secret of the fact that St. Paul and St. Peter, Tertullian, St. Augustine, and St. Ambrose are all consequential to his political theory.[32] Locke, on the other hand, responds with 120 pages of quotes from the Old Testament, and two inconsequential quotes from the New Testament that merely contend with Filmer's use of them.

Thanks are owed to Jeremy Waldron, who troubled to make the page count. As I indicated earlier, Waldron is the only scholar I have found who has written extensively on Lockean political theory, who is truly intrigued by Locke's disproportionate resourcing of the Old Testament, and is equally perplexed by the near absence of New Testamentism in the *Two Treatises*. He chides John Dunn's assertion that the presence of Jesus Christ and St. Paul "can hardly be missed," and that the *Treatises* are "saturated with Christian assumptions,"[33] by caustically observing that the "saturation" is apparently so complete as to render it "invisible."[34] Waldron dedicates a whole chapter, "By Our Saviour's Interpretation," to an attempt to unravel Locke's intention, but admits that, "once again we have circled several times around the question of the absence of New Testament material from the *Two Treatises of Government* without really answering it."[35] In conclusion Waldron confesses, "I have not been able to resolve the question of why Locke offered no *explicit* Christian argument for the specifically individualist way in which he understood man's relation to God's commission and God's purposes."[36] Waldron, though, cautiously ventures an explanation: "I *suspect* – though I have nothing to offer in support of this, and this is the last strand of explanation that

[32] See in particular chapter III of *Patriarcha*.
[33] Dunn writes, "Jesus Christ (and Saint Paul) may not appear in person in the text of the *Two Treatises* but their presence can hardly be missed when we come upon the normative creaturely equality of all men in virtue of their shared species-membership." John Dunn, *The Political Thought of John Locke* (Cambridge: Cambridge University Press, 1969), p. 99.
[34] Waldron, *God, Locke, and Equality*, p. 188.   [35] Ibid, p. 214.   [36] Ibid, p. 215.

I shall venture – that as well as the issue of political strategy, there might also have been some reluctance on Locke's part to entangle his political arguments in the *Treatises*, which were already strange and radical enough by contemporary standards, with the various Christology which we know he was wrestling with in the 1680s."[37]

It appears to me that the logical conclusion of Waldron's *suspicion* is an inescapable Hebraic reading of the *Two Treatises*. If Locke did not want to "entangle his political arguments" with "various Christology," thereby jettisoning the New Testament and embracing only the Old, the implication is surely that the Old Testament could stand alone and be read and interpreted independent of decidedly Christian Biblical exegesis, or simply as the Hebrew Bible.

That having been said, it is important to emphasize that I am not arguing from an exclusivist standpoint suggesting that all of Locke's political ideas are Hebraistic or that those that are, are exclusively so. Greek concepts of natural law are there as is Roman jurisprudence, themes that in turn were embraced by some of the greatest thinkers of the Middle Ages and resulted in, among other things, the doctrine of natural rights. And just as Locke was no stranger to the classics of Aristotle and Cicero, John of Salisbury and Aquinas, he culled knowledge and opinion from some of his seventeenth-century contemporaries such as Bacon, Grotius, Selden, Hobbes, and Milton.

To be sure, despite his eclectic, if not iconoclastic, thinking, Locke was very much part of the long, well-established English tradition that went back to the Magna Carta and was expressed contemporarily in Whig notions of individual freedoms and constitutionalism. These sources of Locke's political thought should not be ignored or downplayed, but neither should his Hebraism.

My first chapter focuses on the *First Treatise*, especially its last chapter, entitled "Who Heir," which reviews most of the arguments made throughout the *Treatise*. This chapter provides the theoretical linchpins for Locke without which much of his *Second Treatise* cannot properly be understood. This, though, is a unique way of reading the *First Treatise*. Because of its overwhelming use of Biblical citation and repetitive style, it has become a text terribly underrated and all but ignored. It certainly is not customarily read as the first and fundamental part of one integral text, as I argue it must.

---

[37] Ibid.

The *First Treatise* serves as a refutation of Robert Filmer's defense of patriarchy as articulated in *Patriarcha*, which Locke read upon its publication in 1680,[38] obviously fearing its potential influence. Here Locke criticizes Filmer in harsh words, writing that, "There was never so much glib nonsense put together in well sounding English," and that he was "mightily surprised, that in a book, which was to provide chains for all man kind, I should find nothing but a rope of sand, useful perhaps, to such, whose skill and business it is to raise dust."[39]

Filmer based his defense of monarchical absolutism on "patriarchalism," the alleged granting in the Book of Genesis of absolute dominion to Adam over all of creation. Filmer argued that the origins of familial and political power are one and the same. Although his theory was by his own admission "naturalist" and conceptually independent of the Biblical narrative, he nevertheless used the Biblical account to argue that since Adam was father and king, in emanating from him, all kings have been divinely granted the absolute and arbitrary power that Adam was granted. And because it is an inviolable duty to honor one's father, it is obligatory in the same measure to honor one's king. Because of the way Filmer understood Adamic dominion, he rejected the notion that humans were or could ever be independent of each other. This reading of the Biblical account of creation meant, in addition, that humans are born into a natural state of inequality and are decidedly not free.

Contrary to Filmer, Locke argues that kings and princes are just metaphorical fathers of their people, and not their real fathers whom they are obligated to always blindly respect and obey. While Filmer wrote that rulers receive their authority to rule directly from the dominion over the world that God gave to Adam, Locke responds that all people descended from Adam and no man can rule any other by claiming divine right.

Locke's multipronged rejoinder does not discard Filmer's arguments by dismissing the relevance of Filmer's stated source, the Bible. Instead, this chapter elucidates Locke's assertion that Filmer's reading of the Bible was simply wrong, and upon the proper reading of Scripture, not only is Filmer debunked but a correct understanding of the origins of political man emerges. It is from the Hebrew Bible that Locke learns that Adam did not have dominion over other human beings in the same sense that he had

---

[38] M. Cranston, *John Locke: A Biography* (Oxford: Longmans, Green and Co., 1985), p. 191.

[39] John Locke, *Two Treatises of Government* (Cambridge: Cambridge University Press, 1964), p. 156.

dominion over other creatures and, hence, familial and political power are not one and the same. It is from the Hebrew Bible as well that Locke establishes the absence of patriarchal political power (hereditary or otherwise), a state of nature in which humans are independent, and a state of natural freedom and equality into which humans are born.

The question then for Locke is not *if* Hebrew Scripture teaches the essence of legitimate political power, but rather *what* that teaching is. These ideas then are crucial for understanding the *Second Treatise*, and in this chapter I show why.

The idea of an original state of nature from which humankind emerges with an inherent embrace of its laws of nature is central to all of Locke's political philosophy. But because the telos of Locke's *Second Treatise* is the justification of rebellion against government's gross violations of natural law, he opens his *Second Treatise* with a discussion of that law. And while natural law theory was popularized by several other seventeenth-century theorists aside from Locke, in *Chapter 2* I demonstrate why his use of it is wholly unique in that it is arbitrated to a large extent by the Hebrew Bible – specifically, the scriptural account of the first murder as well as the postdiluvian prohibition against the spilling of blood as described in the first chapters in the Book of Genesis. Here I focus on how Locke separates himself from most other natural law thinkers whose theories lack a clear source that can serve to induce ubiquitous obligation.

Rather than a concept chronologically restricted to defining prepolitical society, Locke's state of nature is one in which the laws of nature, comprehended by human reason but divinely ordained, are not sustained. The endowment of self-preservation, which also metamorphoses into a more general obligatory overarching human preservation, drives humans out of a state of nature and into civil society in order to ensure obedience to the laws of nature.

This is the result of Locke's granting of what he calls "executive powers" to every individual, a revolutionary idea that he takes directly from his Biblical exegesis. He understands a political process from which government evolves, and rather than receiving its legitimacy through a claim of divine ordination, a government's legitimacy derives from the will of the people who created it with the intent to preserve the laws of nature implanted in humankind by God. Here too, I argue, Locke sets himself apart from other natural law theorists, such as Hugo Grotius, who refused to predicate their understanding of natural law on the existence of a relevant God.

What is critical then for understanding Locke's natural law, and what is generally overlooked together with the ignoring of his Hebraism, is that reason alone is insufficient for a complete comprehension of all natural law stipulates; that it is scriptural revelation of a particularly Hebraic strand that helps make natural law obligatory; and that the human inclination toward self-preservation necessitates complementary religious faith in order for moral political governance to be sustainable. The focus of this chapter has the potential of changing how Locke's theory of natural law is understood and hence how Locke's theory of just rebellion is to be appreciated as well.

Scholarly analyses of Locke's attitude toward human equality, like so many of Locke's ideas on politics, do not generally include an assessment of his critique on Filmer's concept of fatherhood in the *First Treatise*. *Chapter 3* discusses Locke's labeling of Filmerian inequality "as a strange kind of domineering phantom," and proves that it is more than just rhetoric, but rather sets the stage for his equality-guaranteeing, reason-based political construct in the *Second Treatise*.

This is a highly definitive moment for Locke. Humans comprise one community for Locke because they were created as one, not because they are saved in one. This is a creationism that precedes Christ; and in it, men are not brothers in Christ but sons of Adam. In Pauline doctrine equality is theoretically embraceable for all humanity, but only theoretically; it is achievable exclusively for members of the covenanted community, not for those who do not accept the Christian faith.

Examples of this conditional equality in Christ in the New Testament abound, and yet Locke chose to ignore them. Instead, in a tellingly elective move, Locke preferred to establish his theory of inbred human equality on the Hebrew Bible's account of creation. It would be very hard to argue that this exclusion was not a conscious choice, but I go further here and offer proof to the effect that Locke consciously omitted any such references because they stand in opposition to his political theory. Locke believed that only a societal commitment (achieved through the use of human reason – *Second Treatise*) to a nonsectarian creationist doctrine (as elucidated upon in the *First Treatise*) would allow for the establishment of a truly egalitarian society as well as its proper governance.

From this flows Locke's approach to human liberty as well. In the Biblical doctrine of creation humans are born as free as they are equal because everyone is born in the image of God; hence no one has the right to dominion over another. The Biblical concept of *imago dei* is so decisive for Locke that, in contradistinction to many of his contemporaries, he rejected the notion that an individual is permitted to willfully conscript him- or herself into slavery.

Locke's exclusive concentration on the Hebrew Bible is not just to engage Filmer in a polemic on Biblical hermeneutics. Even if Filmer's patriarchal exegesis of the Biblical text had never been made, this book contends that Locke would probably have grounded his theories of human equality and liberty on the Hebrew Bible's account of creation in any case. In it, he found a human equality and liberty that are elemental in their divine ordination, and hence both fundamentally unconditional and unalterable.

America's avowed assurance of "life, liberty, and the pursuit of happiness" is borrowed directly from Locke's definition of the purpose of government as the guarantor of "life, liberty, and property" as he enunciated in the *Second Treatise*. The intention of *Chapter 4* is to present evidence before the reader that in thematically keeping with his philosophical agenda, here too the basis for Locke's thinking was political Hebraism. The importance of this analysis is obvious, for it means that one of the most cherished tenets of the American experience is rooted in the Biblical experience, as mediated through Locke.

Locke extended the personal obligation of self-preservation to society as a whole and with this posited that each individual is endowed with political power. The practical meaning of this extension is that every individual has an obligation to advance the type of government (consensual government) that will ensure the preservation of the life, liberty, and property of all, and oppose the type of government (absolutism) that would compromise those rights.

But from where Locke culled this revolutionary idea is either misunderstood or ignored by Locke scholarship, making its elucidation here so important. Locke in fact cleverly juxtaposed two Biblical concepts in order to make his case. It is from Leviticus, he argues, that we learn the Golden Rule obligation to "love your neighbor like yourself," which stems from inherent human equality. And it is from Genesis that we learn the obligation of self-preservation. Ergo, if part of "loving oneself" is "preserving oneself," and others must be loved as oneself, then it necessarily follows that the other must be preserved, just as the self must be preserved.

Locke famously attributes the acquisition of property to the mixing of one's labor in a substance, but what is less known is the paradigm Locke uses to reach that conclusion. Once again it is the Biblical principle of *imago dei*. Because we are the products of God's workmanship, the mixer of His labor in material substance, we belong to Him and hence we cannot be the property of another created being. And because we were created in His image, when we create by mixing our labor with existing material, we too are workers who acquire and then maintain ownership.

But while God is sole proprietor of His labors, we are not, for nothing becomes ours to the extent that it ceases entirely to belong to God. This results in what has become known as the Lockean proviso, which means that there is no limitation on material acquisition to the extent that no one is deprived of their basic needs. I believe that Locke himself would have been shocked at this concept being referred to as the "Lockean proviso," and demonstrate in this chapter that he himself understood it rather as the Biblical proviso, as delineated specifically in the Hebrew Bible.

This discussion has the potential of adding a new dimension of understanding to the realm of individual and communal responsibility to social welfare in the modern state.

Chapter 5 first surveys Locke's theory of rebellion and then analyzes probable Hebraic influences that helped to shape it. The right to rebel against tyranny is the conclusion and crescendo of the *Two Treatises*.

Because government is predicated on and preserved only through the general consent of individuals, when government violates the very laws it was established by consent to protect, it thrusts society back into a state of nature, public consent is lost, and its legitimacy is forfeited. Here Locke's theoretical legitimization of revolution is crystallized primarily through the Book of Judges account of Jephthah's "appeal to heaven."

Locke's use of Jephthah is repetitive and thematic, not ornamental, and the fact that it has dumbfounded scholarship on the *Two Treatises*, at least that which has bothered to pay attention to its centrality, is an unfortunate outcome of the negation of his Hebraism. Explaining Locke's intent becomes an even greater imperative when it is remembered that the "appealing to the supreme judge" that takes center stage in the American Declaration of Independence is borrowed too from Jephthah, that is, through the mediation of Locke.

Even though it is the Biblical story of Jephthah that Locke explicitly resources, this chapter argues that his reliance on the Hebrew Bible to establish his entire theory on just rebellion is much wider and deeper, and belongs to a long tradition of Protestant Biblicism that negated traditional Christian political docility, relying instead on Old Testament attitudes. This comes to light particularly in the context of the more radical elements of his theory, for example, the limitation Locke puts on what may legitimately constitute "consent." Locke limits the capacity for human consent to that which does not stand in full compliance with natural law. Society, contrary to Grotius and Hobbes, cannot choose to enslave itself of its own volition, or even to passively accept the deprivation of its own freedom. Resistance to such a tyrannical freedom-depriving form of government is not just permissible for Locke, but in essence, obligatory. And this obligation, in another example of Locke's radicalism, belongs to each individual, not just society as a whole. Both of these ideas, albeit to a large extent through the mediation of others, Locke based on Biblical precedent that is decidedly Hebraic.

Chapter 6 is somewhat different in its methodology of analysis than the preceding ones, but I believe no less important. With regard to Locke's theories on natural law, equality, property, and rebellion, the primary focus of my analysis is on the direct use he made of the Hebrew Bible. This is complemented by the places where it appears highly probable that Locke was influenced by Hebraic sources through the mediation of other texts, and yet other places where only a thematic similarity exists between Hebraic texts and the Lockean text. This chapter is distinct insofar as it concerns itself primarily not with what is *included* in his *Treatises* but rather with what is *absent* from Lockean political theory: the Fall and original sin.

Locke, I think it will become clear, did not accept, and indeed could not have accepted, the traditional Christian (predominantly Augustinian) understanding of the Fall that classifies death as punishment, points to a constant state of sin, and denies or at least severely limits human free will, and at the same time advance a theory of natural law that would lead to rebellion against tyrannical government. Because the right to consent to moral government is by definition also the right to *dissent* from amoral government, original sin cannot be understood to preclude the ability to discern the nature of proper conduct and choose it.

The Christological assumption of humanity's natural depravity, endemic to its being as a result of Adam's Fall, could accept a magistrate that enjoys the very divine status that Locke was coming to negate.

This chapter shows that by choosing to define man's post-lapsarian state in terms of human responsibility rather than depravity, Locke kept closely and consciously within the confines of the classical Hebraic reading of the Biblical text, which attributes only the forfeiture of immortality following Adam and Eve's sin while leaving human free will intact. This, along with the "minimalist creed" of Christianity that he came to espouse, put him theoretically well beyond the neo-Thomism and anti-Augustinianism of some of his predecessors.

The primary and most obvious audience for this book is that of Locke studies and scholarship. Few thinkers have generated such an extensive and eclectic written reservoir of scholarship that has sustained the vicissitudes of academic debate and ever-emerging ideas. Interest in Locke in varying academic forums continues to grow, and his political theories remain staple to university courses, both introductory and advanced, all over the world. Because my book proposes an iconoclastic theory bound to generate controversy as it challenges long held and well-entrenched readings of Locke's *Two Treatises*, it is my hope that it will be received beyond the level of yet another scholarly attempt to figure Locke out.

But while *John Locke's Political Philosophy and the Hebrew Bible* is ostensibly a book about the political theory of John Locke, it is really a book about the foundational ideas of Western civilization. And while it appears to be a book specifically focused on Locke's Hebraism, it is actually a book about the persistent relevance of the Biblical political narrative to modernity. For these reasons it is my every hope that the book will not only generate interest among students of Locke and political theory, but include those with special interest in the American founding, readers of philosophy and early modern history, bible study communities, Christians as well as Jews, laypeople as well as scholars.

I

Retrieving the Lost Honor of the *First Treatise*

I should not speak so plainly of a gentleman, long since past answering, had not the pulpit, of late years, publicly owned his doctrine, and made it the current divinity of the times. It is necessary those men, who taking on them to be teachers, have so dangerously misled others, should be openly shewed of what authority this their Patriarch is, whom they have so blindly followed, that so they may either retract what upon so ill grounds they have vented, and cannot be maintained; or else justify those principles which they preached up for gospel; though they had no better an author than an English courtier: for I should not have writ against Sir Robert, or taken the pains to shew his mistakes, inconsistencies, and want of (what he so much boasts of, and pretends wholly to build on) scripture-proofs, were there not men amongst us, who, by crying up his books, and espousing his doctrine, save me from the reproach of writing against a dead adversary. They have been so zealous in this point, that, if I have done him any wrong, I cannot hope they should spare me. I wish, where they have done the truth and the public wrong, they would be as ready to redress it, and allow its just weight to this reflection, viz. that there cannot be done a greater mischief to prince and people, than the propagating wrong notions concerning government; that so at last all times might not have reason to complain of the Drum Ecclesiastic. If any one, concerned really for truth, undertake the confutation of my Hypothesis, I promise him either to recant my mistake, upon fair conviction; or to answer his difficulties.
(From the preface to the *Two Treatises*)

John Locke developed his political theory at a time when the political constructs of much of Western Europe were beginning to metamorphose into forms unprecedented in human history. The Reformation had already torn apart time-weathered political paradigms that centered on the overbearing power of the Roman Catholic Church, resulting in protracted civic and political upheaval from which England was not spared.

Locke sought to mend resultant societal fissures with a revolutionary theory of consensual government.

England's "Glorious Revolution" began in October 1688 when William of Orange left the Dutch Republic and sailed for England accompanied by four hundred ships. In the weeks that followed, the regime of James II collapsed after his forces showed little interest in fighting,[1] and in February 1689, William and Mary were offered the crown of England after Parliament had completed setting a framework for the constitutional future of England. Locke, who had fled to Holland in 1683 to escape the dangers his revolutionary activities brought upon him, was now able to return to his homeland. Fearing that a reversal of the revolution that would return James II to the throne was a real possibility, he immediately began preparing his *Two Treatises* for publication upon his return. Hence his stated objective in publishing the *Two Treatises* was to serve and promote the revolution, as he explained on the first page:

To establish the throne of our great Restorer, our present king William, to make good his title, in the Consent of the people, and justify to the world, the people of England, whose love of their just and Natural Rights, with their resolution to preserve them, saved the Nation when it was on the very brink of Slavery and Ruine.[2]

The *Two Treatises* was authorized for publication on August 23, 1689, with the date 1690 on the cover-page, although Locke's opus actually appeared on sale in December 1689.[3] No author's name appeared on the

---

[1] There were some battles between James's loyalists and revolutionary forces, hence the appellation "bloodless" to the revolution is not entirely accurate. In addition, the "Williamite War" in Ireland cannot be discounted, nor the serious fighting that took place in Scotland. But relative to the English Civil War, which many English people could still remember, and other coups d'etat as they go, the "Glorious Revolution" was "relatively" bloodless. See Christopher Hill, *A Nation of Change and Novelty* (London: Routledge, 1990), pp. 100–101.

[2] Locke, *Two Treatises of Government*, p. 155. Peter Laslett makes the point that, historically speaking, Locke's fears that the revolution would ultimately fail were not unjustified as its legitimacy was subject to intense debate. See Laslett, "Introduction," in *Two Treatises*, p. 65. Elsewhere Locke expressed his fears in almost apocalyptic terms: "We have a war upon our hands of no small weight. We have a potent and vigilant enemy at our doors [who will] ... blow up any doubts or distrusts among us into disorder and confusion." If James were to return, "under what pretences soever, Jesuits must govern and France be our master." James Farr and Clayton Roberts, "John Locke on the Glorious Revolution: A Rediscovered Document," *The Historical Journal*, vol. 28 (Cambridge: Cambridge University Press, 1985), p. 386.

[3] An academic debate rages over when exactly Locke actually wrote the *Two Treatises*. Based upon a meticulous bibliographical and historical inquiry, Peter Laslett suggests that

book, and Locke never publicly acknowledged his authorship. In his own library, the *Two Treatises* was catalogued and placed on the bookshelves with anonymous authors. Locke was quite obsessive about keeping his identity as the author a secret, and the first time Locke did acknowledge his own authorship of the *Treatises* was in his will, written shortly before his death.[4] The second and third editions appeared in 1694 and 1698 respectively, and the fourth edition appeared after his death in 1704. A three-volume edition of Locke's collected works, including the *Two Treatises* printed for the first time under Locke's name, was published in 1713 and was reprinted at regular intervals throughout the nineteenth century. By the beginning of the twenty-first century, the *Two Treatises* had been printed in English more than one hundred times and translated into many different languages, including Arabic, Chinese, Czech, Danish, Dutch, Finnish, French, German, Greek, Hebrew[5], Hindi, Italian,

---

the *Second Treatise* was actually written before the *First*, sometime around 1679, and left unpublished. According to this account Locke left the manuscript of the *Second Treatise* behind when he left England for Holland in 1683 and recovered it upon his return in 1689. It was only prior to the publication of the book in 1689 that Locke wrote the *First Treatise* as a preface to the *Second* and added the introductory passages that were relevant to the Glorious Revolution. Laslett's theory is rejected by other scholars, who argue that both *Treatises* were written as one composition prior to the revolution, sometime around 1680, and then revised and expanded in 1689. It was during the time he spent in Holland that Locke lost more than half of the *First Treatise*. See Peter Laslett, "The English Revolution and Locke's Two Treatises of Government," *Cambridge Historical Journal* 12, 1 (1956), pp. 43–55. Laslett, "Introduction," pp. 3–6. Paul E. Sigmund argues that the *First Treatise* was written in 1680 and the *Second* in 1681–1682 with some updating taking place around the time of its publication. Paul E. Sigmund (ed.), *The Selected Political Writings of John Locke* (London: Norton & Co., 2005), p. xvi. With varying nuances most opinions agree with Sigmund. See Esmond S. de Beer, "Locke and English Liberalism: The Second Treatise of Government in Its Contemporary Setting," in *John Locke: Problems and Perspectives*, J. W. Yolton (ed.) (Cambridge: Cambridge University Press, 1969), pp. 34–36. George T. Manke, "A Research Note and Query on the Dating of Locke's Two Treatises," *Political Theory* 9, 4 (1981), pp. 547–550. J. R. Milton, "Dating Locke's Second Treatise," *History of Political Thought* 16 (1995), pp. 356–390. John W. Yolton, *A Locke Dictionary* (Oxford: Blackwell Publishers, 1993), p. 304. Roger Woolhouse, *Locke: A Biography* (Cambridge: Cambridge University Press, 2007), pp. 181–182, 275–276. John Marshall, *Resistance, Religion and Responsibility* (Cambridge: Cambridge University Press, 1994), pp. 114–118, 223–224. Charles D. Tarlton makes the significant point that even if Peter Laslett's hypothesis that the *First Treatise* was actually written only after the *Second* is correct, "it remains the case that Locke assembled and repeatedly published the two treatises in their particular arrangement." Charles D. Tarlton, "A Rope of Sand: Interpreting Locke's First Treatise of Government," *The Historical Journal* 21, 1 (1978), pp. 47–48.

[4] De Beer, "Locke and English Liberalism," p. 35.

[5] The first Hebrew translation was published in 1948 and the second in 1973, and both included only the *Second Treatise*. The *First Treatise* appeared in Hebrew for the first time

Japanese, Korean, Norwegian, Polish, Portuguese, Russian, Spanish, Swedish, Turkish, and Vietnamese.[6]

THREE SCHOOLS OF THOUGHT AND AN ENDURING ENIGMA

The last four decades have placed John Locke's political theory front, rear, and center in the debates over the essentialities of contemporary liberalism. The emergence of his writings from relative isolation following World War II was followed by the printing of Peter Laslett's critical edition of the *Two Treatises* in 1960. This was just in time for the politically tumultuous 1960s and 70s, heady years of academic debate that were defined by a revived interest in political philosophy, with Lockean liberalism at its fulcrum.

Two diametrically opposed interpretations of Locke's political theory have dominated Lockean scholarship for the past two generations, and both, I believe, do him injustice. One method of interpretation is broad and sweeping, positioning Locke as an avowed secularist whose relevance spans time and place. The other method sees a text written by a devoutly religious author and interprets Locke in a narrow contextualist fashion making him relevant only to his period. More recently a third school has emerged that is indicative of the moderating influence scholarly debate has had over time on both sides of the controversy, as it accepts both the religiosity and modern relevance of Lockean political theory. This last approach probably mirrors best how Locke was understood prior to the contentious investigations into his political philosophy in the second half of the twentieth century.

The first school, chronologically, was initiated by the writings of Leo Strauss, who has remained the predominant figure in this method of

---

in 2008, also as an independent tract. These two separate and partial Hebrew translations are indicative of the bifurcated approach most conventional Lockean scholarship takes toward Locke's political thought. In ignoring the fact that Locke repeatedly published both his *Treatises* together, and in the order in which they appeared, the natural and requisite interdependency of the *Two Treatises* is lost. I will return to this point in greater detail in the following pages. John Locke, *The Second Treatise of Government*, Joseph Ur (trans.) (Jerusalem: The Magness Press, 1973) [Hebrew]. John Locke, *The First Treatise of Government*, Shunamit Lifshitz (trans.) (Tel Aviv: Resling Publishing, 2008) [Hebrew].

[6] www.libraries.psu.edu/tas/locke/bib/lang.html. Laslett, "Introduction," pp. 12–13. J. R. Milton, "Locke, John (1632–1704)," in *Oxford Dictionary of National Biography* (Oxford: Oxford University Press, 2004). www.oxforddnb.com/view/article/16885. De Beer, "Locke and English Liberalism," pp. 34–35.

interpretation. In his landmark *Natural Right and History* (1953), Strauss asserted that Locke's "assumption of a state of nature ... is wholly alien to the Bible," creates a "tension" between his "natural law teaching and the New Testament," and is in fact "not identical with clear and plain meanings of the New Testament or scripture in general."[7] The "tension" he discerned between Locke and Christian revelation led Strauss to conclude that Locke, similar to great philosophers before him, wrote esoterically, with the true meaning of the text hidden between the lines. The impetus for promoting iconoclastic ideas in such a fashion, explained Strauss, was to both avoid persecution by governmental authorities, and prevent dangerous agitation among the masses. Strauss, who had already published this thesis with regard to the writings of Maimonides and Spinoza, argued that because Locke was in a predicament similar to that of his predecessors he chose the same literary tactic.[8]

This meant that the texts were intended exclusively for the savants of the generation who alone could understand which passages were written duplicitously, and this is precisely the method that the Straussian school of thought applies to Locke's use of the Bible in the *Two Treatises*. It is to deliberately conceal his heterodoxy that Locke hides "behind a façade of traditional phrases, ambiguous and designedly confused statements, and pious denials," writes Richard Cox.[9] Cox, who in his *Locke on War and Peace* (1960), "expanded and systemized the Strauss thesis,"[10] argues that Locke quotes the Bible not to draw on its authority, but only to create the impression that this is his agenda, when he really intends to negate its importance and follow a Hobbesian atheism in creating a radically secular view of man and government. According to this theory,

---

[7] Leo Strauss, *Natural Right and History* (Chicago, IL: University of Chicago Press, 1968), pp. 215, 216, 219. Strauss got it only half right and that has created more confusion than getting it all wrong. Locke's "natural law teaching" is in fact "not identical with clear and plain meanings of the New Testament" but is identical to, indeed derived from, "scripture in general": Hebraic Scripture that is, as will be shown as we proceed.

[8] Leo Strauss, *Persecution and the Art of Writing* (Glencoe, IL: The Free Press, 1952). In *Natural Right and History* Strauss writes, "[A]ccording to Locke, cautious speech is legitimate if unqualified frankness would hinder a noble work one is trying to achieve or expose one to persecution or endanger the public peace; and legitimate caution is perfectly compatible with going with the herd in one's outward professions or with using ambiguous language or with so involving one's sense that one cannot easily be understood." Strauss, *Natural Right and History*, pp. 208–209.

[9] Richard Cox, *Locke on War and Peace* (Oxford: Clarendon Press, 1960), p. 27.

[10] Michael Zuckert, *Launching Liberalism: On Lockean Political Philosophy* (Lawrence, KA: University Press of Kansas, 2002), p. 83.

it is only by making this argument that Locke remains relevant for modernity.

Almost four decades later, two of Strauss's important disciples marginally moderated their mentor's approach. In his important work *The Spirit of Modern Republicanism* (1988), Thomas Pangle departs from Strauss's focus on Hobbes and attributes instead Straussian relevance to Lockean theory for the American founding. But despite his differences with Strauss regarding the roots of American republicanism, Pangle remains unambiguous about a requisite Straussian reading of Locke.[11]

In *Launching Liberalism* (2002) and in his earlier work *Natural Rights and the New Republicanism* (1994), Michael Zuckert goes farther than Pangle in forging a newly polemical path through what remains a thoroughly Straussian theoretical field. Like Pangle he accepts the Straussian thesis of Lockean esotericism, but his critique of Strauss's contention that it was really Thomas Hobbes who fathered liberalism with Locke submitting an unoriginal contribution of secondary importance is more explicit and forceful. In addition to crediting Locke with theoretical primacy, Zuckert also goes much farther than Strauss in making Locke pivotally relevant for the evolution of the amalgam of concepts that are comprised by modern America. But on the issue of Locke's use of the Bible, Zuckert remains squarely in the Straussian camp.[12]

The second school of thought finds Strauss's interpretation of Locke far more "strange and striking" than Locke's own composition. It is not Strauss's foundational thesis advancing the notion of esotericism in

---

[11] For example, Pangle writes: "This has required in the first place a constant and careful attention to the many strange and striking things Locke says about the proper way in which a politic writer expresses himself in order to avoid persecution, achieve the greatest influence, and educate the few truly open minded and reflective readers. Only when one's reading is guided by these explicit clues does Locke's radical and shocking intrepidity begin to appear through his well-wrought veil of conventional sobriety and caution. It is then that the excitement, the greatness, and the provocative challenge of Locke as a thinker comes to sight." Thomas L. Pangle, *The Spirit of Modern Republicanism* (Chicago, IL: University of Chicago Press, 1988), p. 276.

[12] This is also the opinion of James Stoner, "Was Leo Strauss Wrong about John Locke?," *The Review of Politics* 66, 4 (2004), pp. 553–563.

See also Zuckert's defense of Strauss in Catherine and Michael Zuckert, *The Truth about Leo Strauss* (Chicago, IL: University of Chicago Press, 2006). See in particular the discussion of Strauss's theory of esotericism, pp. 115–155. Also worthy of mention is Fred Alford's observation that, "Of all the issues with which contemporary Straussians disagree with the master, and there are a number, none arises more frequently than Strauss's interpretation of Locke in *Natural Right and History*." Fred Alford, *Narrative, Nature, and the Natural Law* (New York: Palgrave Macmillan, 2010), p. 156.

political writing that is rejected, but rather his application of it to Locke. A basic historical contention of this school is that even if Locke wrote his political treatise at the time when his fellow Whig activists were being persecuted, or as in the case of Algernon Sidney, executed, he did not publish the tract until *after* the Glorious Revolution and in support of it. Hence he had no reason to fear either governmental persecution or uncontrollable popular passions and he had no reason to publish a document written in a fashion that would prevent general understanding of his political ideas.

This school belongs to the broader "contextualist" school of Cambridge, whose doyens, J. G. A. Pocock and Quentin Skinner argue for a patient and meticulous placing of revolutionary political texts in their strictly literary context and contemporaneous conventions.[13] In total contrast to the Straussians, scholars of the Lockean wing of the Cambridge School, led by John Dunn, present potent arguments to the effect that Locke had no deceptive intent whatsoever, but wrote in a fashion that complemented the period in which he lived and the context of the events he experienced. For Dunn, whose writings on Locke are probably the most influential in advancing the Cambridge School contextualist method of interpretation with regard to the *Two Treatises*, it is because of the Calvinism, and specifically Puritan roots, in Locke's family background that Locke's political discourse closely follows the theological language of his Calvinist contemporaries. In his classic work *The Political Thought of John Locke* (1969), Dunn argues that Locke was a deeply religious man and hence intended every Biblical quote he offered, but it is precisely for this reason that his writings are not relevant to modern-day political thought. Dunn sees in Locke's theses ideas that are exclusively of historical interest precisely because of his religiosity, precisely because his ideas contain intrinsic theological principles that are irrelevant to the modern world, and for that reason one might say, in Dunn's own words, that there is "more that is dead than alive in Locke."[14] On this point – Locke's contemporary irrelevance – Dunn is as strident as Strauss is about

---

[13] See in particular J. G. A. Pocock, *Politics, Language and Time: Essays on Political Thought and History* (New York: Antheneum, 1971), and Skinner, *Liberty before Liberalism*. For a good analysis of the fine differences between Pocock and Skinner, see Mark Bevir, "The Role of Contexts in Understanding Explanation," *Human Studies* 23, 4 (2000), pp. 395–411.

[14] Dunn, *The Political Thought of John Locke*. John Dunn, "What Is Living and What Is Dead in the Political Theory of John Locke," in *Interpreting Political Responsibility*,

Locke's esotericism when he writes that, "I simply cannot conceive of constructing an analysis of any issue in contemporary political theory around the affirmation or negation of anything which Locke says about political matters."[15] Despite their polar differences, both Strauss and Dunn ironically attribute esotericism to Locke: for Strauss it is esotericism in the sense of duplicitous ambiguity, and for Dunn it is esotericism in the sense of distant irrelevance.

Even prior to the formal rise of the Cambridge School, the mainstream milieu of Locke scholarship sharply rejected the Straussian method of interpreting Locke's *Two Treatises*, well demonstrated in a compendium of scholarly articles entitled *John Locke: Problems and Perspectives* (1969).[16] John W. Yolton, for example, argues that Strauss pays "minute attention" to the actual Lockean text, which results in a "violently distorted interpretation" of Locke's theory on natural law. Strauss's esotericism is "insupportable," posits Yolton, who in addition is startled by "the flimsiness of the pretended support and the unscholarly nature of Strauss's analysis."[17]

Another opponent of Strauss, Hans Aarsleff, contends that the Strauss/ Cox "concealment hypothesis rises to comic proportions" and deridingly suggests that, "One might as well argue that the Bible was not only read but indeed written by the devil for his own purposes." On a more reserved note, Aarsleff argues that, "It is much safer and infinitely more useful to argue from what a man does and says than from our opinion of the suspected reason for our view of his omissions."[18]

Two other Lockean scholars who reject Strauss's interpretation are Richard Ashcraft and James Tully, who both contextualize Locke in their specific areas of research. Ashcraft solidifies Locke's reputation as a revolutionary by elucidating Locke's critical role in English politics under the Restoration. While this makes Locke historically pivotal to the revolutionary events of the latter part of the seventeenth century, it severely

---

Essays: 1981–1989, John Dunn (ed.) (Princeton, NJ: Princeton University Press, 1990), pp. 9–25.

[15] Dunn, *The Political Thought of John Locke*, p. x.

[16] John W. Yolton (ed.), *John Locke: Problems and Perspectives* (Cambridge: Cambridge University Press, 1969).

[17] John W. Yolton, "Locke on the Law of Nature," *The Philosophical Review* 67, 4 (1958), p. 478.

[18] Hans Aarsleff, "Some Observations on Recent Locke Scholarship," in *John Locke: Problems and Perspectives*, pp. 264–266.

limits the *Two Treatises* to momentary significance. Concentrating more on Locke's economic influence and intending to counter C. B. Macpherson's attribution of "possessive individualism" to Locke, Tully shows how Locke articulated a defense of Whig landholding practices by emphasizing the responsibilities alongside the privileges anchored in the English law of estate. Again, this is a limited and limiting contextualization of Lockean political thought.[19]

It is important for students of this riveting Strauss/Cambridge donnybrook to bear in mind that while Strauss is a political theorist, the Cambridgers are historians, and it appears that Strauss and some of his disciples have strayed into Cambridge territory far more than the latter have invaded Strauss's theoretical breeding ground. But that having been said, the Cambridge containment policy of Locke appears no less extreme and exaggerated than the Straussian thesis. While Locke's influence on seventeenth-century English politics was undoubtedly less fettered with accumulated historical baggage than his influence on modern politics, a more epistemological approach would focus on the intergenerational discussion of ideas that span not only time, but cultures and civilizations as well. Locke was looking for answers to the same questions about human nature and its governance that Moses, Samuel, Jeremiah, Socrates, Plato, Aristotle, Livy, Augustine, Maimonides, and Aquinas all searched for, and, while it may be logical to suggest that the influence of their writings varies, with some bearing greater timelessness than others, it is not logical to argue that their ideas have no significance beyond their own times and immediate surroundings.

The same is true with regard to John Locke. One might contend that what he has to say about the limitations of power, or the maintenance of consensual government, or the right to revolution, or natural right, is less important than what others have to say. But for a student of ideas, the

---

[19] Richard Ashcraft, "Faith and Knowledge in Locke's Philosophy," in *John Locke: Problems and Perspectives*, pp. 194–223, and Richard Ashcraft, *The Revolutionary Politics of John Locke* (Cambridge: Cambridge University Press, 1987). James Tully, *A Discourse on Property: John Locke and His Adversaries* (Cambridge: Cambridge University Press, 1980), and James Tully, *An Approach to Political Philosophy: Locke in Contexts* (Cambridge: Cambridge University Press, 1993). Jeremy Rayner, "*An Approach to Political Philosophy: Locke in Contexts,* by James Tully," *Canadian Journal of Political Science* 27, 4 (1994), pp. 850–851. C. B. Macpherson, *Political Theory of Possessive Individualism* (Oxford: Clarendon Press, 1962).

suggestion that his thinking has no relevance in toto borders on the incomprehensible.[20]

Complicating matters further for followers of the Cambridge School is the modern resurgence of religion and its role in political life. This is as true of interreligious contentiousness as can be seen in the assault of radical Islam on the Christian West as it is of the intrareligious tensions apparent lately in the religiously cloaked primary campaigns of contenders for the US presidency as well as in regard to some controversial US Supreme Court rulings.

The problems with the Strauss and Cambridge interpretations have spurred the emergence of a third school of thought, which, while I have not seen it characterized as such in academic writing, exists in my opinion as a distinct interpretation of Locke at variance from both of those schools. I call this third approach the "Neo Traditionalist School"[21] because it embraces Strauss's advocacy of Lockean relevance while rejecting the Straussian thesis of obscurantism, and endorses Cambridge's attribution of religiosity to Locke but refuses to accept the extreme contextualist claim of irrelevance. This is a relatively new interpretation of Locke that has developed over recent years but is probably closer to a traditional intellectual approach to Locke that existed prior to Strauss's arrival on the academic scene. These scholars agree with the followers of the Cambridge School that Locke was a committed Christian who believed that human life and governance could not be understood without God and the nature of his interfacing with humankind. For them, Locke clearly drew many of his ideas from the Bible with no ulterior motive or hidden agenda because the Bible serves as a means through which God communicates with his creations. According to these scholars, Strauss miscalculated by a century, as the break with God and the debut of a Godless secularism was the product of the eighteenth century of Hume

---

[20] This point is succinctly made by Pierre Manent: "The political authors who are essential to our investigation, especially Thomas Hobbes, John Locke, and Jean-Jacques Rousseau, are only seen in the 'context' of their time, particularly the religion of their time, without any thought that a first rank mind could liberate itself from the conventions of its time, and think and will something completely novel ... Very often, therefore, those who today expound the great books understand them less well than those who burned them three centuries ago." Pierre Manent, "The Truth, Perhaps," in *Modern Liberty and Its Discontents*, Daniel J. Mahoney and Paul Senton (eds. and trans.) (Lanham, MD: Rowman & Littlefield, 1998), p. 35.

[21] The name I originally used for the third school was the "Eclectic" School. It was at the suggestion of Yoram Hazony, and with gratitude to him, that I chose the more apt dubbing of "Neo Traditionalist" School.

and Kant rather than the seventeenth century of Locke. For Locke, theology was still imperative for analytical justification of any explanation; ideas had to square with God's intentions.[22]

Yet, at the same time, proponents of the Neo Traditionalist School reject the notion that Locke's Biblical focus makes him irrelevant to the modern age. In their opinion, Locke is not to be understood only in a strict contextual sense since he intended to synthesize his Christianity with his ideas on consensual government, making those ideas timeless and relevant.

Jeremy Waldron is an exponent of this third school. In *God, Locke, and Equality*, Waldron is candid about his attempt to "build bridges between Locke's interest in basic equality and our own," and feels altogether comfortable in "lining up John Locke alongside an array of twentieth and twenty first century thinkers." Locke is of acute contemporary importance, suggests Waldron, because his "religious case for equality is that it promises not only to deepen our understanding of equality, but also to enrich our sense of what it is like to make a religious argument in politics." And finally, with slight admonishment for Cambridge thinking, Waldron warns that, "The historians will do well not to underestimate the philosophical agility (by our standards) of a John Locke."[23]

Greg Forster is another Lockean scholar who celebrates contemporary Lockean relevance without diminishing his commitment to scriptural sources and inspiration. The very purpose of his book *John Locke's Politics of Moral Consensus* "is to reintroduce the historically accurate Locke into the discourse of political theory, with his religious views intact, in a way that shows his continuing relevance to politics in our time," and consequentially, Forster is of the opinion that "the ideal separation between religion and politics simply cannot be sustained."[24]

---

[22] In *The Mind of John Locke*, Ian Harris writes: "Locke assumed that theology was important to explanation. That is to say that explanation, to be valid, had to show that it squared with God's intentions – either that it derived from them or was compatible with them ... The great breach with this model was the work of the next century when God was ushered out of reasoned explanation by Hume and Kant. But for the seventeenth century we should emphasize that the idea of God was explanatory." Ian Harris, *The Mind of John Locke: A Study of Political Theory in Its Intellectual Setting* (Cambridge: Cambridge University Press, 1994), p. 13.

[23] Waldron, *God, Locke, and Equality*, pp. 8–12.

[24] Greg Forster, *John Locke's Politics of Moral Consensus* (Cambridge: Cambridge University Press, 2005), pp. 4–5.

In his work *The Biblical Politics of John Locke,* Kim Ian Parker focuses on the syncretic relevance and religiosity of Locke's political thinking. He writes, for example, that Locke: "[C]reates a space for human activity within a world governed by a beneficent deity, a deity who is not interested in condemning humanity so much as directing it toward its own best interests ... Locke courageously sets human freedom on par with the freedom of God at the beginning. In fact, Locke legitimates action and the creation of independent agents. It is almost as if, in Locke's theology, God gave humans reason and left them to make the most of it."[25]

The arguments of this third school of thought are compelling as they solve most of the conundrums that the first two schools identify in each other. But there is one issue that remains enigmatic even for these thinkers and it is an enigma that, for the most part, is not lost on them. And, despite their efforts, no satisfactory solution is forthcoming. (I refer the reader back to the Introduction, where I record how Jeremy Waldron grappled with this question and ultimately admitted that he had not arrived at a satisfactory solution.) The enigma is simply thus: if Christian theology is indeed the backdrop for Locke's theory of consensual government, why then is practically no mention made of Jesus Christ throughout the *Two Treatises,* and why is the New Testament scarcely mentioned while copious references are made to the Old Testament? It is the attempt to solve this conundrum that necessitates the emergence of a fourth school: one that advocates a Hebraic reading of Locke's *Two Treatises.*

But before we go down the road of textual analysis to try and prove that point, it is imperative that we take a brief glance at the role Biblicism played in seventeenth-century English politics generally, in order to appreciate the fact that Locke's Hebraism did not emerge ex nihilo.

THE BIBLE IN SEVENTEENTH-CENTURY ENGLAND AND THE POLITICIZATION OF HEBRAISM

Locke's England was religiously pious. Most English people treated theology as the most serious of businesses and as "the queen of sciences."[26]

---

[25] Parker, *The Biblical Politics of John Locke,* p. 146.

[26] W. M. Spellman writes, "In a highly stratified, overwhelmingly rural and ignorant society where almost half the population was regularly underemployed and earning less than they consumed ... where sickness, death, and disaster were the granite-like constants of everyday life, the interpretive and consolatory role played by official religion was immense. And where natural science and medicine as yet offered no real solution to

Historian Herbert Butterfield writes that, "God was not a mere hypothesis and hell not a speculative affair, the question of right religion tended to be not only the most momentous but also the most immediately urgent thing in life."[27] Because God mediated through the Bible it became an integral part of the intellectual and spiritual life of the English people, making them in their own eyes "the people of the Bible."[28]

The fascination of the English people with the Bible at the time combined with a growing interest in matters that were connected to the Jewish world of ideas and events. This had quite a few historical dimensions, fostered primarily by the theological and political ruptures that the Reformation wrought. The popularization of the Bible in original Hebrew,[29] the glorification of Hebrew as a universal language, the enthusiasm of the Puritan Sabbatarians, the influence of Scripture on different currents of Protestant eschatology and Millennialism,[30] the debate over the lost ten tribes of Israel, the call for the return of Jews to England,[31]

man's daily sufferings, the recognized queen of the sciences, theology, provided men with a fully developed and highly credible interpretation of the whole of life's experiences." W. M. Spellman, *John Locke and the Problem of Depravity* (Oxford: Clarendon Press, 1988), pp. 27–28.

[27] See Herbert Butterfield, *Historical Development of the Principle of Toleration in British Life* (London: The Epworth Press, 1957), pp. 3–4.

[28] See Norman Sykes, "The Religion of the Protestants," in *The Cambridge History of the Bible: The West from the Reformation to the Present Day*, S. L. Greenslade (ed.) (Cambridge: Cambridge University Press, 1963), p. 175, and Christopher Hill, *The English Bible and the Seventeenth-Century Revolution* (London: Penguin Books, 1994), p. 440. Sykes makes the point that the Bible's functional centrality was nuanced: "For the many of the common people it became the source of doctrine and of worship ... the object of close and continuous study on the part of scholars as well as the vade-mecum of ordinary Christian laymen ... it became proof text for systems of government and an outline of knowledge ... in various fields of human interest, historical, geographical and cosmographical." Ibid, p. 175.

[29] David Katz writes that, "By the beginning of the seventeenth century, not only were Hebrew Bibles, grammars and lexicons circulating in England from across the channel, but also separate editions of the rabbinical commentaries, codes of law, Kabbalistic analyses, and Midrash and Talmudic texts." David Katz, *Philo-Semitism and the Readmission of the Jews to England 1603–1655* (Oxford: Clarendon Press, 1982), p. 11.

[30] See Robert M. Healey, "The Jew in Seventeenth-Century Protestant Thought," *Church History* 46, 1 (1977), pp. 74–77.

[31] All these matters are addressed in Katz, *Philo-Semitism and the Readmission of the Jews to England*. See also M. Wilensky, "The Royalist Position Concerning the Readmission of Jews in England," *The Jewish Quarterly Review* 41, 4 (1951), pp. 397–409.

and the interest in the Sabbatai Zevi affair[32] – all contributed to the rise of Hebraism in seventeenth-century England.[33]

Knowledge of the Hebrew language and familiarity with various Hebrew texts expanded at the universities beginning in the late sixteenth and early seventeenth centuries, abetted by the efforts of Jewish converts to Christianity such as John Immanuel Tremellius and the Polish-born Jew Philip Ferdinand, both Hebrew teachers at Cambridge.[34] With the growth of oriental studies at the time[35] came important scholars who stimulated the Hebraic academic effort as well. William Bedwell (1563–1632) was a scholar of Semitic languages and also an expert in Hebrew, both ancient and rabbinic.[36] Thomas Hyde (1636–1703) held a professorship in both Arabic and Hebrew at Oxford and translated a Persian version of the Pentateuch from Hebrew characters back into Persian ones.[37] Edward Pocoke (1604–1691) was known as "the finest European Arabist of his time," and was also well read in rabbinical writings.[38] Locke supposedly said of Pocoke that, "I do not remember

---

[32] Michael Mckeon, "Sabbatai Sevi in England," *AJS Review* 2 (1977), pp. 131–169. For an assessment of the widespread interest the Sabbatai Zevi affair generated in the British Isles, see Richard H. Popkin, "Three English Tellings of the Sabbatai Zevi Story," in *Jewish History*, Lloyd P. Gartner and Kenneth R. Stow (eds.) (Haifa: Haifa University Press, 1994), pp. 43–54, and Michael Heyd, "The 'Jewish Quaker': Christian Perceptions of Sabbatai Zevi as an Enthusiast," in *Hebraica Veritas? Christian Hebraists and the Study of Judaism in Early Modern Europe*, Allison P. Coudert and Jeffrey S. Shoulson (eds.) (Philadelphia, PA: University of Pennsylvania Press, 2004), pp. 234–265.

[33] As I formulated in the Introduction, by "Hebraism" I am referring to the reading of the original Biblical text as belonging to the historical and political experience of the Jewish people, while maintaining relevancy for all humankind through the political, economic, judicial, social, and cultural ideas ensconced within it. My overall focus is obviously on the specifically *political* ideas germane to the Hebraic text(s) that were resourced by Locke; here I'm interested in presenting a brief background of the attention Hebraism received in general in Locke's time.

[34] Katz, *Philo-Semitism and the Readmission of the Jews to England*, p. 11.

[35] About the rise of oriental studies in the seventeenth century, see G. J. Toomer, *Eastern Wisdom and Learning: The Study of Arabic in Seventeenth Century England* (Oxford: Oxford University Press, 1996).

[36] Alastair Hamilton, "Bedwell, William (1563–1632)," *Oxford Dictionary of National Biography* (Oxford: Oxford University Press, 2004, www.oxforddnb.com/view/article/1942).

[37] P. J. Marshall, "Hyde, Thomas (1636–1703)," *Oxford Dictionary of National Biography* (Oxford: Oxford University Press, 2004, www.oxforddnb.com/view/article/14336).

[38] G. J. Toomer, "Pocoke, Edward (1604–1691)," *Oxford Dictionary of National Biography* (Oxford: Oxford University Press, 2004, www.oxforddnb.com/view/article/22430).

that I saw in him any one action that I did, or could in my own mind, blame or think amiss in him."[39]

Pocoke had a son also named Edward Pocoke (1648–1726), who was tutored by Locke in Oxford. Locke and Pocoke junior remained lifelong friends, and one of the latter's scholarly works was a translation of the short treatise "Vessels of the Sanctuary," from Maimonides' *Mishneh Torah* (book 8.3).[40] Henry More and his pupil Anne Conway[41] (1631–1679) were two well-known seventeenth-century philosophers who were attracted to the esoteric and ramified world of Kabbalah.[42] More's close friend Francis Mercury van Helmont (1614–1698) edited the *Kabbala Denudata* (1677–1684), which was the largest collection of Lurianic Kabbalistic texts available to Christians at that time. Van Helmont also wrote *The Alphabet of Nature*, in which he argued for the "naturalness" of the Hebrew language, contending that "Hebrew was the divine language of creation in which words exactly expressed the essential natures of things."[43] Edward Bernard (1638–1696), a professor of astronomy at Oxford, learned Hebrew privately with Issac Abendana and, after mastering the language, made his contribution to Hebraic scholarship by editing the works of Josephus (1680).[44] Abendana (died 1699) was a book collector who secured Hebrew books for the Christian

[39] Richard I. Aaron, *John Locke* (Oxford: Clarendon Press, 1937), p. 5. Aaron is of the opinion that Pocoke had the profoundest of influences on Locke during his early days at Oxford.

[40] G. J. Toomer, "Pocoke, Edward (1648–1726)," *Oxford Dictionary of National Biography* (Oxford: Oxford University Press, 2004, www.oxforddnb.com/view/article/22431).

[41] Sarah Hutton, *Anne Conway: A Woman Philosopher* (Cambridge: Cambridge University Press, 2004).

[42] Aharon Lichtenstein, *Henry More: The Rational Theology of a Cambridge Platonist* (Cambridge, MA: Harvard University Press, 1962), p. 14.

[43] F. M. van Helmont, "Introduction," in *The Alphabet of Nature*, translated with an introduction and annotations by Allison P. Coudert & Taylor Case (Leiden and Boston, MA: Brill Publishing, 2007), p. xii. Van Helmont, who was born Catholic and imprisoned on charges of converting to Judaism, created his Kabbalistic brand of Christianity after an unsuccessful stint at Quakerism. "He was convinced that a union of the mystical teachings of the Jewish Kabbalah and Christianity offered the foundation for a truly universal religion that would embrace Catholics, Protestants, Jews, Moslems, and Pagans. This conviction is very much in evidence in his book on the natural Hebrew alphabet." Ibid. See also Allison P. Coudert, *The Impact of the Kabbalah in the Seventeenth Century: The Life and Thought of Francis Mercury Van Helmont, 1614–1698* (Leiden: Brill, 1998).

[44] Hugh de Queher, "Bernard, Edward (1638–1697)," *Oxford Dictionary of National Biography* (Oxford: Oxford University Press, 2004, www.oxforddnb.com/view/article/2240).

market, and worked at Cambridge translating the Mishnah into Latin (completed in 1679).[45]

Edmund Castell (1606–1686), an Arabic professor at Cambridge, published his lexicon *Heptaglotton Hebraicum, Chaldaicum, Syriacum, Samaritanum, Aethiopicum, Arabicum, et Persicum* (1669), a work that aimed to find the original Hebrew root of Semitic languages.[46] Castell and Thomas Hyde both helped the Biblicist Brian Walton (1600–1661) to prepare one of the great intellectual masterpieces of the time, the *Polyglot Bible* (1652), which included nine languages, among them, of course, Hebrew.[47]

As a churchman and scholar of rabbinical texts, John Lightfoot (1602–1675) was one of the most prominent English Hebraists. His primary works that illuminated different aspects of Biblical and rabbinical texts were *Erubhin, or Miscellanies, Christian and Judaical* (1629), *A Few and New Observations upon the Book of Genesis: the most of them certain; the rest, probable; all, harmless, strange and rarely heard of before* (1642), and *A Handful of Gleanings out of the Book of Exodus* (1643). Lightfoot contributed to Brian Walton's *Polyglot Bible* by drawing a map of Judea and providing notes from the Jerusalem Talmud. In his book *The Temple* (1649–1650), he displayed vast knowledge about archeological, historical, philological, and anthropological aspects of the Biblical era.[48]

John Selden (1584–1654) was the most prominent English Hebraic scholar in the seventeenth century. Selden, who was familiar with at least fifteen languages, worked throughout his life as a barrister in London and took great interest in legal history both in Europe and in England, writing many books in the fields of history and law.[49] The subject that drew most of his attention was the history of the Jews and their literature, both Biblical and rabbinic, throughout the ages. His enquiry led him into

---

[45] David S. Katz, "Abendana, Issac (died 1699)," *Oxford Dictionary of National Biography* (Oxford: Oxford University Press, 2004, www.oxforddnb.com/view/article/37091).

[46] G. J. Toomer, "Castell, Edmund (1606–1686)," *Oxford Dictionary of National Biography* (Oxford: Oxford University Press, 2004, www.oxforddnb.com/view/article/4865).

[47] Katz, *Philo-Semitism and the Readmission of the Jews to England*, pp. 12–13.

[48] Key E. Newton, "Lightfoot, John (1602–1675)," *Oxford Dictionary of National Biography* (Oxford: Oxford University Press, 2004, www.oxforddnb.com/view/article/16648).

[49] Paul Christianson, "Selden, John (1584–1654)," *Oxford Dictionary of National Biography* (Oxford: Oxford University Press, 2004, www.oxforddnb.com/view/article/25052).

expansive research of the Pentateuch, the Talmud, and medieval Jewish commentary. In *De Diis Syris* (1617), Selden drew from ancient Jewish writings as well as classic Jewish commentators such as Abraham ibn Ezra, Levi ben Gershon (Gersonides or Ralbag), Benjamin ben Jona, David Kimchi (Radak), Moses of Copucy, Solomon Yitzhaki (Rashi), and Maimonides.

Selden's magnum opus was *De Jure Naturali et Gentium juxta Disciplinam Ebraeorum* (1640). Comprising seven parts, Selden's book reduced the minimal behavioral requirements of humans to the seven laws, known as the Noachide laws, imposed by God first upon Adam and later upon Noah and his descendants. Selden believed that the Noachide laws represented divinely ordained natural law in the most precise format. He advanced the iconoclastic notion that as one of Shem's descendants (Noah had three sons: Shem, Ham, and Yefet), the Jews preserved the commandments of God more proficiently than any other nation or race. Hence, the rabbinic account of natural law according to Selden stood closer to God's original commandments than the fallible human traditions of other societies.

In *De Anno Civili et Calendario Veteris Ecclesiae seu Reipublicae Judaicae* (1644), Selden related how the lunar and the solar years shaped the rituals and annual festivals of the Jews. In the 622-page treatise *Uxor Ebraica* (1646), Selden examined the nature of marriage and divorce as discussed in the Torah, the Talmud, and the works of later Jewish exegetes. This book, which supported the right of divorce in England based on Jewish law, was to have a substantial influence on John Milton when he set out to advance the struggle to permit divorce in England. Selden's last work, *De Synedriis et Praefecturis Juridicis Veterum Ebraeorum* (1650–1655), was the most detailed of his Judaic works, and dealt with the ruling assembly of the great Sanhedrin and other judicial bodies of the ancient Hebrews.

There was a practical side to Selden that complemented his theoretical work as he was involved in English politics throughout his life, including a stint in Parliament where he was leader of the politically powerful Erastian Party and one of the most outspoken opponents of royal absolutism.[50] He used his extensive historical and juridical knowledge

---

[50] See J. P. Sommerville, *Royalists and Patriots: Politics and Ideology in England, 1603–1640*, 2nd Edition (London: Addison Wesley Publishing Company, 1999), p. 215, and G. P. Gooch, *English Democratic Ideas in the Seventeenth Century*, 2nd Edition (Cambridge: Cambridge University Press, 1954), p. 101.

to support constitutional monarchy and reformed religion. Selden fought against discretionary imprisonment, and was himself arrested by Charles I in 1629 because of his parliamentary responsibility for the tumultuous passage in the House of Commons of a resolution against the illegal levy of tonnage and poundage. Selden was no republican, but he believed that kings owed their power to a grant from the people and was a "staunch believer in the supremacy of the legislature over kingly prerogative or church centered theocracy,"[51] and his work "deeply influenced the deep-end use of Biblical essence in republican discourse."[52] His scholarship and political work were inspired by his belief that the Biblical commonwealth of the Jews was guided by God and was the first juridical state in history. Selden, through his Hebraic work, succeeded in bringing together pure academic scholarship and practical politics in a way that no one else had succeeded in doing up to that time.[53]

It is clear that along with the vast popularity of the Bible among the general English population, the world of English scholarship was rife with Jewish texts. The Mishnah, the Babylonian Talmud, the Jerusalem Talmud, the *Mishneh Torah*, Kabbalistic works, and the writings of Josephus were all an integral part of the literary arsenal of English Hebraists. Many of the products and by-products of this extensive academic effort can be recognized in John Locke's private library. Locke owned dozens of Biblical literary books, including Hebrew versions of the Old Testament, many publications of Biblical studies, several books on the Hebrew language, and a few books about Kabbalah.[54] As for specific Hebraic scholars, Locke owned a copy of Edward Pocoke's commentaries on the books of Hosea, Joel, and Micah[55] and quite a few of the Hebraic works of John Lightfoot and John Selden.[56]

What is of critical importance to emphasize is that this Biblical centrality was not limited to the theoretical. On the long English march from civil war to revolution that involved a deep rivalry between royalists on the one hand and republicans on the other, the holy book served as a source of inspiration and a political paradigm for both sides. Fania Oz-Salzberger suggests that two different levels of Biblical deployment can be identified. On one level, the Bible served political activists as an

---

[51] Ibid, p. 106.   [52] Oz-Salzberger, "Social Justice and the Right of the People," p. 14.

[53] Abraham Berkowitz, "John Selden and the Biblical Origins of the Modern International Political System," *Jewish Political Studies Review* 6, 1–2 (1993), pp. 27–47.

[54] John Harrison and Peter Laslett (eds.), *The Library of John Locke*, 2nd Edition (Oxford: Clarendon Press, 1971), pp. 293–294, 299.

[55] Ibid, p. 212.   [56] Ibid, pp. 174, 229.

"arsenal of quotations, picked and endlessly rehearsed for their rhetorical moving power." On a deeper level, the Bible was not just a "set of quotable phrases, but rather a political theory."[57] Both levels of practical political application, the quotable phrases and the political theory, were employed to the fullest by both sides in the political debate, the royalist and the republican.

THE PRESENCE OF THE HEBREW BIBLE IN SEVENTEENTH-CENTURY ENGLISH POLITICAL THOUGHT: THE ROYALIST CAUSE

The seventeenth-century English monarchs consistently saw their ascent to power as Biblical events and their reign as belonging to a Biblical narrative. King James I based his Divine Rights of Kings theory on the Decalogue's Fifth Commandment, and his son Charles I insisted that his coronation be seen as the making of a new Noah, Moses, or David.[58] On the day of the Stuart restoration in 1660, Charles II was presented with a copy of the Bible from the local mayor when he reached Dover, and responded to the gift by saying that the book was what he "valued above all things."[59] When the Whig struggle threateningly gathered steam in the late 70s and early 80s, the influential poet and supporter of the king John Dryden wrote his parody *Absalom and Achitophel* (1681), in which Charles II was portrayed as King David, and his opponents, the Duke of Monmouth and Lord Shaftesbury, appeared as the rebellious Biblical son Absalom and the evil advisor Achitophel respectively.[60]

Beyond these sporadic and generally symbolic examples of how the Bible was used in defense of monarchical absolutism, political and

---

[57] Oz-Salzberger, "Social Justice and the Right of the People," p. 2.

[58] G. Reedy, *The Bible and Reason: Anglicans and Scripture in the Late Seventeenth Century England* (Philadelphia, PA: University of Philadelphia Press, 1985), pp. 64–65. Charles was not the first English king to be identified with Biblical characters. The young Tudor King Edward VI (1547–1553), for example, was known in the English Protestant tradition as Good King Josiah. See Hill, *The English Bible and the Seventeenth-Century Revolution*, p. 49. Royalist employment of theological models also had a darker side. For example, Robert Wilcher documents how royalist literature compared Charles I to Christ and his detractors to Pontius Pilate and the Jews, claiming that just "as nothing but Christ's Crucifixion would pleas the Jewes of old so nothing by the Kings extinction will satisfie the malic of some in this Age." Robert Wilcher, *The Writing of Royalism 1628–1660* (Cambridge: Cambridge University Press, 2001), p. 269.

[59] Ibid, p. 30.

[60] Harold Fisch, *Jerusalem and Albion* (Tel Aviv: Bar Ilan University Press, 1964), pp. 178–179.

philosophical tracts were written in defense of the royal cause with major reliance on the Bible. Two important spokesmen for that effort, who understood Biblical text as political in nature, were Thomas Hobbes and Robert Filmer.

Thomas Hobbes (1588–1679), the son of a clergyman by the same name, earned his education in Magdalen Hall Oxford, during the first years of the seventeenth century. In those days, Magdalen Hall had a reputation as a stronghold of Puritan and Calvinistic theology. After his years in Oxford, Hobbes spent long periods of time as a tutor in aristocratic households and, simultaneously, his involvement in public or quasipublic affairs grew. Hobbes took several trips to the continent, and it is widely assumed that during one of his trips to Italy he met Galileo. In the early 1630s, Hobbes began to concern himself with philosophy, especially the analysis of religion, politics, and law, and it was during that time that he took deep interest in the writings of Machiavelli, Bodin, Grotius, and Descartes.[61]

During the 1630s, Hobbes participated in meetings of the Great Tew Circle, a group of learned literary men who gathered around Lord Falkland (Lucius Cary, the Second Viscount Falkland, 1610–1643) at his country house near Oxford to discuss such topics as theology, politics, philosophy, and literature. Deeply influenced by the Elizabethan theologian Richard Hooker, Erasmus, and Hugo Grotius, one scholar writes that the members of the Great Tew Circle "belonged to the Renaissance rather than the Reformation,"[62] as they represented a spirit of tolerance, independence, skepticism, critical reason, humanistic scholarship, and active virtue. Hobbes's early works were circulated in manuscript among members of the Great Tew Circle group, and he was a close friend of many of them including William Chillingworth, John Hales Waller, Edward Hyde, and the first Earl of Clarendon, Sidney Godolphin. Many of Hobbes's opinions diverged from those of the group at that time, but this does not seem to have disturbed their personal relations.[63]

[61] Noel Malcolm, "Hobbes, Thomas (1588–1679)," *Oxford Dictionary of National Biography* (Oxford: Oxford University Press, 2004, www.oxforddnb.com/view/article/13400).

[62] Paul G. Stanwood, "Community and Social Order in the Great Tew Circle," in *Literary Circles and Cultural Communities in Renaissance England*, Claude J. Summers and Ted-Larry Pebworth (eds.) (Columbia, MO: University of Missouri Press, 2000) p. 177.

[63] Hugo Trevor Roper, *Catholics, Anglicans and Puritans: Seventeenth Century Essays* (London: Secker & Warburg, 1987), pp. 166–230. M. L. Donnelly, "'The Great

Hobbes's first political work in print (1640) was a treatise in English named *The Elements of Law*, which began with an account of human psychology and went on to offer a powerful analysis of the origins (and the necessity) of the state, mounting into a strong defense of absolute royal authority.[64] From that moment on, Hobbes was known as a hard-line theorist of royal absolutism. When the troubles between Charles I and Parliament began in 1640, Hobbes's royalism came under fierce attack and he fled England for Paris, where he spent the following eleven years.[65] While in Paris, Hobbes worked on his most famous philosophical work, *Leviathan*. Published in English in 1651, *Leviathan* dealt with a gamut of political and religious issues and was obviously Hobbes's response to the anarchy and ongoing chaos he saw in the civil war and in the execution of King Charles I. *Leviathan* was an attempt to present a rational political structure, providing a true understanding of human nature and the requisite form that a secure and stable governmental order must take. Hobbes believed that appetites, desires, fears, and self-interests were the only real powers that motivated human beings. The true nature of all humans was to live only for themselves and to make sure that they survive in a harsh and brutal world. The only way to prevent the never-ending violent struggle for power that normally emerges from this human condition was a civil society that necessitated a powerful sovereign. Hobbes saw the sovereign as a great artificial fear-invoking monster, and believed that it was the only hope and the most effective measure for maintaining societal order and personal security.

In *Leviathan*, Hobbes examined the place of religion in society and concluded that the quest for governmental power had nothing to do with religious beliefs. Religion, he argued, had to be controlled by the state, and by giving the political leader all the power he needed to establish order and stability, Hobbes, in fact, promoted an absolute state. By ignoring any theological justification for power, he led the struggle for a secular concept of politics.[66] It has been reported that when the first Earl

Difference of Time': The Great Tew Circle and the Emergence of the Neoclassical Mode," in *Literary Circles and Cultural Communities in Renaissance England*, Claude J. Summers and Ted-Larry Pebworth (eds.) (Columbia, MO and London: University of Missouri, 2001), pp. 187–209.

[64] Malcolm, "Hobbes, Thomas (1588–1679)."   [65] Ibid.

[66] Thomas Hobbes, *Leviathan*, Richard Tuck (ed.) (Cambridge: Cambridge University Press, 1991). Lorberbaum, "Making Space for Leviathan, p. 83. See also Skinner, *Reason and Rhetoric in the Philosophy of Hobbes*.

of Clarendon, Hobbes's friend from the days of the Great Tew Circle, saw *Leviathan* for the first time, he was shocked by the dedication. The book was dedicated to the memory of one of the key members of the Great Tew Circle – the poet Sidney Godolphin – who had been killed in 1643. It was an insult, said Clarendon, to dedicate a pernicious and erroneous book like *Leviathan* to Godolphin, whose untimely death at the beginning of the conflict symbolized the extent the opposition members of the Great Tew Circle felt toward the very nature of governmental powers that Hobbes was advocating.[67]

The question, though, is why Hobbes chose to present a good deal of his theory of government through the use of Biblical quotations, examples, and ideas. According to Paul D. Cooke, Hobbes had a double aim in using the Bible. On the one hand, he tried to sustain the purely secular power of the sovereign with the prestige of religion, and, at the same time, he wanted to discredit Christianity and ultimately destroy it, while pretending to accept its authority.[68] Contrarily, Paul Dumouchel argues that Hobbes's reading of the Bible in the second half of *Leviathan* is fundamental to his philosophy and it "seeks to liberate the sovereign's authority from the necessity of religious legitimation, which is perceived by Hobbes as a danger to the stability of the commonwealth." According to Dumouchel, the aim of the second half of *Leviathan* (parts III and IV) is to show that Christianity provides historical and theological justification for the separation of the two realms of religion and politics.[69]

Ross Harrison argues that there is no need for God in Hobbes's civil science because it is based exclusively on reason;[70] nevertheless, he contends, Hobbes used the Bible for two reasons. The first was his personality: Hobbes wanted to study, know, and tell people about everything that could be known, whether it was matter, geometry, or theology. The second and more important reason was that the law of nature does not necessarily need God, but it can be established by the Biblical word of God, just as it can be established by human experience or reason.[71]

Suggesting that Hobbes's use of the Bible in *Leviathan* represents his messianic vision, Warren Zev Harvey posits that Hobbes must be featured prominently in the list of seventeenth-century English Hebraists. In

---

[67] Roper, *Catholics, Anglicans and Puritans*, pp. 185–186.
[68] Cooke, *Hobbes and Christianity*.
[69] Dumouchel, "The Political Problem of Religion", pp. 1–27. A. P. Martinich is also of the opinion that Hobbes did not intend his Biblical quotation subversively. Martinich, "The Bible and Protestantism in *Leviathan*," p. 389.
[70] Harrison, *Hobbes, Locke and Confusion's Masterpiece*, p. 59.   [71] Ibid, p. 61.

this vision, it is the task of Jesus to restore the Kingdom of God that was instituted by Moses and rejected by the Israelites when they chose Saul as king. Hobbes's messianic vision differed from his practical politics in that he argued for the absolute rule of a human monarch. Hobbes believed that the Jewish prophetic Kingdom of God was not a metaphorical kingdom but a real one, that it was a political kingdom, and that the ancient Jews who escaped the Egyptian bondage were the freest of all nations that chose the Kingdom of God. In contrast to his practical political thought, which argued for the absolute rule of a human monarch, Hobbes's messianic vision argued that if human beings were truly religious they would need no human sovereign.[72]

Robert Filmer's idea that divine rule of the royal patriarch was the only political formula possible appears unfathomable to the modern mind, but in fact, the ideas that Filmer expressed in *Patriarcha* enjoyed wide currency in seventeenth-century England.[73] The pivotal role that the Church played in influencing the thoughts and world views of individuals contributed greatly to this phenomenon. In its ubiquitous role of having something to say about all aspects of human endeavors, the Church's catechism asserted that ecclesiastical writings concerning politics were clear: the Fifth Commandment of the Decalogue was a direct order to all people to obey the king, just as they were obligated to obey their own father, master, teacher, or minister.[74] This was not a difficult concept for the Church to promote and the people to adopt, because of the strong historical foundation that the patriarchal concept had in English society – a society that was built upon many large English families led by a patriarch.[75] Consequently it was easy for this austere religious concept

---

[72] Harvey, "The Israelite Kingdom of God in Hobbes," pp. 310–327. For more about Hobbes's use of Scripture, see Reventlow, *The Authority of the Bible and the Rise of the Modern World*, pp. 208–222.

[73] Gordon Schochet writes, "It is well to keep in mind that in the late seventeenth century Filmer's theories generally escaped the ridicule they meet today." Gordon J. Schochet, *Patriarchalism in Political Thought: The Authoritarian Family and Political Speculation and Attitudes Especially in Seventeenth-Century England* (Oxford: Basil Blackwell, 1975), p. 120. And see Hill, *The English Bible and the Seventeenth Century Revolution*, p. 194.

[74] Schochet, *Patriarchalism in Political Thought*, pp. 6, 38, 40.

[75] "In pre-restoration England ... families tended to extend to large numbers, including older relatives, cousins, in-laws, servants, apprentices and the like." I. Kramnick, "Children's Literature and Bourgeois Ideology: Observations on Culture and Industrial Capitalism in the Later Eighteenth Century," in *Culture and Politics from Puritanism to the Enlightenment*, P. Zagorin (ed.) (California: University of California Press, 1980), p. 211.

to become the basis for the powerful political agenda that was Filmer's *patriarchalism*. But we will return to Filmer and his political theory shortly.

THE PRESENCE OF THE HEBREW BIBLE IN SEVENTEENTH-CENTURY ENGLISH POLITICAL THOUGHT: THE REPUBLICAN CAUSE

There was another side to the political influence that the Bible had on political agendas and to the seriousness with which the English treated religion. In accordance with this manner of thinking, many English people understood the political teachings of the Bible in a completely different way than the patriarchalists and divine rights theorists, and derived from the Bible a completely different political conclusion.

In his research on the role that the Bible played in seventeenth-century England, Christopher Hill shows how the Biblical text was the source of inspiration for the radical English Protestants in their struggle against the Anglican Church, which defended the absolute monarchy and the patriarchal concept. The Anglican Church had insisted that the masses could not understand the Bible by reading it alone, and worked to ensure that there was an educated clergyman in every parish who could explicate Scripture for the people, hand over the catechisms to the ignorant, and vigilantly try and guarantee that no mistakes were made in the way people understood the requisite religious and political lessons to be derived from the Bible. The Church obviously had a vested power-protecting interest in seeing to it that the divine right of the monarchy and the religion-based legitimacy of patriarchalism remained unchallenged.

The Protestant radicals who arose during the seventeenth century forcefully contested this approach, arguing that it was crucial that English Bibles should be permitted into the "poorest English houses," and that "the simplest man and woman" would "search the Scriptures" unassisted. According to the radicals, the lessons learned from the Biblical text proved that great change ought to be carried out against the monarchy, and against the notion of patriarchy that supported it, and that every English person was able to understand this for him- or herself. This vision advanced exponentially with the ever-increasing availability of popular written texts in the sixteenth century.[76] Obviously, the Protestant argument advocating every man and woman's right to read the Bible independently was not without political calculation. This calculation accompanied the Puritan call for new political and religious ideas as well as the anti-monarchical and revolutionary efforts of the Levellers and later the Whigs.[77] As a supporter of the monarchical cause, Hobbes recognized this threat and wrote in his history of the English Civil War, *Behemoth*, that, "after the Bible was translated into English, every man, nay, every boy and wench, that could read English, thought they spoke with God almighty, and understood the what said."[78]

And Hobbes was probably right. In this dramatically augmented availability of the Bible, and in the frequency with which it was read by all strata of society, lay the basis of the historical role that English Protestantism played in changing political paradigms, as the radical anti-royalist reading of the Bible went on for most of the seventeenth century. It was a world of manifestos and declarations in which for the most part the Hebrew Bible served as the main component in the arsenal of quotations in the service of the political cause. The destructive earthquake of Babylon and the restoration of Zion (taken from Jeremiah 51:24–25), the turning of the great mountain into a plain before Zerubbabel (Zechariah 4:7), and the shattering of the age-old mountains (Habakkuk 3:6) were all signs for opponents of Stuart rule in the first half of the century that great political change in their country was in the offing.[79] Rather than see him as Moses or David, the revolutionaries who opposed Charles I charged that he was more like the evil kings: Pharaoh, Saul, Ahab, Manasseh, Nebuchadnezzar, Absalom, Hazael, Omri, Ahaz, and even the post-Biblical king Herod.[80]

Cromwell himself drew his inspiration for the war against the king from Psalm 110: "He Shall be Judge among the heathen, he shall fill all with dead bodies and smite the head over great countries. He shall drink

[76] Hill, *The English Bible and the Seventeenth Century Revolution*, pp. 12–19, 34–35.

[77] G. E. Aylmer, *The Levellers in the English Revolution* (London: Thames and Hudson, 1975), pp. 71–73. And see Yehoshua Luria, *The Leveller Movement* (Tel Aviv: Poalim, 1978) [Hebrew].

[78] Thomas Hobbes, *Behemoth* (New York: Burt Franklin, 1963), p. 21.

[79] Hill, *The English Bible and the Seventeenth-Century Revolution*, p. 117.

[80] Ibid, p. 103. This was to repeat itself years later when Whig pamphleteers, clamoring against the potential ascension of James Duke of York to the throne, made him synonymous with Saul and Ahab, Judean kings who had abjured God. See John Callow, *The Making of King James II* (Gloucestershire: Sutton Publishing Ltd., 2000), p. 155.

out of the brook in the way, therefore shall he lift up his head."[81] To the Whig writer Samuel Pordage, who wrote his *Azariah and Hushai* (1682) as a riposte to Dryden's *Absalom and Achitophel* (1681), Charles II was a baneful king who "had not cast down Baal's priests, and cut down every grove." James II, who at that time was the Duke of York, was compared to Eliakim, the king of Judea, crowned by the evil Pharaoh. In the year of the Glorious Revolution, another opposition writer, Matthew Meade, compared James II to Abimelech, an example of a king who met a miserable death.[82]

In the arena of political philosophy, the liberal struggle was led by a few great writers; chief among them were John Milton, James Harrington, and Algernon Sidney. These thinkers reflect the role that the Bible played on the seventeenth-century English landscape and on a deeper level – that of the search for Biblical political theory.

In English history, John Milton (1608–1674) is mainly remembered for his great contribution to the world of English literature; he is considered to be one of the greatest writers of English prose and poetry of all times. But Milton's historical role in the shaping of radical political ideas was similarly dramatic, as he was an influential republican, a liberal thinker, a fierce opponent of absolute monarchy, and an advocate of civil liberties.[83]

In the years before the English Civil War, Milton wrote tracts of anti-Episcopal prose in the service of the Puritan and parliamentary cause. The main characters to come under attack by Milton were King Charles I and William Laud, the leader of the High Church Party of the Church of England and the Archbishop of Canterbury.[84] During the Civil War, Milton published his *Areopagitica*, a treatise condemning censorship, and after the parliamentary victory he published *The Tenure of Kings and Magistrates* (1649), a defense of republican principles and popular government. Milton's efforts were highly appreciated by the new English

---

[81] J. Buchan, *Cromwell* (London: Hodder & Stoughton, 1971), pp. 97–129. M. Ashley, *The Greatness of Oliver Cromwell* (New York: Collier, 1962), pp. 41–57.

[82] Hill, *The English Bible and the Seventeenth-Century Revolution*, pp. 108, 393.

[83] In the words of Hugo Trevor Roper: "John Milton cannot be separated from the Puritan revolution. That revolution filled his central years. It drew him away from literature, to which he had resolved to devote his life, distorted his career and transformed his poetry. It made him famous in Europe, and has made it difficult for posterity to judge him even as a poet." Roper, *Catholics, Anglicans and Puritans*, p. 231.

[84] Ibid, p. 249. Laud (1573–1645) was a strong supporter of King Charles I and was deeply committed to the belief in his divine rights. Hugo Trevor Roper goes so far as to compare Milton's harsh writings about the Anglican bishops to Hitler's hysterical hatred of the Jews. Ibid, p. 254.

government, and he was made Secretary for Foreign Tongues, a post that did not prevent him from continuing to produce pro-parliamentarian propaganda (*Pro Populo Anglicano Defensio*, 1652, and *Defensio Secunda*, 1654). He served as one of the main propagandists, certainly one of the most eloquent, of the Commonwealth idea, justifying the revolution in his political writings as a fulfillment of legitimate resistance based on natural law.

After the short-lived English Republic collapsed, Milton held on to his political beliefs. He attacked Erastianism, the idea that the state is responsible for the religious fidelity of its citizens, and argued instead for parliamentary supremacy and civil liberty (*On the New Forces of Conscience under the Long* Parliament, 1645; *A Treatise of Civil Power*; *A Letter to a Friend Concerning the Ruptures of the Commonwealth*; *The Ready and Easy Way to Establish a Free Commonwealth*, all published in 1659).[85] Milton's opposition to Erastianism set him apart from the other English Hebraists such as Selden and Harrington[86] who believed that, as in the Hebrew Commonwealth, the placing of ecclesiastical jurisdiction in the hands of civic authority would foster greater religious toleration, not

[85] Gordon Campbell, "Milton, John (1608–1674)," *Oxford Dictionary of National Biography* (Oxford: Oxford University Press, 2004, www.oxforddnb.com/view/article/18800). In his posthumously published *Explicato Gravissimae Quaetionis* (London, 1589) the German-Swiss theologian Thomas Erastus argued that religious offenses should be punished by civil authority rather than ecclesiastical authority in order to prevent what he saw as a potentially dangerous division of powers. Concomitantly, Erastus restricted his categorization of punishable offenses to a bare minimum, for which he was excommunicated from the new Presbyterian Church system on charges of Socinianism. Milton's *Treatise of Civil Power* came in response to the Savoy Declaration of 1658, which was based in large measure upon *Westminster Confession of Faith*, an Erastian document that used many Old Testament examples to justify civil power over ecclesiastical matters. Milton, while he leaned heavily on New Testament sources to support his anti-Erastianism, felt the need to reconcile the Old Testament texts used by the *Confession* in order to prove that his position did not contradict the Old Testament. See John Milton, "A Treatise of Civil Power," in *The Complete Prose of John Milton*, Revised Edition, vol. VII, 1659–1660 (New Haven, CT: Yale University Press, 1980), pp. 238–272, and William B. Hunter, Jr., preface and notes, ibid, pp. 29–237. Arthur E. Baker contends that Milton's opposition to Erastianism was the result of his "extreme" Puritanism, which brought him to oppose the Presbyterians and Independents as well. See Arthur E. Baker, *Milton and the Puritan Dilemma 1641–1660* (Toronto: University of Toronto Press, 1942, 1955), pp. 91, 228.

[86] Nelson, *The Hebrew Republic*, p. 111, *ft*. 115. For an illuminating discussion of the symbiotic relationship between Hebraism and Erastianism in promoting the rise of toleration, see Ibid, pp. 88–137. Locke followed Milton's anti-Erastianism; see Chapter 3, *ft*. 113, Chapter 5, *ft*. 217, Chapter 6, *ft*. 27.

lesson it. Once the Restoration began, Milton went into hiding, and was captured, briefly imprisoned, and finally pardoned.[87]

Milton's political involvement requires an examination of his poetry through a political prism, not only a literary one. Milton's great literary opuses, *Paradise Lost, Paradise Regained,* and *Samson Agonistes,* were written in the years 1658–1671 and expressed his personal despair at the failure of the revolution. A political reading of his literature would suggest that it was post-revolutionary England that was expelled from paradise and that it was both he himself, the individual freedom fighter, along with the entire English Kingdom that accepted the restoration of Charles II, who were blinded after long years of struggle, defeat, and failure. That having been said, upon pondering the conclusions of his masterpieces, it becomes evident that Milton held an optimistic belief in the abilities of the human race to return to paradise (*Paradise Regained*), despite all difficulties and despair.[88] For Milton, the struggle for liberalism and freedom was bound to succeed, a belief that turned him into one of the founding fathers of the Whig tradition.[89]

What can be gleaned from both his literary and political works is that Milton was deeply concerned with Semitic studies, the Hebrew Bible, and later rabbinical writings. These were important sources of knowledge and inspiration for him, and signs of Milton's use of Biblical sources can even be found in his early writings. In 1648, during the Civil War while Charles was still powerful and threatening, Milton wrote a verse-by-verse translation of a group of nine Psalms, chapters 80–88. The worried poet beseeched God: "Turn us again O Lord of Hosts ... Wilt thou be angry with us for ever?"[90] In his post-parliamentary victory treatise *The Tenure of Kings and Magistrates,* Milton used the following metaphors to describe his political ambitions for England: "there is a direct warrant from God to disembowel the king of Edom, throw the queen of Israel to the dogs, and hew the kings of the Amalekites in pieces before the Lord."[91] We can understand his vehemence when we appreciate that for Milton monarchy is identical with idolatry as defined by the Hebrew

---

[87] John Milton, "Introduction," in *Political Writings,* Martin Dzelzainis (ed.) (Cambridge: Cambridge University Press, 1991), pp. ix–xxv.

[88] Campbell, "Milton, John (1608–1674)."

[89] Roper, *Catholics, Anglicans and Puritans,* p. 233. See also Arthur E. Barker, *Milton and the Puritan Dilemma, 1641–1660* (Toronto: University of Toronto Press, 1964). Christopher Hill, *Milton and the English Revolution* (New York: Viking, 1977). A. N. Wilson, *The Life of John Milton* (Oxford: Oxford University Press, 1983).

[90] Roper, *Catholics, Anglicans and Puritans,* p. 264.   [91] Ibid, p. 266.

Bible, because it replaces the rule of God with that of man. "The union of monarchy and idolatry," writes Eric Nelson in his Hebraic analysis of *Paradise Lost*, "could not be more explicit; human kingship is always illegitimate because it is a sin."[92] It must be emphasized as well that Milton's use of Biblical references to make his case against monarchy should not be mistaken as being of a merely ornamental nature. As Fania Oz-Salzberger has made clear, Milton's use of the Bible throughout his work was critical for establishing a deep-rooted political and theological concept of civil government that was novel.[93]

James Harrington (1611–1677) grew up in a family of aristocracy and wealth, was educated at Trinity College, Oxford, but lived as a private scholar. Despite his friendship with Charles I, he was a republican and spokesman for the parliamentary cause.[94] Harrington was strongly influenced by both Machiavelli and Hobbes but forged his own independent political theory.[95] In his *The Commonwealth of Oceana* (1656) he

---

[92] Nelson, *The Hebrew Republic*, p. 46.

[93] Oz-Salzberger, "Social Justice and the Right of the People," pp. 19–23. Jeffery Shoulson writes that, "After the writers most commonly associated with the English Renaissance – Spencer, Sidney, Shakespeare – seemed to have embraced the classical values of Hellenism, along comes John Milton with all the zealotry of a Puritan preacher thundering forth on God's justice and Christian moral and religious duty. Hebraism, specifically the Hebraism of a Protestant Christian, finds its most eloquent advocate in the poet of *Paradise Lost*, *Paradise Regained* and *Samson Agonistes*." Jeffery S. Shoulson, *Milton and the Rabbis, Hebraism, Hellenism & Christianity* (New York: Columbia University Press, 2001), p. 2.

    Milton was a radical in his religious beliefs; his writings expressed deep religious feelings, but his ideas were far from mainstream Christian concepts. He rejected the Trinity, argued against the classical Augustinian interpretation of the Fall (to be discussed at length in Chapter 6), and believed, like the Socinians, that Jesus was not divine. See William Myers, *Milton and Free Will: An Essay in Criticism and Philosophy* (London: Croom Helm, 1987). William Poole, *Milton and the Idea of the Fall* (Cambridge: Cambridge University Press, 2005). Arthur Sewell, *A Study in Milton's Christian Doctrine* (Hamden, CT: Archon Books, 1967). For further examination of Milton's Hebraism, see Harold Fisch, *The Biblical Presence in Shakespeare, Milton and Blake* (Oxford: Clarendon Press, 2000), pp. 153–205. Harris Francis Fletcher, *Milton's Rabbinical Readings* (Urbana: University of Illinois Press, 1930). Harris Francis Fletcher, *The Use of the Bible in Milton's Prose* (New York: Haskell House Publishers, 1970). Rosenblatt, *Torah and Law in Paradise Lost*. James H. Sims and Leland Ryken (eds.), *Milton and Scriptural Tradition: The Bible into Poetry* (Columbia, MO: University of Missouri Press, 1984).

[94] H. M. Hopfl, "Harrington, James (1611–1677)," *Oxford Dictionary of National Biography* (Oxford: Oxford University Press, 2004, www.oxforddnb.com/view/article/12375).

[95] For an analysis of how Harrington both followed and differed from Machiavelli and Hobbes, see Gary Remer, "After Machiavelli and Hobbes: James Harrington's Commonwealth of Israel," *Hebraic Political Studies* 1, 4 (2006), pp. 440–461.

presents a blueprint for the ideal republic, an imaginary commonwealth dubbed Oceana, which is based on an assessment of the commonwealth of Israel. It calls for an anti-oligarchy parliamentarian system based on a large popular assembly and a system of checks and balances. While attacking Hobbes's *Leviathan*, Harrington argues for the establishment of a commonwealth with citizens who bear a right to legislate and determine social policy; it was, in essence, a plan for a government ruled by the people. And contrary to the anti-Erastian Milton, civic toleration was to be achieved not by separating ecclesiastical from civic jurisdiction, but as in the Hebrew Republic, by uniting jurisdictions and restricting mandatory religiosity while allowing for a wide spectrum of religious belief and practice. Israel's ancient republic as described in the Hebrew Bible was an exemplary one because its structure and dictates were God-given and hence, as Milton argues, infallible. The ultimate unwinding of the Hebrew Republic was due, argues Harrington, not to the imperfection of the polity's divine format but to the failure of the Jewish people to live up to its dictates, and the primary dictate was not to choose the rule of man over the dominion of God.

"They have not rejected thee, but they have rejected me that I should not reign over them." The government of the senate and the people is that only which is or can be the government of laws and not of men, and the government of laws and not of men is the government of God and not of men. "He that is for the government of laws is for the government of God, and he that is for the government of a man is for the government of beasts."[96]

Harrington took special interest in the history of the Old Testament. He was well-versed in contemporary neo-scholastic political theory, and he cited Grotius frequently in his writings, but Scripture stands saliently as his primary authority. Like Milton, he held John Selden in the highest esteem, calling him "the ablest Talmudist of our age or of any,"[97] and in his *The Prerogatives of Popular Government*, Harrington follows Selden's *De Synedriis* in holding up the Sanhedrin as the model for Parliament.[98] He testified, though, to his own limited knowledge of Hebrew and his reliance "for all that is talmudical" on "Selden, Grotius, and their quotations out of the rabbis."[99] In his later writings, *Aphorisms Political* (1659) and *The Rota, or, a Model of a Free State or Equall*

---

[96] Harrington, *Political Works*, p. 574.   [97] Ibid, p. 531.
[98] Rosenblatt, *Renaissance England's Chief Rabbi*, p. 6.
[99] Harrington, *Political Works*, p. 520.

Commonwealth (1660), he defended his interpretation of the Israelite commonwealth and its divine institution.[100] Harrington contends that the ancient Hebrew Commonwealth was a fully historical and political society, on the one hand, and an ideal and immortal society, on the other, which could and should be used as a model for desired civil society.[101]

Algernon Sidney (1623–1683) received much of his early education in France and was devoted to the struggle against the monarchy from a very young age. During the Civil War, he served in the parliamentarian forces, reaching the rank of colonel, and was at one time wounded in one of the battles. Yet it must be mentioned that despite his revolutionary politics, he opposed the execution of Charles I and disapproved of Cromwell's self-appointed post of Lord Protector.[102]

After several diplomatic missions, mainly in Holland and Rome, Sidney left for France after the Restoration and started writing against the restored English monarchy. His first tract, *Court Maxims*, was written in 1665–1666 but was not published until 1996. Predicating his arguments mainly on Grotian ideas, Sidney justified resistance to absolute authority in general and rebellion against Charles II specifically. The monarchical rule of Charles, Sidney wrote, is "the worst evil that can befall a nation."[103] In 1677, after a long exile in France, Sidney returned to England. His homecoming was prompted initially by his father's death and the need to tend to issues of the estate along with other claimants to the inheritance, but it was during his stay that Sidney started participating in politics. He ran as a candidate in parliamentary elections three times, and his ally in these campaigns was the Quaker William Penn.[104] Between 1681 and 1683, Sidney wrote his *Discourses Concerning Government*. Written as a polemical refutation to Filmer's *Patriarcha*, this was a work that had an exceptional impact in England, Europe, and America. The main ideals promoted by Sidney were liberty, reason, virtue, and the natural right of the people to rebellion.

---

[100] Rosenblatt, *Renaissance England's Chief Rabbi*, p. 6.
[101] Remer, "After Machiavelli and Hobbes," pp. 440–461. Oz-Salzberger, "Social Justice and the Right of the People," p. 18.
[102] Jonathan Scott, "Sidney, Algernon (1623–1683)," *Oxford Dictionary of National Biography* (Oxford: Oxford University Press, 2004, www.oxforddnb.com/view/article/25519). And see Jonathan Scott, *Algernon Sidney and the English Republic 1623–1677* (Cambridge: Cambridge University Press, 1988). Jonathan Scott, *Algernon Sidney and the Reformation Crisis 1677–1683* (Cambridge: Cambridge University Press, 1991).
[103] Scott, "Sidney, Algernon (1623–1683)."   [104] Ibid.

Sidney did not limit his ideas to mere political theory, but chose rather a course of radical political action, joining in 1683 with Lord Russell and the Duke of Monmouth in their treasonable Whig maneuvers against the king. In June of that year, Sidney was arrested and some of his writings were confiscated. In prison, Sidney was convinced that he would not in fact be convicted because there was only one witness of his alleged treason. His confidence, however, was a tragic miscalculation. In a famous ruling of the judge that determined that, "To write is to act," Sidney's own political writings were transformed into the second witness against him. On the morning of December 7, 1683, Sidney was beheaded on Tower Hill. Several days before his execution, Sidney wrote that his lifelong struggle was, "To uphold the common rights of mankind, the laws of this land and the true Protestant religion, against corrupt principles, arbitrary power and Popery."[105]

Sidney's Hebraism is most poignantly expressed in his *Court Maxims*, and it was in this book that he presented his version of revolutionary republicanism. The text, Oz-Salzberger writes, is a mixture of "classical and Biblical quotations, along with Machiavellian ideas and elements of the author's aristocratic education."[106] Sidney derived from the Bible that humans were required to use their own reason when attempting to follow the laws of God. This philosophical understanding of Biblical text had a political lesson: the Hebrew Bible that told the story of the Hebrew Republic contained general directives of proper governance for all humankind. Like Milton and Harrington, Sidney believed that monarchy was inherently evil because it necessarily devolves into tyranny and sidelines ultimate divine authority. The Israelite experience teaches that it is both the law of reason and the law of God that obligates total objection to tyrannical forms of government.

The Israelites sinned in desiring a king, let us be deterred by it. God foretold the misery that would follow if they persisted in their wickedness and guilt, and brought upon themselves the deserved punishment thereof. Let their guilt and punishment deter us, let us take warning though they would not. And if we have no communication with Satan, let us have none with those thrones which uphold that which he endeavors to set up against God.[107]

It was this Hebraic anti-monarchical notion that he used to refute Filmer's *Patriarcha* when he wrote his *Discourses Concerning Government*

---

[105] Ibid. [106] Oz-Salzberger, "Social Justice and the Right of the People," pp. 23–24.
[107] Algernon Sidney, *Court Maxims*, Hans Blom, Eco Haitsma Mulier, and Ronald Janse (eds.) (Cambridge: Cambridge University Press, 1996), p. 48.

(published fifteen years after his death).[108] Sidney's ideas were echoed, extended, and promulgated by the more famous and influential John Locke. At about the same time that Sidney was writing his *Discourses*, Locke was busy writing his *Two Treatises of Government*.

The fact that the *Two Treatises* is a text saturated with references to the Hebrew Bible as proof-texts should come then as no surprise when the presence of the Hebrew Bible in the writings of Locke's predecessors and contemporaries in seventeenth-century English politics is considered. But Locke's Hebraism was wider and deeper, and ultimately more influential.

FIRST TREATISE FIRST

Even a cursory reading of the *First Treatise of Government* makes it impossible to ignore the fact that it is a text laden with Biblical references. A more in-depth reading only intensifies the recognition that the quotes are not intended ornamentally, and are specifically, almost exclusively, from the Hebrew Bible. The *First Treatise* serves as a refutation of Robert Filmer's defense of absolute patriarchal monarchy as articulated in *Patriarcha*, and to which Locke feared England would slide back. Hence Locke's critique of Filmer's theory is uncharacteristically harsh. He asserts that, "there was never so much glib nonsense put together in well sounding English," and that he was "mightily surprised, that in a book, which was to provide chains for all man kind, I should find nothing but a rope of sand, useful perhaps, to such, whose skill and business it is to raise dust."[109]

---

[108] Ibid, p. 24.

[109] Locke, *Two Treatises*, p. 156. Many scholars agreed with Locke's derisive evaluation claiming that Filmer's work was "shockingly bad," "absurd," "unusual," and "irrelevant." Only after Peter Laslett published Filmer's political works in 1949 did a new recognition arise, arguing that Filmer held an important place in the development of Stuart political theory. But this new recognition was also not the final word on the issue, for another question arose: Was Filmer's work important standing on its own merits, or was it Locke's refutation that elevated it to an important status? And there is considerable disagreement on the matter. One school maintains that Filmer did not measure up to Hobbes in terms of his public or historical influence on behalf of the royalist cause, and that the only reason he was remembered was because Locke chose *Patriarcha* as the target for his attacks in his *Two Treatises*. A second school argues that Locke had good reason to choose Filmer as his ideological nemesis because of his popularity in Tory propaganda. Mark Goldie contends that, "Filmer's vision did not collapse at the Revolution, for it was rooted in the mentality of a generation of Tory gentlemen, clergy, and publicists, and it would take a generation to purge the effects of

There appears to be solid theoretical ground upon which to connect Robert Filmer's ideas with his life experiences. Born in 1588, Filmer was the oldest of eighteen children, who later married a bishop's daughter. He studied at Trinity College in Cambridge, where he did not receive a degree, but in the 1620s he began to publicly express his dour political opinions. His ideas mirrored those held by the high clergy in England during the decades before the Civil War, most of whom were also powerful, self-interested supporters of the Stuart kings.[110]

During the Civil War, Filmer was well-known as an ideological supporter of the king, and his eldest son, Edward, joined Charles's army. Filmer was in Kent when it fell into the hands of parliamentary forces, and in 1643 an order was issued for his imprisonment. He was subsequently incarcerated in Leeds Castle and released only when the first Civil War was over. During the 1640s, a number of books were published that debated the origins and limitations of both royal and parliamentary authority, and Filmer played an important role in this debate. In 1647, he published his first essay, *Of the Blasphemie against the Holy Ghost*, and in 1648 he published two more pamphlets called *Necessity of the Absolute Power of all Kings* and *The Anarchy of a Mixed or Limited Monarchy*. A book entitled *The Free Holders Inquest*, published under

the astonishingly thorough ideological monopoly held by the high Tories in the 1680's." Goldie, "Introduction," in *The Reception of Locke's Politics*, p. xxxiii. The fact that some other of Locke's contemporaries such as Algernon Sidney and James Tyrell felt the need to forcefully respond to Filmer strengthens the argument that Filmer's influence and historical significance stand on their own merits and were not simply an outcome of the gratuitous attention that Locke showed him. See especially Schochet, *Patriarchalism in Political Thought*, pp. 3–4, 115–158.

See also J. P. Sommerville, *Filmer, Patriarcha and Other Writings* (Cambridge: Cambridge University Press, 1991), pp. xv–xx. John Locke, *Two Treatises of Government*, T. I. Cook (ed.) (New York: Hafner Classics, 1947), p. x. Tarlton, "A Rope of Sand," p. 52.

Locke was apparently fond of the expression "rope of sand" as he used it again, many years later, in a response to the writing of a different intellectual nemesis of his, the Lord Bishop Stillingfleet.

"For I have seen men please themselves with deductions upon deductions, and spin consequences, it mattered not whether out of their own or other men's thoughts; which, when looked into, were visibly nothing but mere ropes of sand." "Mr. Locke's Reply to the Right Reverend the Lord Bishop of Worcester's Answer to His Third Letter," in *Works of John Locke*, vol. 3 (1696, http://oll.libertyfund.org/index.php?option=com_staticxt&staticfile=show.php%3Ftitle), p. 313.

[110] Glenn Burgess, "Filmer, Sir Robert (1588?–1653)," *Oxford Dictionary of National Biography* (Oxford: Oxford University Press, 2004, www.oxforddnb.com/view/article/94.com/view/article/9424).

the pseudonym Richard Royston, was probably authored by Filmer as well. These were all contributions to the royalist efforts to have Charles I return to power after the first stage of the war, efforts that with Charles's execution proved fruitless.[111]After the establishment of the common-wealth, Filmer lapsed into silence, but continued to take interest in the main political essays of the time, writing commentaries on Hobbes's *Leviathan* and on the works of John Milton in defense of England's new government. The following years saw more of Filmer's works in print that addressed a variety of topics such as witchcraft, the Sabbath, marriage, and adultery. The most political of his essays was the *Observa-tion upon Aristotle's Politiques Touching Forms of Government*, in which Filmer attempted to show that the Greek philosopher had favored the doctrine of royal absolutism.[112]

When Filmer died in May 1653, his writings were hardly known to the English public. Filmer's works only acquired popularity when they were republished in 1679–1680 at the time of the great ideological struggle between the Whigs and Tories regarding the Exclusion Bill Crisis. His most important work was *Patriarcha: A Defense of the Natural Power of Kings against the Unnatural Liberty of the People*, which he worked on for many years. It is likely that the entire work predated the Civil War, but it did not appear in print until 1680, twenty-seven years after Filmer died. When *Patriarcha* was finally published, it was intended as Tory propa-ganda and was used in support of Charles's augmentation of his absolut-ist rule. With the publication of *Patriarcha*, Filmer became the most extreme English political theorist using the theory of patriarchalism to support the absolute monarchy of Stuart rule, and, emphasizes Gordon Schochet, his "position very nearly became the official state ideolo-gy."[113]As such, this work attracted significant response from Whig sup-porters such as James Tyrell (*Patriarcha non Monarcha: The Patriarch Unmonarched*, published in 1681) and, as already mentioned, Algernon Sidney (*The Very Copy of a Paper Delivered to the Sheriff*, published in 1683, and *Discourses Concerning Government*, published in 1698).[114]

[111] Ibid.
[112] Sommerville, "Introduction," in *Filmer, Patriarcha and Other Writings*, pp. ix–xxiv.
[113] Schochet, *Patriarchalism in Political Thought*, p. 193. See Sommerville, "Introduction," pp. ix–xxiv, and Perez Zagorin, *A History of Political Thought in the English Revolution* (London: Routledge Kegan Paul, 1954), p. 189.
[114] Filmer was not the only political theorist who supported patriarchalism. Another famous advocate was Sir Thomas Smith, one of Queen Elizabeth's leading diplomats, who was, as Gordon Schochet writes, "The first Englishman who showed more than superficial

Filmer argued that kings derived their power directly from God. The first one to hold this power was the first man who ever lived, Adam, who passed it on to Noah, who in turn left the world to be ruled by his three sons. According to Filmer, all kings and governors in history inherited this authority from Noah's sons, and through the strength of this inheritance ruled over their families, servants, and populations. Filmer argued that the king who inherits his authority to rule from Adam himself is free from all human control and can do as he pleases; his control is absolute and arbitrary. There is no one who can take the king's power away from him or from his descendants, and this state is to continue until the end of the world.[115]

For Filmer, Scripture was an inviolable political authority, and as such a necessary ingredient in the formulation of political theory. In *Patriarcha*, Filmer frequently quotes the Bible and approaches it directly, a fact that caused other Tory writers and patriarchal apologists to rely "more heavily on the fatherly power of Adam, Noah, and the Hebrew patriarchs than they had in the past."[116] In his opinion, the most important political facts contained in Scripture occur in the opening pages of the Book of Genesis where the Bible records that God gave the world to the first man. This divine gift made Adam lord over the earth and gave his descendants the right of primogeniture. Ever since that first stage of history, through the beginning of a new human world after the flood and onward until seventeenth-century England, sovereign authority was attained through divinely granted fatherly authority. According to Filmer, this was an immutable religious and political concept.

Other main concepts that Filmer attempts to draw from the Bible in his *Patriarcha* are:

1) That males have superiority over females (based on Gen. 3:16).
2) That the eldest brother has the right to rule over his other brothers (based on Gen. 4:7).
3) That property, like authority, is entitled only to the sovereign (following the logical assumption that since Adam was granted all

---

familiarity with Aristotle's derivation of the entire social order from the primitive household." Schochet, *Patriarchalism in Political Thought*, p. 50. Other significant advocates were Richard Field in his book *Of the Church* (1606); James Ussher, the Archbishop of Armagh; John Buckeridge, the Bishop of Rochester; Lancelot Andrewes; Thomas Jackson; and Sir Edward Rodney. See Ibid, pp. 94, 112.
[115] Ibid, pp. 115–158.   [116] Ibid, p. 139.

the property of the world and since he was the only sovereign in the world, this must be a never-changing situation. Gen. 1:27–28).

4) That no individual is born free by nature, and that no individual holds the right of self-preservation.[117]

In his *First Treatise* Locke argues in tireless detail that, contrary to Filmer, kings and princes are just metaphorical fathers of their people, and are not their real fathers whom they are obligated to always blindly respect and obey. While Filmer wrote that rulers received their authority to rule directly from the dominion over the world that God gave to Adam, Locke responds that all people descended from Adam and no man can rule any other by claiming divine right.

Locke's *First Treatise of Government* is then an important document in its own right, but it is also central to understanding his overall theory of consensual government. No exegetical discussion of Locke's *Second Treatise* is possible without a thorough reading of the *First Treatise* and consistent referral to it. While it is only logical to assume that an author intends the treatises he writes to be read and understood in a defined sequence, Locke apparently does not want his readers to rely on reason alone to draw that conclusion and chooses instead to hammer the point home. On the title page of his *Two Treatises* he refers to the *First Treatise* as the "former" and the *Second Treatise* as the "latter," clearly two parts of one whole. "In the former the false principles and foundation of Sir Robert Filmer and his followers are detected and overthrown: the latter is an essay concerning the true original, extent, and end of civil government."[118] Echoing Psalmic complementarity, "depart from evil, and do good,"[119] Locke first "overthrows" what he believes to be "false" and goes on to present that which is "true." He then proceeds to remove any doubt regarding his intent of textual integrity by opening his preface to

[117] Sommerville, "Introduction," p. xxi. Parker, *The Biblical Politics of John Locke*, pp. 83–93. For more on the Biblical context of *Patriarcha*, see Hill, *The English Bible and the Seventeenth Century Revolution*, pp. 194–195.
   On a completely side note, I mention the interrelatedness between theological and political absolutism that Debora Kuller Shuger finds in the writings of seventeenth-century poet, preacher, and parliamentarian John Donne. "Both as strategy and substance, then, theology duplicates politics. Donne's God, his preaching, and his king are all analogously related, all participants in absolutist structures of domination and submission." Deborah Kuller Shuger, *Habits of Thought in the English Renaissance* (Los Angeles, CA: University of California Press, 1990), p. 209. An analysis of the same regarding Filmer, as well as other advocates of absolutism, would make a fascinating study.
[118] Locke, *Two Treatises*, p. 153.   [119] Psalms 34:15.

Retrieving the Lost Honor of the First Treatise   61

the *Two Treatises* with, "Thou hast here the beginning and end of a discourse concerning government." Without the *beginning*, there is no *end*.[120]

But this was not enough to convince many Locke scholars of the centrality of the *First Treatise* to Locke's theoretical construct of government. Charles D. Tarlton chidingly delineates three groups of scholars as they relate to the *First Treatise*: 1) Those who offer "some general and scattered examination as a minor chord," 2) Those whose assessments are "extremely brief" and "banish" it to the "depths of oblivion," and 3) Those who never "even mention the *First Treatise*."[121] Tarlton astutely asserts that "it is difficult to summon up an oversight anywhere in the history of political ideas to compare with the muteness, disregard and presumptuousness with which modern scholarship has approached the *First Treatise*."[122] He is right. Despite recent attention paid by some contemporary scholars, little has changed since Tarlton wrote this evaluation.[123]

It is the underlying assumption of this book that Locke wrote the *Two Treatises* with the intent that they be read in the order in which they were published, and likewise, understood in the same manner. Tarlton convincingly emphasizes that even if Peter Laslett's hypothesis that the *First Treatise* was actually written only after the *Second* is correct, "it remains the case that Locke assembled and repeatedly published the two treatises in their particular arrangement."[124]

---

[120] Locke, *Two Treatises*, p. 155. Gordon Schochet was one of the first contemporary scholars to stress the integrity of the *Two Treatises*. "What must be equally understood is that the very logic and structure of the whole of the *Two Treatises* were responses to Filmer. Only through such a realization is it possible both to appreciate Locke's interest in certain problems and to grasp the implications of some of the very fine distinctions that he drew. By looking at his analysis of the relationship between political and paternal authority in these terms, we are able to see how much of Locke's argument was shaped by the need to answer Filmer and to understand the kind of political theory that could serve as an adequate alternative to moral patriarchalism." Schochet, *Patriarchalism in Political Thought*, p. 244.

[121] Tarlton, "A Rope of Sand," pp. 44–47.   [122] Ibid.

[123] Some recent scholarship has begun to pay more attention to the *First Treatise* and treat it as an important text worthy of deciphering. A few good examples are the works of Parker, *The Biblical Politics of John Locke*; Waldron, *God, Locke, and Equality*; and Harris, *The Mind of John Locke*.

[124] Tarlton, "A Rope of Sand," pp. 47–48. Ian Harris cogently explains the *Treatises'* complementary nature thus: "The first of the Two Treatises dealt primarily in arguments about scripture and his second in reason, though Locke deployed both media in each. He criticized absolutism and developed his alternative *pari passu*. For in his attack on Filmer throughout the first book Locke laid down several premises from which his own

What motivated Locke to couch his refutation of patriarchal absolutism in a polemic against its representative may have been the need to make his radical ideas more palatable for his contemporaries. It is ironic that it is precisely this pedagogic approach that made reading his refutation so "tedious" and difficult for moderns. But we must not confuse style and structure with content. The sum and substance of the *First Treatise* include foundational ideas such as natural freedom, the meaning of creation, the meaning of human life, charity, free will, intelligent design, morality, reason and revelation, human potential, forms of government, crime and punishment, war and peace, issues regarding the family nuclei, primogeniture, cannibalism, capital punishment, priesthood, and Biblical hermeneutics. These concepts are central, indeed indispensable, to Locke's political thinking.

Upon what did Locke base his thinking and how did he present it?

Locke begins the *First Treatise* with a quote from the New Testament Book of Hebrews, ends it with an overview of the nature of government of "God's peculiar People" from the time of Egyptian bondage until the Roman destruction of the Second Temple,[125] and in between quotes the

argument about civil government in the second proceeded, whilst that argument itself offered an alternative to the devices of absolutism by explaining another sort of government. The two books of Two Treatises of Government form a continuous treatment of Locke's theme ... They are not merely complementary in subject matter, but also in their manner of treating it. For Locke's First Treatise provided a description of God's purposes which provides a large part of the basis of the Second Treatise. The First is usually conceived as a refutation of one explanation of absolutism, and a rather tedious one at that. This judgment of tedium perhaps obscures the fact that the manner in which Locke executed his attack on Filmer's view of political superiority involved also the rebuttal of Filmer's view of God's purposes: and therefore brought a relocation of His intentions and, conformably, a new explanation of superiority." Harris, *The Mind of John Locke*, pp. 210–211.

Tarlton quotes Herbert H. Rowen, who echoes the imperativeness of the *First Treatise*. "Locke's First Treatise turns out to be an essential portion of his total argument on behalf of the social compact state, and against the dynastic (and potentially absolute) state. Though its argument is negative, the First Treatise is necessary to Locke's major, positive work in the Second Treatise because it clears and defines the ground for it. It therefore deserves more attention than has usually been given to it." Tarlton, "A Rope of Sand," p. 43. See also Herbert H. Rowen, "A Second Thought on Locke's First Treatise," *Journal of the History of Ideas* 17, 1 (1956), pp. 130–132.

[125] I, 168–169, pp. 280–281. Because the latter portion of the *First Treatise* was lost we cannot know exactly how Locke originally intended to conclude his text, but that should not prevent commentary on the text we have before us.

Hebrew Bible more than eighty times.[126] This copious appeal to Hebrew Scripture together with the near total absence of quotes from the New Testament, as well as the total absence of any reference to Christ through-out the *Treatises*, necessarily arouse our attention to the possibility of a requisite Hebraic reading of the text.

There are times when plentiful also means meaningful, instances when quantitative use is also indicative of qualitative intent. Locke was not required to use the Hebrew Bible as extensively as he did if his intent was duplicitous, if, as the school founded by Leo Strauss would have us believe, he really meant to negate Biblical authority in order to present a radically secular philosophy. Such a purpose would have been more cleverly and successfully accomplished if Locke would have limited scrip-tural quotes to no more than the extent that Filmer used the Bible in his *Patriarcha*, and by leaving the use of reason to stand on its own, rather than constantly and consistently juxtaposing it with Biblical revelation.[127] His most potent arguments would still have remained between the lines for exclusive deciphering by intellects and the esoterically inclined. There are simply too many Biblical references in Locke's *Treatises* to argue that Locke meant to undermine the Bible's legitimacy. The possibility that Locke would have forcefully rejected his successors of the Scottish enlight-enment who dethroned God in the public arena, rather than view them as his own natural intellectual heirs, is something the Straussians refuse to entertain.

Clearly, this inescapable fact influenced the thinkers of the Cambridge School and helped lead them to the conclusion that Locke intended every word of the Bible he quoted to be an integral part of his thesis. The cost of this conclusion, though, was to contextualize Locke and depreciate his value as a philosopher by confining his relevance to a very limited time and place. The possibility that Locke intended his political theories to be timeless, while remaining religiously anchored, seems to have escaped their attention.

The reason then that the downplaying and discrediting of the *First Treatise* is as ubiquitous as Tarlton has shown is because it is actually the only issue that unites the Strauss and Cambridge Schools of thought. For

---

[126] See Waldron, *God, Locke, and Equality*, p. 189. Cox, *Locke on War and Peace*, p. 39, *ft*. 2. Arriving at an exact, universally agreed-upon number of Biblical quotations depends on the criteria used for quantification as some quotes are used repetitively and others appear in the context of larger quotations, such as those of Filmer.

[127] As I noted in the Introduction to this thesis, Jeremy Waldron counts 6 pages of Biblical quotes in Filmer versus 120 in Locke. See Introduction, *fts*. 34, 35, 36, 37.

the Straussians, it is the sheer quantity of Biblical sources that makes it intellectually untenable to argue that Locke meant to denigrate the authority or even relevance of religion, revelation, and God to civil society. Richard Cox attempts to escape this quandary by positing that Locke created the *Two Treatises* in a way that showed a gradual depletion of Biblical sources. Not only does the *Second Treatise* contain fewer Biblical sources than the *First*, but within the *Second* as well there is, in his estimate, an incremental decline in the referencing of Biblical sources, with the first half containing more than the second half.[128] However, Cox's view is possible only if the *First Treatise* is minimized exclusively as a riposte to Filmer, and not seen as the foundation of Locke's arguments in the *Second Treatise*, for a theoretical basis is intended to remain ever-present and always relevant once it has been unambiguously articulated, even if it is not constantly and consistently repeated.

To the followers of the Cambridge School, the *First Treatise* presents a different problem. It is not the resourcing of the Bible that they have a need to suppress, but the near exclusive use of the *Hebrew* Bible. The fact that Locke refrained from using New Testament Scriptures in both *Treatises*, choosing instead to quote so copiously from the Hebrew Bible, ties the notion that Locke was writing from a Christological vantage point in theoretical knots. To ignore, or at least downplay, the significance of the *First Treatise* is the natural outcome.

The Strauss and Cambridge Schools are in fact united on a deeper level. Both agree that New Testamentism does not provide sources for governmental authority and does not recommend any preferred form of governmental authority. The Straussian solution for Locke's Biblical quotations is to keep Locke relevant by throwing out the significance of the Bible. Followers of the Cambridge School solve the problem by discarding the significance of Locke. Both overlook the fact that Locke himself specifically stated that he did not find a theory of government in Christian sources.

In his early political treatise, *Two Tracts on Government*, Locke wrote:

[T]he New Testament nowhere makes any mention of the controlling or limiting of the magistrate's authority since no precept appointed for the civil magistrate appears either in the gospel or in the Epistles. In truth it is for the most part silent as to governmental and civil power, or rather Christ himself, often lighting on occasions of discussing this matter, seems to refuse deliberately to involve himself

---

[128] See Cox, *Locke on War and Peace*, pp. 53, 86–88.

in civil affairs and, not owning any kingdom but the divine spiritual one as his own, he let the civil government of the commonwealth go be unchanged.[129]

Locke's use of the Bible then, the *Hebrew* Bible, must have been because he *did* find in it a theory of applied government that could be emulated.

[T]he Scripture speaks very little of polities [i.e., politics] anywhere (except only the government of the Jews constituted by God himself over which he had a particular care) and God doth nowhere by distinct and particular prescriptions set down rules of governments and bounds to the magistrate's authority.[130]

Were the two main schools of Lockean thought to have recognized the concept of political Hebraism, and specifically Locke's appreciation of it, they might have actually ended up agreeing on the nature and relevance of Locke's political philosophy. Followers of the Cambridge School would have agreed that Locke is still relevant, and Straussians would have had no choice but to accept that his relevance is dependent on, rather than devoid of, religious underpinnings. Recognizing that the Hebrew Bible is imperative for the *First Treatise*, and that the *First Treatise* is imperative for the *Second*, both would have agreed that without the Hebrew Bible, Locke's theory of moral government would be impossible. And that, even prior to an analysis of the extensive use of the Hebrew Bible in the *Second Treatise* itself.

CONTINUUM AND DEPENDENCE: *WHO HEIR?*

We can now get more specific. Locke begins the first chapter of his *Second Treatise* with a brief synopsis of the central arguments that he presents in the *First Treatise* against the theory of governmental absolutism advanced by Filmer's *Patriarcha*. This is also a clear indication of the textual dependency of the *Second Treatise* upon the *First*. Locke's synopsis includes four points:

1) That Adam had not, either by natural right of fatherhood or by positive donation from God, any such authority over his children or dominion over the world as is pretended.
2) That if he had, his heirs yet had no right to it.

---

[129] John Locke, *Second Tract on Government*, in *Locke: Political Essays*, Mark Goldie (ed.) (Cambridge: Cambridge University Press, 1997, 2006), p. 72.
[130] Ibid, p. 51.

3) That if his heirs had, there being no law of nature nor positive law of God that determines which is the right heir in all cases that may arise, the right of succession, and consequently of bearing rule, could not have been certainly determined.

4) That if even that had been determined, yet the knowledge of which is the eldest line of Adam's posterity being so long since utterly lost, that in the races of mankind and families of the world there remains not to one above another the least pretense to be the eldest house, and to have the right of inheritance.[131]

If the first point is proven, there is clearly no need to use further argumentation, and indeed Locke spends the first seven chapters of the *First Treatise* (there are a total of eleven) refuting Filmer's understanding of Adamic political power. In actuality, Locke's addressing of this issue is much more exhaustive, as his last chapter, "Who Heir?," mainly reverts back to the issue of original dominion as well. Nevertheless, like a good litigator clinching his or her case through the use of alternative reasoning, Locke asserts that even if primary arguments are to be conceded, the opposing case is weak on all grounds and cannot, in the end, be substantiated.[132]

In order to understand what teachings John Locke found in the Hebrew Bible that were primary to his political theory, I believe, somewhat counterintuitively perhaps, that the place to begin is here, with the last chapter of the *First Treatise*. It is far and away the longest of the *First Treatise* chapters, it repeats many of the arguments made in previous chapters, and it is the chapter that links us to the *Second Treatise*. It is also the chapter especially rife with eclectic references to the Hebrew Bible, which make, or at least should make, standard interpreters of Locke's *Two Treatises* uncomfortable.

---

[131] II, 1, p. 285.
[132] Jeremy Waldron writes, "But his strategy in the First Treatise is that of a lawyer – resisting each step in his opponent's argument, by showing successively that even if the previous step is conceded, the next step does not follow, and so on." Waldron, *God, Locke, and Equality*, p. 178. Daniel Carey makes a similar observation regarding Locke's literary approach in relation to his discussion of "innatism" in the *Essay*. First, suggests Carey, Locke militates against the notion of "universal consent" and then argues that even if there were grounds to grant such consent, it would still not prove innatism. See Daniel Carey, *Locke, Shaftesbury, and Hutcheson: Contesting Diversity in the Enlightenment and Beyond* (Cambridge: Cambridge University Press, 2009), pp. 69–97.

Locke begins by stressing the imperativeness of determining *who* it is that should have political power rather than ignoring qualifying determinants as does Filmer, who focuses entirely on *where* power comes from. To concentrate exclusively on the latter is to choose anarchy and chaos.

What can this do but set Men on the more eagerly to scramble, and so lay a sure and lasting Foundation of endless Contention and Disorder, instead of that Peace and Tranquility, which is the business of Government, and the end of Humane Society.[133]

If Filmer were right, and "the *Assignment of Civil Power be by Divine Institution* " and "*Adam's Heir* be he" "to whom it is thus Assigned," then it would be a "Sacriledge for any one to be King, who was not *Adam* 's Heir." And this Locke deduces from the Jews and their Bible with regard to the divine institution of the priesthood.

Amongst the *Jews*, for any one to have been *Priest*, who had not been of *Aarons* Posterity: For *not only* the Priesthood *in general being by Divine Institution, but the Assignment of it* to the Sole Line and Posterity of *Aaron*, made it impossible to be enjoy'd or exercised by any one, but those Persons, who are the Off-spring of *Aaron*: whose Succession therefore was carefully observed, and by that the Persons who had a Right to the Priesthood certainly known.[134]

In other words, Locke is not willing to accept the potential existence of an alternative paradigm for succession other than the one presented by the Hebrew Bible, for otherwise why would priestly succession, as described by the Bible, be the litmus test for monarchical succession?

What passes along with succession, Filmer posits, is the total domination by the successor of all others. But while it is to be acknowledged that a father has some degree of power over his children, says Locke, what Filmer needs to prove is that an elder brother inherits that power rather than just limited material benefits, especially because the Hebrew Bible suggests otherwise.

The Law of *Moses* gave a double Portion of the Goods and Possessions to the Eldest, but we find not any where that naturally, or by *God's Institution*, Superiority or Dominion belong'd to him, and the Instances there brought by our *Author* are but slender Proofs of a Right to Civil Power and Dominion in the First-born, and do rather shew the contrary.[135]

---

[133] I, 106, p. 237.   [134] I, 107, p. 237.   [135] I, 111, p. 240.

The scriptural proof that Filmer offers is the verse in Genesis (4:7) in which God told Cain of his brother Abel that "his desire shall be Subject unto thee, and thou shalt Rule over him." To read this verse as the granting of a full and supreme right of fatherhood to Cain over his brother Abel is wrong for three reasons, Locke argues. First, the words of the verse "are conditional: *If thou dost well* and so personal to *Cain*, and whatever was signified by them, did depend on his Carriage and not follow his Birth-right." That means that the grant could "by no means be an Establishment of Dominion in the First-born in general." Even prior to the grant, "*Abel* had his *distinct Territories by Right of Private Dominion*," which he could not have had to the prejudice of the heirs title, "*If by Divine Institution, Cain* as Heir were to inherit all his Father's Dominion." Second, Adam had already given birth to additional sons at the time of this grant. "If it was intended by God as the Charter of Primogeniture, and the Grant of Dominion to Elder Brothers in general as such, by Right of Inheritance," then it should have included all his brethren and not just Abel. And last, with reasoning indicative of Locke's opinion of how Scripture is to be read, he argues that this verse is too "doubtful and obscure a place in Scripture" in order to "build a Doctrine of so mighty consequence ... especially when there is nothing else in Scripture or Reason to be found, that favours or supports it."[136] The verse, in fact, Locke goes on to say later, is not referring to Abel at all, but to *sin*. It is sin and the evil inclination that the text is referring to when it says, "thou shalt Rule over him."

God tells *Cain*, Gen. 4. That however sin might set upon him, he ought or might be Master of it: For the most Learned Interpreters understand the words of sin, and not of *Abel*, and give so strong Reasons for it, that nothing can convincingly be inferr'd from so doubtful a text, to our *Author*'s purpose.[137]

Filmer also argues his position based on Isaac's blessing of Jacob, "be Lord over thy Brethren, and let the Sons of thy Mother bow before thee" (Gen. 27:29), and this too meets with three counterattacks. First, Filmer himself acknowledges that "*Jacob bought his Brothers Birth-right*," which must mean that dominion is not a birthright, "unless buying and selling be no compact." Second, Filmer creates the mistaken impression

---

[136] I, 112, pp. 240–241.
[137] I, 118, p. 245. As I will discuss at length in Chapter 6, it is highly significant for his reading of Genesis that it is here, in relation to the crime of homicide, that the term *sin* is first used by the Bible and not in conjunction with the Fall from Eden. Locke, I will argue, rejected widely held Christian dogma on original sin.

that Isaac's blessing immediately followed Jacob's purchase of the birth-right. In fact, Locke points out, there is "no small distance" of time between the two events, as the Scripture "plainly" depicts. In the interim, Isaac had sojourned to Gerar and had transactions with Abimelech. He was young when he married Rebecca, yet "old and decrepit when he blessed Jacob." And furthermore, "*Esau* also complains of *Jacob, Gen. 27. 36.* that *two times* he had Supplanted him, *he took away my Birth-right*, says he, *and behold now he hath taken away my Blessing*; words, that I think signifie distance of time and difference of Action."[138] Finally, Isaac could not possibly have intended that his blessing to Jacob be a result of the latter's purchase of the birthright, for the simple reason that at the time of blessing Isaac thought he was actually blessing Esau! And in the same vein:

> Nor did *Esau* understand any such connection between *Birth-right* and the *Blessing*, for he says, *he hath Supplanted me these two times, he took away my Birth-right, and now he hath taken away my Blessing*: whereas had the *Blessing*, which was to be *Lord over his Brethren*, belong'd to the *Birth-right*, *Esau* could not have complain'd of this second as a Cheat, *Jacob* having got nothing but what Esau had sold him, when he sold him his *Birth-right*: so that it is plain, Dominion, if these words signifie it, was not understood to belong to the *Birth-right*.[139]

That dominion was not understood to be a right of the heir, but only a greater portion of material goods is clear, Locke contends, once again from Scripture. In her choosing Isaac as heir, Sarah says, "Cast out this bond woman and her son, for the son of this bond woman shall not be heir with my son" (Gen. 21:10), "whereby could be meant nothing, but that he should not have a pretence to an equal share of his Father's Estate after his death, but should have his Portion presently and be gone." Later the Bible tells us that, "Abraham gave all that he had unto Isaac, but unto the concubines which Abraham had, Abraham gave gifts and sent them away from Isaac his son, while he yet lived" (Gen. 25:5–6). Clearly Isaac "had no Right to be *Lord over his Brethren*; for if he had, why should *Sarah* endeavour to Rob him of one of his *Subjects*, or lessen the number of his *Slaves*, by desiring to have Ishmael sent away."[140]

Now Locke tells us what Biblical birthright *does* mean. "The Priviledge of Birth-right was nothing but a double Portion ... there was no knowledge, no thought, that Birth-right gave Rule or Empire, Paternal or

---

[138] I, 113, p. 242.   [139] Ibid.   [140] I, 114, pp. 242–243.

Kingly Authority, to any one over his Brethren." For whomever the story of Isaac and Ishmael is not proof enough, Locke turns our attention to the Book of Chronicles (5:1):

Reuben as the first born: but forasmuch as he defiled his father's bed, his birthright was given unto the sons of Joseph, the son of Israel: and the genealogy is not to be reckoned after the birthright, for Judah prevailed above his brethren and him came to chief ruler, but the birthright was Joseph's.

And the blessing Joseph received from his father is explicitly defined as a double portion in Genesis (48:22): "Moreover I have given thee one portion above thy brethren, which I took out of the hand of the Amorite with my sword and with by bow." Dominion then has nothing to do with birthright, Locke concludes, as "*Joseph* had the Birth-right, but *Judah* the Dominion."[141]

It is clear from the Biblical account itself, Locke continues, that Isaac's blessing of Jacob afforded the latter no dominion over Esau.

For 'tis plain in the History, that *Esau* was never subject to *Jacob*, but lived apart in Mount *Seir*, where he founded a distinct people and government, and was himself prince over them, as much as *Jacob* was in his own family.[142]

Furthermore, the plural tense (brethren and sons) that Isaac uses in the blessing cannot be taken literally, as Isaac "knew Jacob had only one brother." Hence the reference to dominion must not be taken literally either, as the text later proves, "for Genesis 32 *Jacob* several times calls *Esau* Lord and himself his Servant, and Genesis 33 *he bowed himself seven times to the ground to* Esau."[143] How then is Isaac's blessing to be understood? Locke turns yet again to textual consistency.

This blessing then of *Isaac* ... signifies no more but what *Rebecca* had been told from God, Genesis 25. 23. *Two nations are in thy womb, and two manner of people, shall be separated from thy bowels, and the one people shall be stronger than the other people, and the Elder shall serve the younger;* And so *Jacob* Blessed *Judah*, Genesis. 49. and gave him the Scepter and Dominion ... Both these places contain only Predictions of what should long after happen to their Posterities, and not any declaration of the Right of Inheritance to Dominion in either.[144]

Having discussed the nature of the inheritance Isaac passed on to Jacob, Locke now goes back to the Biblical account of Isaac's inheritance

[141] I, 115, p. 243.
[142] Locke is referring to the Biblical account of the two brothers parting ways after their long-awaited reunion as depicted in Genesis 33:16–17.
[143] I, 117, p. 244.   [144] I, 118, pp. 244–245.

and in what sense he was heir to Abraham. Had God promised the Land of Canaan to Abraham without determining who would inherit it after him, suggests Locke, one could then perhaps read into the story of Adam a granting of "empire" to Adam's heir. But when it comes to *divine institution*, God defines exactly what and whom he has in mind. Referring to the Book of Leviticus (chap. 18), Locke writes that,

God making it a divine institute that man should not marry those who were near the kin, thinks not enough to say, *None of you shall approach to any that is near of kin to him, to uncover their nakedness*, but moreover, gives rules to know who are those near the kin forbidden by Divine institution.[145]

One must therefore deduce that if God did not define the term *heir* as he did the rules of illicit sexuality, he did not intend that "the next Heir shall Inherit all his Father's Estate and Dominion."

And therefore in Scripture, though the word *Heir* occur, yet there is no such thing as Heir in our *Author*'s Sense, one that was by Right of Nature to Inherit all that his Father had, exclusive of his Brethren. Hence *Sarah* supposes, that if *Ishmael* staid in the House, to share in *Abrahams* Estate after his Death, this Son of a bond woman might be Heir with *Isaac*: and therefore, says she, *cast out this Bond-woman and her Son, for the Son of this Bond-woman shall not be Heir with my Son.*[146]

Next, Locke inveighs against Filmer's use of the Biblical story of Judah and Thamar as told in the Book of Genesis (chap. 38), to prove that the Biblical patriarchs enjoyed a *dominion of life and death*. The fact that "Judah *the Father pronounced Sentence of Death against Thamar his Daughter-in-law for playing Harlot*" does not prove "that Judah had Absolute and Sovereign Authority." That, because a declaration regarding the application of punitive measures indicates a juridical procedure rather than a manifestation of sovereignty.

The pronouncing of Sentence of Death is not a certain mark of Sovereignty, but usually the Office of Inferior Magistrates. The Power of making Laws of Life and Death, is indeed a Mark of Sovereignty, but pronouncing the Sentence according to those Laws may be done by others, and therefore this will but ill prove that he had Sovereign Authority.[147]

[145] I, 128, p. 252.
[146] I, 128, pp. 252–253. The verse appears in Genesis 21:10. This is an extension of the point Locke already made using this verse in I, 114, and cited earlier.
[147] I, 129, pp. 253–254.

Furthermore, Locke argues, the Scripture nowhere suggests that Judah was correct in passing a death sentence against his daughter-in-law.

Our *Author* thinks it is very good Proof, that because he did it, therefore he had a Right to do it; He lay with her also: By the same way of Proof, he had a Right to do that too: If the consequence be good from doing to a Right of doing.[148]

And, were one to entertain the possibility that a scriptural account of the passing of a death sentence was intended to provide Biblical justification for it, then, says Locke, look at the case of Absalom, who "pronounced such a Sentence of Death against his Brother Amnon, and much upon a like occasion, and had it executed too." The Biblical text's rejection of Absalom's behavior is palpable throughout, and clearly the text shows that his father, David, the king and ultimate sovereign power, spurned his son's actions.[149]

Finally, with regard to Judah, Locke wonders how, in accord with Filmer's standards, he could have inherited absolute dominion from Adam, if his father and eldest brother were still alive.

[I]f one so qualified may be Monarch by descent, why may not every man? If *Judah*, his Father and Elder Brother living were one of *Adams* Heirs, I know not who can be excluded from this Inheritance; all Men by Inheritance may be Monarchs as well as *Judah*.[150]

Locke now turns to the issue of war and peace, and Filmer's claim that the right of a ruler to make either proves that he is heir to Adam with absolutist powers. A number of Biblical examples relegate this notion to the absurd.

Abraham *Commanded an army of 318 Souldiers of his own Family, and* Esau *met his brother* Jacob *with 400 men at arms; For matter of Peace;* Abraham *made a League with* Abimelech ... Is it not possible for a Man to have 318 Men in his Family, without being Heir to *Adam*? ... *without the Absolute Dominion of a Monarch, descending to him from Adam.*[151]

---

[148] Ibid.   [149] I, 129, p. 254. See Samuel II, chap. 13.   [150] Ibid.
[151] I, 130, pp. 254–255. That Abraham raised an army of 318 members of his own household in order to free his nephew Lot from captivity is told in Genesis 14:14. When Jacob returned to Canaan from his exile in his uncle Laban's house in Genesis 32:4–33, he was met by his brother Esau, whose anger over having lost his father's blessing to Jacob had not subsided, despite the many years that had passed since Jacob had fled the home of Isaac and Rebecca. The fact that Esau came to greet Jacob "with 400 men" shows that his intent was not pacific. See Genesis 32:7. The pact, what Locke calls "league," that Abraham made with Abimelech is recounted in Genesis 21:22–34.

Locke actualizes for his readers the Abrahamic example by comparing him to a "planter in the West Indies" who might "muster" members of his household and "lead them out against the *Indians*, to seek Reparation upon any Injury received from them."[152] Clearly Locke is implying that no one will mistake the planter for a king just because he can put a small fighting force together in order to protect his interests. The making of war and peace is a mark of sovereignty, but not absolute sovereignty; nor is it a sign of sovereignty over the whole world, and certainly not rights inherited from Adam.

Commonwealths also make war and peace, Locke proceeds to point out, but they are not monarchical powers; hence the making of war and peace cannot serve as a criterion for Filmer's absolute Adamic power. Using syllogistic argumentation Locke confronts Filmer with the obvious rhetorical question.

[I]f your stand to your Argument, and say those that do make War and Peace, as Commonwealths do without doubt, do *inherit Adam's Lordship*, there is an end of your Monarchy, unless you will say, that Commonwealths *by descent enjoying Adam's Lordship* are Monarchies, and that indeed would be a new way of making all the Governments in the World Monarchical.[153]

Locke now oscillates back from reason to Scripture. Having referred to Abraham's domestic fighting force previously, with which the patriarch intended to liberate his captured nephew Lot, Locke picks up on the relationship between these two Biblical figures to show that Abraham had not the powers Filmer attributed to him. The Scripture explicitly treats them as equals, not as king and subject.

If by inheritance he had been King, *Lot*, who was of the same Family, must needs have been his Subject, by that Title before the Servants in his Family: but we see they liv'd as Friends and Equals, and when their Herdsmen could not agree, there was no pretence of Jurisdiction or Superiority between them, but they parted by consent, *Genesis* 13. hence he is called both by *Abraham*, and by the Text *Abraham's Brother*, the Name of Friendship and Equality, and not of Jurisdiction and Authority, though he were really but his nephew.[154]

From Lot, Locke moves swiftly on to the events surrounding another Biblical character intimately involved in Abraham's life, and who *is* referred to as a servant of Abraham: Eliezer. Abraham sends Eliezer to find a wife for his son Isaac, which Eliezer proceeds to do with great

---

[152] Ibid.   [153] I, 133, p. 257.   [154] I, 135, pp. 257–258.

conscientiousness, quoting his master verbatim as to what the potential groom has to offer, and "heir to Adam" is not on the list.[155]

And if our *Author* knows that *Abraham* was *Adam* 's Heir, and a King, 'twas more it seems than *Abraham* himself knew, or his Servant whom he sent a wooing for his Son; for when he sets out the advantages of the Match, 24 Genesis 35. thereby to prevail with the Young-woman and her Friends, he says, *I am Abraham's Servant, and the Lord hath Blessed my Master greatly, and he is become great, and he hath given him Flocks and Herds and Silver and Gold, and Men-Servants and Maid-servants, and Camels and Asses, and Sarah my Masters Wife, bare a Son to my Master when she was old, and unto him he hath given all he hath.* Can one think that a discreet Servant, that was thus particular to set out his Master's Greatness, would have omitted the Crown *Isaac* was to have, if he had known of any such? Can it be imagin'd he should have neglected to have told them on such an occasion as this that *Abraham* was a King, a Name well known at that time, for he had nine of them his Neighbours, if he or his Master had though any such thing, the likeliest matter of all the rest, to make his Errand Successful?[156]

It would also be logical, Locke contends, that if Abraham were king, he would have enough possessions to bury his wife Sarah on his own property, rather than pursue a drawn-out purchase of suitable real estate, as the Bible recounts.

Yet his Estate, his Territories, his Dominions were very narrow and scanty, for he had not the Possession of a Foot of Land, till he bought a Field and a Cave of the Sons of *Heth* to bury *Sarah* in.[157]

Having mentioned Esau once again (in juxtaposing his militia of 400 men with Abraham's outfit of 318), Locke goes back to Filmer's handling of the Biblical account of the two brothers and their contest over their father's inheritance. Filmer claimed that Jacob was supreme because he attained the birthright, while concomitantly asserting that because Esau challenged his brother with 400 fighting men, *he* was heir to Adam and the bearer of the birthright. Nonetheless, both these claims cannot be true.

Esau is brought as a Proof that *Adam* 's Lordship, *Adam's absolute Dominion, as large as that of any Monarch descended by Right to the Patriarchs*, and in this very Chapter ... *Jacob* is brought as an instance of one, that by *Birth-right was Lord over his Brethren* ... So we have here two Brothers Absolute Monarchs by the same Title, and at the same time Heirs to *Adam*: The Eldest Heir to *Adam*, because

---

[155] See Genesis, chap. 24, for the full account of Eliezer's mission.   [156] I, 135, p. 258.
[157] I, 136 p. 258. See Genesis 23 for a full account of Abraham's negotiations with Heth over the purchase of the Cave of Machpela in Hebron.

he met his Brother with 400 Men, and the youngest Heir to *Adam* by *Birth-right*.[158]

Fully engaged in a discussion about Adam's true heirs, Locke goes back chronologically to the story of Noah in order to further explore just how and what was passed from Adam to subsequent generations.

Locke has provided extensive argumentation, showing that Adam did not have the monarchical characteristics that Filmer attributes to him. He now reasons that even if Adam's monarchical powers were theoretically granted, we would have to be told how they were preserved for posterity, yet the Bible says nothing about them surviving the flood.

If he affirms such an Absolute Monarchy continued to the Flood, in the World, I would be glad to know what Records he has it from; for I confess I cannot find a word of it in my Bible.[159]

Having stated what the Bible does not say, Locke, in typical fashion, goes on to say what it *does* say and seem to indicate, and a logical reading of the text is clearly inconsistent with Filmer's notion of an heir to Adamic monarchy. Noah had three sons: Shem, Cham, and Japhet. Did one, perhaps the eldest (Shem), inherit Adam's powers, or did all three sons inherit them? Locke shows how Filmer entangled himself in exegetical knots.

[W]hich of the three was *Adam*'s Heir? If *Adam's Lordship, Adam's Monarchy*, by Right descended only to the Eldest, then the other two could be but his *Subjects*, his *Slaves*; If by Right it descended to all three Brothers, by the same Right, it will descend to all Mankind, and then it will be impossible what he says ... that *Heirs are Lords of their Brethren*, should be true, but all Brothers, and consequently all Men will be equal and independent, all Heirs to *Adam*'s Monarchy, and consequently all Monarchs too.[160]

The confusion that Filmer has sown is not just theoretical for Locke, but inevitably leads to political instability:

Why our *Author* takes such pains to prove the Division of the World by *Noah* to his Sons, and will not leave out an Imagination, though no better than a Dream, that he can find any where to favour it, is hard to guess, since such a *Division*, if it prove any thing, must necessarily take away the Title of *Adam*'s Heir: unless three Brothers can altogether be Heirs to *Adam* ... If *Cham* and *Japhet* were Princes by Right descending to them, notwithstanding any Title of Heir in their Eldest Brother, Younger Brothers by the same Right descending to them are Princes now, and so all our *Authors* Natural Power of Kings will reach no farther than

[158] I, 137, p. 259.   [159] I, 138, p. 260.   [160] I, 139, pp. 260–261.

their own Children, and no Kingdom by this Natural Right, can be bigger than a Family. For either this *Lordship of Adam over the whole World,* by Right descends only to the Eldest Son, and then there can be but one Heir, as our *Author* says ... Or else, it by Right descends to all the Sons equally, and then every Father of a Family will have it, as well as the three Sons of *Noah*: Take which you will, it destroys the present Governments and Kingdoms, that are now in the World, since whoever has this *Natural Power of a King,* by Right descending to him, must have it either, as our *Author* tells us, *Cain* had it, and be Lord over his Brethren, and so be alone King of the whole World, or else as he tells us here, *Shem, Cham* and *Japhet* had it, three Brothers, and so be only Prince of his own Family, and all Families independent one of another; All the World must be only one Empire by the right of the next Heir, or else every Family be a distinct Government of it self, by the *Lordship of Adam's descending to Parents of Families.*[161]

Locke now moves from his discussion of the postdiluvian nature of governmental authority to the next formulating primordial event, as told in Genesis, the generation of the tower of Babel and the dispersion of peoples that ensued. Of this, Filmer had written that, "In the dispersion of Babel, we must certainly find the Establishment of Royal Power, throughout the Kingdoms of the World." Once again Locke begins by demanding a careful reading of the text.

It would have been a hard matter for any one but our *Author* to have found out so plainly in the Text, he here brings. That all the Nations in that dispersion were governed by *Fathers,* and that *God was careful to preserve the Fatherly Authority.* The words of the Text are; *These are the Sons of* Shem *after their Families after their Tongues in their Lands, after their Nations*; and the same thing is said of *Cham* and *Japhet,* after an Enumeration of their Posterities: in all which there is not one word said of their Governors, or Forms of Government; of *Fathers,* or *Fatherly Authority* but our *Author* who is very quick sighted, to spy our *Fatherhood,* where no body else could see any the least glimpses of it, tells us positively their *Rulers were Fathers, and God was careful to preserve the Fatherly Authority*; and why? Because those of the same Family spoke the same Language, and so of necessity in the Division kept together.[162]

Similar to what he asserts here with regard to the Biblical account of the flood, the text should have said something about the intergenerational preservation of fatherly authority, if it was indeed passed on, yet it does no such thing.

The Scripture says not a word of their Rulers of Forms of Government, but only gives an account, how Mankind came to be divided into distinct Languages and

---

[161] I, 142, p. 263.   [162] I, 144, p. 264.

Nations; and therefore 'tis not to argue from the Authority of Scripture, to tell us positively, *Fathers* were their *Rulers*, when the Scripture says no such thing, but to set up Fancies of ones own Brain, when we confidently aver Matter of Fact, where Records are utterly silent.[163]

Conversely, what the Biblical text *does* present is quite different, in fact quite the opposite, from what Filmer reads into it.

As far as we can conclude any thing from Scripture in this matter, it seems from this place, that if they had any Government, it was rather a Commonwealth than an Absolute Monarchy: For the Scripture tells us, *Genesis* 11. *They said*, 'Twas not a Prince commanded the Building of this City and Tower, 'twas not by the Command of one *Monarch*, but by the Consultation of many, a Free People, *Let us build us a City*; They built it for themselves as Free-men, not as Slaves for their Lord and Master: *That we be not scattered abroad*; having a City once built, and fixed Habitations to settle our Abodes and Families. This was the Consultation and Design of a People, that were at liberty to part asunder, but desired to keep in one Body, and could not have been either necessary or likely in Men tyed together under the Government of one Monarch, who if they had been, as our *Author* tells us, all *Slaves* under the Absolute Dominion of a Monarch, needed not have taken such care to hinder themselves from wandering out of the reach of his Dominion. I demand whether this be not plainer in Scripture than any thing of *Adam's Heir or Fatherly Authority*?[164]

Locke is insistent that the Biblical text be taken seriously. It was the people, not an absolute ruler, who said, "Let us build a city," and prevent our being "scattered abroad." It was precisely this social unity that God deemed responsible for the assault against heaven, and hence the resultant divine division of the unitary community into many different peoples and languages. It is hardly conceivable that this human segmentation should include the maintenance of the same fatherly authority that existed prior to the building of the city and tower of Babel.

But if being, as God says Genesis II, 6. one People, they had one Ruler, one King by Natural Right, Absolute and Supreme over them, *what care had God to preserve the Paternal Authority of the Supreme Fatherhood*, if suddain he suffers 72 (for so many our Author talks of) *distinct Nations*, to be erected out of it, under distinct Governors, and at once to withdraw themselves from the Obedience of their Sovereign, this is to entitle God's care how, and to what we please. Can it be Sense to say, that God was careful to preserve the *Fatherly Authority* in those who had it not? For if these were Subjects under a Supreme Prince, what Authority had they? Was it an instance of God's care to preserve the *Fatherly Authority*, when he took away the true *Supreme Fatherhood* of the Natural Monarch?[165]

---

[163] I, 145, p. 265.   [164] I, 146, p. 266.   [165] I, 147, p. 266.

It makes no sense, contends Locke, that Noah's oldest son, Shem, should have exclusive fatherly authority prior to the dispersion of humanity, and then, though still alive, subsequently share the power with tens of other rulers.

> [B]ut this I am sure is impossible to be either proper, or true speaking, that *Shem*, for example (for he was then alive) should have *Fatherly Authority*, or Sovereignty by Right of *Fatherhood* over that one People at *Babel*, and that the next moment *Shem* yet living, 72 others should have *Fatherly Authority*, or Sovereignty by Right of Fatherhood over the same People, divided into so many distinct Governments.[166]

This can be understood only in the form of an either-or formula. Either the seventy-two ruled prior to the dispersion, making the notion of "one people" impossible, or they had fatherly authority potentially only, without being cognizant of it, which is "Strange! That *Fatherly Authority* should be the only Original of Government amongst Men, and yet all Mankind not know it."[167]

Following Filmer, Locke now makes mention of Nimrod, who according to rabbinical and historical legend was the monarch responsible for the tower of Babel.[168] Filmer had written that this Biblical figure, "against Right enlarged his Empire, by seizing violently on the Rights of other Lords of Families," and as a result, "may be said to be the Author and Founder of Monarchy." But, deduces Locke, Nimrod could not have taken away the natural rights of fathers over their children without the father's consent, ergo, contrary to Filmer's assumptions, his monarchy over the people as a whole would necessitate consent of the people as well.

Filmer had gone on to say that the kings who followed Nimrod, the "founder of monarchy," were all sovereign princes as well. To that Locke responds that since the Biblical kings that Filmer mentions all had powers beyond the rule over their own children, they could not possibly all be heirs to the primordial absolute powers of Adam.

> So that if those 12 Dukes of *Edom*; If *Abraham* and the 9 Kings his Neighbours; If *Jacob* and *Esau* and the 31 Kings in *Canaan*, the 72 Kings mutilated by *Adonibeseck*, the 32 Kings that came to *Benhadad*, the 70 Kings of *Greece* making War at *Troy*, were as our Author contends, all of them Sovereign Princes; 'tis evident

---

[166] I, 147, p. 267.   [167] Ibid.
[168] Genesis 10:10 refers to Babel as being "the beginning of his [Nimrod's] kingdom." See also 1 Chronicles 1:10 and Micah 5:6. See also Midrash Bereishit Raba, 38, 7; Midrash Pirke d'Rebbe Eliezer, 24; and Josephus, "Ant.," i. 4:2.

that Kings deriv'd their Power from some other Original *then Fatherhood*, since some of these had Power over more than their own Posterity, and 'tis Demonstration, they could not be all Heirs to *Adam*.[169]

Locke's Biblical accounting now turns to the Israelites under Egyptian bondage, which takes place in the latter part of the Book of Genesis. Filmer had claimed that, "Patriarchal Government continued in Abraham, Isaac, and Jacob, until the Egyptian Bondage," when "the exercise of Supream Patriarchal Government was intermitted, because they were in Subjection to a stronger Prince." But, argues Locke, showing typical concern for strict Biblical chronology, for the 2,290 years from the time of creation until the Egyptian exile, Filmer "cannot produce any one Example of any Person who claim'd or Exercised Regal Authority by right of *Fatherhood*; or show any one who being a King was *Adam*'s Heir."[170] That there were "Fathers, Patriarchs and Kings in that Age of the World" is unarguable,

[B]ut that the Fathers and Patriarchs had any Absolute Arbitrary Power, or by what Title those Kings had theirs, and of what extent it was, the Scripture is wholly silent; 'tis manifest by right of *Fatherhood* they neither did, nor could claim any Title to Dominion and Empire.[171]

The exigent conclusion for Locke is as he "before suspected, *viz.* That Patriarchal Jurisdiction or Government is a fallacious expression, and does not in our Author signifie (what he would yet insinuate by it) Paternal and Regal Power; such an Absolute Sovereignty, as he supposes was in Adam."[172] Filmer's notion then of inherited supreme patriarchal powers was not just "intermitted" with the Egyptian bondage of the Israelites, as Filmer claims, but from that time on was "quite lost in the World, since 'twill be hard to find from that time downwards, any one who exercised it as an Inheritance descending to him from the Patriarchs *Abraham, Isaac* and *Jacob*."[173] Kings did not resurface in the history of the scriptural Jews "till many Years after they were a People: and when Kings were their Rulers, there is not the least mention

---

[169] I, 149, p. 270. For the "Dukes of Edom," see Genesis 36:40–43. For Abraham and the nine kings, see Genesis, chap. 14. For the thirty-one kings of Canaan, see Joshua 12:24. As for the kings mutilated by Adonibeseck, their number appears in Judges 1:7 as being seventy, not the number seventy-two that Locke quotes. Filmer quotes this number correctly in *Patriarcha*, chapter 1, para. 7. The reference to the thirty-two kings who came to Benhadad can be found in 1 Kings 20:1.

[170] I, 150, pp. 270–271.   [171] Ibid.   [172] I, 151, p. 271.   [173] I, 152, p. 272.

or room for a pretence that they were Heirs to *Adam* or Kings by Paternal Authority."[174]

Without saying so in so many words, Locke indicates that he sees something sacrilegious in what Filmer has done with Scripture: "I expected," writes Locke,

talking so much as he does of Scripture, that he would have produced thence a Series of Monarchs, whose Titles were clear to *Adams Fatherhood*, and who as Heirs to him, own'd and exercised Paternal Jurisdiction over their Subjects, and that this was the true Patriarchal Government: whereas he neither proves, that the Patriarchs were Kings, nor that either Kings or Patriarchs were Heirs to *Adam*, or so much pretended to it.[175]

Because the Bible provides no support for his arguments, and any other text could have accomplished the same thing, Filmer had no right to use it in order to buttress his ideas.

I say all these Propositions may be as well proved by a confused account of a multitude of little Kings in the *West-Indies*, out of *Ferdinando Soto*, or any of our late Histories of the *Northern America*, or by our *Authors* 70 Kings of *Greece*, out of *Homer*, as by any thing he brings out of Scripture, in that Multitude of Kings he has reckon'd up.[176]

This passage shows the seriousness with which Locke related to the Biblical text. For if it were otherwise, why would Filmer's quoting the Bible in vain trouble Locke, if he did not view the Bible as a text that must be confronted with the utmost care and respect?

And as long as Locke is dealing with respect and exegetical integrity, he inserts parentheses to show that Filmer showed a similar lack of respect for the philosophers of Greece. Filmer wrote that there are "too many" philosophers and poets who try "to find out such an Original of Government, as might promise them some Title to Liberty, to the great Scandal of Christianity, and bringing in of Atheism." Like Filmer's approach to the Bible, Locke asserts that here too with regard to the philosophers, Filmer quotes them only when it serves his purposes. The result is an affront to Christianity as well by Filmer, whom he derisively dubs "our zealous Christian Politician."

And yet these Heathens, Philosopher *Aristotle*, and Poet *Homer*, are not rejected by our zealous Christian Politician, whenever they offer any thing that seems to serve his turn, whether to the great Scandal of Christianity, and bringing in of *Atheisme*; let him looke. This I cannot but observe in Authors who ('tis visible)

[174] I, 153, p. 272.   [175] Ibid.   [176] Ibid.

write not for truth, how ready zeale for interest and party is to entitle *Christianity* to their design, and to charge *Atheisme* on those who will not without examining, submit to their Doctrines, and blindly swallow their nonsense.[177]

Returning to the Biblical story of the Israelites in Egypt, Locke quotes Filmer as having said that, "after the return of the *Israelites* out of *Bondage*, God out of a special care of them, chose *Moses* and *Joshua* Successively to Govern as Princes in the place and stead of the Supream Fathers." If the Israelites "returned out of bondage," they must, contends Locke, have returned to a state of freedom in which offspring were not treated as possessions, "and disposed of them with as Absolute a Dominion, as they did *their other Goods.*"[178] For this point Locke does not lean exclusively on logic, but as we have grown accustomed to seeing, he identifies Scripture proofs to uphold his argument.

This is evident in *Jacob*, to whom *Reuben* offered his two Sons as Pledges, and *Judah* was at last surety for *Benjamin*'s sage return out of *Egypt*: Which all had been vain, superfluous, and but a sort of mockery, if *Jacob* had had the same Power over every one of his Family as he had over his Ox or his Ass, as *Owner* over his *Substance.*[179]

In another apparent aside that opens more than a vista into Locke's own thinking about the nature of God, he makes reference to Filmer's earlier comment, which included the remark, "God out of a special care of them, the Israelites." On this, Locke comments:

'Tis well that once in his Book, he will allow God to have any care of the People, for in other places he speaks of Mankind, as if God had no care of any part of them, but only of their Monarchs, and that the rest of the People, the Societies of Men, were made as so many Herds of Cattle, only for the Service, Use, and Pleasure of their Princes.[180]

Lastly, with regard to the aforementioned quote from Filmer referring to Moses and Joshua, both sent by God "to govern as princes" in place of the "Supream Fathers," Locke reminds us that Moses belonged to the tribe of Levy, and Joshua to the tribe of Ephraim, "neither of which had any Title to *Fatherhood.*"[181]

Following Moses and Joshua, Filmer claimed, God "raised up Judges, to defend his People in time of peril," but it was only with the giving of kings to the Israelites that he reestablished "the ancient and prime Right of Lineal Succession to Paternal Government."[182] Yet there is no

---

[177] I, 154, p. 273. [178] I, 154, pp. 273–274. [179] I, 155, p. 274.
[180] I, 156, p. 274. [181] I, 157, p. 274. [182] I, 158–159, p. 275.

scriptural mention of this "positive command," emphasizes Locke. And, "To re-establish *de facto* the Right of Lineal Succession to Paternal Government, is to put a Man in Possession of that Government which his Fathers did enjoy, and he by Lineal Succession had a Right to." In order to test whether or not this was the case, one need only to check whether or not the supposed initial bearers of regal power indeed had anything of the sort, and in light of everything we have studied to this point, the answer, Locke says, is obvious.

[W]hether *Isaac* and *Jacob* had the same Power, that the Kings of *Israel* had, I desire any one, by what has been above said, to consider, and I do not think they will find that either *Abraham, Isaac,* or *Jacob* had any Regal Power at all.[183]

From this point to the end of the *First Treatise* Locke focuses on scriptural proof that the history of the Israelites tells nothing of a *fatherly authority* that is passed on through *lineal succession*, but shows rather that the opposite is the case.

Saul the first King that God gave the *Israelites*, was of the Tribe of *Benjamin*. Was the *Ancient and Prime Right of Lineal Succession Re-established* in him? The next was *David* the Youngest Son of *Jesse*, of the Posterity of *Judah, Jacob's third* (sic) Son. Was the *Ancient and Prime Right of Lineal Succession to Paternal Government Re-established* in him? Or in *Solomon* his younger Son and Successor in the Throne? Or in *Jeroboam* over the ten *Tribes*? Or in *Athaliah* a Woman, who reigned six Years an utter Stranger to the Royal Blood?[184]

In spite of these stark Biblical examples, Filmer is not prevented from suggesting that a divine grant of regal power to a father also includes his *issue* even though it is only the father who is mentioned in the grant. "[B] ut *Solomon*," Locke retorts, "who succeeded *David* in the Throne, being no more his Heir than *Jeroboam*, who succeeded him in the Government of the ten Tribes, was his Issue."[185] Jeroboam did not inherit David, though, despite the fact that he was his issue. This means, concludes Locke, that the grant of monarchy to an individual is entirely dissimilar to the grant of that which is given also to one's seed, such as the Land of Canaan to Abraham and his seed.

For if the Regal Power be given by God to a Man and his *Issue*, as the Land of *Canaan* was to *Abraham* and his Seed, must they not all have a Title to it, all share in it? And one may as well say, that by God's Grant to *Abraham* and his Seed, the Land of *Canaan* was to belong only to one of his Seed exclusive of all others, as by

[183] I, 160, p. 276.   [184] I, 161, p. 276.   [185] I, 162, p. 277.

God's Grant of Dominion to a man and his *Issue*, this Dominion was to belong in peculiar to one of his *Issue* exclusive of all others.[186]

Moses and Joshua themselves, Locke now reminds us, were not succeeded by any of their issue, and this was a phenomenon that persisted throughout the period of the judges right up until the times of the kings.

[S]ince from their coming out of *Egypt* to *David*'s time, 400 Years, the *Issue* was never *so sufficiently comprehended in the Person of the Father*, as that any Son after the death of his Father, succeeded to the Government amongst all those Judges that judged *Israel*. If to avoid this, it be said, God always chose the Person of the Successor, and so transferred *Fatherly Authority* to him, excluded his Issue from succeeding to it, that is manifestly not so in the Story of *Jephtha*, where he Articled with the People, and they made him Judge over them, as is plain, *Judges*. II.[187]

The story of Jephthah, who was appointed by popular demand to lead the people, shows that it was not because the judges were appointed by God that their issue did not succeed them. The conclusion that must be drawn then is that regal authority did not proceed to offspring in the Book of Judges, because that was, contrary to Filmer, not the nature of the divine grant.

[W]e find the Authority, the Judges had, ended with them, and descended not to their *Issue*, and if the Judges had not *Paternal Authority*, I fear it will trouble our *Author* or any of the Friends to his Principles, to tell who had then the *Paternal Authority*, that is, the Government and Supream Power amongst the *Israelites*; and I suspect they must confess that the chosen People of God continued a People several hundreds of Years, without any Knowledge of Thought of this *Paternal Authority*, or any appearance of Monarchical Government at all.[188]

That there was no paternal authority among God's chosen people for "several hundreds of years" can be seen, Locke exegetically explains, from the last three chapters of the Book of Judges, which tell of heinous social crimes surrounding the "concubine of Givah" incident, and how these were handled by the people.

[T]he the story of the *Levite*, and the war thereupon with the *Benjamites*, in the 3 last *Chapt*. of *Jud*.: and when he finds, that the *Levite* appeals to the People for Justice; that it was the Tribes and the Congregation, that debated, resolved, and directed all that was done on that occasion.[189]

---

[186] Ibid.   [187] I, 163, p. 278.   [188] I, 164, pp. 278–279.   [189] I, 165, p. 279.

From the absence of any paternal authority set in motion in this story, one is drawn to the fact that it is actually absent from the entire historical period in which the Book of Judges is set.

[I]t will seem very strange and improbable that God should ordain *Fatherly Authority* to be so Sacred amongst the Sons of Men, that there could be no Power or Government for them, and therein, prescribes Rules to the several States and relations of Men, this Great and Fundamental one, this most material and necessary al the rest should be concealed, and lye neglected for 400 Years after.[190]

What is true for judges must also be true for kings, Locke now goes on to argue. Filmer is wrong to say that, "The Issue is comprehended sufficiently in the Person of the father"; on the contrary, where God intended the seed to inherit, he said so explicitly.

And yet God, when he gave the Land of *Canaan* to *Abraham*, *Gen.* 13. 15. thought fit to put *his Seed* into the Grant too. So the Priesthood was given to *Aaron and his Seed*; And the Crown God gave not only to *David*, but *his Seed* also: And however our Author assures us that *God intends, that the issue should have the benefit of it, when he chooses any Person to be King*, yet we see that the Kingdom which he gave to *Saul*, without mentioning his Seed after him, never came to any of his *Issue*; and why when God chose a Person to be King, he should intend that his *Issue* should have the benefit of it, more than when he chose one to be Judge in *Israel*, I would fain know a reason; or why does a Grant of *Fatherly Authority* to a King more comprehend the *Issue*, than when a like Grant is made to Judge?[191]

The last two paragraphs of Locke's *First Treatise* encapsulate in many ways much of Locke's argumentation throughout his work. Filmer used Scripture in order to establish a theoretical and quasi-theological basis for his notions of monarchical absolutism and patriarchalism. But the relevant Scripture for determining mankind's nature and hence the requisite nature of its government contains a narrative that tells a very different story than the one Filmer sought. It is the narrative of the Jewish people in which paternal authority in the Filmerian sense is totally absent, and the right of lineal succession is of short duration and of minor import.

This is what the Old Testament does not contain. But as we have seen throughout this chapter, Locke attempts to adumbrate upon what underlying principles the Hebrew Bible does contain and advocate. Because he will move from critique in his *First Treatise* to advocacy in the *Second*, and that advocacy will be predicated in no small measure on the Hebrew Bible as well, it is significant that the *First Treatise* functionally ends with

---

[190] Ibid.   [191] I, 167, p. 280.

a brief account of the Israelite Biblical narrative. A narrative of the people of the book in question.

> But since our *Author* has so confidently assured us of the care of God to preserve the *Fatherhood*, and pretends to build all, he says, upon the Authority of the Scripture, we may well expect that the People whose Law, Constitution and History is chiefly contained in the Scripture, should furnish him with the clearest Instances of God's care of preserving of the Fatherly Authority, in that People who 'tis agreed he had a most peculiar care of. Let us see then what State this *Paternal Authority* or Government was in amongst the *Jews*, from their beginning to be a People, It was omitted by our *Author*'s confession, from their coming into *Egypt*, till their return out of that Bondage, above 200 Years. From thence till God gave the *Israelites* a King about 400 years more, our *Author* gives but a very slender account of it, nor indeed all that time are there the least Footsteps of Paternal or Regal Government amongst them. But then says our Author *God re-established the Ancient and Prime Right of Lineal Succession to Paternal Government.*[192]
> What a *Lineal Succession to Paternal Government* was then Established, we have already seen. I only now consider how long this lasted, and that was to their Captivity about 500 Years: From thence to their Destruction by the *Romans*, above 650 years after, the Ancient *and Prime Right of lineal Succession to Paternal Government* was again lost, and they continued a People in the promised Land without it. So that of 1150 Years that they were God's peculiar People, they had hereditary Kingly Government amongst them, not one third of the time, and of that time there is not the least Footstep of one moment of *Paternal Government, nor the Re-establishment of the Ancient and Prime Right of Lineal Succession to it*, whether we suppose it to be derived, as from its Fountain, from *David, Saul, Abraham*, or, which upon our *Author* Principles is the only true; From *Adam*.[193]

The Bible tells the story of a people under divine guidance, and that story is decidedly not one of paternal government, Adamic or otherwise, and that Locke believes should guide us. Here the Lockean text abruptly ends, the contents lost owing to the author's transient years in hiding. Did Locke continue here with his Biblical exegesis in this section, which he testified was longer than all the rest? Did he offer ever more proof of the reverence in which he held the political teachings of the Hebrew Bible? Barring some earthshaking discovery we will probably never know. But what we have before us is convincing enough, that which we have already seen, and particularly that which we are about to see.

---

[192] I, 168, pp. 280–281.   [193] I, 169, p. 281.

2

Locke's Unusual Natural Law

When in the Course of human events, it becomes necessary for one people to dissolve the political bands which have connected them with another, and to assume among the powers of the earth, the separate and equal station to which the Laws of Nature and of Nature's God entitle them, a decent respect to the opinions of mankind requires that they should declare the causes which impel them to the separation. (From the Declaration of Independence)

In transgressing the law of nature, the offender declares himself to live by another rule than that of reason and common equity, which is that measure God has set to the actions of men, for their mutual security; and so he becomes dangerous to mankind, the tye, which is to secure them from injury and violence, being slighted and broken by him. (From the *Two Treatises*, ST 8)

In the *First Treatise* Locke defined for us what political power is *not*; now, at the outset of his *Second Treatise* he declares what legitimate political power truly *is*:

Political power, then, I take to be a right of making laws with penalties of death and, consequently, all less penalties for the regulating and preserving of property, and of employing the force of the community in the execution of such laws, and in the defence of the commonwealth from foreign injury, and all this only for the publick good.[1]

"Such laws" are those laws that are compatible and complementary with the natural law, and that fix the state of war that emerges from the breakdown of society in its unsustainable pre-political state of nature.

---

[1] II, 3, p. 286.

The idea of an original state of nature from which humankind emerges with an inherent embrace of its laws of nature is central to all of Locke's political philosophy. But because the telos of Locke's *Second Treatise* is the justification of rebellion against government's gross violations of natural law, he opens his *Second Treatise* with a discussion of that law. And while natural law theory was popularized by several other seventeenth-century theorists aside from Locke, his use of it is wholly unique in that it is arbitrated to a large extent by the Hebrew Bible – specifically, the scriptural account of the first murder, as well as the postdiluvian prohibition against the spilling of blood as described in the first chapters in the Book of Genesis. Locke separates himself from most other natural law thinkers whose theories lack a clear source that can serve to induce ubiquitous obligation.

Rather than a concept chronologically restricted to defining pre-political society, Locke's state of nature is one in which the laws of nature, comprehended by human reason but divinely ordained, are not sustained. The endowment of self-preservation, which also metamorphoses into a more general obligatory overarching human preservation, drives humans out of a state of nature and into civil society in order to ensure obedience to the laws of nature.

This is the result of Locke's granting of what he calls "executive powers" to every individual, a revolutionary idea that he takes directly from his Biblical exegesis. He understands a political *process* from which government *evolves*. Rather than receiving its legitimacy through a claim of divine ordination, a government's legitimacy derives from the will of the people who created it with the intent to preserve the laws of nature implanted in humankind by God. Here too, Locke sets himself apart from other natural law theorists, such as Hugo Grotius, who refused to predicate their understanding of natural law on the existence of a relevant God.

What is critical then for understanding Locke's natural law, and what is generally overlooked, is that reason alone is insufficient for a complete comprehension of all natural law stipulates; that it is scriptural revelation of a particularly Hebraic strand that helps make natural law obligatory; and that the human inclination toward self-preservation necessitates complementary religious faith in order for moral political governance to be sustainable.

THE HISTORICAL DEVELOPMENT OF NATURAL LAW

The concept of natural law, or the law of nature, played an important role in Greek and Roman philosophy as well as some Christian theology long before it emerged, reconceptualized, in the sixteenth and seventeenth centuries. The Reformation triggered a crisis in natural law philosophy, which was responsible for the development of a modernized natural law tradition within both the context of Protestantism and seventeenth-century rationalism.[2]

Beginning in the fifth century BCE classical Greek theory philosophically contrasted those things that are true by nature (*Physis* φύσις) and those things that are true by convention (*nomos* Nομός).[3] Later, Aristotle, concerned primarily with the legal implications of the issue, asserted that, "there is in nature a common principle of the just and unjust that all people in some way divine, even if they have no association or commerce with each other."[4]Aristotle distinguished between laws humanly enacted, which may or may not be good, and laws enacted by a higher law of nature, which are necessarily the best. Aristotle goes on to quote from Sophocles' *Antigone*, in which an appeal to a justice outside local convention or momentary norms is made.[5] Because Aristotle believed that humans have a natural tendency to be good, natural law could be discerned through human instinct and the use of reason.[6]

[2] As will become readily apparent from my discussion of Locke's natural law later, there is strong evidence pointing to a natural law doctrine in the Hebrew Bible, in which case it would be more accurate, chronologically at least, to begin my discussion there. I have chosen nevertheless to simplify matters at this stage by beginning my brief assessment of natural law history with its traditionally held starting point, Ancient Greece. For a partial analysis of natural law in the Hebrew Bible and in rabbinic exegeses, see David Novak, *Natural Law in Judaism* (Cambridge: Cambridge University Press, 1998), and especially Yoram Hazony, *The Philosophy of Hebrew Scriptures* (Cambridge: Cambridge University Press, 2012). The central argument of Hazony's work is that natural law is at the core of Tanach; that the law of Moses is the first known formulation of natural law; the entire "history of Israel" narrative from Genesis through Kings is designed to advance a natural law argument; and that Jeremiah should be considered a natural law theorist.

[3] See Martin Oswald, *From Popular Sovereignty to the Sovereignty of Law: Law, Society, and Politics in Fifth-Century Athens* (Berkeley, CA: University of California Press, 1986), pp. 260–273. See also J. L. Adams, "The Law of Nature in Greco-Roman Thought," *Journal of Religion* 25 (1945), pp. 97–118.

[4] Aristotle, *The Art of Rhetoric*, John Henry Freese (ed.) (Cambridge, MA: Harvard University Press, 1967), p. 39.

[5] "Thus," writes Susan Wiltshire, "for Aristotle, natural law has an existence apart from the conventional or positive laws that human beings enact to deal with matters of everyday justice. "Susan Ford Wiltshire, *Greece, Rome, and the Bill of Rights* (Norman, OK and London: University of Oklahoma Press, 1992), p. 12.

[6] See Ibid, p. 13.

Following Aristotle, the Stoics further developed the idea of natural law by augmenting the defining scope of individuals from the city to the cosmos, by emphasizing individuals as moral agents, and by creating a structure for natural law that subsequent doctrines could build upon.[7] Brian Tierney writes that, "Stoic thinkers conceived of natural law as an expression of divine reason pervading and ordering the whole cosmos, and they envisioned a natural law inherent in humankind as one aspect of this pantheistic world-view."[8]

This is an established reading of natural law's early evolution, and as Helmut Koester has written, "Established and dignified assumptions are not easily challenged," but challenge them he does.[9] "There is, in fact, very little evidence for the occurrence of the term 'law of nature' in classical Greek texts," asserts Koester. In pre-Socratic Greek thought, "[O]ne does not find ... the appeal to nature as the source of law." For the Sophists, "Law and Nature are mutually exclusive"; and for Aristotle, in stark contrast to what we saw previously, "no virtues for moral and political action can be derived from nature." Indeed, "The Sophists, Plato and Aristotle agree that anything like a law of nature would be absurd."[10]

Koester posits that it was not the Stoics either who advanced the natural law concept; they searched for harmony with the existing order of nature, not agreement with something higher and on the outside as with laws of nature. "Stoicism would not attempt to produce any independent set of moral values and would not establish the claim to possess the knowledge of the law of nature in any way whatsoever."[11]

It was instead, Koester contends, Philo Judaeus of Alexandria who "created" natural law by fusing the Greek concept of nature "with the belief in a divine legislator and with a doctrine of the most perfect (written!) law," thereby overcoming "the Greek dichotomy of the two realms of law and nature."[12] This Koester calls Philo's "genuinely Jewish contribution," as,

There can be no doubt that for Philo the law of nature is the Torah, and that the new term "law of nature" was designed to express a new concept which did not

---

[7] See Ibid, p. 17.

[8] Brian Tierney, *The Idea of Natural Rights: Studies on Natural Rights, Natural Law, and Church Law 1150–1625* (Grand Rapids, MI: William B. Eerdmans Publishing Company, 1997), p. 45.

[9] Helmut Koester, "*Nomos Phuseos*: The Concept of Natural Law in Greek Thought," in *Religions in Antiquity: Essays in Memory of Erwin Ramsdell Goodenough*, Jacob Neusner (ed.) (Leiden: Brill, 1968), pp. 521–541.

[10] Ibid, p. 526.   [11] Ibid, p. 528.   [12] Ibid, p. 540.

exist before in the Hellenistic world: "that the Father and Maker of the world was in the truest sense also its lawgiver" and "that he who would observe the laws (of Moses) will accept gladly the duty of following nature and live in accordance with the ordering of the universe" (Vit. Mos. II 48).[13]

The primary example of life that follows nature for Philo is that of the "men of old," i.e., those who preceded Moses the lawgiver, especially Abraham, who "was not taught by written words, but by unwritten nature ... [T]he more universal laws are those which existed before the written legislation of Moses. They are the originals of the particular laws given through Moses, which Philo calls their copies."[14]

In this key paragraph Koester most clearly delineates the difference between Philonic thought and the Greek thinking on nature that preceded him.

But on the whole, this Philonic identification of Torah, divine order, and nature's law is rooted in his understanding of the unity of all realms of human experience. The Greek concept of the world assigned fundamentally different qualities to the two realms of human experience, to the realm of man's activity – the law – on the one hand, and to the world of nature on the other; and even the monistic system of the Stoics was unable to overcome this dichotomy, or, rather: the Stoics sacrificed large portions of the realm of law, since they declared that the region of political and social involvement was ultimately irrelevant. Philo, on the contrary, knows only one realm of human experience, which can be variously characterized either through his concept of God, or through the investigation of nature, or through the interpretation of the legislation of Moses. But in every case, the one and only unifying principle remains the Torah, the law par excellence.[15]

Koester, though, leaves us dangling on the question of how the Philonic doctrine of natural law continued to develop. As for the Roman concept of *lex naturalis*, he suggests it evolved separately, "by a productive misunderstanding and mistranslation of a Greek Stoic concept." And while this *misconceived* Roman invention influenced the early Church it was Philo's syncretic theoretical construct that had the greatest impact. We will return momentarily to Philo when we discuss the thinking of Hugo Grotius on natural law, but in the absence of research on Philo's immediate influence, we must return to the traditional reading of natural law history and move on to the Roman contribution.

The Romans, who endowed Western culture with the belief in the rule of law and the scientific structuring of that law, found in Stoicism (misunderstood or not) the theoretical framework for contending with

[13] Ibid, p. 533.   [14] Ibid, p. 535.   [15] Ibid, p. 536.

their expansive empire. When the Roman jurist Gaius (130–180 AD) created the distinction between *ius civile*, the particular law of each people, and *ius gentium*, the general law understood through natural reason and observed by everyone, the concept of universal reason through which a higher universal law was understood was initialed into a corpus of civil law.[16]

It was through the teachings of Panaetius, Plybius, and Posidonius in the second century BCE that Stoicism was incorporated into Roman thought, but the greatest influence was brought to bear by Marcus Tullius Cicero.[17] Cicero (106–43 BCE) believed that humans were bound to observe the *ius naturale*, the law of nature, which they could discern through the use of an innate force he called *vis innata*.[18] Like the Stoics, Cicero claimed in his *Laws* that certain fundamental principles are so universal that, in this respect, a person can be viewed not as a citizen of a particular locale, but as "a citizen of the world as [if] it were a single city."[19] "True law," he writes, "is right reason in agreement with nature; it is of universal application, unchanging and ever-lasting; it summons to duty by its commands, and averts from wrong-doing by its prohibitions ... there will be one master and one ruler, that is, God, over us all, for he is the author of this law, its promulgator,

---

[16] Wiltshire writes, "The power of Roman law was greatly enhanced by its marriage with Stoic philosophy and especially with the doctrine of natural law ... Stoicism furnished the philosophical basis that, over a long period of time, transformed the *ius gentium* from an exception into a rational system flexible enough to embody a system of equity for all of Western society ... As Rome assumed a role of administering jurisdiction over the world it had conquered, it needed a broader conception of law to confirm and justify such a role. Stoic philosophy as adapted by the Romans and most especially by Cicero was perfectly suited for this function." Wiltshire, *Greece, Rome, and the Bill of Rights*, pp. 19–20. It is important to point out that the term *ius* was used to connote different concepts at different times during Roman and post-Roman history. It was used, for example, in both the context of *right* and *law* indicating that they were perceived for the most part as two sides of the same conceptual coin. For a short etymological discussion regarding *ius*, see Tuck, *Natural Rights Theories*, pp. 7–13; and for a much more exhaustive one, see Tierney, *The Idea of Natural Rights*, pp. 25, 43–77, *passim*. Tierney contends that Michel Villey was mistaken to credit William of Ockham with being "the first philosopher to understand the word *ius* in the sense of a subjective right." Ibid, p. 105. Instead, Tierney argues for thematic historical consistency from the Greco-Roman period through the medieval period up to the early modern and modern ages.
[17] See Wiltshire, *Greece, Rome, and the Bill of Rights*, p. 22.
[18] Tierney, *The Idea of Natural Rights*, p. 46.
[19] Cicero, *De Legibus*, Clinton Walker Keyes (ed.) (Cambridge, MA: Harvard University Press, 2000), p. 323.

and its enforcing judge."[20] What motivated Cicero to develop his concept of natural law was the conviction that positive laws were alone insufficient for maintaining social stability and what they needed was a higher moral law upon which they were to be based in order to ensure compliance.[21]

More than a millennium and a half later, the observations, and conclusions, of John Locke on the political turmoil of his own times were not dissimilar to those of Cicero, as we shall see later.[22] Natural law still had a long process of development to undergo until it was reconstituted and used to defend the Glorious Revolution, but the initial Greco-Roman contribution, promoting reason to reveal nature's truth, was crucial. It made the universality of justice palatable and practicable.[23]

The Roman notion of *ius naturale* or *lex naturalis* was committed to perpetuity in the opening of the massive and final compilation of Roman jurisprudence called the *Digest*, or *Corpus iuris civilis*, written at the behest of the emperor Justinian in the mid-sixth century.[24] But its contributive longevity is also due in large measure to its appropriation for Christian purposes by fathers of the church. Of this, A. P. d'Entreves writes:

As far as the "formal" continuity of the notion is concerned, there is no doubt that medieval natural law is the progeny of the Greeks and the Romans. To medieval eyes the idea of the law of nature appeared surrounded by the glamour of the Roman

---

[20] Cicero, *Republic*, Clinton Walker Keyes (ed.) (Cambridge, MA: Harvard University Press, 2000), p. 200.

[21] See Wiltshire, *Greece, Rome, and the Bill of Rights*, p. 24. Cicero was followed by a number of Roman Stoics, Seneca (4 BCE–65 AD), who later was quoted extensively by Augustine, John of Salisbury, and Aquinas, being the most notable among them. Ibid, p. 32.

[22] Neal Wood is of the opinion that Cicero's influence on Locke exceeded all other influences (barring that of Francis Bacon) despite the lack of attention it has received by commentators. Neal Wood, *The Politics of Locke's Philosophy: A Social Study of "An Essay Concerning Human Understanding"* (Berkeley, CA: University of California Press, 1983), p. 29. See also Aaron, *John Locke*, p. 8.

[23] Ross Harrison captures this Greco-Roman contribution well: "We are citizens of the world; the city that frames our ethical life is universal; our home is wider than our first home. Right things will not just be right in Rome or Jerusalem but right everywhere ... If there is such law, such universal justice, then its truths obviously cannot come from the particular actions of particular peoples in particular places. It has to come from nature ... It has to be innate in us, or at least accessible on the basis of our innate, natural qualities ... People are, by nature, rational animals. They, universally, are reasonable creatures, able to use reason in the discovery of truth." Harrison, *Hobbes, Locke and Confusion's Masterpiece*, p. 29.

[24] Tierney, *The Idea of Natural Rights*, pp. 26, 41, 111.

legal inheritance. It had however, received as it were the necessary christening by being accepted and embedded in the teaching of the Christian Fathers.[25]

These Church Fathers were, most notably, St. Ambrose (340–397) and St. Augustine (354–430), and while their teachings served to "accept and embed" natural law, their embrace of it was limited and problematical. Ambrose found Stoic ideas of natural law useful to promote his ethics, but only in the sense of "posing and arguing issues"; he had no interest in trying to bring Stoicism into systematic accord with the Gospel.[26] Indeed, it was not easy to reconcile the materialistic basis of Stoic philosophy, which saw even divine providence as material substance, with the abstract nature and idealism of Christian thought. In addition, Christianity championed notions of original sin and natural human depravity; Stoicism, on the other hand, thought that humans were born good and inclined to goodness. Hence, while Augustine lauded Roman greatness, Roman achievements were not a fulfillment of Christian aspirations; the true Christian rather pursued a different world, a "Heavenly City" in which the need for human institutions was obviated. In his *The City of God*, Augustine wrote, "Our City is as different from theirs [the Romans] as heaven from earth, as everlasting life from passing pleasure, as solid glory from empty praise, as the company of angels from the companionship of mortals."[27] For Augustine, the natural law was indeed innate to man from the birth of Adam, but original sin had corrupted man's judgment so that this law of conscience was wholly insufficient to lead man to a moral life and to salvation. Hence the necessity of the *City of Man*, insubordinate to a natural law, to punish man in his fallen state. So, while it formally incorporated natural law, this Augustinian otherworldliness was not conducive to its continued evolution and development.[28]

---

[25] A. P. d'Entreves, *Natural Law: An Introduction to Legal Philosophy*, 2nd Edition (London: Hutchison, 1970), pp. 38–39.

[26] Marcia L. Colish, *The Stoic Tradition from Antiquity to the Early Middle Ages*, vol. 2 (Leiden: E. J. Brill, 1985), p. 302.

[27] St. Augustine, *City of God*, 5.17, Vernon J. Bourke (ed.) (New York: Image Books, 1958). It is not surprising that Augustine was harshly critical of the supremacy Cicero granted to human reason. See Ibid, chapter 9.

[28] Augustine's consistent and unswerving support for autocratic rule served to trump any possible notion of subordinating a ruler to natural law. Evil rulers were as ordained by God as moral ones and had to be obeyed and loved as such. As Herbert A. Deane writes, "[W]e must never forget that [for Augustine] the wicked or unjust man who exercises rule is in every way as legitimate and as much entitled to absolute obedience as the most pious or just ruler. The goodness or badness, piety or impiety, justice or injustice of the ruler has nothing at all to do with his title to rule and to be obeyed." Herbert A. Deane, *The

Later, the political realities of the early Middle Ages also contributed to the decline of natural law. Theorists had little interest in set principles of justice because the times dictated that justice was at the authority and discretion of a lord. Prevailing feudalism made authority highly decentralized and concentrated it in the hands of local counts and community courts. Decentralized authority made for decentralized justice, so the structuring of justice around a single and constant principle was not considered.[29]

The "renaissance" of the early twelfth century, also referred to often as the "medieval renaissance," shook natural law thinking out of stagnation. As a result of the Crusades and extensive urban development, there was a recovery of Greek science and philosophy, a vigorous revival of Latin classics and poetry, and emergence of Europe's first universities.[30] A newfound sense of individualism and humanism in both philosophy and theology emerged as well.[31] Of particular import is the fact that at the start of this period, the lost corpus of Roman law was recovered in total, and church law canonized in the *Decretum* of Gratian.[32]

Political and Social Ideas of St. Augustine (New York: Columbia University Press, 1963), p. 134. For an additional thorough study of Augustine's social and political thought that demonstrates his aversion to the temporality of politics, see R. W. Dyson, *The Pilgrim City: Social and Political Ideas in the Writings of St. Augustine of Hippo* (Suffolk, UK: Boydell Press, 2001).

[29] See Harrison, *Hobbes, Locke and Confusion's Masterpiece*, pp. 106, 108–109. Geoffrey Koziol adds that, "In the early middle ages ... no political or legal treatise made extensive use of the concept (of natural law) after the seventh century ... It forms no part of the numerous political tracts of the Carolingian age, including those of Hincmar of Reims, Sedulius Scotus, and Jonas of Orleans. Indeed, an exhaustive catalog of references to such terms as *ius naturale* and *lex naturalis* in early medieval writings has produced no more than a handful of instances." Geoffrey Koziol, "Lord's Law and Natural Law," in *The Medieval Tradition of Natural Law*, Harold J. Johnson (ed.) (Kalamazoo, MI: Western Michigan University, 1987), p. 103.

[30] See the pioneering study of the period by Charles Homer Haskins, *The Renaissance of the 12th Century* (Cleveland and New York: World Publishing Co., 1927). In a more recent study, R. N. Swanson delineates this period of change between the years 1050 and 1250, dubbing it the "long twelfth century." R. N. Swanson, *The Twelfth Century Renaissance* (Manchester and New York: Manchester University Press, 1999), p. viii.

[31] Ibid, p. 103.

[32] Brian Tierney writes that, "Among all the 'renaissances' of the twelfth century the one most significant for us was the revival of legal studies, first the recovery of the whole corpus of Roman law, then the reordering of the confused mass of church law that had accumulated over many centuries in the *Decretum* of Gratian (c. 1140)." Tierney, *The Idea of Natural Rights*, p. 56. The natural law that Gratian and the canonists included in the *Decretum*, Tierney goes on to explain, took on "a decisive shift of meaning and

This rekindled interest, but changed perception of natural law was also expressed by leading theologians of northern France such as Anselm of Laon (died 1117), Peter Abelard (1079–1142), and Hugh of St. Victor (1096–1141).[33] Nature was now perceived as having its own "substantive reality" and possessing its own "equilibrium" that functioned independently, without divine or human interference. That necessarily led to positing "laws of nature" that offered twelfth-century theorists "a way of anchoring human laws in universal principles that were fixed and constant."[34]

But it was not until Thomas Aquinas (1225–1274) that Aristotelian thought with its natural law philosophy was fully rehabilitated. Because Aristotle, to whom Aquinas referred as "the philosopher," had been shunned by Augustine and embraced by Muslim philosophers, his political and ethical thought remained relatively unknown in the West.[35] Aquinas insisted that Aristotle could be reconciled with church teachings, and not only was he unintimidated by the assimilation of Aristotle into Islamic thought, he did not hesitate himself to draw from the great Muslim thinkers who preceded him, in particular: al-Farabi (870–950), Avicenna (Ibn Sina) (980–1037), and Averroes (Ibn Rushd) (1126–1198). Aquinas was also greatly influenced by Maimonides (1135–1204), or "Rabbi Moses" as he always referred to him, who "was an important link on the chain that brought the ontological theory of Aristotle to the attention and consideration of Christian thinkers in Europe."[36] The common thread connecting these thinkers was their focus on forging a synthesis between

emphasis." "For some of the Stoics and for Cicero there was a force in man through which he could discern *ius naturale*, the objective natural law that pervaded the whole universe; but for the canonists *ius naturale* itself could be defined as a subjective force or faculty or power or ability inherent in human persons." Ibid, p. 65.

[33] Koziol, "Lord's Law and Natural Law," pp. 103–104.   [34] Ibid, pp. 104–106.

[35] R. W. Dyson, "Introduction," *Cambridge Texts in the History of Political Thought: Aquinas, Political Writings* (Cambridge: Cambridge University Press, 2002), pp. xxii–xxiv. Dyson adds: "Not surprisingly, the Church regarded the 'recovery' of Aristotle with hostility. Apart from his own paganism, the fact that Aristotle had been so much handled by Arab scholars was enough to infect him with the taint of Islam." Ibid, p. xxiii.

[36] David Novak, "Maimonides and Aquinas on Natural Law," in *St. Thomas Aquinas and the Natural Law Tradition: Contemporary Perspectives*, John Goyette, Mark S. Latkovic, and Richard S. Myers (eds.) (Washington, D.C.: The Catholic University of America Press, 2004), p. 44. Novak is of the opinion that without "belittling the metaphysical influence," the "influence of Maimonides on Aquinas was far more extensive in the area of practical reason, which covers the joint area of ethics and politics." Ibid. It is important to emphasize here the Maimonidean embrace of Aristotle's theory of human sociability. In *The Guide* Maimonides writes, "It has already been fully explained that man is

faith and reason; it was Aquinas who provided an ethical basis for Christianity that need not be based exclusively on faith and grace.

There are four kinds of law in Aquinas's typology: eternal law, natural law, human law, and divine law. The concept of eternal law is general, embracing the entire universe that was created through divine wisdom and is subject to the rational pattern of God's mind. Natural law is specific; it is the human ability, through the use of reason, to decipher eternal law and choose good over evil in specific circumstances. Human law encompasses the civil norms established by particular communities at a particular time, and divine law is religious law, received through revelation rather than self-revealed through reason.[37] The critical importance of natural law to Aquinas's philosophy becomes readily apparent, for without it eternal law would remain indecipherable. This is what Aquinas means when he writes that, "natural law is nothing other than the sharing in the eternal law by rational creatures."[38] On the other side of the equation, human law is mutable and must match up to the standards of the natural law, while natural law itself is permanent and unalterable.[39] Aquinas wrote in the scholastic tradition, arguing for a natural law that was part and parcel of God's creation. God did not create anything for naught, and since everything was implanted in nature with a purpose, the

naturally a social being, that by virtue of his nature he seeks to form communities; man is therefore different from other living beings that are not compelled to combine into communities." Maimonides, *The Guide for the Perplexed*, M. Friedlander (trans.) (New York: Dover, 1956), part Ii, chap. XL, p. 232. See also part I, chap. 72, and part III, chap. XXVII.

Regarding the influence of Islamic philosophy on Maimonides himself: while it is clear that Maimonides held both Avicenna and Averroes in high esteem, their works were most probably not known to him before the completion of *The Guide to the Perplexed*. The same cannot be said of al-Farabi, in whom Maimonides found great interest and whose writings he assessed as superior to those of his successors. Two other Islamic philosophers thought to have influenced Maimonides are al-Ghazali (d. 1111) and Ibn Bajja (d. 1138). See Shlomo Pines, "Translator's Introduction: The Philosophical Sources of *The Guide to the Perplexed*," in his Moses Maimonides, *The Guide to the Perplexed* (Chicago, IL: The University of Chicago Press, 1963), pp. lix, lx, ciii–cviii, cxxvi–cxxxi.

[37] This last category, divine law, Aquinas divides into two subheadings: Old Law – pre-Christian revelation of divine law to the Jewish people – and New Law – divine law revealed by Christ to the Church. David Novak points to the inordinate amount of space Aquinas counterintuitively dedicates to the Old rather than the New Law. Novak, "Maimonides and Aquinas on Natural Law," pp. 45–46.

[38] Thomas Aquinas, *Summa Theologica* (Westminster, MD: Benziger Bros., 1981); Dyson, *Cambridge Texts in the History of Political Thought: Aquinas, Political Writings*, p. 86.

[39] In Aquinas's words: "Hence every human law has the nature of law in so far as it is derived from the law of nature. But if it is in any respect at odds with the law of nature, it will then no longer be law, but a corruption of law." Ibid, p. 130.

objective of reason is for humankind to participate in God's wisdom, which made the universe. For Aquinas, natural law is a divinely given privilege that allows humans to reflect on God's infinite purposes with their finite minds, a reflection that can direct them to natural good. This is what Aquinas means when he defines it as "the participation of the rational creature in the eternal law."[40] Aquinas's greatest contribution, philosophical and theological, was in the forging of a modus vivendi between faith and philosophy, reason and revelation, between natural law and divine law, and it was due to him that natural law thinking became a distinguishing feature of church theology.[41]

Aquinas's thinking on natural law remained predominant until the Protestant Reformation triggered a crisis in the natural law tradition. While some Reformers such as Philipp Melanchthon, "the most prominent intellectual amongst Luther's early disciples,"[42] saw no problem with natural law, Martin Luther did, and Luther is particularly interesting because he presented a theoretical undoing of Thomistic synthesis. Contrary to Aquinas, yet in keeping with Augustine, he divided society into two parts, the Kingdom of God, where only good was to be found, and the kingdom of the world, where the necessary evils of the world were located, including the secular state. When he refers to the Golden Rule as natural law, it is specifically "the natural law which Christ announces,"[43] meaning that for Luther natural law emanates and can be understood only through God, and not by human reason. Luther rejected the Aristotelian/Thomistic concept of natural law on two theological grounds. First, he could not accept the requisite connection

---

[40] Ibid. See also Sommerville, *Royalists and Patriots*, p. 13, and J. Budziszewski, *Written on the Heart: The Case for Natural Law* (Downers Grove, IL: Inter Varsity Press, 1997), pp. 56–57.

[41] Susan Wiltshire writes: "Aquinas's great achievement was to provide a rational basis for both ethics and politics, the very institutions that earlier Christians considered hopelessly mired in sin and subject only to the remedy of grace. His momentous discovery was that natural law provided a medium by which to incorporate Aristotelian/Stoic ethics and politics into a Christian view of life. Once again human beings could be conceived of as political animals, and life in community could be seen as a place for the harmonious integration of individual lives. That the Christian community can be based on natural law, human reason, and political institutions as well as on God's will is a great breakthrough in human thought." Wiltshire, *Greece, Rome, and the Bill of Rights*, pp. 38–39.

[42] Quentin Skinner, *The Foundations of Modern Political Thought*, vol. II (Cambridge: Cambridge University Press, 1978), p. 31.

[43] Martin Luther, *Luther's Works*, 55 vols., J. Pelikan (ed., vols. 1–30) and H. Lehmann (ed., vols. 31–55) (Philadelphia, PA: Concordia Press, 1958–1967), vol. 45, pp. 233–310.

between nature and reason. Following man's fall from Eden, he argued, reason can only help guide humankind to what is proper, not supply absolute knowledge of correct conduct. That is something only the gift of grace can do. Similarly, a person's actions cannot alter his or her innate state of corruption; only divine grace can accomplish that. Humans were obligated instead, according to Luther's doctrine of justification, to live "by faith alone" (*sola fide*) because their corrupt nature eclipsed their ability to reason.[44]

Reason is also closely associated with the idea of individual free will, which Luther forcefully rejected, arguing that free will for humankind meant a limitation of God's freedom. The nominalist view, that people could choose their own identity, was for Luther tantamount to denying God's existence.[45]

---

[44] H. Brown stresses the contrast between Aquinas and Luther: "For Aquinas, reason is the keystone of natural law, but for Luther it is at best a guide which lacks certainty. The distinction, then, is in the inability of the reason to discover truth due to man's corrupt nature outside of a state of grace." Harvey Owen Brown, "Martin Luther: A Natural Law Theorist?," in *The Medieval Tradition of Natural Law*, Harold J. Johnson (ed.) (Kalamazoo, MI: Medieval Institute, 1987), p. 19.

[45] Owen Brown writes: "Luther's view of man is such that no theory of individual liberty is likely where men are commanded to submit to authority for fear of defying an unknown and unknowable will. While it is true that salvation is removed from the clutches of the priesthood and made an individual matter between man and God, the method is to remove man's ability to play a conscious role in the process, and no individualist view of society can exist where men cannot make free choices about their destinies." Brown, "Martin Luther: A Natural Law Theorist?," p. 18.

The issue of free will was the subject of Luther's great argument with Erasmus (1466–1536), who wrote *The Freedom of the Will*, to which Luther responded with *The Bondage of the Will* (1525). Quentin Skinner stresses that the free will of Erasmus that Luther vehemently contested was not the idea that humans can choose simple matters of human conduct, but rather the notion that through the use of human will salvation can be earned. Skinner also points out that Luther followed the voluntarism of Ockham, insisting that God's laws must be obeyed not because human intellect can comprehend their justness, but merely because they are God's commandments. Skinner, *The Foundations of Modern Political Thought*, pp. 5–6. Martin van Gelderen makes the following interesting observation about the perceived differences between Erasmus and Luther: "even though Erasmus eventually denounced Luther in public, it was hard for contemporaries to discern the sometimes rather subtle differences between Erasmian and Lutheran ideas. For a number of decades a situation of perplexing questions and slowly proliferating answers persisted. For, even if the points of controversy were clear, the answers were certainly not. Religious identities were still very much in the process of formation and formulation. During the first half of the sixteenth century there was simply no instant, clear-cut choice between well-defined versions of traditional Roman Catholicism, Christian humanism, Lutheranism, Anabaptism and Calvinism." Martin van Gelderen, *The Political Thought of the Dutch Revolt 1555–1590* (Cambridge: Cambridge University Press, 1992), p. 65.

The second problem Luther had with natural law related to equality. Luther believed that God made some individuals superior to others: some were gifted with the grace of God and others were not, and only those who received grace were equal. Natural law, on the other hand, posited that all people are equally rational and hence by nature equal.[46]

Luther's New Testament supremacy[47] and exclusively faith-based theology were in no need of a natural law to direct human moral obligations, as those duties were both infinite and unfulfillable. The ramifications for Luther regarding a requisite attitude toward secular power were obvious, as Quentin Skinner articulates.

Luther's major political tracts may thus be said to embody two guiding principles, both of which were destined to exercise an immense historical influence. He treats the New Testament, and especially the injunctions of St Paul, as the final authority on all fundamental questions about the proper conduct of social and political life. And he claims that the political stance which is actually prescribed in the New Testament is one of complete Christian submission to the secular authorities, the range of whose powers he crucially extends, grounding them in such a way that their rule can never in any circumstances be legitimately resisted. The articulation of these principles involved no appeal to the scholastic concept of a universe ruled by law, and scarcely any appeal even to the concept of an intuited law of nature: Luther's final word is always based on the Word of God.[48]

The outcome, concludes Skinner, and this is key, was deep and widespread Lutheran justification for monarchical absolutism.

[T]here is no doubt that the main influence of Lutheran political theory in early modern Europe lay in the direction of encouraging and legitimating the emergence of unified and absolutist monarchies. Luther's doctrines proved so useful for this purpose that his most distinctive political arguments were

---

[46] Knud Haakonssen summarizes the effect Luther had on early Protestantism with regard to natural law: "For Protestant thinkers the starting point was the complete discontinuity between God and man, a discontinuity which made it impossible to give a rational account of human morality by reference to God and his eternal law. Only faith could bridge the gulf between humanity and its creator. This led to a continuing ambiguity in Protestantism towards natural law as a rational account of morals." Knud Haakonssen, *Natural Law and Moral Philosophy: From Grotius to the Scottish Enlightenment* (Cambridge: Cambridge University Press, 1996), p. 25.

[47] Skinner writes: "[F]or Luther ... it is always essential to understand the commands of the law in the light of the gospel, not the gospel in the light of the law." Skinner, *The Foundations of Modern Political Thought*, p. 10.

[48] Ibid, p. 19.

eventually echoed even by the leading Catholic protagonists of the divine right of kings.[49]

The Catholic Counter-Reformation, which extended approximately from the pontificate of Pope Pius IV in 1560 to the close of the Thirty Years' War in 1648, brought with it a revival of the natural law tradition known as the "second scholasticism." Perhaps its greatest exponent was the Jesuit Francis Suarez (1548–1617), who in his *De legibus, ac Deo legislatore* (1612) leans heavily on Aquinas while presenting a classical synthesis of scholastic moral-legal theory culled from earlier natural law doctrines. Suarez embraced the idea that through a "dictate of reason" or "judgment of the mind" natural law "dwells in the human mind to distinguish the righteous from the evil."[50] Suarez is particularly known for attempting to reconcile the two sides of the scholastic debate regarding natural law, that of the "intellectualists" (the supremacy of reason) led by Gregory of Rimini (1300–1358) and Aquinas, and that of the "voluntarists" (supremacy of God's will) led by John Duns Scotus (1265–1308) and William of Ockham (1288–1348).[51]

Suarez strongly rejected Luther's antinomianism; good works, not just faith, can make a difference in narrowing the gap between material human and the divine, he posited. With Aristotle and Aquinas in mind, Suarez argued that the sociability of the human condition naturally drives humans into groups wider than the family unit.[52] Natural law, found in

---

[49] Ibid, p. 113.   [50] *De legibus*, 1:1.3.9,44; 3:2.5.12,71; 2.5.12,72.

[51] Haakonssen, *Natural Law and Moral Philosophy*, pp. 19–24. The "second scholasticism" was advanced by the founding of the Society of Jesus (the Jesuits) in 1540, of which, in addition to Suarez, Gabriel Vasquez (1549–1604), also of Spain (and quoted extensively by Grotius), and Robert Bellarmine (1542–1621), of Italy, were leading advocates. Josef Bordet, "Late Scholasticism," in *The Oxford International Encyclopedia of Legal History* (New York: Oxford University Press, 2009). It was Vasquez who had a decisive influence on Hobbes's thesis equating natural liberty with natural right. See Quentin Skinner, *Hobbes and Republican Liberty* (Cambridge: Cambridge University Press, 2008), p. 39. Skinner sees Ockham as one of the important forerunners of Lutheranism because he believed that papal authority was not absolute but conditional on its use to benefit the faithful, and because of his insistence on keeping spiritual and temporal jurisdictions sharply divided from each other. Skinner, *The Foundations of Modern Political Thought*, p. 38. For a full and fascinating survey of Luther's forerunners who fought against unlimited papal powers, see Ibid, pp. 20–64. For the differences in the theologies of Scotus and Ockham, see Denis R. Janz, "Late Medieval Theology," in *The Cambridge Companion to Reformation Theology*, David Bagchi and David C. Steinmetz (eds.) (Cambridge: Cambridge University Press, 2004), pp. 8–13.

[52] Brian Tierney's explanation of Suarez's pursuit of synthesis is well stated. "The Spanish scholar himself did not think it necessary to choose between these alternatives; rather he sought to balance them against one another in an inclusive synthesis ... Suarez chose a middle course. The natural law discerned by reason, he held, both indicated what was intrinsically

human reason and in the Decalogue, exists to direct and monitor the requisite working arrangements in the resultant social structure so that the common good will be sought and maintained. Suarez presented a legal typology similar to that of Aquinas and argued that natural law could not conflict with the "law of scripture" or "eternal law." Humanity's fallen status does not prevent human reason from defining natural law, as Luther had argued; it only makes its discernment more difficult.[53]

Suarez believed that political governance was established through the will of the people but once the people granted power to the ruler they could not reclaim it at will. In turn, the ruler was not obligated to seek consent of the people in order to legislate or levy taxes. Tyrannical rule could be opposed by the people in the context of self-defense, and the only right the individual had with regard to tyranny was personal self-defense. There was much in Suarez's writing that Locke would pick up on, but in contradistinction to what Locke would later develop, the individual, as far as Suarez was concerned, had no political power.[54]

Following Suarez, and in the context of the historical transformation from the medieval to early modern era, the development of natural law doctrine that had been dominated by Catholic theologians was taken over by Protestant theorists; the central figure linking the periods was Hugo Grotius of the United Provinces.[55]

---

good or evil and also commanded the one and forbade the other. But, in discerning natural law, reason also discerned the will of God for humankind. Since God chose to create humans as creatures endowed with reason, we can know that he intended them to act in accord with the dictates of their rational nature." Tierney, *The Idea of Natural Rights*, pp. 302, 305.

[53] Haakonssen explains how Suarez's theology translated into a critique of the Reformers' political thinking: "This view of society, political authority and legislation as necessary responses to the needs of human nature is clearly directed against the Reformers' political ideas. Social life and political governance are not to be seen as necessary means of compensating for fallen man's loss of moral self-government. They are in fact part of the fulfillment of human nature. Original sin just makes it harder to achieve fulfillment in these as in other aspects of the moral life." Haakonssen, *Natural Law and Moral Philosophy*, p. 18.

[54] Tierney, *The Idea of Natural Rights*, pp. 312–313.

[55] Grotius praised the Jesuit Suarez as a theologian and philosopher of such depth, breadth, and penetration that "he hardly had an equal." Hugo Grotius, Letter of October 15, 1633 (2001: 194, http://plato.stanford.edu/entries/suarez/).

Of Grotius's pivotal historical importance Brian Tierney writes that, "The idea of natural rights grew up among Catholic jurists and theologians during the medieval era. The further development of the doctrine in the early modern world was almost entirely the work of Protestant political theorists. Between the two worlds, linking them together, stood the figure of the great Dutch scholar, Hugo Grotius." Tierney, *The Idea of Natural Rights*, p. 316. To be sure, interpretations over Grotius's exact historical role differ. Richard Tuck, for example, sees in Grotius's writing a fundamentally new theory of

Writing his *De Juri Belli ac Pacis* at the time of the Thirty Years' War and attendant continental religious conflicts, one of which affected him personally, the questions he went about answering were decidedly practical. He was looking for an independent moral truth that could be applied to all parties in a conflict, without reducing this truth to mere custom. The personal persecution Grotius experienced, the result of ending up on the losing side of a vociferous religious-political debate, had a profound influence on his thinking. The Synod of Dort (1618) declared Arminianism to be heresy because contrary to strict Calvinism it took a less rigid approach to predestination and to the severe limitation of human free will, and accused its Remonstrant leadership of siding with the enemy in the Dutch war with Spain. Grotius, himself an Arminian who had sided with the Remonstrants, was imprisoned, and had it not been for his daring escape to Paris, would have probably ended his life on the guillotine, as did Remonstrant leader Johan van Oldenbarnevelt.[56]

natural law (and rights) that breaks with his predecessors. See Richard Tuck, "Grotius and Selden," in *The Cambridge History of Political Thought, 1450–1700,* J. H. Burns (ed.) (Cambridge: Cambridge University Press, 1991), pp. 499–529. Tuck's pivotal placing of Grotius is clear from the following quote: "It is in many ways reasonable to view Hobbes as someone who was trying to provide a persuasive theoretical foundation to the ethical ideas put forward by Grotius, and in the process transforming those ideas (at least to some extent); it is plausible to see Pufendorf and Locke as engaged in a similar task." Richard Tuck, "Hobbes," in *Great Political Thinkers* (Oxford: Oxford University Press, 1992), p. 208. Conversely, Brian Tierney sees Grotius's genius in his ability not in changing traditional notions of natural law but in presenting them in a fashion that placed them in the relevant context of his era. "Grotius was in fact using the medieval tradition of thought about natural law and natural rights to sustain a new vision of the world and the church. Many Catholic authors – though by no means all – had given up the view of the medieval hierocrats who held that the pope was temporal lord of the whole world. But Catholic thinkers still commonly maintained that the pope possessed at least an 'indirect' power by virtue of which he could intervene in temporal affairs to attain spiritual ends. Through his indirect power the pope could release subjects from oaths of allegiance, depose a heretical monarch, launch wars to extend or defend the Christian faith. The Catholic ideal was a world order in which the pope was supreme in spiritual affairs and had a considerable authority to regulate temporal matters also. In contrast to this, Grotius envisaged a world made up of free sovereign states, Christian and non-Christian, owing allegiance to no external superior. It was a world in which commercial rivalries as well as religious conflicts had become a major cause of wars. A degree of order and harmony in such a world could be maintained, Grotius thought, not by an appeal to some overriding spiritual authority, but by the common consent of all nations to the code of international conduct that he had diligently worked out for them." Tierney, *The Idea of Natural Rights,* pp. 339–340. Tierney understands it to be Pufendorf who, mistakenly, invented the idea that Grotius was "uninfluenced by any vestiges of previous scholarship" and "made a complete break with the past." Ibid, p. 318.

[56] Tuck, *Natural Rights Theories,* p. 64.

Often considered the father of modern natural law, Grotius refused to restrict universal rules to mere prudence and instead pursued a natural law construct that provided a more robust definition of universal civic justice – a natural law "that is true for all times, peoples and places, and whose truth follows from the nature of humanity (Christians would add, as created by God)."[57] In this regard, Grotius closely follows Suarez's approach in determining the roots and intentions of natural law, as he does in combining elements of both rationalist and voluntarist thought.[58] But he broke ranks with Suarez in discounting the Decalogue as a source of natural law[59] and in granting political power to the individual.[60]

At the core of natural law for Grotius are those precepts minimally imperative for people to live in peace with each other. The preliminary requirement is keeping agreements, whether tacit or explicit, because social order cannot otherwise be maintained. What is Grotius's source? It was not revelation. Grotius sought a natural law that was not dependent on a special revelation of God's will, a natural law paradigm that "would have a degree of validity even if we should concede that which cannot be conceded without the utmost wickedness, that there is no God, or that the affairs of men are of no concern to him."[61] Instead,

---

[57] Harrison, *Hobbes, Locke and Confusion's Masterpiece*, p. 135.

[58] Of the general stylistic and substantive similarity between Grotius's writing with that of Suarez, Tierney writes: "[I]n considering his work, one seems to be reading Suarez transposed into a different idiom." And, "When he came to give a formal definition of *ius naturale* Grotius, like Suarez, combined both elements of thought, rationalist and voluntarist." Tierney, *The Idea of Natural Rights*, pp. 316, 327.

[59] Haakonssen, *Natural Law and Moral Philosophy*, p. 29.

[60] Tuck, *Natural Rights Theories*, pp. 62–63.

[61] Hugo Grotius, *The Rights of War and Peace*, with an introduction by Richard Tuck (ed.) (Indianapolis, IN: Liberty Fund, 2005), Preliminary Discourse, XI, p. 89. Tierney makes the important observation that Grotius himself "qualified his hypothesis at once by adding that there was indeed a God and that God's free will was 'another source of law besides the source of nature.' (De jure belli, Prolegomena, 3) In the subsequent pages of his work there were more references to the Bible than to any other source. One can hardly call this a 'secularist' approach." Tierney, *The Idea of Natural Rights*, p. 320. Tierney is clearly correct in his assessment of Grotius's rhetorical intent regarding God's existence, in light of what Grotius himself wrote a bit later in *De Jure Belli ac Pacis*. "[T]he Law of Nature is so unalterable, that God himself cannot change it ... as God himself cannot effect, that twice two should not be four; so neither can he, that what is intrinsically Evil should not be evil ... God suffers himself to be judged of according to this Rule, as we find, *Gen.* xviii. 25. *Isa.* V. 3. *Ezek.* xviii. 25. *Jer.* ii. 9. *Mich.* vi. 2. *Rom.* ii. 6. iii. 6. Chap. 1, X, 6." pp. 155–156. Grotius uses no less than six Biblical sources, five from the Hebrew Bible and one from the New Testament, in order to prove that God's natural law is inviolable and unchangeable. Grotius makes it clear that it is *God himself* who teaches us that he is not above the law.

Grotius found his source in the inherent rationality and sociability of humankind.[62]

Because human nature draws humans into agreements, it becomes elementary that the obligation to honor agreements creates the right not to have them violated. And once an agreement is violated, it is an injustice that creates a license for redress, even if the result is war. Natural law, Grotius wrote, means "that 'tis the first Duty of every one to preserve himself in his natural State, to seek after those Things which are agreeable to Nature, and to avert those which are repugnant."[63] While Grotius theorizes that the human propensity toward self-preservation as well as social contracting are elemental to the composition of natural law, he puts far more emphasis on the latter. Though it would appear that in doing so he distances himself from the possible advent of governmental absolutism, the end result was very similar to the Leviathan that Thomas Hobbes would soon create. Because Grotius believed that humanity's natural propensity for making agreements included the individual's right to contract him- or herself into slavery, society, he argued, could do the same and contract itself into domination by an absolute ruler.[64] Because governmental absolutism is only one possible result for Grotius (as opposed to Hobbes's exclusivist position, as we shall presently see), it leaves his theory of natural law somewhat deficient when it comes to the issue of obligation. What is it that makes natural law compulsory upon the individual? Grotius responded to this question by addressing the happiness involved in doing good deeds and emphasized the dictates of "conscience" and "public opinion,"[65] but these are hardly concepts upon which juridical imposition can be based.[66]

---

[62] Knud Haakonssen explains: "According to Grotius individuals with natural rights are the units of which all social organization is made. They are people who balance pure self-interest and social inclinations by entering in contractual relations with others about property and about modes of living together, especially about authority. They consider it a right to enforce the obligations arising from such arrangements, that is, to punish their transgression. Over and above this, and to varying degrees, they may or may not do good to others by honoring 'imperfect rights.'" Haakonssen, *Natural Law and Moral Philosophy*, p. 28.

[63] Grotius, *The Rights of War and Peace*, 1.2.1., p. 180.   [64] Ibid, 2.5.26, pp. 555–556.

[65] See particularly the last chapter of *The Rights of War and Peace*.

[66] Richard Tuck aptly sums up this problem in Grotius's philosophy. "[G]rotius's achievement was a remarkable one ... it was nevertheless incomplete in a number of important respects. In particular, it stressed individuality in the area of rights, but communality in the area of obligation, and though that might be logically coherent there was a certain psychological implausibility in it. Grotius's men were fiercely

As with our brief discussion of Aristotle and natural law earlier, it can be said that this reading of Grotian natural law follows the traditional approach; Grotius more or less followed Aquinas and the scholastics, while his innovation was confined to the creation of a synthesis between natural law and international law.[67] But this reading of Grotius has not gone unchallenged; Meirav Jones has proposed a thesis that is as original as it is convincing, and it connects with the untraditional reading of early natural law by Helmut Koester, who placed Philo Judaeus at the pivot of the story rather than the early Greeks.[68]

Jones points to the copious references Grotius makes to Philo in his *De Jure Belli ac Pacis*, indeed quoting him more than any other source, a fact overlooked by most scholars. This turn to Philo was as much a turn to Hebraism as it was a turn away from scholasticism. As in Philo and in contradistinction to Aquinas, for Grotius "right reason" attains the status of natural law because it is in complete harmony with the will of God; it is willed into the world through the nature of humankind from whom natural law proceeds.

Jones shows that in addition to custom and agreement among peoples, Grotius employed Mosaic Law, even those parts that clearly belong to the "volitional law of the Jews" category. The most pronounced case in point is his proof that there are wars that do not violate natural law because "as god could not have legislated against natural law, and the Hebrews engaged in lawful wars, there must be wars that do not violate natural law." To be sure, Jones assures us, Mosaic Law is not binding on Christians, according to Grotius, but anything contrary to Mosaic Law would be contrary to natural law. The Gospel comes to add or alter Mosaic Law, but it must maintain the "same purport as the laws of Moses."[69]

---

defensive of their original rights, and capable of so far controlling their own lives that they could commit themselves to slavery; and yet their moral world was informed by the principle of sociability with its distributive and unindividualistic implications, and in extremis their more harmful commitments could be disregarded." Tuck, *Natural Rights Theories*, p. 82.

[67] See, for example, Heinrich A. Rommen, *The Natural Law: A Study in Legal and Social History and Philosophy*, Thomas R. Hanley, OSB, PhD (trans.) (Indianapolis, IN: Liberty Fund, 1998), pp. 62–66.

[68] Meirav Jones, "Philo Judaeus and Hugo Grotius's Modern Natural Law," *Journal of the History of Ideas* 74, 3 (2013, http://muse.jhu.edu/journals/jhi/summary/v074/74.3.jones.html), pp. 339–359.

[69] Ibid, p. 356.

Dubbed by Grotius "The Glory of England,"[70] John Selden drew much from Grotius in formulating his own thinking on natural law, and as Jones points out, was quick to identify the Hebraic strand in Grotius's thinking on natural law.[71] But Selden sensed an inherent deficiency in Grotius's philosophy and hence refused to leave natural law exclusively to human rationality; contrary to Grotius, for Selden natural law without a God who takes an active interest in human affairs was impossible. In his *Table Talk*, Selden could not have been more explicit.

I cannot fancy to myself what the law of nature means, but the Law of God. How should I know I ought not to steal, I ought not to commit adultery, unless somebody had told me so? 'Tis not because I think I ought not to do them, nor because you think I ought not; if so, our minds might change; whence then comes the restraint? From a higher power; nothing else can bind. I cannot bind myself, for I may untie myself again; nor an equal cannot bind me, for we may untie one another. It must be a superior, even God Almighty.[72]

The superior naturally has the power to punish as well, for without the threat of punishment, obligation would be meaningless.

The idea of a law carrying obligation irrespective of any punishment annexed to the violation of it ... is no more comprehensible to the human mind than the idea of a father without a child.[73]

Despite the power of human rationality, not all of natural law could be understood without a higher authority dictating it, according to Selden.[74] In addition, even that which could be comprehended through unaided reason would not be binding without divine ordinance, since nothing can be binding unless it includes the threat of punishment. Those divine positive laws appear in the form of the precepts given to the sons of Noah, the *praecepta Noachidarum*, as delineated in the Book of Genesis and as extrapolated in the Babylonian Talmud of Sanhedrin. It was precisely because of the extent of man's autonomous free will that

---

[70] Gooch, *English Democratic Ideas*, p. 101.   [71] Jones, "Philo Judaeus," pp. 339–340.

[72] John Selden, *Table Talk*, Sir Fredrick Pollock (ed.) (London: Quaritch, 1927), p. 101.

[73] Ibid, p. 106.

[74] J. P. Sommerville on Selden: "Selden confirmed his thesis that unaided reason was insufficient to tell us our natural obligations logically entailed penalties. An obligation was something for the non-fulfillment of which a superior would punish us. 'Pure, unaided reason merely persuades or demonstrates, it does not order, nor bind any one to do their duty, unless it is accompanied by the authority of someone who is superior to the man in question'. In the case of the natural law, this superior was God." J. P. Sommerville, "John Selden, the Law of Nature, and the Origins of Government," *The Historical Journal* 27, 2 (1984), p. 442.

Selden granted that he had to insist on the divine promulgation of natural law.[75]

The centrality Selden places on the direct divine source of obligation to natural law leads Richard Tuck to the conclusion that, "Selden's theory of obligation had taken him much further along the road to absolutism than ever Grotius had gone." And in relation to Hobbes, "In some ways, paradoxically enough, the timorous Hobbes was a more liberal theorist than the brave fighter for Parliamentary rights."[76] This assessment is difficult to accept. While admittedly Selden's theory is paradigmatically not a blueprint for the abolition of governmental absolutism, at least in relation to both Grotius and Hobbes, it contains more, not less, of an impediment to limitless governmental power. Precisely because Grotius's source of obligation is amorphous and ill-defined, ample room is left for unlimited governmental absolutism to evolve, and as for Hobbes, as we shall presently see, such absolutism in the form of a Leviathan is actually advocated from the outset. In both cases government is as arbitrary as it is absolute. This is decidedly not the case with Selden's theory in which ultimate authority is anything but humanly arbitrary or absolute, but is rather a clearly defined, divinely delineated natural law.

Like Selden, Thomas Hobbes was significantly influenced by Grotius.[77] Guided by scientific thought, Hobbes's challenge was to form a construct of human reason in an age of skepticism. Hobbes was motivated to formulate his theory of natural law while exposed to the thinking of French skeptics such as Michel de Montaigne (1533–1592) and Pierre Charron (1541–1603) during his exile in Paris in the 1630s. Because the skeptics, despite their variant opinions, found it difficult to achieve general agreement on what constituted justice, they concluded that objective

[75] Knud Haakonssen writes: "Selden took the idea of man's natural freedom from moral laws a great deal further than Grotius, so far in fact, that according to him the only way in which moral community could be understood was as an effect of God's positive imposition and enforcement of the moral law as promulgated in the precepts given to the sons of Noah." Haakonssen, *Natural Law and Moral Philosophy*, pp. 29–30. Jason P. Rosenblatt similarly stresses that for Selden the de rigueur of natural law is to be found in the Hebraic Noachide commandments. "Selden identified natural or universal law as the *praecepta Noachidarum*, uttered by God at a specific moment in historical time, when he made plain to humankind what he would punish them for." Rosenblatt, *Renaissance England's Chief Rabbi*, p. 172. Rosenblatt's illuminating discussion of attitudes toward the Noachide precepts among Selden and his contemporaries shows the degree to which Talmudic and other rabbinic writings were known and of consequence (or not) to thinkers such as Selden, Grotius, Milton, and Barbeyrac. See especially pages 135–157.
[76] Ibid, pp. 97, 100.   [77] Haakonssen, *Natural Law and Moral Philosophy*, p. 30.

and universal justice does not exist and denied the natural sociability of humankind. The authority that laws have for these thinkers stems exclusively from *custom*. For example, Charron writes that, "laws and customs are maintained in credit, not because they are just and good, but because they are laws and customs: this is the mystical foundation of their authority, they have no other."[78] This skeptical deconstruction of Aristotelian thinking left intact one universal principle of human conduct, that of self-preservation. Hobbes followed the skeptics on this account, engaging in what Quentin Skinner has termed "a frontal assault on Aristotle's governing assumption that ... 'man is naturally a sociable and civil creature,'"[79] but he countered the skeptics by refusing to ground the notion of self-preservation in mere custom; he was looking, in Tuck's words, to "transcend the skeptics."[80]

The fundamental axiom of his science is that humans do everything to prevent harm to themselves, "to preserve body and limbs from death and pain."[81] This is not a moral assessment of human nature, but a prudential or utilitarian one.[82] The next step in his scientific definition of natural law is the pursuit of peace, which he determines by reason: it is the state that will be most conducive to self-preservation. In *Leviathan*, Hobbes writes that natural law is "a precept or general rule found out by reason by which a man is forbidden to do that which is destructive of his life or taketh away the means of preserving the same."[83] Hence, "the first and fundamental law of nature ... is to seek peace and follow it."[84] This human inclination toward self-preservation was a natural law that Hobbes turned into a human right. Hobbes solves the problem of making natural law binding on the individual by placing it in the hands of the state through governmental coercion. Because the Leviathan, the powerful absolute state authority, has the power to punish, it pays for the individual to listen, cooperate, and keep his or her side of the deal.

[78] Ibid, p. 40.   [79] Skinner, *Hobbes and Republican Liberty*, p. 41.

[80] See Tuck, "Hobbes," pp.122–125. Tuck is also of the opinion that finding a natural law that transcended the skeptics was what Grotius was pursuing as well, an argument that is contended by Tierney. See Tierney, *The Idea of Natural Rights*, pp. 321–324.

[81] Thomas Hobbes, *The Elements of Law, Natural and Politic*, Ferdinand Tonnies (ed.) (London: Frank Cass and Company Limited, 1969), chapter 14, section 6, p. 71.

[82] Tuck writes that, "Utilitarians, and particularly ... James Stuart Mill, came to see some of Hobbes's philosophy as anticipating their own." Tuck, "Hobbes," p. 211.

[83] Hobbes, *The Elements of Law*, 14.3, p. 64.

[84] Hobbes, *The Elements of Law*, 14.4, p. 64.

Hobbes ended up limiting personal liberty exclusively to the freedom of movement.[85]

For Hobbes then, the state of nature (a term that he probably invented[86]) is a state of war, in which the complete natural freedom of each individual engenders constant strife over opposing interests and competition over limited resources. "The desperate paradox on which Hobbes's political theory is grounded," as Quentin Skinner so aptly puts it, "is that the greatest enemy of human nature is human nature itself." In total contrast to Aristotle's theory of human sociability, explains Skinner, for Hobbes, "There is no possibility ... that a multitude of individuals living in a state of mere nature would ever be able to cooperate with each other in amity and peace."[87] It is the natural law of self-preservation that tames human nature and brings humankind peace and tranquility through the evolution of a strong and controlling sovereign, a Leviathan. It is true that Leviathan could abuse its power, but that for Hobbes would never be as bad as the absence of absolute governmental powers. Hobbes also believed that the word of God did not sanction sedition, and, in this respect, he was very much on the same page with Augustine and the Lutheran Reformers, who quoted the famous text in Romans (13:1–4) to the effect that God was represented by the powers that be, no matter how oppressive they were.

---

[85] Skinner is of the opinion that Hobbes arrived at this conclusion between the publication of *De cive* and his writing of *Leviathan* following the shock he experienced upon learning of the execution of Charles I. Skinner, *Hobbes and Republican Liberty*, pp. 126–131, 211. Skinner suggests that Hobbes developed his theory that, "To be free is simply to be unhindered from moving in accordance with one's natural powers ... in conscious reaction to the republican theory of liberty." Skinner sums up the contrast between the two theories so poignantly that it is worth quoting him in full. "According to the republican theorists, human freedom is subverted not merely by acts of interference, but also and more fundamentally be the existence of arbitrary power. The mere presence of relations of domination and dependence within a civil association is held to reduce us from the status of *liberi homines* or 'free-men' to that of slaves. It is not sufficient, in other words, to enjoy our civic rights and liberties as a matter of fact; if we are to count as free-men, it is necessary to enjoy them in a particular way. We must never hold them merely by the grace or goodwill of anyone else; we must always hold them independently of anyone's arbitrary power to take them away from us. For Hobbes, by contrast, freedom is undermined not by conditions of domination and dependence but only by overt acts of interference. So for Hobbes it *is* sufficient for us to count as free-men that we enjoy our civic rights and liberties as a matter of fact; the mere presence of arbitrary power within a civil association does nothing to subvert our liberty." Ibid, pp. 211–212.

[86] Harrison, *Hobbes, Locke and Confusion's Masterpiece*, p. 70.

[87] Skinner, *Hobbes and Republican Liberty*, pp. 42, 94.

Hobbes used the Hebrew Bible to develop his arguments, but as Ross Harrison emphasizes, even "if the religious elements in his thought were to be removed or refuted, this would not lead to the inevitable collapse of the rest."[88] Natural law had to be something that would neutralize all strife and argument, and because the Bible could be explained in diverse manners, Hobbes thought it could not be the basis of natural law. He thought the classics of Greece and Rome led to sedition as well.[89]

By his own admission, Samuel Pufendorf (1632–1694) "fought against Hobbes at close quarters,"[90] and intended his political thought to be an antidote to the methodical individualism in Hobbes's natural law science, which he found "cynical and excessive."[91] Pufendorf, born in the Lutheran principality of Old Saxony, was an inveterate traveler who divided his time mostly between Germany and Sweden. Although he was one of the few seventeenth-century natural law theorists who wrote at a time of relative calm, it was during a stay in Denmark, after he accepted a position as tutor to the family of the Swedish minister to Denmark and relations between the two countries soured, that he was incarcerated in a Danish prison. It was under these conditions of politically motivated incarceration that he wrote his first major work, *Elementorum jurisprudentiae universalis libri duo* (Elements of Universal Jurisprudence), which was published in 1660 following his release. After teaching philosophy at the University of Heidelberg for almost a decade he wrote his most important work, *De jure naturae et gentium* (On the Law of Nature and of Nations) as a member of the faculty at the University of Lund in Sweden, which was followed by a much heralded short summary entitled *De officio hominis et civis*

---

[88] Harrison, *Hobbes, Locke and Confusion's Masterpiece*, p. 54.

[89] Ibid, 57. Skinner posits that it was Aristotle's *Politics* that Hobbes found most troubling (as opposed to Thucydides' *History*), and as for Rome it was Tacitus's "immortal account" in the *Annals* of how ancient governments were swept away that Hobbes found to be dangerously seditious and dangerous. Skinner, *Hobbes and Republican Liberty*, pp. 64–68. See also Gooch, *English Democratic Ideas*, pp. 150–151. Fittingly, Herbert A. Deane draws attention to the probable strong influence that Augustine and the centrality of fallen man in his ontology had on Hobbes's dour appreciation of human nature and his resultant advocacy of absolutism. Deane, *The Political and Social Ideas of St. Augustine*, pp. 46–47, 234–237.

[90] Samuel Pufendorf, *De jure naturae et gentium*, Gottfried Mascovius (ed.), Michael J. Seidler (trans.) (Lausanne and Geneva: Marcus-Michael Bousquet, 1744), vol. 2, p. 341.

[91] See Craig L. Carr (ed.), "Editor's Introduction," *The Political Writings of Samuel Pufendorf* (Oxford: Oxford University Press, 1994), p. 3.

juxta legem naturalem (On the Duty of Man and Citizen According to Natural Law).[92]

For Pufendorf, humanity's natural state was not the Hobbesian one of perpetual war but rather the Grotian one of natural sociability.[93] In Hobbes, humans *choose* to enter into society in order to preserve themselves; in Pufendorf, humans merge into society by nature.[94] Referencing what he calls the "infallible scripture," Pufendorf turns to the Hebrew Bible in order to prove the error in Hobbes's thought.[95]

[T]here is an opposite point of view based chiefly on the origins of humankind as taught us by the infallible authority of Sacred Scripture, which represents men's natural state as peaceful rather than warlike ... Accordingly, when the first man had been divinely brought forth from the earth, there was joined to him a companion whose matter was taken from himself, so that he might immediately embrace her with a tender love as someone taken from his own flesh and bones ... Since all mortals are descended from this pair, the human race is understood to be associated not only by an ordinary friendship that can spring from natural similarity ... but also by ... a common lineage and blood relationship. Though awareness of it has nearly faded ... anyone who puts it aside and adopts a hostile attitude toward others must be deemed to have fallen away from his primeval and natural state.[96]

Following his Dutch counterpart Grotius, Pufendorf also crafted a natural law theory based on the supremacy of reason and independent from theology, but he could not countenance Grotius's claim that natural laws would be valid even without the existence of God. For Pufendorf,

[92] Ibid, pp. 3–5. Locke thought the *De Jure* to be the "best of that kind." John Locke, "Thoughts Concerning Reading and Study for a Gentleman," in *Locke: Political Essays*, Goldie (ed.), p. 352.

[93] Haakonssen, *Natural Law and Moral Philosophy*, p. 42. Although he accepted the notion of natural sociability, Pufendorf rejected the Aristotelian structuring of humans as "political animals." "[M]an is so far from being by nature a political animal, or from being fitted immediately through birth to play the part of a good citizen, that instead, barely a few of them are by long discipline somehow brought to that point." Pufendorf, *De jure naturae et gentium*, in Carr (ed.), *The Political Writings of Samuel Pufendorf*, p. 205.

[94] Craig Carr writes succinctly: "Social life, in short, is not an artifact of human choice in Pufendorf's judgment; it is a necessary feature of the human condition ... By insisting on humankind's basic sociality, Pufendorf blocks the reduction to methodical individualism. And by fashioning human sociality in moral terms, he blocks the inclination to divorce civil association from its larger moral context." Carr, "Editor's Introduction," p. 20.

[95] There is a plethora of references to God in Pufendorf's writings, as "the good and great creator" or "wise creator," as well as to the "sacred scriptures," but there are almost no direct quotations from the Bible (to be precise, other than some scant references to "Roman Lawyers," there are practically no quotations at all).

[96] Pufendorf, *De jure naturae et gentium*, in Carr (ed.), *The Political Writings of Samuel Pufendorf*, pp. 144–145.

this was an "impious and absurd hypothesis," and if anyone were to conceive "the human race to have sprung from itself, then those dictates of reason could in no way have the force of law, as this necessarily supposes a superior."[97] Pufendorf argued that God created a moral world with certain permanent features that were discoverable by human reason, just as he did in the physical world.[98] Contrary to the Lutherans, for example, Pufendorf posited that humans could indeed attain rational knowledge of God's nature and therefore participate in God's eternal law, but, in agreement with Grotius, he viewed this attainment and participation as a Godless scientific process. Pufendorf differed with Grotius in insisting that recognition of God was necessary to force human obligation to natural law, but he did not elaborate on just how the belief in God translates into obligation. Hence, like Grotius, Pufendorf's theory fell short when it came to the issue of obligation.

Pufendorf tried to improve on the Grotian toleration of governmental absolutism by advocating the possibility of a civil pact that would, from the initial stage of public consent, limit the scope of magisterial power, but he in no way was willing to go so far as to countenance rebellion against what he called "supreme sovereignty."[99] Pufendorf also went beyond Grotius in attributing the root of morals to God's will, and in his categorization of the rest of morals (the branches) as human creations, he is considered a forerunner to Locke.[100] But on the whole, despite the similarities between the two, it was John Selden's Hebraic derivation of natural law that Locke, as I shall presently demonstrate, followed most closely.

[97] Ibid, pp. 154–155. See *ft.* 61 in this chapter for an explanation of Grotian intent. What Pufendorf called "impious and absurd" (the denial of God), Algernon Sidney similarly, based on Scripture, referred to as "foolish and wicked." "Wise and good in a scriptural sense are the same thing, so are the wicked man and the fool, else the psalmist would not have said: The fool, but the wicked man has said in his heart there is no God; for the denying of God is certainly the height of wickedness." Sidney, *Court Maxims*, pp. 30–31.

[98] Haakonssen, *Natural Law and Moral Philosophy*, p. 39.

[99] For example, Pufendorf wrote that, "a people that has given itself into servitude, or rather subjected itself to the absolute sovereignty of one person has no more of a right to reclaim its freedom by force than I do to seize again by force a thing that has already been handed over to another by means of a contract." Pufendorf, *De jure naturae et gentium*, in Carr (ed.), *The Political Writings of Samuel Pufendorf*, p. 240. That having been said, Craig Carr makes the important observation that Pufendorf is "one of the first to entrust the sovereign with the affirmative responsibility both for maintaining a degree of economic and social welfare and for overseeing the social and moral development of the citizenry." Carr, "Editor's Introduction," p. 17.

[100] Ibid, pp. 51–53. For further discussion regarding how Pufendorf's rendering of the state of nature influenced Locke, see Marshall, *Resistance, Religion and Responsibility*, pp. 201–204.

NATURAL LAW AND LOCKE'S STATE OF NATURE

Locke begins his *Second Treatise* discussion on "the state of nature" by establishing that the "state all men are naturally in" is one of "perfect freedom to order their actions and dispose of their possessions and persons as they think fit." It is also a state of full equality, "wherein all the power and jurisdiction is reciprocal, no one having more than another." Freedom in the state of nature is limited only by "the bounds of the law of nature," and the sole limitation on equality is the "will" of "the lord and master," who may with "manifest declaration ... set one above another, and confer on him by an evident and clear appointment an undoubted right to dominion and sovereignty."[101]

The state of nature for Locke is decidedly not a Hobbesian state of lawlessness. "The *State of Nature* has a Law of Nature to govern it, which obliges every one: And Reason, which is that Law, teaches all Mankind, who will but consult it, that being all equal and independent, no one ought to harm another in his Life, Health, Liberty, or Possessions." The law of nature prevents human freedom from extending to the right to harm others and even forbids the harming of oneself (e.g., suicide), "but where some nobler use, than its bare Preservation calls for it." And, conversely, it binds one *"to preserve himself"* and *"to preserve the rest of mankind."*[102] This natural law forbidding harm to person or property produces the natural *right* of the individual not to be the recipient of harm.

Because human behavior is naturally inclined to deteriorate into transgression of the law of nature and in order that "men may be restrained from invading others' rights and from doing hurt to one another," the law of nature, "which willeth the peace and preservation of all mankind ... put into every man's hands, whereby everyone has a right to punish the transgressors of that law."[103] Without this ubiquitous executive power to punish violators of natural law, which may be implemented only "to such a degree as may hinder its violation," the "law of nature would, as all other laws that concern men in this world, be in vain."[104] In what he admits will seem to be a "strange doctrine," Locke declares that the right to punish he who "becomes degenerate and

---

[101] II, 4, p. 287. And see Philip Vogt, "Locke, Eden and Two States of Nature: The Fortunate Fall Revisited," *Journal of the History of Philosophy* 35, 4 (1997), p. 523.

[102] II, 6, p. 289. John Yolton suggests that, for Locke, the law of nature defined morality. See Yolton, "Locke on the Law of Nature," pp. 481–482.

[103] Ibid.   [104] II, 7, p. 289.

declares himself to quit the principles of human nature and to be a noxious creature" belongs to every person, not just to the immediate victim.[105]

Locke is keenly aware of the interpersonal conflict to which this state of affairs leads: "The state of war is a state of enmity and destruction" that evolves in the state of nature. It occurs when a "design upon another man's life," one form of which includes the attempt "to get another man into his absolute power," is confronted with the right, guaranteed under the law of nature, "to destroy that which threatens" and preserve one's own being.[106] In the state of nature, humankind is ruled by reason – "the common rule and measure God hath given to mankind" – and in the state of war, humankind has "renounced reason."[107] What is true of both states, though, is that neither have a "common superior on earth" – no one "to judge between them" in the state of nature, and no one "to appeal to for relief" in the state of war.[108]

Because heaven does not customarily adjudicate human conflicts and thus cannot serve as "the remedy of those evils which necessarily follow from men's being judges in their own cases," Locke can "easily grant that civil government is the proper remedy for the inconveniences of the state of nature."[109] The state of nature then is jettisoned when government is formed.

And this *puts Men* out of a State of Nature *into* that of a *Commonwealth*, by setting up a Judge on Earth, with Authority to determine all the Controversies, and redress the Injuries, that may happen to any Member of the Commonwealth; which Judge is the Legislative, or Magistrate appointed by it. And where-ever there are any number of Men, however associated, that have no such decisive power to appeal to, there they are still *in the State of Nature.*[110]

---

[105] II, 9, 10, pp. 290–291.   [106] II, 3, 16, 17, pp. 286, 296, 297.

[107] II, 11, pp. 291–292.

[108] II, 3, 19, pp. 298–299. Locke, in an apparent indictment of Hobbes's state of nature, warns against "confounding" the two states, which "are as far distant, as a State of Peace, Good Will, Mutual Assistance, and Preservation, and a State of Enmity, Malice, Violence, and Mutual Destruction are one from another." Ibid, p. 298. See also Cox, *Locke on War and Peace*, p. B. It is important to note that the critics of Hobbes's warlike state of nature predicated their disagreement with Hobbes on the fact that the scriptural description of creation militated against his description. See Helen Thornton, *State of Nature or Eden? Thomas Hobbes and His Contemporaries on the Natural Condition of Human Beings* (Rochester, NY: Rochester University Press, 2005), pp. 70–86.

[109] II, 13, pp. 293–294.

[110] II, 89, p. 343. Similarly, Locke will later write that the individual "and all the rest of *Mankind are one Community*, make up one Society distinct from all other Creatures.

But if the government does not abide by the laws of nature that it was in essence established to uphold, society reverts back to a state of nature and individuals retrieve their original right of self-preservation, which allows them to endeavor to replace tyranny with legitimate government.

We can now appreciate the importance of understanding Locke's theory of natural law. For Locke, humankind's state of nature is an anarchic state that is ruled by the laws of nature, but because these laws cannot ensure a person's protection in the state of nature, humanity must enter into a compact state in which these laws of nature remain intact. If creation of the state by compact results in the violation of the laws of nature, then the compact state loses its legitimacy and its right to exist, resulting in the obligation to form a new governmental system in which the laws of nature are honored. Clearly Locke's theory of civil government, which includes the right to rebel against uncivil government, is predicated on his understanding of natural law, hence the requisite introduction of the *Second Treatise* with a discussion of natural law.

LOCKE'S NATURAL LAW AND LOCKE'S GOD

Locke establishes his understanding of natural law on the existence of God, which in the *Second Treatise* he takes entirely for granted. Some scholars have detected this in Locke's other writings, but they seem to have missed that it is in the *Two Treatises* itself where Locke positions his proof-of-God-by-design theory, and he does so following his (repeated) insistence on properly interpreting the Biblical text.[111] Here is how he does it.

And were it not for the corruption, and viciousness of degenerate Men, there would be no need of any other; no necessity that Men should separate from this great and natural community, and by positive agreements combine into smaller and divided associations." II, 128, p. 370.

[111] J. Budziszewski, for example, states that, "[Y]ou can see that Locke stakes his entire argument for natural law and natural rights on the existence of God. But how do we know that God exists? Locke answers in his other writings that we know him by his works. The universe shows magnificent order and design; however, design presupposes a designer." Budziszewski, *Written on the Heart*, p. 105. Locke was not committed to proof-by-design exclusivity but believed rather that "no arguments that are made use of to work the persuasion of a God into men's minds, should be invalidated." The reason he gave for this was that, "the different make of men's tempers and application of their thoughts, some arguments prevail more on one, and some on another, for the

In his argument against patriarchalism in the *First Treatise*, Locke disproves Filmer's contention that all of God's powers were transferred to Adam at creation, that Adam in effect took God's place with the transference of God's regal power over all living things to Adamic regal power over children. Filmer's version of fatherhood was granted in concurrence with the birth of offspring, which meant in effect that human thralldom was also elemental to human existence. Thus writes Filmer:

Not only Adam, but the succeeding Patriarchs had by Right of Fatherhood Royal Authority over their Children ... That every Man that is born is so far from being free, that by his very Birth he becomes a Subject of him that begets him.[112]

Locke proceeds to point out that Filmer claims to derive this idea from Grotius, who teaches that fathers have power over their children by virtue of begetting them. (Could Filmer have turned to Grotius for support because he realized he could not rely on the Hebrew Bible to support his claim?) What is certain, stresses Locke, is that nowhere did Grotius himself define this parental power as *supreme power*, similar to the power of a master over a slave, which includes the power of life and death.

Grotius tells us not here how far this *jus in liberos*, this Power of Parents over their Children extends; but our *Author* always very clear in the point, assures us, 'tis *Supreme Power*, and like that of Absolute Monarchs over their Slaves, Absolute Power of Life and Death. He that should demand of him, How, or for what Reason it is, that begetting a Child gives the Father such an Absolute Power over him, will find him answer nothing: we are to take his word for this as well as several other things, and by that the Laws of Nature and the Constitutions of Government must stand or fall.[113]

Even if one were to assume "that *Fathers have a Power over the Lives of their Children, because they give them Life and Being,*"[114] a claim for which we have already seen that Filmer offers no proof, no logical deduction exists to assert that the power to give also contains a correlative power to confiscate. It should be clear rather "that every one who gives another any thing, has not always thereby a Right to take it away again."[115] However, Locke is not satisfied in predicating his arguments on reason alone, and goes on to formulate a far more theological grounding for his position denying absolute

confirmation of the same truth." Locke, *The Works of John Locke*, vol. 3 (1696, http://oll.libertyfund.org/index.php?option=com_staticxt&staticfile=show.php%3Ftitle), p. 40.
[112] I, 50, p. 194.   [113] I, 51, p. 195.   [114] I, 52, p. 196.   [115] I, 52, p. 196.

sovereignty to the notion of fatherhood. His argument is one of *intelligent design*.

> They who say the *Father* gives Life to his Children, are so dazzled with the thoughts of Monarchy, that they do not, as they ought, remember God, who is *the Author and Giver of Life:* '*Tis in him alone we live, move, and have our being.* How can he be thought to give Life to another, that knows not wherein his own Life consists? Philosophers are at a loss about it after their most diligent enquiries; And Anatomists, after their whole Lives and Studies spent in Dissections, and diligent examining the Bodies of Men, confess their Ignorance in the Structure and Use of many parts of Mans Body, and in that Operation wherein Life consists in the whole. And doth the Rude Plough-Man, or the more ignorant Voluptuary, frame or fashion such an admirable Engine as this is, and then put Life and Sense into it? Can any Man say, He formed the parts that are necessary to the Life of his Child? Or can he suppose himself to give the Life, and yet not know what Subject is fit to receive it, nor what Actions or Organs are necessary for its Reception or Preservation?[116]

The design of human life is simply too intricate, argues Locke, for humankind to take exclusive credit for creation. Humankind can hardly be considered its own sole or even primary creator because it cannot comprehend its own existence. For Filmer, God transferred his creative powers to Adam, and Adam, in a sense, then inherited God's powers. For Locke, God's limitless creative powers remained intact and God continued as primary creator, even after humankind became partners with him in the perpetuation of its species.

> If he made it, let him, when it is out of order, mend it, at least tell wherein the defects lie. *Shall he that made the Eye not see?* Says the Psalmist, *Psalm* 94. 9. See these Mens Vanities: The Structure of that one part is sufficient to convince us of an All-wise Contriver, and he has so visible a claim to us as his Workmanship, that one of the ordinary Appellations of God in Scripture is, *God our Maker,* and *the Lord our Maker.*[117]

At the very beginning of the first chapter of his *Essays on the Law of Nature*, entitled "Is There a Rule of Morals, or Law of Nature Given to Us? Yes," he is unequivocal that, in contradistinction to Grotius and in accord with Selden and Pufendorf, everything he has to say about natural law derives from the existence of God.

---

[116] I, 52, p. 196. It is not just "in other writings" as Budziszewski suggests, but in the *Two Treatises* itself.
[117] I, 53, p. 197.

Since God shows himself to us as present everywhere and, as it were, forces himself upon the eyes of men as much in the fixed course of nature now as by the frequent evidence of miracles in time past, I assume there will be no one to deny the existence of God, provided he recognizes either the necessity for some rational account of our life, or that there is a thing that deserves to be called virtue or vice. This then being taken for granted, and it would be wrong to doubt it, namely, that some divine being presides over the world – for it is by his order that the heaven revolves in unbroken rotation, the earth stands fast and the stars shine, and it is he who has set bounds even to the wild sea and prescribed to every kind of plants the manner and periods of germination and growth; it is in obedience to this will that all living beings have their own laws of birth and life; and there is nothing so unstable, so uncertain in this whole constitution of things as not to admit of valid and fixed laws of operation appropriate to its nature – it seems just therefore to inquire whether man alone has come into the world altogether exempt from any law applicable to himself, without a plan, rule, or any pattern of his life. No one will easily believe this, who has reflected upon Almighty God, or the unvarying consensus of the whole of mankind at every time and in every place, or even upon himself or his conscience.[118]

Through their intellect ("reflection upon Almighty God"), humans can reach the understanding that it is unreasonable to assume that there is a divine law for every creation, as demonstrated in the sublime order and design, yet "man alone has come into the world altogether exempt from any law applicable to himself, without a plan, rule, or any pattern of his life." In the fourth chapter of his *Essays on the Law of Nature*, entitled "Can Reason Attain to the Knowledge of Natural Law through Sense Experience? Yes," Locke reiterates the unambiguous connection between God and the natural law he bestows on humankind and touches upon subjects that he will later use in his *Second Treatise*.

Hence it is undoubtedly inferred that there must be a powerful and wise creator of all these things, who has made and built this whole universe and us mortals who are not the lowest part of it. For, indeed, all the rest of it, inanimate things and brute beasts, cannot create man who is far more perfect than they are. Nor, on the other hand, can man create himself; for that we do not owe our origin to ourselves is surely undisputed, not merely for the reason that nothing is its own cause – for obviously this axiom does not prevent us, if we are willing to acknowledge God, from believing that something exists which does not depend upon another – but also because man does not find in himself all those

---

[118] John Locke, *Essays on the Law of Nature*, W. von Leyden (ed.) (Oxford: Oxford University Press, 1954), p. 81.

perfections which he can conceive in his mind. For ... if man were the maker of himself, able to give himself being, then he who could bring himself forth into the world of nature would also give himself an existence of everlasting duration ... After the case has been put thus it necessarily follows that above ourselves there exists another more powerful and wiser agent who at his will can bring us into the world, maintain us, and take us away. Hence, having inferred this on the evidence of the senses, reason lays down that there must be some superior power to which we are rightly subject, namely God who has a just and inevitable command over us and at his pleasure can raise us up or throw us down, and make us by the same commanding power happy or miserable. And since he has himself created the soul and constructed the body with wonderful art, and has thoroughly explored the faculties and powers of each ... it appears clearly that, with sense perception showing the way, *reason can lead us to the knowledge of the lawmaker or of some superior power to which we are necessarily subject*give himself an existence of everlasting duration ... After the case has been put thus it necessarily follows that above ourselves there exists another more powerful and wiser agent who at his will can bring us into the world, maintain us, and take us away. Hence, having inferred this on the evidence of the senses, reason lays down that there must be some superior power to which we are rightly subject, namely God who has a just and inevitable command over us and at his pleasure can raise us up or throw us down, and make us by the same commanding power happy or miserable. And since he has himself created the soul and constructed the body with wonderful art, and has thoroughly explored the faculties and powers of each ... it appears clearly that, with sense perception showing the way, *reason can lead us to the knowledge of the lawmaker or of some superior power to which we are necessarily subject.*[119] (Italics added.)

---

[119] Ibid, pp. 103–104. The same intellect, driven by "sense perception," that allows humankind to comprehend the existence of a relevant God also dictates, according to Locke, the existence of an afterlife, the nature of which is determined by human action. Later, in chapter V of *Essays on the Law of Nature*, Locke writes: "Even if God and the soul's immortality are not moral propositions and laws of nature, nevertheless they must be necessarily presupposed if natural law is to exist. For there is no law without a lawmaker, and law is to no purpose without punishment." Ibid, p. 113.

Locke also elaborates on this in a journal entry on the "extent and measure of knowledge" written during his travels in France in 1677. "Another use of his knowledge is to live in peace with his fellow-men, and this also he is capable of. Besides a plenty of the good things of this world, with life, health, and peace to enjoy them, we can think of no other concernment mankind hath that leads him not out of it, and places him not beyond the confines of this earth; and it seems probable that there should be some better state somewhere else to which man might arise, since, when he hath all that this world can afford, he is still unsatisfied, uneasy, and far from happiness. It is certain, and that all men must consent to, that there is a possibility of another state when this scene is over; and that the happiness and misery of that depends on the ordering of ourselves in our actions in this time of our probation here. The acknowledgment of a God will easily lead any one to this, and he hath left so many footsteps of himself, so many proofs of his being in every creature, as are sufficient to

Interestingly, Locke, who nowhere predicated the substance of his natural law on universal consent, nevertheless attributes the belief in a consequential God to the faculty of human reason, which *is* of a universal nature.

convince any who will but make use of their faculties that way – and I dare say nobody escapes this conviction for want of sight; but if any be so blind, it is only because they will not open their eyes and see ... It being then possible, and at least probable, that there is another life, wherein we shall give an account of our past actions in this to the great God of heaven and earth; here comes in another, and that the main concernment of mankind, to know what those actions are that he is to do, what those are he is to avoid, what the law is he is to live by here, and shall be judged by hereafter; and in this part too he is not left so in the dark, but that he is furnished with principles of knowledge, and faculties able to discover light enough to guide him; his understanding seldom fails him in this part, unless where his will would have it so." John Locke, *The Life and Letters of John Locke: With Extracts from His Journals and Commonplace Books*, Peter King (ed.) (London: H. Colburn & R. Bentley, 1830), pp. 89–90.

King also writes that it was the world to come that preoccupied Locke's attention during his last hours of life. "To Lady Masham, who remained with him, he said that he thanked God he had passed a happy life, but that now he found that all was vanity, and exhorted her to consider this world only as a preparation for a better state hereafter." Ibid, p. 267.

In *An Essay Concerning Human Understanding*, Locke writes thus regarding human accountability in the next world: "But in the great day, wherein the secrets of all hearts shall be laid open, it may be reasonable to think, no one shall be made to answer for what he knows nothing of; but shall receive his doom, his conscience accusing or excusing him." John Locke, *An Essay Concerning Human Understanding*, Roger Woolhouse (ed.) (London: Penguin Books, 2004), p. 310.

And lastly, in his third letter of response to Bishop Stillingfleet's attacks on the *Essay*, Locke writes of his own appointment with destiny with a distinct air of serenity: "I am going, my lord, to a tribunal that has a right to judge of thoughts, and being secure that I there shall be found of no party but that of truth (for which there is required nothing but the receiving truth in the love of it) I matter not much of what party any one shall, as may best serve his turn, denominate me here." "Mr. Locke's Reply to the Right Reverend the Lord Bishop of Worcester's Answer to His Second Letter," in Locke, *The Works of John Locke*, vol. 3, http://oll.libertyfund.org/index.php?option=com_staticxt&staticfile=show.php%3Ftitle), p. 190.

See also Marshall, *Resistance, Religion and Responsibility*, p. 192, who writes that, "Behind Locke's argument that there had to be another life because men were uneasy in this once again stands both a tacit reluctance to adopt a theory of solely terrestrial self-interest and a notion that God was bountiful, not making men to be unhappy ... According to Locke, the acknowledgment of a God led directly to this view." See also ibid, p. 441. In this, as in so many other ideas, Locke took issue with Hobbes, who, as A. P. Martinich writes, "was notorious for being a materialist and for denying the immortality of the soul." Martinich, "The Bible and Protestantism in *Leviathan*," p. 378.

It is worth noting that the concept of an afterlife, the nature of which is determined by human conduct in temporal reality, is a basic Hebraic tenet, included by Maimonides as one of the requisite Principles of Faith. See Maimonides' Thirteen Principles of Faith, Introduction to Commentary on Mishnah, BT Sanhedrin, Principle 11.

To this your question, my lord, I answer, that I think, amounts to thus much, that the vastly greater majority of mankind have, in all ages of the world, actually believed a God; that the majority of the remaining part have not actually disbelieved it, and consequently those who have actually opposed the belief of a God, have truly been very few. So that comparing those that have actually disbelieved with those who have actually believed a God, their number is so inconsiderable, that in respect of this incomparably greater majority of those who have owned the belief of a God, it may be said to be the universal consent of mankind.[120]

Clearly then, for Locke there is a natural law that can be perceived by human reason, the same reason that ubiquitously perceives the existence of the God who is the arbiter of that law. But the big question is: *From where did Locke derive that?*

THE SOURCES OF NATURAL LAW

For source material on his presentation of natural law, Locke quotes the Hebrew Bible three times, the English ecclesiastic Richard Hooker twice, and the historian Garcilaso de la Vega once.[121] I will soon demonstrate a far

---

[120] "Mr. Locke's Reply to the Right Reverend the Lord Bishop of Worcester's Answer to His Third Letter," p. 366.

[121] Richard Hooker (1554–1600) was an Anglican priest and theologian. His most well-known work, *Of the Laws of Ecclesiastical Polity*, was published in 1594–1597 and argued for a middle way (*Via Media*) between the Roman Catholic Church and the Puritans. According to Hooker, the Bible commanded political authority, and so it was based both on piety and reason that supplemented divine revelation. Locke always refers to Hooker as "the Judicious Hooker" (II, 5, 15, 61, pp. 288, 295, 327), and it is quite clear that he was close to Hooker's search for a via media in the context of a compromise or synthesis between reason and revelation, religion and government. See Robert K. Faulkner, "Reason and Revelation in Hooker's Ethics," *The American Political Science Review* 59, 3 (1965), pp. 680–690. Hooker wrote under Queen Elizabeth when the church and state had been "safely" restored to the Protestantism of her father, King Henry VIII, from the Catholic rule of her sister, Mary. King Henry, it must be remembered, had taken both secular and ecclesiastical jurisdiction into his own hands while dismissing the authority of the Pope. Hence it was convenient for Hooker to argue that for a Christian people, church and state were not two separate institutions. What is of special import, as Eric Nelson has shown, is that Hooker was following Erastus in arguing that any Christian polity must follow the commonwealth of the Hebrews, which "recognized no distinction between civil and ecclesiastical law or authority." Hooker believed, Nelson continues, that, "the constitutional design of ancient Israel retains authority in the Christian world because God himself was its author. Hooker's basic defense of the Elizabethan settlement is thus that it replicates this divinely-sanctioned arrangement." Nelson, *The Hebrew Republic*, pp. 94–96. In an interesting aside, Hooker was a Hebrew lecturer at Corpus Christi College from

more copious reliance on the Hebrew Bible than immediately meets the eye, but my analysis must begin with the Biblical passages he quotes explicitly.

The first quote, "Whoso sheddeth man's blood, by man shall his blood be shed," Locke calls "that great law of nature";[122] he juxtaposes it to the second quote, Cain's (chronologically earlier) entreaty to God, "Every one that findeth me, shall slay me,"[123] a plea "so plain" that it was "writ in the hearts of mankind."[124]

These quotes demonstrate the centrality of the Hebrew Bible, specifically the Book of Genesis, to several aspects of Locke's thinking. First, Locke is not satisfied with the use of one single verse to make his point. It would appear that Cain's entreaty is sufficient to show the legitimacy of two concepts that Locke places at the center of his theory of natural law: capital punishment for murder and "individual executive power." (By this latter expression Locke refers to the political power of retributive justice with which he believes every individual is endowed. I will presently discuss this concept at length.) Locke, however, does not deem Cain's plea sufficient and instead precedes the Cain entreaty with the postdiluvian admonition against shedding human blood. Why is this additional verse needed? The answer, I believe, may be found through a careful reading of Locke's text. The sentence in which the quote appears reads, "And upon this is grounded

1577–1580. John S. Marshall, *Hooker and the Anglican Tradition* (London: Adam & Charles Black, 1963), p. 37.

Inca Garcilaso de la Vega (1539–1616) was a Spanish poet and historian who wrote a history of Peru.

[122] Genesis 9:6. Milton similarly wrote, "The first express Law of God giv'n to mankind, was that to *Noah*, as a law in general to all the Sons of men. And by that most ancient and universal Law, *whosoever sheddeth mans blood, by man shall his blood be shed.*" John Milton, "Eikonoklastes," *The Complete Prose Works of John Milton*, Don M. Wolfe (gen. ed.), 8 vols., vol. III (New Haven, CT: Yale University Press, 1953–1982), p. 586.

[123] Genesis 4:14.

[124] II, 11, p. 292. "Writ in the hearts" is an apparent reference to Paul in Romans 2:15, with regard to gentiles who know nothing of Moses or Christ but may nonetheless show by their deeds "that the requirements of the Law are written on their hearts, their consciences also bearing witness, and their thoughts now accusing, now even defending them." It might be significant that Locke chose not to quote this New Testament support for natural law. For the followers of the Cambridge School, this quote appears contextually obligatory for a Christian theorist on natural law, and for the Straussians it is a source that Locke should be most interested in subverting. It is also worth noting that Paul was preceded by Jeremiah, who used a similar expression: "The guilt of Judah is inscribed with a stylus of iron, engraved with an adamant point on the tablet of their hearts." Jeremiah 17:1. Of worthy note as well is the use of the expression in Proverbs 3:3 where the "writing on heart" is taken to be a human endeavor.

that great law of nature, 'Whoso sheddeth man's blood, by man shall his blood be shed.'" Locke specifically labels this Biblical verse a *great law of nature*. But what is this law, divine or natural? Locke has already defined the law of nature as the law of *reason*.[125] Is it not reason then, rather than divine ordinance, that the criminal renounces?

The synthesis that Locke forges between reason and revelation will be discussed later. At this juncture, it suffices to say that Locke's intention was apparently to use the Biblical account of the first recorded murder to prove his understanding of natural law. "[A]nd when they were in the field, Cain set upon his brother Abel and killed him. The Lord said to Cain, 'Where is your brother Abel?' And he said 'I do not know. Am I my brother's keeper?' Then He said, 'What have you done? Hark, your brother's blood cries out to me from the ground.'"[126] In these verses, God confronts Cain over the murder of his brother Abel as if the postdiluvian admonition against murder had already been given to humankind. Because it had not yet been given, the conclusion that must be drawn from God's indictment of Cain is that he is responsible because he should have known through reason, divinely implanted within him, that murder is forbidden and warrants accountability. What Locke has done then is cleverly use Scripture itself, the very revelation that would seem to obviate reason, to prove the existence of a ubiquitous reason-based natural law, installed and relevant from the time of creation.[127]

INDIVIDUAL POLITICAL POWER

Locke also uses these verses from the Book of Genesis to prove his doctrine of "the executive power of the law of nature," which he himself dubs a "strange doctrine."[128] The doctrine

---

[125] "The *State of Nature* has a Law of Nature to govern it, which obliges every one: And reason, which is that law, teaches all Mankind, who will but consult it, that being all equal and independent, no one ought to harm another in his Life, Health, Liberty, or Possessions." II, 6, p. 289.

[126] Genesis 4:8–10.

[127] Grotius seems to hold a similar view regarding the significance of Cain's response, albeit less developed than Locke's. Grotius writes: "From a sense of this natural justice, Cain knowing himself guilty of his brother's blood said, 'whosoever finds me shall kill me.'" Grotius, *The Rights of War and Peace*, book I, chapter 2, p. 5.

[128] II, 13, p. 293.

is, that every Man in the State of Nature, has a power to kill a Murderer ...
who, having renounced Reason, the common Rule and Measure, God hath
given to Mankind, hath, by the unjust Violence and Slaughter he hath committed upon one, declared War against all Mankind, and therefore may be
destroyed as a *Lyon* or a *Tyger*, one of those wild Savage Beasts, with whom
Men can have no Society nor Security: And upon this is grounded that great
Law of Nature, *Who so sheddeth Mans Blood, by Man shall his Blood be
shed.* And *Cain* was so fully convinced, that every one had a Right to
destroy such a Criminal, that after the Murder of his Brother, he cries out,
Every one that findeth me, shall slay me; so plain was it writ in the Hearts of
Mankind.[129]

The idea of political power belonging to the individual is obviously
fully consonant with Locke's concept of individual natural freedom and is
consistently at odds with Filmer's notion of the individual's natural state
of subjection.[130] What makes Locke's idea so "strange" is how iconoclastic it was for the times; philosopher and Locke scholar James Tully writes,
"[I]t is one of the major conceptual innovations in early modern political
thought."[131] Tully goes on to say that until Locke:

No one was willing to grant that the people either individually or collectively had
the capacity to exercise political power themselves. In positing political individualism or individual popular sovereignty Locke thus repudiates 500 years of elite
political holism and reconceptualizes the origins of political power in a radically
populist way.[132]

---

[129] II, 11, p. 292. David Novak sees in the events subsequent to Cain's entreaty Biblical
precedent and justification for humankind's (Aristotelian) sociability. "When Cain
protests to God that his punishment of being 'a wanderer (*na ve-nad*) in the world' is
'more than I can bear' (Genesis 4:12–13), since he will be vulnerable to destruction as
was his now dead brother, God promises protection. Cain then starts his own family,
and 'builds a city' (Genesis 4:17) ... The city itself would seem to be Cain's protection,
both from those who would murder him and from his own homicidal temptations that
seriously wounded a life worthy of human participation. What could be inferred from all
this is that without socialization, humans are left unprotected from being both the
victims and the perpetrators of violent death by natural forces as well as by their own
hands. A justly ordered society is a requirement of human nature if human beings are to
survive, let alone flourish." Novak, *Natural Law in Judaism*, p. 36. See also John
Milton, "The Tenure of Kings and Magistrates," in Milton, *Political Writings*,
pp. 8–9.

[130] See James Tully, "Locke," in J. H. Burns (ed.), *The Cambridge History of Political
Thought, 1450–1700* (Cambridge: Cambridge University Press, 1991), p. 620. Tully
points out that, "Locke explicitly places the Two Treatises in the tradition of natural
freedom and in opposition to natural subjection"; see Locke, *Two Treatises on
Government*, I.i.3–5, pp. 160–161, I.ii.6, p. 162, I.ii.15, p. 169, II.ii.4, p. 287, II.
vii.95, pp. 348–349 *ft*. 3.

[131] Tully, "Locke," p. 620.   [132] Ibid, p. 622.

Tully, though, does not say whence Locke culled this revolutionary idea, despite the significant textual evidence pointing to the Hebrew Bible.

It is not that Locke invented the concept of individual natural freedom. The idea of natural freedom has been traced back to Roman law as well as to political theorists of the seventeenth century such as Grotius, Hobbes, and Pufendorf. These thinkers, however, asserted that natural freedom is limited to individuals' right to defend themselves and their possessions from attack, and that it must, in any case, be completely abdicated to the executive power. In his early *Two Tracts* Locke belonged to this group as well, when he wrote:

That the subject is bound to passive obedience under any decree of the magistrate whatever, whether just or unjust, nor on any ground whatsoever may a private citizen oppose the magistrate's decrees by force of arms ... Nor can anyone deny that all indifferent actions, of whatsoever sort they may be, lie under the power of him to whose discretion are delivered the liberty, fortunes and the life itself of every subject.[133]

In his *Two Treatises*, however, Locke defines individual natural freedom for the first time in terms of political power. Hence, rather than lead to a defense of absolutism as it did for many of his predecessors and contemporaries, it leads Locke to the advocacy of limited government and inviolable individual rights.[134] Because individual political power is the source of communal power for Locke (and communal power for governmental power), the individual and his or her rights never entirely dissipate. Individual power, which has been sidelined or placed in deep freeze in order to facilitate the insurances that only socialization can guarantee, is thawed and reconstituted when the very objectives of socialization are violated by the abuses of government. Locke's predecessors, such as Aquinas and Suarez, who did not believe that communal power emanated from individual power but was rather a creation of the community itself, could naturally not have advocated a resurfacing of individual power in

---

[133] Locke, *Locke: Political Essays*, pp. 61–62, 70.

[134] Tully, "Locke," p. 621. Ross Harrison astutely describes the differences between Hobbes and Locke with regard to the place human freedom occupies in the social construct. "Hobbes wrote in and after a civil war. The known political world had fallen apart: Hobbes in reaction makes a plea for unity, strong government, absolute authority. Locke wrote in a period of strong government, absolute authority that he thought was taking England in the wrong direction. It is in reaction to this a plea for resistance, rebellion, war, for things (temporarily) falling apart." Harrison, *Hobbes, Locke and Confusion's Masterpiece*, p. 169.

the face of governmental abuses, and hence it is not surprising that they showed very limited and muddled support for rebellion against egregious governmental abuses, as we saw earlier.

Michael Zuckert is troubled by Locke's categorization of this doctrine as "strange" because "his signals about the natural executive power stand in stark contrast to the overall tone of the early parts of the *Second Treatise*, where Locke for the most part suggests that his position is anything but novel, claiming agreement with Hooker, and through Hooker with a long tradition of Christian natural law philosophy going back at least to Thomas Aquinas."[135] Contrary to Zuckert's suggestion, though, Locke does not claim agreement with Hooker on the issue of individual executive power in a pre-political state. Locke's two quotes from Hooker in his discussion of the state of nature deal first with the idea of natural equality and then with the reason humans unite to create political societies. The quotes from Hooker indicating marginal agreement with the notion of individual executive power are not cited by Locke himself, and with good reason, as Zuckert himself goes on to argue that Hooker's version of individual executive power is a truncated one allowing for this power only under certain limited conditions.

For Hooker, it is decidedly not a sweeping, natural, and inherent right of each individual that then metamorphoses into a collective and communal responsibility within political society, but remains poised for potential reemergence if that political society should revert back to the state of nature by succumbing to tyranny, as it is for Locke. While Hooker, in his limited recognition of the existence of a pre-political society and individual executive power within it, had moved beyond natural law classicists such as Aquinas and Suarez, he is still far from Locke's iconoclastic presentation of these ideas. It is possible that Locke uses Hooker in his chapter on the state of nature to create an image of moderation, or what John Dunn calls "a claim to respectability,"[136] in order to engender a proper hearing for his "strange" doctrine, but it is clearly not because he predicates his thinking on this subject on Hooker's philosophy.

The question that naturally arises is: Upon what basis *does* Locke postulate his idea of individual executive power in pre-governmental society? Is it a concept simply of his own creation? Even if we posit that the idea is his own, Locke is clearly uncomfortable presenting it as such

[135] Michael P. Zuckert, *Natural Rights and the New Republicanism* (Princeton, NJ: Princeton University Press, 1998), p. 222.
[136] Dunn, *The Political Thought of John Locke*, p. 169.

and chooses instead to base it upon the authority of the Hebrew Bible. Other than the two quotes from Hooker that do *not* address his groundbreaking natural law concept, the quotes from Genesis are the only quotes that Locke offers in his chapter on natural law, and they explicitly suggest the very same argument that Locke is trying to make. The world that Cain and Abel inhabit is a pre-political world where the right to utilize individual executive power is self-evident, as demonstrated in Cain's appeal to God for protection. Cain's supplication is meant to forestall the retribution of pre-political society in which it is "writ in the hearts," meaning naturally understood by all, that everyone has the right, and the political power, to destroy the man like a "lion or tiger," since in murdering another, he has "declared war against all mankind."[137]

Based on this similarity of quotation, Richard Tuck finds Locke's doctrine identical with Grotius's understanding of individual freedom, and the quote he brings from Grotius seems to verify it.[138] Grotius wrote, "From a sense of this natural justice, Cain knowing himself guilty of his brother's blood said, 'whosoever finds me shall kill me.'"[139] Zuckert, too, suggests that Grotius is Locke's source.[140] Yet Grotius's idea of individual political power clearly does not lead him in the same direction as Locke's does, because, as mentioned earlier, he was "to become notorious after the publication of the *De Jure Belli* for his permissive attitude towards absolutism."[141] Second, and most relevant, Grotius himself brings the Biblical quote of Cain, "whosoever finds me shall kill me," as proof of the individual executive power idea – a point that appears to have gone unnoticed by Tuck and Zuckert.[142] Clearly, this revolutionary concept is grounded in the Hebrew Bible, and its advocates refuse to equivocate about its source.

Surely it seems strange then to acknowledge Grotius as Locke's source, while at the same time declaring the one source cited by both men to be insignificant for Locke, or worse, using it as part of an

---

[137] II, 11, p. 292.   [138] Tuck, *Natural Rights Theories*, pp. 62–63.
[139] Grotius, *The Rights of War and Peace*, book I, chapter II, V. Tuck does not bring an earlier quote of Grotius that seems to serve as further verification. "And before Civil Laws were made, every one was at Liberty to right himself by force." Chapter I, X, 7, p. 157.
[140] Zuckert, *Natural Rights and the New Republicanism*, pp. 126, 222.
[141] Tuck, *Natural Rights Theories*, p. 63.
[142] See Grotius, *The Rights of War and Peace*, I.ii.5; II.xx.3, 7, 8, 9. For more about Grotius and his Jewish sources, see Lachs, "Hugo Grotius' Use of Jewish Sources," and Isaac Husik, "The Law of Nature, Hugo Grotius and the Bible," *HUCA* 2 (1925), pp. 381–417.

attempt to argue the very opposite, as Leo Strauss would have us believe. (That would de facto place Grotius in the same esoteric camp as Locke, a suggestion that to the best of my knowledge has not been made by the Straussians.)

The Cambridge School, though, does not fare much better than its opposition on this issue. Quentin Skinner suggests that Locke actually borrowed the idea of individual political power from the early-sixteenth-century French theologian and opponent of papal absolutism Jacques Almain, who postulated that "each individual in his pre-political state must be pictured as the 'executioner of the law of nature', with the right to wield the sword of justice on his own behalf."[143] But the Lockean power of individual sovereignty went beyond the right to "wield the sword of justice on *his own behalf*" and was instead on "everyone's behalf." That is precisely what Tully found to be Locke's "repudiation of 500 years of elite political holism" and his "reconceptualization of the origins of political power."

John Dunn admits that it was Hebrew Scripture (not Almain or anyone else) that Locke drew from, but he projects bafflement over the fact that Locke uses Scripture at this particular juncture of his writing. "It is profoundly significant," writes Dunn, "that it is at the point where Locke makes the central claim of his entire argument and makes it in words which constitute the most explicit flouting of the epistemological criteria which he had adopted ever since the *Essays on the Law of Nature*, that he should desert a plausible naturalism so bluntly for the record of divine positive law."[144] Dunn is correct in saying that Locke's use of the Bible at this point is "profoundly significant" but not for the reason he provides.[145] The naturalism that

---

[143] Skinner, *The Foundations of Modern Political Thought*, pp. 43, 119.
[144] Dunn, *The Political Thought of John Locke*, p. 168, *ft.* 3.
[145] In Locke's use of the Biblical text, Dunn finds a severe limitation on individual executive power, entirely restricted to an immediate and closed social unit, and not to all of humankind. "When force without right disrupts the proper peace of the state of nature every man's hand is justly against the aggressor, not because of the universality of the threat in natural terms but because the aggressor has violated the Hebraic unity of the tribal family and bears in consequence the brand of Cain. It is not a naturalistic individualism which gives to all men the executive power of the law of nature in others' cases, but the Hebraic simplicity of ... 'tribal brotherhood' as opposed to 'universal otherhood.'" Dunn, *The Political Thought of John Locke*, pp. 168–169. Dunn's interpretation here of Locke is most troubling. Locke, in the paragraph in question itself (II, 11, p. 292), is in no way referring to a limited tribal unit when he licenses an individual with executive power. On the contrary, he writes specifically, "And thus it is, that every Man in the State of Nature, had a Power to kill a Murderer ... who having

is "plausible" for Locke is one that is rooted in Biblical authority, an authority that shows that Cain was responsible for his actions not just because of "divine positive law" but because his actions contravened a natural law that he could and should have understood even without divine directive.

Kim Ian Parker makes the point that Dunn is needlessly bothered by Locke's turn to Scripture at this point because, "Locke is very reliant on Genesis at critical moments in his political thought." Parker argues that it is Locke's intention here to show that, "once God reveals to Cain the violation of the law of nature, Cain is intellectually convinced of the truth of God's statement."[146] While Parker is on surer ground than the Straussian and Cambridge scholars, it is not just at "critical moments" that Locke relies on Genesis, and for that matter not only on Genesis, but other parts of the Hebrew Bible as well. Scripture is not just a kind of epistemological fallback position for Locke. Locke uses the Bible rather as a fundamental source, in both the chronological and foundational senses. One must go farther than Parker with regard to Locke's understanding of what the Hebrew Bible says about natural law. It is not just a matter of Cain being "intellectually" predisposed to God's "revelation" of "the truth." Rather, as I have argued, Locke brings these verses at this "critical" juncture in order to prove that humans can and must know through their own, God-given perception that murder is wrong. God then does not "reveal" this truth, as Parker suggests, but announces Cain's responsibility for "keeping" his brother and his accountability for not doing so.[147]

An observation made by David Novak, who has written extensively on natural law in Judaism, is worthy of mention here, although it was made with no relation to Lockean political philosophy. Novak highlights a temporal logic that sits well with a Grotian and Lockean sense of responsibility and due punishment. He points out that it is not only the antediluvian divine indictment of Cain that proves the Bible's authentication of natural

---

renounced Reason ... God hath given to Mankind hath by the unjust Violence and Slaughter he hath committed upon one, **declared War against all Mankind**" (emphasis added). The "declaration of war" of a murderer is, according to Locke, not a declaration against his social unit alone, but against all of mankind. This is elementary reading of the Biblical text as well. In the early chapters of Genesis there are as yet no peoples, clans, or tribes, let alone Jews. There is no "Hebraic simplicity" of "tribal brotherhood," but only a "universal otherhood." How Dunn could have read both texts, the Biblical and the Lockean, as he did is puzzling.

[146] Parker, *The Biblical Politics of John Locke*, p. 182, *ft*. 16.

[147] I will address the complementarity of reason and revelation in Lockean thought later.

law theory, but also the postdiluvian admonition, "Whoso sheddeth the blood of man, by man shall his blood be shed." This indicates a preexistent ordinance against murder, as it is not written as a directive – "thou shall not" – but merely states the punishment for murder, which must therefore already have been prohibited. "Even the prescription of capital punishment for murder (Gen. 9:5–6) presupposes a prohibition of murder already in place. To employ a Talmudic question: If the punishment has been heard, so where is the prohibition to be found?"[148] We are thereby provided, Novak makes clear, with a sound historiographic basis for elemental natural law, which is also a moral constant in Biblical ethical thought.

In light of what I have shown to be his position on natural law as expressed in the *Second Treatise*, it seems highly likely that Locke asked the same question: "If Cain knew that he was punishable for the crime he had committed, how did he come across this piece of ethical knowledge?" It is also likely that Locke offered the same answer: "Cain was supposed to understand through the use of his own reason that murder was prohibited by divine law implanted in nature."[149]

PENAL PROPORTIONALITY AND BIBLICAL INJUNCTION

Fundamental to the limitations natural law places on political power is the concept of proportionality in punishment. Hence it is no surprise that Locke makes it a crucial point of his discussion on natural law. "Executive" power indeed belongs to each individual in the state of nature. But while the individual has the right, indeed the duty, to exact criminal punishment against social miscreants, the punishment must nevertheless be proportionate to the transgression.

And thus in the State of Nature, *one Man comes by a Power over another*; but yet no Absolute or Arbitrary Power to use a Criminal when he has got him in his hands, according to the passionate heats, or boundless extravagancy of his own will, but only to retribute to him, so far as calm reason and conscience dictates, what is **proportionate to his Transgression**, which is so much as may serve for

---

[148] See BT, *Tractate Sanhedrin*, 54b. Novak, *Natural Law in Judaism*, p. 34, *ft.* 28.

[149] It is worth noting here that R' David Kimche (Radak, 1160–1235) uses the second part of Genesis 9:6 "for in the image of God has God made man" to establish that the essence of *imago dei* means the human capacity for reason. "For man has the greatest dignity of all the lowly creations in that God created him in his image; that is with the ability to reason which he bestowed upon him." Radak, Commentary on Genesis, 9:6. Later, in the discussion of reason and revelation, we shall see that Maimonides, a contemporary of Radak, also interprets *imago dei* as the capacity for reason.

Reparation and Restraint; for these two are the only reasons why one man may lawfully do harm to another, which is that we call *punishment*.[150] (Emphasis added.)

... Each Transgression may be *punished* to that *degree*, and with so much *Severity* as will suffice to make it an ill bargain to the Offender, give him cause to repent, and terrifie others from doing the like.[151]

Human beings, however, cannot be trusted to adhere to the proportionality proviso because:

it is unreasonable for Men to be Judges in their own Cases, that Self-love will make Men partial to themselves and their Friends. And on the other side, that Ill Nature, Passion and Revenge will carry them too far in punishing others. And hence nothing but confusion and disorder will follow.[152]

... In the State of Nature there wants a *known and indifferent Judge*, with Authority to determine all differences according to the established Law. For every one in that state being both Judge and Executioner of the Law of Nature, Men being partial to themselves, Passion and Revenge is very apt to carry them too far, and with too much heat, in their own Cases, as well as negligence, and unconcernedness, to make them too remiss, in other Mens.[153]

Because of humankind's self-love, the requisite proportionality degenerates into an illicit partiality that can be avoided only by the emergence of civil society.

Thus mankind, notwithstanding all the Privileges of the state of Nature, being but in an ill condition, while they remain in it, are quickly driven into Society ... The inconveniences, that they are therein exposed to, by the irregular and uncertain exercises of the Power every Man has of punishing the transgressions of others, make them take Sanctuary under the establish'd Laws of Government, and therein seek *the preservation of their Property*. 'Tis this makes them so willingly give up every one his single power of punishing to be exercised by such alone as shall be appointed to it amongst them; and by such Rules as the Community, or those authorised by them to that purpose, shall agree on. And in this we have the original *right and rise* of both *the Legislative and Executive Power*, as well as of the Governments and Societies themselves.[154]

If, however, the government that has emerged shall revert to "irregular and uncertain exercises of power," then it has violated the very proportionality in punishment that it was originally created to guarantee. By extension, Locke will later argue in the closing chapter of the *Second*

[150] II, 8, p. 290. [151] II, 12, p. 293. [152] II, 13, p. 293. [153] II, 125, p. 369.
[154] II, 127, p. 370.

Treatise, this triggers the right to revolt against such a government and depose it.

Locke does not explicitly offer a source for his use of proportionality, but, as we saw earlier with regard to his doctrine of individual political power, scholars such as Richard Tuck and Michael Zuckert credit Grotius with being Locke's source, and it is viable to argue here as well that a Grotian impact is highly likely.[155] Indeed, in the very paragraph where Grotius quotes Cain's supplication, "whosoever finds me shall kill me" as proof of the individual executive power idea, Grotius mentions the concept of proportionality as well: "it is not unjust, according to the principles of nature that any one should suffer **in proportion** to the evil he has done"[156] (emphasis added). Later in his work, when Grotius begins his discussion on punishment, he emphasizes the importance of proportionality, and supports his claim with at least one source from the Hebrew Bible, providing, in effect, the missing link between Locke and Hebrew Scripture.

For that which is simply and in the first Place intended, is an Equality between the Offence and the Punishment ... And it is to this that the Divine Law, *Deut.* xxv. And *Leo* 's Novell have a Regard. [157]

It is interesting to note that Grotius does not quote a specific verse but refers instead to the "Chapter of Deuteronomy." Indeed, the juridical principle of proportionality runs throughout the entire chapter. The first three verses are perhaps the most telling:

If there be a controversy between men, and they come to judgment, that the judges may judge them; then they shall justify the righteous, and condemn the wicked. And it shall be, if the wicked man be worthy to be beaten, that the judge shall cause him to lie down, and he shall be beaten in his presence, according to his fault, by a certain number. Forty stripes he may give him, and not exceed: lest, if he should exceed, and beat him above these with many stripes, then thy brother shall be thus made vile before thee.[158]

---

[155] Tuck, *Natural Rights Theories*, pp. 62–63. Zuckert, *Natural Rights and New Republicanism*, pp. 126, 222.

[156] Grotius, *The Rights of War and Peace*, book I, chapter V.

[157] Grotius, *The Rights of War and Peace*, book II, chapter 20, paragraph 2, pp. 951–952.

[158] Deuteronomy 25:1–3. It is worth noting that this basic concept of the limitations of penal jurisprudence is a Talmudic axiom based on Deuteronomy 25:3: "Forty stripes he may give him, and not exceed." The axiom is explained in the BT, *Tractate Makot*, 22b. See also Eliyahu Ben Zimra, "Considerations of Punishment in Jewish Criminal Law as Reflected in Responsa Literature," *Annual of the Institute for Research in Jewish Law* VIII (1981), pp. 8–42 [Hebrew].

While Locke does not openly draw here from Deuteronomy, it is clear that an indispensable component of Locke's theory on government is also a critical element of Biblical justice. While this does not provide the same level of proof of Locke's Hebraism as do the cases of Locke's own direct Biblical quotation, nevertheless, there still appears to be strong evidence of Hebraic influence on Locke, in the very least indirectly, through the mediation of Grotius.

There is an additional point that is worthy of consideration regarding Locke's Biblicism, and while it is not proof of any direct or indirect impact on Locke, it is nonetheless significant. In paragraph 13 of the *Second Treatise*, in which Locke first introduces the idea that the state of nature is unfit for the implementation of proportional punishment and hence necessitates an emergence into society and government, Locke also emphasizes that this conclusion depends on what *kind* of government is at work:

Absolute Monarchs are but Men, and if Government is to be the Remedy of those Evils, which necessarily follow from Mens being Judges in their own Cases, and the State of Nature is therefore not to be endured, I desire to know what kind of Government that is, and how much better it is than the State of Nature, where one man commanding a multitude has the Liberty to be Judge in his own Case, and may do to all his Subjects whatever he pleases, without the least liberty to any one to question or controle those who Execute his Pleasure? ... **Much better it is in the State of Nature, wherein Men are not bound to submit to the unjust will of another:** And if he that judges, judges amiss in his own, or any other Case, he is answerable for it to the rest of Mankind.[159] (Emphasis added.)

Here Locke is once again establishing the theoretical backdrop for his advocacy of rebellion against tyrannical government that will come toward the end of his *Treatises*. This concept, that government-sanctioned evil is worse than the interpersonal evil that the anarchical state of nature brings, is an idea easily found in Hebraic literature. For example, the question has been posed as to why the Benjaminites of Giv'a were not sentenced to the same end as that of Sodom and Gomorrah. As depicted in the Book of Judges (chap. 19), the citizens of Giv'a behaved similarly to the Sodomites, yet God annihilated Sodom and Gomorrah but did not treat the Benjaminites in the same manner. The Biblical commentator R. Yitzchak Arame, a Spanish Jewish scholar (1420–1494), suggests that the answer is to be found in this very same idea. In Sodom and Gomorrah, torture, cruelty to strangers, decadence, and debauchery were products of the courts. In Giv'a, the citizens behaved in a disgusting manner, but it

[159] II, 13, p. 294.

was momentary depravity, and not juridically sanctioned evil.[160] At the end of the *First Treatise*, Locke himself uses these "Concubine in G'iva" passages in order to prove the absence of *fatherly authority* in the political realm.[161]

LOCKE'S STATE OF WAR AND THE HEBREW BIBLE

In presenting an example of what the state of war looks like for the individual in the state of nature, Locke ostensibly contradicts his own proportionality proviso. The individual, because of her executive power, has the right to kill a thief even though the thief has given no indication whatsoever that he intends to harm his victim. The entire quote reads as follows:

This makes it Lawful for a Man to *kill a Thief*, who has not in the least hurt him, nor declared any design upon his Life, any farther than, by the use of Force, so to get him in his Power, as to take away his Money, or what he pleases, from him: because using force, where he has no Right, to get me into his Power, let his pretence be what it will, I have no reason to suppose, that he, who would *take away my Liberty*, would not when he had me in his Power, take away every thing else. And therefore it is Lawful for me to treat him, as one who has put *himself into a state of War* with me, *i.e.* kill him if I can; for to that

---

[160] R. Yitzchak Arame, *Akeidat Yitzchak* (Jerusalem: Laor, 1961), chapter 20 [Hebrew].

[161] See I, 164–165, pp. 278–279. A few decades after Arame, Thomas More similarly stressed the imperativeness of proportional punishment in a well-organized and moral state while drawing support from the "Mosaic law." "[T]his way of punishing thieves is neither just in itself (capital punishment) nor is it beneficial to the public. It is too severe a punishment for this crime. Neither does it serve as an effective deterrent. Simple theft is not such a grave crime that it demands capital punishment, nor does it restrain a person who has no other means of livelihood ... almost everyone in this world seems to imitate those bad schoolmasters who would rather punish their students than instruct them. Cruel and severe punishments are inflicted upon the thief when it would be much better to provide him with the means of making a living instead of forcing him out of sheer necessity to steal rather than die.

"The Mosaic law is severe and, intended as it was for an enslaved and stubborn people, nevertheless punished theft with a fine rather than death. Let us not think that God in his new law of mercy, whereby he assumes the role of a father toward a son, has given us a broader license for eliminating one another. For these reasons I think it is illegal, and there is no one, in my opinion, who does not realize the need to make the punishment fit the crime." Thomas More, *Utopia and Other Essential Writings of Thomas More*, James J. Greene and John P. Dolan (eds.) (New York: New American Library, 1984), pp. 34, 39.

hazard does he justly expose himself, whoever introduces a State of War, and is *aggressor* in it.[162]

Locke's example is curious for two reasons. First, it hardly seems to stand up to the proportionality standard already stipulated; and second, there seem to be better examples one could give to depict an attempt by one person to subjugate another. But Locke here sounds very much like a case described in the Hebrew Bible.

If a thief be found breaking up, and be smitten that he die, there shall no blood be shed for him. If the sun be risen upon him, there shall be blood shed for him; for he should make full restitution; if he have nothing, then he shall be sold for his theft.[163]

The Talmudic explanation of these verses makes it plain that the thief is not a "dead man walking" because thievery does not warrant the death penalty.[164] Rather, writes the classic Biblical commentator Rashi (1040–1105), "the thief is well aware that a person will not just stand by and watch his property being stolen and remain quiet, therefore it is clear that he came with the thought that should the owner present opposition, he will kill him."[165] The Bible's teaching here then is consistent **with its own** proportionality clause. It is in the defense of one's life, not one's possessions, that it is permitted to take a life. But that, of course, is on condition that the threat to life is unequivocal. For if the "sun be risen upon him," meaning it is clear that the thief will under no circumstances also take a life, then proportionality forbids the taking of the thief's life. Rashi continues:

[The sun rising] is just an example. If it is completely clear to you that he (the thief) is at peace with you, like the sun that symbolizes peace in the world, so it is clear to you that he has not come to kill even if the property owner will stand against him, like a father trying to steal the money of his son, for it is known that a father will always have mercy on his son and has not come to take a life.[166]

As with the concepts of penal proportionality and individual political power, this is once again not a case of explicit Biblical referencing by Locke, but rather one where Biblical influence flows to Locke by way of Grotian resourcing. Grotius uses the "thief by night" account in Exodus in order to

---

[162] II, 18, pp. 297–298.   [163] Exodus 22:1–3.
[164] BT, *Tractate Sanhedrin*, 72b. If "one comes to *kill* you, you may kill him first," not, "if one comes to *rob* you, you may kill him first."
[165] Rashi (based on the Talmud) on Exodus; ibid.

prove that "all private war is not made repugnant to the law of nature." Referring to "Jewish Law" (by which he means Mosaic Law) Grotius writes:

This therefore is that Presumption which is allowed in favour of him who has killed Thief by Night; but if Witnesses should chance to be present, by whom Proof could be made, that the person who thus slew the other, was far from being in Danger of his own Life, then should we presume no longer in his Favour, but account him guilty of Murder.[167]

Grotius then concludes with a citation of Maimonides as well: "And as *Moses Maimonides* observes, *No private Person is permitted to kill another, except in defence of that which, if once lost, is irreparable, as* Life *and* Chastity."[168]

It is significant that Locke similarly seems to try and resemble the Biblical state of war concept when he writes that, "because using force, where he has no right to get me into his power, let his pretence be what it will, I have no reason to suppose that he who would take away my liberty would not, when he had me in his power, take away everything else."[169] The "sun be risen" means in effect that he had reason to suppose the thief would *not* take his life or liberty away. Locke, like Grotius, appears to choose this example precisely because it brings Biblical authority to his understanding of the state of nature. And it is not just any example; rather it is one that depicts a state of nature not as

---

[166] Ibid.   [167] Grotius, *The Rights of War and Peace*, book II, chap. I, XII, 3, p. 412.

[168] Ibid, book II, chap. I, XII, 4, p. 4123. Grotius ends up taking a view much different than the Biblical one, a fact that might have provided an explanation as to why Locke chose not to refer to Grotius directly. Grotius asks, "What shall we then say of the Gospel in this Affair? Does it allow the same that he Law of *Moses* did? Or does it, as it is in other Things more perfect than the *Mosaick* Law, require something *more* of us in this Respect also?" Grotius answers his rhetorical question in the affirmative. "In my Opinion it is not to be questioned but that it does." Ibid, XIII, p. 413. He then concludes that the Christian attitude is far more circumspect on establishing the parameters of legitimate self-defense than the Hebrew Bible followed by Maimonides. "Therefore, when the Law acquits that Man who has killed Thief, it may be understood to take off the Punishment, but not to give him a real Right to the Act itself." Ibid, XIV, p. 415.

[169] II, 18, pp. 297–298. Brian Calvert concludes from Locke's treatment of a thief in the state of nature that, "It almost seems as if in the state of nature every offence could become a capital offence." That means that according to Calvert, Locke set no proportionality injunction on punishment within the natural context in pre-governmental society. Aside from overlooking Locke's specific references to proportionality, Calvert's most fundamental misreading of Locke stems from ignoring Locke's implicit resourcing of the Hebrew Bible with regard to the "thief" situation, showing the circumstances under which the natural law of proportionality is abandoned in the state of nature. See Brian Calvert, "Locke on Punishment and the Death Penalty," *Philosophy Journal of the Royal Institute of Philosophy* 68, 264 (1993), pp. 211–229.

a pre-societal (chronological) phenomenon, but that exists alongside or within the context of political society.[170] That this is Locke's intention becomes clear in his next paragraph.

Thus a *thief*, whom I cannot harm but by appeal to the Law, for having stolen all that I am worth, I may kill, when he sets on me to rob me, but of my Horse or Coat: because the Law, which was made for my Preservation, where it cannot interpose to secure my Life from present force, which if lost, is capable of no reparation, permits me my own Defence, and the Right of War, a liberty to kill the aggressor, because the aggressor allows not time to appeal to our common Judge, nor the decision of the Law, for remedy in a Case, where the mischief may be irreparable. *Want of a common Judge with Authority, puts all Men in a State of Nature: Force without Right, upon a Man's Person, makes a State of War*, both where there is, and is not, a common Judge.[171]

There are times, argues Locke, even in the context of political society, when individuals have no "common judge" to turn to who can arbitrate or adjudicate their issues. Rather than being at a loss in such circumstances, people can turn to natural law, as directed by both reason and revelation to guide them. This, as we will see later, can lead people to revolt against the very authority that was originally intended to protect them. The interconnectedness Locke creates between natural law, reason, and revelation, the rule of human preservation, human depravity, and government, is well summarized by K. I. Parker:

Since humans in some sense renounce their reason by not acting in accord with natural law (as pointed out in Locke's example of the Cain and Abel story, 11, 10), they may be punished, that is, treated like the animals over whom they are said to have dominion. For, according to Genesis 1:28, if humans have dominion over the irrational animals, they can, by extension, have dominion over those who act irrationally in the state of nature. They can invoke the executive power of the law of nature over those who have acted irrationally in not following the natural law. Locke once again cites the story of Cain and Abel and focuses on Cain's fear that he would be killed for violating the law of nature (Genesis 4:14), to show the "strange doctrine's" compatibility with the Genesis account. The example of Cain

---

[170] "The state of nature is in effect an analytical device in Locke, a way of understanding certain kinds of situations rather than any sort of historical or more generally descriptive device. It is understood by definition: if a situation fulfills certain conditions, then it is a 'state of nature.'" Harrison, *Hobbes, Locke and Confusion's Masterpiece*, p. 175.

[171] II, 19, pp. 298–299. The suggestion that Locke's belief that the state of natural law exists alongside or within the context of political society is in direct contradiction to John Dunn's interpretation that the state of nature for Locke "has literally no transitive empirical content what so ever." Dunn, *The Political Thought of John Locke*, p. 103. And see Vogt, "Locke, Eden and Two States of Nature," p. 523, *ft.* 2.

also comes up indirectly when Locke points out that one cannot be trusted to use the executive power of the law of nature justly and equitably; "Who was so unjust as to do his Brother an Injury, will scarce be so just as to condemn himself for it" (11, 13). Thus there needs to arise an independent judge to settle conflicts and thereby to take humans out of the state of nature.[172]

Parker's description of Lockean thinking here is right on the money, but I believe he doesn't go quite far enough. Locke's citing of the Cain and Abel story is not just to show that his "strange doctrine" is "compatible with the Genesis account" but is rather from where Locke in fact drew the very concept of individual executive power. The "strange doctrine" is not originally his; it is rather borrowed from the Book of Genesis, and Locke practically says so much.

REASON AND REVELATION

Until this point my analysis has focused on the direct influence that the Hebrew Bible had on Locke's natural law theory, as well as its highly probable indirect influence through the writings of thinkers from whom, it is likely, he drew. There are, in addition, instances where Lockean ideas are marked with a stark resemblance to Hebraic ones in which no explicit or implicit citation is made, and while I do not suggest that this is proof of Locke's dependence on Hebraic precedent, I believe that they serve to underscore the cases of direct and indirect (but apparent) impact. At the very least they help to point at a consistency in Locke's thinking, such that if it were absent, doubt might be cast upon the ostensibly obvious cases of the Hebrew Bible's influence on Locke. This clarification is necessitated by the forthcoming discussion on Locke's understanding of the relationship between reason and revelation, and the need for both.[173]

Despite the pivotal importance he places on reason, Locke does not by any means discard the importance he attributes to revelation as well.[174]

---

[172] Parker, *The Biblical Politics of John Locke*, p. 145.

[173] This clarification will be of particular importance once again with regard to my analysis of Locke and "the Fall" (Chapter 6).

[174] To the contrary, in fact, Locke actually attributes primacy to revelation. In the postscript to his reply to the Lord Bishop of Worcester, Locke concludes with a revealing paragraph regarding how he believed his own ideas had to properly mesh with scriptural revelation. And while it was written specifically in relation to his *Essay Concerning Human Understanding*, there is no reason to assume that his attitude was any different with regard to the *Two Treatises*. "The holy scripture is to me, and always

As we have already seen, Locke identifies a necessary complementarity between reason and revelation. The prohibition against murder is something one is to comprehend by oneself, proof of which is brought from Scripture. And despite the fact that one is to know it through one's own reason, one is nevertheless admonished against it by Scripture. The same is true regarding the law of preservation. Although it is divinely planted in human nature at inception, it is also divinely commanded to humankind through scriptural revelation. In fact, throughout the *Two Treatises*, Locke refers to reason and revelation in a complementary and sometimes even interchangeable fashion.[175] He does not see the two concepts as exclusive or contradictory, contrary to some of his contemporaries and certainly many of his successors. Locke seems to depend on the synthesis of reason and revelation in order to achieve what Waldron calls "the democratic intellect,"[176] a common denominator at the root of human equality that enables the human mind to sufficiently use reason in order to discover God's existence and decipher his moral law. Divine revelation is

will be, the constant guide of my assent; and I shall always hearken to it, as containing infallible truth, relating to things of the highest concernment. And I wish I could say, there were no mysteries in it: I acknowledge there are to me, and I fear always will be. But where I want the evidence of things, there yet is ground enough for me to believe, because God has said it: and I shall presently condemn and quit any opinion of mine, as soon as I am shown that it is contrary to any revelation in the holy scripture. But I must confess to your lordship, that I do not perceive any such contrariety in any thing in my Essay of Human Understanding." *The Works of John Locke*, vol. 3 (1696, http://oll .libertyfund.org/index.php?option=com_staticxt&staticfile=show.php%3Ftitle), p. 73.

[175] "For that 'them' should signify Adam singly, exclusive of the rest that should be in the world with him, is against both *Scripture and all reason* " (I, 30, p. 180). "Because reason and revelation offer them" (I, 60, p. 202). "Having been planted in him as a principle of action by God himself, *reason*, 'which was the *voice of God in him*'" (I, 86, p. 223). "Determined by the *law of nature or the revealed law of God*" (I, 124, p. 250). "The state of nature has a *law of nature* to govern it which obliges every one; and *reason*, which is that law" (II, 6, p. 289). "Having renounced *reason*– the common rule and measure God *hath given to mankind*" (II, 11, p. 292). "*God, who hath given* the world to men in common, *hath also given them reason*" (II, 26, p. 304). "These are the bounds which the trust that is put in them by the society and the *law of God and nature* " (II, 142, p. 381). "For having quitted *reason, which God hath given* to be the rule betwixt man and man" (II, 172, p. 401).

But in the beginning of chapter V, Locke uses reason and revelation alternatively rather than interchangeably. "Whether we consider natural reason, which tells us that men, being once born, have a right to their preservation, and consequently to meat and drink and such other things as nature affords for their subsistence; or revelation, which gives us an account of those grants God made of the world to Adam, and to Noah and his sons" (II, 25, pp. 303–304).

[176] This is the title of Waldron's fourth chapter in *God, Locke, and Equality*, pp. 83–107, which I discuss at greater length in Chapter 3.

necessary for those truths that cannot be understood through reason alone, and reason, a form of revelation itself, is better for understanding those truths that, though they can also be revealed and in some cases are revealed, can be comprehended through human intellect.

We must first recall that for Locke the defining characteristic of the Biblical concept of *imago dei* is human intellect, the discerning power of reason. "God makes him *in his own Image after his own Likeness*, makes him an intellectual Creature, and so capable of Dominion,"[177] notes Locke in the *First Treatise*. From this we can understand, explains Kim Ian Parker, that, "For Locke, it is not so much that reason should be distinguished from revelation, as that reason is a capacity that God gave us in the beginning. In other words, it is a specific form of revelation."[178] Quoting the *Essay*, Parker goes on to establish that Locke's "reason" is not defined by "syllogisms or mathematical logic," but "is natural *revelation*, whereby the eternal Father of Light, and fountain of all knowledge, communicates to mankind that portion of truth, which he has laid within the reach of their natural faculties."[179] This "faculty" is what

---

[177] I, 30, p. 180.   [178] Parker, *The Biblical Politics of John Locke*, p. 39, *ft. 3.*
[179] Ibid, p. 39. Locke, *An Essay Concerning Human Understanding*, p. 616. After defining *reason*, Locke then goes on in the second part of the paragraph to define *revelation*. "*[R]evelation* is natural *reason* enlarged by a new set of discoveries communicated by GOD immediately, which *reason* vouches the truth of, by the testimony and proofs it gives, that they come from GOD." Having explained the importance of revelation, Locke concludes the paragraph with a warning to religious enthusiasts who might think that, with revelation, reason is obviated. "So that he that takes away *reason*, to make way for *revelation*, puts out the light of both, and does much what the same, as if he would persuade a man to put out his eyes the better to receive the remote light of an invisible star by a telescope." Ibid.
  See also Nicholas Wolterstorff, "Can Belief in God Be Rational If It Has No Foundations," in *Faith and Rationality: Reason and Belief in God*, Alvin Plantinga and Nicholas Wolterstorff (eds.) (Notre Dame, IN: Notre Dame Press, 1983), pp. 135–186. On page 177 Wolterstorff writes: "And what, lastly, about the enthusiasts who so vexed Locke? Locke was persuaded that the enthusiasts claiming private revelations were irrational and, accordingly, irresponsible. They were acting in disobedience to their Creator. But if we do not demand of everyone in the field of religion good evidence for their convictions, said Locke, then we will simply have to acknowledge that anything goes. The concept of rational belief will simply have to be discarded. So Locke undertook to provide good evidence for his Christian convictions, and he challenged the enthusiasts to act likewise."
  And lastly, in his discussion of Locke's critical attitude toward religious enthusiasts, Michael Heyd makes an important general observation that, "reason as conceived by the late seventeenth and early eighteenth centuries had a social role to play in the critique of enthusiasm ... [E]nthusiasm was viewed as dangerous to the social order because of its subjective and idiosyncratic character." Michael Heyd, *Be Sober and Reasonable: The*

distinguishes humans from all other creatures; it is what makes a human a human, in the "image of God" and "a little lower than the angels." This is a recurrent theme for Locke. In the *Essay* he writes:

> *The word reason in the English language has different Significations* ... But the consideration I shall have of it here, is in a signification ... as it stands for a faculty in man, that faculty, whereby man is supposed to be distinguished from beasts, and wherein it is evident he much surpasses them.[180]

Concomitantly, when people behave like beasts and do not utilize reason, they are no longer divine, as they have repudiated their Godlike image.

> And thus it is, that every Man in the State of Nature, has a Power to kill a Murderer ... *to secure* Men from the attempts of a criminal who, having **renounced Reason**, the common Rule and Measure, God hath given to mankind, hath by the unjust Violence and Slaughter he hath committed upon one, declared War against all Mankind, and therefore may be destroyed as a *Lyon or a Tiger*, one of those wild Savage Beasts with whom men can have no Society nor Security. (Emphasis added.)
> ... And one may destroy a Man who makes War upon him, or has discovered an Enmity to his being, for the same Reason, that he may kill a *wolf* or a *lyon*; because such Men are not under the ties of the **Common Law of Reason**.[181]
> (Emphasis added.)

Locke's defining of reason as itself a form of revelation, as "the voice of God in man," is commensurate with Hebraic thinking and even terminology on the subject. Commenting on the Mishnaic adage that "anyone who does not respect the honor of his creator, it would have been best had he not been created,"[182] Maimonides defines disrespect for "the honor of his creator" as disrespect for his own intellect:

> In their saying, "anyone who does not respect the honor of his creator," they meant to say "anyone who does not have respect and have mercy on his own intellect, for human intellect is the honor of God, and anyone who does not know its measure that has been bestowed upon him, is given over to his desires and is to be compared to an animal."[183]

Critique of Enthusiasm in the Seventeenth and Early Eighteenth Centuries (Leiden: Brill Academic Publishers, 1995), p. 182.

[180] Locke, *An Essay Concerning Human Understanding*, book IV, chapter XVII; 1, p. 590.

[181] II, 11,16, pp. 291–292, 296–297. In II, 172, Locke again uses the same expression with identical intent. "For having quitted reason, which God hath given to be the rule betwixt man and man"; p. 401.

[182] BT, *Tractate Hagigah*, chap. 2, Mishnah 1.

[183] Maimonides, *Peirush Hamishnaiyot, Hagigah*, chap. II, Mishnah I. Maimonides is basically following a Talmudic tradition of thought in regard to the centrality of

Maimonides offers a similar definition in his *Guide*:

[T]he intellect which was granted to man as the highest endowment, was bestowed on him before his disobedience. With reference to this gift the Bible states that "man was created in the form and likeness of God." On account of this gift of intellect man was addressed by God, and received His commandments, as it is said: "And the Lord God commanded Adam" (Gen. ii. 16) – for no commandments are given to the brute creation or to those who are devoid of understanding. Through the intellect man distinguishes between the true and the false.[184]

Once one is created with the potential to use one's intellectual capacity to reason, it is only one's use of the intellect as expressed in deed and not merely in theory that sets one apart from the rest of creation. Hence, God expects people to use their intellectual potential whenever possible, even though scriptural revelation may be applicable as well. Regarding the benefits of human reason, Locke writes:

reason alongside revelation. Talmudic references to the complementary relationship between reason and revelation abound; for example: "Lame li k'ra, sevarah hu?" (why do I need scripture – to prove the point – it's logical). BT, *Ketuboth*, 22a; BT, *B Kama*, 46b; BT, *Niddah*, 28a. "Ei bayit aimah k'ra, ei bayit aimah sevarah" (the question can either be answered through scripture or through logic). BT, *Berachot*, 4a; BT, *Yevamot*, 38b. "Miltah d'ati m'sevarah, tarach v'katav la k'ra" (an issue that can be understood from logic, was nevertheless written down in scripture). BT, *B. Metzia*, 61a. In his introduction to the Babylonian Talmud R. Nissim Gaon (990–1050) writes: "All the divine commandments that are dependent on logic and the rationality of the heart, everyone is already obligated by them from the day God created Adam, he and his seed after him for all generations to come." R. Joseph Karo (1488–1575) follows through on this theme that locates the human soul in the capacity to reason. See *Shulchan Aruch, Orach Hayim*, 25.

Abraham Joshua Heschel summarizes medieval Jewish thinking on the subject of reason and revelation complementarity in a manner it appears Locke would not contest. "That there can be no true conflict between the teachings imparted to us by revelation and the ideas acquired by reason was a prevalent opinion of the great Jewish thinkers of the Middle Ages … What is contained in the divine message can neither misrepresent reality nor contradict any truths taught by science, since both reason and revelation originated in the wisdom of God who created all reality and knows all truth." Abraham Joshua Heschel, *Man Is Not Alone* (New York: Farrar, Straus and Giroux, 1976), pp. 172–172. See also Norbert M. Samuelson (ed.), *Reason and Revelation as Authority in Judaism* (Philadelphia, PA: Congregation Rodeph Shalom, 1981).

[184] Maimonides, *The Guide for the Perplexed*, part I, chapter II. Bearing this idea in mind, that reason is a form of revelation, and, as we shall see, divine laws are sometimes revealed through both the human capacity to reason and overt divine revelation, I am not sure David Novak is correct to define natural law as "a reality that is less exalted than direct divine revelation." Novak, *Natural Law in Judaism*, p. 3. Locke authoritatively quotes Maimonides' *Guide for the Perplexed* in *The Reasonableness of Christianity* (p. 92). See my discussion in Chapter 6 on Locke's use of Maimonides' rule of hermeneutics.

For whatsoever Truth we come to the clear discovery of, from the knowledge and contemplation of our own ideas, will always be certainer to us, than those which are conveyed to us by *traditional revelation*. For the Knowledge, we have, that this *revelation* came at first from GOD, can never be so sure, as the knowledge we have from the clear and distinct perception of the agreement, or disagreement of our own ideas.[185]

Locke goes on in the *Essay* to say that, "Reason must be our last Judge and Guide in every Thing,"[186] and in the *First Treatise* refers to reason as "our only star and compass."[187] In a correspondence of his later years, Locke stressed the same theme:

The first requisite to the profiting by books is not to judge of opinions by the authority of the writers. None have the right of dictating but God himself, and that because he is truth itself. All others have a right to be followed as far as I have, and no farther, i.e. as far as the evidence of what they say convinces, and of that my own understanding alone must be judge for me, and nothing else.[188]

So Locke refers to human reason as "the last judge and guide," "our only star and compass," and that which "alone must be judge," but Locke is also keenly aware of the limitations of human reason. God can "dictate," in apparent contradistinction to human understanding, because "he is truth itself." And, as an obvious extension of that maxim, there are truths that reason simply cannot confirm.

But since GOD in giving us the light of *reason* has not thereby tied up his own hands from affording us, when he thinks fit, the light of *revelation* in any of those matters, wherein our natural faculties are able to give a probable determination, *revelation*, where GOD has been pleased to give it, *must carry it, against the probable conjectures of reason.*[189]

Much earlier, during his travels in France, Locke made the following entry in his journal in the context of a brief note on "knowledge, its extent and measure," which similarly describes the limitations of human intellectual prowess and hence the need for divine revelation.

God having made the great machine of the universe suitable to his infinite power and wisdom, why should we think so proudly of ourselves, whom he hath put into

---

[185] Locke, *An Essay Concerning Human Understanding*, book IV, chap. XVIII; 4, p. 609. Clearly Locke is here coming to counter Catholic notions of "infallible certitude" and "apostolic succession" as well as the Protestant concept of *sola fide*.

[186] Ibid, IV. XIX; 14, p. 621.   [187] I, 58, p. 200.

[188] "A Letter from Mr. Locke to Mr. Samuel Bold," in *The Works of John Locke*, vol. 9 (Letter and Misc. Works) (1685, http://oll.libertyfund.org/title/1726/18681), p. 3.

[189] Locke, *An Essay Concerning Human Understanding*, IV. XVIII. 8, p. 612.

a small canton, and perhaps the most inconsiderable part of it, that he hath made us the surveyors of it, and that it is not as it should be unless we can thoroughly comprehend it in all the parts of it? It is agreeable to his goodness, and to our condition, that we should be able to apply them to our use, to understand so far some parts of that we have to do with, as to be able to make them subservient to the convenience of our life, as proper to fill our hearts with praise of his bounty. But it is also agreeable to his greatness, that it should exceed our capacity, and the highest flight of our imagination, the better to fill us with admiration of his power and wisdom; besides its serving to other ends, and being suited probably to the use of other more intelligent creatures which we know not of. If it be not reasonable to expect that we should be able to penetrate into all the depths of nature, and understand the whole constitution of the universe, it is yet a higher insolence to doubt the existence of a God because we cannot comprehend him – to think there is not an infinite Being because we are not so. **If all things must stand or fall by the measure of our understandings, and that denied to be, wherein we find inextricable difficulties, there will very little remain in the world, and we shall scarce leave ourselves so much as understandings, souls, or bodies.** It will become us better to consider well our own weakness and exigencies, what we are made for, and what we are capable of, and to apply the powers of our bodies and faculties of our souls, which are well suited to our condition, in the search of that natural and moral knowledge, which, as it is not beyond our strength, so is not beside our purpose, but may be attained by moderate industry, and improved to our infinite advantage.[190] (Emphasis added.)

Expanding further on the limitations of reason, Locke argues that while reason can lead the individually wise and virtuous to the proper conclusions, it cannot prevail upon the masses to acknowledge one God and his moral law.

Hence we see that *Reason*, speaking never so clearly to the Wise and Virtuous, had never Authority enough to prevail on the Multitude; and to perswade the Societies of Men, that there was but One God, that alone was to be owned and worshipped.[191]

---

[190] King, *The Life and Letters of John Locke*, pp. 91–92. In the same vein, Alexis de Tocqueville was later to write: "I am ignorant of his designs, but I shall not cease to believe in them because I cannot fathom them, and I had rather mistrust my own capacity than his justice." Alexis de Tocqueville, *Democracy in America*, with an introduction by Alan Ryan (New York: Knopf, 1972, 1994), p. 13.

[191] Locke, *The Reasonableness of Christianity*, p. 192. This appears prima facie to lie in stark contradiction with the quote from Locke's letter to Stillingfleet to the effect that "the belief of a God, it may be said to be the universal consent of mankind." "Mr. Locke's Reply to the Right Reverend the Lord Bishop of Worcester's Answer to His Third Letter," p. 366.

I think, though, that Locke draws a distinction between the general belief in God and the more specific belief in *one God* as emphasized in this quote from *The Reasonableness*. The same is true for the quote in footnote 193: "The Belief and

And similarly he notes that,

'tis too hard a task for unassisted Reason, to establish Morality in all its parts upon its true foundations; with a clear and convincing light. And 'tis at least a surer and shorter way, to the Apprehensions of the vulgar, and mass of Mankind, that one manifestly sent from God, and coming with visible Authority from him, should as a King and Lawmaker tell them their Duties; and require their Obedience; than leave it to the long, and sometimes intricate deductions of Reason, to be made out to them.[192]

Locke then goes on to offer proof from the Israelite experience in Egypt, as well as from the reality of Athens, that only revelation can engender faith among the multitude.

The Belief and Worship of One God, was the National Religion of the *Israelites* alone: And if we will consider it, it was introduced and supported amongst that People by *Revelation*. They were in *Goshen*, and had Light; whilst the rest of the World were in almost *Egyptian* Darkness, *without God in the World*.[193]

Worship of One God, was the National Religion of the *Israelites* alone." If it was "of the Israelites alone" it could hardly belong in the category of "universal consent," but apparently Locke is speaking specifically of the emergence of monotheism.

[192] Ibid, p. 195.

[193] Ibid, p. 192. Locke refers here to the Biblical account of the plague of darkness brought to bear on the Egyptians. Exodus 10:22–23 reads: "And Moses stretched forth his hand toward heaven; and there was a thick darkness in all the land of Egypt three days; they saw not one another neither rose any from his place for three days; but all the children of Israel had light in their dwellings." It is interesting to note that despite his principled adherence to a literal reading of Biblical texts, Locke does not shy away from allegorical explanation where he deems fit. Locke would certainly not deny that the absence of light in Egypt is to be understood in the literal sense, but that does not prevent him from interpreting it as Godlessness as well. This may be due to Locke's familiarity with Midrashic exegesis on the subject, because that is precisely how all the Midrashic literature interprets the passage. Literally, the passage indicates that there was already "darkness" upon Egypt prior to the plague itself, and the plague of darkness activated and added to that original darkness. In explaining what that original darkness was, Midrashic exegesis posits that it was the darkness of idolatry and Godlessness. This, Midrash goes on to say, was why the angels agreed to plague the Egyptians with additional darkness when God broached the subject with them. See *Midrash Raba*, Exodus, 14a; *Midrash Tanchumah, Bo*, A; *Yalkut Shimoni*, Exodus, 186; *Yalkut Shimoni*, Psalms, 863.

Elsewhere Locke used the notion of a "return to Egypt" in a similar allegorical fashion, referring to those clerics who wrest proofs from Scripture in order to justify self-serving political gain. He attacked those who "got the right use of Scripture, and the knack of applying it with advantage, who can bring God's word in defence of those practices which his soul abhors and do already tell us we are returning to Egypt." John Locke, *Two Tracts of Government*, Philip Abrams (ed.) (Cambridge: Cambridge University Press, 1967), pp. 159–160.

And as for Athens:

> There was no part of Mankind, who had quicker Parts, or improved them more; that had a greater light of Reason, or followed it farther in all sorts of Specula- tions, than the *Athenians*: And yet we find but one *Socrates* amongst them, that opposed and laughed at their Polytheism, and wrong Opinions of the Deity; And we see how they rewarded him for it. Whatsoever *Plato*, and the soberest of the Philosophers thought of the Nature and Being of the One God, they were fain, in their outward Professions and Worship, to go with the Herd, and keep to the Religion established by Law.[194]

Finally, the use of human reason alone is perilous, for human reason as expressed through human custom can deteriorate into the immoral.

> They who allege the Practice of Mankind, for *exposing or selling* their Children, as a Proof of their Power over them, are with Sir *Rob*. happy Arguers, and cannot but recommend their Opinion by founding it on the most shameful Action, and most unnatural Murder, humane Nature is capable of.[195]

The fact that it has become human practice to "expose" or "sell" or even "murder" children proves nothing with regard to the legitimate power parents have over children. Custom cannot militate against God's Biblical injunction against murder. "Doth God forbid us under the severest Pen- alty, that of Death, to take away the Life of any Man, a Stranger, and upon Provocation?"[196]

Humankind, though, can choose not to utilize reason and thereby ignore God's command, despite the severity of the resultant penalty that accompanies its descent from its near angelic state.

> Thus far can the busie mind of Man carry him to a Brutality below the level of Beasts, when he quits his reason, which places him almost equal to Angels. Nor can it be otherwise in a Creature, whose thoughts are more than the Sands, and wider than the Ocean, where fancy and passion must needs run him into strange courses, if reason, which is his only Star and compass, be not that he steers by.[197]

This paragraph is rife with Biblical references. As we saw earlier (I, 30), "almost equal to angels" is a quote from the Book of Psalms (chap. 8) and refers to God's creating humankind in his image. As for the phrase "More

---

[194] Locke, *The Reasonableness of Christianity*, p. 192.

[195] I, 56, pp. 198–199. Grotius similarly attributes the need for revealed divine law to the natural deterioration of human custom. "Therefore, both the Law of *Moses*, and the Law given to *Noah*, tend rather to explain and renew the Law of Nature, obscured, and, as it were, extinguished by wicked Customs, than to establish any Thing new." Grotius, *The Rights of War and Peace*, book I, chap. II, V, p. 190.

[196] I, 56, p. 199.   [197] I, 58, p. 200.

than the sands and wider than the ocean," both sand and ocean or sea are used repeatedly throughout the Hebrew Bible as metaphors to describe plenty.[198] And as for reason, it is a specific form of revelation in humankind that emanates from the divine. It is also the divine that keeps reason in check and prevents it from deteriorating to the worst forms of brutality and immorality, as described in the de la Vega story of Peruvian cannibalism.[199] Reason alone can become identified with that which is socially acceptable, and reason cannot stop that which has become socially acceptable from existing, no matter how immoral it may be. There must be an objective standard of right and wrong guiding reason and steering those who have left reason – objectively measured – back to moral behavior.[200] Hence, in the same "star and compass" paragraph celebrating human reason, Locke draws once again on the Hebrew Bible to make his point about the need for revelation:

The Psalmist tells us *Psalm* cvi. 38. *They shed innocent bloud even the bloud of their sons and of their daughters when they sacrificed unto the Idols of Canaan.*[201]

The fact that it was a corrupted use of reason that led to the making of idols to which children were then sacrificed in popular worship did not make it acceptable.[202] Locke goes on to quote the Scripture in which the Canaanite ritual, believed acceptable by the Israelites, is condemned.

The land was polluted with bloud, therefore was the wrath of the Lord kindled against his people in so much that he abhorred his own inheritance.[203]

And so, Locke concludes:

---

[198] See, for example, Genesis 22:17, Genesis 32:12, Genesis 41:49, Job 11:9.

[199] In I, 57, pp. 199–200, just before the aforementioned reference to "a brutality below the level of beasts," Locke quotes de la Vega's account of Peruvian cannibalism.

[200] Locke made this point clear in his *Essays on the Law of Nature*: "Even if God and the soul's immortality are not moral propositions and laws of nature, nevertheless they must be necessarily presupposed if natural law is to exist. For there is no law without a lawmaker, and law is to no purpose without punishment." Locke, *Essays on the Law of Nature*, p. 113.

[201] I, 58, p. 201.

[202] In *Essays on the Law of Nature* Locke notes similar brutal customs such as: "There is a custom in Sardinia that children kill their aged fathers by beating them with sticks, and then bury them, believing that it would be wrong if those who are already too old remained alive any longer." Locke, *Essays on the Law of Nature*, p. 112.

[203] I, 58, p. 201.

The killing of their Children, though it were fashionable, was charged on them as *innocent bloud*, and so had, in the account of God, the guilt of murder, as the offering them to Idols had the guilt of Idolatry. [204]

For Locke, reason is the "only star and compass" when it not only keeps religious enthusiasts in check but is also kept in check by Biblical instruction. Gregg Forster puts it well: "When Locke says reason is our star and compass for successfully navigating the strong waters of depraved human desires, he intends reason to include rational faith in the Bible's moral teachings."[205] That this symbiosis of reason and revelation includes "rational faith in the Bible's moral teachings" becomes clear from Locke's own words:

> Be it then as Sir *Robert* says, that *Anciently*, it was *usual* for Men *to sell and Castrate their Children*, O. 155 [231]. Let it be, that they exposed them; Add to it, if you please, for this is still greater Power, that they begat them for their Tables to fat and eat them: If this proves a right to do so, we may, by the same Argument, justifie Adultery, Incest and Sodomy, for there are examples of these too, both Ancient and Modern: Sins, which I suppose, have their Principal Aggravation from this, that they cross the main intention of Nature, which willeth the increase of Mankind, and the continuation of the Species in the highest perfection, and the distinction of Families, with the Security of the Marriage Bed, as necessary thereunto.[206]

For the Deist who believes that God exists but has no interest in human affairs, it is only reason that can determine moral behavior. But since reason alone may deteriorate into the immoral, the unconcerned God of the Deists is entirely unreasonable. Reason, therefore, necessitates a consequential God, as Waldron emphasizes: "Locke thinks reason refutes the deist's claim that God might have no concern with human affairs."[207] The

---

[204] Ibid.

[205] Forster, *John Locke's Politics of Moral Consensus*, p. 210. Neal Wood makes the interesting observation that, "the only circumstance under which Locke ever condones immoderation" is in pursuit of the truth for which he quotes Locke as writing we must be "zealous champions." Neal Wood, *The Politics of Locke's Philosophy* (Los Angeles, CA: University of California Press, 1983), p. 124.

[206] I, 59, p. 201.

[207] Waldron, *God, Locke, and Equality*, p. 96. Waldron then quotes from Locke's "Of Ethick in General" in order to explain what follows from this line of thought: "The next thing then to show is, that there are certain rules ... which it is his will all men should conform their actions to and that this will of his is sufficiently promulgated and made known to all mankind." That divine law ("certain rules" to which "all men should conform their actions") is conveyed through both reason and revelation, and that both evoke reward for compliance and punishment for noncompliance, Locke writes plainly in the *Essay*: "The *divine* law, whereby I mean, that law which God has set to the actions of men, whether promulgated to them by the light of nature, or the voice of revelation.

use of Psalms here contributes to Locke's countering of Deist thinking as well, for only a living and caring God would have his "wrath kindled against his people." Reason and revelation then are presented here as wholly syncretic. When man "quits his reason" and allows reason to be "laid aside," he is also laying aside the precepts of a God for whom human behavior matters.

The notion of a consequential God who instructs and judges one's use of reason as a necessary component for the creation and preservation of moral society is put forward by Hugo Grotius, who, as we have already seen, served as a probable resource for Locke. Grotius is of the opinion that there exists a "true religion" at the base of all religions, at all times, and upon which every society must rest. This ubiquitous faith paradigm comprises four "fundamental principles":

[T]he first is that there is a GOD, and but one GOD only. The second, that GOD is not any of those Things we see, but something more sublime than them. The third, that **GOD takes Care of human Affairs, and judges them with the strictest Equity.** The fourth, that The same GOD is the Creator of all Things but himself.[208]
(Emphasis added.)

That it is these principles *only* that are absolutely imperative and that any other religious doctrines must be tolerated by the civil sovereign, Grotius proves from the Biblical experience of ancient Israel.

The Law of GOD, tho' delivered to a Nation [Israel], which by the concurrent Proof of Prophecies and Miracles, either seen or transmitted to them by incontested Authority, was infallibly assured of the Truth of these Notions, tho' it

That God has given a rule whereby men should govern themselves, I think there is nobody so brutish as to deny. He has a right to do it, we are his creatures: He has goodness and wisdom to direct our actions to that which is best: and he has power to enforce it by rewards and punishments, of infinite weight and duration, in another life; for nobody can take us out of his hands. This is the only true touchstone of *moral rectitude*; and by comparing them to this law, it is that men judge of the most considerable *moral good* or *evil* of their actions; that is, whether as *duties, or sins*, they are like to procure them happiness or misery from the hands of the ALMIGHTY." Locke, *An Essay Concerning Human Understanding* (2.28.8), p. 317. This notion, God's power to reward and punish compliance with his moral law, is in fact the central idea of Locke's article "Of Ethick in General," quoted earlier by Waldron. See Victor Nuovo (ed.), *John Locke: Writings on Religion* (Oxford: Oxford University Press, 2002), pp. 9–14. It is of particular note that medieval Jewish philosophy placed the concept of reward and punishment among the basic tenets of Jewish faith. See especially Maimonides' *Thirteen Principles of Faith, Introduction to Commentary on Mishnah*, BT Sanhedrin (Principle 11), and Spanish Jewish philosopher R. Yosef Albo (1380–1444), *Sefer Haikarim* (Book of Principles), part IV, chapters 32, 33 (Principle 3).
[208] Grotius, *The Rights of War and Peace*, book II, xlv, 1.

utterly detested the Adoration of False Gods, did not sentence to Death every Offender in that Case, but such only whose Crime was attended with some particular Circumstance; as, for Instance, one who was the Ringleader and Chief in seducing others, *Deut.* xii.1, or a City that began to serve Gods unknown before, *Deut.* iii.12, or him who paid divine Honour to any of the Host of Heaven, hereby cancelling the whole Law, and entirely relinquishing the Worship of the true GOD, *Deut.* xvii.2 ... Nor did GOD himself think the Canaanites, and their neighboring Nations, tho' long addicted to vile Superstitions, ripe for Punishment, till by an accumulation of other Crimes they had enhanced their Guilt, *Gen.* xv.16.[209]

In order to further appreciate the role that reason plays in Lockean thought, and just how compatible it is with Hebraic thought, it must be remembered that for Locke the capacity for human reason does not just *allow* for the existence of God, the source of revelation, but actually *obligates* recognition of his existence, as I showed earlier in my discussion of Lockean natural law. In fact, Locke even argues that it is only reason, as opposed to what he refers to as "inspiration," that forces an acceptance of a consequential God, and that anything about God or from God must conform to reason.

Religion being that homage and obedience which man pays immediately to God, it supposes that man is capable of knowing that there is a God, and what is required by, and is acceptable to Him, thereby to avoid his anger and procure his favour. **That there is a God, and what that God is, nothing can discover to us, nor judge in us, but natural reason.** For whatever discovery we receive any other way, must come originally from inspiration, which is an opinion or persuasion in the mind whereof a man knows not the rise nor reason, but is received there as a truth coming from an unknown, and therefore a supernatural cause, and not founded upon those principles nor observations in the way of reasoning which makes the understanding admit other things for truths. But no such inspiration concerning God, or his worship, can be admitted for truth by him that thinks himself thus inspired, much less by any other whom he would persuade to believe him inspired, any further than it is conformable to reason; not only because where reason is not, I judge it is impossible for a man himself to distinguish betwixt inspiration and fancy, truth and error; **but also it is impossible to have such a notion of God, as to believe that he should make a creature to whom the knowledge of himself was necessary, and yet not to be discovered by that way which discovers everything else that concerns us,** but was to come into the minds of men only by such a way by which all manner of errors come in, and is more likely to let in falsehoods than truths, since nobody can doubt, from the contradiction and strangeness of opinions concerning God and religion in this world, that men are likely to have more

---

[209] Ibid, xlvii, 2, 3.

frenzies than inspirations. Inspiration then, barely in itself, cannot be a ground to receive any doctrine not conformable to reason.[210] (Emphasis added.)

The scriptural account of the experiences of the first monotheist does not indicate a profound sense of human discovery of the divine through the use of rational faculties. In Abraham's primeval connection to the God who calls upon him to "Get thee out of thy country, and from thy kindred, and from thy father's house, to the land that I will show thee,"[211] Abraham appears to be discovered by God rather than vice versa, and it is through that divine revelation that Abraham comes to know God's will. But the Maimonidean account of Abrahamic monotheism, based on Talmudic and Midrashic exegetical interpretation, provides a very different view, one that Locke it appears came to champion as well.

The wise men among them would think that there is no God other than the stars and spheres ... The world continued in this fashion until ... Abraham – was born. After this mighty man was weaned, he began to explore and think ... How is it possible for the sphere to continue to revolve without having anyone controlling it? Who is causing it to revolve? Surely, it does not cause itself to revolve. He had no teacher, nor was there anyone to inform him ... [However,] his heart was exploring and [gaining] understanding.

... He realized that there was one God who controlled the sphere, that He created everything, and that there is no other God among all the other entities. He knew that the entire world was making a mistake. What caused them to err was their service of the stars and images, which made them lose awareness of the truth.

... Abraham was forty years old when he became aware of his Creator. When he recognized and knew Him, he began to formulate replies to the inhabitants of Ur Kasdim and debate them, telling them that they were not following a proper path ... When he overcame them through the strength of his arguments, the king desired to kill him. He was [saved through] a miracle and left for Charan. [There,] he began to call in a loud voice to all people and inform them that there is one God in the entire world and it is proper to serve Him. He would go out and call to the people, gathering them in city after city and country after country, until he came to the land of Canaan – proclaiming [God's existence the entire time] – as [Genesis 21:33] states: "And He called there in the name of the Lord, the eternal God."

---

[210] King, *Life and Letters of John Locke*, pp. 124–125. Locke wrote this in 1681, at around the same time he began working on the *Two Treatises*. The same theme can be detected in *An Essay Concerning Human Understanding* (quoted later) in his discussion of the advantages of human self-perception.

[211] Genesis 12:1.

... When the people would gather around him and ask him about his statements, he would explain [them] to each one of them according to their understanding, until they turned to the path of truth.[212]

Close attention must be paid to the sequence of events as described by Maimonides. Abraham searches for meaning and, by use of his rational faculties, concludes that there is a God who created the world and continues to maintain it. By the same use of reason he convinces many others, and when his iconoclastic activities prove life-threatening he suddenly enjoys divine intervention and is miraculously saved. But even after he emerges from his brush with death, it is not by bearing testimony to the miracle that he experienced that he wins minds to monotheistic faith, but still by the exclusive use of reason (bottom up). Indeed, Maimonides is as emphatic as he is consistent on the limited role miracles (top down) play in inducing religious faith. Earlier in his *Mishneh Torah*, when enumerating the laws pertaining to the *Fundamentals of Torah*, Maimonides makes it clear that 1) the miracles Moses performed in Egypt were circumscribed both in time and significance, and 2) any apparent miracles subsequent to Sinaitic revelation that intend to alter the laws given at Sinai must be false and hence utterly rejected.

Israel did not believe in Moses ... on account of the tokens he showed. **For when one's faith is founded on tokens, a lurking doubt always remains in the mind that these tokens may have been performed with the aid of occult arts and witchcraft.** All the signs Moses showed in the Wilderness, he performed because they were needed, and not to support his prophetic claims ... What then were the grounds of the faith in him? The Revelation on Sinai which we saw with our own eyes, and heard with our own ears, not having to depend on the testimony of others.

... After the Revelation on Sinai, all Israel became witnesses for him; and there was no need for him to show them any further sign. The Almighty indicated this to Moses at the beginning of the latter's career, when He gave him signs which he was to perform in Egypt, and said to him, "They shall hearken to thy voice" (Ex. 3:18). Moses realized that belief based on signs leaves lurking doubts and is followed by musings and speculation ... Hence one may conclude with regard to every prophet after Moses, that we do not believe in such a prophet because of the signs he shows ...

Hence too, if a prophet were to arise and perform signs and wonders, and seek to deny the prophetic character of Moses ... we would not have to listen to him and would be clearly certain that those signs were wrought by secret arts and witchcraft. For Moses' authority as a prophet is not founded upon signs, in which case we might have weighed the signs of one prophet against those of another. But with our eyes we saw and with our ears we heard the divine Voice ... The Torah

---

[212] Maimonides, *Mishneh Torah, Hilchot Avodat Cochavim, Laws of Idol Worship*, New Corrected Edition (New York: Feldheim Publishers, 1981), chapter 8, laws 1–3.

accordingly ordains that even if the sign or token takes place, you are not to listen to the words of such a prophet; since he shows a sign and token in order to deny what you saw with your own eyes ... how shall we, on the strength of such a sign, accept a man as a prophet, who seeks to repudiate Moses' prophecy for the truth of which we have the evidence of our own eyes and ears?[213] (Emphasis added.)

Regarding false prophecy, Maimonides refers to the verses in Deuteronomy that read:

If there arise among you a prophet, or a dreamer of dreams, and he give thee a sign or a wonder, and the sign or the wonder come to pass, of which he spoke to thee, saying, Let us go after other gods, which thou hast not known and let us serve them; thou shalt not hearken to the words of that prophet, or that dreamer of dreams: for the Lord your God puts you to the proof, to know whether you love the Lord your God with all your heart and with all your soul.[214]

Referring to the scriptural account of the miracles performed by Moses in Egypt, and their limitations, Locke similarly pares down the importance of miracles in a way that smacks of the Maimonidean argument. Locke first posits that the miracle cannot supplant reason "because reason must be the judge what is a miracle and what not." He then stresses that humankind's ability to reason is itself a miracle; hence in the case of a miracle that stands opposed to reason, it is "at best ... but one miracle against another, and the greater still on reason's side." Lastly and most importantly, miracles are not always commensurate with God's truth, but may on the contrary come to challenge it, and thus must be ignored.

Because man does not know whether there be not several sorts of creatures above him, and between him and the Supreme, amongst which there may be some that have the power to produce in Nature such extraordinary effects as we call miracles, and may have the will to do it, for other reasons than the confirmation of truth; for the magicians of Egypt turned their rods into serpents as well as Moses; and since so great a miracle as that was done in opposition to the true God, and the revelation sent by Him, what miracle can have certainty and assurance greater than that of a man's reason?[215]

---

[213] Maimonides, *Mishneh Torah, Hilchot Yesodai Hatorah, The Book of Knowledge*, New Corrected Edition (New York: Feldheim Publishers, 1981), chapter 8, laws 1–3.

[214] Deuteronomy 13:2–4.

[215] King, *Life and Letters of John Locke*, pp. 125–126. Locke then concludes his miracles vs. reason discussion with a reference to the same admonition in Deuteronomy against false prophecy, and adds two New Testament sources. God may at times use a miracle as a confirmation of faith, argues Locke, but it is only such if it is verified by doctrine; it is not the miracle that verifies the doctrine. "I do not hereby deny in the least that God can do, or hath done, miracles for the confirmation of truth; but I only say that we cannot think he should do them to enforce doctrines or notions of himself, or any worship of

Here Locke is not negating the potency of the miracles performed by the Egyptian magicians; he is suggesting rather that reason simply cannot tolerate the attribution of decisive significance to them because they contravene the truth. Elsewhere Locke suggests that the requisite rejection of the miracles performed by Pharaoh's magicians is due rather to their inferior supernatural status.

The producing of serpents, blood, and frogs, by the Egyptian sorcerers and by Moses, could not to the spectators but appear equally miraculous: which of the pretenders then had their mission from God, and the truth on their side, could not have been determined, if the matter had rested there. But when Moses's serpent eat up theirs, when he produced lice which they could not, the decision was easy. It was plain Jannes and Jambres acted by an inferior power, and their operations, how marvelous and extraordinary soever, could not in the least bring in question Moses's mission; that stood the firmer for this opposition, and remained the more unquestionable after this, than if no such signs had been brought against it.[216]

Later, in a gloss of the Biblical text, Locke goes on to point out that it is God himself who directs humankind as to how miracles are to be judged and interpreted.

When God send Moses to the children of Israel with a message, that now according to his promise he would redeem them by his hand out of Egypt, and furnished him with signs and credentials of his mission; it is very remarkable what God himself says of those signs, Exod. Iv. 8, "And it shall come to pass, if they will not believe thee, nor hearken to the voice of the first sign," (which was turning his rod into a serpent,) that "they will believe the voice of the latter sign" (which was

him not conformable to reason, or that we can receive such for truth for the miracle's sake: and even in those books which have the greatest proof of revelation from God, and the attestation of miracles to confirm their being so, **the miracles are to be judged by the doctrine, and not the doctrine by the miracles,** *v.* Deut. xiii. 1; Matt. xiv. 24. And St. Paul says, 'If an angel from Heaven should teach any other doctrine,' &c. &c." Ibid (emphasis added). Locke's (Maimonidean) thinking here had deep theological implications, a good example being his rejection of transubstantiation; Locke insists that reason does not allow for any confusion between flesh and bread. "It is a thing we exercise our senses and knowledge on and not our faith, and so clear that there is not room to doubt. For the reality and essence of bread being in respect of us nothing but a collection of several simple ideas, which make us know it, distinguish it from flesh, and call it bread, it is as impossible for a man, where he finds that complex idea to know it to be flesh or receive it to be such, as it is to believe himself a loaf ... [God never] made use of invisible miracles to destroy the testimony of our senses, overturn all our knowledge, and confound all measures of faith and reason." Locke, MS Journal, 1676, pp. 422–423, 424, quoted in Woolhouse, *Locke*, p. 127.

[216] John Locke, *The Works of John Locke in Nine Volumes*, 12th Edition (London: Rivington, 1824), vol. 8, chapter: "A Discourse of Miracles," http://oll.libertyfund.org/title/1444/81473 on 2013-02-04, p. 5.

the making his hand leprous by putting it in his bosom). God farther adds, v. 9, "And it shall come to pass, if they will not believe also these two signs, neither hearken unto they voice, that thou shalt take of the water of the river and pour upon the dry land: and the water which thou takest out of the river shall become blood upon the dry land." Which of those operations was or was not above the force of all created beings, will, I suppose, be hard for any man, too hard for a poor brick-maker, to determine; and therefore the credit and certain reception of the mission, was annexed to neither of them, but the prevailing of their attestation was heightened by the increase of their number; two supernatural operations showing more power than one, and three more than two. God allowed that it was natural, that the marks of greater power should have a greater impression on the minds and belief of the spectators.[217]

The interconnectedness between reason and revelation that emerges from these quotes is ineluctable. For Locke, reason is itself a form of divine revelation that also measures the validity of revelation, and revelation is necessary for those laws that cannot be ascertained through reason. The result of this complementarity is a healthy tension that humankind is challenged to moderate, to understand when it is reason that must dominate and when its limitations must give way to the boundless reason of God. Locke himself conveys the nature of this tension best in his third letter to Lord Bishop Stillingfleet, in which he draws from the words of Solomon in Ecclesiastes.

Does God propose anything to mankind to be believed? It is very fit and credible to be believed, if reason, if reason can demonstrate it to be true. But, if human reason comes short in the case, and cannot make it out, its credibility is thereby lessened: which is in effect to say, that the veracity of God is not a firm and sure foundation of faith to rely upon, without the concurrent testimony of reason; i.e. with reverence be it spoken, God is not to be believed on his own word, unless what he reveals be in itself credible, and might be believed without him …

It is not for me to judge how far your lordship's speculations reach; but finding in myself nothing to be truer than what the wise Solomon tells me, (Eccles. Xi. 5.) "as thou knowest not what is the way of the spirit, nor how the bones do grow in the womb of her that is with child; even so thou knowest not the works of God who maketh all things," I gratefully receive and rejoice in the light of revelation, which sets me at rest in many things, the manner whereof my poor reason can by no means make out to me: omnipotency, I know, can do any thing that contains in it no contradiction; so that I readily believe whatever God has declared, though my reason find difficulties in it, which it cannot master. As in the present case, God having revealed that there shall be a day of judgment, I think that foundation enough to conclude men are free enough to be made answerable for their actions,

---

[217] Ibid, p. 7.

and to receive according to what they have done; though how man is a free agent, surpass my explication or comprehension.[218]

But as we shall now see there is more to this requisite tension. Revelation also makes the moral law achieved through philosophical reasoning *obligatory*, something reason alone is incapable of doing.

REVELATION AND OBLIGATION

The concept of "obligation" was a serious point of contention between Locke and Hobbes, since the latter believed that other than under conditions of safety, natural law did not obligate.[219] Locke disagreed, but was misunderstood and accused of being a "Hobbesian," at which he took great umbrage.[220] But Locke also rejected the idea held by other contemporaries that natural law by itself obligates.

'tis too hard a task for unassisted Reason, to establish Morality in all its parts upon its true foundations; with a clear and convincing light ... 'tis plain in fact, that human reason unassisted, failed Men in its great and Proper business of *Morality*. It never, from unquestionable Principles, by clear deductions, made out an entire body of the *Law of Nature*.[221]

And:

Did the saying of *Aristippus*, or *Confutius*, give it an Authority? Was *Zeno* a Lawgiver to Mankind? If not, what he or any other Philosopher delivered, was but a saying of his. Mankind might hearken to it, or reject it, as they pleased; or as it suited their interest, passions, principles or humors. They were under no Obligation: the Opinion of this or that Philosopher, was no Authority ... [T]hese incoherent apothegms of Philosophers, and wise Men, however excellent in themselves, and well intended by them; could never make a Morality, whereof the

---

[218] "Mr. Locke's Reply to the Right Reverend the Lord Bishop of Worcester's Answer to His Third Letter," pp. 351–352, 363–364.

[219] Locke's sixth chapter in his *Essays on the Law of Nature*, entitled "Are Men Bound by the Laws of Nature? Yes," begins with an apparent reference to Hobbes; albeit he does not refer to him by name. "Since there are some who trace the whole law of nature back to each person's self-preservation and do not seek its foundations in anything greater than that love and instinct wherewith each single person cherishes himself and, as much as he can, looks to his own safety and welfare, and since everyone feels himself zealous and industrious enough in self-preservation, it seems worth our labour to inquire what and how great is the binding force of the law of nature." Locke, *Essays on the Law of Nature*, p. 116.

[220] Harris, *The Mind of John Locke*, p. 275.

[221] Locke, *The Reasonableness of Christianity* (para. 265–268), pp. 195–196.

World could be convinced, could never rise to the force of law, that mankind could with certainty depend on.[222]

In his "Of Ethick in General" Locke similarly writes of the arbitrariness and relativity of unaided human reason:

And however Aristotle or Anacarsis, Confucius or any amongst us shall name this or that action a virtue or vice their Authoritys are all of them alike & they exercise but what power every one has which is to shew what complex Ideas their words shall stand for. For without shewing a law that commands or forbids them Morall goodnesse will be but an empty sound, & those Actions which the schools have called virtues or vices, may by the same authority be cald by contrary names in an other country, & if there be noe thing more than their decisions & determinations in the case they will be still neverthelesse indifferent as to any man's practice, which will by such kinde of determinations be under noe **obligation** to observe them ... (Emphasis added.)

To establish morality therefore upon its proper basis & such foundations as may carry an obligation with them we must first prove a law which always supposes a law maker one that has a superiority & right to ordeyne & also a power to reward & punish according to the tenor of the law established by him. This Soverain Law maker who has set rules & bounds to the actions of men is god their maker whose existence we have already proven.[223]

And much earlier, in his *Essays on the Law of Nature,* Locke writes:

For, ultimately, all obligation leads back to God, and we are bound to show ourselves obedient to the authority of His will because both our being and our work depend on His will, since we have received these from Him, and so we are bound to observe the limits He prescribes.[224]

---

[222] Ibid (para. 269–270), p. 196.

[223] Locke, "Of Ethick in General," in *John Locke: Writings on Religion*, pp. 12, 14.

[224] Locke, *Essays on the Law of Nature*, p. 183. Peter A. Schouls summarizes Locke's thinking on obligation and the limitation of reason as follows: "[R]eason by itself has no compelling force: Locke holds that knowing truth or goodness does not necessarily lead to action in accordance with such knowledge, that we can consciously and persistently disobey the dictates of our reason. Such disobedience results in degeneracy." Peter A. Schouls, *Reasoned Freedom: John Locke and Enlightenment* (Ithaca, NY: Cornell University Press, 1992), p. 55. Similarly, W. M. Spellman writes: "Moral right and wrong would be unintelligible for him (Locke) without the existence of God, the command of a superior will being an absolute necessity before the moral 'ought' could be considered truly obligatory ... Cudworth believed that the intrinsic moral worth of certain actions perceived by reason would be sufficient to obligate men; Locke would have none of this. That man was created a rational being, he would not deny: that most men would exercise reason and remain faithful to its dictates, he emphatically denied." Spellman, *John Locke and the Problem of Depravity*, pp. 56–57. Based on what we have seen here, though, Spellman was wrong to suggest that it was only after 1693, four years after the *Two Treatises* had been published, "that he would return to Scripture to lead men into obedience." Ibid, p. 126.

Locke does not provide us with a source for his insistence that reason as the basis of moral law alone is insufficient to obligate humankind, necessitating complementary divine command for the same law. But it is important to note that the relatively oft-quoted ("judicious") Hooker of the *Second Treatise* makes the identical point.

[B]e they plain of themselves or obscure, the evidence of God's own testimony added unto the natural assent of reason concerning the certainty of them, doth not a little comfort and confirm the same ... requisite it cannot but seem the rule of divine law should herein help our imbecility, that we might the more infallibly understand what is good and what evil. The first principles of the law of nature are easy, hard it were to find men ignorant of them: but concerning the duty which nature's law doth requite at the hands of men in a number of things particular, so far hath the natural understanding even of sundry whole nations been darkened, that they have not discerned no not gross iniquity to be sin.[225]

Without intending to suggest that he provided a source for either Hooker or Locke, it is interesting to note that they were both preceded by

---

[225] Richard Hooker, *Of the Laws of Ecclesiastical Polity*, book I, chapters 12.1–12.2, Cambridge Texts in the History of Political Thought, Arthur Stephen McGrade (ed.) (Cambridge: Cambridge University Press, 1989), p. 108. Pointing at his source for this concept, Hooker footnotes Josephus (*Against Apion*, book 2, chapter 37), paraphrasing him extensively while adding support sources of his own from Augustine and Aquinas. Because of its substantive and stylistic similarity with the Lockean quote earlier referring to the insufficiency of Athenian reason to ensure morality (p. 276) or that of Confucius as well (p. 287), it might have provided Locke with his source. "Are not the Lacedemonians to be reprehended for their inhospitality and their neglect of the marriage covenant? And the Elienses and Thebians, indeed, for practicing sexual union of men with men, an act which is obviously shameless and against nature, but which they thought right and useful? And since they performed these things, they threw even their own laws into confusion. See Thomas ... The law of nature was so corrupt among the Germans that they did not consider robbery a sin. Augustine or whoever is the author ... Who is ignorant of what is fitting for a good life, or who does not know that what one does not will to happen to himself he should not at all do to others? But where natural law has disappeared, vanished because of overwhelming custom, then it is necessary that it be manifest in the Scriptures, so that all men may hear the judgment of God and so that it be not completely obliterated. But since all men were cut off from the great authority of the natural law, idolatry was pursued, there was no fear of God in the land, fornication was practiced, and there was avid lust for the neighbor's possession. Therefore, the law has been given so that those things which were known might have authority, and so that those things which had begun to disappear might become manifest." Ibid. An examination of the Josephusean text will show that while Hooker chose to highlight the Lacedemonians of chapter 37, the very next chapter (38) uses the Athenian example of reason gone immoral, the very same example Locke chose to use in both *The Reasonableness* and "Of Ethick in General" as quoted in full earlier. This suggests that in this case Josephus might have been Locke's direct source without the mediation of Hooker.

the twelfth-century Jewish judge and philosopher Bahia ibn Pakuda, who also confronted the question of why "there was any need for revelation of the moral law, since it was already given through reason." He solves the theological dilemma by arguing that, "the people who received the Sinaitic revelation was so full of corporeal desires, and so weak in its power of discernment, that it was necessary to impart to it even the rational law, and not only the religious law, via revelation."[226] This argument, needless to say, is quite similar to the arguments of Hooker and Locke.

Jeremy Waldron expands on the limitations of reason as they relate to Locke's Christianity, the relevance of which will become readily apparent. Waldron writes:

Locke believed that there were certain elements of morality which are just not accessible to reason in the ordinary way ... Locke's prescription ... was not a prescription for more and better philosophy ... What was needed was not more expert philosophy, or more studious attention to the deliverances of good philosophy by those who were capable only of bad. What was needed was something different altogether: that people should be told their duties by "one manifestly sent from God, and coming with visible authority from him."
(RC: 143–144)[227]

The specific resource which, according to Locke, affords the clearest basis for our knowledge of and obedience to natural law and morality, is the Christian religion, the teachings of Jesus Christ, underwritten by the miracles that demonstrate His credentials, inspired by the example of His life and ministry, and taught as by "one having authority." (RC: 139)[228]

But Waldron is troubled enough by the role the Hebrew Bible played in Locke's theological paradigm that he footnotes the following:

So far as the revelation to ancient Israel was concerned, Locke says, that "that revelation was shut up in a little corner of the world, amongst a people, by that very law, which they received with it, excluded from a commerce and communication with the rest of mankind," whereas "our savior, when he came, threw down this wall of partition" between Jews and Gentiles.[229]

---

[226] See Bahia, *Hovot HaLevavot (The Book of Direction to the Duties of the Heart)*, part III, chap. 3, Ziphroni (ed.), M. Mansoor (trans.) (London: Routledge & Paul, 1973), p. 224. Quoted in Leo Adler, *The Biblical View of Man* (Jerusalem: Urim Publications, 2007), p. 101. For a deeper glance at the historical and philosophical context of this issue see Eliezer Berkovits, "Law and Morality in Jewish Tradition," *Essential Essays on Judaism*, David Hazony (ed.) (Jerusalem: The Shalem Center, 2002), pp. 8–9, 15–17.

[227] Waldron, *God, Locke, and Equality*, pp. 102–103.   [228] Ibid, p. 103.

[229] Ibid, pp. 137–138.

In other words, the obligatory nature of natural law was inherently clear to the standard bearers of the Hebrew Bible, but the exclusivity of its primary bearers prevented its universal application. It was the job of Jesus, and the Christianity that he spawned, to accomplish the universal implementation of God's law. This point seems to be of considerable importance to Locke, as he makes it rather unambiguously in his *Reasonableness of Christianity*. In stating that the role of Jesus Christ was to banish polytheism and idolatry by making the "One Invisible True God known to the world," Locke explains why that theological imperative "which the *Mahometan* Religion had derived and borrowed from it" could not be achieved through the Mosaic Law alone:

If it be asked, whether the Revelation to the *Patriarchs* by *Moses*, did not teach this, and why that was not enough? The Answer is obvious; that however clearly the Knowledge of One Invisible God, maker of Heaven and Earth, was revealed to them; Yet that Revelation was shut up in a little corner of the World; amongst a People by that very Law, which they received with it, excluded from a Commerce and Communication with the rest of mankind. The Gentile World in our Saviour's time, and several Ages before, could have no Attestation of the Miracles, on which the *Hebrews* built their Faith, but from the *Jews* themselves; A People not known to the greatest part of mankind; Contemned and thought vilely of by those Nations that did know them; And therefore very unfit and unable to propagate the Doctrine of *One God* in the World, and diffuse it through the Nations of the Earth, by the strength and force of that Ancient Revelation, upon which they had received it. But our Saviour, when he came, threw down this Wall of Partition; And did not confine his Miracles or Message to the Land of *Canaan*, or the Worshippers at *Jerusalem*.[230]

Locke's approach here cannot be said to differ significantly from the Hebraic viewpoint as articulated by Maimonides. It is in the context of his theological negation of Jesus as Messiah that Maimonides credits Jesus and Christianity with fostering true belief in God and with being the harbingers of the true messianic age.

---

[230] Locke, *The Reasonableness of Christianity*, pp.193–194. The words of Blaise Pascal (1623–1662), who also referred to God's revelation to the Jews as being locked up "in a distant corner of the earth," are worth mentioning here. Pascal, a Catholic French theologian writing around the same time as Locke, echoed the idea that Christianity's purpose is to bring to the entire world divine moral truths that were underexposed due to the natural state of Jewish isolationism. Blaise Pascal, *Pensees*, translated into Hebrew with an introduction and notes by Joseph Ur (Jerusalem: Magnes Press, The Hebrew University, 1976), p. 134 [Hebrew].

For the thoughts of the creator of the world are incomprehensible to the human mind ... and all of these things of Jesus the Christian and of the Ishmaelite who followed him are only to prepare the path for the Messiah and fix the entire world to serve God in oneness.[231]

In conclusion, Locke joined with Hobbes, Grotius, and Pufendorf against the position of the French skeptics, who posited that there was no universal concept of justice and that human social structure had to rely exclusively on custom. He joined with Grotius and Pufendorf, who thought natural law to be universal and obligatory, against Hobbes, who thought natural law was not inherently obligatory but was rather prudential and utilitarian.[232]And though he did not explicitly indicate adherence to the codex of Noachide laws, it was nonetheless the classical Hebraist John Selden with whom Locke joined in arguing that natural law could not be obligatory without divine revelation. Locke and Selden thus opposed Grotius, who searched for an obligatory formula without God.[233]

Locke's ideas on the power of human rationality rest on solid Hebraic ground when he defines the centrality of reason to moral behavior.

[231] Maimonides, *Mishneh Torah, Book of Judges, The Laws of Kings and War*. R. Judah Halevi, in his classic philosophical work *Kuzari*, is also fully in tandem with this view. See *Kuzari*, part IV, paragraph 23. A millennium later, the great Jewish historian Yosef Klausner ended his seminal work by crediting Paul with the same Maimonidean attribution. Yosef Klausner, *From Jesus to Paul* (Tel Aviv: Mada, 1951), p. 305 [Hebrew].

[232] "Locke also differs importantly from Hobbes in the general principles on which he draws, particularly in his understanding of the law of nature. Here he is much more like Grotius and Pufendorf than Hobbes. Although, as we saw, Hobbes talks of a 'law of nature,' he did not think that it was a real law but merely advice; he took its content to be prudential. By contrast, both Grotius and Pufendorf think that the law of nature is a real law, and that it produces real obligation. Here, Locke is like them rather than Hobbes. He also has a real law, offering obligatory commands rather than prudential advice." Harrison, *Hobbes, Locke and Confusion's Masterpiece*, p. 169.

[233] To be sure, Selden did not only depend on revelation for making natural law obligatory but for ascertaining what the law comprised to begin with as a result of man's diverse and deficient use of reason. In his notes (1616) to John Fortesque's *De Laudibus Legum Angliae* Selden stressed "the diverse opinions of interpreters [of the law of nature] proceeding from the weakness of man's reason." Later, in book 1 of his *Iure Naturali et Gentium juxta Ebraeorum* (1640) Selden wrote of the "uncertainty and inconsistency [that] appear in the unrestrained use of pure and simple reason ... so intrinsically inconsistent and dissimilar among men that it would be better for nothing to be derived from it." John Fortesque, *De Laudibus Legum Angliae* (London, 1775), Selden's notes to chapter 17, p. 51; *De Iure et Gentium*, book 1, chapter 7. I am indebted to Steven Grosby for these sources. See Grosby, "Reading the Talmud in the Tower of London."

Because once it is recognized that reason originates with God, is monitored by a consequential God, and is complemented by binding revelation, only then does reason have the legitimacy to identify what is true and then serve as "the only star and compass" of humankind's moral behavior.

3

Equality and Liberty

The Role of Imago Dei *vs. Domineering Phantom*

We hold these truths to be self-evident, that all men are created equal, that they are endowed by their Creator with certain unalienable Rights, that among these are Life, Liberty and the pursuit of Happiness. – That to secure these rights, Governments are instituted among Men, deriving their just powers from the consent of the governed, – That whenever any Form of Government becomes destructive of these ends, it is the Right of the People to alter or to abolish it, and to institute new Government, laying its foundation on such principles and organizing its powers in such form, as to them shall seem most likely to effect their Safety and Happiness.
(From the Declaration of Independence)

The *state of nature* has a law of nature to govern it, which obliges every one: and reason, which is that law, teaches all mankind, who will but consult it, that being all *equal and independent*, no one ought to harm another in his life, health, liberty, or possessions: for men being all the workmanship of one omnipotent, and infinitely wise maker; all the servants of one sovereign master, sent into the world by his order, and about his business; they are his property, whose workmanship they are, made to last during his, not one another's pleasure: and being furnished with like faculties, sharing all in one community of nature, there cannot be supposed any such *subordination* among us, that may authorize us to destroy one another, as if we were made for one another's uses, as the inferior ranks of creatures are for our's. (From the *Two Treatises*, ST 6)

In arguing against tyrannical forms of government, which by their very nature negate human equality and deprive humans of their liberty, Locke had to present a theory fundamentally supportive of the natural equality of humans and their undeniable right to personal liberty. He did so by predicating his argument on the fact that humans were all created by God, were by his will equal, and hence subordinate to him alone.

Because God is the source of human equality there is little toleration for atheists in Locke's philosophy, as any absence of God, in his assessment, must lead ultimately to inequality. Being created by God also means being "made in his image," which Locke understands as the human ability to think rationally and choose freely; indeed, a life guided by reason is what makes humans free. Despite the palpable presence of the Hebrew Bible in these ideas, some explicit and others implicit as we shall presently see, scholarly debate over Locke's theory of equality runs through a theoretical tension field in which Locke's Hebraism is curiously absent. The fact that some scholars interpret Locke's equality as a purely secular theory, while others put it in an exclusively Christian perspective, is here particularly contentious; the battle lines between the different schools of Lockean thought discussed earlier (Chapter 1) are especially salient. This chapter demonstrates the centrality of Hebraic ideas to Locke's theory of equality and will serve, I believe, to diffuse some of those tensions.

THE TRUE NATURE OF PRIMORDIAL HUMAN DOMINION

Anyone claiming that John Locke was a political Hebraist could not have asked for a better first reference to Scripture than the one Locke made at the opening of his *First Treatise*, and it is there that any analysis of Locke's conceptions of equality and liberty must begin.

In referring to the structure of Robert Filmer's arguments in support of patriarchalism, Locke writes, "and that from thenceforth our *Author*'s short Model was to be the Pattern in the Mount, and the perfect Standard of Politics for the future."[1] Peter Laslett sites Locke's source as the New Testament Book of Hebrews (8:5), "itself a reference to God's Commandments on Sinai."[2] The full text in Hebrews reads, "This is why Moses was warned when he was about to build the tabernacle: 'See to it that you make everything according to the pattern shown you on the mountain.'" Locke does not just open his treatise with a quote from Hebrews, but with a quote from Hebrews that speaks of the Sinaitic revelation to the Jews, the substance of which he will refer to consistently throughout his writing. It is this "Pattern in the Mount" that serves as well as the pattern for the construction of his theory of consensual government.

[1] I, 2, p. 160.   [2] Ibid, *ft.* 2.

Locke's choice to begin his scriptural quoting with a New Testament reference to the revelation of the Hebrew Bible can be viewed in two ways. Theoretically, it could be argued that the Hebraic quotes that follow must be seen through the prism of New Testamentism, or conversely one may contend that the following quotes stand on their own merit, quite distinct from any Christological reinterpretation. It is my contention that Locke's quantitative usage of Hebrew Scripture defines his qualitative intentions as well. The fact that subsequent New Testament quotations are so textually and theoretically, quantitatively and qualitatively, insignificant indicates that his primary usage of Hebrews was a fundamental contextual copula for understanding his foundational use of Hebrew Scripture throughout the *Two Treatises*.

Filmer's "Pattern in the Mount" was a "system" that "lies in a little compass, 'tis no more but this, *That all Government is absolute Monarchy*, and the Ground he builds on, is this, *That no Man is Born free*."[3] Locke wants his readers to make no mistake about what the absence of human freedom and absolute monarchy add up to – slavery. He therefore opens his first chapter with the defining declaration that, "slavery is so vile and miserable an Estate of Man, and so directly opposite to the generous temper and courage of our Nation; that 'tis hardly to be conceived, that an *Englishman*, much less a *Gentleman*, should plead for it."[4] Locke continues his opening broadside against the Filmerian paradigm by charging that it would "provide chains for all Mankind," "blind the people," "draw ... into bondage," and because "they have denied Mankind a Right to natural freedom" and proposed that "we are all born as Slaves," provide only a life of "Thralldom" and "subject us to the unlimited Will of another."[5] Concerned the reader will not concur with him that Filmer intended that slavery be deduced from the no-freedom-plus-absolute-monarchy equation, Locke closes his chapter with a quote from Filmer that could not be more specific:

Men are not born free and therefore could never have the liberty to choose either Governors or forms of government. Princes have their power absolute and by divine rights, for slaves could never have a right to compact or consent. Adam was an absolute monarch, and so are all princes since.[6]

From the Biblical account of Adam, it is clear to Filmer that humans are not born into a state of natural freedom, and hence the only form of

[3] I, 2, p. 10.   [4] I, 1, p. 158.   [5] I, 1, 2, 3, 4, pp. 159–161.   [6] I, 5, p. 161.

legitimate government is absolute monarchy. Before embarking on his rebuttal, Locke critically cites how Filmer derives these ideas from the Biblical character of Adam.

> Sir R.F.'s great position is, that *Men are not naturally free*. This is the Foundation on which his absolute Monarchy stands, and from which it erects it self to an height that its Power is above every Power, *Caput inter nubila* (head in the clouds), so high above all Earthly and Human Things that Thought can scarce reach it; that Promises and Oaths, which tye the infinite Deity cannot confine it. But if this Foundation fails, all his Fabric falls with it, and Governments must be left again to the old way of being made by contrivance, and the consent of Men making use of their Reason to unite together into Society.[7]

Thus Locke opens his second chapter of the *First Treatise* already adumbrating a bit on his modus operandi for positing a different conceptual structure than Filmer's in the *Second*. The foundation that Locke will proceed to collapse is that which is predicated on Adam, not the Biblical Adam per se, but Filmer's particular understanding of him. He will not differ with Filmer with regard to the centrality of the Biblical Adamic character to the human condition; rather, his understanding will not negate reason; it will not exist in a place where "thought can scarce reach it." As he does on many occasions, here Locke engages us with his approach to hermeneutics. The Bible is not discounted; quite the reverse, it is as foundational for Locke as it is for Filmer, but contrary to Filmer, it is relevant and understood only when read with reason. This is how Locke proceeds throughout his presentation of Filmer's thesis. As he drops hints of his full-blown later-to-come critique he does not discount the Biblical narrative but indicates why Filmer's reading of it is illogical.

For Filmer, Adam teaches a concept of fatherhood in which "*Men are born in subjection to their Parents*, and therefore cannot be free."[8] Locke goes on to say that the names Filmer gives to this parental authority are *Royal Authority, Fatherly Authority*, and *Right of Fatherhood*.[9] Filmer's fatherhood, which Locke dubs a "strange kind of domineering phantom," began with Adam, and:

> continued its course, and kept the World in order all the time of the *Patriarchs* till the Flood, got out of the Ark with *Noah* and his Sons, made and supported all Kings of the Earth till the Captivity of *the Israelites* in *Egypt*, and then the poor *Fatherhood* was under hatches, till *God* by giving the Israelites Kings Re-established the ancient and prime Rights of the Lineal Succession in Paternal Government.[10]

---

[7] I, 6, p. 162.   [8] I, 6, p. 162.   [9] Ibid.   [10] I, 6, p. 163.

Filmer's idea of fatherhood began with Adam and continued through the Books of Genesis, Exodus, Joshua, Judges, Samuel, and Kings, as depicted in the political life of the Hebrews. Locke does not yet challenge this reading, but rather asks what exactly Filmer meant by *Fatherly Authority* and on what basis he equates the powers of fathers and kings.

Sir Robert should have told us, what his *Fatherhood* or *Fatherly Authority* is, before he had told us, in whom it was to be found ... But perhaps Sir Robert found, that this *Fatherly Authority*, this Power of Fathers, and of Kings, for he makes them both the same ... would make a very odd and frightful Figure ... and very disagreeing, with what either Children imagine of their Parents, or Subjects of their Kings ... and therefore like a wary Physician, when he would have his Patient swallow some harsh or *Corrosive Liquor*, he mingles it with a large quantity of that, which may dilute it; that the scatter'd Parts may go down with less feeling, and cause less Aversion.[11]

Quoting Filmer at length without any "dilutions," Locke, drawing from his medical studies and experience for the use of the "corrosive liquor" metaphor, goes on to demonstrate just how "frightful" the figure that emerges from Filmer's fatherly authority actually is.

A perfect kingdom is that, wherein the king rules all things according to his own will. Neither common nor statute laws are, or can be, any diminution of that general power which kings have over their people by right of fatherhood. Adam was the father, king and lord over his family, a son, a subject, and a servant or slave, were one and the same thing at first. The father had power to dispose or sell his children or servants.[12]

Further defining Filmer's position, Locke writes:

This *Fatherly Authority* then, or *Right of Fatherhood*, in our *Author*'s sence is a Divine unalterable Right of Sovereignty, whereby a Father or a Prince hath an Absolute, Arbitrary, Unlimited, and Unlimitable Power, over the Lives, Liberties, and Estates of his Children and Subjects; so that he may take or alienate their Estates, sell, castrate, or use their Persons as he pleases, they being all his Slaves, and he Lord or Proprietor of every Thing, and his unbounded Will their Law.[13]

Filmer's denial of natural human freedom is unfathomable for Locke without some form of proof, and that he asserts is not provided by Filmer.

For it is scarce credible that in a discourse where he pretends to confute the *Erroneous Principle* of man's natural freedom he should doe it by a bare supposition of Adam's authority without offering any proof of that authority.[14]

Locke goes on to site the one proof source he has discovered in *Patriarcha*.

[11] I, 7, p. 164. [12] I, 8, p. 165. [13] I, 9, pp. 165–166. [14] I, 11, p. 167.

[B]ut what is strange in all his whole *Patriarcha* I find not one Pretence of a Reason to establish this his great Foundation of Government; not any thing that looks like an Argument, but these words: *To confirm this Natural Right of Regal Power, we find in the Decalogue, that the law which injoyns Obedience to Kings, is delivered in the Terms, Honour thy Father, as if all Power were Originally in the Father.*[15]

On this single recorded source of Filmer, Locke caustically comments:

And why may I not add as well, That in the *Decalogue*, the Law that enjoyns Obedience to Queens, is delivered in the Terms of *Honour thy Mother*, as if all Power were originally in the Mother? The argument, as Sir *Robert* puts it, will hold as well for one as t'other. But of this, more in its due place.[16]

For Locke then it is not that Filmer resources the Decalogue that is the problem, but that he does not resource it properly. The Biblical command makes no distinction between father and mother with regard to their honor; hence Filmer has no license to do so, unless, of course, he chooses not to lean on Biblical authority, which we have already seen is not the case. And so it is with regard to Filmer's understanding of the Biblical story of creation and the first man. As Locke will presently show, it tells us of nothing like that which Filmer would have us believe. Before moving on to explain how the Hebrew Scriptures *should* be read, Locke quotes Filmer in order to point to the aggregate misreading of his arguments.

If God Created only Adam, and of a piece of him made the Woman, and if by Generation from them two, as parts of them all Mankind be propagated: If also God gave to Adam not only the Dominion over the Woman and the Children that should Issue from them, but also over the whole Earth to subdue it, and over all the Creatures on it, so that as long as Adam lived, no Man could claim or enjoy any thing but by Donation, Assignation or Permission from him ... Here we have the sum of all his Arguments, for *Adam's Sovereignty*, and against *Natural Freedom*, which I find up and down in his other Treatises; and they are these following; *God's Creation* of *Adam*, the *Dominion* he gave him *over Eve*; And the *Dominion* he had as *Father over his Children*, all which I particularly consider.[17]

Here Locke indicates why he goes on to spend so great an effort on proving that the Bible does not support Filmer's claim that familial

[15] I, 11, p. 167.
[16] Ibid. Its "due place" is chapter VI, "OF Adam's Title to Sovereignty by Fatherhood," where Locke discusses parental authority at length.
[17] I, 14, p. 168.

dominion was granted to Adam by virtue of his creation. It is because it provides "the sum of all his arguments."

Sir Robert ... tells us, *A Natural Freedom of Mankind cannot be supposed without the denial of the Creation of Adam.*[18]

Locke does not denigrate the importance of Adam having been created by God as per the Biblical account. What he refuses to acknowledge is that there is a connection between the fact that Adam was created and the denial of human freedom.

I cannot see, nor consequently understand, how a *Supposition of Natural Freedom is a denial of* Adam's *Creation* ... For I find no difficulty to suppose the *Freedom of Mankind*, though I have always believed the *Creation of Adam*; He was created, or began to exist, by God's immediate Power, with the Intervention of Parents or the pre-existence of any of the same Species to beget him, when it pleased God he should.[19]

Divine creation does not of itself obligate dominion. The lion, Locke goes on to argue, also came into being through "the same Creating Power of God," but that hardly grants him "as good a Title to it as he (Adam)." This point is apparently what forces Filmer to double back and admit that it was not *creation* through which Adam was granted dominion over all other creations but *appointment*.

No! for *Adam* had his Title *by the Appointment of God*, says our author in another place. Then bare *Creation* gave him not Dominion, and one might have *supposed Mankind Free* without *denying the Creation of Adam* since 'twas God's *Appointment* made him Monarch.[20]
Adam, says he, *being Commanded to Multiply and People the Earth and to subdue it, and having Dominion given him over all Creatures, was thereby the Monarch of the whole World, none of his Posterity had any Right to possess any thing but by his Grant or Permission, or by Succession from him.*[21]

Echoing his belief that Scripture must be read with logic and with fidelity to what actually appears in the text, Locke attacks Filmer's argumentation on two levels.

The original Grant of Government, which not being till after the Fall, when *Adam* was somewhat, at least in time, and very much, distant in condition from his *Creation*, I cannot see how our Author can say in this Sense, that *by God's Appointment, as soon as* Adam *was Created he was Monarch of the World*.

---

[18] I, 15, p. 169.   [19] I, 15, p. 169.   [20] I, 15, p. 169.   [21] I, 16, p. 170.

Secondly, Were it true that God's actual Donation appointed Adam *Monarch of the World as soon as he was Created*, yet the Reason here given for it would not prove it, but it would always be a false Inference, that God, by a positive Donation *appointed* Adam *Monarch of the World, because by Right of Nature it was due to* Adam *to be Governor of his Posterity*: for having given him the Right of Government by Nature, there was no need of a positive Donation, at least it will never be a proof of such a Donation.[22]

Locke is forcing Filmer to stand up to the scrutiny of objective logic, a logic that allows for an unbiased reading of the Biblical text. God's directive to Adam to "multiply and people the earth" came quite a while after his own creation; ergo creation and appointment could not have been concurrent. And if God's creation of Adam included dominion there was no need to follow creation later with a positive donation.

Filmer, Locke recognizes, was cognizant of this contradiction and attempts an explanation, an explanation that also fails the test of reason.

To this foreseen Objection, our Author answers very Logically, *He was Governor in Habit, and not in Act*: A very pretty way of being a Governor without Government, a Father without Children, and a King without Subjects ... *Adam*, as soon as he was Created, had a *Title only in Habit, and not in Act*, which in plain *English* is, He had actually no Title at all.[23]

Having introduced the reader to the Filmerian argument he is determined to counter, Locke seals his third chapter of the *First Treatise* with a re-clarification as to why he quoted his intellectual nemesis at length.

For though this assertion, that *Adam was King from his Creation*, be true in no Sense ... though in truth it be but a bare assertion joyn'd to other assertions of the same kind, which confidently put together in words of undetermined and dubious meaning, look like a sort of arguing, when there is indeed neither Proof nor Connection ... having given the reader a taste here, I shall, as much as the Argument will permit me, avoid touching on hereafter, and should not have done it here, were it not to let the World see, how Incoherencies in Matter, and Suppositions without Proofs put handsomely together in good Words and a plausible Style, are apt to pass for strong reason and good Sense, till they come to be look's into with Attention.[24]

It is "bare assertions" with "dubious meaning," as well as "incoherencies in matter" and "suppositions without proofs," that Locke is coming to negate, not Scripture. We already know that Locke accepts fully the

---

[22] Ibid, p. 171.   [23] I, 18, pp. 171–172.   [24] I, 20, p. 173.

authority of the Hebrew Bible and that hermeneutically it must be read with both textual integrity and the logic it incurs.

Basing his arguments on the Biblical text, Locke is very specific regarding the two points he intends to prove Filmer wrong about: 1) that Adam was not granted "monarchal" rule, and 2) that the dominion he was granted was not private.

First Locke quotes the verse from Genesis upon which Filmer predicates his argument.

And God Blessed them, and God said unto them, be Fruitful and Multiply and Replenish the Earth and subdue it, and have Dominion over the Fish of the Sea, and over the Fowl of the Air, and over every living thing that moveth upon the Earth.[25]

Contrary to Filmer's perverted use of this verse, Locke writes that he shall show:

1. That by this Grant, 1 *Gen.* 28. God gave no immediate Power to *Adam* over Men, over his Children, over those of his own Species, and so he was not made Ruler, or *Monarch* by this Charter.
2. That by this Grant God gave him not *Private Dominion* over the Inferior Creatures, but right in common with all Mankind; so neither was he *Monarch*, upon the account of the Property here given him.[26]

Referring repeatedly to the Hebrew language and the Bible's vernacular, Locke demonstrates etymologically why humankind cannot be included in that which man was given dominion over. The words used to describe terrestrial beings simply cannot connote rational man. Furthermore, Filmer's suggestion flies in the face of the Biblical sequence of creation, the obviation of which naturally leads to the absurd.

All the Terrestrial irrational Creatures are enumerated at their Creation, *ver.* 25. under the Names, *Beasts of the Earth, Cattle, and creeping things*, but Man being

---

[25] Genesis 1:28. I, 23. Locke later refers to this verse as the "great and primary Blessing of God Almighty ... which contains in it the improvement too of Arts and Sciences, and the conveniences of Life." I, 33, pp. 182–183. Because the absolute monarchy advocated by Filmer does not allow for these "improvements" and "conveniences" it runs counter to the "great and primary Blessing of God Almighty." Locke writes this clearly later in the *First Treatise* (I, 41) where he says that one need just look at the "Absolute Monarchies of the World" to "see what becomes of the Conveniences of Life, and the Multitudes of People." This adumbrates on the centrality Locke places on the idea of private property in his philosophy of consensual government as expounded in the fifth chapter of the *Second Treatise*.

[26] I, 24, p. 175.

not then Created, was not contained under any of those Names, and therefore, whether we understand the *Hebrew* words right or no, they cannot be supposed to comprehend Man in the very same History, and the very next Verses following, especially since that *Hebrew* word רמש which if any in this Donation to *Adam*, *Ch.* 1. 28. must comprehend Man, is so plainly used in contradistinction to him, as *Gen.* 6. 20; 7. 14. 21. 23; *Gen.* 8. 17, 19. And if God made all Mankind slaves to Adam and his Heirs, by giving Adam Dominion over every living thing that moveth on the Earth, Chap. 1. 28. as our A____ would have it, methinks Sir *Robert* should have carried his Monarchical Power one step higher, and satisfied the World, that Princes might eat their Subjects too, since God gave as full Power to *Noah* and his Heirs, *Chap.* 9. 2. to eat *every Living thing that moveth*, as he did to *Adam* to have Dominion over them, the *Hebrew* words in both places being the same.[27]

Having used Scripture itself to prove just how illogical Filmer's reading of monarchical rule into God's grant of dominion to Adam is, Locke now moves on to dispose of the notion that the dominion granted to Adam was to Adam the individual, rather than to Adam the representative of humankind.

That this Donation was not made in particular to *Adam*, appears evidently from the words of the Text, it being made to more than one, for it was spoken in the Plural Number, God blessed *them*, and said unto *them*, Have Dominion. God says unto *Adam* and *Eve*, Have Dominion; *thereby* says our Author, *Adam was Monarch of the World.*[28]

Filmer argued that those who assert absolute power have received it from God in that he, at the time of creation, explicitly made some individuals superior to others. This Filmer predicated on Genesis 1:28, which reads:

God blessed them and God said to them, be fertile and increase, fill the earth and master it, and rule the fish of the sea, the birds of the sky, and all the living things that creep on earth.

For Filmer and the governmental absolutism he was coming to defend, this verse means a divine granting to Adam of dominion over the entire world, including other human beings. This is precisely the notion that Locke dedicates most of the *First Treatise* to refuting. In the previously cited verse, Locke argues that "Them" plainly refers to both man *and* woman as representatives of humanity. The verse follows the two verses that present the Hebrew Bible's idea of *imago dei*, that humans are equal because they were created in the image of God.[29] Adam is not to be considered as a

---

[27] I, 27, p. 178.   [28] I, 29, p. 179.
[29] The Hebrew Bible returns to the concept of *imago dei* following the postdiluvian admonition against bloodshed made to Noah and his sons discussed earlier: "Whoever

singular phenomenon, but rather as the beginning of a higher creature, whose intelligence and rationality are what earn its *dominion* over other species. The Scripture itself, reminds Locke, presents the elixir of all theology, God's plan to design a creature *in his image.*

The word *Them* in the Text must include the Species of Man, for 'tis certain *Them* can by no means signifie *Adam* alone. In the 26th Verse, where God declares his intention to give this Dominion, it is plain he meant, that he would make a Species of Creatures, that should have Dominion over the other Species of this Terrestrial Globe: The words are, *And God said, Let us make Man in our Image, after our likeness, and let them have Dominion over the Fish, & c. They* then were to have Dominion. Who? Even those who were to have the *Image* of God, the Individuals of that Species of *Man* that he was going to make, for that *Them* should signifie *Adam* singly, exclusive of the rest, that should be in the World with him, is against both Scripture and all Reason: And it cannot possibly be made Sense, if *Man* in the former part of the Verse do not signifie the same with *Them* in the latter, only *Man* there, as is usual, is taken for Species, and *them* the individuals of that Species: and we have a Reason in the very Text. God makes him *in his own Image after his own Likeness*, makes him an intellectual Creature, and so capable of *Dominion.* For wherein soever else the *Image of God* consisted, the intellectual Nature was certainly a part of it, and belong'd to the whole Species, and enabled them to have *Dominion* over the inferiour Creatures; and therefore *David* says in the 8th *Psalm* above cited, *Thou hast made him little lower than the Angels, thou hast made him to have Dominion.* 'Tis not of *Adam* King David speaks here, for *Verse* 4, 'tis plain, 'tis of *Man, and the Son of Man*, of the Species of Mankind.[30]

What is true for the reading of Genesis is equally true for the reading of Psalms. Just as Genesis does not speak of an exclusive Adamic dominion, the reference in Psalms to the creation, which is a "little lower than the Angels," does not refer just to King David, but to "man, the son of man," i.e., *all* humans.

Filmer had referred to another verse in Psalms as well in order to prove his concept of a monarchical fatherhood. *"The Earth, saith the Psalmist, hath be given to the Children of Men, which shews the Title comes from Fatherhood."*[31] Here too, Locke charges, it is only a spurious reading of the text that can eventuate Filmer's conclusion.

These are Sir *Robert*'s words in the Preface before cited, and a strange Inference it is he makes, *God hath given the Earth to the Children of Men*, ergo *the Title*

---

sheds the blood of man, By man shall his blood be shed; For in His image Did God make man." Genesis 9:6.
[30] I, 30, p. 180.   [31] I, 21, p. 174.

comes from Fatherhood. 'Tis pity the Propriety of the *Hebrew* Tongue had not used *Fathers of Men* instead of *Children of Men*, to express Mankind.[32]

Filmer ignores not only the more general "children" of Psalms, but the specific children of Noah as well. Similar to his exclusivist claim regarding Adamic dominion, Filmer argues that upon their exit from the ark, God granted Noah alone dominion over all living creatures. The verses regarding God's postdiluvian blessing to Noah read:

And God blessed Noah and his sons, and said to them, Be fruitful, and multiply, and replenish the earth. And the fear of you and the dread of you shall be upon all that move upon the earth, and upon every bird of the air, upon all that moves upon the earth, and upon all the fishes of the sea; into your hand are they delivered. Every moving thing that lives shall be food for you; even as the green herb have I given you all things.[33]

Once again Locke draws the reader's attention to the *plain reading* and meaning of the text.

What *Warrant* our *Author* would have, when the plain express words of the Scripture, not capable of another meaning, will not satisfie him, who pretends to build wholly on Scripture, is not easie to imagine. The Text says, *God blessed* Noah *and his Sons, and said unto them,* i.e. as our *Author.* would have it, *unto him: For,* saith he, *although the Sons are there mentioned with* Noah *in the Blessing, yet it may best be understood, with a Subordination or Benediction in Succession* ... The sum of all his reasoning amounts to this: God did not give to the Sons of *Noah* the World in common with their Father, because 'twas possible they might enjoy it under, or after him. A very good sort of Argument, against an express Text of Scripture: but God must not be believed, though he speaks it himself, when he says he does any thing, which will not consist with Sir *Robert*'s Hypothesis.[34]

Locke goes on to reveal an additional implausibility of Filmer's reading, a reading as sequentially problematic as it is contextually untenable.

This part of the Benediction, as appears by the sequel, concerned not *Noah* himself at all: for we read not of any Children he had after the Flood, and in the following Chapter, where his Posterity is reckon'd up, there is no mention of any, and so the *Benediction in Succession,* was not to take place till 350 Years after, and to save our *Author*'s imaginary *Monarchy,* the Peopling of the World must be deferr'd 350 years.[35]

The granting of dominion to Noah included the benediction of posterity. How then can one part refer to Noah alone and the other to his sons as well?

---

[32] I, 31, p. 180.   [33] Genesis 9:1–3.   [34] I, 32, pp. 182–183.   [35] I, 33, p. 182.

Why is it not either-or? And if indeed both parts were intended for Noah alone, were his children to wait until he died in order to procreate? The same is true, argues Locke, for the divine promise that Noah will be feared by the other living creatures; it defies all logic to suggest that the reference is to Noah alone.

The fear of you, and the dread of you, says God, *shall be upon every Beast*, & c. Will any Body but our *Author* say, that the Creatures feared and stood in awe of *Noah* only, and not of his Sons without his leave, or till after his death? And the following words, *into your hands they are delivered*, are they to be understood as our *Author* says, if your Father please, or they shall be deliver'd into your hands hereafter.[36]

Locke concludes with a summation of his understanding of the textual intent of Genesis 1:28, which demonstrates once again his fidelity to the Biblical teaching.

Thus we have Examined our *Author*'s Argument for *Adam*'s *Monarchy*, founded on the Blessing pronounced, I *Gen*. 28. Wherein I think 'tis impossible for any sober Reader, to find any other but the setting of Mankind above the other kinds of Creatures, in this habitable Earth of ours. 'Tis nothing but the giving to Man, the whole Species of Man, as the chief Inhabitant, who is the Image of his Maker, the Dominion over the other Creatures ... To conclude, this Text is so far from proving *Adam* Sole Proprietor, that on the contrary, it is a Confirmation of the Original Community of all things amongst the Sons of Men, which appearing from this Donation of God, as well as other places of Scripture; the Sovereignty of *Adam*, built upon his *Private Dominion*, must fall, not having any Foundation to support it.[37]

Relying on the same scriptural source that Filmer uses to establish his notion of Adamic patriarchy, Locke shows that Adam is not granted

---

[36] I, 34, p. 183.

[37] I, 40, p. 187. The following observation by Joshua Mitchell is in close keeping with what we have spelled out here. Against Filmer, who claims that Adam is *one* man who inherits the right of rule over other human beings, Locke claims that Adam is *all human beings* who inherit the right to rule over all creatures. In Locke's view, all are equal in Adam; in Filmer's view, God ordained *difference* among human beings with Adam ... Adam's right to rule was the right of *all* human beings to rule over the creatures of the earth. Made in the image of God, human beings were set above all creatures and given the right of property in common that they may secure through its use 'subsistence and comfort' in this life. The truth of Adam does not establish legitimate difference between human beings, as Filmer claims, but rather establishes a legitimate basis for differentiating the human community *as a whole* from everything else created, and for the dominion over all those things created." Joshua Mitchell, *Not by Reason Alone: Religion, History, and Identity in Early Modern Political Thought* (Chicago, IL: University of Chicago Press, 1993), pp. 80–81.

dominion by God over Eve,[38] and using the Biblical verses in Genesis regarding Noahic dominion, he proves the very same regarding children.[39] Locke does not take the approach that Filmer had merely defied reason alone in *Patriarcha*, but rather that he did not read Scripture properly, that he twisted Scripture to justify his position. Filmer's argument "is against both Scripture and all Reason," Locke asserts, not abandoning Scripture to make his argument but continuing rather with Filmer's reliance on it. He agrees with Filmer on the authority of the Bible but argues against Filmerian interpretation. "What is fundamental to remember however," K. I. Parker observes, "is that although Locke attacked Filmer's scriptural absolutism, he did not attack the Bible itself – only Filmer's interpretation of it. The Biblical baby was not thrown out with the patriarchal bathwater."[40]

I argue that the "Biblical baby" was actually the authoritative adult in charge of the bath. It is evident from Locke's harsh critique of Filmerian hermeneutics that he believed Filmer had not shown the Biblical text enough respect. Locke refers to Filmer's "ill-grounded" and "improbable" interpretations[41] and prescribes that when reading the Bible one must pay close

---

[38] In the *First Treatise*, Locke proves that the Bible makes no distinction between man and woman with regard to their equality, nor is there a distinction between father and mother with regard to the honor they deserve from their children. See I, 11, p. 167 and I, 15, p. 169. For more about Locke and his contribution to gender equality, see Susan Kingsley Kent, "Gender Rules: Law and Politics," in *A Companion to Gender History*, Teresa A. Meade and Merry E. Wiesner-Hanks (eds.) (Malden, MA: Blackwell Publishing, 2006), p. 93. Here the doctrine that emerged from Locke's ideas is celebrated and described as one that would "provide 19th and 20th century feminists throughout the world with the ammunition they would need for their battles to bring women into the world of politics and gain for them recognition and respect as political actors."

In addition, there is a connection between Locke's belief of equality and his rejection of the idea of the Fall as analyzed in Chapter 6. According to William Poole, those who followed the strict doctrine of the Fall and predestination did not accept the idea of equality, in this case equality between men and women: "Lack of any political and legal rights for women, again was all because of the Eve. Reflecting on the curse delivered to Eve in *Genesis*, 3:16, one lawyer explained: 'See here the reason ... that woman have no voyse (sic) in Parliament. They make no lawes, (sic) they consent to none, they abrogate none. All of them are understood either married or to be married and their desires or (sic) subject to their husband, I know no remedy though some women can shift it well enough. The common law here shaketh hands with divinity." Poole, *Milton and the Idea of the Fall*, p. 10.

[39] I, 32–39, pp. 181–186.   [40] Parker, *The Biblical Politics of John Locke*, p. 96.
[41] I, 36, p. 183.

attention to the "plain express words of Scripture,"[42] "the direct and plain meaning of the Words,"[43] and "an ordinary understanding"[44] of the passage. Parker points to the fact that, "Locke's principles for reading scripture in the *Two Treatises* are founded on a very literal, empirical, and commonsensical interpretation of the meaning of the words."[45] And Locke, it would appear, never veered from this approach to reading Scripture. Later in his life, in response to Stillingfleet's attacks on *The Essay*, Locke wrote:

[I]n matters of revelation, I think it not only sagest, but our duty, as far as any one delivers it for revelation, to keep close to the words of the scripture; unless he will assume to himself the authority of one inspired, or make himself wiser than the Holy Spirit himself.[46]

LOCKE'S CREATIONIST EQUALITY

Having predicated his negation of human inequality on proper Biblical exegesis, Locke begins his *Second Treatise* discussion on the state of nature by declaring that humans are naturally in a state:

of *Equality*, wherein all the Power and Jurisdiction is reciprocal, no one having more than another: there being nothing more evident, than that Creatures of the same species and rank promiscuously born to all the same advantages of Nature, and the use of the same faculties, should also be equal one amongst another without Subordination or Subjection.[47]

And again, all humans are:

equal to the greatest, and subject to no Body.[48]

What sort of equality is Locke advancing? Is it an equality that rests on a theological or completely secular substructure? For the Straussians, of course, Locke's notion of human equality was exclusively secular and it is only that secularity that makes it relevant for modernity.[49]

---

[42] I, 32, p. 182.   [43] I, 36, p. 184.   [44] I, 80, p. 220.
[45] Parker, *The Biblical Politics of John Locke*, p. 46.
[46] "Mr. Locke's Reply to the Right Reverend the Lord Bishop of Worcester's Answer to His Third Letter," p. 247.
[47] II, 4, p. 287.   [48] II, 123, p. 368.
[49] K. I. Parker points out that, "Both C.B. Macpherson and Leo Strauss maintain that although Locke was at least partially responsible for enshrining the values of freedom and equality in modern liberal democracies, he was able to maintain the plausibility of his notions of freedom and equality only by subverting other values such as religion and Biblical morality." Parker, *The Biblical Politics of John Locke*, p. 100. Parker couldn't be more correct, if though somewhat understated, when he says that, "Macpherson's and

On the other side of the theoretical spectrum, John Dunn understands Locke's equality as "a Christian egalitarianism" in the context of the Protestant doctrine of *the calling*. According to this doctrine individuals are "put into this world in particular social situations" and "They are called by God to fill a particular role."[50] It is their Christianity that makes them equal.

Jeremy Waldron seems to have been caught for some time between these two extremely divergent positions. He admits to having been initially troubled by an assertion made by Alasdair Macintyre to the effect that, "the arguments of John Locke concerning basic equality and individual rights were so imbued with religious content that they were not fit, constitutionally, to be taught in the public schools of the United States of America."[51] Waldron testifies that he was of the opinion that Macintyre was mistaken when he heard him make this claim, thinking "that the theology [in the *Second Treatise*] could be bracketed out of Locke's theory and that, if it was, a defensible secular conception of equality would remain." Seventeen years after hearing Macintyre's remarks he "had second thoughts about that bracketing possibility"[52] and concluded that Macintyre was right.

Locke's equality claims are not separable from the theological content that shapes and organizes them. The theological content cannot simply be bracketed off as a curiosity. It shapes and informs the account through and through; the range property on which Locke relies is simply unintelligible apart from these religious concerns. And so there is no way round it – Lockean equality is not fit to be taught as a secular doctrine; it is a conception of equality that makes no sense except in the light of a particular account of the relation between man and God.[53]

I believe Waldron's conclusive reassessment is correct, but I think that it still calls for greater precision, as the "particular account of the relation between man and God" that Waldron detects appears to be the one found specifically in the Hebrew Bible. Equality for Locke is indeed inseparable from theology, but where Waldron sees a decidedly Christian theology, I detect a Hebraic one. Locke, as if to preclude Waldron's initial

Strauss's interpretations are suspect; they lack textual sanctity and seem to contradict Locke's own express intentions and views on the Bible." Ibid, p. 102.

[50] Dunn, *The Political Thought of John Locke*, pp. 220–222. Toward the end of this chapter I will expand a bit more on Dunn's theory and why I believe it is distant from what Locke had in mind.

[51] Waldron, *God, Locke, and Equality*, p. 44. Waldron heard Macintyre's remarks in 1982 when the latter gave the Carlyle lectures at Oxford. Macintyre, a political philosopher, later incorporated these lectures in his book *Whose Justice, Which Rationality* (1988).

[52] Ibid.   [53] Ibid, p. 82.

assumption about the possibility of "bracketing out" any "particular account of the relation between man and God," explains why equality is the natural state of humankind.

For Men being all the Workmanship of one Omnipotent, and infinitely wise Maker; All the Servants of one Sovereign Master, sent into the World by his order, and about his business, they are his Property, whose Workmanship they are, made to last during his, not another's Pleasure. And being furnished with like Faculties, sharing all in one Community of Nature, there cannot be supposed any such *Subordination* among us, that may Authorize us to destroy one another, as if we were made for one anothers uses, as the inferior ranks of Creatures are for ours.[54]

For Locke, humans are equal because they were created equal by "one omnipotent and infinitely wise Maker" and because that Maker had furnished them "with like faculties." Attributing equality to natural law alone would allow for every separate society to attribute natural law equality to its own particular culture. Attributing natural law equality to the concept of creation, on the other hand, does not allow for the limiting of equality to a specifically prescribed community. The creation of humankind sets humans apart from other (lower) species, but not from each other, and were it not for the human propensity for moral corruption there would be no need for humans to divide themselves into smaller groupings and separate societies, which clears the way for claims of inequality.

[B]y which Law common to them all, he and all the rest of *Mankind are one Community*, make up one Society distinct from all other Creatures. And were it not for the corruption, and vitiousness of degenerate Men, there would be no need of any other; no necessity that Men should separate from this great and natural Community, and by positive agreements combine into smaller and divided associations.[55]

Humans, for Locke, compose one community because they were created as one, not because they are saved in one. This is a creationism that precedes Christ; and in it, men and women are not brothers and

---

[54] II, 6, p. 289.

[55] II, 128, p. 370. In a paragraph unrelated to Locke, but one that I think helps explain his intent, David Novak writes of what Biblical creationism does for human equality. "Here is where the doctrine of creation comes in because it does not allow any member of the covenanted community to ignore the world beyond the community facing her. It must be taken with utmost seriousness. (The minimization of that political reality very much correlates with a weak or nonexistent theology of creation.)" Novak, *Natural Law in Judaism*, pp. 189–190.

sisters in Christ but children of Adam. In Pauline doctrine equality is theoretically embraceable for all humanity, but only theoretically, as it is achievable exclusively for members of the *covenanted community*, not for those who do not accept the Christian faith.[56] In Corinthians, for example, it is baptism that makes for equality: "For by one Spirit are we all baptized into one body, whether Jews or Greeks, whether slaves or free – and we were all given the one spirit to drink."[57] And similarly, in Galatians: "There is neither Jew nor Greek; there is neither slave nor free; there is no 'male and female'; for all of you are One in Jesus Christ."[58] Contrary to the creationism of Genesis, which is featured prominently, these are absent from the *Treatises*. Locke's choice to establish his theory of innate human equality on the Hebrew Bible's account of creation is a telling elective move insofar as he did not include any Christian Scripture referring to conditional equality in Christ. It would be very hard to argue that this exclusion was not a conscious choice.[59]

The question may be posed as to why Locke chooses not to use the account of creation in Genesis at the beginning of his *Second Treatise* discussion of equality to ground this point, but the answer, as we have

[56] Similarly (although in regard to Luther), Joshua Mitchell writes: "Locke's *political vision,* then, rests first and foremost on Adam and not on Christ. Notably, he derives the equality of all human beings from the truth about Adam not Christ, unlike Luther." Mitchell, *Not by Reason Alone*, p. 199, *ft.* 31.

[57] Corinthians 12:13.   [58] Galatians 3:28.

[59] See Gordon J. Schochet, "John Locke and Religious Toleration," in *The Revolution of 1688–1689: Changing Perspectives*, Lois G. Schwoerer (ed.) (Cambridge: Cambridge University Press, 1992), pp. 147–164. Matthew H. Kramer makes the following, complementary, observation: "Locke's egalitarianism tended more to *overthrow* the priorities and the foci of the New Testament than to *recapitulate* them. When Jesus and especially Paul underscored the profound commonalities among human beings as creations of the Almighty, they did so in order to discount the significance of values such as equality or hierarchy within this vale of tears. Exactly because they portrayed the Christians in earthly bondage as freedmen of the Lord, and portrayed the Christians possessing earthly freedom as the Lord's slaves, they felt no qualms about instructing their faithful comrades that '[e]very one should remain in the state [such as slavery] in which he was called' (91 Corinthians 7:20). To be sure, this bland acceptance of hierarchy by Paul and Jesus was not a preordained consequence of their metaphysical holism; furthermore, these two men were sometimes less than unalloyedly quietistic in their remarks about the inegalitarian practices of sublunary life. But the center of their concern lay in an otherworldly level of human similitude, a level that generally overcame their interest in pushing for equality at the level of mundane institutions." Matthew H. Kramer, *Locke and the Origins of Private Property* (Cambridge: Cambridge University Press, 1997), p. 39.

seen, is that he has already done precisely that in his *First Treatise*.[60] Predicating an understanding of equality on the doctrine of creation as depicted in the Hebrew Bible results in a definition of humankind for Locke that is dependent on its ability to perceive, through the use of reason, the God of creation.[61] After all, those to be included in humankind's state of equality are defined by Locke as:

All the Servants of one Sovereign Master, sent into the World by his order and about his business, they are his Property, whose Workmanship they are, made to last during his, not one anothers Pleasure. And being furnished with like Faculties, sharing all in one Community of Nature.[62]

Throughout the *Two Treatises* Locke projects a take-it-for-granted attitude with regard to which creatures are defined as "man,"[63] this despite the fact that in *An Essay Concerning Human Understanding* Locke refrains from presenting a delineated taxonomy that can easily define the proper classification of species. In his search for a Lockean threshold above which a rational creature enters into the category of humankind and hence into the Biblically guided equality imperative of natural law, Jeremy Waldron detects a Lockean directional at the beginning of the *Essay* that, coupled with his copious references to God as "creator of man" and "master of his being" in the *Second Treatise*, elucidates for us Locke's definition of humankind. "[T]hey have Light enough to lead them to the Knowledge of the Maker," says Locke, "For the visible marks of extraordinary Wisdom and Power appear so plainly in all the Works of Creation, that a rational Creature, who will but seriously reflect on them, cannot miss the discovery of a *Deity*."[64] Waldron's conclusion is salient and inadvertently challenges Lockean scholarship that either denudes Lockean thought of its religious underpinnings or pigeonholes it to an exclusively Christian orientation.

---

[60] This is precisely a point that Richard Cox uses in order to negate Biblical centrality of Lockean thought, but Cox totally ignores Locke's *First Treatise* resourcing of Genesis. See Cox, *Locke on War and Peace*, p. 49.

[61] John Dunn emphasizes that, "Whenever he began to sketch out the contours of an ethic and searched for the fundamental form which it must take, the touchstone which he set up was always the relation between Creator and created." Dunn, *The Political Thought of John Locke*, p. 26.

[62] II, 6, p. 289.

[63] See Waldron's discussion of the relevant *Essay* texts: *God, Locke and Equality*, pp. 49–76.

[64] Quoted ibid, p. 79. For more about the value of the *Essay* in understanding religious Lockean concepts, see David C. Snyder, "Faith and Reason in Locke's Essay," *Journal of the History of Ideas* 47, 2 (1986), pp. 197–223. W. M. Spellman, "The Christian Estimate of Man in Locke's Essay," *The Journal of Religion* 67, 4 (1987), pp. 474–492.

Anyone with the capacity for abstraction can reason to the existence of God, and he can relate the idea of God to there being a law that applies to him both in his conduct in this world and as to his prospects for the next.[65]

Waldron then identifies two steps in Locke's ontology. The first identifying trait of humanity is the capacity for rational abstraction that can reason the existence of God. Emphasizing his inveterate opposition to innatism (a theory claiming inbred knowledge of God – a topic I will discuss presently), Locke disagrees with those who claim that God had imprinted this "idea of His being directly on our minds," explains Waldron, but had rather "conferred on those whom He intends to serve Him the rational power that is required for easy recognition of His existence."[66] The second characteristic defined by Locke is that people's comprehension of God leads them to the understanding that God relates to them and expects certain behavior from them, behavior that is defined in a law that guides them in this world and determines their place in the next. Waldron continues:

The content of that law may not be available to everyone's reason, but anyone above the threshold has the power to relate the idea of such a law to what is known by faith and revelation about God's commandments, and is in a position therefore to use such intellect as he has to follow and obey those commandments. Moreover, he can think of himself, abstractly, as a being that endures from moment to moment, and as the same being that may commit a sin today and have to account to the Almighty for it tomorrow: in short he has the minimal capacity to think of himself as a *person* ... [T]he fact that one is dealing with an animal that has the capacity to approach the task one way or another is all-important, and it makes a huge difference to how such a being may be treated in comparison to animals whose capacities are such that this whole business of knowing God and figuring out his commandments is simply out of the question.[67]

It appears highly probable then to conclude that, "Lockean equality ... is a conception of equality that makes no sense except in the light of a particular account of the relation between man and God."[68] But it is specifically the

---

[65] Waldron, *God, Locke and Equality*, p. 79.   [66] Ibid.   [67] Ibid, pp. 79– 80.

[68] Ibid, p. 82. It was apparently this "particular account" that also enabled Locke to overcome his own subjective sense of social elitism. W. M. Spellman writes that, "Locke, like most men of his particular social station, cared little for the vast majority, the ninety per cent of the population that he often referred to in language which seems, to our ears, cruelly insensitive. But cruel towards his social inferiors he was not, nor even contemptuous in any meaningful sense of the word." Spellman, *John Locke and the Problem of Depravity*, pp. 206–207. Spellman earlier recorded similar views about Locke held by E. J. Hundert, "The Making of *Homo Faber*: John Locke between Ideology and History," *Journal of the History of Ideas* 33 (1972), pp. 3–22, and Macpherson, *Political Theory of Possessive Individualism*, pp. 222–223. But Locke nevertheless did not forget that his own high social status was not the loftiest and that above him was a God who

God of creation that Locke links with equality, not Christ. Locke's exclusive concentration on the Hebrew Bible is not just to engage Filmer in a polemic on Biblical hermeneutics. Even if Filmer's patriarchal exegesis of the Biblical text had never been made, Locke would have grounded his theory of human equality on the Hebrew Bible's account of creation in any case. In it, he found a human equality that is innate in its divine ordination, and hence fundamentally unconditional and unalterable.[69]

ATHEISM AND INNATISM

Because Locke predicated his theory of equality on the human capacity to reason God's existence, his near total intolerance of nonbelievers and forceful rejection of theories claiming an inborn conception of the divine were axiomatic. In denying God's existence, the atheist denies the commonality of humankind established at creation; while the innatist, in rejecting human reason as the source of comprehension of the divine, leaves humanity devoid of a classification that elevates it over other species.

As for atheism, two levels of opposition can be discerned in Locke's writing, which reveal a gap between his cognitive understanding and his political theory; the individual-theoretical and the societal-practical.[70] On the individual level he could not understand how an unbiased mind

created all humans completely equal, no matter their social standing. Spellman concludes: "His (Locke's) bifurcated conception of human roles did not, however, mean that Locke was inconsistent on the subject of human nature." Spellman, *John Locke and the Problem of Depravity*, p. 209.

[69] See Mitchell, *Not by Reason Alone*, p. 81.

[70] Atheism, it should be pointed out, did not always refer to a denial of God's existence, and in the sixteenth century the term was actually used quite heterogeneously. Hooker, for example, distinguished between a small group of people who did not believe in God and a much larger group who lived as if God did not exist. (See E Pol. book V: ii, 1) For some, atheism meant a denial of God's providence, the immortality of the soul, and an afterlife, and for others, negative traits such as haughtiness, promiscuity, greediness, and stubbornness constituted atheism. It was not until the eighteenth century, which produced philosophies that not only tolerated but encouraged the denial of God, that atheism came to exclusively mean the denial of God's existence. The seventeenth century was a turning point regarding the meaning attributed to atheism and its usage, and the denial of God's existence is clearly what Locke was opposing. For an interesting compilation of sixteenth-century writers who used the terms *atheist* or *atheism* to describe beliefs or behaviors they were critical of, see Karen Armstrong, *A History of God* (New York: Ballantine, 1993), p. 288. See also Lucien Febvre, *The Problem of Unbelief in the Sixteenth Century: The Religion of Rabelais*, Beatrice Gottlieb (trans.) (Cambridge, MA: Harvard University Press, 1982).

In this regard it is of special interest to note Pierre Bayle's defense of Hobbes, about whom he claimed: "a great slander has therefore been committed by those who accused him of being guilty of atheism." Bayle made the following general observation about

could deny God's existence, at one time calling atheism a "crime" and "madness."[71] Furthermore, even if the atheist could find reason to defend her position, were she proven wrong the ramifications would be ominous, whereas if the believer is ultimately shown to be mistaken, nothing is lost. "Infinite misery ... will certainly overtake the atheist" if she is wrong, whereas even if the believer is wrong and fails to achieve "everlasting happiness," the worst that can happen to her is "eternal insensibility."[72] On the societal level, Locke's intolerance of atheists was more practical. In his *Letters Concerning Toleration*, Locke writes: "those are not at all to be tolerated who deny the Being of a God. Promises, Covenants, and Oaths, which are the Bonds of Humane Society, can have no hold upon an Atheist. The taking away of God, tho but even in thought, dissolves all."[73] Earlier, in "The Fundamental Constitutions of Carolina," Locke went so far as to make citizenship dependent on belief in God. "No man

atheism: "It is undeniable that no accusation has been more seriously abused than that of atheism. Many small minds and people of malice bestow it upon all who – drawing on sound metaphysics and the general doctrines of the Scriptures – put limits upon claims about great and sublime truths." Pierre Bayle, "Hobbes," in *Political Writings*, Cambridge Texts in the History of Political Thought, Sally L. Jenkins (ed.) (Cambridge: Cambridge University Press, 2000), p. 89. Compare Bayle's take on Hobbes with that of contemporary historian Bishop Gilbert Burnet, who wrote of Henry More that he was "an open-hearted, sincere Christian philosopher, who studied to establish men in the great principles of religion against atheism, that was then beginning to gain ground by the help of a very wicked book with a very strange title, 'The Leviathan,' that Hobbes, in the late times of confusion, had ventured to publish." Bishop Gilbert Burnett, *History of His Own Time*, abridged by Thomas Stackhouse, introduction by David Allen (London: Everyman's Library, 1979), p. 44. Bayle himself was in fact condemned for defending atheism and had formal charges leveled against him at the instigation of his old friend Pierre Jurieu (1637–1713, who taught theology and Hebrew at the Academy of Sedan, where Bayle held the chair in philosophy). On the controversy with Jurieu, see ibid, p. 311. This having been noted, Bayle himself did not refrain from forcefully attacking Spinoza for his pantheism, which Bayle understood as an extreme form of atheism. Pierre Bayle, *Historical and Critical Dictionary*, Selections, translated and notes by Richard H. Popkin with assistance of Craig Bush (New York: Bobbs-Merrill Co. Inc., 1965), pp. 288–338.

[71] Locke, "A Vindication of the Reasonableness of Christianity," in *John Locke: Writings on Religion*, p. 211. Yolton, *A Locke Dictionary*, p. 23.

[72] MS Locke Journal, 1676, pp. 369–370, *ft.* 1, quoted in Woolhouse, *Locke*, p. 127. This reasoning sounds very much like Pascal's famous "wager." Pascal, though, did not believe that reason could decide the question of God's existence because "infinite chaos separates us," and in this he was, of course, very different than Locke. Locke saw the "wager" logic as part of the rationale proving God's existence, whereas Pascal used it in a more utilitarian sense to guide human behavior. See Blaise Pascal, *Pensees*, A. J. Krailsheimer (trans.) (London: Penguin, 1966), section II, series II, "The Wager," pp. 149–155.

[73] John Locke, *A Letter Concerning Toleration*, James Tully (ed.) (Indianapolis, IN: Hackett Publishing, 1983), p. 51. Fania Oz-Salzberger writes: "Locke held that promises will not be kept without God, and that no social contract and no civil society can be maintained without keeping promises." Fania Oz-Salzberger, "The Jewish Roots of Western Freedom," *Azure* 13

shall be permitted to be a freeman of Carolina, or to have any estate or habitation within it, that does not acknowledge a God, and that God is publicly and solemnly to be worshipped."[74] Clearly, Locke believed that if God and the law he wills for humanity are the basis for equality among humankind, the atheist destroys that very foundation.[75]

(2002), pp. 105–106. In Chapter 5, "On Rebellion," I discuss the emphasis Locke places on *trust* in order to legitimate consensual government, and trust, he believed, could only be engendered through a belief in God. In this regard it is worth taking note of Abraham's response to Abimelech when the latter chided him for not telling him the truth about Sarah being his wife. "And Abraham said, because I thought, 'Surely the fear of God is not in this place' and they will slay me for my wife's sake." Genesis 20:11. The ensuing rationale of Abraham's justification is that without the fear of God and his laws, reasoned societal norms are not enough to ensure the prevention of serious iniquity between men.

[74] Locke, "The Fundamental Constitutions of Carolina," in *Locke: Political Essays*, p. 177.

[75] Jeremy Waldron notes: "Someone in denial of or indifferent to the existence of God is not going to be able to come up with anything like the sort of basis for equality that Locke came up with … The atheist may pretend to ground our equality in our rationality, but he will be at a loss to explain why we should ignore the evident differences in people's rationality. He will be at a loss to defend any particular line or threshold, in a non-question-begging way." Waldron, *God, Locke, and Equality*, p. 81. Later, Waldron adds: "Maybe John Dunn puts it a little too strongly when he writes that Locke saw atheism 'as a sort of spiritual equivalent of AIDS in the most hysterical contemporary understandings.' But Locke did see atheists as some sort of all-purpose menace, and this precisely because of what they did and did not believe." Ibid, p. 223. Waldron goes on to explain that in contrast to his attitude regarding Catholics, Locke's "refusal of toleration to atheists is as explicit as one could wish." Ibid. Waldron contests, correctly I believe, Richard Ashcraft's view that Locke remained practically as well as theoretically intransigent with regard to toleration for Catholics. Locke did express, particularly in his *Essay on Toleration*, rather harsh criticism of Catholicism for possessing some doctrines that were "absurd" and even contained "secret evil," and that Catholics were a subversive entity as they showed more loyalty to the Pope than to any magistrate, but he nevertheless did not practically exclude Catholics from the requisite social and political toleration he advocated. This mitigated attitude may have had its influence in Locke's later exposure (nearly a decade after the *Essay on Toleration* was written) to French Catholics during his travels in France. About them Locke wrote: "[T]he Catholic religion is a different thing from what we believe it in England. I have other thoughts of it than when I was in a place that is filled with prejudices, and things are known only by hearsay. I have not met with any so good-natured people, or so civil, as the Catholic priests, and I have received many courtesies from them, which I shall always gratefully acknowledge." King (ed.), *The Life and Letters of John Locke*, p. 15. In his discussion regarding Locke's conception of freedom, Raymond Polin draws the same conclusion with regard to atheists: "[F]or him (Locke), freedom is fundamentally a moral freedom, man a moral man, and we must certainly admit that, within the frame of his system, those who do not believe in God can neither think nor act in conformity with the law of human nature, which is a moral law." Raymond Polin, "John Locke's Conception of Freedom," in *John Locke: Problems and Perspectives*, John Yolton (ed.) (Cambridge: Cambridge University Press, 1969), p. 17. This seems to present a winning argument against the Straussians. If Locke's use of God and the Bible in formulating his political philosophy were actually

What is of essential note, however, is that Locke does not express his fear of and antipathy toward atheists in his *political* treatise. While his focus and philosophical dependency on the divine are explicit, his negation of atheism is implicit. He apparently wants the message that atheism is dangerous to consensual government understood, but at the same time when it comes to political practicalities, Locke does not deem the problem of atheism as insuperable. Locke, it must be emphasized, does not say so in so many words, but by simply ignoring the issue of atheism in his political treatise, the dangers of which he had already forcefully expressed in earlier writings, it seems fair to deduce that he did not think the menace of atheism in the public square implacable. Locke's reference to the "unbeliever" in his *Two Tracts* is particularly noteworthy here as it clearly indicates that even in his early writing his defense of absolutism was intended to preserve social harmony, which he recognized must be inclusive even of those who did not believe in God.

I know not therefore how much it might conduce to the peace and security of mankind if religion were banished the camp and forbid to make arms, at least to use no other sword but that of the word and the spirit, if ambition and revenge were disrobed of that so specious outside of reformation and the cause of God, were forced to appear in their own native ugliness and lie open to the eyes and contempt of all the world, if the believer and **unbeliever** could be content as Paul advises to live together, and use no other weapons to conquer each other's opinions but pity and persuasion, if men would suffer one another to go to heaven every one his own way, and not out of a fond conceit of themselves pretend to greater knowledge and care of another's soul and eternal concernments than himself.[76] (Emphasis added.)

One could read into Locke's silence on atheism in the *Second Treatise* that it is the *number* of atheists society comprises that is of crucial significance. Such a reading reconciles his epistemological assault on atheism with his political quietism on the subject. Locke, I suggest, is

intended to achieve the deprecation of the divine in the public square, why then the intolerance of atheists that, for Locke, was to have practical implications? Are we to believe that that too was part of the ruse?

James Harrington, it is worth noting, was unambiguous about the need for the civic exclusion of Catholics because of their extra-national loyalties. See Harrington, *The Political Works of James Harrington*, p. 681. For more about Locke and his attitude toward atheists see Locke, "Atheism," in *Locke: Political Essays*, pp. 245–246; Yolton, *A Locke Dictionary*, pp. 23–24; and especially Waldron's entire chapter entitled "Tolerating Atheists?" in Waldron, *God, Locke, and Equality*, pp. 217–243.

[76] Locke, *Two Tracts*, p. 161.

saying that government must be predicated on God and his divine laws as revealed through the use of reason, and as long as that remains paramount, atheism is but a theoretical challenge and atheists can be included in the societal consensus.[77] Where Locke would have difficulty in the practical political realm is with a governmental system (such as Marxism or Fascism) that rejects a priori any concept of the divine.[78]

As for believers in innatism, a philosophical-theological doctrine that holds that the mind is born with ideas and knowledge and is not a blank slate, Locke metes out similar treatment to that of the atheists. The belief in innatism, which can be traced to Plato's dialogue *Meno*, was primarily adopted and advanced in the seventeenth century by Rene Descartes.[79] Other major advocates of innatist thinking of the period included Malebranche and Leibniz on the continent and Newton and Bishop

[77] Paul Anthony Rahe posits that it is doubtful that Locke "really believed atheism dangerous to human society" but does not suggest how to reconcile Locke's strident wording in the *Letters Concerning Toleration* with the absence of any discussion on the matter in the *Second Treatise*. The dichotomy I suggest between theory and practice may provide the missing answer. See Paul Anthony Rahe, *Republics, Ancient and Modern* (Chapel Hill, NC: The University of North Carolina Press, 1992), pp. 465–466.

[78] I believe Jeremy Waldron is suggesting the same idea when he writes that Locke's "conviction that a society inhabited by a **significant number** of people who deny the existence of God is running a grave risk with its public morality." Waldron, *God, Locke, and Equality*, p. 235 (emphasis added). See also Alex Schulman, "The Twilight of Probability: Locke, Bayle, and the Toleration of Atheism" (http://harvard.academia.edu/AlexSchulman/Papers/). We will see later (Chapter 5) why atheism also negates Locke's theory on revolution, and in that regard as well, the determinative factor will be a quantitative one. It is important to note that Grotius too expressed concern about the potential dangers of atheists to society and rather than call for their banishment stressed the need for their being "restrained." "That there is a Deity, (one or more I shall not now consider) and that this Deity has Care of human Affairs, are Notions universally received, and are absolutely necessary to the Essence of any Religion, whether true or false … *Aelian* remarks, that none, even of People the most unpolite and uncivilized, did ever sink so low as to entertain and profess Atheism, but that a Divinity, and a Providence, were allowed and affirmed by all … Wherefore even out of mere Necessity, as it were, that these two Notions have for so many Ages been preserved among all the People of the known World … It is my judgment therefore, that those who first attempt to destroy these Notions, ought, on the Account of human Society in general, which they thus, without any just Grounds, injure, to be restrained." Grotius, *The Rights of War and Peace*, book II, chapter XX, XLVI, pp. 1035–1037.

[79] G. A. J. Rogers refers to the seventeenth-century disagreement over innatism as, "the great debate … between the Rationalists and the Empiricists, of whom the protagonists are traditionally identified as Descartes on the one side and Locke on the other." G. A. J. Rogers, "Innate Ideas and the Infinite: The Case of Locke and Descartes," *The Locke Newsletter* 27 (1996, www.luc.edu/philosophy/LockeStudies/articles/rogers-infinity .htm).

Stillingfleet in England.[80] It presented a significant challenge for Locke because innatists believed that the divine implantation of ideas in the minds of humans prevents the full use of reason to discover true beliefs. In one of his most famous philosophical arguments that are comprised by book I of his *Essay Concerning Human Understanding*, Locke opposed this concept and argued instead that every human mind is a blank slate – tabula rasa – at birth.[81] Locke was harshly criticized for challenging popular religious dogma; the denial of innatism was considered one step away from atheism. Because it was charged that the rejection of innatism negates proof of the human soul's immortality and spirituality as well as the existence of a divinely ordained moral law, it was seen as tantamount to rejection of God's existence.[82] But as in regard to the Fall and original sin, as we shall see in Chapter 6, Locke was not afraid to reject a major philosophical doctrine widely accepted to be true by Christian theorists across the Catholic-Protestant divide.[83]

But by the absence of any reference to innatism in the *Second Treatise* Locke appears to leave room for innatists in his polity, for the political realm is not the forum to contend with innatist ideas; hence his negation of innatism takes place in the *Essay*. This silence about atheists and

---

[80] G. A. J. Rogers makes the point that although Descartes had fewer disciples in England than on the continent, "few thinkers of any note remained untouched by his arguments." The Cambridge Platonists, many of whom were Locke's intellectual peers, were in particular "sympathetic readers" of Descartes even though "none of them could be described as a Cartesian." Ibid. Richard I. Aaron reached a similar conclusion: "the theory of innate knowledge had gained in favour during the seventeenth century both on the continent and in England, and Locke felt that the time was ripe for a thorough re-examination of it ... Locke's polemic was meant for the Cartesians, for the schoolmen, for certain members of the Cambridge Platonists, and for those others ... who advocated the theory of innate ideas in any way." Aaron, *John Locke*, pp. 83, 94.

[81] See Locke, *Essay Concerning Human Understanding*, pp. 59–74. Neal Wood suggests that Locke might have borrowed the term from Bacon and that it was actually from Bacon's scientific method that Locke drew his opposition to innatism. His more significant argument is that opposition to innatism naturally leads to a social theory of human equality, for if knowledge is not inbred, all people and all peoples start off equal (equally with a blank slate) and it is only education and societal norms that shape inequality. See Wood, *The Politics of Locke's Philosophy*, esp. pp. 109–148. Locke, though, was very specific regarding his source for human equality: "For Men being all the Workmanship of one Omnipotent, and infinitely wise Maker." II, 6.

[82] Newton, for example, charged Locke with "striking at the roots of morality." *The Correspondence of John Locke*, 8 vols., E. S. de Beer (ed.) (Oxford: Clarendon Press, 1976–1989), p. 1659.

[83] Rogers, "Innate Ideas and the Infinite."

innatists is crucial to understanding Locke's theory of equality. Even those whose ideas might interfere with the ability to ensure equality are still inherently equal, and this understanding of equality is entirely based on the equality of the Hebrew Bible as told in the account of creation. Here we witness another example of Lockean genius with regard to theoretical synthesis. It is not only the atheist who is not left out of Locke's consensus. Indeed, the *Second Treatise* does not explicitly exclude anyone from civil society or from the general polity. Or better framed as a syllogism: if a political doctrine utterly dependent on and suffused with references to God and his laws is nonetheless inclusive of atheists, it is elementary that no one, regardless of religion, denomination, or lack of either, is to be excluded from the social consensus.

Even though Locke has already made his Biblical case for human equality in the *First Treatise*, his presentation of equality and its practical ramifications are still influenced by Biblical references in the *Second*. Between his assertion that humans are born naturally in a state of equality and that they are "the workmanship of one omnipotent and infinitely wise Maker," Locke quotes Richard Hooker at length. Hooker associates human equality with the "Golden Rule" first uttered in the Hebrew Bible: "Love your neighbor as yourself."[84]

The like natural inducement, hath brought Men to know that it is no less their Duty, to Love others than themselves, for seeing those things which are equal, must needs

---

[84] II, 5, p. 288. The Golden Rule appears in Leviticus 19:18. Why Locke could not do without a reference to the Golden Rule in the context of his discussion of natural law will become clear in our forthcoming discussion of Locke's theory of self-preservation in Chapter 4. As to why he chose to use Hooker to make the point, it is beyond the scope of this thesis to try and ascertain why and where Locke leans on Hooker to convey his points. It is nonetheless worth mentioning here that Richard Cox, in his attempt to prove Locke's break with religion and establish his subversive use of Scripture, argues that Locke's equality has nothing in common with Hooker's. Cox, *Locke on War and Peace*, pp. 58–63. Michael Zuckert agrees and asserts that, "None of the other critics of the Strauss thesis has objected to Cox's demonstration of what Locke has done here." Zuckert, *Launching Liberalism*, p. 91. This is simply not true. See Harris, *The Mind of John Locke*, pp. 222–223, who sees consistency in Locke's quoting of Hooker here, and Waldron, *God, Locke, and Equality*, pp. 154–156, who quite accurately submits that, "This invocation of Hooker ... is also not just window dressing on Locke's part." (p. 155). W. M. Spellman makes an interesting observation regarding Hooker's theoretical opposition to Puritan thinking that lends some understanding as to why Locke chose to use him whenever appropriate. "The puritans, we know, would go on to claim for the Bible equal authority in questions concerning every aspect of life – modes of conduct, the order of worship, the form of temporal government – while Anglicans, led by Richard Hooker, insisted that such an extreme position would only abrogate the limited and legitimate role of God-given reason and natural law in settling matters of lesser import." Spellman, *John Locke and the Problem of Depravity*, p. 37. The

all have one measure; If I cannot but wish to receive good, even as much at every Man's hands, as any Man can wish unto his own Soul, how should I look to have any part of my desire herein satisfied, unless my self be careful to satisfie the like desire, which is undoubtedly in other Men, being of one and the same nature? to have any thing offered them repugnant to this desire, must needs in all respects grieve them as much as me, so that, if I do harm, I must look to suffer, there being no reason that others should shew greater measure of love to me, than they have by me, shewed unto them; my desire therefore to be lov'd of my equals in nature, as much as possible may be, imposeth upon me a natural Duty of bearing to themward, fully the like affection; From which relation of equality between our selves and them, that are as our selves, what several Rules and Canons, natural reason hath drawn for direction of Life, no Man is ignorant. Eccl. Pol. Lib. I.[85]

Reference to human equality in the context of the Biblical directive "Love thy neighbor as thyself" was imperative for Locke's theory of natural law. If, as Locke believed, a basic natural law is that of self-preservation and a Biblical injunction requires treating others as one would treat oneself, ergo *each individual has an obligation to preserve humankind as a whole.* Basic human equality then, as ordained by God at creation and as dictated by the divine command to treat others equally, "as yourself," is foundational for Locke's natural law. With this idea, Locke goes well beyond the natural law imperatives of Grotius or Hobbes, both of whom did not expand the law of self-preservation to include an obligation to preserve humankind.[86]

NATURAL LIBERTY AND *IMAGO DEI*

Basic human equality must be complemented with a belief in essential human liberty, as slavery can only be the result of inequality. Yet Locke is apparently not satisfied with such deductive reasoning because he chooses to anchor his concept of freedom on the Biblical notion of *imago dei*. He

rejection of reason by Calvinist pietists was also what drove Hooker to challenge the rigid Calvinist doctrine of predestination. Hooker accepted a much more limited notion of predestination that included but a small number of elect and totally rejected predestination of the reprobate. See Peter O. G. White, *Predestination, Policy and Polemic*, (Cambridge: Cambridge University Press, 1992), pp. 124–139. Here too Locke found much in Hooker, as Locke (as I will show in Chapter 6) did not believe in Augustinian notions of original sin, and championed the idea of human free will while totally rejecting predestination.

[85] II, 5, p. 288.

[86] I will expand in Chapter 4 on Locke's augmentation of the law of self-preservation where the importance of the quote from Hooker and his use of the Golden Rule are of critical importance.

begins his short chapter on slavery with the following declaration regarding human liberty:

The *Natural Liberty* of Man is to be free from any Superior Power on Earth, and not to be under the Will or Legislative Authority of Man, but to have only the Law of Nature for his Rule.[87]

It should be remembered that this too is how Locke began his discussion on the *state of nature*. Once created, a human begins his or her life in a "State all Men are naturally in, and that is, a *State of perfect Freedom*, to order their Actions, and dispose of their Possessions, and Persons as they think fit."[88] Clearly then, just as Locke links human equality with the God of creation and not with Christ, he does the same with human freedom. It was after all St. Paul himself who limited human freedom exclusively to believers in Christ's ministry when he said that people were free "with the freedom wherewith Christ has made us free."[89]

But, just as he will later open his chapter on slavery (chap. III), Locke qualifies this natural freedom, relegating it to "within the bounds of natural Law of Nature."[90] Natural law does not limit freedom in the sense that were it not for that law man would be freer. On the contrary, for Locke, human freedom is a result of *imago dei*. What endows humans with the image of God is their capacity to reason and it is that same capacity without which humans cannot be free. In violating the use of reason, either by ignoring or corrupting it, humans deplete not only their Godlike image but their own freedom as well. Hence, as shown earlier, the most elemental component of Locke's state of nature is humankind's most primordial political state, "a state of perfect freedom." K. I. Parker makes this point:

To be created in the image of God was, as Locke had argued in the *First Treatise*, to be created rational (I, 30), and if human beings are created with a capacity for reason, they are born with a capacity for freedom. Their freedom, in other words, is dependent upon their being rational, which is in turn dependent on being in the image of God, as Locke succinctly phrases it in the *Second Treatise*, "We are *born Free*, as we are born Rational" (II, 61). In the Lockean world of Biblical politics,

---

[87] II, 22, p. 301.

[88] It is important here to note Quentin Skinner's observation that, "The notion of a state of nature, and the claim that this condition is one of perfect freedom, were assumptions wholly foreign to the Roman and Renaissance texts." Skinner, *Liberty before Liberalism*, p. 19.

[89] Galatians 5:1.   [90] II, 4, p. 287.

then, to be in the image of God (that is, endowed with reason) is to be born into a state of freedom.[91]

On behalf of governmental absolutism Filmer totally negated the notion of natural human freedom because he believed that natural freedom meant the opposite of order, an anarchic humanity. Contrary to this belief, Locke teaches that without law, freedom cannot exist.

Freedom then is not what Sir R. F. tells us, O.A. 55. [224]. *A Liberty for every one to do what he lists, to live as he pleases, and not to be tyed by any Laws*: But *Freedom of Men under Government* is to have a standing Rule to live by, common to every one of that Society, and made by the Legislative Power erected in it; A Liberty to follow my own Will in all things, where the Rule prescribes not; and not to be subject to the inconstant, uncertain, unknown, Arbitrary Will of another Man. As *Freedom of Nature* is to be under no other restraint by the Law of Nature.[92]

Reason and freedom emerge from the womb together with the creation that is capable of utilizing and upholding these two attributes. The former permits humankind to delineate the obligatory contours of the law of nature, and the latter allows it to choose compliance. Compliance with the law, however, is by no means a limitation on natural freedom, as Locke elaborates later in his chapter on *paternal power*:

[T]he end of Law is not to abolish or restrain, but *to preserve and enlarge Freedom*: For in all the states of created beings capable of Laws, *where there is no Law, there is no Freedom*. For *Liberty* is to be free from restraint and violence from others which cannot be where there is not Law: But Freedom is not, as we are told, *A Liberty for every Man to do what he lists*: (For who could be free, when every other Man's Humour might domineer over him?) But a *Liberty* to dispose, and order, as he lists, his Person, Actions, Possessions, and his whole Property, within the Allowance of those Laws under which he is; and therein not to be subject to the arbitrary Will of another, but freely follow his own ... For God having given Man an Understanding to direct his Actions, has allowed him a

[91] Parker, *The Biblical Politics of John Locke*, p. 124. This theme, that freedom has meaning only in the context of reason, is also stressed by Raymond Polin: "Since reason constitutes the comprehension of the world order and is identified with it in the end, it is evident that, for Locke, freedom acquires meaning only when it is related to an order, to the order of the world itself, which is the order of reason ... Our freedom is indeed, as we have seen, a freedom of beings capable of reason, in a world organized in such a way that, with the power of reason and freedom given to us by God, we are capable of accomplishing a meaningful duty, that obligation for eternal happiness which happens to be the motive of our creation and the principle of our temporal existence. Polin, "John Locke's Conception of Freedom," pp. 3–5.
[92] II, 22, pp. 301–302.

freedom of Will, and liberty of Acting, as properly belonging thereunto, within the bounds of that Law he is under.[93]

Our discussion in Chapter 6 regarding Locke's rejection of the classical Augustinian interpretation of the Fall that jettisons the idea of human free will to choose between good and evil must be mentioned here, as it demonstrates the consistency of Locke's thinking. The "understanding to direct his actions" that "God has given man" and that allows "him a freedom of will and liberty of acting" has never been taken away from him. Depravity has not replaced reason in the human psyche as a result of Adam's choice to transgress the original divine command and perform the original sin. Humankind remains capable of assessing, through the use of reason, what is truly necessary for attaining happiness and of postponing the immediate gratifications that stand in the way of achieving it. Freedom then for Locke sounds very much like what Erich Fromm calls *freedom from* rather than *freedom to*.[94] Only when human beings refrain from the use of reason and allow themselves subservience to momentary material satisfaction are they naturalistically determined and not free. In *Some Thoughts Concerning Education* Locke writes: "[T]he principle of all virtue lies in a power of denying ourselves the satisfaction of our own desires, when reason does not authorize them."[95] Once action on initial

---

[93] II, 57 and 58, p. 324. Here Locke sounds much like the classic rabbinic tenet regarding the issuance of the Ten Commandments: "do not read 'charut' (engraved) on the tablets," but "cheirut" – liberated – on the tablets, to teach that no one is really free but the person who occupies oneself with the Torah (law). *Mishnah Avot*, 6:2.

[94] Fromm writes: "Human existence begins when the lack of fixation of action by instincts exceeds a certain point; when the adaptation to nature loses its coercive character; when the way to act is no longer fixed by hereditarily given mechanisms. In other words, *human existence and freedom are from the beginning inseparable*. Freedom is here used not in its positive sense of 'freedom to' but in its negative sense of 'freedom from,' namely freedom from instinctual determination of his actions." Erich Fromm, *Escape from Freedom* (New York: Avon Books, 1971), p. 48. In his well-known monograph *Two Concepts of Liberty*, Isaiah Berlin also makes a distinction between "freedom to" and "freedom from," but his intention is somewhat different than Fromm's. The "negative liberty" that Berlin defends is a liberty that ensures freedom from outside interference on a person's life, while "positive liberty" or "freedom to" means that a person must participate in a form of social control that will serve to liberate the "true self."

[95] John Locke, "Some Thoughts Concerning Education," *The Clarendon Edition of the Works of John Locke*, John W. Yolton and Jean S. Yolton (eds.) (Oxford: Oxford University Press, 1989), #38. Similarly, Neal Wood writes: "We have already seen that for Locke the individual possesses liberty only insofar as he is not the unthinking creature of his desires. Liberty is not license, but consists in the power of suspending the realization of our desires." Wood, *The Politics of Locke's Philosophy*, p. 145.

desire is held in abeyance in order for reason to determine whether or not it is a virtuous action, true human freedom is attained. On the other hand, the absence of "all Moral Rules whatsoever," Locke asserts in the *Essay*, denies "freedom to Mankind" making "Men no other than bare Machines."[96] Upon analyzing extensive quotations from the *Essay* Raymond Polin makes this point:

Through faith in eternal happiness, our freedom acquires the power of suspending the course of our desires, of interrupting the determination of the will by that permanent uneasiness produced in us by the flight and disappearance of everything present and immediate. By suspending in such a way the pressure of our desires, we become able to examine and judge by ourselves in an impartial and loyal manner.[97]

And following a survey of quotations from *Concerning Education* and the *Essay* Peter A. Schouls writes similarly that an:

[a]ttentive reading of Locke's discussion of freedom reveals his conclusion that a human being is naturalistically determined unless guided by reason; or more positively, that there is freedom, truly human action, whenever a person's reason guides.[98]

The restraints induced by natural law that foster human freedom must obviously include the rule of self-preservation, and for Locke, self-preservation is not just a right but an obligation.[99] As divine creations,

---

[96] Locke, *Essay Concerning Human Understanding*, 1.3.14, p. 84.

[97] Polin, "John Locke's Conception of Freedom," p. 4.

[98] Schouls, *Reasoned Freedom*, p. 126.

[99] I refer the reader to the argument toward the end of my discussion on natural law that Locke followed Selden in contending an obligatory divine origin of natural law and to my discussion in Chapter 4 in regard to self-preservation and property. This is the place to take note of Peter A. Schouls's particularly important observation that according to Locke it is *obligation* with regard to the moral choices that ensures self-preservation, which separates humans from other sentient beings. Schouls points to the *Essay* (2.21.51), where Locke wrote: "[W]e are by the necessity of preferring and pursuing true happiness as our greatest good, *obliged* to suspend the satisfaction of our desire in particular cases." And further (2.21.52): "For the inclination, and tendency of their nature to happiness is an obligation, and motive to them, to take care not to mistake, or miss it; and so necessarily puts them upon caution, deliberation, and wariness, in the direction of their particular actions, which are the means to obtain it." On this Schouls writes: "Corporeal sentient creatures other than human beings are under the *natural* necessity to act in ways that enhance self-preservation. For human beings this necessity is of a moral kind: they have a genuine choice whether or not to act in ways that enhance their preservation." Schouls, *Reasoned Freedom*, p. 151.

humans are also divine property, and as such do not have the right to forfeit their lives or compromise their freedom. They cannot commit suicide nor sell themselves into slavery.

This *Freedom* from Absolute, Arbitrary Power, is so necessary to, and closely joyned with a Man's Preservation, that he cannot part with it, but by what forfeits his Preservation and Life together. For a Man, not having the Power of his own Life, *cannot*, by Compact, or his own Consent, *enslave himself* to any one, nor put himself under the Absolute, Arbitrary Power of another, to take away his Life, when he pleases. No body can give more Power than he has himself; and he that cannot take away his own Life, cannot give another power over it.[100]

There is nothing about Locke's negative attitude on suicide that, at least on the surface, appears novel, but an observation is nevertheless in order. Locke does not invoke the use of Biblical quotation to support his position on suicide as he does regarding slavery (which I will presently examine). The writings of Augustine and Aquinas on the subject make the classic Christian view of suicide similar to that of Judaism, as they assert that suicide is absolutely forbidden. But while Christianity's great guiding lights draw the prohibition from the Sixth Commandment of "thou shall not murder," Hebraic sources relate the prohibition to the verse in Genesis 9:5: "But for your own life-blood I will require a reckoning; I will require it of every beast; of man, too, will I require a reckoning for human life, of every man for that of his fellow man."[101] This verse precedes the one used by Locke in his discussion on the state of nature analyzed at length earlier: "Whoever sheds the blood of man, by man shall his blood be shed" (Genesis 9:6). This exegetical distinction, coupled with the fact that certain streams of Christianity have taken a more liberal view of suicide, may be the reason Locke avoids the use of Biblical sourcing.[102]

---

[100] II, 23, p. 302. See George Windstrup, "Locke on Suicide," *Political Theory* 8, 2 (1980), pp. 169–182.

[101] Babylonian Talmud, *Tractate Baba Kama*, 91b. See also Maimonides, *Hilchot Rotziach*, chap. 2:2–3.

[102] For example, suicide was not included in the Justinian code. In addition, the English cleric and poet John Donne (1572–1631) wrote an entire treatise, first published in the 1640s, in defense of the Christian permissibility of suicide. See *Biathanatos a declaration of that paradoxe or thesis, that selfe-homicide is not so naturally sinne that it may never be otherwise: wherein the nature and the extent of all those lawes, which seeme to be violated by this act, are diligently surveyed written by John Donne* (London, 1644). Deborah Kuller Shuger suggests that Donne's theology was not "markedly different from the mainstream of English Protestantism." Shuger, *Habits of Thought in the English Renaissance*, p. 158. To be sure, whether or not he is representative with

More than just being a command in the sense of "thou shall not," the verse in Genesis is explanatory and bespeaks precisely what Locke intends to convey, that humankind is the *image* of God and the *property* of God.[103]

SLAVERY AND THE ABSENCE OF ENTITLEMENT

That all men are by nature equally free and independent and have certain inherent rights, of which, when they enter into a state of society, **they cannot, by any compact, deprive or divest their posterity**; namely, the enjoyment of life and liberty, with the means of acquiring and possessing property, and pursuing and obtaining happiness and safety. (From the Virginia Declaration of Rights; emphasis added.)

Tellingly, Locke opens his *Two Treatises* with the declaration that, "Slavery is so vile and miserable an Estate of Man, and so directly opposite to the generous Temper and Courage of our Nation; that 'tis hardly to be conceived, that an *Englishman*, much less a *Gentleman*, should plead for't."[104] On this Jeremy Waldron comments that, "In general opposition to slavery is the leitmotiv of Locke's *Two Treatises*."[105] Locke reasons that just as humans are obligated to preserve their life, they are prohibited from forfeiting it as well. And just as humans are not allowed to give up their life, they are likewise prohibited from giving up their God-granted freedom.

---

regard to suicide as well is a question. Augustine apparently also countenanced suicide under certain conditions. See Frederick Vaughan, *The Tradition of Political Hedonism* (New York: Fordham University Press, 1982), p. 58.

[103] Because of the inviolability of material property that Locke will go on to stress (and as I shall discuss later), it is imperative for him to establish proprietorship on the basis of humans themselves being "all the workmanship of one omnipotent and infinitely wise Maker."

[104] I, I, p. 159. Already in the *Two Tracts*, despite his defense of authoritarianism, Locke decried slavery. "Besides the submission I have for *authority* I have no less a love of *liberty* without which a *man* shall find himself less happy than a *beast*. *Slavery* being a condition that robs us of all the benefits of life, and embitters the greatest blessings, reason itself in slaves (which is the grand privilege of other men) increasing the weight of their chains and joining with their oppressions to torment them." Locke, *Two Tracts*, p. 120.

[105] Waldron, *God, Locke, and Equality*, p. 199.

In contrast to Aristotle,[106] Locke does not accept that people can be slaves by their nature,[107] but not only, not by their nature. For Locke, in pointed contradistinction to other natural law thinkers such as Francisco Suarez, Hugo Grotius, and Thomas Hobbes, it is equally impossible for a person to choose slavery by right or by contractual choice.[108] "Nobody can give more power than he has himself; and he that cannot take away his own life cannot give another power over it." And again: "no Man can, by agreement, pass over to another that which he hath not in himself, a Power over his own Life."[109] Locke will go on to say even more succinctly:

For no Body can transfer to another more power than he has in himself; and no Body has an absolute Arbitrary Power over himself, or over any other, to destroy his own Life, or take away the Life or Property of another. A Man, as has been proved, cannot subject himself to the Arbitrary Power of another...[110]

Any contract then through which people would exceed "an agreement for a limited Power on the one side, and Obedience on the other" but would rather abandon their life to the arbitrary power of another or consent to their own servitude would be null and void, for no master can justify his or her authority with the claim of the slave's consent.[111] Freedom is not something that people can contract away, because it is simply not theirs to dispense with. Jeremy Waldron writes that, "Locke is

---

[106] Aristotle, "The Household and the City," in *Politics* (Oxford: Oxford University Press, 1995), book I, chapters 4–7, pp. 13–20. Waldron points out that Filmer also rejected Aristotle's notion of slavery being appropriate for some people by nature. Waldron, *God, Locke, and Equality*, p. 199.

[107] Referring to despotic power, Locke writes later that, "This is a Power, which neither Nature gives, for it has made no such distinction between one Man and another; nor Compact can convey, for Man not having such an Arbitrary Power over his own Life, cannot give another Man such a Power over it." II, 172, p. 400.

[108] Tuck, *Natural Rights Theories*, pp. 54–57, 69–71, 119–127. Sommerville writes: "most natural law theorists were perfectly willing to allow that private persons could sell or give themselves into slavery." Sommerville, *Royalists and Patriots*, p. 70. A good example is Grotius, who writes: "To every man it is permitted to enslave himself to any one he pleases for private ownership ... Why, then, would it not be permitted to a people having legal competence to submit itself to some one person, or to several persons, in such a way as plainly to transfer to him the legal right to govern, retaining no vestige of that right for itself?" Grotius, *The Rights of War and Peace*, pp. 261–262.

[109] II, 23, 24, pp. 302–303. [110] II, 135, p. 375.

[111] II, 24, pp. 302–303. Locke also makes reference here to "the perfect condition of slavery, which is nothing else but 'the state of war continued between a lawful conqueror and a captive.'" Waldron sees this as the only case of justified slavery for Locke. See Waldron, *God, Locke, and Equality*, p. 200.

adamant that it is because we are, each of us, responsible to God for our own freedom that we are not entitled to sell ourselves into slavery, i.e. to alienate the stewardship of our freedom to anybody else."[112] Here it is John Milton whom Locke follows. In his *Defence* Milton attacks the notion that humans can voluntarily commit to slavery.

Our liberty is not Caesar's, but is a birthday gift to us from God himself. To give back to any Caesar what we did not receive from him would be most base and unworthy of the origin of man. For if upon beholding the face and countenance of a man, someone should ask whose image is that, would not anyone freely reply that it was God's? Since then we belong to God, that is, we are truly free and on that account to be rendered to God alone, surely we cannot, without sin and in fact the greatest sacrilege, hand ourselves over in slavery to Caesar, that is to a man, and especially one who is unjust, wicked and tyrannical.[113]

Although Locke recognizes the existence of slavery, he attributes it to humankind's underdeveloped capacities or its decline to a subhuman level. Raymond Polin posits that:

For Locke ... it is not even possible that a man could be a slave by right – and this doctrine is a very new one – but he admits however that there may in fact exist, such is the weakness, the frailty and the depravity of mankind, a slavery *de facto*, actual human beasts consenting to their slavery. This situation corresponds to the principle that, for Locke, men are born with capacities and under a specific obligation, but that they have to mature and to develop themselves, and that they can remain undeveloped or can destroy and corrupt what they have been able to achieve. Consequently, human creatures happen to exist who, not being fully

---

[112] Ibid, p. 198. This idea is embedded in the Biblical (Leviticus 25:55) expression "For to me the children of Israel are servants," upon which the Talmud comments: "They are my servants and not servants to servants" (BT, *Baba Metziah*, 10a).

[113] John Milton, *A Defence of the People of England* (EEBO Editions, ProQuest, 2011), p. 108. This is one of three cardinal issues upon which Locke sides with Milton against most other seventeenth-century philosophers. Locke also adopted Milton's anti-Erastianism, and he embraced the Miltonian notion that individuals, and not just "inferior magistrates" or the people as a whole, have the right to rebel against tyrannical government.

  Locke may have very well developed his anti-Erastianism during the years of the "Exclusion" crisis, as Erastianism and Exclusion appeared mutually exclusive. Accepting Erastianism for Locke, who was deeply involved in trying to prevent a Catholic ascent to the throne (James II in this particular instance, but opposition to Catholic rule was fundamental and total), would also mean accepting "popery" (which for him was synonymous with "slavery") should a Catholic attain the throne. As a result of that fear, Locke came to favor complete separation between religious and basic civic concernments. See Marshall, *Resistance, Religion and Responsibility*, pp. 110–112. As for following Milton on the right of the individual to rebel, see Chapter 5.

developed, having failed to make a reasonable and constant use of their liberty, live below the level of mankind, at the level of brute beasts.[114]

While Polin categorizes Locke's doctrine here as "very new," Locke himself did not think it was too new, as he goes on to anchor his thinking regarding slavery on the Israelite experience and the Hebrew Bible.

> I confess, we find among the *Jews*, as well as other Nations, that Men did sell themselves; but, 'tis plain, this was only to *Drudgery, not to Slavery*. For, it is evident, the Person sold was not under an Absolute, Arbitrary, Despotical Power. For the Master could not have power to kill him, at any time, whom, at a certain time, he was obliged to let go free out of his Service: and the Master of such a Servant was so far from having an Arbitrary Power over his Life, that he could not, at pleasure, so much as maim him, but the loss of an Eye, or Tooth, set him free, *Exod.* XXI.[115]

Locke refers to "the Jews as well as other nations" but does not go on to reference any of the texts of the "other nations." In addition, the chapter from Exodus to which Locke refers is so complementary to his attitude on slavery that it is impossible to deem the Biblical reference as merely coincidental or ornamental. The chapter begins with the placing of a strict limitation on the amount of time for which a contractual relationship between master and slave may be brokered. Locke's statement to the effect that, "For, if once *Compact* enter between them, and make an agreement for a limited Power on the one side, and Obedience on the other, the State of War and *Slavery* ceases, as long as the Compact endures"[116] appears to be a reflection of this concept. The "compact" between slave and master that is permitted may not exceed six years "and in the seventh he shall go out free, for nothing."[117] Should the sabbatical year precede the seventh year, then the slave is released prior to the full six-year maximum period.[118] The Hebrew Bible frowns upon any extension of the period of servitude but allows for it only under circumstances that demonstrate the self-deprecatory nature of the slave's decision. "And if the servant shall plainly say, I love my master, my wife, and my children; I will not go out free: then his master shall bring him to the judges; he shall also bring him

---

[114] Polin, "John Locke's Conception of Freedom," p. 8.

[115] II, 24, p. 303. The contrast with Augustinianism could hardly be greater. Augustine saw slavery as flowing from original sin and hence a necessary state of retribution and discipline that is not to be challenged. The fact that the Jews freed slaves after a given time, argues Augustine, is not applicable to Christians, while Locke, on the other hand, drew the opposite conclusion from the Hebraic example, as we have seen. See Deane, *The Political and Social Ideas of St. Augustine*, pp. 113–114.

[116] Ibid, p. 302.   [117] Exodus 21:2.   [118] Leviticus 25:52.

to the door, or to the door post; and his master shall bore his ear through with an awl; and he shall serve him for ever."[119]

In the Book of Leviticus the Bible's attitude toward slavery is made plain:

If your brother under you continues in straits and must give himself over to you, do not subject him to the treatment of a slave. He shall remain under you as a hired or bound laborer, he shall serve you only until the Jubilee year. Then he and his children with him shall be free of your authority, he shall go back to his family and return to his ancestral holding. For they are My servants, whom I freed from the land of Egypt, they may not give themselves over into servitude. You shall not rule over him ruthlessly, you shall fear your god ... for it is Me that the Israelites are servants, they are My servants, whom I freed from the land of Egypt, I the Lord your God.[120]

---

[119] Exodus 21:5–6. Even "forever" here is not really forever but until the jubilee year. See Leviticus 25:10. Rabbinic interpretation identifies this chapter in Exodus as referring to a thief who is sold in order to make restitution for his theft. As for the impoverished who sells himself, the Bible deals even more stringently with regard to the respect that must be paid him, as he is referred to as "brother" and so must be treated. See Leviticus 35:39. As to why the ear was chosen, the classical Biblical commentator Rashi offers the following Talmudic explanation. "Why was the ear, among all the organs of the body, selected for perforation? Asked the pupils of Rabban Yochanan ben Zakkai. He answered 'The ear that heard the Divine utterance, *for unto Me the children of Israel are servants (Leviticus, 25:55)* and yet preferred a human master, let that ear be bored.'" J. H. Hertz offers an additional explanation: "The drilling of the ear to the door of the house may also have symbolized the attaching of the slave to the household, and may have served as permanent evidence that the slave had remained in service of his own free will. This boring of the ear was thus something altogether different from the inhuman custom in modern times of branding slaves by a red-hot iron, marked with certain letters, and them pouring ink into the furrows to make the inscription more conspicuous." J. H. Hertz (ed.), *Pentateuch and Haftorahs*, 2nd Edition (New York: Soncino Press, 1972), p. 307.

[120] Leviticus 25:39–43, 55. Locke was drawing from what is contextually a revolutionary text with regard to slavery. J. H. Hertz writes: "The system of slavery which is tolerated by the Torah was fundamentally different from the cruel systems of the ancient world, and even of Western countries down to the middle of the last century. The Code of Hammurabi has penalties only for the master who destroys the tooth or eye of *another man's* slave. It orders that a slave's ear be cut off, if he desires freedom; while to harbour a runaway slave was considered a capital offence. As to Greece, a slave was deemed 'an animated tool', and he could claim no more rights in his relationship to his master than a beast of burden. Agricultural labourers were chained. If at any time it was thought that there were too many slaves, they were exterminated, as wild beasts would be. Athens was an important slave market, and the State profited from it by a tax on the sales. So much for 'the glory that was Greece'. The 'grandeur that was Rome' was even more detestable. The slave was denied all human rights, and sentenced to horrible mutilation and even crucifixion at the whim of his master. Sick slaves were exposed to die of starvation, and there was *corporate*

And in Deuteronomy, the Bible adds directives for exactly how and under what circumstances the slave is to be freed when the time arrives:

And when thou sendest him out free from thee, thou shall not let him go away empty: thou shalt furnish him liberally out of thy flock, and out of thy threshing floor, and out of thy winepress: of that with which the Lord thy God has blessed thee thou shalt give him. And thou shalt remember that thou wast a bondman in the land of Egypt and the Lord thy God redeemed thee: therefore I command thee this thing today.[121]

The Talmudic apothegm "he who takes a slave for himself, takes a master upon himself"[122] emphasizes the Hebraic approach toward slavery.[123] In its "other-worldly-ness," the Christological view of slavery

responsibility for slaves: Tacitus records that as late as the Empire the 400 slaves of one household were all put to death because they had been under their master's roof when he was murdered. Worlds asunder from these inhumanities and barbarities was the treatment accorded the Hebrew slave. The position of Eliezer in Abrahams' household (Gen. xxiv) enables us to realize the nature of servitude in the ancient Hebrew home. Kidnapping a man or selling him as a slave was a capital offence. Cruelty on the part of the master that resulted in injury to an organ of the body secured the slave's freedom (Exod. xxi, 26); and if a slave ran away, he must not be surrendered to his master (Deut. XXIII, 16). A Fugitive Slave Law, such as existed in America, with the tracking of runaway slaves by blood hounds, would have been unthinkable to the Israelite of old." Hertz, *Pentateuch and Haftorahs*, pp. 537–538.

While Hertz's commentary refers specifically to *Hebrew* as opposed to *heathen* slaves the contrast he makes with other nations of antiquity remains precisely within the context of "thy brother be waxen poor." Ideas that change moral human perceptions advance in historical stages. *Heathen* slaves were generally members of a subdued populace, the result of successful military campaigns (not mere social and financial destitution), and were not in the frame of reference that included something even remotely close to a notion of "thy brother." This did not prevent Maimonides from writing the following directive in his codification of the Laws of Slavery: "A heathen slave may be worked harshly. But even though the law is such, the way of the righteous and the wise is to be merciful and to pursue justice, not to overbear the yoke upon his slave, not to cause him pain, and to provide him with proper food and drink … he must not shame him verbally or otherwise … and he must not raise his voice in anger against him, but rather must speak to him with compassion and listen to his complaints." Maimonides, *Mishneh Torah, Hilchot Kinyan, Book of Acquisition, The Laws of Slaves* (New York: Feldheim Publishers, 1981), chapter 9, law 9.

[121] Deuteronomy 15:13–15.   [122] BT, *Tractate Kiddushin*, 21a.

[123] In his classic *Justice and Righteousness in Israel and the Nations*, Moshe Wienfeld shows how the specific idea of equality separated the Israelites from their neighboring nations in the ancient Near East. Justice, righteousness, and equality were not only the right way to conduct a social and political structure in ancient Israel, but a human reflection of God's cosmic order and a vision of a future redemption for all humanity. Moshe Wienfeld, *Justice and Righteousness in Israel and the Nations: Equality and Freedom in Ancient Israel in Light of Social Justice in the Ancient Near East* (Jerusalem: The

is tellingly more complicated and provides ample reason for Locke to avoid any mention of it in his discussion on the subject. In Corinthians, for example, Paul says:

Let every man abide in the same calling wherein he was called. Art thou called being a servant? Care not for it: but if thou mayest be made free, use it rather. For he that is called in the Lord, being a servant, is the Lord's freeman: likewise also he that is called, being free, is Christ's servant. Ye are bought with a price; be not ye the servants of men.[124]

In *A Paraphrase and Notes on the Epistles of St. Paul*, Locke paraphrases Paul, presenting what John Dunn determines as akin to the Protestant doctrine of *the calling*, the theological foundation for ordering humankind to reconcile itself to the position life has prepared for it. Locke writes:

Wert thou called being a slave, think thy self not the less a Christian for being a slave: but prefer freedom to slavery if thou canst obtain it. For he that is converted to Christianity being a bond-man is Christ's freed-man. And he that is converted being a free man, is Christ's bond-man under his command and dominion.[125]

Dunn, whose thesis proposes that Locke here uses "Christianity as a balm to sooth the pain" that his "theories on society" had elicited, defines the doctrinal "calling" thus:

Men are put into the world in particular social situations and with particular individual talents. They are called by God to fill a particular role, and they can discern what this role is to be by conscientious reflection on the relationship between their genetic endowment and the social situation into which they are born. When they have construed this divine provision correctly, they will have

Magnes Press, The Hebrew University of Jerusalem, 1985) [Hebrew]. For notions of human equality as derived from the Hebrew Prophets in general and from the social and political work of Ezra the Scribe in particular, see Yoram Mayshar, *In His Image: The Idea of Equality from Ezra to Nietzsche* (Jerusalem: Carmel, 2007) [Hebrew].

[124] Corinthians 7:20–23. Henry Chadwick emphasizes that the Church was not indifferent to slavery; rather it placed the importance of public subordination to political authority above the cons of slavery. "What made the Church conservative about slavery as an institution was no political indifference but respect for the State and for Law as laid down in Romans xiii. That any one would possess property rights over another was recognized as an evil, and therefore held to be a consequence of the fallen state of humanity since Adam. According to St Paul slavery is like a mixed marriage in which the Christian partner should not take the initiative in seeking for its dissolution." Henry Chadwick, *The Early Church* (London: Penguin Books, 1993), p. 59.

[125] John Locke, *A Paraphrase and Notes on the Epistles of St. Paul to the Galatians, 1 and 2 Corinthians, Romans, Ephesians*, Arthur W. Wainwright (ed.) (Oxford: Oxford University Press, 1987), Volume I, pp. 201–202.

identified their "particular calling." The calling is thus a summons from God, but it is a summons for the interpretation of which each adult individual is fully responsible. Chronic indecision over the choice of an appropriate calling was morally suspicious and the stubborn refusal to settle down to any particular calling was morally outrageous ... The problem of the world is the problem of its enticements, of its deflections of energy from religious aspiration to self-satisfied consumption ... The calling, by rejecting such unequivocal behavioral norms, forced men to nerve themselves to the most unrelenting moral exertion ... The only available touchstone within the structure of the theory must be their own sense of their authentic and total subjection to the demands of their religious role. They had to discipline their lives so that these felt totally subordinated to the fulfillments of this purpose. Any sense of emerging insouciance in their attitudes had to be met by undertaking some unambiguously taxing practical duty. Physical labour for any man ... could serve as such concrete tokens of dutifulness.[126]

With terms like "genetic endowment," "social situation," "totally subordinated," "unambiguously taxing practical duty," and "physical labor" helping to define the doctrine of *calling*, it is not hard to imagine just how easy it might be to see slavery as a legitimate "calling." But is Dunn right about attributing this doctrine of Christian quietness and resignation to Locke? Jeremy Waldron, for one, forcefully rejects Dunn's interpretation.

I am certain there is nothing at all of that flavor in his note on the passage from I Corinthians. For what Locke says there is the exact equivalent of what he said about the passage from Romans 13: civil slavery, he says, was "not dissolved by a man's becoming a Christian" (P&N: i.202n). And in general, Locke goes on, Paul tells us that "noething in any man's civil estate or rights is altered by his becoming a Christian" (ibid.). This is quite different from the idea of a calling ... It is a pure negative. *If* slavery is legitimate, then Christians may be slaves ... But if slavery is illegitimate, then Christians, like everyone else, may not be slaves and need not and probably should not obey their *de facto* masters ... If moral and political theory could establish that they already owed no obedience to their masters, then that would remain their position after the coming of, or their conversion to, Christianity.[127]

To conclude, judging from what we have discussed earlier, Waldron is clearly correct in arguing that Locke does not champion the Protestant doctrine of *the calling*, but he could have made a stronger case had he

---

[126] Dunn, *The Political Thought of John Locke*, pp. 221, 222–224.
[127] Waldron, *God, Locke, and Equality*, p. 198. Earlier, Waldron makes the critical observation that Locke's gloss on Romans 13: 1–5 in his *Paraphrase and Notes* rejects the commonly held opinion that Paul intended to sanction blind obedience to every authority. See ibid, pp. 195–197.

considered Locke's Hebraism. In doing so he could have turned to Locke's foundational reference to the Hebrew Bible with regard to slavery, which rejects in total any complacent acceptance of slavery as part of its social teleology. Locke brings the scriptural injunction against slavery and the people of the book's experiential shunning of slavery in order to substantiate categorical rejection of slavery by nature or by choice. Indeed, by nature, humans are equal and free as taught by the Hebrew Bible, and because equality and freedom are of divine origin and divinely maintained, humans may not even choose to jettison it. Any reference to a moral or religious credo inclusive of doctrinal tolerance of slavery would be impossible for Locke.

4

Property and Charity

The Biblical Contours of Lockean Economics

The great and chief end, therefore, of men's uniting into common-wealths, and putting themselves under government, is the preservation of their property. To which in the state of nature there are many things wanting. (From the *Two Treatises*, ST 124)

The reason why men enter into society, is the preservation of their property; and the end why they chuse and authorize a legislative, is, that there may be laws made, and rules set, as guards and fences to the properties of all the members of the society, to limit the power, and moderate the dominion, of every part and member of the society: for since it can never be supposed to be the will of the society, that the legislative should have a power to destroy that which every one designs to secure, by entering into society, and for which the people submitted themselves to legislators of their own making; whenever the legislators endeavour to take away, and destroy the property of the people, or to reduce them to slavery under arbitrary power, they put themselves into a state of war with the people, who are thereupon absolved from any farther obedience, and are left to the common refuge, which God hath provided for all men, against force and violence. (From the *Two Treatises*, ST 222)

In terms of his writing and the publication of his works, the time from Locke's return to England until his death was a prolific one, but he did not limit his endeavors to the printed word. Upon his return, Locke immediately voiced concern over England's standing overseas, which probably was the reason William offered him important diplomatic postings abroad, possibly including an appointment as Secretary of State. Locke, though, who it appears was always torn between his desire for leisurely study and his sense of duty to country, respectfully declined these overtures, claiming a personal demeanor unfit for diplomacy, and, as in the past, poor health.[1]

So, while he rejected diplomatic postings abroad he nevertheless sought positions in public service, and these, it so happened, were in the economic and fiscal realm. As a result, in these later years of his life Locke paid an unusually high level of attention to economic issues, the foundational concepts of which are to be found in his *Second Treatise*.

The first position he accepted was as a Commissioner of Appeals for Excise. It was secured through his friend Lord Charles Mordaunt (3rd Earl of Peterborough and 1st Earl of Monmouth), who due to his Whig activism had been in Dutch exile together with Locke (and had been one of those who appealed to William to invade England), and was now a Treasury Lord. Soon afterward, Locke was appointed a Commissioner for Greenwich Hospital, and later by the king himself as a Commissioner in the reconstituted Council of Trade.[2]

One of the major issues was the question of interest rates. After England had entered the war against France soon into William's reign, there had been a considerable rise in the legal interest rate, which followed with calls for its official reduction. Locke firmly believed that sound economic policy required that the government not interfere with the dictates of the market and hence opposed what he considered to be an artificial reduction of the rate. This would cause an incongruity between the market rate and the legal rate that was unsustainable because it would foster illicit lending practices. The banks would take money on deposit at the lower legal rate and then lend it out at the higher market rate, he warned. In addition, it was unfair to those who had all their assets in money rather than land as their assets would suddenly undergo devaluation.

Locke had already addressed this principled policy question in response to a request from Shaftesbury in 1668 and now expanded what he had written then into a pamphlet entitled *Some Considerations of the Consequences of the Lowering of Interest and Raising the Value of Money*. The work was published anonymously but used extensively in Parliament by Locke's good friend Edward Clark, who like Shaftesbury had sought Locke's advice on the issue. Although Locke's position was initially rejected, it ultimately won the day when the bill calling

---

[1] Woolhouse, *Locke: A Biography*, pp. 266–268, 400–401.   [2] Ibid, pp. 348, 361.

for the lowering of the legal interest was lost when Parliament was prorogued.[3]

Another economic issue of serious national consequence that Locke addressed related to the devaluation of currency due to the illegal "clipping" of coins. At that time coins were not simply fiduciary tokens but took their value from their weight in valuable metal. The edges of the coins were being cut for the value of the clippings resulting in a de facto lower value of the coin itself. Here again the recommended popular solution to the problem was an artificial one, the issuing of new coins with raised prices without consideration of their weight in precious metal, and here too Locke was opposed. He argued that by merely calling something what it was in fact not did not turn it into what it was now being called; whatever they were being labeled, either the coins had the recognized weight or they did not. The proper way to deal with the problem, Locke thought, was to intensify legal pressure against coin clipping. Once again it was Clarke who turned to Locke for advice following the publication of a pamphlet favoring the devaluation entitled *For Encouraging the Coinage of Silver Money in England*, probably authored by Thomas Neale, Master of the Mint. Locke, suggesting that Neale would benefit personally from the re-coinage, responded in a short piece to Clarke that was published only two years later (1695) when Parliament had to deal with the serious effects clipping was having on domestic trade. Locke's article was published anonymously under the title *Short Observations on a paper, entitled, "For Encouraging the Coinage of Silver Money in England, and after for keeping it here."*[4]

As the troubles and ensuing debates over clipping intensified, Locke answered separate requests by both William Trumbull, Secretary of State, and William Lowndes, Secretary of the Treasury, to address the issue. Locke responded with a series of three articles entitled *Guineas, Money*, and *Further Considerations concerning the Value of Money* in which he argued that the profit from clipping had to be denied by making it illegal for clipped money to be exchanged at its face value, but rather only by its actual weight in silver.[5]

Locke also wrote on the "poor law," arguing that assistance to the poor had been improperly applied because it did not differentiate between those who were destitute because they chose not to work though they

---

[3] Ibid, pp. 290–294, 304–305. [4] Ibid, pp. 294–296, 322, 347.
[5] Ibid, pp. 355–356, 359.

were physically able, who should not be the recipients of help, and those who wanted to work but were physically impaired and hence unable to do so, who should be helped.[6] These debates over economic policy were rancorous, and as time wore on, Locke began to express a growing weariness over the pivotal involvement that his published ideas had forced upon him. At the root of these issues was the question of property, its origins and the rights it engenders, and nowhere was that explained better, as Locke confidently testified, than in the *Two Treatises*. "Property, I have no where found more clearly explain'd than in a Book intituled, *Two Treatises of Government*. " A book, whose author was still unknown to everyone but Locke.[7]

THE COSMIC RAMIFICATIONS OF SELF PRESERVATION

And 'tis not without reason, that he seeks out, and is willing to joyn in Society with others who are already united, or have a mind to unite for the mutual *Preservation* of their Lives, Liberties and Estates, which I call by the general Name, *Property*.[8]

The nature of property and the process of its acquisition are fundamental to Locke's *Second Treatise*. It is not only acquired material, though, that humans can call their own, but their very own life and liberty are their property as well. Once Locke established that the purpose of government is to preserve the life, liberty, and estates of individuals, all of which cannot be properly preserved in the state of nature, it became imperative for him to define the individuation of property holding.[9] That, because "no body has originally a private Dominion, exclusive of the rest of Mankind" in the world that "God ... hath given ... to Men in common."[10]

---

[6] Ibid, pp. 396–397.
[7] Regarding this quote, Laslett writes: "This remark was made by John Locke in 1703, not much more than a year before he died. It must be a rare thing for an author to recommend one of his own works as a guide to a young gentleman anxious to acquire 'an insight into the constitution of the government, and real interest of his country.' It must be even rarer for a man who was prepared to do this, to range his own book alongside Aristotle's Politics and Hooker's Ecclesiastical Polity, to write as if the work were written by some body else, somebody whom he did not know." Laslett, "Introduction," *Two Treatises of Government*, p. 3.
[8] II, 123, p. 368.
[9] The terminology Locke uses with regard to property is inconsistent, but his intention is always the same. For example, in some places Locke refers to property as "goods" (II, 6, p. 289), "estate" (II, 87, p. 341), and "possession" (II, 135, p. 375).
[10] II, 26, p. 304.

The rights, though, of other individuals, contends Locke, are "excluded" from an object in nature the moment an individual mixes his labor in that object and "thereby makes it his *property*."[11] Locke calls this idea the "original Law of Nature for the *beginning of property*,"[12] which follows from the natural law of self-preservation. But it is not a limitless license of acquisition that Locke grants, as God always maintains a degree of original title. This concept of divine limitation, coupled with the idea that the law of self-preservation is augmented to include the duty to preserve humankind, as we saw earlier with regard to human equality,[13] creates an individual obligation of charity.

Locke begins his chapter on property with the acknowledgment that the individual right of self-preservation is dictated by both reason and revelation.

Whether we consider natural *Reason*, which tells us, that Men, being once born, have a right to their Preservation, and consequently to Meat and Drink ... Or *Revelation*, which gives us an account of those Grants God made of the World to *Adam*, and to *Noah*, and his Sons, 'tis very clear, that God, as King *David* says, *Psal. CXV. xvi. has given the Earth to the Children of Men*, given it to Mankind in common.

Self-preservation, though, as Locke has already made clear, is not just a *right* but a *duty*: "Every one as he is *bound to preserve himself*, and not to quit his station willfully." Humans are under divine ordinance to preserve themselves because they are the "Workmanship of one Omnipotent, and infinitely wise Maker," which prevents them from even agreeing to a subservient status to anyone other than their creator. For the same reason humans must preserve themselves because being the "workmanship of God" they are not autonomous to the degree that they may choose otherwise. This obligation to preserve oneself, Locke contends, becomes a duty to preserve humankind as a whole.

Every one as he is *bound to preserve himself*, and not to quit his Station willfully; so by the like reason when his own Preservation comes not in competition, ought he, as much as he can, *to preserve the rest of Mankind*, and may not, unless it be to

---

[11] II, 27, pp. 305–306. Neal Wood observes that Locke "is the first major political thinker to make labor the cornerstone of his edifice of ideas." Wood, *The Politics of Locke's Philosophy*, p. 34.

[12] II, 30, p. 307.

[13] I refer specifically to Locke's application of the Golden Rule through the Hooker quote in II, 5, p. 288, upon which I will expand discussion later.

do Justice to an Offender, take away, or impair the life, or what tends to the Preservation of the Life, the Liberty, Health, Limb or Goods of another.[14]

The personal obligation of every individual to preserve humankind is closely connected, Locke emphasizes, to the concept of individual executive power, explored at length earlier in the context of our discussion of natural law. If I have an obligation to preserve others, I must have the political power to do so.

[E]very man upon this score, by the Right he hath to preserve Mankind in general, may restrain, or, where it is necessary, destroy things noxious to them, and so may bring such evil on any one who hath transgressed that Law, as may make him repent the doing of it and thereby deter him, and by his Example others, from doing the like mischief. And in this case, any upon this ground, *every Man hath a Right to punish the Offender, and be Executioner of the Law of Nature.*[15]

It is only logical that individual executive power should be a natural extension of the obligation that each individual has to preserve all of humankind. The question, though, is: From where does Locke cull his notion of individual responsibility for human preservation? Once again, a thorough understanding of Locke's references in the *Second Treatise* is dependent on a close reading of the *First Treatise*. In the latter, we learn the origins of Locke's idea of self-preservation as well as how he understands its practical applicability, and then in the *Second Treatise* we learn how self-preservation is augmented by Locke to include society and humankind.

In the Biblical verse (Genesis 1:28) showing general human equality (discussed in Chapter 3), Locke also sees "the great design of God" put forward, which establishes a Biblical basis for the requisite preservation of humankind.[16] Not only are humans charged to "subdue the earth and have dominion over creatures," humankind is also graced with the

---

[14] II, 6, p. 289. The fact that Locke follows the term *bound* with "Workmanship of one Omnipotent, and infinitely wise Maker" obviates the possibility of reading *bound* as *prone* to as opposed to *obligated*.

[15] II, 8, p. 290. Later, Locke writes: "The first and fundamental natural law which is to govern even the legislative itself is the preservation of the society." II, 134, pp. 373–374. For further clarification it should be pointed out that when Locke refers to the "right" one has "to preserve mankind" at the beginning of the quote, he does not mean "right" as opposed to "obligation," but rather, as at the end of the quote, he refers to the right of the individual (executive power) to "punish the offender."

[16] I, 21, p. 174 and I, 41, pp. 187–188. Locke's emphasis on procreation as part of "Gods great design" smacks of Isaiah 45:22: "For thus said the Lord, The Creator of heaven who alone is God, Who formed the earth and made it, Who alone established it – He did not create it a waste But formed it for habitation."

directive to "increase and multiply." For Locke, this was the "great and primary Blessing of God Almighty: Be fruitful and multiply, and replenish the earth."[17] God's "great design" is his creation of a species in "his image" whose "intellectual nature" allows him to partner with God in creation.[18]

Enlarging the human race numerically is to be matched with and include its evolving perfection, what Locke calls "the improvement, too, of arts and sciences and the conveniences of life."[19] Humanity's betterment then is part of the "Thou hast made him a little lower than angels" *imago dei* formula that Locke has already made central to his philosophy.[20] Humanity's intellectual superiority over all other creations does not just grant dominion over them, but saddles humans with the responsibility to multiply in quantity and improve in the quality of life. Similar to the prohibition against murder that is naturally known by humans and is yet repeated in a direct divine admonition, the Lockean rules of self-preservation through procreation are both built into the characteristics of human nature *and* revealed through divine commands. Because Locke, unlike Filmer, refuses to read Genesis 1:27 and 28 as referring to Adam alone, but rather as intending mankind as a whole, Locke concludes that:

[17] I, 33, p. 182.

[18] I, 30, p. 180. That for Locke Genesis provides the theological underpinnings for his unique theory of human preservation in the context of natural law is summed up well by K. I. Parker: "While it is true that natural law supplied a philosophical foundation for Locke's ideas of freedom and equality, it is also true that Genesis provided the theological foundation for the doctrine of natural law. Genesis shows a God who has created humanity with certain purposes in mind – initially spelled out in the command to be fruitful, multiply, fill the earth, and have dominion over certain creatures that inhabit the earth and seas. In the most elemental sense, God is interested in the propagation and preservation of humanity. Humanity is part of God's workmanship suited for his purposes, which can be discerned by using God's gift of reason (that image of God in man; I, 30)." Parker, *The Biblical Politics of John Locke*, p. 144. This is clearly a classical Hebraic concept. Isaiah, for example, said in his prophesy: "For thus said the Lord, the creator of heaven who alone is God, Who formed the earth and made it, who alone established it, he did create it a waste, but formed it for habitation." (Isaiah 45:18).

[19] I, 33, p. 182. And in the words of Parker: "Locke's overriding concern, based on his reading of scriptures, to improve the lot of humanity surfaces very early in the *First Treatise*, and is a recurring motif throughout his political work. Locke's theological views once again provide the basis of his political structure." Parker, *The Biblical Politics of John Locke*, pp. 110–111.

Neal Wood shows how this theme consistently repeats itself in the *Essay*. See Wood, *The Politics of Locke's Philosophy*, p. 128.

[20] Psalms 8. I, 30, p. 180, and I, 58, pp. 200–201. See also my discussion in Chapter 2 on "Reason and Revelation."

God having made Man, and planted in him, as in all other Animals, a strong
desire of self-preservation, and furnished the World with things fit for Food and
Rayment and other Necessaries of Life, Subservient to his design, that Man should
live and abide for some time upon the Face of the earth, and not that so curious
and wonderful a piece of Workmanship by its own Negligence, or want of
Necessaries, should perish again, presently after a few moments continuance ...
For the desire, strong desire of Preserving his Life and Being having been Planted
in him, as Principle of Action by God himself, reason, *which was the Voice of God
in him*, could not but teach him and assure him, that pursuing that natural
Inclination he had to preserve his Being, he followed the Will of his Maker ...
The first and strongest desire God Planted in Men, and wrought into the very
Principles of their Nature being that of Self-preservation ... But next to this, God
Planted in Men a strong desire also of propagating their Kind, and continuing
themselves in their Posterity. [21]

Locke first lays out the Biblical sources for the law of self-preservation
and then explains that what humankind is later commanded is in fact
"planted" in its nature at inception.[22] In other words, it proceeds logically
that Locke needs the Biblical description of creation, including the concept of *imago dei*, to establish his concept of mankind's natural inclination toward self-preservation.[23]

Now we can move back to the *Second Treatise* and ask: Just how then
does Locke see this elemental law of self-preservation, reasoned and
revealed, metamorphosed into an individual right and obligation to preserve all of humankind? Indeed, Locke does not leave it in the general
context of procreation. It must be remembered that Locke juxtaposes the
idea of self-preservation with the Golden Rule as quoted in the passage
from Hooker that he brings to prove the natural equality of God's
creations, and that he then follows with the assertion that humans are
obligated to preserve each other.

*The like natural inducement, hath brought Men to know that it is no less their
Duty, to Love others than themselves, for seeing those things which are equal,
must needs all have one measure; If I cannot but wish to receive good, even as
much at every Man's hands, as any Man can wish unto his own Soul, how
should I look to have any part of my desire therein satisfied, unless my self be
careful to satisfie the like desire, which is undoubtedly in other Men, being of*

---

[21] I, 86, 88, pp. 222–223, 224–225.
[22] I, 21, 30, 33, 41, pp. 174, 179–180, 182–183, 187–188.
[23] Jeremy Waldron notes that, "The Lockean moral world ... involves not only a
recognition that the source of the normativity of self-preservation in your case is similar
to the source of the normativity of self-preservation in my case, but also a recognition of
the fact that the source in the two cases is literally *the same*." Waldron, *God, Locke, and
Equality*, pp. 157–158.

one and the same nature? To have any thing offered them repugnant to this desire, must needs in all respects grieve them as much as me, so that if I do harm, I must look to suffer, there being no reason that others should shew greater measure of love to me, than they have by me, shewed unto them; my desire therefore to be lov'd of my equals in natuer, as much as possible may be, imposeth upon me a natural Duty of bearing to themward, fully the like affection; From which relation of equality between our selves and them, that are as our selves, what several Rules and Canons, natural reason hath drawn for direction of Life, no Man is ignorant. " (Eccl. Pol. Lib. 1.)[24]

From Leviticus we learn the Golden Rule obligation to "love your neighbor like yourself," which stems from inherent human equality, and from Genesis we learn the obligation of self-preservation. Ergo, if part of "loving oneself" is "preserving oneself" and others must be loved as oneself, then it necessarily follows that the other must be preserved, just as the self must be preserved.[25]

This conjugation of rules does not only produce a directive in the negative sense of what is to be refrained from doing, i.e., harming others, but what people are positively obligated to do to or for others. God then makes preserving mankind a duty in which he wishes "people to act in a manner *incompatible* with absolutism."[26] Absolutism means that some people exist for "another's pleasure" and results in "subordination" and

---

[24] II, 5, 6, pp. 288–289. Hooker, *Of the Laws of Ecclesiastical Polity*, p. 80. It is of particular interest to note that here Locke lifts the Hooker quote from the middle of a sentence that begins by making reference to Jesus ("our Saviour"). Hooker quotes Matthew 22:38, where Christ credits the Biblical imperative of *"Thou shalt love the Lord thy God with all thy heart, with all thy soul, and with all thy mind "* (Deuteronomy 6:6), and that of, *"You shall love your neighbor as yourself "* (Leviticus 19:18), as both being the "First and the great Commandment." Locke chose to present the Hooker reference to the Golden Rule without referencing Jesus or the New Testament despite the fact that it meant beginning the quote from mid-sentence.

[25] Ian Harris explains this Lockean teleology and how it amounts to an obligating paradigm. See Harris, *The Mind of John Locke*, pp. 219–222. Precisely because Locke is so in tandem with Hebraic instruction on the subject of human preservation, it is a bit puzzling that he did not use the neighboring verse to the Golden Rule, which Locke resources through Hooker: the Bible clearly commands, "Thou shalt not stand idly by your brothers' blood" (Leviticus 19:16). Rabbinical exegetes in the Talmud understood this verse as an obligation to save another human being from the threat of death or injury. Examples offered are victims of drowning, wild animals, and violent thieves. The obligation not to withhold testimony on a defendant's behalf is also included in this Biblical dictum. Lastly, the necessity of killing a would-be murderer in order to protect his victim is also derived from this verse. See *Sefer Hachinuch*, Mitzvah 244. One might conjecture that once Locke chose to use Biblical verse at this juncture through the mediation of Hooker he also chose not to turn to Scripture that Hooker did not use.

[26] Ibid, p. 223.

in the "authorization" to "destroy another." This is exactly contrary to what the equality of the Golden Rule meshed with the rule of self-preservation prescribes, and this is what Locke intends when he writes:

This *Freedom* from Absolute, Arbitrary Power, is so necessary to, and closely joined with a Man's Preservation, that he cannot part with it, but by what forfeits his Preservation and Life together.[27]

In the *non-absolute* government that must emerge from the state of nature in order to protect the laws of nature, the rights and duties of preservation, individual and societal, are mediated by the positive laws created by the legislative power of that government.

The first *Power, viz. of doing whatsoever he thought fit for the Preservation of himself*, and the rest of Mankind, *he gives up* to be regulated by Laws made by the Society, so far forth as the preservation of himself, and the rest of that Society shall require; which Laws of the Society in many things confine the liberty he had by the Law of Nature.[28]

Until this point we have seen that society is the best guarantor of human life; the same is true, Locke teaches, for liberty and material possessions. The entering into society and government better ensures the natural law obligating the preservation of private property, and government maintains its legitimacy only as long as it fulfills that expectation.

But though Men when they enter into Society, give up the Equality, Liberty, and Executive Power they had in the State of Nature, into the hands of the Society, to be so far disposed of by the Legislative, as the good of the Society shall require; yet it being only with an intention in every one the better to preserve himself his Liberty and Property; (For no rational Creature can be supposed to change his condition with an intention to be worse) the power of the Society, or *Legislative* constituted by them, *can never be suppos'd to extend farther than the common good*; but is obliged to secure every ones Property by providing against ... that made the State of Nature so unsafe and uneasie.[29]

Such a society, which guarantees the life and property of its individuals, is itself to be preserved by those individuals as well.

[A]s the first and fundamental natural law, which is to govern even the Legislative it self, is the preservation of the Society, and (as far as will consist with the publick good) of every person in it.[30]

---

[27] II, 23, p. 302. [28] II, 129, pp. 370–371. [29] II, 131, p. 371.
[30] II, 134, pp. 373–374.

In concluding this section it is important to point to the theoretical progression in Locke's philosophy. As we have seen, he begins with the Genesis-rooted idea of self-preservation (which includes life, liberty, and property), and how, through the Golden Rule in Leviticus, it metamorphoses into the duty to preserve humankind in general. This ubiquitous obligation then emerges into a narrower charge to preserve one's own specific society. While the preservation of these three typologies might always appear poised in potential conflict, it is the conformity with God's natural law that prevents this from occurring. For Locke, it is only when positive law stands in opposition to natural law that individual preservation and societal preservation are at odds with each other as well.[31] It is now for us to see how the individual's duty of his or her own self-preservation and obligation toward the preservation of society practically materialize in the concepts of property and charity. But before proceeding to that discussion, it is important to digress momentarily in order to expand on what Locke means by the "strong desire" that is "planted in man" to "preserve his life and being"[32] that we saw earlier, as it serves as a great source of controversy among scholars of Lockean thought.

AN INTERIM CRITIQUE OF SCHOLARLY ATTITUDES ON LOCKE'S IDEA OF SELF-PRESERVATION

For the desire, strong desire of Preserving his Life and Being having been Planted in him, as Principle of Action by God himself, reason, *which was the Voice of God in him*, could not but teach him and assure him, that pursuing that natural Inclination he had to preserve his Being, he followed the Will of his Maker.[33]

In a note to this paragraph in his critical edition of the *Two Treatises*, Peter Laslett suggests that here, Locke, with his idea that self-preservation is a law of nature "planted by God in man," seems to contradict his rejection of innatism as enunciated in his *Essay Concerning Human Understanding*. Laslett quotes a line from the *Essay* where Locke writes: "Nature, I confess, has put into man a desire of happiness and an aversion

---

[31] See Parker, *The Biblical Politics of John Locke*, pp. 127–128. See also Ruth Grant, *John Locke's Liberalism* (Chicago, IL: The University of Chicago Press, 1991), pp. 99–100, 129. Parker also refers to James Tully's explanation that can be traced to Suarez and Pufendorf, which suggests that, "since humans have a duty to preserve their species, and since God wants them to join society, it follows that humans should preserve society." See Tully, *A Discourse on Property*, pp. 48–49.

[32] I, 86, 88, pp. 222–223, 224–225.　　[33] I, 86, p. 223.

to misery: these indeed are innate practical principles"[34] and uses it to let Locke off the hook by granting that, "the language here is very close to the exception he makes for the 'desire for happiness' an 'innate practical principle.'"[35] For Laslett then the apparent contradiction is resolved by assuming that:

1) Locke accepts innatism when it comes to the pursuit of happiness.
2) Self-preservation is like the pursuit of happiness.

Similarly, and consistent with his overarching theory that Locke, like Hobbes, drives a wedge between the law of reason and the law of God, Leo Strauss uses the same quote from the *Essay* to prove that Locke's state of nature in the *Second Treatise* intends to present self-preservation as a *right*, not a *duty*, and (as for Laslett) an extension of the innate drive to attain happiness. Strauss writes:

> The desire for happiness and the pursuit of happiness to which it gives rise are not duties ... The desire for happiness and the pursuit of happiness have the character of an absolute right, of a natural right. There is, then, an innate natural right, while there is no innate natural duty ... It is a right antedating all duties for the same reason that ... establishes as the fundamental moral fact the right of self-preservation: man must be allowed to defend his life against violent death because he is driven to do so by some natural necessity which is not less than that by which a stone is carried downward ... Since the right of nature is innate, whereas the law of nature is not, the right of nature is more fundamental than the law of nature and is the foundation of the law of nature.[36]

In the light of my discussion in Chapter 2 regarding reason and revelation, it is imperative to make a few observations regarding Strauss's argument. First, it is hard to understand how Strauss asserts that natural right is more fundamental than natural law, as a *right* is by definition forfeitable, whereas *law* is by definition obligatory. Second, Locke specifically refers to self-preservation in the *Second Treatise* as being not just a right, but an obligation. For example, Locke writes: "Every one, as he is *bound* [italics added] to preserve himself and not to quit his station willfully."[37] Third, Strauss completely ignores Locke's move from self-preservation to societal preservation. (Were Strauss to acknowledge

---

[34] Chapter III of book I is entitled "No Innate Practical Principles."   [35] I, 86, p. 223.

[36] Strauss, *Natural Right and History*, pp. 226–227.

[37] II, 6, p. 289. And as mentioned earlier, Locke will go on to write that, "the first and fundamental natural law which is to govern even the legislative itself is the preservation of society, and, as for as will consist with the public good, of every person in it." II, 134, pp. 373–374.

Locke's notion of societal preservation, would he deem it a *right* rather than an *obligation* as well?) Lastly, Strauss totally ignores the Biblical basis upon which Locke establishes his theory of self-preservation in the *First Treatise*.[38]

John Yolton takes Strauss to task, but not because of the aforementioned arguments. He chastises Strauss for not quoting fully the sentence he brings from Locke's *Essay*, something Yolton sees as "an odd kind of perversity on Strauss's part," for in doing so he would have discovered "that Locke meant to contrast desires and aversions with impressions of truth upon the understanding." For Locke, "only the latter," Yolton argues, "are properly called 'innate practical principles,' for the sentence concludes by saying that the desire for happiness and the aversion to pain are 'inclinations of the appetite.'"[39]

While Yolton, in his critique of Strauss, is referring only to innatism as it relates to the pursuit of happiness and not to the Lockean concept of self-preservation, Strauss did connect the two. Hence we can deduce that if Yolton is right about Locke's attitude toward the pursuit of happiness, then Strauss is wrong about self-preservation. It is interesting to note, though, that the same continuation of the Locke quote that proves for Yolton that Strauss is wrong proves for Michael Zuckert the validity of Strauss's contention.[40] Despite their considerable differences, all these Lockean scholars are united in one thing: they all detect a prima facie contradiction between Locke's description of humankind's natural inclination for self-preservation in the *Second Treatise* and his rejection of innatism in the *Essay*. While Laslett proffers that both self-preservation and the pursuit of happiness are innate, Yolton argues that neither is, and Strauss (with Zuckert at his defense) claims that they are not obligations but rights.

Jeremy Waldron offers a completely different, and what appears to me to be a more compelling, reading of Locke. While he is referring specifically to Laslett's aforementioned note, his criticism is relevant to Locke's other critics as well.

---

[38] The last point is, of course, Strauss's original sin. Had he understood Locke as having meant what he actually wrote rather than its very opposite, he would not have ignored the obligation for self-preservation, would not have set right above duty, and would not have forgotten about Locke's idea about preserving humankind. It is also fair to assume that he would have jettisoned his idea that Locke was in agreement with Hobbes regarding the law of nature.

[39] Yolton, "Locke on the Law of Nature," p. 490.

[40] Zuckert, *Launching Liberalism*, pp. 39–40.

Unfortunately Laslett has not read the passage (I, 86) carefully enough. Locke does not infer rightness directly from the existence of a natural inclination. He says humans find themselves with all sorts of inclinations: some of them nice, some of them nasty: "Nor can it be otherwise in a Creature, whose thoughts are more than the Sands, and wider than the ocean" (I, 58). As beings endowed with reason, we have to sort through our impulses and relate them to some rational understanding of our being and some experiential knowledge of our nature. Then and only then are we in a position to draw normative conclusions from the fact of their existence. Far from any inconsistency with Locke's philosophical argument, this is more or less exactly the point that is made in the discussion of innate ideas in the *Essay*. That discussion acknowledges the existence of natural inclinations:

"I deny not that there are natural tendencies imprinted on the Minds of Men, and that from the very first instances of Sense and Perception, there are some things that are grateful and others that are unwelcome to them, some things that they incline to, and others that they fly: but this makes nothing for innate Characters on the Mind, which are to principles of knowledge, regulating our practice ... Principles of Actions indeed there are lodged in Men's Appetites, but these are so far from being innate Moral Principles that, if they were left their full swing, they would carry Men to the over-turning of all Morality." (*Essay*: I.3.3 and 13).

What we need, before we think it right to follow such an innate appetite, is some assurance that it guides us as we ought to be guided, and that assurance can only come from the exercise of our intellect. In the present context, we find that it is safe (and indeed requisite) to rely on our survival instinct only by relating it rationally to ideas like God, creation, and purpose. These are not given in the inclination themselves; they have to be brought to it by reason.[41]

Though human inclinations are indeed "principles of actions" that are "lodged in men's appetites," they are not as such inherently innate moral principles. When Locke speaks about God having "planted" in human-kind "a strong desire of self-preservation" he also speaks of reason as "the voice of God in him," because reason, the outcome of the "intellect" that defines humankind's "likeness to God" in "God's great design," rationally brings "God, creation and purpose" to humankind's survival instinct. This distinction Waldron discerns in the Lockean text between innate knowledge (which Locke rejects) and the truths that humans can grasp through their use of God-given reason (which Locke endorses) is a distinction that Locke himself makes in his *Essays on the Law of Nature*, as if to preempt the scholarly debate on the subject. Locke could not have been clearer in rejecting all readings of his work other than that of Waldron.

---

[41] Waldron, *God Locke, and Equality*, p. 161.

We do not maintain that this law of nature, written as it were on tablets, lies open in our hearts, and that, as soon as some inward light comes near it (like a torch approaching a notice-board hung up in darkness), it is at length read, perceived, and noted by rays of that light. Rather, by saying that something can be known by the light of nature, we mean nothing else but that there is some sort of truth to the knowledge of which a man can attain by himself and without the help of another, if he makes proper use of the faculties he is endowed with by nature.[42]

As has already been demonstrated earlier in the chapter on natural law, it was from the Hebrew Bible, specifically from the account of the first murder and the subsequent admonishment against the spilling of blood, that Locke adduced that there are truths "which a man can attain himself ... if he makes proper use of the faculties he is endowed with by nature." Locke turns to Biblical revelation in order to prove and then establish the primacy of reason. A proper appreciation of this concept would, I think, obviate much of the scholarly debate over what Locke meant when he wrote that God "planted in man" a desire to preserve life.

Lastly, it seems appropriate to make note of what strongly appears to be a Talmudic attitude toward innatism. In its discussion on the conscious state of a fetus, the Talmud (in the name of R' Simlai) compares "a fetus in its mother's womb" to a "folded notebook" who is "taught the entire Torah." But when the baby is born (literally – "goes out to the air of the world") "an angel comes and strikes him on the mouth causing him to forget everything he learned" (BT, *Tractate Nidah*, 30b). While this passage seems to reject an innatist epistemology, it appears to qualify its rejection with an acceptance of natural inclination. The knowledge attained in the womb decidedly does not carry on through birth, but it is nevertheless significant because it creates an inclination or predisposition toward divine-given knowledge. Without suggesting that Locke might have been served by this passage in the formulation of epistemology, the similarity of his conceptual framework is of interesting note.[43] It is also not unfair to wonder if this Talmudic "folded notebook" could not be the original reference to the notion of tabula rasa.

---

[42] Locke, *Essays on the Law of Nature*, p. 89.
[43] No less interesting is speculation on the similarities and differences between this Talmudic idea and Plato's "Theory of Recollection."

FILMER'S FAULTY CONCEPTION OF HUMAN CONCEPTION

Locke is insistent that God maintains the title of *Maker* beyond Adam. One facet of God's human creation is the designing of humans such that their proclivity for sexual relations will make them partners with the divine in the perpetuation of their own species. But they remain junior partners, as their primary interest is the satisfaction of their own pleasure.

But had Men Skill and Power to make their Children, 'tis not so slight a piece of Workmanship, that it can be imagined they could make them without designing it. What Father of a Thousand, when he begets a Child, thinks farther then the satisfying his present Appetite? God in his infinite Wisdom has put strong desires of Copulation into the Constitution of Mankind, which he doth most commonly without the intention, and often against the Consent and Will of the Begetter. And indeed those who desire and design Children, are but the occasions of their being, and when they design and wish to beget them, do little more towards their making, than *Ducalion* and his Wife in the Fable did towards the making of Mankind, by throwing Pebbles over their Heads.[44]

But even this limited partnership is not the lot of woman any less than of man.

Our *Author* indeed is of another mind; for he says, *We know that God at the Creation gave the Sovereignty to the Man over the Woman, as being the Nobler and Principal Agent in Generation* ... I remember not this in my Bible, and when the place is brought where God at the *Creation* gave the Sovereignty to Man over

---

[44] I, 54, pp. 197–198. It is important to point out here just how far Locke has departed from the Augustinian notion of sin that is attributed to the carnal act of procreation. For Augustine every child is born in sin because it is through the lust and concupiscence of fallen mankind that he or she is conceived. That, as opposed to Christ alone, who was born through an immaculate conception. For Locke, conversely, mankind's passion for sexual relations is telling of "God's infinite wisdom." "God in his infinite Wisdom has put strong desires of Copulation into the Constitution of Mankind, which he doth most commonly without the intention, and often against the Consent and Will of the Begetter."

Locke's words here bear a stark resemblance to those of one Thomas Hunt, another, albeit much lesser known, harsh critic of Filmer. Hunt writes that God planted in mankind "powerful and irresistible instincts to procreation," but when they obey his command to increase and multiply they are "gratifying their own Natures." And hence, "What from all this can give them a right over their Child?" Rather than give us life, parents "hand it over to us from the fountain of being, the Universal Father of all things." Thomas Hunt, *Mr Hunts Postscript for Rectifying Some Mistakes in the Inferior Clergy* (London: 1682), pp. 62–63, quoted in Schochet, *Patriarchalism in Political Thought*, p. 198.

The idea that it is corporeal desire rather than altruism that is at the basis of the preservation of the human species is consonant with Hebraic teaching. In a Talmudic discussion regarding the "evil inclination" a suggestion is made that the corporeal desire be eliminated as was the desire for idol worship. The idea is rejected because doing so would result in the elimination of humanity. See BT, *Tractate Yoma*, 69b.

the Woman, and that for this Reason, because *he is the Nobler and Principal Agent in Generation*, it will be time enough to consider and answer it: But it is no new thing for our *Author* to tell us his own Fancies for certain and Divine Truths, though there be often a great deal of difference between his and Divine Revelations: for God in the Scripture says, *his Father and his Mother that begot him.*[45]

For Locke, Filmer's grossly selective reading of Scripture is intellectually insolvent and distorts the word of God and the reality it intended to foster.

To the same purpose, the same Law is cited by our *Author* in several other places, and just after the same Fashion, that is, *and Mother*, as Apocriphal Words, are always left out; a great Argument of our *Author* 's ingenuity, and the goodness of his Cause, which required in its Defender Zeal to a degree of warmth, able to warp the Sacred Rule of the Word of God, to make it comply with his present occasion; a way of proceeding, not unusual to those, who imbrace not Truths, because Reason and Revelation offer them; but espouse Tenets and Parties, for ends different from Truth, and then resolve at any rate to defend them: and so do with the Words and Sense of Authors, they would fit to their purpose, just as *Procrustes* did with his guests, lop or stretch them, as best fit them to the size of their Notions: And they always prove like those, so served, Deformed, Lame, and useless.[46]

It is not just any text that Filmer truncates, but the "sacred rule of the word of God" that he distends, which, to Locke's thinking, is an infraction more serious than the mere bastardization of any standard text. Locke goes on to prove that the "constant tenor of the Scripture" is to "set up the *Mother* equal with him, and injoyn'd nothing but what was due in common, to both Father and Mother," by listing all the places in Scripture where they appear together.[47]

Honour thy Father and thy Mother, Exod 20.
He that smiteth his Father or Mother, shall surely be put to Death, 21.
He that Curseth his Father or Mother, shall surely be put to Death, Ver. 17.
Repeated *Lev.* 20. 9. and by our Saviour, *Matth.* 15. 4.[48]
Ye shall fear every Man his Mother and his Father, Lev. 19. 3.
If a Man have a Rebellious Son, which will not Obey the Voice of his Father, or the Voice of his Mother; then shall his Father and Mother, lay hold on him, and say, this our Son is Stubborn and Rebellious, he will not Obey our Voice, Deut. 21; 18, 19, 20, 21.
Cursed be he that setteth Light by his Father or his Mother, 27. 16.[49]

---

[45] I, 55, p. 198. Laslett points us to Zechariah 13:3.   [46] I, 60, p. 202.
[47] I, 61, p. 203.
[48] This is an example of the secondary and ornamental usage Locke makes of a New Testament verse.
[49] This verse is usually translated more simply: "Cursed is the man who dishonors his father or his mother."

My Son, hear the Instructions of they Father, and forsake not the Law of thy Mother, are the words of Solomon a King, who was not ignorant of what belonged to him, as a Father or a King, and yet he joyns *Father* and *Mother* together, in all the Instructions he gives Children quite through his Book of *Proverbs* ...

Wo unto him, that sayeth unto his Father, what begettest thou, or to the Woman, what hast thou brought forth, Isa. 45. ver. 10.

In thee have they set Light by Father or Mother, Ezek. 22. 7.

And it shall come to pass, that when any shall yet Prophesie, then his Father and his Mother that begat him, shall say unto him, thou shalt not live, and his Father and his Mother that begat him, shall thrust him through when he Propheseith, Zech. 13. 3.

In order that one not assume the existence of an obverse approach in the New Testament, Locke emphasizes that Old and New Testament views are identical on this matter. Parental entitlement to honor in the Bible is intended in equal measure to both mother and father.

Here not the Father only, but Father and Mother joyntly, had Power in this Case of Life and Death. Thus ran the Law of the Old Testament, and in the New they are likewise joyn'd, in the Obedience of their Children, *Eph.* 6. 1. The Rule is, *Children Obey your Parents*, and I do not remember, that I any where read, Children *Obey your Father* and no more.[50]

The Hebrew Bible has even placed mother *before* father, Locke stresses.

Nay, the Scripture makes the Authority of *Father* and *Mother*, in respect of those they have begot, so equal, that in some places it neglects, even the Priority of Order, which is thought due to the Father, and the *Mother* is put first, as *Lev.* 19. 3. From which so constantly joining Father and Mother together, as is found quite through the Scripture, we may conclude that the Honour they have a Title to from their Children, is one common Right belonging so equally to them both, that neither can claim it wholly, neither can be excluded.[51]

The Decalogue's Fifth Commandment then clearly does not grant any more parental power to the father than to the mother, and the power that is granted is not monarchical power. Hence the father has not the right to neutralize the child's obligation to honor his or her mother either, even though, as Locke notes, the Bible did grant the right of divorce to the Jews.

Can the Father, by this Sovereignty of his, discharge the Child from paying this *Honour* to his *Mother*? The Scripture gave no such License to the Jews, and yet

---

[50] Ibid.   [51] I, 61, pp. 203–204.

there were often Breaches wide enough betwixt Husband and Wife, even to Divorce and Separation.[52]

Locke points out another inherent contradiction in Filmer's thinking. How can a father have absolute dominion over his child if his own father retains the jurisdiction that he had over his son now turned father? Who under such a circumstance would have ultimate authority, father or grandfather? The case in point that Locke offers is Biblical. If Adam was granted supreme political power over his offspring, "and yet *his Children*, viz. *Cain and Seth*, have a Paternal Power over their Children at the same time,"[53] the unreasonable result is that, "Here then are two Absolute Unlimited Powers existing together, which I would have any body reconcile one to another, or to common Sense."[54]

By our *Author*'s Doctrine, the Father having Absolute Jurisdiction over his Children, has also the same over their Issue, and the consequence is good, were it true, that the Father had such a Power: And yet I ask our *Author* whether the Grandfather, by his Sovereignty, could discharge the Grand-child from paying to his Father the Honour due him by the 5th Commandment. If the Grandfather hath by *right of Fatherhood*, sole Sovereign Power in him, and that Obedience which is due to the Supreme Magistrate, be Commanded in these Words, *Honour thy Father*, 'tis certain the Grandfather might dispense with the Grand-sons Honouring his Father, which, since 'tis evident in common Sense, he cannot, it follows from hence that, *Honour the Father and Mother*, cannot mean an absolute Subjection to a Sovereign Power, but something else.[55]

Were the commandment to honor one's parents of a political nature, Locke posits, the "magistrate" who is the ultimate political authority could invalidate the obligation on political grounds.

The right therefore which Parents have by Nature, and which is confirmed to them by the 5th Commandment, cannot be that political Dominion, which our *Author* would derive from it: For that being in every Civil Society Supreme somewhere, can discharge any Subject from any Political Obedience to any one of his fellow Subjects. But what Law of the Magistrate, can give a Child liberty, not to *Honour his Father and Mother*? 'Tis and Eternal Law annex'd purely to the relation of Parents and Children, and so contains nothing of the Magistrates Power in it, nor is subjected to it.[56]

The consequence of Filmer's granting sovereign power to every father yields a situation that is as untenable as it is absurd.

[52] I, 62, p. 204.   [53] I, 68, p. 209.   [54] I, 69, p. 210.   [55] I, 64, p. 205.
[56] I, 64, p. 205.

If therefore this Command, *Honour thy Father and Mother*, concern Political Dominion, it directly overthrows our *Author*'s Monarchy; it being since to be paid by every Child to his Father, even in Society, every Father must necessarily have Political Dominion, and there will be as many Sovereigns and there are Fathers: besides that the Mother too hath her Title, which destroys the Sovereignty of one Supreme Monarch. But if *Honour thy Father and Mother* mean something distinct from Political Power, as necessarily it must, it is besides our Author's buisiness, and serves nothing to his purpose.[57]

The conclusion Locke draws from his objective and rational reading of the Bible is central to his thinking, even without its relevance to his vitiation of Filmerian thought, and with an eye toward future generations long freed from such stifling thought. In absence of any parental political license, humanity is born into a state of natural freedom and, as a result, can be governed, as explicated in the *Second Treatise*, only through its consent.

If all this be so, as I think, by what has been said, is very evident, then Man has a *Natural Freedom*, not withstanding all our *Author* confidently says to the contrary, since all that share in the same common Nature, Faculties and Powers, are in Nature equal, and ought to partake in the same common Rights and Priviledges, till the manifest appointment of God, who is *Lord over all, Blessed for ever*, can be produced to shew any particular Persons Supremacy, or a Mans own consent subjects him to a Superior.[58]

Locke's rationale for negating his nemesis's notions of primogeniture will similarly prove to have contemporary relevance when he comes to elucidate his theory of property. Locke goes on to concisely debunk Filmer's position that property rights over the world and the absolute and sovereign rights of a father over his children are transferred to the eldest son upon the father's demise. Filmer had argued that, *"every Man that is born, by his very Birth becomes a Subject to him that begets him,"*[59] and when the begetter dies, his sovereign right over his offspring is inherited by his oldest son.

Here 'tis obvious to demand which of these two (Cain or Abel) after *Adam*'s Death, was Sovereign? *Cain*, says our *Author* ... By what Title? *As Heir; for Heirs to Progenitors, who were Natural Parents of their People, are not only Lords of their own Children, but also of their Brethren, says our Author.*[60]

Locke attacks this idea once again using both reason and Scripture. First, if the criterion for parental sovereignty is "begetting," then how can

[57] I, 65, p. 206.   [58] I, 67, p. 208.   [59] I, 74, p. 214.   [60] I, 76, p. 215.

the eldest brother inherit the parental right of complete dominion, not having begotten his brother? It simply stands to reason:

That a Man by his Birth cannot become a Subject to his Brother, who did not beget him: unless it can be suppos'd that a Man by the very same Title can come to be under the *Natural and Absolute Dominion* of two different Men at once, or it be Sense to say, that a Man by Birth is under the *Natural Dominion* of his father, only because he begat him, and a Man by Birth also in under the *Natural Dominion* of his Eldest Brother, though he did not beget him.[61]

Scripture, as depicted through the sons of both Adam and Noah, clearly complements this logic.

What was *Cain* Heir to? Not the entire Possessions, not all that which *Adam* had *Private Dominion* in, for our *Author* allows that *Abel* by a Title derived from his Father, *had his distinct Territory for Pasture by Right of Private Dominion.* What then *Abel* had by *Private Dominion* was exempt from *Cain's* Dominion. For he could not have *Private Dominion* over that, which was under the Private Dominion of another, and therefore his Sovereignty over his Brother is gone with this *Private Dominion*, and so there are presently two Sovereigns, and his imaginary Title of *Fatherhood* is out of doors, and *Cain* is no Prince over his Brother.[62]

The same inconveniences he runs into about *the three Sons of Noah*, who, as he says, *had the whole World divided amongst them by their Father.* I ask then in which of the three shall we find *the Establishment of Regal Power* after *Noah's* Death? If in all three, as our *Author* seems to say; then it will follow, that Regal Power is founded in Property of Land, and follows *Private Dominion*, and not in *Paternal Power* or *Natural Dominion*, and so there is an end to Paternal Power as the Fountain of Regal Authority, and the so much magnified *Fatherhood* quite vanishes ... For his Grant to *Cham* and *Japhet* was little worth if *Shem*, notwithstanding this Grant, as soon as *Noah* was dead, was to be Lord over them.[63]

Using the first two historical Biblical families, Locke has shown why it is impossible to suggest that original property and fatherhood were passed on to one of the offspring at the expense of the others. This right that children have belongs to all children, not just the eldest sibling. Locke admits that he has gone to lengths to explain this because there are countries where, since they have laws granting the whole possession of land to the firstborn, they have been "deceived into an Opinion, that there was Natural or Divine Right of Primogeniture, to both *Estate* and *Power*; and that the Inheritance of both *Rule* over Men and *Property* in things, sprang from the same Original."[64] This mistake leads them to a second fundamental error and that is that government is "inherited by the same

[61] I, 74, p. 214.   [62] I, 76, p. 216.   [63] I, 77, p. 216.   [64] I, 91, p. 227.

Title that Children have to the Goods of their Father." But, writes Locke, predicating his position on his previous discussion of the Biblical account of creation:

The Right of a Son has to be maintained and provided with the necessaries and conveniences of Life out of his Fathers Stock, gives him a Right to succeed to his Father's *Property* for his own good, but this can give him no Right to succeed also to the *Rule*, which his Father had over other Men.[65]

The source of a ruler's authority must first be identified, argues Locke, in order to determine the legitimacy of his successor. If it was the "consent of Men" that "first gave a Scepter in to any ones hand, or put a Crown on his Head," then consent must "direct its descent and conveyance."[66] The same is true if original authority was a grant of God, as demonstrated through the Biblical account of Israel's primordial monarchies.

If God by his positive Grant and revealed Declaration, first gave *Rule* and *Dominion* to any man, he that will Claim by that Title, must have the same positive Grant of God for his Succession … Primogeniture can lay no Claim to it, unless God the Author of this Constitution hath so ordained it. Thus we see the pretensions of *Sauls* Family, who received his Crown from the immediate Appointment of God, ended with his Reign; and *David* by the same Title that *Saul* Reigned, *viz.* Gods Appointment, succeeded in his Throne, to the exclusion of *Jonathan*, and to pretensions of Paternal Inheritance. And if *Salomon* had a Right to Succeed his Father, it must by some other Title, then that of Primogeniture.[67]

Perhaps in order to emphasize the importance he places on the Biblical sources he brings, Locke now points to the fact that, obversely, Filmer makes no Biblical references to support his notion of monarchical inheritance. "For I find not that our *Author* brings one word of Scripture to prove the Right of such an Heir he speaks of."[68] It is clear from this then that Locke did not resource the Bible only in response to Filmer's usage. If at the opening of the *First Treatise* Locke offered a step-by-step rebuttal of Filmer's Biblical exegesis, Locke proceeds to invalidate Filmer's ideas by using his own Biblical sources.

Having already discredited the familial Filmerian notion of Adamic absolute monarchical sovereignty that is transmitted to select progeny, Locke proceeds to very briefly confute the idea that these powers, were they to exist, could be channeled from the world's first human down to each and every monarch. In doing so, Locke quotes no Biblical sources,

---

[65] I, 93, p. 228.   [66] I, 94, p. 229.   [67] I, 95, p. 229.   [68] I, 101, p. 233.

nor does he use Biblical characters to prove his point, though he speaks of Filmer's supposed *Heirs* to Adam that are to rule the earth. Instead he hones in on the contradictions inherent in Filmer's own arguments. Filmer is quoted as having said that:

All Kings either are, or are to be reputed, the next Heirs to those first Progenitors, who were at first the Natural Parents of the whole People ... There cannot be any Multitude of Men whatsoever, but that in it, consider'd by its self, there is one Man amongst them, that in Nature hath a Right to be the King of all the rest, as being the next Heir to Adam.[69]

And yet, argues Locke, when Filmer comes to show exactly how one man rises above his brethren to rule them as the natural heir to Adam, he presents a number of modi operandi for the effectuation of this inheritance, which stand in contradiction to one another.

[B]y making sometimes *Inheritance* alone, sometimes only *Grant or Inheritance*, sometimes only *Inheritance or Usurpation*, sometimes all these three, and at last *Election*, or *any other means*, added to them, the ways whereby *Adam*'s Royal *Authority*, that is, his right to Supreme Rule, could be convey'd down to future Kings and Governors, so as to give them a Title to the Obedience and Subjection of the People.[70]

What appears to be even more startling in Filmer's argumentation is that he contradicts his very own idea of providing an explanation for this inheritance by stating in effect that by the mere fact of his rule the monarch enjoys the supreme powers that originally belonged to Adam.

And he might have spared the trouble of speaking so much, as he does, up and down of Heirs and Inheritance, if to make any one properly a King, needs no more but *Governing by Supreme Power, and it matters not by what Means he came by it.*[71]

Indeed, if the means via which a monarch "came by" his power "matters not," it is more than just an impression that Filmer was trying to justify absolutism at any expense, something Locke sensed was at the essence of governmental absolutism, indeed its very nature. It is here that Filmer, and as far as Locke was concerned Filmer was speaking for all would-be defenders of freedom-depriving governments, inadvertently let the cat out of the bag.

[69] I, 78, p. 218.   [70] I, 80, p. 219.   [71] I, 78, p. 218.

THE ORIGINS OF PROPERTY

Locke begins his *Second Treatise* chapter "Of Property" with a description of the origins of property, and he then goes on to discuss the centrality of property to the human condition.[72] Property is attained through labor, and human labor is an extension of divine creation. Locke has already taught us that, "men being all the workmanship of one omnipotent and infinitely wise Maker ... they are his property whose workmanship they are."[73] God's laboring at the creation of mankind makes mankind God's property, and because mankind is the property of God, it cannot escape its owner and be the property of anyone else, as previously delineated with regard to slavery. Hence, in order for mankind, like God, to have property, it must labor (it must be a "maker" even if it is not "infinitely wise"), and that labor allows for a similar exclusive entitlement to material goods.[74]

---

[72] Paul Rahe writes: "Thus, what begins as an account of the origins of property swiftly turns into a paean of praise for human acquisitiveness and industry and for the 'invention and Arts' that have so much 'improved the conveniences of Life.'" Rahe, *Republics, Ancient and Modern*, p. 503.

[73] II, 6, p. 289.

[74] James Tully refers to this explanation of how property ownership materializes as the *workmanship model*. Tully, *A Discourse on Property*, pp. 35–42. Tully writes that, "the workmanship model is a fundamental feature of all Locke's writings." Ibid, p. 4. See also Gopal Sreenivasan, who nuances the workmanship model somewhat differently. Gopal Sreenivasan, *The Limits of Lockean Rights in Property* (Oxford: Oxford University Press, 1995), pp. 62, 74–81.

The Talmudic discussion regarding whether or not "an artisan gains a title to the improvement of the utensil" ("Oman koneh b'shevach keli") is worthy of mention here. The question relates to material (such as wood) placed in the hands of an artisan (such as a carpenter) to construct a particular artifact (such as a cabinet). If the wood was destroyed while in the hands of the artisan, he would be responsible for reimbursing his customer for the value of the wood. But what if what was destroyed in the artisan's possession was the ordered product (the cabinet) that he had not yet transferred to his customer? Does his own labor in the material earn the artisan possession of the finished product, in which case he would have to reimburse only the value of the wood? Or does his labor not earn him ownership of the cabinet, in which case he would have to pay the entire value of the finished product? BT, *Tractate Baba Kama*, 98b–99a, and *Tractate Kiddushin*, 48b. Maimonides rules that the artisan does not gain title to the product through his labor. See Maimonides, *Mishneh Torah, Hilchot Sicherut, The Laws of Rent*, New Corrected Edition (New York: Feldheim Publishers, 1981), chap. 10, law 4. But a large number of rabbinic authorities disagree and are of the opinion that the efforts of the artisan and the *labor* he put into the artifact do earn him ownership in it. See *Talmudical Encyclopedia* (Jerusalem: Yad Harav Herzog, 1998), p. 310 [Hebrew].

In the Hebrew Bible, when God as part of his "great design"[75] gives "the earth to the children of men,"[76] humans born into natural freedom and equality, he intends that the earth be used by them for their self and communal preservation; ergo to refrain from labor is to go against God's design. This granting of the earth to mankind then creates not only a right but a duty to labor and preserve. As James Tully writes: "[Locke] wishes to emphasize that labor is the most suitable means for a rational animal to perform the first phase of his duty to preserve mankind."[77] Jeremy Waldron also makes this reading of Locke eminently clear:

> Each person is directed "to the use of those things, which [are] serviceable for his Subsistence" (I, 86). Each is required to help himself. And so his having the right to help himself to natural resources is intelligible not just in the light of his own purposes for himself, but in the light of God's purposes for him ... Laboring is not just something we happen to do to resources ... it is the appropriate mode of helping oneself to resources given what resources are *for*. Being permitted to help oneself is not a divine indulgence of the self-interested inclination of an acquisitive being. It is the naturally requisite next step following our creation once we accept that we were created subservient to God's design "that Man should live and abide for sometime upon the Face of the Earth, and not that so curious and wonderful a piece of Workmanship by its own Negligence, or want of Necessaries, should perish again, presently after a few moments continuance."[78]

It is interesting to point out that the Fourth Commandment of the Decalogue, "Remember the Sabbath day to keep it holy," begins not with the command to rest on the seventh day, but with echoing God's work during the six days of creation, with the obligation to labor during the six days leading up to the seventh. "Six days shalt thou labour, and do all thy work; but the seventh day is a Sabbath unto the LORD thy

---

[75] II, 41, p. 188.   [76] Psalms 106:16.   [77] Tully, *A Discourse on Property*, p. 131.

[78] Waldron, *God, Locke, and Equality*, p. 160. Here again the departure from Augustinian thought could not be starker: for Locke, labor and property acquisition follow creation; for Augustine they are the result of the Fall. The notion of inalienable right to private property follows the creation narrative, while the patristic idea that it is the rulers who determine the parameters of property ownership belongs to the belief that the fallen man narrative is predominant. See Deane, *The Political and Social Ideas of St. Augustine*, pp. 104–108. Quoting from Augustine's *Confessions*, book XIII, chap. 23, p. 332, Joshua Mitchell writes: "Dominion [for Augustine] means the possession of *spiritual gifts* which differentiate human beings from the created world. There is no theory of property deriving from Augustine's reading of Genesis; his intention, like Luther's, was to show how the Old already prefigured the New, how even in the creation of the world the spiritual domain which supersedes it is *already there*." Mitchell, *Not by Reason Alone*, p. 200, *ft.* 34.

God, in it thou shalt not do any manner of work."[79] While Locke did not quote from the Fourth Commandment of the Decalogue here, he did deal extensively with the Fifth, "Honor thy father and mother," in his rejoinder to Filmer over the latter's patriarchalist interpretation of it. And although it clearly cannot be asserted that Locke was influenced by the Decalogue's apparent celebration of human labor, it is important nonetheless to emphasize that he is at least in keeping with Biblical direction on the subject.

Labor, for Locke, is not just a means to an end, the end-goal of production. Labor is itself an intentional, Godlike occupation in resources, resources that were created to be labored in. Idleness, therefore, is a destructive force to be rejected even when there is no need for subsistence, as in the case of the rich, for example.

Nor indeed can man believe ... that all this equipment for action is bestowed on him by a most wise creator in order that he may do nothing, and that he is fitted out with all these faculties in order that he may thereby be more splendidly idle and sluggish.[80]

Through labor in the creations that God gave "men in common" (II, 26), humans fulfill their natural duty as defined by both reason and revelation to preserve themselves and their fellow humans and at the same time turn the fruits of labor into their own private property.[81]

---

[79] Exodus 20:8–10. This theme is poignantly taken up by rabbinic commentary. See, for example, *Avot d'Rebbe Natan*, chapter 11: "Shemaiyah and Abtalyon took over from them, Shemaiyah says: Love work, hate lordship, and seek no intimacy with the ruling powers ... Rabbi Tarfon says: The Holy One, blessed be He, likewise did not cause His Shekinah to rest upon Israel before they did work, as it is said, 'And I let them make Me a sanctuary, then shall I dwell among them' (Exodus 25:8) ... Rabbi Judah ben Bathyra says: If a man has no work to do, what should he do? If he has a run-down yard or run-down field let him go and occupy himself with it, for it is said, Six days shalt thou labor, and do all they work (Exodus 20:9). Now, why does the verse say, And do all thy work? To include him who has run-down yards and fields – let him go and occupy himself with them!" There are literally dozens of additional Talmudic and Midrashic sources praising industrious human labor as behavior endorsed by God, and apparently intended as well to counterbalance negative Greek and Roman attitudes on the subject. See Abraham Arazi, "Work in the Eyes of the Rabbis," *Machnayim* (91, 5724, www.daat.ac.il/daat/kitveyet/mahanaim/arazi-3.htm) [Hebrew].

[80] Locke, *Essays on the Law Nature*, p. 105.

[81] As I showed at the beginning of this chapter, in the previous paragraph (II, 25), Locke, drawing from Psalms 115:25, states that God "has given the Earth to the Children of Men, given to Mankind in common." Tully's exhaustive study on Locke's theory of property shows that Locke was not alone with his "commonality" concept. Cumberland,

[T]he Hare that any one is Hunting, is thought his who pursues her during the Chase. For being a Beast that is still looked upon as common, and no Man's private Possession; whoever has imploy'd so much *labour* about any of that kind, as to find and pursue her, has thereby removed her from the state of Nature, wherein she was common, and hath *begun a Property*.[82]

The exclusivity of possession that ensues from labor is manifested in regard to other people, but not to God. Based on the Hebrew Bible's "case of the Israelites when they departed from Egypt and journeyed to Palestine [Exodus 12:35]," which included the confiscation of Egyptian property by their fleeing ex-slaves, Locke concludes in his *Essays on the Law of Nature* that, "the goods of fortune are never so much ours that they cease to be God's: that the supreme lord of all things can, without doing wrong, give of his property to anyone as he pleases by his sovereign will."[83] Since mankind remains God's property, mankind's property is linked to divine dominance as well as in a kind of joint ownership between mankind and God, and hence ultimately remains always under the guidelines of God's moral law.[84] Those guidelines, according to Locke, include the ironclad stipulation of charity.

Grotius, Pufendorf, Selden, and Suarez all differed with regard to the "consent" problem (if everyone is an owner in common, how can the individual attain proprietorship without consent of his or her "partners"?), but all agreed more or less with regard to common ownership. What is less clear is whether or not these thinkers also predicated their notion of commonality on the Psalms as well, something Tully does not discuss.

[82] II, 31, p. 308.

[83] Locke, *Essays on the Law of Nature*, p. 126. The scriptural text in Exodus 12:35–36 reads: "And the children of Israel did according to the word of Moses; and they asked of the Egyptians jewels of silver, and jewels of gold, and raiment. And the LORD gave the people favour in the sight of the Egyptians, so that they let them have what they asked. And they despoiled the Egyptians."

In his discussion of "egalitarianism and assets" in the Hebrew Bible, Joshua Berman points out that it is precisely the dichotomous relationship between the inalienability of property and its concurrent divine ownership that is the central theme of Leviticus 25. "In Leviticus 25 ... the inalienability of property is presented with theological overtones. The ultimate owner of the land is God, and He grants rights to it to His people, Israel, as an everlasting holding, or in the legal terminology of the ancient Near East, as a land grant." Berman, *Created Equal*, pp. 90–91.

[84] A great deal has been written about the apparent contradiction between Locke's basic theory of God's proprietorship of mankind and his statement here (II, 27) that, "every man has a property in his own person. This nobody has a right to, but himself." Patrick Coby sees a total contradiction, and Zuckert concludes that, "Locke's shift in terminology must be either the product of very loose thinking or the expression of a shift in conception of some significance." See Patrick Coby, "The Law of Nature in Locke's Second Treatise: Is Locke a Hobbesian?," in *Political Theory*, Joseph Losco and Leonard Williams (eds.) (New York: St. Martin's Press, 1992), pp. 301–303. Zuckert, *Natural Rights and the New Republicanism*, p. 221. But, of course, Locke meant that, "every man has a propriety in

The primary limitation God sets on mankind's material accumulation is the obligation to give charity to the destitute, which Locke presents in the *First Treatise*.

But we know God hath not left one Man so to the Mercy of another, that he may starve him if he please: God the Lord and Father of all, has given no one of his Children such a Property in his peculiar Portion of the things of this World, but that he has given his needy Brother a Right to the Surplusage of his Goods; so that it cannot justly be denied him, when his pressing Wants call for it. And therefore no Man could ever have a just Power over the Life of another, by Right of property in Land or Possessions; since t'would always be a Sin in any Man of Estate, to let his Brother perish for want of affording him Relief out of his Plenty.

---

his own person" in regard to other men, but with regard to God he is still ultimately and everlastingly under God's proprietorship. See Grant, *John Locke's Liberalism*, pp. 69–70.

Our interpretation suggesting a continued divine link to the products of human labor is somewhat different than Tully's interpretation. In II, 27, Locke writes that, "*Labour* of his Body, and the *Work* of his Hands, we may say, are properly his." From this Tully concludes that, "His body and his limbs are God's property: the actions he uses them to make are his own." Tully, *A Discourse on Property*, pp. 108–109. Clarifying Tully's point, Sreenivasan writes: "What God enjoys, therefore, is a property in man, whereas what man enjoys is a property in his own person and labour." Sreenivasan, *The Limits of Lockean Rights in Property*, p. 66. See also how Sreenivasan concludes that there is no justification for dichotomizing between "creating" and "making" to the effect that it is God who performs the former and mankind the latter (ibid, pp. 74–77).

I believe my interpretation, though, explains more poignantly the limitations of divine orientation that always remain tied to the property that mankind accumulates through its labor. In addition, it obviates the potential to adduce contradiction with Locke's negation of Filmer's theory of parental ownership of their children. Locke argues that parents do not create their children alone because mankind has not the knowledge and skill "to frame and make a living Creature" (I, 53). Furthermore, argues Locke, at the time of procreation mankind does not think "farther then the satisfying of his present Appetite" (I, 54). It is therefore not just an extension of God that is making something new to which God is ultimate proprietor, but God is full (perhaps primary) partner in the creation itself. Hence parenting does not grant parents proprietorship of their children.

It is also worth mentioning on a related matter that Robert Nozick poses what Sreenivasan admits is a "real difficulty" (Sreenivasan, *The Limits of Lockean Rights in Property*, p. 85) with Locke's reasoning, that because mankind cannot understand its own origins it cannot be considered the real bearer of another life. To Nozick, Locke's refutation "seems to depend upon the view that one owns something one makes only if one controls and understands all parts of the process of making it. By this criterion, people who plant seeds on their land and water them would not own the trees that then grow ... Yet in many such cases, Locke does want to say that we own what we produce." See Robert Nozick, *Anarchy, State, and Utopia* (New York: Basic Books, 1974), p. 288. Nozick overlooks the fact that Locke is speaking of one very specific instance, that of giving human life: "How can he be thought to give Life to another, that knows not wherein his own Life consists (I, 52)?" Individuals need not know how a seed grows into a sapling in order for them to take credit for watering and weeding it. But for creating a replica of the rational creature and for being the potential creator that they themselves are, they cannot take exclusive credit without becoming God themselves.

As *Justice* gives every Man a Title to the product of his honest Industry, and the fair Acquisitions of his Ancestors descended to him; so *Charity* gives every Man a Title to so much out of another's Plenty, as will keep him from extream want, where he has no means to subsist otherwise; and a Man can no more justly make use of another's necessity, to force him to become his Vassal, by with-holding that Relief, God requires him to afford to the wants of his Brother, than he that has more strength can seize upon a weaker, master him to his Obedience, and with a Dagger at his Throat offer him Death or Slavery.[85]

Bearing this *First Treatise* quote in mind it will be impossible to reach the conclusion asserted by Gopal Sreenivasan that, "[N]either of the characteristic elements of Locke's argument (regarding private property) requires a belief in God's existence."[86] But a brief interlude for a procedural discussion of why Locke does not include this charity proviso in the *Second Treatise* must precede our more substantive assessment of Locke's theory on charity because it will directly contribute to our understanding of Locke's approach to the entire subject.

The absence of any mention of charity in the *Second Treatise* discussion of property does prima facie indicate that Locke has abandoned the doctrine by the time he reaches the *Second Treatise*, a reading, of course, that Laslett's assertion that the writing of the *First Treatise* actually followed the *Second* would militate against.[87] It is not just Locke's silence, though, that raises the question of what Locke actually believed when writing the *Second Treatise*, but the passages that beg for its reference if it is indeed still relevant. For example, in his discussion of the development of unequal possession due to the advent of money, Locke writes:

This I dare boldly affirm, That the same *Rule of Property*, (viz.) that every Man should have as much as he could make use of, would hold still in the World, without straitning any body, since there is Land enough in the World to suffice

---

[85] I, 42, p. 188. Regarding Locke's use of the expression "honest industry" in this paragraph, Laslett believes that Locke "hints at the labour theory of property, stated at length in Second Treatise." Laslett, "Introduction," p. 188, *ft.* 11–14.

[86] Sreenivasan, *The Limits of Lockean Rights in Property*, pp. 6–7.

[87] This is precisely the argument made by Thomas Pangle: "Locke does not define or characterize charity as a duty at all: Lockean charity is a right, a conditional right, of the starving (and only them) to some of the 'surplusage' (and only the surplusage) of the 'rich,' or of those who possess 'Plenty' (and only those). Or, as Locke also makes clear in this section, what he means by 'charity' is just a subdivision of justice: an expression, in desperate circumstances, of the inalienable right and undeniable urge to self-preservation (cf. II 183) ... (Locke drops charity from his discussion of property in the *Second Treatise*)." Pangle, *The Spirit of Modern Republicanism*, p. 144. I believe the forthcoming evidence will remove any doubt that Pangle is completely mistaken about Locke abandoning his commitment to charity in the *Second Treatise*.

double the Inhabitants had not the *Invention of Money* ... introduced (by Consent) larger Possessions, and a Right to them.[88]

Jeremy Waldron seems correct in commenting on this paragraph that:

The clear implication is that some people *are* "Straitned" by the inequality that money introduced. If so, it seems odd not to mention the natural law doctrine of charity by which such straitening might be mitigated. Sure, this does not actually contradict the charity doctrine; but the passage is remarkable for the omission of the doctrine, if we assume it was one that Locke had in mind when he wrote it.[89]

Nevertheless, Waldron reaches the conclusion that there is a "substantive case for importing the *First Treatise* doctrine of charity into the *Second Treatise* ... around the premises of Lockean natural law."[90] As has already been extensively shown, a foundational idea of Locke's natural law is the duty to preserve mankind, not just a right or a duty to preserve oneself, but an obligation to preserve as many other individuals as possible. "Everyone as he is *bound to preserve himself* ... so by the like reason when his own Preservation comes not in competition, ought he, as much as he can, *to preserve the rest of Mankind*."[91]

It will be recalled that Locke begins his chapter on the acquisition of property by quoting from Psalms 106:16 that God "has given the earth to the children of men." The verse states that the earth is "given to mankind in common" by God in order to facilitate the human preservation upon which all natural law depends. Echoing Waldron, Gopal Sreenivasan cogently makes this point:

The right of charity exists to succour the *disabled* poor and needy, a group comprising the naturally disabled and those who, through poverty or misfortune, suffer from temporary disability. This right derives from the fundamental law of nature, which is the preservation of mankind (II, 6, 16, 135). The earth and the inferior creatures were given to mankind in common by God for the purpose of bringing about this preservation (I, 86–87, 97; II, 25, 172); indeed, the whole matrix of natural rights is subordinated to this end. In the case of disabled,

[88] II, 36, p. 311.   [89] Waldron, *God, Locke, and Equality*, p. 183.
[90] Ibid, p. 184. Waldron is, of course, correct: Locke's theory of property cannot be fully understood without a prior appreciation for his doctrine of charity. But, as I maintain throughout this book, Waldron does not go quite far enough, for it is not just his theory of property that needs the *First Treatise* but the *Second Treatise* in its entirety that cannot be fully understood in absence of the *First* or in isolation from it. It is for this reason that I think Waldron's use of the term *import* to be misplaced; one can import an idea from one book to another, but ideas that are conceptually linked to one another in the very same text, the *Two Treatises*, cannot really be considered "importation."
[91] II, 6, p. 289.

however, God's intention must obviously be fulfilled in some other way – whence the obligation of charity.[92]

An individual's labor allows for his or her obligatory preservation, hence the person who cannot labor is to be supported through charity, which is the manifestation of mandatory interpersonal preservation. We have then a Biblically rooted natural law of human preservation; a Biblically rooted theory of human equality; and a Biblically anchored theory of labor and property, all but making obvious the mandatory nature of charity. But Waldron, quite appropriately I believe, goes on to discover more in Locke's thinking on charity.

I think it is extremely significant that Locke's language in paragraph 42 of the *First Treatise* involves a denial that property-owners have the right to *withhold* their surplus goods from the poor. In other words, he seems to be committed not to a view about *giving* but to the view that neither the rich nor civil society on their behalf is entitled to *resist* the poor when the poor attempt to seize their surplus goods for themselves. It is not a question of forcing the rich to do anything: it is enough that they be compelled simple to stand back and let the poor take what (an account of their "pressing Needs") is rightfully theirs. The needy have a right to surplus goods, and the rich have no right to withhold them. Though Locke does not talk at this stage of the role of the state in these matters, it is clear that what he has in mind are not so much affirmative charitable obligations (which, once introduced into the picture, might have to be enforced) but unjust and uncharitable withholding and denying (which may have to be prevented by the state).[93]

In his *First Treatise* paragraph on charity (42), Locke twice refers to the "title" that the needy of subsistence have in the "surplusage" of another. In other words, there is a duty on the part of the self-sufficient to feed the needy, as well as a religious prohibition against withholding charity, which Locke calls a "sin." Locke actually posits that the obligation is of a juridical nature, establishing an inherent legal right that the disabled and needy have in the surplus property of the able-bodied and the self-sufficient.

Although I began my discussion with the assumption that the obligation of charity appears exclusively in the *First Treatise*, the discerning eye will detect just such a reference in the *Second Treatise* as well. Locke states that:

---

[92] Sreenivasan, *The Limits of Lockean Rights in Property*, pp. 103–104.
[93] Waldron, *God, Locke, and Equality*, p. 185. See also Waldron's article "Enough and as Good Left for Others," in which he expands the argument that for Locke charity is a matter of natural right. A rich person who does not give anything to the poor is violating his or her rights.

[H]e who gathered as much of the wild fruit, killed, caught, or tamed as many of the beasts as he could ... by placing any of his labour on them, did thereby acquire a property in them; but if they perished in his possession without their due use, if the fruits rotted or the venison putrified, before he could spend it, he offended against the common law of nature, and was liable to be punished; he invaded his neighbor's share, for he had no right farther than his use called for any of them, and they might serve to afford him conveniences of life.[94]

Mankind's labors serve to acquire for it exclusive ownership of what its efforts produce and it cannot be confiscated from mankind without its consent because the title it has in it cannot be compromised. But the surplus part of its produce engenders the entitlement of the needy, an entitlement so strong that the laborer cannot withhold that part of his or her produce, and were the laborer to take it he or she would be held accountable for "invading his neighbor's share" even though it is of his or her own making. Like Waldron, James Tully detects a strong hint at this obligation of charity in the *Second Treatise*:

It should be noted as well that the positive duty of charity is not inconsistent with Locke's definition of property as that which cannot be taken without the proprietor's consent. The inclusive rights of each refer to the goods of a given society, and these are held individually because this serves the function of preserving mankind. If a case of need arises then, *ipso facto*, one man's individual right is overridden by anther's claim, and the goods become his property. By failing to hand over the goods, the proprietor invades the share now belonging to the needy and is liable to punishment (2. 37). The necessary goods "cannot justly be denied him" (I. 42). Individual ownership provides the means by which a moral agent may exercise his choice in performing his duties to others. However, in a manner similar to that of Pufendorf's analysis, if the duty is not discharged voluntarily, the claim right of the needy imposes the duty. As Lady Masham quotes Locke, the needy, like everyone else, have "a right to live comfortably in the world."[95]

Neither Tully nor Waldron suggest where Locke may draw his unique concept of entitlement from, as it is not original. This concept of the statutory right that the impoverished have in the property of the more solvent members of society is a strong motif in the Hebrew Bible's teaching on charity, and it appears reasonable to assume that this might have served as Locke's inspiration, particularly in light of the fact that the Christian directives on charity are a bit different, as will be demonstrated presently. The laws of *Pe'ah* (corner of the field), *Leket* (produce that falls to the ground at the time of reaping), and *Shichicha*

---

[94] II, 37, pp. 312–313. Thomas Pangle ignores this paragraph.
[95] Tully, *A Discourse on Property*, p. 132.

(forgotten produce), for example, are obligations the field owner has toward the destitute and rights that the destitute have in the produce of the field owner.

> And when ye reap the harvest of your land, thou shalt not wholly reap the corner of they field, neither shalt thou gather the gleaning of thy harvest. And thou shalt not glean thy vineyard, neither shalt thou gather the fallen fruit of thy vineyard; thou shalt leave them for the poor and for the stranger: I am the LORD your God.[96]

> When thou reapest thy harvest in thy field, and hast forgot a sheaf in the field, thou shalt not go back to fetch it; it shall be for the stranger, for the fatherless, and for the widow; that the LORD thy God may bless thee in all the work of thy hands.[97]

It is readily apparent that each Biblical commandment is actually a double one, to give and to not hold back from giving,[98] which translates into a title that the poor person has in the surplus property of the rich person. Thus, writes Maimonides in his legal codification regarding "Gifts to the Poor," if the owner of the field forgets to leave any of these divinely ordained gifts in the field, he must return them to the poor even if they have already been "ground and baked." And in a more sweeping identification of the nature of the title that the poor have, he writes: "All the obligatory gifts to the poor include no benefit to their owners (the donors). Rather the paupers come and take them (the gifts) even against the wishes of the owners."[99]

The fallacy of Strauss's assertion that, "Locke explicitly justifies man's natural right to appropriate and to own without concern of the needs of

---

[96] Leviticus 19: 9–10. [97] Deuteronomy 24:19.

[98] See Jeremy Waldron's article "Welfare and the Images of Charity," in which he speaks of two models of charity: 1) active charity – giving and helping others, and 2) passive charity – allowing others to help themselves to the resources one has (p. 471).

[99] Maimonides, *Mishneh Torah, Hilchot Matnot Aniyim, The Laws Concerning Gifts to the Poor*, New Corrected Edition (New York: Feldheim Publishers, 1981), chap. 1, laws 4 and 8. The Biblical verse reads: "If there is among you a poor man, one of thy brethren within any of thy gates in thy land which the Lord thy God gives thee, though shalt not harden thy heart, nor shut thy hand from thy poor brother ... [but thou shalt open thy hand wide to him, and shalt surely lend him sufficient for his need, in that which he lacks]." Deuteronomy 15:7–8. It is important to point out the following qualification with regard to the rights the poor person has in another's charity. In contradistinction to the laws of agrarian charity, the poor person does not have the right to take tithed money without the permission of the giver. In this case it is the religious courts that force every able giver to tithe and donate their tithing to the poor. See Maimonides, ibid, chap. 7, law 10.

others"[100] is clear. Locke's "doctrine of charity"[101] is in its granting of a statutory right of surplusage to the needy so entirely un-Hobbesian that Strauss could not have recognized it and its Biblical antecedents, and continued to maintain his general thesis regarding the Hobbesian nature of Lockean thought. Locke "explicitly justifies man's natural right to appropriate," but he does not do so "without concern of the needs of others."

Mankind's right to private property is anchored throughout the Book of Genesis. The reason Scripture gives for the flood is that, "The earth became corrupt before God; the earth was filled with lawlessness,"[102] with "corruption" and "lawlessness" understood in traditional rabbinic commentary as primarily the absence of any respect for private property.[103] Abraham recommends territorial separation from his nephew Lot so that their individual property rights will be respected.[104] The entire story of Abraham's purchase of a burial site for Sarah is an account of a financial transaction.[105] Isaac confronts Philistines who close the wells that his father had dug (*labored* over);[106] Jacob purchases a field upon arrival in Schechem;[107] and Joseph nationalizes the private property of Egyptians at a time of famine.[108]

But the more contentious side of the Lockean equation is his doctrine of charity, hence the need to use language more indicative of Biblical precedent than in his justification of property. We have already seen the

---

[100] Strauss, *Natural Right and History*, p. 239.
[101] See Waldron, *God, Locke, and Equality*, p. 186.   [102] Genesis 6:11.
[103] Rashi, on Genesis 6:13. The verdict of the generation of the flood was determined because of their thievery. Rashi's commentary here is based on the Talmud, BT, *Sanhedrin*, 108a: "So said R. Yohanan, come and see how serious is the power of thievery, for the generation of the flood transgressed every injunction but were not sentenced to the destruction of the flood until they stretched their hand out in thievery."

In conjunction with what was discussed earlier in regard to the merits of human labor, another Talmudic passage suggests that the Biblical flood was due to an indolent lack of industriousness. See JT, *Ma'asrot* B, 6.

The inherent connection for Locke between private property and the concept of injustice is worth noting here. In discussing how he believed children should be inculcated with a sense of honesty, he recommended that, "The first tendency to any injustice that appears must be suppressed with a shew of wonder and abhorrence ... but because children cannot well comprehend what injustice is, till they understand property, and how particular persons come by it, the safest way to secure honesty, is to lay the foundations of it in early liberty, and as easiness to part with to others whatever they have or like themselves." Locke, "Some Thoughts Concerning Education," part vii, section 110, p. 126.
[104] Genesis 13:5–18.   [105] Ibid, 23:1–20.   [106] Ibid, 26:1–30.   [107] Ibid, 33:18–20.
[108] Ibid, 47:13–26.

substantive theoretical sources for Locke's thinking in the Hebrew Bible, but a close reading of Locke's *First Treatise* focusing on charity reveals textual similarities as well. Locke begins his paragraph on charity (I, 42, p. 188) with "But we know God hath not left one man so to the mercy of another," but from where exactly *we know* this moral rule Locke does not say. That God wills human charity is known to all from the Biblical books of Leviticus and Deuteronomy. Those two books have in them God's command to give charity and to take care of the poor, and in both places when the poor man in need of charity is mentioned he is called *brother*, the same term Locke uses no less than three times in his paragraph on charity.

If your brother, being in straits, comes under your authority, and you hold him as though a resident alien, let him live by our side. Do not exact from him advance or accrued interest, but fear your God. Let him live by your side as your brother. Do not lend him money at advance interest, or give him your food at accrued interest. I the LORD am your God, who brought you out of the land of Egypt, to give you the land of Canaan, to be your God. If your brother under you continues in straits and must give himself over to you, do not subject him to the treatment of a slave.[109]

Another textual similarity with the Hebrew Bible is to be found toward the beginning of his *Second Treatise* discussion of property. In what Lockean scholarship calls the *sufficiency limitation*, Locke writes: "For this labour being the unquestionable Property of the Labourer, no Man but he can have a right to what that is once joined to, at least where there is enough, and as good left in common for others."[110] What Locke means is that individuals are required to leave enough for the use of others and that which they leave must be qualitatively on par with what they labored for, in order for their labor to generate their property in the product. We have seen the use of similar terminology before. When the Hebrew Bible issues the directives obligating the agricultural gifts to the poor that were noted earlier, it says: "thou shalt *leave* them for the poor."[111] It is perhaps not entirely incidental that where Locke is speaking of the requirement to supply the poor with the surplus of one's labor he too uses the terminology "*left* in common for others."[112]

---

[109] Leviticus 25:35–39.   [110] II, 27, p. 306.   [111] Leviticus 19:10.

[112] I suggest that this terminological observation here is relevant, albeit less so, even according to Waldron's reading of the "enough and as good" clause. Waldron argues that Locke intended no limitation on appropriation (no "sufficiency limitation") but was rather describing reality at the early history of mankind. See Jeremy Waldron, "Enough and as Good Left for Others," *Philosophical Quarterly* 29, 117 (1979), pp. 319–328.

This theoretical consistency and textual similarity with the Hebrew Bible makes it a far more plausible resource for Locke than the New Testament's Luke 11:41, as suggested by Peter Laslett.[113] That verse reads: "But rather give ye alms of such things as ye have; and behold, all things are clear unto you," and Jeremy Waldron justifiably argues that there is "no textual basis for this attribution."[114] It should also be emphasized that if a New Testament imperative is what Locke has in mind, his *we know* would be limited to Christians, something that would severely limit the scope of the *Two Treatises* and, as we have been arguing throughout, would go against the grain of his ubiquitous intent in his theory of government. It is curious that even though Waldron identifies the uniqueness of Locke's teaching on charity, in which he aptly classifies the "title" of the needy in surplusage as both a religious and statutory right, he does not suggest probable attribution of it to what is a solid Hebraic convention and for which a textual basis is apparent.

Waldron also inadvertently provides us with another reason as to why Locke shuns referencing the New Testament to present his doctrine of charity. Waldron quotes Locke from *The Reasonableness of Christianity* to the effect that charity is enforceable, this in contradistinction to belief in Jesus as Messiah, which his *Letter Concerning Toleration* argued is unenforceable. Waldron goes on to quote Locke's interpretation of the very specific kind of charity found in the New Testament and then offers his comments on it.

[L]ocke presents Jesus' commandment to the rich young man "sell all you have and give to the poor" (Matthew 19:21) as a test only. It is Christ's test to see whether the young man in question really would be willing to follow his commandments, not a genuine imperative addressed to all of us ... Selling all you have and giving it to the poor would be a form of what I want to call *radical* charity – giving away what you actually have a moral right to keep, giving away enough to impoverish yourself. This is not what Locke is arguing for; it goes way beyond the charity which he argues for in the *First Treatise* – the charity that he thinks should be enforced. Radical charity may be a particular requirement imposed on particular people, but it is not intended as a general command.[115]

For a full treatment of Waldron's unique approach to the subject, see Sreenivasan, *The Limits of Lockean Rights in Property*, pp. 37–41.

[113] I, 42, *ft.* 5, p. 188.   [114] Waldron, *God, Locke, and Equality*, pp. 179–180.

[115] Ibid, p. 182. Waldron goes on to point out in a footnote that the young man in question significantly seems to have failed the test, for the text continues: "[W]hen the young man heard that saying, he went away sorrowful: for he had great possessions" (Matthew 19:22).

Locke chooses to interpret the passage in Matthew as a test for a specific individual at a specific juncture and not as a general commandment, because he is, as Waldron argues, unequivocally opposed to the very notion of radical charity. Furthermore, for our discussion of charity in the context of the *Two Treatises* it must be clarified that a creed that sanctions if not advocates radical charity is absolutely not a creed that Locke can draw from. What Waldron does not point out, though, is that in this regard Locke is very much, once again, in tandem with Hebraic teaching. The general verse commanding the giving of charity in the Hebrew Bible reads:

If there be among you a poor man, one of thy brethren within any of they gates in thy land which the LORD thy GOD gives thee, thou shalt not harden thy heart, nor shut thy hand from thy poor brother: but thou shalt open thy hand wide to him, and shalt surely lend him sufficient for his need, in that which he lacks.[116]

Rabbinical exegesis on these verses is very clear. One is obligated to "lend him sufficient for his need," but one is not commanded to make him rich.[117] On the contrary, Maimonides actually limits the amount the donor is permitted to give and rules that the "sufficiency" clause cannot surpass one-fifth of one's possessions.[118] Locke then is well grounded in his reductionist interpretation of Matthew and his avoidance of New-Testamentism on the subject in the *Two Treatises*.[119]

We have now come full circle and are able to answer our initial question of why Locke chooses not to mention charity once again in

---

John Bossy makes the important point that up until the sixteenth century the "act" of charity was associated with the "state" of charity. This assumed a requisite religious connection between the giver and recipient of charity, such as the latter's praying for the soul of his or her benefactor. England's Poor Law of 1530 began the process of depersonalizing the concept of charity and removing it from the religious context of a state of charity. John Bossy, *Christianity in the West: 1400–1700* (Oxford: Oxford University Press, 1985), pp. 143–146. This could provide additional insight as to why Locke might have shunned the formulation of his doctrine on charity in a Christological context.

[116] Deuteronomy 15:7–8.
[117] "Our Rabbis taught: '*Sufficient for his need*' [implies] you are commanded to maintain him, but you are not commanded to make him rich; 'in that which he wanteth' [includes] even a horse to ride upon and a slave to run before him." BT, *Tractate Ketubot*, 67b.
[118] Maimonides, *Mishneh Torah, Matnot Aniyim*, (Laws Concerning Gifts to the Poor), chap. 7, 5.
[119] See Alan Ryan, *Property and Political Theory* (Oxford: Basil Blackwell, 1984), pp. 18–19.

his discussion of property in the *Second Treatise*. Waldron might be right in interpreting Locke as one who believes that the religious imperative of charity includes a requisite enforceability, but this enforceability is by the church and not by the state. In a treatise approving the separation of church and state, Locke is more than reserved about suggesting governmental enforcement of religious obligation even if he believes fulfillment of that religious requirement is necessary for the moral functioning of society. In the *Second Treatise*, Locke proposes his theory of government in which he believes that government must ensure the freedom to accumulate wealth for both moral and economic reasons. But it is not the job of government to enforce the religious duties of the individual, even if they are vital for the success of the very form of government he is advocating. Because charity is too important an issue to go unmentioned, it is stated in his *First Treatise*, the basis for the *Second*, where he sets the parameters for how the pursuit of private property must be guaranteed.

EMPLOYMENT AS THE BEST FORM OF CHARITY

We began this chapter with mention of Locke's preoccupation with economic issues in the years prior to his death, and that at the center of these efforts was his very practical influence on England's poor law. In his recommendations for the reformation of the poor law, Locke wrote that, "Everyone must have meat, drink, clothing and firing. So much goes out of the stock of the kingdom, whether they work or no."[120] No one in society may be left to perish for want of food or

---

[120] John Locke, "A Report to the Board of Trade to the Lords Justices 1697, Respecting Relief and Unemployment of the Poor," in H. R. Fox Bourne, *The Life of John Locke*, vol. 2 (New York: Harper and Brothers Publishers, 1876), p. 382. In this report Locke also proposed the establishment of "working schools" for children, the intention of which was not to exploit the unprotected for cheap labor but rather to help them break the cycle of poverty and dependency. See Woolhouse, *Locke: A Biography*, pp. 394–397, and Schouls, *Reasoned Freedom*, pp. 180–181, ft. 4. After Locke's death, Damaris Masham wrote that his personal habits of charity complemented the principled kind of charity he had advocated in theory. "[H]is charity was always directed to encourage working, laborious, industrious people, and not to relieve beggers ... People who had been industrious, but were through age or infirmity passed labour, he was very bountiful to; and used to blame that sparingness with which such were ordinarily relieve ... they had (she said) a right to live comfortably." Roger Woolhouse (ed.), "Lady Masham's Account of Locke," *Locke Studies* 3 (2003), pp. 190–191. In addition, his burial was plain and his coffin unadorned, with the

shelter, but the responsibility of society is to ensure the integration of the poor into the work force. It is a responsibility that must be taken with the utmost seriousness, for "if any person die for want of due relief in any parish in which he ought to be relieved, the said parish [must] be fined according to the circumstances of the fact and the heinousness of the crime."

Hence Locke's proposal intended "to consider of some proper methods for setting on work and employing the poor of this kingdom, and making them useful to the public, and thereby easing others of that burden." He was interested in compulsory employment for those seeking financial relief "as far as they are able to work." This, "rightly considered, shows us what is the true and proper relief to the poor. It consists in finding work for them, and taking care that they do not live like drones upon the labour of others."[121] Already in the *First Treatise*, shortly after his mention of the charity obligation, Locke outlines the course he believes charity should take, which he bases on the Book of Genesis.

God sets him to work for his living, and seems rather to give him a Spade into his hand, to subdue the Earth, then a Sceptre to Rule over its Inhabitants. *In the Sweat of thy Face thou shalt eat thy Bread*, says God to him, *ver.* 19. This was unavoidable, may it perhaps be answered, because he was yet without Subjects, and had no body to work for him, but afterwards … he might have People enough, whom he might command, to work for him; no, says God, not only whilst thou art without other help, save thy Wife, but as thou livest shall thou live by thy Labour. *In the sweat of they Face, shalt thou eat they Bread, till thou return unto the Ground, for out of it wast thou taken, for dust thou art, and unto dust shalt thou return, v. 19.*[122]

It is on this basis that Gopal Sreenivasan observes that Locke was careful about the terminology he used when speaking of those with a right to benefit from charity.

It is therefore at best misleading to refer, as is common practice, to the bearers of Locke's right of charity as the "poor" or "needy," since this completely obscures the fact that there are needy individuals who do not enjoy any such right, namely, able-bodied ones.[123]

---

money saved going to the deserving poor, as he directed in his will. Woolhouse, *Locke: A Biography*, p. 325. Cranston, *John Locke*, p. 480.
[121] Locke, "A Report to the Board of Trade," p. 382.   [122] I, 45, pp. 190–191.
[123] Sreenivasan, *The Limits of Lockean Rights in Property*, p. 45.

Sreenivasan then goes on to show how Locke's proposals for reforming the poor law were intended to get as many people as possible to support themselves through their own labor. Conjointly, Waldron makes the interesting point that, for Locke, giving charity to the indolent is a second form of radical charity, which he opposes.

This would be charity to someone who refuses to work when he *could* work, charity to someone who does not make any efforts to provide for himself or work to subsidize the cost of his provision. And Locke is no more in favor of enforcing this than he is of enforcing the other sense of radical charity – "sell all thou hast and give to the poor."[124]

Locke's doctrine of charity is also very much in keeping with the Hebraic concept of charity, which focuses on creating a society in which everyone who is able to work and support his or her self is able to do so, without falling into a state of dependency on others. The highest form of charity, then, is providing the destitute with employment, enabling them to labor and profit, preventing their idleness, and allowing them to be Godlike by creating their own property. In his discussion of the Biblical obligation of charity, Maimonides establishes eight levels, the highest degree of which is "to strengthen that person's hand, so that she or he will have no need to beg from others."

The highest degree, than which there is no higher is the one who upholds the hand of an Israelite reduced to poverty by handing that person a gift or loan, or by entering into a partnership with him, or by finding that Israelite work in order to strengthen that person's hand, so that he will have no need to beg from others.[125]

Everyone would agree that to ignore Lockean thinking on "property" would mean to ignore Locke. But, curiously, few scholars of Locke who admit to the centrality of his thinking on the nature and limitations of human acquisitiveness attribute to him a "Doctrine of Charity," as Jeremy Waldron aptly did. But even Waldron overlooks the salient

[124] Waldron, *God, Locke, and Equality*, p. 187.
[125] Maimonides, *Mishneh Torah, Matnot Aniyim* (Laws Concerning Gifts to the Poor), chap. 10, 7. Maimonides draws here from Talmudic teaching on the subject. Regarding the Biblical account of the dove returning to Noah's ark, "and, lo, in her mouth was an olive leaf plucked off" (Genesis 8:11), the Talmud recounts that the dove said before God, "Creator of the universe: may my sustenance be bitter like this olive leaf and dependent on you, rather than sweet like honey and dependent on my fellow man." BT, *Eruvin*, 18b. See also BT, *Berachot*, 6b, regarding the negative effects of human dependency.

Hebraic nature of that doctrine in Locke's world view. Locke's natural law of human preservation; his theory of human equality that forces a sweeping obligation to preserve humankind; and his theory of labor and property; all enjoy, albeit different levels of, Biblical influence and precedent, making obvious the mandatory nature of charity and the form it is to take.

5

On Rebellion

What Makes a Revolution Glorious?

But when a long train of abuses and usurpations, pursuing invariably the same Object evinces a design to reduce them under absolute Despotism, it is their right, it is their duty, to throw off such Government, and to provide new Guards for their future security. Such has been the patient sufferance of these Colonies; and such is now the necessity which constrains them to alter their former Systems of Government. The history of the present King of Great Britain is a history of repeated injuries and usurpations, all having in direct object the establishment of an absolute Tyranny over these States. To prove this, let Facts be submitted to a candid world. (From the Declaration of Independence)

But if a long train of Abuses, Prevarication, and Artifices, all tending the same way, make the design visible to the People, and they cannot but feel, what they lie under, and see, whither they are going; 'tis not to be wonder'd, that they should then rouze themselves, and endeavour to put the rule into such hands, which may secure to them the ends for which Government was at first erected; and without which, ancient Names, and specious Forms, are so far from being better, that they are much worse, than the state of Nature, or pure Anarchy; the inconveniences being all as great and as near, but the remedy farther off and more difficult.
(From the *Two Treatises*, ST 225)

The right to revolution, to rebel against tyranny, is the conclusion and crescendo of the *Two Treatises*. For the Revolution of 1688 to succeed, it needed theoretical justification potent enough to prevent any recidivism to monarchical absolutism.

Such was Locke's intent. Everything he argued prior to his final chapter intended to explain when and why it is legitimate to bring about the "Dissolution of Government" (Chapter XIX). The laws of nature could not be maintained in a pre-social world where every individual enjoyed political power. Natural equality and freedom, the right of self-preservation, the duty to preserve others, and the right of material acquisition needed to be mediated by government in order to ensure social equity and stability. But if the potential abuses of nature's laws in the state of nature carry over to the state of government, the outcome is worse than that which the formation of government originally came to fix, and the ensuing bad government must be dissolved. The political power of the people, qua individuals, that is held in abeyance as long as government functions properly is retrieved and utilized in order to reassemble the social contract from the temporary state of nature that has emerged.

Up to this point we have analyzed the probable influences of the Hebrew Bible and Hebraic thinking on these elemental ideas, which if properly addressed obviate the need for rebellion. But when there is sustained abuse of these concepts, "a long train of abuses," rebellion may become necessary, even obligatory. Through an analysis of possible Hebraic influences that helped to shape it, this chapter surveys Locke's theory of legitimate rebellion, with what it was consistent and with what it broke.

THE MAKING OF REVOLUTIONARY LOCKE

Before an examination of the influences over Locke's theory of rebellion and their Biblical antecedents it is essential to remember that in practice, in his real-life experience, Locke was himself a rebel. Richard Ashcraft has extensively documented Locke's radical political activities, and argues that Locke's political theory of rebellion must be understood in that biographical context.[1]

The English Civil War was the first major historical event witnessed by Locke. Born in 1632, he was ten years old when it erupted, and his father, a Puritan of the same name, joined the parliamentary forces and

---

[1] To my mind, Ashcraft is right to criticize those scholars who treat Locke's theory of rebellion as an abstract issue removed from its historical context and Locke's personal involvement. See Richard Ashcraft, *Revolutionary Politics & Locke's Two Treatises of Government* (Princeton, NJ: Princeton University Press, 1986), p. 304, *ft.* 80.

served as captain in the regiment commanded by his employer, Alexander Popham.[2] After attending Westminster School,[3] Locke entered Christ Church College, Oxford.[4] As a student at Oxford, Locke was loyal to Cromwell, and his first appearance in print was a salute to the "Lord Protector" on his bringing the First Anglo-Dutch War to a close with the signing of the Treaty of Westminster in 1653.[5]

It was during the first years (1660–1661) of the reign of Charles II that Locke wrote in his *Two Tracts on Government*: "I no sooner perceived myself in the world but I found myself in a storm which has lasted almost hitherto, and therefore cannot but entertain the approaches of a calm with the greatest joy and satisfaction."[6] Yearning for the storm to end, and concerned primarily with the prevention of societal anarchy following the Restoration, Locke developed in the *Two Tracts* a traditionalist and authoritarian attitude with regard to political life.[7] In the *Tracts* Locke

---

[2] In later years Locke wrote about his father, who had suffered considerable financial loss as a result of the war: "a captain in the Parliamentary army ... [he was] by that means a private sufferer in those public calamities which probably was the sole cause of his fortunes being impaired." Woolhouse, *Locke: A Biography*, p. 10.

[3] It is worth noting that the curriculum at Westminster included the study of Hebrew and that Locke became proficient enough to prepare and deliver an oration in Hebrew. Cranston, *John Locke: A Biography*, p. 24, and Woolhouse, *Locke: A Biography*, pp. 11, 14. Later, Locke achieved a high enough level of Hebrew to enable him to judge the aptitude of others. When Nicholas Toinard, a French Catholic scholar whom Locke befriended during his time in France, presented him with a copy of a book he had written attempting to harmonize parts of the New Testament discovered in early Greek texts, Locke inscribed it with reference to Toinard's "deeply versed ... Greek and Hebrew scholarship." See ibid, p. 140.

[4] Popham was instrumental in ensuring Locke's acceptance to Oxford as a payback to Locke senior. Ibid, pp. 14–15. See also J. R. Milton, "Locke in Oxford," in *Locke's Philosophy: Content and Context*, G. A. J. Rogers (ed.) (Oxford: Clarendon Press, 1994), pp. 29–48, and W. N. Hargreaves-Mawdsley, *Oxford in the Age of John Locke* (Norman, OK: University of Oklahoma Press, 1973). Despite his education at so venerable an institution of higher learning, Locke felt more indebted to himself for his educational achievements than to his instructors. His experience was formative in his later-expressed attitudes on education in which he emphasized the determinant importance of an individual's "relish of knowledge" and "love and credit of doing well" whether "with teachers or without." See King, *Life and Letters of John Locke*, pp. 4–5.

[5] It was soon after the establishment of the "Barebones Parliament" in July 1653 that Cromwell was sworn in as "Lord Protector," a position he was to hold for life according to the new constitution that was called "Instrument of Government." Cranston, *John Locke: A Biography*, pp. 16–17, 36.

[6] Locke, *Two Tracts*, p. 119.

[7] Laslett, "Introduction," *Two Treatises*, p. 21. John Marshall writes that, "The primary shaping fear of the *Two Tracts* was unquestionably that of 'anarchy.'" Marshall, *Resistance, Religion and Responsibility*, p. 20.

argued that the magistrate must have absolute and arbitrary power over all the "indifferent" actions of his people.[8]

[A]nd this, methinks, obliges me both in duty and gratitude to endeavour the continuance of such a blessing be disposing men's minds to obedience to that government, which has brought with it the quiet settlement which even our giddy folly had put beyond the reach not only of our contrivance but hopes; and I think men would be persuaded to be so kind to their religion, their country, and themselves, as not to hazard again the substantial blessings of peace and settlement, in an over-zealous contention about things which they themselves confess to be little, and at most are but indifferent.[9]

Following the Hobbesian theme of *bellum omnium contra omnes*, Locke explained that without obedience to government, the life of every person would be with "no peace, no security, no enjoyments, enmity with all men and safe possession of nothing, and those stinging swarms of miseries that attend anarchy and rebellion."[10] This authoritarian approach to government was no doubt the result of the way Locke fearfully understood the turbulent times in his country.[11] At this point in his life, he was still very far from the revolutionary ideas he would later express in the *Two Treatises of Government*.

In 1664, when he was Censor of Moral Philosophy at Christ Church, Locke gave a series of lectures on the law of nature to undergraduates who were going on to be clerics in the reestablished Church of England. For some time Locke considered revising and publishing these lectures on ethics but never did. It was only some three hundred years later, in 1954, that the lectures were published by Dr. Wolfgang von Leyden, who translated the Latin manuscripts into English and published them under the title *Essays on the Laws of Nature*.[12] In these essays Locke argued for a syncretic approach to understanding human rationality and

---

[8] The pamphlet was entitled "Question. Whether the civil magistrate may lawfully impose and determine the use of indifferent things in reference to religious worship." Woolhouse, *Locke: A Biography*, p. 39.

[9] Locke, *Two Tracts*, p. 119–120.

[10] Ibid, p. 156. Compare with Hobbes, *Leviathan* I, chap. 13, section 62, p. 89.

[11] "Locke's letters to his father at that time express a profound disenchantment with visionary politics and a strong desire for peace and security. He welcomed the Restoration and contributed a poem full of flattery for the King in a university collection named *Britannia Rediviva*." Milton, "Locke, John (1632–1704)." For more about this development, see Robert P. Kraynak, "John Locke: From Absolutism to Toleration," *The American Political Science Review* 74, 1 (1985), pp. 53–69.

[12] Locke, *Essays on the Law of Nature*.

divine will. Locke presupposes a divine lawgiver whose will is deciphered and then expressed through the faculties of human conscience. In such an understanding, the rational foundations of morality do not contradict the will of God but define it. Locke's ideas in these essays served as theoretical antecedents to his later, much longer work, *An Essay Concerning Human Understanding.* Here Locke already lays the foundations for his rejection of Cartesian *innatism* on the one hand and Grotian *common consent* on the other as potential bases of natural law. Contrary to Descartes, who posited that humans are born with ideas, including moral knowledge, Locke argues that ideas are acquired through the combination of sense experience and the use of reason. And as opposed to Hugo Grotius, who saw natural law defined in what humans commonly consent to, Locke insisted on the divine origins and objectivity of natural law. Reason, presses Locke, does not in and of itself constitute natural law, but it is rather the God-given device for discovering and deciphering natural law.[13]

In 1665, after holding the post of Censor of Moral Philosophy for a year, Locke moved from academia to diplomacy, serving as secretary to

---

[13] See Goldie, "Introduction," *Locke: Political Essays,* pp. xix–xxi. Goldie suggests that Locke followed Thomas Aquinas and Francis Suarez in forging a middle way between voluntarism, which saw moral dictates confined exclusively to God's will, and rationalism, which restricted morality to human reason. But in his attempt at striking the right balance between voluntarism and rationalism Maimonides might have been no less an influence on Locke. In *The Guide,* part III, chapter 26, Maimonides reconciles a passage in *Midrash Raba* that smacks of a voluntarist approach to God's commandments with his own insistence that none of the commandments are without reason other than simply God's will. The Midrash (*Br' Raba*; 44.a) states: "What difference does it make to the Holy One Blessed be He, whether (the animal) is slaughtered at the throat or at the neck? But it is necessary to conclude that the commandments were given to try men, as it is written (Psalms 18, 31) 'the word of the Lord is tried'." Maimonides suggests that the Midrash is by no means negating the functional benefit of each commandment, but is rather explaining why that benefit, potentially comprehensible to human reason, is not provided and left unknown. Locke, whose familiarity with and usage of *The Guide* I show later, may have been exposed to the Midrash through the mediation of *The Guide.* In his *A Letter Concerning Toleration,* published the same year as the *Two Treatises,* he uses language strikingly similar to the Midrash in order to explain what must not be considered "indifferent" in regard to worship of the divine. Locke writes: "But these things, how indifferent soever they be in common uses, when they come to be annexed unto divine worship, without divine authority, they are as abominable to God as the sacrifice of a dog. And why is a dog so abominable? *What difference is there between a dog and a goat, in respect of the divine nature, equally and infinitely distant from all affinity with matter, unless it be that God required the use of one in His worship and not of the other?*" (Italics added.) For a fuller discussion of Locke's natural law and how he chooses to reconcile reason and revelation, see Chapter 2, "Locke's Unusual Natural Law."

Sir Walter Vane. Vane was sent by Charles on a diplomatic mission to Cleves, home to the Elector of Brandenburg, whose territory bordered Holland.[14] His assignment was to convince Brandenburg to side with England, or at least stay neutral, in England's war against the Dutch. Locke's diplomatic abilities were apparently more successful than the mission itself because though the mission failed and was curtailed after only three months, the king's court offered Locke a second diplomatic posting to Spain. Locke declined, and was, some months later, offered a diplomatic post in Sweden.

Locke, though, chose to halt his diplomatic career and return to Oxford, in order to go back to his studies in medicine and the physical sciences, upon which he had embarked following the conclusion of his MA in 1658. Locke had a keen interest in medicine and related scientific matters that began early, even before he entered Oxford, and persisted throughout his life. His reading of medical authors was extensive and he made his own notations of their findings, and his pursuit of knowledge in the fields of anatomy, chemistry, and physiology, for example, related specifically to their application to medicine (or "physic" as it was customarily referred to at the time).[15] Locke's interest was always practical: he collected and recorded remedies for common ailments, observed the circulation of blood in a frog stripped of its skin, participated in postmortem examinations of deceased individuals, studied the growth and culture of grapes and olives and the process of baking bread, inquired about a method for preserving and embalming insects, investigated towing engines for riverboats and routinely observed weather patterns, studied different standards of measurement and methods for bleaching linen, searched for the proper solution for the watering of fruit trees, and experimented with the burning of rapeseed oil for street lamps.[16]

---

[14] Woolhouse says that it is not clear how exactly Locke's appointment came about, whether via intermediary or by the king himself. Woolhouse, *Locke: A Biography*, p. 60. See also Cranston, *John Locke: A Biography*, pp. 81–87; and Laslett, "Introduction," *Two Treatises*, p. 23.

[15] Woolhouse, *Locke: A Biography*, p. 34. Several of Locke's notebooks show that already in the late 1650s he had started taking extensive notes from a large number of medical works. Milton, "Locke, John (1632–1704)." About Locke the physician, see Cranston, *John Locke: A Biography*, pp. 88–104; Patrick Romanell, *John Locke and Medicine* (New York: Prometheus Books, 1984); Kenneth Dewhurst, *John Locke, 1632–1704: Physician and Philosopher, a Medical Biography* (London: The Wellcome Historical Medical Library, 1963); Woolhouse, *Locke: A Biography*, pp. 23–69.

[16] Woolhouse, *Locke: A Biography*, pp. 30–31, 67–68, 70, 160–161, 172, 174–175, 201, 278, 305, 307, 333, 334, 402, 428–429, 439, 445–446.

Locke suffered throughout his life from bouts of asthma and this might have been the reason he found so much interest in pursuing medicine and medically related subjects. Of the importance of medicine Locke wrote: "Length of life, with freedom from infirmity and pain ... is of so great concernment to mankind that there can scarce be found any greater undertaking than the profession to cure diseases."[17] His own medical infirmaries may have had much to do with Locke's consistent refusal to accept diplomatic postings abroad,[18] and might also explain why he ultimately decided not to make a career of medicine,[19] although toward the end of his life he did express some regret for not having done so.[20]

Locke's affinity for the world of medicine and empirical science must be understood in the context of the rise of these fields of study in England at the time. The Restoration helped to foster support for the scientific revolution that had begun decades earlier and was now popularized by the philosophical writings of, among others, Francis Bacon, whose influence was not lost on Locke. Bacon (1561–1626), a well-respected lawyer and jurist who also served some time as a parliamentarian (albeit on the king's behalf), wrote extensively in defense of the scientific breakthroughs of his age, insisting that they did more to advance humankind than any "empire, sect, or star."[21] Harvey's discovery of the circulation of blood

---

[17] *De Arte Medica*, in Bourne, *The Life of John Locke*, pp. 222–227.

[18] Woolhouse, *Locke: A Biography*, p. 267. Locke rejected suggestions of ecclesiastical appointments abroad as well. See ibid, pp. 73–74.

[19] Ibid, pp. 96–97, 410. Woolhouse suggests that Lord Ashley, though kept alive by Locke's medical prowess, also helped deter Locke from pursuing a medical career, insisting that his greatest contribution would be in the field of politics. Ibid, pp. 87–88.

[20] Ibid, p. 277. Peter King quotes a Mr. D. Stewart to the effect that Locke's "study of medicine formed one of the best preparations for the study of the mind," referring, of course, to the *Essay Concerning Human Understanding*. See King, *Life and Letters of John Locke*, p. 177.

[21] Woolhouse, *Locke: A Biography*, p. 413. G. A. J. Rogers claims that Locke was influenced by the natural philosophy of the Baconian school through the mediation of Robert Boyle. Rogers, "Innate Ideas and the Infinite." The strongest argument for Locke's Baconianism is made by Neal Wood, who presents a thorough and convincing thesis that Bacon's influence on Locke was decisive, both directly (only the number of Cicero's books exceeded that of Bacon's in Locke's library) and through Boyle and Syndenham. See Wood, *The Politics of Locke's Philosophy*, esp. pp. 65–93.

In one of his letters Locke makes a direct reference to one influence that Bacon had on him: "You say you lose many things because they slip from you. I have had experience of that myself, but for that my lord Bacon had provided a sure remedy. For, as I remember, he advises somewhere never to go without pen and ink, or something to write with, and to be sure not to neglect to write down all thoughts of moment that come into the mind, I must own I have omitted it often, and often repented it. The thoughts that come often unsought, and, as it were, drop into the mind, are commonly the most valuable of any we

that obtained prominence after 1640, Robert Boyle's works in chemistry during the middle of the century, and above all the discoveries of Sir Isaac Newton marked the beginning of a new era in the search for scientific knowledge. It is important to emphasize that this scientific revolution was not intended to counterbalance or replace theology, as many of these leading scientists were men of the Bible for whom "the harmony of science and religion was the basic proposition."[22] With empirical thinking uppermost in his mind, Locke, a close friend of Boyle,[23] and later in his life a good friend of Newton (to whom he referred as "the incomparable Mr. Newton"[24]), wanted to be a participant in this new world of scientific discovery, and Oxford was the place to pursue this goal. As a result of the Civil War, the university itself was going through

have, and therefore should be secured, because they seldom return again." Locke, "A Letter from Mr. Locke to Mr. Samuel Bold," *Works of John Locke*, p. 3.

For Bacon's general long-term influence see C. Drinker Bowen, *Francis Bacon: The Temper of a Man* (Boston, MA: Little Brown and Company, 1963); Margaret C. Jacob, *Scientific Culture and the Making of the Industrial West* (Oxford: Oxford University Press, 1997); and Julian Martin, *Francis Bacon: The State and the Reform of Natural Philosophy* (Cambridge: Cambridge University Press, 2007).

[22] R. S. Westfall, *Science and Religion in Seventeenth Century England* (New Haven, CT: Yale University Press, 1958), p. 194.

[23] John Marshall suggests that the source for Locke's rejection of innatism rests in his collaboration with Boyle on scientific experimentation, which moved Boyle from scholasticism to empiricism. Marshall, *Resistance, Religion and Responsibility*, p. 30. Maurice Cranston contends that there were many physical and lifestyle resemblances between Locke and Boyle that may have deepened their lifelong friendship. Cranston, *John Locke: A Biography*, pp. 7–77. See also Woolhouse, *Locke: A Biography*, pp. 34–35.

Harold Fisch refers to Boyle as "a devout naturalist whose proximity to Hebraism, both in its Biblical and post-Biblical manifestations, has never been fully appreciated." Fisch goes on to say that, "The fact that Boyle did not find any opposition developing between his scientific and his religious interests is to be explained by his stress on the Hebraic rather than the evangelical elements in his religious tradition." Fisch, *Jerusalem and Albion*, pp. 132–150. See also B. J. Shapiro, *Probability and Certainty in Seventeenth Century England* (Princeton, NJ: Princeton University Press, 1983), pp. 15–73. B. Willey, *The Seventeenth Century Background* (New York: Doubleday, 1934).

[24] Locke, "Epistle to the Reader," in *Essay Concerning Human Understanding*, p. 11. Regarding the relationship between Locke and Newton, see Cranston, *John Locke: A Biography*, p. 337. J. L. Axtell, "Locke, Newton and the Two Cultures," in *John Locke: Problems and Perspectives*, J. W. Yolton (ed.) (Cambridge: Cambridge University Press, 1969), pp. 165–182. G. A. J. Rogers, *Locke's Enlightenment: Aspects of Its Origin and Impact of His Philosophy* (Zurich: Goerg Olms Verlag, 1998), pp. 93–111. About Newton, Locke wrote: "Mr. Newton is really a very valuable man, not only for his wonderful skill in mathematics, but in divinity too, and his great knowledge of the Scriptures, wherein I know few his equals." King, *Life and Letters of John Locke*, p. 263.

revolutionary changes with regard to its chief personnel, turning the institution for the first time in history into a leading center of scientific activity.[25]

Fatefully it was his medical knowledge that secured for Locke the fortuitous position that was to permanently change his life by putting it on revolutionary footing: that of confidant, friend, political aide, and personal physician to Anthony Ashley Cooper, or Lord Ashley, who was later to become the famous Earl of Shaftesbury. The two met for the first time in Oxford during the summer of 1666, and as Ashley's grandson wrote many years later, Locke appeared to his grandfather "as a genius." Locke in turn was charmed by the charismatic baron from London.[26] The great fire that destroyed London during September of that year served as an excuse for Lord Ashley to invite Locke to his home, Exeter House, asserting that the situation "will certainly occasion great business for physicians."[27] As fate would have it, during the spring of 1668 Locke operated on Lord Ashley's abscessed liver, and the successful outcome led the grateful patient to believe that his physician and new friend had saved his life.[28]

The close lifelong friendship between them evolved into a political bond of mutual dependency that was to help change England. Lord Ashley, ten years Locke's senior, was one of the most influential figures in the court of Charles II. A member of Parliament from the age of nineteen, and a skilled politician and administrator, he served as Chancellor of the Exchequer (1667–1672), and as member of a coterie that advised the king known as the "Cabal Ministry," a group of five ministers who directed government

---

[25] Christopher Hill, *The Century of Revolution, 1603–1714* (London: Van Nostrand Reinhold Co, Ltd., 1991), p. 154.

[26] Lord Ashley's grandson, the Third Earl of Shaftesbury, who went on to become an important moral philosopher in his own right, wrote that Locke was his "friend and foster-father." Woolhouse, *Locke: A Biography*, p. 97.

[27] Ibid, pp. 71–72.

[28] Locke's medical knowledge and abilities were held in the highest esteem by leading contemporary medical experts. Dr. Syndenham, who Sir Peter King refers to as "the greatest authority of his time," said of Locke's medical expertise that, "if we consider his genius, and penetration, and exact judgment, has scarce any superior, and few equals now living." See King, *Life and Letters of John Locke*, p. 9. For a period of time Locke accompanied Syndenham on his visits to patients and studied his methods of treatment, particularly his treatment of smallpox. Woolhouse, *Locke: A Biography*, p. 80. Ashley's grandson wrote thus of Locke's medical prowess: "at that time a student in physic ... though he had never practiced physic, yet appeared to my grandfather to be such a genius that he valued him above all his other physicians." Woolhouse, "Lady Masham's Account of Locke," *Locke Studies* 3, pp. 167–193.

policy at home and abroad. The Cabal did not last long, though (roughly from 1668 to 1674), due to the ideological divide that erupted between those members who saw Parliament as the main seat of power (the group to which Shaftesbury belonged) and those who advocated monarchical supremacy. In 1672, the king granted Ashley an English title of Peerage, First Earl of Shaftesbury, following his ascent to the position of Lord Chancellor, the most powerful minister in the government. As such, he served as Charles's liaison to Parliament and to the general public. Shaftesbury defended, for example, the Declaration of Indulgence, in which Charles extended toleration for all denominations of Protestant dissent. Shaftesbury was unaware that lurking behind the declaration hid the Treaty of Dover, a secret deal that, with the encouragement of his Catholic brother James, Charles signed with France's Louis XIV intending to restore Catholicism as England's official religion, and subsequently, together to declare war on the Dutch. This began Shaftesbury's break with Charles and the beginning of his active opposition to the throne. Within a few years, he became one of the key leaders of the organized opposition to the monarch, and one of the founders of the Whig Movement.[29]

Locke's new domicile in the heart of London introduced him to a broader intellectual world than the one he had been exposed to at Oxford. He increasingly grew involved in Lord Ashley's personal life, cultural circles, and business affairs. One of Locke's major contributions to his patron was his participation in the writing of the *Fundamental Constitutions of Carolina* (1663), a legal codex that delineated a set of laws for the new English settlers who set out for the North American colonies. That contribution, though, was not the only interest Locke took in Colonial affairs, as he also developed a financial interest in the Bahamas Company and the Royal African Company.[30] In 1668, in another step toward joining the English scientific elite, Locke was elected to join the meetings of the Royal Society of London for the Improving of Natural Knowledge.[31] When Shaftesbury was promoted Lord Chancellor, he appointed Locke Secretary of Presentations, which involved the oversight of all ecclesiastical matters that fell under the Lord Chancellor's jurisdiction. Soon afterward Shaftesbury appointed Locke to an additional

---

[29] Tim Harris, "Cooper, Anthony Ashley, First Earl of Shaftesbury (1621–1683)," *Oxford Dictionary of National Biography* (Oxford: Oxford University Press, 2004, www .Oxforddnb.com/view/article/6208). Woolhouse, *Locke: A Biography*, pp. 110–115.

[30] Milton, "Locke, John (1632–1704)." Woolhouse, *Locke: A Biography*, p. 111.

[31] Ibid, p. 109.

official role, that of Secretary of the Council of Trade and Plantations, a position in which Locke wrote and advised Shaftesbury on economic matters, such as interest and exchange rates, and trade balances. When Shaftesbury began to openly oppose Charles and the anti-Popish *Test Act* was published by Parliament, the latter dismissed him as Lord Chancellor, and subsequently Locke was removed from his position as Secretary of Presentations. Later, the Council of Trade was dissolved as well.[32] Throughout this period Locke served Shaftesbury as medical consultant and economic advisor, assisted in speech writing, and helped structure his patron's political standing. But the relationship was not one-sided as Locke's theoretical scope benefited from his practical political experiences as well as from Shaftesbury's functional opposition to monarchical excesses and abuses. This made for Shaftesbury's formidable influence on the development of Locke's political ideas during the seventeen years they worked together.[33]

The first major tract that Locke wrote after beginning his collaboration with Shaftesbury, then Lord Ashley, was his *Essay Concerning Toleration*, written in 1667. This was the first indication of Locke's departure from the Hobbesian spirit of the *Two Tracts*, because it was here that he began to establish a theoretical demarcation line between the religious sphere and what he referred to as "civil concernments."[34] In this essay, with the last part written as if intended to be introduced to the king himself, it is clear to Locke that the Church of England had become too restrictive in its doctrinal and ceremonial requirements. Here Locke argued that the civil ruler carried no responsibility for the human soul, and that personal morality was exclusively God's concern. "[T]he whole trust, power, and authority of the magistrate is vested in him for no other purpose but to be made use of for the good, preservation, and peace of men in that society over which he is set, and therefore ... this alone is and ought to square and proportion his laws, model and frame his government."[35] For the first time Locke drew a fundamental distinction between human action that affected other people and could under circumstances deemed necessary for the public good be circumscribed, and those that did not affect others and

---

[32] Ibid, pp. 113–115.
[33] Ashcraft, *Revolutionary Politics*, pp. 83–87. Cranston, *John Locke: A Biography*, pp. 105–128, 214–230.
[34] Locke, "An Essay on Toleration," in *Locke: Political Essays*, pp. 134–159.
[35] Ibid, p. 135.

hence could not be compromised. The duty of the magistrate, he argued, was only to keep the peace, safety, and security of his people. It was a strong initial expression of the requisite separation between civil politics and religious matters that Locke was beginning to champion.[36]

Locke's decision to leave England for France, where he was to spend the next three and a half years, had more to do with his ill health than the souring of his (and Shaftesbury's) political fortunes.[37] But while the French air was apparently much better for his chronic cough, it did him no harm to distance himself from the political climate at home that was now as hostile to his politics and public standing as it was to his lungs. During his three and a half years of travel in France, Locke seems to have deepened his interest in the thought of Descartes and met some important philosophers as well, such as the Cartesian philosopher Pierre Regis (1632–1707), and Francois Bernier (1625–1688), the disciple of the Epicurean philosopher-scientist Pierre Gassendi (1592–1655).[38] Locke also took notes on varied topics (this was his method for many years) such as descriptions of the countryside, and local modes of agricultural and industrial production, and translated some of the philosophical essays of distinguished French writer and controversialist

[36] Locke's experience in Cleves, where he witnessed for the first time different religious denominations living in relative harmony, as well as Shaftesbury's influence, was no doubt at least partially responsible for his change of mind. Woolhouse, *Locke: A Biography*, pp. 82–86. Here Locke was still nevertheless insistent that toleration should not be extended to Catholics. "Papists are not to enjoy the benefit of toleration, because, were they have power, they think themselves bound to deny it to others." Ibid, p. 152. His attitude in regard to Catholics by the time the *Two Treatises* was written is discussed in Chapter 4.

[37] J. Lough (ed.), *Locke's Travels in France 1675–1679* (Cambridge: Cambridge University Press, 1953). Cranston, *John Locke: A Biography*, pp. 160–183. Woolhouse, *Locke: A Biography*, pp. 115–118.

[38] Regarding the philosophical predominance of Epicurean hedonism in France during this period, Frederick Vaughan writes that, "No European country, not even Italy, openly espoused hedonism with as much public acclaim as did France. For the better part of the sixteenth and seventeenth centuries, France was the undisputed haven of Epicureans." Vaughan, *The Tradition of Political Hedonism*, p. 43. Locke had studied Descartes's and Gassendi's philosophies at Oxford during the 1650s and read some of Gassendi's *Syntagma Philosophicum* in the early 1660s. That he held Descartes in the highest esteem is clear. Woolhouse, *Locke: A Biography*, pp. 18, 35. Milton, "Locke, John (1632–1704)." The thesis of Peter A. Schouls contends that it was Locke's reading of Descartes that metamorphosed his thinking in the mid-1660s and that it his adoption of Cartesian methodology that explains his revolutionary thinking. Schouls, *Reasoned Freedom*.

Pierre Nicole (1625–1695), who together with Blaise Pascal (1623–1662) contributed much to the evolution of French prose. Locke also had a number of opportunities to put his medical skills to use, particularly in treating English citizens attached to England's embassy in Paris. Later, Shaftesbury asked Locke to act as a tutor and guardian of Caleb Banks, the son of one of his rich associates with whom Locke ended up traveling all over France, meeting French intellectuals, doctors, scientists, and theologians.[39]

When Locke returned to England in mid-1679, he immediately resumed his position alongside Shaftesbury, who had been reappointed by Charles to an official position, that of Lord President of the Privy Council.[40] It is not that the king had found any new love for Shaftesbury, but it was a time of acute public agitation and political unrest, particularly following Charles's torpedoing of Parliament's Exclusion Bill (the legislative attempt to keep James from succession) and the revelation of the "Popish Plot." Shaftesbury, who used the circumstances to drum up anti-Catholic sentiment, enjoyed a resurgent popularity, which forced the king to bring him back to public office. But it was not to last for long, as in the summer of 1681 Shaftesbury was accused of encouraging witnesses to testify falsely with regard to the plot. Shaftesbury was arrested, charged with high treason, and sent to the Tower of London. There is evidence that upon his release in September 1682, Shaftesbury was involved in the plotting an insurrection or even the assassination of the king and his Catholic brother, which resulted in his going into hiding. By 1683, he was forced to flee to Holland, where he soon died.[41]

Throughout these years Locke wrote on his observations from his time in France and tried to return to his academic, mostly medical pursuits, but admitted that he did not find time enough to do so, because he was primarily preoccupied with Shaftesbury and his political activities.[42] It was at this time that Robert Filmer's *Patriarcha* in defense of Charles's absolutism was published (1680), and it was at this time too (1680–1681) that Locke probably wrote his *Two Treatises*, which was to be completed and published only much later following the Glorious Revolution.[43]

---

[39] Woolhouse, *Locke: A Biography*, pp. 119–152. John Marshall believes that Locke's preoccupation with translation of Nicole's works had a profound influence on his evolving liberal ideas on toleration. See Marshall, *Resistance, Religion and Responsibility*, pp. 89, 131–138.

[40] Woolhouse, *Locke: A Biography*, pp. 153–154.   [41] Ibid, p. 179.   [42] Ibid, p. 155.

[43] For a detailed discussion about the time and setting surrounding the writing of the *Two Treatises*, see Chapter 1, *ft.* 3.

Shortly after Shaftesbury died his political peers engaged in plans to assassinate the king and his brother at Rye House, which was on the road they were to take upon return from the horse races. Because the royal party left unexpectedly early the plot failed, and some of its more noted organizers, such as Lord William Russell and Algernon Sidney, were tried by the king's court and executed. The failure of the Rye House Plot provided Charles II with an opportunity to move against his enemies. Many politicians and political writers were arrested, and ominous political clouds now moved in Locke's direction as well, as he too was suspected of taking part in the clandestine maneuvers against the king.[44] In Oxford, where he had returned seeking peace and quiet after the death of Shaftesbury, Locke was soon placed under surveillance, and students were passing information about him to governmental circles. On July 21, 1683, the last book burning in English history took place at Oxford. It was a violent act of the politically loyal academic establishment against the literature of the king's opposition, and ideas included in Locke's *Two Treatises*, although as yet unpublished, could easily qualify among the "damnable doctrines" that were condemned to the flames. Many of the books that were burned could be found in Locke's own library as well. Locke, who had spent long and important periods of his life in Oxford, sensed impending danger and left the university a few weeks later, never to return.[45]

Like his patron Shaftesbury had been, Locke was now a fugitive in exile, escaping to Holland, the favorite exilic domicile for Whig agitators, where he lived under the pseudonym Dr. Van der Linden. When James II assumed the throne upon Charles's death in February 1685, Locke's threatened status remained unchanged. There is no doubt that he was under the surveillance of the monarchy's long arm, even after the king himself promised one of Locke's friends that Locke might safely return to England. Maintaining a low profile and moving frequently between several different Dutch cities, Locke concerned himself with questions

---

[44] Cranston, *John Locke: A Biography*, pp. 184–230. Laslett, "Introduction," *Two Treatises*, pp. 31–32. Philip Milton argues against Ashcraft's claim that Locke was deeply involved in the Rye House Plot (Ashcraft, *Revolutionary Politics*) and suggests that he deliberately stayed out of the way; see Philip Milton, "John Locke and the Rye House Plot," *The Historical Journal* 43, 3 (2000), pp. 647–668.

[45] Ibid, pp. 190–196. Cranston, *John Locke: A Biography*, p. 228. Laslett, "Introduction," *Two Treatises*, pp. 23–24.

regarding the development of knowledge and religion,[46] and it was during this period that he wrote his *Essay Concerning Human Understanding*.[47] But even while in Holland he continued to take part in additional conspiracies against the king, and there are signs that in September 1685, Locke might have even taken part in the failed attempt by supporters of James Scott, the 1st Duke of Monmouth, to overthrow James II in what became known as the *Monmouth Rebellion*.[48]

Over the next few years James made no secret of his Catholic agenda. He infiltrated Catholics into public office, defended his prerogative to act without Parliament, and sought ways to discipline Anglican clergy who attacked Catholicism. As public consternation over James's encroaching Catholic advocacy increased, so grew support for the Whig agenda – a Protestant monarchy that would give Parliament its due. This process resulted in an invitation to William of Orange, the Protestant husband of James's daughter Mary, by senior Whig statesmen, to come from Holland

---

[46] Milton, "Locke, John (1632–1704)."

[47] Woolhouse, *Locke: A Biography*, pp. 223–229. One of those cities Locke spent time in was Rotterdam, which makes for a mandatory reference to Pierre Bayle (1647–1706), the Huguenot French philosopher who spent a large part of his life in Rotterdam as a refugee from Catholic persecution. I have not found any evidence of Bayle and Locke having met even though their time spent in Rotterdam seems to have overlapped to some degree. This might have been due to the fact that Bayle, whom John Marshall refers to, in addition to Locke, as "*the* [italics added] other major theoretician of toleration in the Netherlands" (Marshall, *Resistance, Religion and Responsibility*, p. 366) supported James's toleration of Protestants and Catholics and, contrary to Locke, opposed resistance. Locke, though, was clearly familiar with Bayle's work, as he contributed a book review of Bayle's *Commentaire Philosophique* in Jean le Clerc's prestigious *Bibliotheque Universelle et Historique* (ibid, p. 330) and refers to him respectfully in a letter requesting that the *Essay* be given to Bayle for intellectual appraisal (Cranston, *John Locke: A Biography*, p. 455). Locke's library also contained the 1697 edition of Bayle's *Dictionnaire historique et critique* (Harrison and Laslett, *Library of John Locke*, p. 82). As for Bayle's familiarity with Locke's work, he did read at least book I of the *Essay* in either French or Latin (he was not fluent in English) and contended with Locke over issues in Cartesian metaphysics. Bayle mostly followed Descartes's theories with regard to the functions of matter, hence his critique of Locke's epistemology, which rejected Cartesian innatism. Based on the same theoretical concern, Bayle is also said to have followed the Locke/Stillingfleet donnybrook with great interest. Todd Ryan, *Pierre Bayle's Cartesian Metaphysics* (London: Routledge, 2009), pp. 50–62.

[48] Ibid, pp. 217–219, 229–230. Peter King contends that Locke's actual extradition was demanded of the Netherlands. He writes that, "The persecution which had driven Locke from his country, the tyranny which had illegally deprived him of his situation at Oxford, did not cease after his retreat to Holland; the King's minister at the Hague demanded amongst several others named in his memorial, that Locke should be delivered up, describing him as secretary to the late Earl of Shaftesbury, a state crime worthy of such extraordinary interposition." King, *Life and Letters of John Locke*, p. 154.

with an army strong enough to save England from "Popery and Slavery." In December 1688 James fled England,[49] and William and Mary assumed the throne. In the hope that this would encourage Locke to return to England one friend wrote to the exiled philosopher/physician that what transpired was "no less than the Israelites' deliverance from Egypt by the hand of Moses."[50]

William's position, though, was somewhat less unequivocal than that of Moses at the Egyptian exodus. William had initially been invited to pressure James into respecting Parliament and protecting Protestantism, not necessarily to inherit the throne; hence it was not clear that with James's departure the throne was now automatically his. Even though James had fled, it was not evident to all that he was not in fact still king. And even if one were to argue that his vacating the post meant that his absence was tantamount to legal abdication, it was not to be ruled out that the throne belonged to the next in line of hereditary succession, James's infant son.[51] William, in any case, was not willing to assume the throne as a surrogate king, but insisted on constitutional legitimacy and recognition. To that end he called for a parliamentary convention, which concluded its deliberations with a Declaration of the Rights of Parliaments, in which William and Mary were jointly offered and accepted the throne.

On that same day (the beginning of February 1689) Locke, who had been waiting for favorable weather conditions in order to make the sea journey back home, arrived in London following a five-year exile.[52] He immediately sensed that even following Parliament's decision and William and Mary's formal ascension to the throne, England's new political constellation was still precarious. Parliament had completed setting a framework for the constitutional future of England, but fears, uncertainty, and disagreement about the future did not abate. Locke was anxious that a diluted legitimacy of the new throne made James's return

---

[49] James was taken in by Louis XIV and warmly hosted by the Catholic monarch, who encouraged him to launch an expedition to Ireland for the purpose of establishing a royal government there. See John Callow, *King in Exile, James II: Warrior, King, and Saint, 1989–1701* (Gloucestershire: Sutton Publishing Ltd., 2004), pp. 61–65.

[50] Woolhouse, *Locke: A Biography*, pp. 261–262.

[51] For a full account of this period of monarchical instability and uncertainty, see Callow, *King in Exile*, pp. 1–65.

[52] Ibid, pp. 262–263, 275. Woolhouse also makes the observation that if Locke had not survived that winter sea journey from Holland back to England, his written works would have probably been almost completely unknown. Most of them were published after he reached England. Ibid, pp. 1–2.

and/or a Williamite slide back toward Stuart-type absolutism real possibilities.[53]

In order to ward off the worst, Locke lost no time in preparing his *Two Treatises* for publication. The opus, the basis of which had most probably been written eight to nine years earlier,[54] argued for the exclusive legitimacy of consensual government, and the right of revolution to attain it. In order to serve and promote the revolution it was now needed, as he stated on the opening page:

To establish the throne of our great Restorer, our present king William, to make good his title, in the Consent of the people, and justify to the world, the people of England, whose love of their just and Natural Rights, with their resolution to preserve them, saved the Nation when it was on the very brink of Slavery and Ruine.[55]

His intention in publishing it immediately after the revolution was then, on the one hand, to strengthen William in the face of a potential renewed claim by James and his supporters to the throne, and, on the other hand, to remind William that the strength of his own legitimacy rested in the continued consent of the people.

But why was Locke so concerned about political recidivism? Why wasn't the notion of consensual government obvious and irreversible? What was it exactly that made the seventeenth century a historical turning point, and what political crisis was Locke in essence looking to resolve?

---

[53] Peter Laslett emphasizes that, historically speaking, Locke's fears that the revolution would ultimately fail were not unjustified as its legitimacy was subject to intense debate. See Laslett, "Introduction," *Two Treatises*, p. 65. Elsewhere Locke expressed his fears in almost apocalyptic terms: "We have a war upon our hands of no small weight. We have a potent and vigilant enemy at our doors [who will] ... blow up any doubts or distrusts among us into disorder and confusion." If James were to return, "under what pretences soever, Jesuits must govern and France be our master." Farr and Roberts, "John Locke on the Glorious Revolution," p. 386.

Charles Tarlton argues that the real intention of the publication of the *Two Treatises* was not to criticize the absolutism of the Stuart kings but rather to communicate with the nascent government of William III, when a possibility of recidivism arose and when Locke feared that the new king was sliding toward the adoption of the Stuart way of monarchy. See C. Tarlton, "The Rulers Now on Earth: Locke's Two Treatises and the Revolution of 1688," *The Historical Journal* 28, 2 (1985), pp. 279–298.

[54] I have already discussed the intense academic debate that rages over precisely when Locke actually wrote the *Two Treatises*. See Chapter 1, *ft*. 3. What concerns us here is that Locke decided to publish the contents for the first time and in the order in which he did, immediately following the revolution.

[55] Locke, *Two Treatises*, p. 155.

CHRISTIANITY AND GOVERNMENTAL AUTHORITY
UP TO THE REFORMATION: MAJOR TRENDS

It is generally true that up to the beginning of the sixteenth century, Western Europe maintained a fine-weathered tradition in which religion and politics were interdependent. With the advent of the Protestant Reformation, though, this tradition was ruptured. The surge of new religious currents that the Reformation unleashed, together with the spread of Renaissance-induced secular rationalism, philosophy, and science, served to bifurcate the church-crown duality and challenge long-entrenched Catholic traditions. This evolving phenomenon turned the seventeenth century into a pivotal transitional period that shaped the future of the European continent and beyond. Political theorists of the era such as Locke wrote under the influence of the internecine struggles that the fissures in Christianity created. Theirs was a search for a new sociopolitical order.

The interrelatedness of Christianity and secular politics was always complex and took on different forms since the birth of Christianity and the advent of Christian power. Early Christians, who removed themselves from the heathen society surrounding them and kept away from all that seemed corrupt and hostile to God, had no interest in partaking of the mundane aspects of corporeal life such as the preoccupations with labor, trade, slave possession, and warfare. This climate of otherworldliness in which the here and now had little significance also affected attitudes toward the philosophy of government and its institutions.[56] A theological polar opposite of the classical Greek attitude toward the state emerged: rather than a promotional instrument of the good and virtuous civic life, the principal function of the state was seen as that of repression and retribution for human iniquity. There was certainly no religious obligation to participate in the state as it played no role in the salvation of humanity. This led to an attribution of irrelevance to the nature of government and to a de facto acceptance of even its most repressive forms. The view of political life of these early Christians was mirrored in the attitude articulated by Paul of Tarsus in which the requisite attitude of those ruled toward their government is made clear with religious clout:

---

[56] See Elazar, *Covenant & Commonwealth*, pp. 25–29. See also T. M. Parker, *Christianity and the State in Light of History* (London: Adam and Charles Black, 1955), pp. 18–19.

Let every soul be subject unto the higher powers. For there is no power but of God: the powers that be are ordained of God. Whosoever therefore resisteth the power, resisteth the ordinance of God: and they that resist shall receive to themselves damnation. For rulers are not a terror to good works, but to the evil. Wilt thou then not be afraid of the power? do that which is good, and thou shalt have praise of the same: For he is the minister of God to thee for good. But if thou do that which is evil, be afraid; for he beareth not the sword in vain: for he is the minister of God, a revenger to execute wrath upon him that doeth evil. Wherefore ye must needs be subject, not only for wrath, but also for conscience sake. For this cause pay ye tribute also: for they are God's ministers, attending continually upon this very thing. Render therefore to all their dues: tribute to whom tribute is due; custom to whom custom; fear to whom fear; honour to whom honour. Owe no man any thing, but to love one another: for he that loveth another hath fulfilled the law.[57]

Paul's incentive for advocating total political commitment, though, was not just theological; it had a practical political side as well. *Fear*, suggests S. S. Wolin, was a primary motivational factor. The early Christians realized that if they were to turn their backs on civic duties, no matter their moral substance, the order that held society together would unravel, leaving everyone vulnerable and the very agenda of the Church in jeopardy. This concern, Wolin argues, had a history prior to the advent of Christianity.

This belief, that the Roman Imperium was all that stood between civilization and anarchy, was not original with the early Christians. It formed, instead, a continuation of an old theme which had been prominent, for example in the literature of the Augustan age. Virgil, Horace, Tacitus, and, later, Seneca constantly invoked the frightened imagery of a tottering world whose sole salvation depended on the *providentia* of its ruler. The emperor came to be praised as the *restitutor orbis*, the rejuvenator of a dying system. Although the bitter rivalries among the political factions of the late republic undoubtedly contributed to these apprehensions and made men ready to reference authority, these tendencies were hurried along by the growing threat of barbarian pressures at the extremities of the Empire. The barbarian invasions shocked the Romans into fearful consciousness of an

---

[57] Romans 13:1–8. A similar indication of implicit New Testament tolerance for tyrannical rule can be found in Matthew 5:45: "God makes his sun to rise on the good and the evil." This kind of approach can be traced to Greek Epicureanism and Stoicism, philosophic trends preceding Paul, which promoted the idea that an individual can be self-sufficient, with little need for business interactions with the surrounding world. This concept was profoundly alien to earlier Greek thought. John Bowle, *Western Political Thought: A Historical Introduction from the Origins to Rousseau* (New York: University Paperbacks, 1961), p. 70.

"outside," of a restless and alien force, constantly probing for weakness and threatening to engulf the civilized world.[58]

There was an inherent tension, though, that no matter how latent couldn't be escaped. If the early Christians did not break with their Greek predecessors in their fear of anarchy, they most certainly did part ways when it came to an alternative rationale for political order; and in doing so they not only embraced an alternative society but actually insisted on its superiority by claiming its redemptive exclusivity.

The Christian ... could entertain meaningful doubts about political obligation and membership, because his response was not governed by a hard choice between membership in a political society and membership in no society at all. He could choose because already he belonged to a society that surpassed any existing one in the things that mattered most; he belonged to a society that was "an outpost of heaven."[59]

From a historical perspective, however, this tension was short-lived, as in the fourth century, Constantine (270–337 AD) became the first Roman emperor to embrace Christianity. This resulted in a complete overhaul of relations between Christianity and secular government. Being a *Christian* emperor, Constantine ushered a new political-religious coalition into Western European history, that of an alliance of the monarchical secular state system with the Christian Church.[60] This phenomenon is well depicted in the change Constantine made in the military oath of his soldiers, which included: *"By GOD, and CHRIST, and the HOLY GHOST, and the Majesty of the Emperor, which, next to GOD, ought to be loved and reverenced by Mankind."*[61] And to be sure, Church leaders saw Constantine's conversion clearly as a divine act intended to place Christianity in the seat of political power in order to further extend its reach.[62]

---

[58] S. S. Wolin, *Politics and Vision* (Princeton, NJ: Princeton University Press, 2004), p. 93.
[59] Ibid, p. 92. Wolin also points to the inescapable political dilemmas and processes within the Church itself. Decisions regarding schismatic groups, for example, were by nature dominated by political questions: to take an inclusive approach would mean the watering down of dogma, but to go the route of doctrinal purism meant to raise the requisite level of coercion. This is an example of what Wolin calls *primary conflicts* of the political realm. *Secondary conflicts* would include political issues such as the allocation of official positions and the disbursement of Church funds. See ibid, pp. 103–108.
[60] See Charles M. Odhal, *Constantine and the Christian Empire* (London: Routledge, 2004).
[61] Quoted by Grotius, *The Rights of War and Peace*, book I, chap. II; X, p. 233.
[62] Chadwick, *The Early Church*, p. 71.

This new alliance then catalyzed a dual historical metamorphosis from which hitherto unfamiliar tensions emerged. Christianity, originally predicated on exclusively spiritual ideas and pursuits, now evolved into a political religion governing the mundane and the terrestrial as well; in the hands of the Church government could no longer be seen as irrelevant to human salvation. At the same time, the body holding political power, which had previously been an earthly and irreligious institution, transfigured into a quasi-religious entity that made little distinction between the spiritual and the materialistic realms of life.[63]

In the fourth and fifth centuries, the power of the Roman Empire waned, and correlatively, the Church Fathers set about establishing the foundations of Christian belief. These two processes were the backdrop for the life and work of Augustine of Hippo (354–430 AD). St. Augustine presented a corpus of religious-political thought in his book *City of God* (*De Civitate Dei*), which was written during the years 413–427 AD following the march into Rome of the Visigoth King Alaric I (355–410 AD) and a hundred years after Constantine's conversion. Rome's defeat took place at a time when Augustine was pondering the reasons for the already divided Roman Empire (Rome and Byzantium), which was now crumbling under the pressure of the Goths, the Visigoths, the Vandals, the Picts, the Franks, and the Burgundians. For the North African Church Father, there was no doubt that the future of Roman culture depended on Christianity. In his eyes, the earthly city of Rome was a living hell filled with pride, lust, sin, and evil. Only the *City of God*, symbolized by Augustine as Biblical Jerusalem, which was concerned exclusively with belief in God and a Christian love of God, could survive to replace the lost city.[64]

In comparison to early Christian thought, there was an important development in Augustine's political theology. Like the early Christian founders, he viewed the need for social institutions as part of humankind's eternal punishment following original sin. For Augustine, a wicked or unjust ruler is as legitimate as one who is just, and most importantly,

---

[63] This process was temporarily impeded by the efforts of Julian the Apostate (361–363 AD) to have Rome revert back to its pagan roots. With the reign of Theodosius, who followed him to the throne, however, Christianity was elevated to the position of the official religion of Rome. See Samuel N. C. Lieu (ed.), *The Emperor Julian: Panegyric and Polemic* (Liverpool: Liverpool University Press, 1986), and Stephen Williams, *Theodosius: The Empire at Bay* (New Haven, CT: Yale University Press, 1994).

[64] St. Augustine, *City of God*.

temporal government qua government can never really be just.[65] Legitimate rulers and just governments are not terms relevant for humanity's fallen status. But at the same time, Augustine also believed, conversely, that there was an obligation for humans to do good in the here and now social and political frameworks. He argued that governmental institutions were important for preserving social order and keeping people secure, and hence brought with them a religious obligation to respect them. Even if earthly politics were temporary in a world that was waiting for the Kingdom of God, it was still important to maintain a positive attitude about these politics. Augustine's approach toward the role of Orthodox Christianity within the temporal setting created a new perspective on the fiction between asceticism and the pursuit of the Divine on the one hand, and the obligation to be involved in corporeal life on the other.[66]

This Augustinian development contained another dimension as well: because Christians believed that they had a mission to bring Christian love through conversion to all people, they came to understand, as did most followers of salvation movements throughout history, that this mission necessitated a structure of civil polity and political rules that could *compel* compliance. This was yet another step on the path that left behind the original climate of Christian otherworldliness and led to an ever-increasing involvement of the Church within the realms of authoritarian politics and government.[67] It became increasingly clear to Augustine that practicality required the enlisting of political power to advance Christianity's heavenly cause despite the inherent paradox. Augustine, explains S. S. Wolin, was pragmatic in making peace of these seemingly conflicting values.

To a surprising degree, Augustine rested the case for compulsion on pragmatic grounds. Since persuasion had proved unavailing in inducing the vast majority of men to enter the Church, sheer numbers could be brought in only by power, and hence the pragmatic test: did coercion in fact increase the number of Christians inside the Church?

This tough-minded view of power seems incongruous in the great exponent of Christian love. Yet the paradox is an important one, because it shaped a theory of power that has exerted a powerful influence in the West. Augustine consistently

---

[65] See extensive quotes in Deane, *The Political and Social Ideas of St. Augustine*, pp. 116–153.

[66] Robert A. Marcus, *History and Society in the Theology of St. Augustine* (Cambridge: Cambridge University Press, 1988). Henry Paolucci (ed.), *The Political Writings of St. Augustine* (Chicago, IL: Gateway, 1962).

[67] Elazar, *Covenant & Commonwealth*, pp. 34–35.

held that love and power were not of necessity mutually inconsistent: "righteous persecution" must be distinguished from "unrighteous persecution." Compulsion was righteously used when it was informed and motivated by a spirit of charity; to neglect those souls who had strayed from correct belief was greater cruelty than punishment, because it forever condemned them to darkness. "Terrible but salutary laws" administered in a "spirit of love," and a deep concern for the souls of others, took the stigma from power. In short, love dictated compulsion.[68]

The tensions that this duality fostered were an integral part of Christian thought for the millennia following Augustine and increased with the growth of the Church itself. It was Augustine's consolidation of Christian love and political power that medieval Popes would metamorphose into a theocratic theory of state and the leaders of the Reformation were to grapple with when political power was wrested from the Church a thousand years later.[69]

The centuries that passed during and after the decay of the Roman Empire saw the Church augment its economic, political, and cultural powers within the kingdoms of Western Europe. When Attila the Hun (434–453) attacked Italy in 451, it was not the weak Roman Emperor Aetius who set out to stop him, but the Pope, Leo the Great (440–461).[70] This was a clear indication that the days of the great Roman Empire were coming to an end and that a new power was emerging. As Augustine predicted in his *City of God*, only the Church had the vitality and the organizational power to take over the bankrupt society of decaying Rome.

From the ashes of the great empire, a number of smaller kingdoms emerged. The name Rome was now officially used only in the Eastern European Roman Empire of Byzantium, and it was mostly thanks to the spirit of Christianity that the culture that Rome established was preserved in Western Europe. The Church clergy touched the lives of people in

[68] Wolin, *Politics and Vision*, p. 107. On this, Augustine's fusion of love and coercion, Herbert A. Deane writes: "More terrible and less easy to understand than his change of attitude is his use of the doctrine of love in defense of the policy of coercion. To defend the Church's appeal to the State to punish heretics and schismatics by imprisonment, fines, and exile as a labor of love toward errant sinners, to argue for this policy on the basis of the analogy with a father's loving correction of his son, to speak of the successful results of the state's coercion as 'conquests of the Lord' – all these demonstrate the grim conclusions to which even a very wise man can be led by zeal for the promotion of orthodoxy." Deane, *The Political and Social Ideas of St. Augustine*, p. 220.
[69] Ibid, p. 215.
[70] For a detailed account of this encounter, see Patrick Howarth, *Attila, King of the Huns: The Man and the Myth* (London: Constable, 1994).

thousands of communities, bringing under their cloak most of the tribal populations throughout Western Europe. The form of Christianity that these new Christians took upon themselves was not the original limited humble practice of the first Christians who had no interest in monetary wealth and political power. Despite the rise of monasticism, Christianity by this time had drifted far away from its prototype religious world view regarding corporeal life and instead had become very involved in all issues of social concern.

Most Western European kings were Christians, but none of them brought cooperation and interdependence with the Papacy to such a high level as did the Carolingian Frankish rulers. When, on Christmas of 800 AD, Pope Leo III (795–816) first prostrated himself at the feet of Charlemagne (742–814), and then placed a crown on the head of the Frankish monarch, it became abundantly clear which power emerged predominant from the political-religious merger begun by Constantine. By making Charlemagne the successor of the ancient Caesars, Leo essentially laid the foundations of the Holy Roman Empire. Never before was the control of a great empire under such decisive Christian supervision, making it one of the greatest pushes forward Christianity would ever receive during its expansion throughout Europe.[71]

The Crusades of the eleventh through thirteenth centuries showed how deep the Church's influence had become on Western European modes of thinking. The clarion call of the different Popes to liberate the Holy Land fostered a strong Christian fellowship between different and sometimes hostile Western European kingdoms. The Crusades had quite a few motives, some political and some economic in nature, but it is of particular interest that leaders of the Christian faith had the power to inspire armies that operated thousands of miles away from home. It was a faith that was energized and augmented when wedded with political power. Centuries later, following the wane of Christian political power, Joseph Stalin would be able to derisively ask "how many divisions the pope had," but during the Crusades the Pope had the power to influence the

---

[71] Until that event, the Eastern Roman emperor residing in Constantinople had been recognized, even in Western Europe, as the holder of the highest secular office; with the coronation of Charlemagne and the subsequent weakened Papacy that changed as well. Constantinople tried for a time to hold on to its independent status, but twelve years later Charlemagne received the Byzantine acknowledgment of emperor he was looking for. See Matthias Becher, *Charlemagne* (New Haven, CT: Yale University Press, 2003), pp. 7–17, 95–97.

European political agenda in a profound way, as kings and armies did belong to the Pope in many respects.[72]

Many of the Popes of the Middle Ages, though, were not merely religious authorities that subdued monarchs, but were rather not far from being kings and emperors themselves. During the eighth century, an agreement with the Franks granted political independence to the Papacy, officially turning the Popes into heads of states with large armies under their command. With the passing of time, many of the Popes saw themselves as the leaders of a great international institution with absolute authority and total independence. This situation reached its zenith during the tenure of the thirteenth-century Pope Innocent III (1198–1216), who had extensive political control over Western Europe. Innocent described his office as one that is midway between God and mankind; he saw himself less than God but more than mankind, the judge of all people and judged by none.[73] This powerful Pope declared that it was his business to look after the interests of the Roman Empire, since the empire derived its origin and its final authority from the Papacy.[74]

Thomas Aquinas's contribution to the reconciliation of Greek philosophy and Christianity was mainly a philosophical effort, but it had political ramifications as well. Like Augustine, Aquinas posited that it was Adam's

---

[72] Holy war gradually became part of the papal program during the eleventh century when papal reformers tried to secure church autonomy by enforcing canonical rules. The opposition this engendered necessitated papal support for those who would physically ensure compliance. Such support necessitated a religious dimension as well in order to legitimate the enforcer's moral status; hence, the conflicts were called *bellum dei*, war of God. The Popes most responsible for this development were Leo IX (1048–1054) and Gregory VII (1073–1085). See Christopher Tyerman, *Gods War: A New History of the Crusades* (Cambridge, MA: Harvard University Press, 2006), pp. 44–51. Because of the power it wielded, crusading emerged as a papal instrument for intervention in the secular political world, even though its original purpose was ostensibly the liberation and defense of the Holy Land. See Peter Lock, *The Routledge Companion to the Crusades* (London: Routledge, 2006), pp. 289–306.

[73] See V. H. H. Green, *Renaissance and Reformation* (London: Edward Arnold, 1970), p. 15.

[74] Pope Innocent's political power was so robust that historians have dubbed him "the true emperor" (*versus imperator*): meaning, true heir to Emperor Henry VI, king of Germany and then the Holy Roman Empire, as opposed to Henry's son Frederick II. See Jane E. Sayers, *Innocent III: Leader of Europe, 1198–1216* (London: Longman, 1994), pp. 49–50. See also Brian Pavlac, "Emperor Henry VI (1191–1197) and the Papacy: Similarities with Innocent III's Temporal Policies," in *Pope Innocent III (1160–1216): To Root Up and to Plant*, John C. Moore (ed.) (Durham, NC: Ashgate Publishing Co., 1999), p. 266. Pavlac contends that Innocent III's political power overreached himself, and as a result of his secular politics the moral authority of the Church was weakened. Ibid, p. 268.

original sin and the resultant fall of humankind that necessitated political institutions and organized government. At the same time, though, he embraced the Aristotelian belief that the human being is a social animal and that the political state is a natural phenomenon that belongs to the eternal realm of reason. Aquinas agreed that although the Church was superior to all institutions, the secular down-to-earth governmental framework was important in its own right and should be viewed in a positive light. Aquinas did not challenge the notion of papal supremacy but did restate the Augustinian notion that Christianity was not a call exclusively for otherworldliness.[75]

Feudalism, the triangular social system with the emperor at the apex, had been one of the main political frameworks in Western European medievalism.[76] To the feudal system and its ruler, the medieval church offered a governmental framework based on the idea of a universal Christian commonwealth that included the social structure of the state (*regnum*) and the religious structure of the Church (*sacerdotium*), with the latter of superior stature, for it was considered the highest spiritual authority. The analogy was that of the sun and the moon: the Pope's light shined on the inferior satellite, the emperor.[77]

There were emperors, though, who did not accept the supreme power that the Popes demanded for themselves, and the conflict between the two sides led to some major rivalries. In England, for example, it led to the murder of the Archbishop of Canterbury Thomas Becket, by Henry II (1170).[78] On the continent, it led to such rivalries as those between King

---

[75] Brian Shanley, *The Thomist Tradition* (Boston, MA: Kluwer Academic Publishers, 2002), pp. 30–32, 101–102, 128–129. See also John Finnis, *Aquinas: Moral, Political, and Legal Theory* (Oxford: Oxford University Press, 1998).

[76] Clifford Backman asserts that, historically speaking, it is more correct to refer to this social framework in the medieval social setting as *feudal relations* rather than *feudalism*, because while stratified relations of mutual obligation and service evolved, they were not part of a cogent and conscious plan that the appellation *feudalism* requires. Clifford Backman, *The Worlds of Medieval Europe* (New York: Oxford University Press, 2003), pp. 220–225.

[77] Michael Curtis (ed.), *The Great Political Theories: From Plato and Aristotle to Locke and Montesquieu* (New York: Avon Books Division, 1961), p. 151. Yves Renouard explains how feudal structure was used by the Papacy to augment its power. "Papal sovereignty was reinforced by the whole system of feudal submission of vassal kingdoms to the Holy See, which was further developed by Innocent III in an attempt to build up Christendom into a sort of feudal pyramid with the pope at its head and the various kings bound to him by personal oaths of loyalty." Yves Renouard, *The Avignon Papacy 1305–1403*, Denis Bethell (trans.) (London: Faber and Faber, 1970), p. 124.

[78] Becket was actually murdered by a mob at the instigation of Henry. The two had been longtime friends, and it was Henry who appointed Becket Archbishop of Canterbury. (This, despite the fact that Becket had been a fighter, leading men in bloody battles with the

Henry IV and Pope Gregory VII (eleventh century),[79] King Frederick Barbarossa and Pope Alexander III,[80] Frederick II and Pope Innocent IV (twelfth century),[81] King Philip IV and Pope Boniface VIII (thirteenth century),[82] and King Louis IV and Popes Clement V, John XXII, and Clement VI (fourteenth century).[83] These conflicts demonstrated that the political power of the Church could be challenged and sometimes even

French.) Becket, though, was of an independent mind, and an unbridgeable divide developed between the two over questions of superiority. This led to charges of treachery against Becket, which culminated in his murder in the Canterbury Cathedral. Pope Alexander III, who was anxious about Becket's increasing independence (from Rome as well as from Henry, who was loyal to Rome), supported Henry in confrontation with Becket, but bestowed him with sainthood nonetheless following the murder. William Urry, *Thomas Becket: His Last Days*, with an introduction by Peter A. Rowe (ed.) (Gloucestershire: Sutton Publishing Ltd., 1999), esp. pp. 1–30, 127–149. For further reading, see Frank Barlow, *Thomas Becket* (Berkeley, CA: University of California Press, 1990), and David Knowles, *Archbishop Thomas Becket: A Character Study* (Oxford: Oxford University Press, 1970). In an interesting side note: when Becket was appointed archbishop he recruited a body of *eruditi* as "headquarters staff." Chief among them was John of Salisbury, who in his *Politicraticus* justified organized political opposition to illegitimate monarchy, forcing policies on the throne that culminated in the issuance of the Magna Carta. This makes him a precursor of Locke's theory of just rebellion. Urry, *Thomas Becket*, p. 8.

[79] Henry IV initially refused to accept the legitimacy of Gregory's election to the pontificate, recognizing instead an anti-Pope. Gregory in turn excommunicated the king, depriving him of his royal authority. Realizing he had overstepped the limitations of his power, Henry traveled to the Pope, who was residing at a castle in Canossa, to beg for forgiveness and absolution. After he kept the king waiting, barefoot in the snow, for three days, the Pope granted the desired absolution and revoked the excommunication. But it was Henry who had the last word, when he later stormed Rome, deposed and exiled Gregory, and appointed his anti-Pope in Gregory's stead. Brian Tierney, *The Crisis of Church and State 1050–1300* (Englewood Cliffs, NJ: Prentice-Hall, Inc., 1964), pp. 53–57.

[80] Frederick, like Henry IV before him, refused to recognize Alexander's election as Pontiff and supported the claims of an anti-Pope instead. When Frederick's military campaigns against the Pope's supporters proved fruitless, he acquiesced, and in the Peace of Venice accepted the Papacy of Alexander III. Ibid, pp. 110–111.

[81] In this papal-monarchical confrontation, legitimacy of papal election was not a factor. Frederick II recognized Innocent's legitimacy but rejected his right to limit the physical boundaries of his kingdom, which Innocent, on the other hand, was convinced was included in his purview. Here too the Pope's persistence paid off, as he gained supremacy by not allowing Frederick a military victory, and by outliving him. Ibid, pp. 140–141.

[82] See *ft.* 87.

[83] Louis IV was known as the "uncrowned" Holy Roman Emperor because Clement V and his successor John XXII refused to approve his election (he was elected because his predecessor's son, John of Luxembourg, was still a child). Louis set up an anti-Pope, Nicholas V, in retaliation, and was later deposed by the next Pope, Clement VI. Louis received support from Marsilius of Padua (circa 1275–circa 1342) through his important work *Defensor pacis* and from William of Ockham. www.britannica.com/EBchecked/topic/348803/Louis-IV.

defeated. What is important to remember, though, is that the real issue at the heart of all these titanic struggles was the source and legitimacy of political power.[84]

During the fourteenth and fifteenth centuries the Papacy fell on hard times. Critically popular movements that challenged the Church, such as the Lollardy in England and the Hussites in Bohemia, opposed the terrestrially focused, politically powerful, monetarily rich, and, by now, morally corrupt Church.[85] Subsequently, the Avignon Papacy (1305–1378) and the Great Schism (1378–1417) threatened to split the Church apart, and the great power that controlled Europe for hundreds of years began to lose power.[86]

---

[84] Curtis, *The Great Political Theories*, pp. 166–170.

[85] "Lollardy" began in the 1370s as a set of beliefs held by Oxford-trained clerics who were keenly interested in the teachings of John Wycliffe; they attacked clerical celibacy, indulgences, and pilgrimages. The Lollardys probably owed their appellation to the Dutch word Lollard, meaning a mumbler of prayers. Anne Hudson, *The Premature Reformation: Wycliffite Texts and Lollard History* (Oxford: Oxford University Press, 1988). Alister McGrath attributes the spurring of the English Reformation to the Lollardy movement. The Lollardys wanted the Bible available to every layperson in the vernacular, opposed the excessive authority of the Pope, and rejected the doctrine of transubstantiation. Alister E. McGrath, *Reformation Thought: An Introduction*, 3rd Edition (Oxford: Blackwell Publishers, Ltd., 1988, 1993, 1999), p. 36. The Hussites, who fought for reforms in the Catholic Church, for the advancement of social issues, and for Czech nationalism, followed the teachings of the reformer Jan Hus (1369–1415), who was himself influenced by John Wycliffe. Jiri Kejr, *The Hussite Revolution* (Orbis Press Agency: Prague, 1988).

[86] The Papacy of Avignon was the result of a harsh quarrel over temporal supremacy between King Philip IV (the Fair) of France and Pope Boniface VIII. Before Boniface could excommunicate him, the king arrested the Pope by force. He was quickly released due to public pressure, but the toll had been taken and the Pope died a few weeks later. As a result, a Papacy was established in Avignon, France that lasted from 1305 to 1378, in which seven Popes, all French, served under secular monarchical French domination. Philip's actions resonated throughout Europe, as the subordination of papal power to temporal power had lasting ramifications on the nature of political power as whole. "Philip the Fair brutally called the whole system into question when he attacked Boniface VIII ... The King of France had vindicated the temporal authority of the princes of Europe; he had claimed to speak in the name of the faith itself when he accused Boniface of heresy." Renouard, *The Avignon Papacy*, p. 124. For a detailed account of the Crusades during the Avignon Papacy, see Norman Housley, *The Avignon Papacy and the Crusades, 1305–1378* (Oxford: Clarendon Press, 1986). As for the "Great Schism": after the Papacy returned from Avignon to Rome in 1378 it split again over rival papal claims, with the followers of Clement VII challenging Urban VI and breaking away to the city of Anagni while reestablishing the Avignon Papacy. This schism ended with the Council of Constance, which formally made the emperor the Pope's superior; claims for the totality of the unassailable rights of the Vicar of Christ would no longer be relevant. Renouard, *The Avignon Papacy*, p. 131.

The decline of the Church's power by the end of the Middle Ages is explained in the classical theory of the English historian Richard W. Southern.[87] According to Southern, the Church had grown into a powerful international corporation with the Pope's power emanating from his unique persona, which symbolized a holy representative of God on earth, coupled with the status of the ultimate all-powerful mortal king and supreme judge. The irony of history is that the overwhelming political power, gained by the Church with its Pope at the helm, was exactly the factor that, in a kind of imperial overstretch, led to its collapse. In the eyes of the common believers, the Church's authority had divine and mystical roots, but the simple truth was that its practical power and authority were achieved through political agreements based on compromises between the Church and many local authorities throughout Europe. The local authorities did not have sufficient power to rule without the Church's spiritual legitimization, and, concomitantly, the Church depended on the cooperation of the local ruling systems to guarantee day-to-day social and economic stability. This mutually beneficial agreement, with its theoretical roots in Augustinian synergy, was a down-to-earth, realistic, and practical political system cloaked in supernatural and holy disguise. Alister McGrath emphasizes, in addition, the rise of anti-clericalism and doctrinal pluralism that preceded the Reformation, the result of a deficient clergy and a more educated laity that saw a growing disparity between what the Church was and what it could be. The Pope could not implement reform because of his enervated stature, and the secular authority that continued to grow in strength assumed responsibility for ecclesiastical matters as well.[88]

From the fourteenth through the sixteenth centuries the feudal system was fading away as far-reaching social changes were taking place in Europe. Population growth, coupled with the expanding metropolitan centers based on commercial trade, paved the way for the introduction of much more independent, non-clerical local governmental authorities. These secular authorities, whose activities laid the basis for the first national European states, were growing rich and powerful and were no

---

[87] R. W. Southern, *The Making of the Middle Ages* (New Haven, CT: Yale University Press, 1961). R. W. Southern, *Western Society and the Church in the Middle Ages* (New York: Penguin Books, 1970).

[88] McGrath, *Reformation Thought*, pp. 26–35. For an example of the doctrinal pluralism that preceded the Reformation, McGrath cites the great divide between the rationalist school of Thomas Aquinas and the voluntarist school of John Duns Scotus.

longer in need of the Church's support. They soon challenged the Church's unlimited political power, and, as a result, the Church started to lose its exclusive governing role.[89] The most salient example of this new willingness to challenge Church authority is undoubtedly Henry VIII's struggles with the Papacy over the issue of his divorce from Catherine of Aragon, which ultimately resulted in the official break with Rome and the establishment of the Church of England.

The Renaissance also contributed to the deterioration of Church power. It is interesting to note that the term *Renaissance* was not used prior to 1835 to denote an era in European history. In fact, the people living in Italy during the fifteenth century had no idea that they were participating in one of the most pivotal periods in Western history. But it was, nevertheless, a time in which the arts flourished and many Europeans reclaimed the long lost cultural treasures of ancient Greece and Rome. Christian holy politics fell under serious attack as human reason and the pursuit of knowledge turned primarily to Greek philosophy for inspiration in order to try and master the art of government and proper social organization.[90]

A good example of the new Renaissance attitude toward Christian politics can be found in Niccolo Machiavelli's *The Prince*. Machiavelli (1469–1527), the Italian political philosopher who played a significant role in the war between the Florence city republic (which he served) and the Medici family, was one of the most important Renaissance writers to lead an assault on Christianity and, more specifically, Christian politics. Because of his for-the-time iconoclastic ideas, Machiavelli was imprisoned and tortured by his opponents. In his short book *The Prince*, which was published five years after his death and has won significant popularity ever since, Machiavelli searched for a practical governmental structure in which the supreme goal of the head of state was to maintain his own authority. He believed that the use of power by a head of state – including the use of violence when necessary – was a legitimate means of maintaining this authority. In doing so he shifted away from the Christian concept of "pure goodness," arguing instead that there is a much thinner line between good and evil than is generally understood and that definitions

[89] For a thorough analysis of the important thinkers during this period who challenged the notion of unlimited papal power, see Skinner, *The Foundations of Modern Political Thought*, pp. 20–64.
[90] Green, *Renaissance and Reformation*, p. 29. See also Levi Anthony, *Renaissance and Reformation: The Intellectual Genesis* (New Haven, CT: Yale University Press, 2002).

depend entirely on the circumstances in which they are observed. Only one thing can define any deed as good or evil, cruel or compassionate: Did it or did it not help the prince to maintain his authority?[91] Machiavelli criticized the Church as an antiquated and politically deleterious organization, which, he argued, was a historical burden on the way a governmental system was to operate. But his criticism was far less radical than that of a contemporary recusant German priest, which followed.

THE REFORMATION: FROM RELIGIOUS TO POLITICAL REBELLION

When Martin Luther (1483–1546) nailed his list of ninety-five theses to the door of Wittenberg Castle in 1517, calling out the Church on what he saw as its theological errors and institutional iniquities, he unleashed what would come to be known as the Protestant Reformation, a movement that quickly tore apart the already disintegrating Church/state relationship within Europe. The Reformation was a direct response to the religious, political, and financial corruption that had spread unabated in the Roman Church, and its aftershock affected almost every aspect of European life. To be sure, the Reformation was rebellion against a religious order, but because that order was so politically entrenched its effects on governmental structure were no less dramatic. The modern world was born as politics, foreign affairs, economics, societal norms, and communal cohesion would never and could never be the same again.[92]

The old Roman-Christian alliance had granted the Church a status of supreme spiritual and political power. The Popes represented God, and while they were supposedly above all temporal issues, they did not let go of their earthly political power. They demanded that Europeans live in accordance with the teachings of Christianity and, at the same time, demanded obedience from all the kings of Western Europe. The Papacy, then, was the highest authority governing European life, and in many respects the only such authority. Whatever the drawbacks this arrangement may have presented, it was *the* millennia-plus political paradigm that provided certainty and stability to the people of Europe. The

[91] Niccolo Machiavelli, *The Prince*, William J. Connell (ed. and trans.) (Boston, MA: Bedford St. Martin's, 2005).
[92] See Steven Ozment, *The Age of Reform: An Intellectual and Religious History of Late Medieval and Reformation Europe* (New Haven, CT and London: Yale University Press, 1980), pp. 182–222.

subsequent political and social instability that ensued was twofold. First, long lasting imperial-Christian unity was fissured by an alternative and inviting religious credo, and, second, this credo had to identify what the new nature of political power should be.

During the first few decades after Luther's dramatic move against the Pope, Protestant beliefs spread swiftly throughout Europe, as leaders of the Lutheran movement quickly allied themselves with the strands of opposition to papal pretensions of absolutism that were already in existence. Quentin Skinner writes that:

The emphasis which the early Lutherans placed on their continuities with this historical background can be shown to have played a definite role in helping to further the cause of their own reform movement. For their propaganda helped to encourage most of the surviving Lollard and Hussite communities to link up with the wider movement of the Reformation, a development which in turn helped to widen the basis of its support and in this way to increase its influence.[93]

For millions of new Protestants in Germany, Switzerland, France, Bohemia, and the Scandinavian Kingdoms, the Pope was no longer the supreme power, neither in the realm of religion, nor in politics. The old combination of Christianity and empire forged by Constantine suddenly collapsed, and a new paradigm to explain government and the source of its legitimate power was required. The question that needed answering was: Now that the Pope is no longer the highest authority in the land, from where does the authority of government issue?[94] Luther, and most of the early reformers, followed Augustine in the belief that secular political government had a religious justification: keeping order and preventing chaos, for the sake of Christian love. Disobedience is then unthinkable iniquity. Philipp Melanchthon (who through his educational reforms of schools and universities earned the title Praeceptor Germaniae, "teacher of Germany")[95] wrote, for example: "deliberate disobedience against the worldly authority, and against true or reasonable laws, is deadly sin, sin which God punishes with eternal damnation if we

---

[93] Skinner, *The Foundations of Modern Political Thought*, pp. 49–50.
[94] Owen Chadwick, *The Reformation: The Pelican History of the Church* (London: Penguin Books, 1966), pp. 391–397.
[95] Sachiko Kusukawa, "Melanchthon," in *The Cambridge Companion to Reformation Theology*, David Bagchi and David C. Steinmetz (eds.) (Cambridge: Cambridge University Press, 2004), p. 57.

obstinately continue it."[96] Although he was to change his opinion in the early 1530s, initially Luther even supported a theory that held that the sovereign has the duty to maintain the true religion by force. In all instances as far as he was concerned, there was no place for disobedience toward government, even if the source and nature of its power are secular.[97] Skinner writes of Luther's secular political empowerment that:

Luther's theological premises not only committed him to attacking the jurisdictional powers of the Church, but also of filling the power-vacuum this created by mounting a corresponding defence of the secular authorities. He first of all sanctioned an unparalleled extension of the range of their powers. If the Church is nothing more than a *congregatio fidelium*, it follows that the secular authorities must have the sole right to exercise all coercive powers, including powers over the Church.[98]

Almost a generation after Luther, Calvin too saw the possibility of some elements of God's kingdom in the non-clerical political framework. He initially believed that the Church and the civil government were separate powers, but in a theoretical slide back to pre-Reformation governmental structures, he argued that they still had an obligation to exist in harmony for the sake of social order and the glory of God. Functionally, this meant the abandonment of any attempt to distinguish between secular and spiritual matters, putting immense power in the hands of the magistrate.[99] Under the strict leadership of Calvin in Geneva, the

[96] Phillipp Melanchthon, "Common Topics in Theology," in *Melanchthon on Christian Doctrine*, Clyde L. Manschreck (ed. and trans.) (New York: Oxford University Press, 1965), p. 333.

[97] See James Martin Estes, *Peace, Order and the Glory of God: Secular Authority and the Church in the Thought of Luther and Melanchthon 1518–1559* (Leiden: Brill, 2005), and Harro Hopfl (ed.), *Luther and Calvin on Secular Authority* (Cambridge: Cambridge University Press, 1991), pp. ix–xxiii.

[98] Skinner, *The Foundations of Modern Political Thought*, pp. 14–15. Alister McGrath sees a connection between Luther's deficiencies in political theory and his deference to secular authority. "Luther was no political thinker, and his limited and deficient experiments in this field are best regarded as an attempt to accommodate himself to the political realities of his time. For the consolidation of the German Reformation, the full support of the German princes and magistrates was essential. Luther appears to have been prepared to lend these rulers religious dignity in return for their continued support for the Reformation. The end justified the means. Luther appealed to a specific power group; but had a different group held political power, he would almost certainly have appealed to that group instead and justified *its* existence." McGrath, *Reformation Thought*, p. 227.

[99] "Just as Luther inclined to the providentialist view that Romans 13 refers to whomever we find equipped with power, and that Christians have no business curiously inspecting the titles of those they find in authority, so did Calvin." Hopfl, *Luther and Calvin on Secular Authority*, p. xxi. Because of his unwavering commitment to remodeling the

Calvinistic movement drew larger and larger numbers of adherents even though it was a new system based on severe discipline and obedience that maintained thorough control over the life of every man and woman. For a short while then in the heart of Europe, governmental rule was completely in the hands of a religious authority, with no significant interference by a secular power.[100] Conversely, there were radical circles within the Protestant movement, such as the Anabaptists, no less committed to Biblical literalism, which allowed for no connection between religious covenant and political institution, and actively militated against any attempt to create such a religious-political affiliation; theirs was an attempt to practice the original ancient Christian formula.[101]

The approaches of Luther and Calvin to the question of political power left behind a Central European legacy of religious patriarchal society and unchallenged all-powerful government. This Protestant-caused attenuation of a Church-dominated government transformed the structure of government into something new, but it was very different from the more liberal ethos presented by the Protestant Whigs who lived in England almost one hundred years later. Alister McGrath argues that the differences rest in how the English Reformation distinguished itself from the Reformation on the continent, and makes two important observations in this regard. First, whereas the continental reformers turned to secular rulers for added authority to their ecclesiastical cause, in England it was the secular ruler (Henry VIII) who established the reformed Church of England to begin with. Second, having been established by the king,

---

world to conform to theological certainties, Calvin went beyond Luther, and came to accept only that form of government that furthered that goal, creating a revolutionary fervor unique to Calvinism. This process is best explained by Michael Walzer, *The Revolution of the Saints: A Study in the Origins of Radical Politics* (New York: Atheneum, 1968), especially pp. 58–59. Similarly, G. P. Gooch writes: "as we trace the development of the theory and practices of resistance ... we shall convince ourselves that, despite his guarded reservations, the teaching of Calvin ... made steadily for popular right." Gooch, *English Democratic Ideas in the Seventeenth Century*, p. 7. The issue of resistance will be discussed at length in Chapter 6.

[100] Philip Benedict, *Christ's Churches Purely Reformed* (New Haven, CT: Yale University Press, 2002), pp. 82–109. Ronald Stewart Wallace, *Calvin, Geneva, and the Reformation: A Study of Calvin as Social Reformer, Churchman Pastor and Theologian* (Edinburgh: Scottish Academic Press, 1988). Elazar, *Covenant & Commonwealth*, pp. 149–150.

[101] Michael Heyd, "Charisma and Establishment: The Crises of the Reformation and Its Influence on the Church-State Relationship," in *Priesthood and Monarchy: Studies in the Historical Relationships of Religion and State*, Isaiah Gafni and Gabriel Motzkin (eds.) (Jerusalem: The Zalman Shazar Center For Jewish History, 1987), pp. 149–163 [Hebrew].

fundamental theological issues were less important for the English Reformation because the Anglican Church had no need to define itself in opposition to Rome. Conversely, in Germany, for example, the Lutheran Church "was obliged to define and defend its existence and boundaries at the level of religious ideas because it had broken away from the medieval Catholic church – a church which continued to exist around Lutheran regions, forcing Lutheranism to carry on justifying its existence by defending its ideas."[102]

In the meantime, the ineluctable fact was that the Holy Roman Empire, which dated back to the Charlemagne–Pope Leo III entente in the year 800 AD, was torn apart during the powerful religious earthquake that stretched across Western Europe during the Reformation and transformed the empire into a patchwork of Catholic, Lutheran, Anabaptist, and Calvinist areas of dominance.[103] It did not take long for wars to erupt, tainting the continent with violence for decades. These internecine hostilities always had political and economic antecedents to them, but the seemingly endless intracontinental bloodshed was primarily a result of incendiary religious antagonisms.[104]

The longest and most destructive of these wars of religion was the Thirty Years' War, which persisted from 1618 to 1648 as a continent-wide clash involving Germany, Bohemia, Sweden, France, Spain, England, Hungary, and Denmark, and which reduced the population of Central Europe by an estimated 30 percent.[105] The reasons behind this

---

[102] McGrath, *Reformation Thought*, p. 22.

[103] In 1512 the name officially adopted for the empire was the Holy Roman Empire of the German Nation, which unraveled only in 1806 during the Napoleonic wars. See Peter H. Wilson, *The Holy Roman Empire, 1495–1806* (London: Macmillan Press, 1999), pp. 2, 17.

[104] The Religious Peace of Augsburg, accepted as law of the empire in 1555, defused post-Reformation religious tensions by recognizing Protestantism as one of the two religions (in addition to Roman Catholicism) that could be practiced in Germany. But the recognition was not individualistic, as it granted religious toleration only to princes and estates, with the inhabitants of specific principalities left with the choice of accepting the local ruler's confessional choice, or emigrating. This was not a situation conducive to long-term political calm and stability. In addition, with both denominations still wedded to the idea of an exclusive ecclesiastical truth, local political disputes could not remain separated from political problems of the empire. Tensions simmered in the beginning of the seventeenth century and finally erupted in Germany in 1618, then spreading throughout most of the Holy Roman Empire. See Ronald Asch, *The Thirty Years War: The Holy Roman Empire and Europe, 1618–1648* (New York: St. Martin, 1997), pp. 9–17.

[105] Historians have set the 30% mark as a rough average, but it was probably closer to 40%. The carnage ravaged more than two-thirds of the territory controlled by the Holy

drawn-out campaign were many, but it primarily involved a great cataclysm between Catholics and Protestants over political power. The Peace of Westphalia that was signed in 1648 put an end to the carnage by recognizing the legitimacy of diverse forms of religious worship, and by delineating more defined areas of national jurisdiction based on the population's religious persuasion, which in effect determined the political borders of the emergent European nations. Westphalia was incorporated by virtually all European powers, making it the fundamental law of the empire (still the Holy Roman Empire) and a central element of the European system of states.[106]

But Westphalia did not provide an answer to the cardinal question regarding the source of political authority within European states.[107] And so, Europe found itself in a state of transitional crisis due to the civil strife and political confusion that escorted the collapse of Catholic control and the emergence of many different religious currents that engulfed Europe with the violence that ensued. This demanded that new ways of thinking about the relationship between religion and politics emerge and that political thinkers of the age meet the challenge.

The main questions they addressed were: How and why could there be peace and order? What are the source and nature of authority? What are the roles of states, kings, and governors? What is a citizen? What is the proper relationship between public and private spheres? Can the authorities take their denizens' lives? Can the authorities force citizens to fight wars? Do the authorities enjoy executive privileges that other individuals do not? Should there be a state at all?[108] The responses that these thinkers provided to these questions formed the bases of their political philosophies.

It is worthy of particular note that many of these political thinkers suffered personally during this period of crisis. Grotius's *Rights of War and Peace* was published while he was in exile in Paris, and Hobbes's

---

Roman Empire, with Germany sustaining the worst devastation. In some parts of Germany, the northeastern areas in particular, the loss of the prewar population went as high as 60% and 70%, and it took more than a hundred years for most areas to regain their prewar population, for some, three hundred years. The devastating economic effects of such severe population loss were also protracted. Ibid, pp. 185–186.

[106] The exception was the Pope (Innocent X), who forcefully rejected the peace because of what he thought were excessive concessions to the Protestants. Ibid, p. 148.

[107] Ibid, pp. 134–149. See also Henry Kissinger, *Diplomacy* (New York: Simon & Schuster, 1994), pp. 21, 65, 68.

[108] See Harrison, *Hobbes, Locke and Confusion's Masterpiece*, pp. 7–42.

Leviathan was also written while he was in his Parisian exile. Pufendorf read Hobbes and Grotius while imprisoned by the Danes. John Milton went into hiding after the Restoration, was later imprisoned, and narrowly escaped the death penalty. Algernon Sidney was not as lucky, and was executed for his political beliefs. And, John Locke was forced to spend considerable time on the run in Holland as a result of his political activity, fearing for his life even in exile. His theoretical approach then to the notion of rebellion was born in the practical realm and it is a direct extension of his Hebraic understanding of what legitimate government is and is not.

LOCKE'S CONCEPT OF REBELLION, FROM PERSONAL PRACTICE TO GENERAL THEORY

Prudence, indeed, will dictate that Governments long established should not be changed for light and transient causes; and accordingly all experience hath shewn, that mankind are more disposed to suffer, while evils are sufferable, than to right themselves by abolishing the forms to which they are accustomed. (From the American Declaration of Independence)

Having defined the human state of nature and the incontrovertibility of the law of nature, in the first part of the *Second Treatise*, Locke proceeded to his conclusive and primary agenda: the justification and legitimation of rebellion in the face of egregious governmental abuse. In the second part of the *Second Treatise* Locke describes how and why a political society can deteriorate into tyranny and why every individual of that society has the right, indeed obligation, to rebel against it.

In Locke's political world view, the foundational idea of an established political society fully emerged from the state of nature is *consent*. Primordially, individuals are in a state of nature in which they are not subject to any central authority with political power. This elemental state of human affairs metamorphoses, and civil society develops with the creation of a voluntary mechanism of consent that joins individuals together in political society. Locke asserts that, "Politick Societies all began from a voluntary Union, and the mutual agreement of Men freely acting in the choice of their Governours, and forms of Government."[109] And, "the *Governments* of the World, that were begun in Peace, had their beginning laid on that foundation, and were *made by the consent of the people*."[110] And

---

[109] II, 102, p. 353.   [110] II, 104, p. 354.

again, "the beginning of *Politick Society* depends upon the consent of the Individuals to join into and make one society."[111]

In the *First Treatise*, Locke has already hinted at the fact that ultimate political power rests with the people as a result of their consent, and he turned to the Hebrew Bible for proof. In his broadside against the Filmerian notion that every king is naturally entitled to the absolutism that Adamic paternal authority supposedly brings, Locke refers the reader to the last three chapters of the Book of Judges, to the story of Benjamites and the concubine of Giv'a, where "the *Levite* appeals to the People for Justice; that it was the Tribes and the Congregation, that debated, resolved, and directed all that was done on the occasion."[112] In the *Second Treatise* consent becomes a cornerstone of his political theory, the mainstay of political power; sometimes popular consent is mistakenly ignored, but, Locke contends, it can fundamentally never be discarded.

Though Governments can originally have no other Rise than that beforementioned, nor *Politics* be *founded* on any thing but *the Consent of the People*; yet such have been the Disorders Ambition has fill'd the World with, that in the noise of War, which makes so great a part of the History of Mankind, this *Consent* is little taken notice of: And therefore many have mistaken the force of Arms, for the consent of the People; and reckon Conquest as one of the Originals of Government. But *conquest* is as far from setting up any Government as demolishing an House is from building a new one in the place. Indeed, it often makes way for a new Frame of a Commonwealth by destroying the former, but, without the **Consent of the people,** can never erect a new one.[113]

For no Government can have a right to obedience from a people who have not **freely consented** to it: which they can never be supposed to do, till either they are put in a full state of Liberty to choose their Government and Governors, or at least till they have such standing laws, to which they have by themselves or their Representatives given, their free consent.[114] (Emphasis added.)

---

[111] II, 106, p. 355.   [112] See I, 164–165, pp. 278–279.   [113] II, 175, pp. 402–403.

[114] II, 192, p. 412. The author of the anonymously published text *Vindiciae, Contra Tyrannos*, which carries many Hebraic references and which I will suggest later had an important influence on Locke and his theory of rebellion, refers to *consent* as "constitution by the people." "[T]he people constitutes kings, confers kingdoms, and approves the election by its vote [*suffragio*]. Indeed, God willed that it should be done in this way, so that whatever authority and power they have, should be received from the people after Him; and that thus they would apply all their care, thought, and effort to the welfare of the people [*utilitas populi*]. Nor would they consider themselves to preside over other men by some excellence of nature, as men do with sheep or cattle. Rather, they should remember that they are born entirely by the same lot as other men, and they are elevated from the ground to their positions by the votes and, as it were, on the shoulders of the people, in order that the burdens of the commonwealth should henceforth, for the most part, rest on their shoulders." The author's proofs of the

The stability and permanence of the political society, the "one body Politick," depend on the consent of every individual, i.e., his or her obligation to the government.[115] Hence, emphasizes Locke, if this condition comes to an end, so too is the legitimacy of government terminated. This happens when a government that is "limited to the natural good and preservation of society"[116] enslaves or plunders its citizens, turning it into a tyranny. Locke defines tyranny as "the exercise of Power beyond Right, which no body can have a Right to. And this is making use of the Power any one has in his hands, not for the good of those, who are under it, but for his own private separate Advantage."[117] According to Locke, "tyranny begins were law ends,"[118] and because the tyrant does not enjoy the consent of the people, he does not have the right or the authority to harm his subjects; if he does, they have the right to oppose him.[119] This natural right to opposition means that ultimate political authority belongs to the people.

necessity of such a "constitution" are examples taken from the Hebrew Bible: first and foremost the divine command to Moses to appoint a king upon entering the promised land *after the people demand it* – "Let me constitute a king over myself, like the other nations round about," "that his heart be not lifted above his brethren" (Deuteronomy 17:15–20) – Samuel's anointment of Saul and then David; the coronation of Solomon; and the appointment of Rehoboam as well as the kings who followed. George Garnett (ed.), *Vindiciae, Contra Tyrannos* (Cambridge: Cambridge University Press, 1994), pp. 68–71.

H. J. Laski and George Garnett, both editors of modern *Vindiciae* editions, favor the theory that the book was a collaborative effort between Hubert Languet and Philip de Mornay (the Huguenot "Pope"). Michael Walzer contends that the "Calvinist spirit" that "pervades the whole book" suggests a single author, and "for convenience' sake" credits De Mornay as the sole author. See *Vindiciae contra Tyrannos* (org. published 1576; English ed. 1689; repr. with intro. by H. J. Laski, New York: n.d.), pp. 71ff; Garnett (ed.), *Vindiciae, Contra Tyrannos*, pp. lv–lxxvi; and Walzer, *The Revolution of the Saints*, p. 80, ft. 35. In the Garnett edition the word *Vindiciae* is followed by a comma and all three words are capitalized. In the Laski edition the "c" of *contra* is left lowercase and no comma follows *Vindiciae*. V. H. H. Green attributes authorship exclusively to Hubert Languet and has all first letters capitalized with no comma following *Vindiciae*. A French edition of Librairie Droz Genève (1797) capitalizes only the "V" of *Vindiciae*, leaving "c" and "t" lowercase, and has no comma following *Vindiciae*. Here I follow the Garnett edition as it is the most recent.

[115] II, 97–99, pp. 350–351. In what is a relatively lengthy piece at the end of the Fourth Dialogue in his *Court Maxims*, Algernon Sidney also predicates the legitimacy of monarchical rule on public consent, basing it on an analysis of the Israelite leaders as described in the Hebrew Bible. See Sidney, *Court Maxims*, pp. 55–65. Earlier, Sidney wrote that there is no better source from which to draw guidance on the subject of legitimate and illegitimate government than the Hebrew Bible. Ibid, p. 39.

[116] II, 135, p. 376.   [117] II, 199, pp. 416–417.   [118] II, 202, p. 418.
[119] Ibid, pp. 418–419.

Though in a Constituted Commonwealth, standing upon its own Basis, and acting according to its own Nature, that is, acting for the preservation of the Community, there can be but *one Supream Power*, Which is *the Legislative*, to which all the rest are and must be subordinate, yet the Legislative being only a Fiduciary Power to act for certain ends, there remains still *in the People a Supream Power* to remove or *alter the Legislative*, when they find that the Legislative act contrary to the **trust** reposed in them.[120] (Emphasis added.)

The idea of *trust* is thematic in Locke's concluding chapters as it provides the basis for *consent*; consent is a natural extension and concomitant of trust.

[A]nother way whereby *governments are dissolved*, and that is; when the Legislative, or the Prince, either of them, act contrary to their **Trust** ... The *legislative acts against the **Trust*** reposed in them, when they endeavour to invade the Property of the Subject, and to make themselves, or any part of the Community, Masters or Arbitrary Disposers of the Lives, Liberties, or Fortunes of the People.[121] (Emphasis added.)

Whensoever, therefore, the *Legislative* shall transgress this fundamental Rule of Society; and either by Ambition, Fear, Folly, or Corruption, *endeavour to grasp* themselves, *or put into the hands of any other, an Absolute Power* over the Lives, Liberties, and Estates of the People; By this **breach of Trust** they *forfeit the Power*, the People had put into their hands, for quite contrary ends, and it devolves to the People, who have a Right to resume their original Liberty, and by the Establishment of a new Legislative (such as they shall think fit) provide for their own Safety and Security, which is the end for which they are in Society ... To prepare such an Assembly as this, and endeavour to set up the declared Abettors of his own Will, for the true *Representatives* of the People, and the Law-makers of the Society, is certainly as great a **breach of trust**, and as perfect a Declaration of a design to subvert the Government, as is possible to be met with.[122] (Emphasis added.)

When trust is compromised, consent is revoked, government is dissolved, and a return to a *state of war* is the result. And as Locke has already shown us extensively, it is from this recurrent primeval state of war that civil society based on trust and consent must reemerge. This recalibration of consensual government is so entirely essential for human

---

[120] II, 149, pp. 384–385.   [121] II, 221, p. 430.
[122] II, 222, pp. 430–431. See also II, 239, pp. 442–444. Peter Laslett makes the important observation that Locke did not mean to use the idea of *trust* as "a formal trust deed for government" despite the "legal overtones" that flow from his text. Rather, "The concept is obviously intended to make it clear that all actions of governors are limited to the end of government, which is the good of the governed, and to demonstrate by contrast that there is no contract in it – a fiduciary relationship, that is all." Laslett, "Introduction," *Two Treatises*, pp. 112–113.

preservation that it is justifiable to face the force of despotic government
with the necessary counterforce to depose it.

I say using Force upon the People without Authority, and contrary to the Trust
put in him, that does so, is a state of War with the People who have a right to
reinstate their *Legislative in the Exercise* of their Power. For having erected a
Legislative, with an intent they should exercise the Power of making Laws, either
at certain set times or when there is need of it; when they are hindr'd by any force
from what is so necessary to the Society, and wherein the Safety and preservation
of the People consists, the People have a right to remove it by force. In all States
and Conditions, the true remedy of *Force* without Authority, is to oppose *Force* to
it. The use of *force* without Authority, always puts him that uses it into a *state of
War*, as the Aggressor, and renders him liable to be treated accordingly.[123]

Locke was not cavalier in his defense of a right to rebellion but rather
offered a circumspect and carefully articulated definition of the requisite
circumstances validating that right: "That Force is to be opposed to
nothing but to unjust and unlawful Force, whoever makes any opposition
in any other case, draws on himself a just Condemnation both from God
and Man."[124] The act of rebellion by the people, the supreme power, is
justified when the prince puts himself into a "state of war with his people,
dissolve[s] the government and leave[s] them to that defense, which
belongs to every one in the state of nature."[125] The circumstances that
Locke believes to *justify* rebellion are in fact the same circumstances that
for Locke *obligate* rebellion.[126]

---

[123] II, 155, pp. 388–389. Locke leaves room for the exercise of *prerogative* or what might be
called in modern terms *executive privilege* by the ruler, but the key component that may
guide the use of prerogative is once again *trust*. "This power whilst employed for the
benefit of the Community, and suitably to the trust and ends of Government, *is
undoubted Prerogative*, and never is questioned. For the people are very seldom, or
never scrupulous, or nice in the point: they are far from examining *prerogative*, whilst it
is in any tolerable degree employ'd for the use it was meant; that is, for the good of the
People and not manifestly against it. But if there comes to be a *question* between the
Executive Power and the People, *about* a thing claimed as a *Prerogative*; the tendency of
the exercise of such *prerogative* to the good or hurt of the People, will easily decide that
Question." II, 161, p. 393.
  And later Locke writes: "For as a good prince, who is mindful of the trust put into his
hands, and careful of the good of his People cannot have too much *Prerogative*." II, 164,
p. 395. On the issue of *prerogative* Locke sounds very much like the author of *Vindiciae*
as well (see *ft.* 114). "From time to time they might supplement the law with certain
principles derived from natural equity, because it had not been able to foresee every
eventuality." Garnett (ed.), *Vindiciae, Contra Tyrannos*, p. 96.
[124] II, 204, p. 420.   [125] II, 205, p. 420.
[126] David Snyder writes: "And since we sometimes have a duty to protect the rights of
ourselves or others (II, 6), this implies that for Locke revolution may sometimes be a

In chapter XIX of *Of the Dissolution of Government*, Locke begins by distinguishing between the *dissolution of society*, which is always calamitous and can be brought about only by a force *from without*, and the *dissolution of government*, which must be accepted under the right circumstances and materializes *from within*.[127] He then goes on to list five examples delineating situations in which the government that has "the force, Treasure, and offices of state to imploy"[128] is responsible for the termination of popular consent: 1) "when arbitrary will is practiced in place of laws";[129] 2) "when the Legislative is prevented of assembling in its due time, or prevented of acting freely";[130] 3) "when the governmental power stands in 'contrary to the common Interest of the People'";[131] 4) "when the people are delivered by their rulers into the subjection of a foreign power";[132] and 5) "when he who has the supream Executive Power, neglects and abandons that charge, so that the laws already made can no longer be put in execution." This situation leads to the state in which "People become a confused Multitude, without Order or Connexion."[133] Each one of these situations justifies the resistance of the people. Locke explains:

> The reason why men enter into society, is the preservation of their property, and the end why they chuse and authorize a Legislative, is, that there may be Laws made, and Rules set as Guards and Fences to the properties of all the Members of the Society, to limit the power, and moderate the Dominion of every Part and Member of Society ... *whenever the Legislators endeavour to take away, and destroy the Property of the People*, or to reduce them to Slavery under Arbitrary Power, they put themselves into a **state of War** with the People, who are thereupon absolved from any farther Obedience, and are left to the common refuge, which God hath provided for all men, against force and violence.[134] (Emphasis added.)

As far as who shall decide whether or not "the legislators" have in fact endeavored to "take away, and destroy the property of the people, or reduce them to slavery," Locke is specific and unyielding. It is the people themselves who shall decide if there has been a breach of trust and a state of war entered into, just as the individual has the political power and law

---

duty." David C. Snyder, "Locke on Natural Law and Property Rights," in *Locke and Law*, Thom Brooks (ed.) (Hampshire: Ashgate, 2007), p. 12.

[127] II, 211, pp. 424–425.   [128] II, 218, p. 428.   [129] II, 214, p. 426.
[130] II, 215, p. 427.   [131] II, 216, p. 427.   [132] II, 217, p. 427.   [133] II, 219, p. 429.
[134] II, 222, p. 430.

of natural right (obligation of self-preservation) to exact punishment on an aggressor who would threaten his or her person or possessions.[135]

Here, 'tis like, the common Question will be made, *Who shall be judge* whether the Prince or Legislative act contrary to their trust? This, perhaps, ill-affected and factious Men may spread amongst the People, when the Prince only makes use of his due prerogative. To this I reply, *The people shall be judge*; for who shall be *Judge* whether his Trustee or Deputy acts well and according to the Trust reposed in him, but he who deputes him, and must, by having deputed him, have still a Power to discard him, when he fails in his Trust? If this be reasonable in particular Cases of private Men, why should it be otherwise in that of the greatest moment; where the Welfare of Millions is concerned, and also where the evil, if not prevented, is greater, and the Redress very difficult, dear, and dangerous?[136]

In stark contrast to some of his predecessors who also advanced the notion of *consent* in one form or another (Hobbes immediately comes to mind) Locke was not overly concerned that this right of the public to oppose tyranny would easily be abused and deteriorate into chaos, at least not to the extent that he was willing to negate such a right and thereby sanction a "Leviathan"-type government. Locke first points to history and life experience, showing that people will not suffer the consequences of arbitrary rule under any circumstances for very long, and rebellion against it is ultimately going to occur in any case.

But 'twill be said, this *Hypothesis* lays a *ferment* for frequent *Rebellion*. To which I Answer ... No more than any other *Hypothesis*; For when the *People* are made *miserable*, and find themselves *exposed to the ill-usage of Arbitrary power,* cry up their Governors, as much as you will for sons of *Jupiter*, let them be Sacred and Divine, descended, or authoriz'd from Heaven; give them out for whom or what you please, the same will happen. *The people generally ill treated*, and contrary to right, will be ready upon any occasion to ease themselves of a burden that sits heavy upon them. They for the opportunity, which in the change, weakness, and accidents of human affairs seldom delays for long to offer it self.[137]

That having been said, the people, Locke believed, would show responsible restraint for two reasons: the first practical, and the second principled. On the practical level individuals are not eager to pay the painful price that revolution requires. Only following a careful cost-benefit analysis would the public, as a last resort, choose rebellion against tyrannical governmental authority.

---

[135] I refer the reader back to Chapter 2 and my discussion of Locke's "strange doctrine" of individual political power and its exegesis from the Hebrew Bible.
[136] II, 240, pp. 444–445.   [137] II, 224, pp. 432–433.

[S]uch *Revolutions happen* not upon every little mismanagement in public affairs. *Great mistakes* in the ruling part, many wrong and inconvenient laws, and all the *slips* of human frailty will be *born by the people* without mutiny or murmur. But if a long train of Abuses, Prevarications, and Artifices, all tending the same way, make the design visible to the People, and they cannot but feel, what they lie under, and see, whither they are going; 'tis not to be wonder'd that they should then rouze themselves, and endeavour to put the rule into such hands, which may secure to them the ends for which Government was at first erected, and without which, ancient Names, and specious forms, are so far from being better, that they are much worse, than the state of Nature, or pure anarchy; the inconveniences being all as great as near, but the remedy farther all and more difficult.[138]

Nor let any one say, that mischief can arise from hence, as often as it shall please a busie head, or turbulent spirit, to desire the alteration of the Government. 'Tis true, such men may stir, whenever they please, but it will be only to their own just ruine and perdition; for till the mischief be grown general, and the ill designs of the Rulers become visible, or their attempts sensible to the greater part, the people who are more disposed to suffer than right themselves by Resistance are not apt to stir ... I grant, that the pride, Ambition, and Turbulency of private Men have sometimes caused great Disorders in Commonwealths, and Factions have been fatal to States and Kingdoms. But whether the *mischief* hath *oftener* begun *in the people's wantonness* and a Desire to cast off the lawful Authority of their Rulers; or *in the Rulers' Insolence*, and Endeavours to get, and exercise an Arbitrary Power over their people; whether Oppression or Disobedience gave the first rise to Disorder, I leave it to impartial History to determine.[139]

The second, more principled reason for public restraint in a move toward rebellion is the nature of the popular appeal: it is an "appeal to heaven," to "a tribunal that cannot be deceived." The ramifications of unjustified rebellion are therefore ominous and daunting, and hence inherently preventative.

[H]e that *appeals to heaven*, must be sure he has Right on his side; and a Right to that is worth the Trouble and Cost of the Appeal, as he will answer at a Tribunal, that cannot be deceived and will be sure to retribute to every one according to the Mischiefs he hath created to his Fellow-Subjects, that is, any part of Mankind.[140]

---

[138] II, 225, p. 433.   [139] II, 230, pp. 435–436.

[140] II, 176, p. 404. This paragraph provides further evidence of Locke's belief in an afterlife. See Chapter 2, *ft.* 119. Reference must be made here as well to my discussion in Chapter 3 regarding Locke's understanding of freedom in order to fully appreciate the synthesis of Lockean thought with regard to his theory of rebellion. Freedom, it must be remembered, is for Locke decidedly not unbridled license, but rather a "negative" freedom, a right not to be dominated by others with the laws of nature (God's laws) always remaining predominant. Rebellion in pursuit of freedom, then, must be in order to attain and maintain the practice of those laws. It is worth quoting John Marshall at length in this regard: "Locke was very clear at all points in the *Two Treatises* that this

Once again we witness the importance Locke attributes to belief in a consequential God. People will not hastily interpret government actions as a breach of trust warranting a revocation of their consent, because they fear the consequences of divine judgment. It is the absence of such belief that Locke fears, as we saw earlier with regard to atheists.[141] Locke adopts his notion of an "appeal to heaven" from the Biblical story of Jephthah, and it is a reference that he makes repeatedly. This is a topic that I will address at greater length later.

HEBRAIC ATTITUDES AND INFLUENCES ON THE RIGHT OF REBELLION

Yoram Hazony has lucidly documented how the roots of the Western tradition of disobedience and rebellion are to be found in the Hebrew Bible.[142] Beginning with the Biblical story describing Abraham's separation from the great tyrannical empires of Mesopotamia and Egypt in search of ideological and political independence, the Bible initiates theological-political imperatives that include the beliefs that:

1) There is definite objective justice, a natural and higher law of God, which the laws of state cannot annul or override.
2) A government forfeits its right to govern if it does not act with justice and in consonance with God's law.

---

liberty of acting in ways uncoerced by others was only a liberty of acting within the bounds of the law of nature. Men had a right to liberty of action but not to license. Liberty of action was restricted by the second, 'positive' conception of liberty in the Two Treatises, of men being made 'free' in being directed to their true interests. Where they wished to transgress the law of nature they were made 'free' by being coerced to obey the law. Thus, being directed by the government to follow the law of nature was not a restriction of freedom, but its enhancement. It was appropriate for men to be free from others' command because they were capable of knowing the rules that they were to follow, but they did not have the right to be free from command when they did not follow these rules, and they were made free when they were made to follow these rules." Marshall, *Resistance, Religion and Responsibility*, p. 18.

[141] See Chapter III for my discussion on Locke's attitude toward atheism and innatism. A Hebraic maxim connecting belief in God with the social imperative of trust is particularly worthy of note: "A person does not betray his friend unless he has first abandoned belief in God." Tosefta, *Tractate Shavuoth*, 3:6.

[142] Yoram Hazony, "The Jewish Source of the Western Disobedience Tradition," in *Disobedience and Democracy*, Y. Weinstein (ed.) (Jerusalem: Shalem Press, 1999), pp. 13–36 [Hebrew]. The following examples are gleaned from Hazony's introductory chapter.

3) Individual disobedience and civil rebellion are justified, in cases of egregious excesses by despotic regimes.

The lives of the Biblical patriarchs tell the story of independent leaders pondering the essence of civilization from without, not as city dwellers caught up by the dictates of temporal overlords, but as shepherds on the hilltops, separate, distinct, and prepared to entertain iconoclastic ideas. The story of Moses, the recalcitrant midwives, and the Israelite exodus from Egypt set the standard for disobeying the unjust, opposing tyranny, and rebelling against despotism. Balaam's ass, who refuses his master's orders, tells, suggests Hazony, of a tyrant struck by blindness because he is unused to disobedience, and knows only to resort to self-defeating violence under such circumstances.[143] The prophet Samuel's warnings to the Israelites about the pitfalls of monarchy focus on the dangers of governmental excesses, the result of arbitrary or absolute governance. The people ignore Samuel's admonitions and he nevertheless sanctions the crowning of kings because it is the will of the people, and consent must be at the core of government, meaning that once consent is revoked governmental legitimacy is revoked as well.[144] Despite King Saul's death sentence against David, the former's children, Jonathan and Michal, disobey the king and save David from monarchical harm's way.[145] The prophets fearlessly railed against the injustices of their kings: Elijah against Ahab,[146] Elisha against Jehu,[147] and Jeremiah against Zedekiah[148] are but a few examples. Even after the destruction of the Temple and exile of the Jews to Babylon and Persia the canonized stories of the Jews are of disobedience to unjust and immoral rule.[149] In contradistinction to the rest of antiquity the Hebraic experience separated the roles of king and high priest, preventing a necessary a priori association of the *good* and holy with *political power*. The role of political power was to help ensure the implementation of good, not to define it.

Inherently a revolutionary movement, early Christianity was not alien to this Hebraic idea but was functionally unable to promote it because the

[143] Numbers 22:28–32.
[144] 1 Samuel 8:10–20. It is important to point out that the "Mishpat Hamelech" – literally, the "law of the king" – as articulated by the prophet Samuel to the Israelites can be interpreted as both advocating monarchical absolutism and harshly opposing it. Both approaches can be found in Hebraic exegesis of the issue and indeed were both used in the seventeenth-century debate between the monarchists and the republicans. See Nelson, *The Hebrew Republic*, pp. 23–56.
[145] 1 Samuel 19, 20. [146] 1 Kings 17. [147] 2 Kings 9:10–29. [148] Jeremiah 38:2.
[149] The Books of Daniel and Esther are of particular import in this regard.

resultant confrontation with the Roman Empire upon which it was dependent for survival would have spelled its doom.[150] Instead the followers of Jesus sublimated their theoretical embrace of the Hebraic dichotomy between justice and political power into a Platonic-like distinction between what was true in the spiritual world above and the corporeal world below. Hence total submission to political power was the theological outcome, as St. Paul made clear.

Let every soul be subject unto the higher powers. For there is no power but of God: the powers that be are ordained of God. Whosoever therefore resisteth the power, resisteth the ordinance of God: and they that resist shall receive to themselves damnation. For rulers are not a terror to good works, but to the evil. Wilt thou then not be afraid of the power? Do that which is good, and thou shalt have praise of the same.[151]

---

[150] Henry Chadwick writes: "The paradox of the Church was that it was a religious revolutionary movement, yet without a conscious political ideology; it aimed at the capture of society throughout all its strata, but was at the same time characteristic for its indifference to the possession of power in this world ... this non-political, quietist, and pacifist community had it in its power to transform the social and political order of the empire." Chadwick, *The Early Church*, p. 69.

[151] Romans 13:1–3. See also the First Epistle General to Peter 2:13, 18–22.

S. S. Polin writes: "That Paul felt it necessary to come down heavily in defense of political authority ... was evidence of a deep unease in the relationships between the Christians and the political order. This is to be explained partly by the psychological difficulties experienced by a beleaguered and persecuted sect in a hostile society. Paul would not have had to put the case for political obedience in such emphatic language had the Christians felt a natural and spontaneous loyalty to their Roman rulers." Wolin, *Politics and Vision*, p. 89.

Not surprisingly, the debate over Locke's political theories, often centered on how Romans 13 should be understood. Mark Goldie writes that, "It is striking how often ... opinions for and against Locke are mediated through sermons on Romans 13, St. Paul's injunction to obey the 'powers that be.'" Goldie, *The Reception of Locke's Politics*, p. xxiv.

Erich Fromm suggests that Roman tyranny and oppression of the early Christians forced a fundamental change in Christian theology. While the early Christians were filled with eschatological expectation about future redemption, which naturally included a revolutionary streak marked by the fervent cry that "The kingdom is at hand," second-century dogma refocused from the future to the past, to the death of Jesus rather than his anticipated return, thereby making peace with the mortal kingdom of the present no matter the nature of governance. "The decisive event had already taken place. The appearance of Jesus had already represented the miracle. The real, historical world no longer needed to change; outwardly everything could remain as it was – state, society, law, economy – for salvation had become an inward, spiritual, unhistorical, individual matter guaranteed by faith in Jesus. The hope for real, historical deliverance was replaced by faith in the already complete spiritual deliverance. The historical interest was supplanted by the cosmological interest. Hand in hand with it, ethical demands

Augustine further defined the ramifications of Paul's words with regard to disobedience; no evil, he believed, could match the evil innate to rebellion or disobedience. Because human government is necessitated only as a result of humanity's fallen stature the excesses of the authoritarian are punishments for human iniquity. Governmental rules need not be commensurate with divine rules because that is part of the price humanity pays for its sinfulness. The ruler is in place as an emissary of the divine, and for the post-lapsarian depraved and sinful to rebel against him would be to rebel against God. What Augustine did in effect was place his non-Hebraic reading of the Fall and subsequent human depravity above the Hebraic advocacy of legitimate humanly arbitrated opposition to illegitimate government. (The Fall, its full political ramifications, and Locke's rejection of it will be discussed at length in Chapter 6.) Of Augustine's theological-political theory Herbert Deane writes:

One of his [Augustine's] favorite examples of God's Providence operating to control the actions of evil men as well as of the good is His granting temporal power and earthly rule to good and bad men and to various nations. It is God alone who has power to give kingship or domination over other peoples or to remove it ... Even the most wicked, cruel, and tyrannical rulers receive their power from God alone ... this view has direct consequences for Augustine's doctrine that subjects owe complete obedience to their rulers.[152]

As far as I have been able to discover, in none of the works written during the remaining forty years of his life does Augustine ever state that positive law must conform to God's eternal law or to the law of nature if it is to be valid ... He does not say that if the ruler is unwise or evil and fails to take the eternal law into account when he frames temporal laws, these laws have no validity and the subjects have no obligation to obey them; nor does he say that the subjects have the right to determine for themselves, by reference to the natural or eternal law, whether or not such a temporal law invalid and tis to be obeyed.[153]

Augustine condones disobedience only when the edicts of the ruler directly contravene the ordinances of God, but even then the disobedient

---

faded away ... Very closely connected to the renunciation of the original rigorous ethical practice was the growing reconciliation of Christians with the state ... It now sufficed to have God in one's heart and to confess faith in Him when a public confession before the authorities was unavoidable ... The Church adopted this attitude everywhere after the beginning of the third century. The state thereby gained numerous quiet, dutiful, and conscientious citizens who, far from causing it any difficulty, supported order and peace in society." Erich Fromm, *The Dogma of Christ* (New York: Routledge, 1963, 2004), pp. 53–54.
[152] Deane, *The Political and Social Ideas of St. Augustine*, pp. 68–69.   [153] Ibid, p. 90

must not expect to escape punishment, as the punishment for disobedience is always justified.[154]

Augustine's blanket rejection of legitimate rebellion begins to find challenge only much later, in the writings of John of Salisbury, author of *Politicraticus* (1159), who predicated his appeal against non-legitimate monarchy on the Old Testament. In opposition to Augustine he establishes that the "positive law" of the prince must be consonant with the "higher law" of God if it is to be valid. He bases this entire chapter on Deuteronomy 17:14–20 and on Job 29.[155] "There is wholly or mainly this difference between a tyrant and a prince," he wrote, "the latter obedient to law, and rules his people by will that places itself at their service."[156] On the other hand, "the tyrant is, therefore, one who oppresses the people by violent domination," and "it is just for public tyrants to be killed and the people thus set free for the service of God."[157] It was Salisbury's writing that spurred the revolt of the barons, and forced

---

[154] Ibid, p. 147.

[155] See in particular *Politicraticus*, IV: 2. See too VIII: 20 where he justifies tyrannicide almost exclusively through the books of Judges and Kings. John of Salisbury, *Politicraticus*, Cary J. Nederman (ed. and trans.) (Cambridge: Cambridge University Press, 1990).

[156] Ibid, IV: 1, p. 28.

[157] Ibid, VIII: 17, p. 190. On this Quentin Taylor writes that, "John's doctrine of removing a tyrant, by violence if necessary, is perhaps the best known feature of his political thought." Quentin Taylor, "John of Salisbury, the Politicraticus, and Political Thought," *Humanitas* XIX, 1&2 (2006), p. 153.

  Elsewhere, though, Salisbury takes a far more circumspect approach to disobedience and that too he bases on Biblical precedent, specifically the story of David's rise to kingship, where David endured Saul's oppression rather than depose him. "For even David, the best of the kings about whom I have read and one who (except for his plot against Uriah the Hittite) advanced blamelessly in all his affairs, endured the most grievous of tyrants. Although he enjoyed frequent opportunities to destroy the tyrant, David preferred to spare him, trusting in the compassion of God who could free him without sin. He therefore decided to wait patiently to the end that the tyrant might be visited by God with a return to chastity or might fall in battle or might otherwise be extinguished by the just judgment of God. For indeed his patience can be distinguished in the fact that, at the time when David had cut off his cloak in the cave and on the other occasion when, entering into camp by night, he found fault with the negligence of the guards, the king himself was compelled to admit that David acted upon the more just cause. And this method of eradicating tyrants is the most useful and the safest: those who are oppressed should humbly resort to the protection of God's clemency and, raising pure hands to the Lord in devoted prayer, the scourge with which they are afflicted will be removed." Ibid, p. 209.

  This is an interesting ideational tension that can be found as well in the reversals of Luther and particularly of Calvin on the issue (discussed later).

King John to recognize certain rights of his subjects, a process that ultimately led to the issuance of the Magna Carta.[158]

John of Salisbury might have also influenced Thomas Aquinas, who argued that when governmental power becomes tyrannical in nature, it might be resisted. "Man," wrote Aquinas, "is bound to obey the secular princes insofar as the order of justice requires. And so if princes have a ruling power which is not just but usurped, or if they command what is unjust, their subjects are not bound to obey them."[159] Furthermore, argues Aquinas, "if some sinful act is commanded contrary to the virtue which the ruler is ordained to foster and preserve ... not only is one not bound to obey the ruler, but one is bound not to obey him."[160] This idea led Lord Acton to name Aquinas *the first Whig.*[161] But the Thomistic view of right to rebellion was far from unequivocal and remained quite nuanced. Susan Wiltshire stresses that for Aquinas, "While resistance to the state might sometimes be necessary, there is in his thought no call to revolution against the state."[162] Another scholar of Aquinas, R. W. Dyson comments that, "What action St. Thomas thinks them entitled to take is not entirely clear, at least partly because he himself does not think the question amenable to a straightforward answer. Some commentators have thought him inconsistent or pusillanimous on this issue." And following a survey of Aquinas's quotes on the matter, though, Dyson tellingly concludes that, "His remarks, taken together, add up to an intelligible position of cautious conservatism which recognizes that

---

[158] Natalie Fryde writes: "John of Salisbury made the idea that the king is subject to the law accessible ... John of Salisbury's ideas also inspired the Magna Carta." Natalie Fryde, *Why Magna Carta?: Angevin England Revisited* (Munster: Lit Verlag, 2002), pp. 110–111. Cary J. Nederman concurs that John of Salisbury's influence played an important role in the creation of the Magna Carta, but contrary to Fryde contends that his influence stemmed from his defense of the freedom of the Church rather than the distinction he drew between the king and the tyrant. Cary J. Nederman, "The Liberty of the Church and the Road to Runnymede: John of Salisbury and the Intellectual Foundations of the Magna Carta," *PS. Political Science and Politics* (Cambridge: Cambridge University Press, 2010), pp. 457–461, published online by CUP June 30, 2010. See also J. C. Holt, *Magna Carta* (Cambridge: Cambridge University Press, 1992), p. 89.

[159] *Summa Theologiae*, IIaIIae 104, Dyson (ed. and trans.), *Cambridge Texts in the History of Political Thought: Aquinas, Political Writings*, pp. 71–72.

[160] *Scripta super libros sententiarum*, II:44:2:2, ibid, p. 74.

[161] For an interesting analysis of this *first Whig* concept see Michael Novak, *This Hemisphere of Liberty: A Philosophy of the Americas* (Washington, D.C.: American Enterprise Institute, 1992), pp. 107–120.

[162] Wiltshire, *Greece, Rome, and the Bill of Rights*, p. 39. On this, Wiltshire draws from D'Entreves, *Natural Law*.

extreme measures may be justified sometimes but should be avoided if at all possible."[163]

The words then of Paul and Peter sanctioning strict civic obedience to political power, whatever form it took, carried the day in Christian Europe. Most Christian thinkers continued to follow Augustine's belief that social institutions were part of humankind's punishment after the Fall and shunned any notion of legitimate rebellion.

The forebearer of the Reformation, Martin Luther, at least initially, followed this vein; secular government had a religious justification in terms of keeping social order for the sake of Christian love, and rebellion, even under the most extenuating circumstances, was out of the question. In his commentary on Psalms 82 Luther writes: "Let no one undertake to judge the gods [rulers], to punish them, or to correct them. But be quiet, keep the peace, be obedient, and suffer."[164] The origin of civil authority is always divine; it "is not a matter of human will or devising, but God himself appoints and preserves all authority, and He no longer held it up, it would all fall down, even though all the world held it fast."[165] During the violence of the German Peasants' War in 1524–1525, Luther supported the princes and summoned them to slay the rebels.

> The peasants have taken upon themselves the burden of three terrible sins against God and man; by this they have abundantly merited death in body and soul ... Therefore let everyone who can, smite, slay, and stab, secretly or openly, remembering that nothing can be more poisonous, hurtful or devilish than a rebel. It is just as when one must kill a mad dog; if you do not strike him he will strike you, and a whole land with you.[166]

For Luther, authority is not served because the individual is under a *political* obligation to do so; rather, it is a fundamental *religious* obligation to succumb in total to authority.

> To omit to do it would not be the act of a Christian; it would be contrary to [the Christian duty of] love, and would give a bad example to [Unchristian]; they too would refuse to submit to authority, although they are unchristian. And all this

[163] Dyson, "Introduction," *Cambridge Texts in the History of Political Thought: Aquinas, Political Writings*, pp. xxix–xxx.

[164] Luther, *Luther's Works*, vol. 13, Psalms 82, *Selected Psalms II*, Jaroslav Pelikan (ed.) (St. Louis, MO: Concordia Publishing House, 1956), p. 45.

[165] Ibid, 13:44.

[166] Luther, *Luther's Works*, "Against the Murdering Thieving Hordes of Peasants," American Edition, vol. 46, *The Christian in Society III*, Robert C. Schultz (ed.), Helmut T. Lehman (gen. ed.) (Philadelphia, PA: Fortress Press, 1967), pp. 49–50.

would bring the gospel into disrepute, as if it taught rebellion and created selfish people unwilling to be of use or service to anyone, whereas the Gospel makes the Christian a servant to everyone.

The words of Christ are *not*: you are not to serve the power, nor be subject to it but rather: "you shall not resist evil," as if to say: so conduct yourself as to suffer all things, so that you have no need for those in power to help or serve or be of use to you; on the contrary, *you* are to help, serve and be indispensable to them. I will have you be of such a noble and honorable status as not to need them; rather they shall need you.[167]

Luther's attitude was a considerable withdrawal from John of Salisbury's theoretical approach to political authority, as well as from Aquinas's scholasticism and theological-political world view.[168] Reverting back to Augustine, cardinal to Luther's thought was the Pauline directive of submission to political authority without concern for the ethical nature of its governance. Quentin Skinner describes the impact of Luther's thinking.

Luther could scarcely be more explicit in acknowledging that all political authority is derived from God. The text to which he constantly recurs, and which he regards as the most important passage in the whole Bible on the theme of political obligation, is the injunction of St Paul ... that we should submit ourselves to the highest powers, and treat the powers that be as ordained of God. Luther's influence helped to make this the most cited of all texts on the foundations of political life throughout the age of the Reformation.[169]

Skinner goes on to explain the pivotal effect Luther's attribution of divinity to secular power had on the rise of theories advocating governmental absolutism. Because Luther and his Protestant reformers: 1) eliminated the Catholic Church as a possible mediator of monarchical power, 2) insisted that secular rulers, no matter how tyrannical, ruled by divine providence, and 3) negated natural law as a yardstick of moral right, they contributed greatly to the legitimization of absolutism.

The political theories of the early Lutherans played a vital role in helping to legitimate the emerging absolutist monarchies of northern Europe. By arguing that the Church is nothing more than a *congregatio fidelium*, they automatically assigned the exercise of all coercive authority to kings and magistrates, and in this

---

[167] Martin Luther, "On Secular Authority," in *Luther and Calvin on Secular Authority*, Hopfl (ed. and trans.), p. 14.
[168] Estes, *Peace, Order and the Glory of God.* Hopfl (ed. and trans.), *Luther and Calvin on Secular Authority*.
[169] Skinner, *The Foundations of Modern Political Thought*, p. 15.

way crucially extended the range of their powers. This in turn led them to reject one of the traditional limitations on the authority of secular rulers: they explicitly denied the orthodox Catholic claim that a tyrant may be judged and deposed by the authority of the Church. Secondly, they introduced a new note of passivity into the discussion of political obligation. By insisting that all the powers that be must be treated as a direct gift of God's providence, they committed themselves to saying that even tyrants rule by divine right, and that even when they do manifest wrong it must still be blasphemous to oppose them. They thus withdrew the other traditional limitation on the authority of secular rulers: they rejected any suggestion that the law of nature may be used as a touchstone for condemning or even questioning the behavior of our superiors.[170]

Some scholars are of the opinion that Luther's position changed over time. W. D. J. Cargill Thompson, for example, divides Luther's life into three phases: the first phase (until 1530), in which he categorically rejected the possibility of legitimate rebellion in both theory and practice; the second phase (1530–1536), in which he entertained the possibility of rebellion in theory but not in practice; and the last phase (after 1536), which was marked by support for rebellion due to visceral threats that the Reformation faced from Charles V (and the drifting of his Reformation colleagues in that direction).[171] Similarly, Gary M. Simpson sees the second phase marked by the "Torgau Declaration" penned by Luther and Melanchthon, which acknowledged a natural right law of self-defense within the existing positive law – meaning armed resistance was constitutionally mandated in cases of egregious moral violations.[172] In the third phase it was agreed that armed resistance could be sanctioned without falling to positive law, but here Simpson agrees with Thompson that Luther never actually made that explicit in his writings.[173] This is probably the reason that many other scholars do not discern any such

---

[170] Ibid, p. 73.
[171] W. D. J. Cargill Thompson, *Studies in the Reformation: Luther to Hooker*, C. W. Dugmore (ed.) (London: Athlone Press, 1980), p. 6.
[172] Gary M. Simpson, "Toward a Lutheran 'Delight in the Law of the Lord': Church and State in the Context of Civil Society," in *Church & State: Lutheran Perspectives*, John R. Stumme and Robert W. Tuttle (eds.) (Minneapolis, MN: Fortress Press, 2003), pp. 40–41.
[172] Gary M. Simpson, "Toward a Lutheran 'Delight in the Law of the Lord': Church and State in the Context of Civil Society," in *Church & State: Lutheran Perspectives*, John R. Stumme and Robert W. Tuttle (eds.) (Minneapolis, MN: Fortress Press, 2003), pp. 40–41.
[173] Ibid, *ft.* 45.

metamorphosis in Luther's thinking.[174] But Quentin Skinner, agreeing with Thompson and Simpson, concludes that Luther's thinking did indeed change and for the same reasons that Calvin's did. But in Calvin's case the change appears more obvious.

In his writing on how secular authority is to be understood, Jean Calvin (1509–1564), leader of the second-generation of reformers, enlisted Scripture to prove that all political leaders, including tyrants, belonged to the realm of the divine will and was initially as resolute as Luther on the impermissibility of rebellion.

[A]ll those who hold the office of magistrate are called gods (Exodus 22.8; Ps. 82, 1 and 6). This title is not to be reckoned as having little importance, for it shows that they have a commission from God, that they are endowed with divine authority, and that they in fact represent his person, acting in a certain sense in his place ...

For we are to be subject not only to the authority of those princes who do their duty towards us as they should, and uprightly, but to all of them, however they came by their office, even if the very last thing they do is to act like [true] princes. For even though the Lord declares that the [office of] magistrate is the greatest gift of his goodness for the preservation of mankind, and although he himself sets the boundaries within which they are to confine themselves, nonetheless he also declares at the same time that whatever they are (and however they govern), it is from him alone that they derive their authority. Those who govern for the public good are true examples (mirrors) and signs of his goodness; those who govern unjustly and intemperately have been raised up by him to punish the iniquity of the people.

Hence, if we are tormented by a cruel ruler, if we are fleeced by a rapacious and extravagant one, if we suffer neglect from an indolent one or are afflicted for [our] godliness by an impious and sacrilegious one, let us first recall to mind our sins, for it is those without a doubt which God is punishing by such scourges ... And let us summon this reflection to our assistance: it is not for us to remedy such evils; all that is left to us is to implore the help of the Lord, for the hearts and princes and alterations of kingdoms are in his hands (Prov. 21.1).[175]

While Calvin's words here leave little room for doubt as to the legitimacy of political absolutism he concludes the piece with ideas that open the

[174] Simpson himself critically refers to Ernst Troeltsch, J. N. Figgis, Reinhold Niebuhr, and William Shirer. Ibid, p. 41.
[175] Jean Calvin, "On Civil Government," in *Luther and Calvin on Secular Authority*, Hopfl (ed. and trans.), pp. 51, 76, 81. Glenn Moots makes this important contribution: "Calvin will ascribe tyranny to the will and arrangements of God much in the same way that he related the Fall to the will and arrangement of God's sovereignty." Moots, *Politics Reformed*, p. 58. I come back to the Fall and its weighty influence on political theory in the next chapter.

Pandora's box of rebellion against what he calls "insolent kings" with "bloodstained scepters" and "unbearable tyrannies." First, tyrants do not have a divine license to act immorally and they will incur God's wrath upon themselves to be sure. But legitimate opposition to them is not constrained to the celestial realm, for while it is individuals who cannot rebel against kingly oppression there are those in leadership positions who can.

And even if the punishment of unbridled tyranny is the Lord's vengeance [on tyrants], we are not to imagine that it is we ourselves who have been called upon to inflict it. All that has been assigned to us is to obey and suffer. Here as always, I am speaking about private persons. It may be that there are in our days popular magistrates established to restrain the licentiousness of kings ...

If there are such [popular magistrates established], then it is no part of my intention to prohibit them from acting in accordance with their duty, and resisting the licentiousness and frenzy of kings; on the contrary, if they connive at their unbridled violence and insults against the poor common people, I say that such negligence is a nefarious betrayal of their oath; they are betraying the people and defrauding them of that liberty which they know they were ordained by God to defend.[176]

So lower magistrates can rebel against higher kings; can these magistrates organize the people to come to their aid? Can individuals encourage the magistrate to lead the rebellion? Calvin, it appears, leaves things vague enough for affirmative answers to both questions. And in the very next paragraph he makes it rather explicit where the individual doesn't have to wait for a magistrate to lead him or her – in cases where the edicts of the king contravene the will of God as taught in the Book of Daniel.

But there is always one exception to that obedience which, as we have established, is due to (the authority of) superiors, and it is this that must be our principal concern; we must never allow ourselves to be diverted from our obedience to the one to whose will the desires of every king must be subjected, to whose decrees all their commands give place, and before whose majesty they must lay down their own insignia. Would it not be an absurdity to give contentment to [mere] men [by obeying them], but thereby to incur the wrath of him on whose account alone [any human being at all] must be obeyed? The Lord is the king of kings. When his sacred mouth has spoken, it alone and no one else is to be heard. We are subject to those who have been placed over us, but only in him. If they command anything against [his will], It must be as nothing to us. And in this instance we must ignore all that dignity that magistrates possess. There is no injustice in compelling it to be subordinate to the true, unique and supreme power of God. It is for this reason that Daniel (Dan. 6.22) denied that he was guilty of any offence against the king when he disobeyed an ungodly law the

---

[176] Ibid, pp. 82–83.

latter had made: for the king had transgressed the bounds set to him [by God] and had not only wronged men, but had raised his horns against God, thereby abrogating his own power.[177]

Calvinism's insistence on the strict obedience to repressive governmental powers was overshadowed by an even greater insistence that those repressive governmental powers be true representations of God's repressive will.[178] Hence it should come as no surprise that once notions of disobedience were unleashed, many of the Protestant followers would not share the commitment to strict civil obedience, because disobedience was also ipso facto the will of God. Thus the early modern call for civil disobedience rose from radical Protestant thought, based on the Hebraic-Biblical demand for resistance in the pursuit of justice.[179]

Quentin Skinner also points to Calvin's concept of the "covenanting community," which is created through the swearing of an oath to abide by the Ten Commandments, and allows "for a group of godly men

---

[177] Ibid, p. 83.

[178] This apparent inherent theoretical contradiction between Calvinistic suppression and revolutionary fervor is rivetingly analyzed by Michael Walzer. He describes the evolution of this phenomenon thus: "Here is what Calvin meant by obeying God. He sought to organize the *noblesse de la religion* at home and so to impose a Christian commonwealth upon the French. If the saints held office – and Calvin had already described even feudal lordship as a vocation – their day-to-day activity would transform ordinary repression into godly discipline. It was something like this that Calvin preached to the young noblemen who asked his advice. He did not demand of them any spontaneous activity, any purely personal courage; he probably thought martyrdom naïve. Calvinist conscience was collective and it would be acted out, as long as Calvin himself was in control, in an orderly, disciplined, and systematic fashion. But suppose the French king forbade such activity? Given Calvin's vindication of secular authority, it is difficult to see how he could justify any kind of political opposition, however godly in intention. If the established powers were indeed divinely ordained and therefore always legitimate, then Calvin's French followers could do nothing but pray to God for the king's conversion. A tyrannical or even a heretical monarch would appear to them as God's scourge; they would search natural and political history for omens of further punishment or merciful relief. Bred to activism and diligence in the church, the saints would be passive in the state. But this was not the conclusion that Calvinists drew from the theory of God's sovereign power. For the view of political reality as the embodiment of divine will had this fundamental ambiguity: the divine will must be active in any group of men actively in revolt, manifest in revolutionary organizations as much as in the institutions of government. And did not the Calvinist saints know themselves to be instruments of that will? God had put his mark upon them and that mark was conscience, a piece of divine willfulness implanted in man. Conscience would be the saint's warrant to free himself from political passivity and success would be the divine sign justifying whatever he did." Walzer, *The Revolution of the Saints*, pp. 58–59.

[179] Hazony, "The Jewish Source of the Western Disobedience Tradition," pp. 49–50. See also Walzer, *The Revolution of the Saints*, p. 98.

formally to reaffirm their contractual relationship with God" as a source
for the evolution of Calvinist advocacy of popular revolution.[180] Skinner
points to just how total this theological reversal of the reformers was: they
reversed "the most fundamental assumption of orthodox reformation
political thought: they assure the people not that they will be damned if
they resist the powers that be, but rather that they will be damned if they
fail to do so, since this will be tantamount to breaking ... the 'league and
covenant; which they have sworn with God himself.'"[181] Skinner shows
that the seismic shift in both Luther's and Calvin's thinking from support
for unconditional obedience to advocacy of the duty to resist ungodly
tyrannical regimes was due to the historical progression of events. The
inherent tension in their theologies, which had always existed, ruptured
into full-fledged advocacy of resistance when, "[A]fter years of vacillation
and compromise, the Catholic rulers of northern Europe had turned with
violence against the reformers," and the advance of the Protestant agenda
was placed in serious jeopardy. The absence of a theological volte-face on
the part of the reformers would have spelled their defeat. It is of particular
note that in their repudiation of strict Augustinianism and justification for
lawful resistance the reformers drew from concepts such as self-
preservation and natural law.[182]

[180] Skinner, *The Foundations of Modern Political Thought*, p. 236. On Calvin's use of
covenant theory to justify popular resistance, see also Moots, *Politics Reformed*,
pp. 60–68. Moots goes on to suggest that it was Calvin who "enabled John Bradshaw
to say at the trial and execution of Charles I, almost one hundred years later, 'Resistance
to Tyrants is Obedience to God.'" Ibid, p. 62.

[181] Ibid, p. 238. Because of his unwavering commitment to remodeling the world to
conform to theological certainties, Calvin went beyond Luther, and came to accept
only that form of government that furthered that goal, creating a revolutionary fervor
unique to Calvinism. See Walzer, *The Revolution of the Saints*, especially pp. 58–59.
G. P. Gooch writes: "as we trace the development of the theory and practices of
resistance ... we shall convince ourselves that, despite his guarded reservations, the
teaching of Calvin ... made steadily for popular right." Gooch, *English Democratic
Ideas in the Seventeenth Century*, p. 7.

[182] Ibid, pp. 203, 208. For a thorough analysis of all the theoretical justifications the
reformers used to explain their contradictory and sudden support for resistance, see
Skinner, *The Foundations of Modern Political Thought*, pp. 189–238. Note should also
be made of Skinner's disagreement with Walzer over the influence of scholasticism on
Calvin, which Walzer discounts and upon which Skinner places great importance. See
ibid, pp. 318–323. As noted earlier, many scholars would not lump Luther and Calvin
together and see rather Luther's shift as far more limited, if at all, than that of Calvin.
See, for example, Martin van Gelderen, who shows instances where Calvinists supported
rebellion even when Luther's followers continued with unswerving obedience. Van
Gelderen, *Political Thought of the Dutch Revolt*, pp. 86–88.

The violent Huguenot rebellion in France and the anti-Spanish Dutch rebellion, both in the sixteenth century, were promoted by and subsequently further advanced the call for civil disobedience and rebellion in pursuit of political liberties. This movement reached its zenith with the Protestant-led anti-monarchical struggles of seventeenth-century England and later in the spirit of revolution and rebellion among the founders of the United States of America. And while Calvin would have recoiled at what he would have considered excessive and dangerous anarchism in these movements, his own Bible-based "revolution of the saints" served as a pivotal historical linchpin in their evolution.[183]

DIRECT AND INDIRECT INFLUENCES ON LOCKE'S THEORY OF REBELLION

Ostensibly Locke does not predicate his theory of rebellion on the Hebrew Bible. His chapters on "Prerogative," "Conquest," "Usurpation," "Tyranny," and the "Dissolution of Government" are not as rife with Biblical quotation and resourcing as are his preceding chapters. Locke, though, does make repeated use of Jephthah's appeal to heaven in a manner that is crystal clear and highly effective. The last mention of Jephthah appears at the conclusion of his work, and its particular location appears indicative of a literary strategy; it is in a crucial paragraph indicating the bottom line of his entire argument. In answer to the question of "*Who shall be Judge?*" and of whether or not "another has put himself into a State of War with him, and whether he should appeal to the Supreme Judge, as *Jephtha* did," Locke concludes that "*every Man is Judge* for himself," and it is precisely this conclusion that set Locke apart from most other contemporary theorists, as I shall presently show.[184] Another Biblical source he refers to is Hezekiah's revolt against Assyrian conquest in his justification of rebellion against foreign subjugation.[185] But in light of the centrality of the right to rebellion in the Hebrew Bible as shown earlier it is curious that Locke chose not to lace his arguments supporting the right of rebellion with more strands of Hebraic thought and example. One explanation might be the fact that because rebellion

---

[183] Walzer calls sixteenth- and seventeenth-century Calvinism "an agent of modernization, an ideology of the transition period." Walzer, *The Revolution of the Saints*, p. 300. See too Moots, *Politics Reformed*, who discerns the modernizing contribution of Reformed political thinking in the covenantal theology.
[184] II, 241, p. 445.   [185] 2 Kings 18:7. II, 196, pp. 414–415.

was the one practical and immediately functional aspect of Locke's *Two Treatises*, and because the Bible was being enlisted by both sides in the struggle over the monarchy to advance each respective cause, Locke might have felt that direct Biblical quotation would do more to confuse the issue than clarify it.[186] Whatever the explanation might be, though, while references to the Hebrew Bible are fewer they are not less compelling. It remains the case that Locke's thinking on rebellion and the legitimate dissolution of government is consistent with the teachings of the Hebrew Bible and that it is reasonable to assume that Locke came under its decisive influence, at the very least through the consistent mediation of other theorists, in crafting his theory.

One probable source to have impacted Locke on the right of rebellion is the book *Vindiciae, Contra Tyrannos*. Written during the French Wars of Religion, this anonymously published work was one of the most radical texts justifying rebellion of the sixteenth and seventeenth centuries. The book was an attempt to provide a systematic validation of resistance against absolute political authority, and it was naturally accepted with hostility by those who felt threatened by it.[187] At the beginning of the work the author lists the questions he sets about confronting.

---

[186] A salient illustration of this phenomenon is what Nevada Levi DeLapp calls "Davidic social imagery" by sixteenth- and seventeenth-century thinkers. King David's image was used by both those who favored rebellion as well as those who opposed it under any circumstances to prove their position. The former found in David a fomenter of rebellion against Saul, the sitting king, while the latter saw in David the epitome of nonresistance as he patiently suffered exile despite having been anointed by God's prophet. DeLapp understands Calvin as having embraced both aspects of the Davidic imagery (and especially how a king should behave once in power), which explains the tension in Calvin's thought between quietism for fear of anarchy and divine-driven rebellion. For DeLapp it was Calvin's successors, especially Theodore Beza, who came down decisively in favor of David's revolutionary imagery. See Nevada Levi DeLapp, *The Reformed David(s) and the Question of the Resistance to Tyranny: Reading the Bible in the 16th and 17th Centuries* (London: Bloomsbury, 2014). See in particular pp. 30–54.

[187] It was threatening enough, for example, to be subject to a public burning during the reign of James I at Cambridge University in 1622. White, *Predestination, Policy and Polemic*, pp. 207–208. White does not specify which edition was burned as a full English edition was not published until 1648. In 1588 an English translation of the fourth question was published under the title *A Shorte Apologie for Christian Souldiours*, but White's reference is to the full book, making it more likely to have been a copy in the original Latin published in Basle in 1576 or a full French edition published in Toulouse in 1614. Garnett (ed.), "Introduction," *Vindiciae, Contra Tyrannos*, pp. xi, xii, xix, xx, lxxxiv–lxxxvii. Of the *Vindiciae*'s pathbreaking significance, G. P. Gooch writes: "It is the first work in modern history that constructs a political philosophy on the basis of certain inalienable rights of man. For this reason its relevance was not confined to France. It was utilized by, even if not specifically composed for, the United Provinces, was quoted

1) Whether subjects be bound, or ought, to obey princes who command anything against the law of God.
2) Whether it be lawful to resist a prince wishing to abrogate the law of God and devastate the church: also by whom, how, and to what extent.
3) Whether, and to what extent, it be lawful to resist a prince who is oppressing or ruining the commonwealth: also by whom, how, and by what right it may be allowed.
4) Whether neighboring princes may be right, or ought, to render assistance to subjects of other princes who are being persecuted on account of pure religion, or oppressed by manifest tyranny.[188]

The author of the *Vindiciae* provides his answers to these questions with direct references and extensive evidence gleaned from the Hebrew Bible. While the life of Christ and direct quotes from the New Testament appear frequently as well, such citations are usually aimed to show that Christian ideas are consonant with the evidence offered from the Hebrew Bible.[189] The book was in Locke's library,[190] and it is reasonable to assume that he used it in architecting his justificatory approach toward the right of rebellion. On the issue of the right to disobey, decrees that violate the laws of God, the author writes:

---

to justify the trial and execution of Charles I, and reprinted to justify the Revolution of 1688." Gooch, *English Democratic Ideas in the Seventeenth Century*, p. 14.

[188] Garnett (ed.), *Vindiciae, Contra Tyrannos*, p. 5. J. P. Sommerville writes that in the three decades following the publication of the *Vindiciae*, "Catholics likewise printed many works permitting resistance to heretical or tyrannical rulers," but does not list them by name or describe their content. An assessment of these works in comparison to Protestant ones with particular emphasis on their use or non-use of Old Testament sources would make for an interesting comparative study.

[189] The primacy of the Hebrew texts is demonstrated, for example, by commentary of political scientist Eric Voegelin. After questioning "why anybody should care about the Hebrew covenants in a discussion of matters of public law in a Western kingdom in the sixteenth century," Voegelin suggests that the author of *Vindiciae* "does not want to support his argument by a secular philosophy of natural law; he wants a scriptural basis ... the acceptance of a historical, legal construction, endowed with scriptural sanction, as valid positive law ... The (Hebrew) covenants are assumed to be a positive law for mankind, outlasting by their validity the existence of the Israelite polity, and obligatory not only for Christians but also for pagans." Eric Voegelin, *History of Political Ideas*, vol. V, with introduction by James L. Wiser (ed.) (London: University of Missouri Press, 1998), p. 53. Without saying so in so many words, Voegelin is associating *Vindiciae*'s natural law with the positive law of the Hebrew Bible. But Voegelin does feel the need to explain, as Locke did (possibly following the lead of *Vindiciae*), how natural law, understood through reason, is squared with divine positive law, which is absorbed through revelation. (Discussed in Chapter 2.)

[190] Harrison and Laslett, *The Library of John Locke*, p. 95.

But indeed, if it be a crime to injure a neighbour, and it is deemed a grievous sin to attack a prince, what name shall we attribute to so great and atrocious a crime as assaulting the majesty of the supreme Lord of all? In short, just as it is far more serious to injure the creator than the creature, or a man than his image, and since in law [*ius*] the penalty is heavier for one who has harmed the royal majesty than for someone who breaks a statue dedicated to it, so there is no doubt that a much graver and more terrible punishment awaits those who violate the first table of the law rather than the second (although one depends on the other). And so we must be still more careful with regard to the first than the second.[191]

Clearly, just as servants are not bound to obey masters if they command anything contrary to the directives of the king, so also subjects are not obliged to obey kings, if they order anything against the law of God.[192]

Those who would argue this point by bringing the writings of Peter and Paul, which indicate the contrary, the author calls "impious,"[193] but the proofs he offers for his position are culled from the Hebrew Bible: Samuel's harsh criticism of King Saul for not strictly following the word of God; the prophet Obadiah's concealment and feeding of the prophets who King Ahab had ordered killed; Elijah's criticism of King Ahab for obliging sacrifice to Baal; Shadrach, Meshach, and Abednego's refusal to obey King Nebuchadnezzar; Daniel's repudiation of Darius; and the Hasmonean Eleazar's rejection of the Greek Antiochus.[194]

Despite its advocacy of popular consent, limited royal prerogative, and the right to disobey, *Vindiciae, Contra Tyrannos* did not go so far as to support the right of *individuals* to rebel against repressive regimes – be they legitimate or illegitimate – an idea that was to find ample space in Locke's revolutionary mosaic. The right of individuals to rebel was reserved, according to the author of *Vindiciae*, exclusively to one to whom God had expressly appeared with clear sanction for rebellion. Moses versus the Egyptian Pharaoh, Ehud versus King Eglon of Moab, and Jehu versus King Joram are the proofs that the author of *Vindiciae* offers to defend his position.[195]

---

[191] Garnett (ed.), *Vindiciae, Contra Tyrannos*, p. 31   [192] Ibid, p. 33   [193] Ibid.
[194] Ibid, pp. 31–34.
[195] Ibid, pp. 59–63. "But when God has neither spoken with his own mouth nor, extraordinarily, through the prophets, we should be especially sober and circumspect in this matter. For if anyone lays claim to that authority for himself, as though he were inspired by the divine spirit, he should certainly make sure that he is not puffed up with pride, that he is not God to himself." Ibid, p. 62. See also Fania Oz-Salzberger, "Social Justice and the Right of the People: The Seventeenth Century Reads the Hebrew Bible," p. 20.

In light of the point made earlier as to why Locke chose not to laden his theory of rebellion with Biblical sources, what we have just seen in *Vindiciae* gives reason for pause and question. Might Locke have preferred to leave his argument in favor of an individual's right to rebellion un-resourced with Biblical argument (that is, of course, aside from his references to Jephthah, which will be discussed at length later) because of *Vindiciae*'s position on the matter? Locke was after all going well beyond the parameters of sanctioned rebellion as prescribed by *Vindiciae*, and perhaps by Biblical example as well, by relying on human reason and natural human reluctance with regard to rebellion. Locke, who was fearful of religious enthusiasts, might not have wanted to unleash the potentiality of individuals claiming to be acting in rebellion as a result of the direct word of God.

Human reason as the guidepost for legitimate rebellion was at the center of another work published the same year as the *Vindiciae* by the name of *De Iure Regni apud Scotos Dialogus* (A Dialogue on the Law of Kingship among the Scots), which, contrary to the *Vindiciae*, put rebellion in the hands of individuals as well. Its author, George Buchanan (1506–1582), Quentin Skinner refers to as "the most radical of all the Calvinist revolutionaries" as well as the "most important theorist" to advance the idea that the people could repudiate a legitimate prince. Skinner has dubbed Buchanan's work "remarkable," and H. J. Laski has written that it was "the most influential political essay of the sixteenth century."[196] It is difficult to ascertain what level of that influence was carried into the seventeenth century, but it is known that copies of the book were included in the Oxford book burnings of 1683,[197] making it an important enough work not to be

---

[196] Skinner, *The Foundations of Modern Political Thought*, pp. 301, 339. H. J. Laski (ed.), *A Defence of Liberty against Tyrants* (London: Cambridge University Press, 1924), p. 5. In support of Laski's assertion one could point to II, 233, where Locke quotes Barclay (whom he is coming to refute), who forbids an "inferior from rebelling against a superior" and specifically posits Buchanan as the "only" exception. Ironically, Buchanan was boyhood tutor of James I (then James VI, King of Scotland, following his mother Mary's forced abdication), but not much of his teacher's advice on kingly duties to one's subjects rubbed off on the soon-to-become Divine Rights of Kings theorist. See Jane Rickard, "Mover and Author: King James VI and I and the Political Use of the Bible," in *The Oxford Handbook of: The Bible in Early Modern England, c. 1530–1700*, Kevin Killeen, Helen Smith, and Rachel Willie (eds.) (Oxford: Oxford University Press, 2015), pp. 371–383.

[197] Roger A. Mason and Martin S. Smith, "Introduction," in *A Dialogue on the Law of Kingship among the Scots*, A Critical Edition and Translation of George Buchanan's *De Iure Regni apud Scotos Dialogus* (London: Ashgate, 2004), p. xv. G. P. Gooch writes of *De Jure Regni*: "this was that 'criminal book' of which, a century after its appearance, the royalist historian of the Civil Wars could not speak without fear. Denounced by Blackwood in 1581 and by Barclay in 1600, it remained dangerous enough to be burnt

overlooked by Locke, even though he did not maintain a copy of it in his library. In stark contrast to the author of the *Vindiciae*, Buchanan does not heavily laden his text with scriptural proof of the right to rebel against tyranny, but he is nevertheless unafraid to go so far as to place that right in the hands of individuals. "Now when a war has once been undertaken against an enemy for a just cause, it is the right not only of the people as a whole but also of individuals to kill the enemy."[198] Interestingly, just a few lines before these, Buchanan makes reference to the right of the individual to kill a thief at night (but not during the day) because of the immediate danger he or she presents, without a requirement of due process.[199] It should be recalled that, as I showed earlier (Chapter 2), Locke used this Biblical teaching in order to help establish his theory of "individual executive power," which gives the individual political power that is never fully abandoned, but is rather held in abeyance as long as organized government fulfills its obligations and renders the individual power unnecessary. When government reneges on that responsibility, that individual power resurfaces and can be practically applied until legitimate government is re-created. Locke's similarity here with Buchanan cannot be overlooked. And despite the more secular structure of Buchanan's text as compared with that of the *Vindiciae*, Buchanan is concerned enough with some Biblical passages to pass commentary on them. For example, with regard to the prophet Jeremiah's exhortations to the Jews to follow the dictates of the tyrant Assyrian king, Buchanan insists that it was the exception; only to *that* tyrant were they to be obedient, but decidedly not to others.[200]

The Levellers are another highly probable source of influence on Locke's understanding of the individual and rebellion. Led by John "Freeborn" Lilburne, the Levellers were in the foreground of the radical Protestant struggle in favor of natural freedom and equality during the mid-seventeenth century. Lilburne was well known for his love of the Bible and for the use he made of its ideas to promote his ideology. The Levellers consistently advanced an idea of rebellion against any kind of tyranny and unjustified governmental control over individuals, and had a

---

by the University of Oxford in 1683." Gooch, *English Democratic Ideas in the Seventeenth Century*, pp. 39–40.

[198] Ibid, p. 153, (p. 97 in original Latin ed.).
[199] Ibid, p. 151 (p. 96 in original Latin ed.).
[200] Ibid, p. 117 (pp. 75–76 in original Latin ed.).

significant influence over the Whig struggle against the Stuarts in the following years.[201]

Leveller ideology, like that of its parent Puritan theology,[202] had deep roots in the Hebrew Bible. The members of the movement, most of them common people, enjoyed no schooling, and the only text they used for an ideological platform was the popular Bible. In Leveller books, pamphlets, letters, and speeches one can find many references to the Bible, justifying and inspiring their struggle for equality and freedom.[203] The similarities between Locke's theories and Leveller thinking are significant; Prasanta Chakravarty tellingly writes: "The Levellers ... were thinking like Locke before Locke."[204] The Levellers rejected original sin (to be discussed in Chapter 6), and John Lilburne himself entirely ignored the Fall. When Socinian leader John Bidle got into trouble for publicly denying original sin and the doctrine of eternal torment, it was the Levellers who spoke up for him.[205] Very much like what Locke would later contend, the Levellers argued forcefully that political liberty was a prerequisite for religious liberty,[206] and that the end (purpose) of all of government was for the protection of private property.[207]

---

[201] William Haller and Godfrey Davies, "Introduction," in *The Levellers Tracts 1647–1653*, William Haller and Godfrey Davies (eds.) (New York: Columbia University Press, 1944), pp. 1–50. G. P. Gooch stresses that those in the movement were "Levellers only so far as they (were) against any kind of tyranny." They did not promote a social agenda of wealth redistribution. See Gooch, *English Democratic Ideas in the Seventeenth Century*, p. 119. Gooch also submits that Leveller influence waned considerably after Cromwell's ascent to power. Ibid, p. 125.

[202] "The beginnings of the Leveller movement, and the main secret of its strength, are to be looked for in the popular and unorthodox forms of Puritanism which sprang up in the wake of the reform movement in the English church." Haller and Davies, "Introduction," *The Levellers Tracts*, p. 39.

[203] Ibid, p. 72. See also John Lilburne, *Come Out of Her My People* (London: 1639). See also Andrew Bradstock, "Digging, Levelling, and Ranting," in *The Oxford Handbook of: The Bible in Early Modern England*, Killeen, Smith, and Willie (eds.), pp. 397–411. Bradstock points to the change in attitude of scholarship that originally interpreted Leveller ideas as essentially "secular" and "modern."

[204] Prasanta Chakravarty, *Like Parchment in the Fire: Literature and Radicalism in the English Civil War* (London: Routledge, 2006), p. 88.

[205] Christopher Hill, *The World Turned Upside Down: Radical Ideas during the English Revolution* (New York: The Viking Press, 1972), pp. 132–138.

[206] John Morrill, *The Nature of the English Revolution* (New York: Longman Publishing, 1993), p. 385.

[207] H. N. Brailsford, *The Levellers and the English Revolution*, Christopher Hill (ed.) (London: The Crescent Press, 1961), p. 151. Richard Ashcraft discusses the relation between Locke's political theory and that of the Levellers, rejecting a commonly held view among Locke scholars that there was no connection between the two:

The Levellers were actually the first political movement to embed certain inalienable individual rights into a proposed constitution. Their proposal later found its way into the political mainstream when it ultimately became Whig doctrine through the writing of Locke. Lawrence Stone argues that, "The verbal and philosophical parallels between the two descriptions of man in the state of nature are too striking to be mere coincidence."[208] Stone continues:

In 1646 the Leveller Richard Overton wrote:

To every individual in nature is given an individual property by nature, not to be invaded or usurped by any: for everyone as he is himself, so he hath a self propriety, else he could not be himself ... For by natural birth all men are equally and alike born to like propriety, liberty and freedom.[209]

"The relationship of Locke's argument in the Two Treatises to the language used by the Levellers merits much more serious consideration than has been heretofore given by interpreters of Locke's political ideas." Ashcraft, *Revolutionary Politics*, p. 150. And: "I have throughout this work placed Locke in much closer proximity to the Levellers and to the radical political theory they developed than has previously been supposed." Ibid, pp. 164–165. Explaining his rejection of the commonly held view, Ashcraft writes: "[T]he revolutionary natural law position, with appeals to equality, freedom by natural birth, political power in the hands of the people, the free consent of every individual, and so forth, was a distinctively radical language associated with the Levellers ... If historians have tended to forget just how much the form of the Levellers argument rankled their opponents, this is no excuse for supposing that when the same concepts and language reemerged in the radical Whig political tracts of the 1680s, they had somehow become the common property of an amorphous body of moderate Whigs. On the contrary ... both the form of argument and the social composition of the audience to whom such arguments were directed, suggested to contemporaries that the Shaftesbury-led Whigs were attempting to revive the Levellers' movement." Ibid. Ashcraft emphasizes further that, "It is worth stressing this point since one might gain the impression from reading some of the secondary literature on Locke ... that this language of natural rights, equality, consent of individuals, right of resistance, power in the people, etc., was simply the common coin of political thinkers. This is not the case." Ibid, p. 164, *ft*. 144.

[208] Lawrence Stone, "The Results of the English Revolutions of the Seventeenth Century," in *Three British Revolutions: 1641, 1688, 1776*, J. G. A. Pocock (ed.) (Princeton, NJ: Princeton University Press, 1980), p. 35. Prasanta Chakravarty concurs that the idea of natural law was "at the core of their political philosophy ... from which evolve their radical ideas about property and electoral rights." Chakravarty, "Like Parchment in the Fire," p. 66.

[209] Stone, "The Results of the English Revolutions." On the difference between Overton and Hobbes and the former's similarity with Locke, Chakravarty writes: "While in both Hobbes and Overton the powers of the magistrate do not originate immediately from God but are mediated via the represented to the representatives, in Overton the covenant is negotiable and renewable by the common people. In fact, unlike Hobbes there is no schema of an explicit covenant between the represented and the representative in Overton so that the liberty and political freedom of every man lies within himself and

When, more than thirty years later, Locke wrote his *Second Treatise of Government*, he used almost identical language:

All men are naturally in ... a state of perfect freedom to order their actions and dispose of their possessions and persons as they think fit, within the bounds of the law of nature, without asking the leave or depending upon the will of any other man.

It is highly probable then that it was due to Leveller influence, in addition to Buchanan's, that Locke adopted the individualistic idea of the right each person has to him- or herself oppose tyranny.[210] Following the spirit of the Levellers, Locke argued that the right and duty to revolt against tyranny are the responsibility of every member of society. He admitted that it "will seem a very strange doctrine to some men,"[211] that "every man hath a right to punish the offender, and be executioner of the law of nature."[212] But he believed nonetheless that the act of rebellion need not emerge exclusively from an organized army opposing the tyrant (as was the case in the time of the Civil War) or any other kind of political party or group. It was rather the responsibility of any individual that was part of "the body of the people"[213] to oppose infractions against his or her person and/or property, and it was from this individual right that the people as a whole drew their right of rebellion.

Locke's attitude sanctioning popular resistance that extends to everyone could have also been influenced by the political writings of the mid-century political moderate George Lawson.[214] Julian Franklin has examined the influence of Lawson on Locke and suggests that Lawson's main contribution as expressed in his *Politica sacra et civilis* (completed in 1657) was the concept that the ultimate power in the state does not belong to the king or to the parliament but to the people who alone are entitled to constitute a new authority. Lawson argued that when individuals found themselves confronted by the dissolution of government they owed their allegiance not to any specifically constituted entity but to the community, and the enforcement of natural justice was

---

is not surrendered to any authority in order to safeguard one's economic security. Overton's individualism is rather Lockean in the sense that one's individual rights cannot be transferred. It follows that, for Overton, any man was authorized to resist when magistrates themselves become a threat to self-preservation." Chakravarty, "Like Parchment in the Fire," pp. 72–73.

[210] Peter Laslett is of the opinion that Locke probably never read Lilburne and the other Levellers but admits still, that by working with Shaftesbury he continued their political tradition. Laslett, "Introduction," *Two Treatises*, p. 22.

[211] II, 9, p. 290.   [212] II, 8, p. 290.   [213] II, 242, p. 242.

[214] Ashcraft, *Revolutionary Politics*, pp. 310–311.

the obligation of every person. Franklin posits that this approach was adopted by Locke.[215]

Lawson, though, was hardly the only English political thinker promoting the idea of the individual's right to rebellion in the seventeenth century, and he was not a Hebraist. There were others whose influence over Locke was far greater, most predominant among them John Milton and Algernon Sidney. As we have already seen, both were political Hebraists deeply influenced and motivated by the Hebrew Bible.

At the time he wrote *A Defense of the People of England*, a justification of the execution of Charles I in 1649 and the legitimacy of the Puritan revolution, John Milton was at the apex of his political career.[216] It was the Bible, as Fania Oz-Salzberger explains, that allowed Milton to develop his radical anti-monarchical theory. According to Oz-Salzberger, in Milton's understanding of the Bible, rebellion was an act based upon natural justice and divine guidance. The stories of the Bible set good examples and solid theoretical background for him when he justified the rebellion of the common English person against the king. There appears to be an absence of theoretical and historical research regarding the influence of Milton's political theory on Locke; nevertheless, Oz-Salzberger suggests that the two have much in common when it comes to the Biblical justification of rebellion.[217] In particular, salient in his thought on justifiable rebellion is that, in pointed contradistinction to the position of the author of *Vindiciae*, it is a right that belongs to the individual.

The Biblical freelance tyrannicides, he said, were acting purely upon natural justice; direct divine guidance, when they got it, was merely an affirmation of an act already made legitimate through natural law ... Milton relied on Jewish legalism to reject the extreme Calvinist concept of God's incomprehensible will ... In sum, the Book of Judges and the Books of Kings afforded Milton the sustenance for his idea of the right of the people (rather than their magistrates,

[215] Julian H. Franklin, *John Locke and the Theory of Sovereignty: Mixed Monarchy and the Right of Resistance in the Political Thought of the English Revolution* (Cambridge: Cambridge University Press, 1978). Locke had a copy of Lawson's book in his library; see Harrison and Laslett, *The Library of John Locke*, p. 170.
[216] John Milton, "A Defence of the People of England," in *John Milton: Political Writings*, Dzelzainis (ed.).
[217] Oz-Salzberger, "Social Justice and the Rights of the People," p. 22. Oz-Salzberger appears to be on steady ground as this would not be the only example of Locke following Milton: as I showed earlier (Chapter 3, *ft.* 113) Locke incorporated Milton's anti-Erastianism into his political philosophy, as opposed to the Erastianism of Selden and Harrington, and we also saw how Locke sides with Milton in negating the notion of consensual enslavement, against such theorists as Suarez, Grotius, and Hobbes.

including the English Parliament) to dispose of a monarch turned tyrant. A reasonable man, even without magisterial status or a divine command, can oust the oppressor when guided "by the very principles of nature in him." (Milton, "Tenure," 17) The people themselves, having "the liberty and right of free born Men to be govern'd as seems to them best" (Ibid, 13) can change their rulers as often as they see fit.[218]

It is especially interesting that Milton bases his defense of a reasonable man's right to rebellion in large measure on the very same Biblical precedent that for the author of *Vindiciae* assumed the very opposite. One example is Milton's use of the Book of Judges account of the assassination of Eglon the King of Moab at the hands of Ehud to show the veracity of his theory. Where the author of *Vindiciae* claimed that Ehud was justified only because of exclusive divine order, Milton puts forward that it was God's natural law that motivated Ehud, and hence was lauded by God after the fact. As if responding specifically to the author of *Vindiciae*, Milton writes:

Truly Ehud who killed him is believed to have done it by the advice of God. What could be a better recommendation for a deed of this kind? For God usually encourages men to do deeds that are honourable and praiseworthy, not unjust, treacherous and cruel. But nowhere do we read that he had an express command from God.[219]

Milton finds further scriptural proof of the individual's right to take matters into his or her own hands in the struggle against tyranny in the story of Samson.

If Ehud slaughtered Eglon justly, we have justly punished Charles. Yes, and that hero Samson, though even his countrymen blamed him – Judg. 15;11, "Did you not know that the Philistines rule over us?" – yet made war alone on his masters and killed not one but many of his country's tyrants at one stroke, whether at the instigation of God or of his own courage. And he made prayers beforehand to God to Help him. So it didn't seem impious but pious to Samson to kill his masters, the tyrants of his country, when the majority of the citizens did not decline to be slaves.[220]

---

[218] Ibid, pp. 20–21. See also in general Don M. Wolfe, *Milton in the Puritan Revolution* (London: Cohen & West, 1963).

[219] Milton, "A Defence of the People of England," chap. IV, p. 131. Of Ehud and Eglon, Milton writes similarly, but less explicitly, in "The Tenure of Kings and Magistrates," *Political Writings*, p. 17.

[220] Ibid. In the next paragraph Milton goes on to make the fascinating assertion that because the Biblical David was a "private person," the fact that he chose not to kill Saul is not a lesson for posterity to be followed. It is fair then for the Milton reader to conclude that Milton did not hold an individual's right of rebellion and that of the

Evident justification of rebellion based on Biblical sources can also be found in the political writings of Locke's contemporary Algernon Sidney. In his *Court Maxims*, Sidney argues that the right attitude toward any monarch must be learned from the ancient Hebrews, who never allowed their kings to enjoy a divine status.[221] In his *Discourses Concerning Government* Sidney could not have been clearer when he bases the right of the people to rebel against a tyrant on the Hebrew Bible.

> The rights therefore of kings are not grounded upon conquest, the liberties of nations do not arise from the grants of their princes, the oath of allegiance binds no private man to more than the law directs, and has no influence upon the whole body of every nation: Many princes are known to their subjects only by the injuries, losses and mischiefs (sic) brought upon them ... Rebellion being nothing but a renewed war, can never be against a government that was not established by war, and of itself is neither good nor evil, more than any other war, but is just or unjust according to the cause or manner of it. Besides the rebellion which by Samuel is compar'd to witchcraft, is not of private men, or a people against the prince, but of the prince against God: The Israelites are often said to have rebelled against the law, word, or command of God, but tho (sic) they frequently opposed their kings, I do not find rebellion imputed to them on that account, nor any ill character put upon such actions.[222]

There is much shared by Sidney and Locke both biographically and intellectually. Both had comparable contempt for Filmerian ideas, and both wrote rebuttals to those ideas at about the same time. Like Locke, Sidney spent formative years in France, experienced the practical side of political theory in the context of government service, and was a key Whig theorist. Sidney was executed for his role in the Rye House Plot to dethrone Charles II, and Locke had to flee England for the same

---

people wholly comparable, and, despite his radical advocacy of resistance, was still more circumspect when it came to the individual's right to rebel. The text reads as follows: "But David the king and prophet refused to kill Saul, the anointed of God. Not that we are necessarily obliged to refuse to do whatever David refused. David refused as a private person. Will it be necessary that a council, a parliament, a whole nation refuses it at once? David refused to kill his enemy by treachery; shall a magistrate then refuse to punish a criminal by law? David refused to kill a king; shall the senate then refuse to punish a tyrant? David had a religious scruple about killing one anointed by God; so then shall a nation have scruples about condemning to death their own anointed, especially one who was smeared with the blood of citizens and who had blotted out that unction whether sacred or civil by such long enmity?" Ibid, 131–132.

[221] Sidney, *Court Maxims*, pp. 38–65.

[222] Algernon Sidney, *Discourses Concerning Government*, Thomas G. West (ed.) (Indianapolis, IN: Liberty Classics, 1990), pp. 522–523.

reason.[223] Both were Hebraists who anchored many of their ideas on political theory such as popular consent, limited government, natural equality and liberty, and the right to rebellion, on ideas that originated in the Hebrew Bible.[224] Most importantly, Sidney, like Milton, though a bit more cautious perhaps than Locke, agreed that the right of rebellion when justified rested not just with the people as a whole but with each aggrieved individual.

But if the ill administration be such as proceeds not from ignorance but malice; not in some small circumstances, but in such as destroy the end, for which the Law was made, so that the people, which sought justice thereby, falls under oppression; the trust is broke; all acts done upon pretence of powers given are void; and those that exercise them become enemys and traytors to their masters that intrusted them.[225]

Locke's self-proclaimed "strange doctrine" then, a doctrine that guaranteed the right of an individual to disobey state-sponsored injustice and revolt against it, was not strange enough to be advocated by no one other

---

[223] "Locke was exposing himself like Sidney to the penalties of treason, by imagining and compassing a civil war that had not happened yet." J. A. G. Pocock, "The Significance of 1688: Some Reflections on Whig History," in *The Revolutions of 1688*, Robert Beddard (ed.) (Oxford: Clarendon Press, 1991), p. 274.

[224] A comparison between Sidney and Locke on many political issues, including rebellion, can be found in Alan Craig Houston, *Algernon Sidney and the Republican Heritage in England and America* (Princeton, NJ: Princeton University Press, 1991). Locke's library's catalog shows that he owned a copy of Sidney's *Discourses Concerning Government*, but it was the 1698 edition. If Locke had read Sidney's political writings during the 1670s and early 1680s it was, most probably, done in secrecy.

John Marshall makes the important observation that Locke was more circumspect than Sidney (as well as Milton and the Leveller Richard Overton) in rejecting "an expansively revocable consent based on equal rights. He stood apart from Sidney's vision of establishing the best possible society to make men as good as they could be molded to be ... Political society was not set up to be a revocable consent in the name of greater social justice, or of other conceptions of a better (more virtuous) society ... Rather, it was set up with a much more minimal conception of government as a trust to establish security and protect property, whereby only the violation of that trust would dissolve government and allow the people to then re-establish the government." Marshall, *Resistance, Religion and Responsibility*, pp. 270.

[225] Sidney, *Court Maxims*, p. 116. See also Sidney, *Discourses Concerning Government*, p. 315. Alan Craig Houston agrees that here Sidney is not as unambiguous and as forceful as Locke's statement that, "every Man is Judge for himself," but that the sum of Sidney's writing on the subject amounts to the same. "Sidney was less explicit, but the collective weight of various observations and arguments in his writings tips the balance in favor of the conclusion that he, too, assigned this momentous right to private individuals." Houston, *Algernon Sidney and the Republican Heritage*, p. 214.

than himself. It was a view shared by several other noted seventeenth-century philosophers, who in large measure anchored their position on case histories of the Hebrew Bible.

THE JEPHTHAH AFFAIR

In every stage of these Oppressions We have Petitioned for Redress in the most humble terms: Our repeated Petitions have been answered only by repeated injury. A Prince whose character is thus marked by every act which may define a Tyrant, is unfit to be the ruler of a free people ...

We, therefore, the Representatives of the united States of America, in General Congress, Assembled, **appealing to the Supreme Judge of the world** for the rectitude of our intentions, do, in the Name, and by Authority of the good People of these Colonies, solemnly publish and declare, That these United Colonies are, and of Right ought to be Free and Independent States; that they are Absolved from all Allegiance to the British Crown, and that all political connection between them and the State of Great Britain, is and ought to be totally dissolved; and that as Free and Independent States, they have full Power to levy War, conclude Peace, contract Alliances, establish Commerce, and to do all other Acts and Things which Independent States may of right do. And for the support of this Declaration, with a firm reliance on the protection of divine Providence, we mutually pledge to each other our Lives, our Fortunes and our sacred Honor. (From the American Declaration of Independence; emphasis added)

Where Locke appears to set himself apart, even from other thinkers with whom he was in fundamental agreement, is in his use of the Biblical story of Jephthah; and this was clearly not lost on the founders of America.

At the end of his discussion on *the state of war*, Locke quotes the story of Jephthah[226] in order to explain what he means by "an appeal to heaven" in a situation where no authority exists to adjudicate contentious issues among mankind.

For wherever violence is used, and injury done, though by hands appointed to administer Justice ... the end whereof being to protect and redress the innocent, by an unbiased application of it, to all who are under it; wherever that is not *bona fide* done, *War is made* upon the Sufferers, who having no appeal on Earth to right them, they are left to the only remedy in such Cases – an appeal to Heaven.[227]

---

[226] Judges 11:12   [227] II, 20, p. 299.

Just as an individual possesses a right to kill a thief whose actions pose a risk to his or her life, because at the immediate time of the threat the individual has no authority to which to turn other than the law of nature, so too a nation threatened with war by another has no adjudicating authority from which it can demand justice other than from heaven. Locke illustrates this point by using the Biblical account of Jephthah's confrontation with the Ammonites, and in order to accommodate my later discussion I will quote the paragraph in its entirety.

To avoid this State of War (wherein there is no appeal but to Heaven, and wherein every the least difference is apt to end, where there is no Authority to decide between the Contenders) is one great *reason of Men's putting themselves into Society*, and quitting the State of Nature. For where there is an Authority, a Power on Earth, from which relief can be had by *appeal*, there the continuance of the State of War is excluded, and the Controversie is decided by that Power. Had there been any such Court, any superior Jurisdiction on Earth, to determine the right between *Jephtha* and the *Ammonites*, they had never come to a State of War, but we see he was forced to appeal to *Heaven. The Lord the Judge (says he) be Judge this day between the Children of* Israel, *and the children of* Ammon, Judg. II. 27. and then Prosecuting, and relying on his *appeal*, he leads out his Army to Battle: And therefore, in such Controversies, where the question is put, *who shall judge?* It cannot be meant, who shall decide the controversie; every one knows what *Jephtha* here tells us, that *the Lord the Judge* shall judge. Where there is no Judge on Earth, the *Appeal* lies to God in Heaven. That Question then cannot mean, who shall judge? whether another hath put himself in a State of War with me, and whether I may as *Jephtha* did, appeal to Heaven in it? Of that I myself can only be Judge in my own Conscience, as I will answer it at the great Day to the supream Judge of all Men.[228]

Later in the *Second Treatise*, in chapter XVI, entitled "Of Conquest," when Locke elucidates his understanding of a conquest that is deemed unjust, he sends the subjugated, which have "no arbitrator on earth to appeal to," to "appeal to heaven," and once again he draws from the Jephthah experience:

That the *Aggressor*, who puts himself into the state of War with another, and *unjustly invades* another Man's right, *can*, by such an unjust War, *never* come to *have a right over the Conquered*, will be easily agreed by all Men, who will not think, that Robbers and Pyrates have a Right of Empire over whomsoever they have Force enough to master; or that Men are bound by promises, which unlawful Force extorts from them. Should a Robber break into my House, and with a Dagger at my Throat, make me seal Deeds to convey my Estate to him, would this

---

[228] II, 21, p. 300.

give him any Title? ... The Injury and the Crime is equal, whether committed by the wearer of the Crown, or some petty Villain ... But the Conquered, or their Children, have no Court, no Arbitrator on Earth to appeal to. Then they may *appeal*, as *Jephtha* did, *to Heaven*, and repeat their *Appeal*, till they have recovered the native Right of their Ancestors ... he that *appeals to Heaven*, must be sure he has Right on his side ... as he will answer at a Tribunal, that cannot be deceived, and will be sure to Retribute to every one according to the Mischiefs he hath created to his Fellow-Subjects.[229]

Locke's final deployment of the Jephthah story comes near the end of the *Second Treatise* and is intended to make the same fundamental point.

But farther, this Question, (*Who shall be judge?*) cannot mean, that there is no Judge at all. For where there is no Judicature on Earth, to decide Controversies amongst Men, *God* in Heaven is *Judge*: He alone, 'tis true, is Judge of the Right. But *every Man is Judge* for himself, as in all other Cases, so in this, whether another hath put himself into a State of War with him, and whether he should appeal to the Supreme Judge, as *Jephtha* did.[230]

Locke makes two complementary arguments. The first is that because there are times when no legitimate earthly authority to adjudicate contentious human situations exists, an appeal must be made to the ultimate source of justice, God and his law. And second, because the appeal to God is before "a tribunal that cannot be deceived" mankind will itself rule judiciously as to when such an appeal is justified and will not abuse this license.

Both of these points are poignantly made in the Jephthah story. The Ammonites approach the Israelites with a territorial claim backed up with the threat of bloodshed. Because there is no higher authority to turn to, Jephthah speaks the truth as he understands it to the Ammonite threat of war. His argument is a detailed rebuttal of the Ammonite contention that they have a right to retrieve territory now in possession of the Israelites. Because Jephthah is convinced of the justness of his case he can defend the justness of his willingness to fight the Ammonites, rather than surrender, as well. He also believes that because he is in the right, God will vindicate him and his people in the course of an evolving history. It follows simply that where an argument as convincing as Jephthah's does not exist, there is consequently no justification for "appealing to heaven" and fear of heaven prevents abuse of the privilege to make heavenly appeals. Locke's repeated reference to the Jephthah story seems to be a rather straightforward appeal to a Biblical source that explains an elemental phase in the

[229] II, 176, pp. 403–404.   [230] II, 241, p. 445.

state of nature and the emergence of human governance.[231] If the Judges of the Hebrew Bible are the transitional phase between the prophetic leadership of Moses and Joshua and the Kings, then Jephthah is the linchpin connecting the two primordial phases of Israelite governance. Jephthah is not only countenanced for leadership by God as were his predecessors, but he is the first leader to be drafted by the people to lead them as well (as I will presently expand upon). And it is he, having emerged to lead through popular consent, who "appeals to heaven" in his pursuit of justice. Locke's ultimate focus on Jephthah is because an "appeal to heaven" can work both ways: to establish just government and dissolve unjust government. Jephthah was precisely what Locke needed to justify the English Revolution, because the revolution went down the same ladder Jephthah went up; both were "appealing to heaven," to a higher authority and law. To descend the ladder meant to retrace the constructive steps of Jephthah, to move temporarily from bad government into the state of nature in order to ascend into good government. I sense that this is the understanding of Locke that Peter Laslett has in mind when he writes that, "Locke evidently regarded the story of Jephthah as crucial to the scriptural foundations of his case about civil society and justice."[232]

But Locke's conception of the Jephthah affair has been used as a test case polemic calling into question the validity of the entire academic enterprise of Hebraism. A scholarly article on the subject by Andrew Rehfeld finds Locke's repeated references to the Biblical Jephthah so troubling that it must, he argues, force a more sober approach to political Hebraism, which he contends is a field "dominated by an uncritical cataloguing."[233] Rehfeld presents a number of what he clearly believes to be formidable questions that contradict the Biblical narrative with Locke's arguments.

The problem is that adjusting this story to Locke's own theory would require far more effort and far more deviations from the "plain meaning of words" than Locke himself advises for interpreting the Bible. The alternative explanation that

---

[231] There are another two references to Jephthah, one in the *First Treatise* and one in the *Second*, that we have not yet mentioned because they are used in a different context. They will be discussed later, separately.

[232] Laslett, "Introduction," *Two Treatises*, p. 282, *ft. 17*.

[233] Andrew Rehfeld, "Jephthah, the Hebrew Bible, and John Locke's 'Second Treatise of Government,'" *Hebraic Political Studies* 3, 1 (2008), p. 62. It is precisely because Rehfeld uses the Jephthah issue in Locke to call Hebraism as a whole into question that I think it important to address his specific arguments at length.

the narrative simply contradicts Locke's own theory is much more clearly supported. Even if a very careful parsing of the text might explain how these problems fit, why would Locke choose such a story in a work so focused on limiting paternal authority and individual consent? And ... why would he include such a peculiar reading in a work that was published anonymously and thus could not be referenced back to him for clarity? Whether or not the story *could be* accommodated through interpretation, the central question remains: why draw on a narrative that creates so many problems so prominently in a work ... whose argument requires no Biblical authority and in which, indeed, Biblical references are so sparse?

Rehfeld on the whole, however, provides no answers to his queries, leaving one to conclude that:

1) Locke does not know his Bible (a conclusion he correctly dismisses).
2) Locke is a sloppy writer (another conclusion he correctly dismisses).
3) Locke's views are, as John Dunn claims, "grossly incoherent" (a conclusion he does not dismiss).[234]
4) Locke's use of Jephthah is Straussian, meaning to ridicule the Biblical text and suggest its opposite (also a conclusion he does not dismiss).
5) "If nothing else the sacrifice of Jephthah's daughter and the chaos that follows his short rule caution of the harm that an appeal to heaven might bring on those who invoke it."[235]

At this point it is necessary to tackle Rehfeld's general argument against Locke's Hebraic inspiration and questioning of Hebraism in general. Though finishing on an inconclusive note, Rehfeld cites his contribution as one that goes beyond an attempt to clarify Locke's Jephthah problem itself, and instead could be "a useful case study for those attempting new projects in political Hebraism, particularly because of the prominence of the Two Treatises in the history of Western political thought."[236] But Rehfeld's arguments appear unfree of their own "uncritical cataloguing," making it seemingly difficult for them to be put into the service of "new projects in political Hebraism." At the very opening of his paper Rehfeld states:

---

[234] Ibid, p. 84. Dunn, *The Political Thought of John Locke*, p. 95. Rehfeld also resources David Foster, "The Bible and Natural Freedom in John Locke's Political Thought," in *Piety and Humanity: Essays on Religion and Early Modern Political Philosophy*, Douglas Kries (ed.) (New York: Rowman & Littlefield, 1997), p. 181.

[235] Rehfeld, "Jephthah," p. 93.   [236] Ibid, p. 91.

References to the Hebrew Bible are relatively scarce in John Locke's "Second Treatise on Government" – relative, that is, to their prominence in Locke's "First treatise." Even if Locke's argument in the "Second Treatise" depends on God and natural law, it does not depend on the authority of scripture. On the contrary, the argument is an original one, mapping out the implications of natural law for political authority. Why then does Locke refer to the Biblical story of Jephtha throughout the work.[237]

These comments need clarification. The fact that Biblical citation in the *Second Treatise* is considerably less frequent than in the *First* does not necessarily suggest that the citations are infrequent. In fact, as I have shown earlier, nothing is quoted with any comparable frequency as the Hebrew Bible in the *Second Treatise*. Rehfeld also treats the *Two Treatises* as if they are two independent works rather than two parts of one holistic theoretical construct. The "repeated" quotes from Jephthah, therefore, must be seen in that context. There are some twenty-five quotes from the Hebrew Bible in the *Second Treatise*, and only four of them relate of Jephthah. It appears disingenuous then to present a discussion as "the Hebrew Bible and John Locke's *Second Treatise* of Government" when it is restricted to the Jephthah story.[238] The same would be true for an isolated discussion of Biblical Adam in the context of a discourse on Locke and the Hebrew Bible, even though Adam is no less an important Biblical character for Locke than is Jephthah. Furthermore, Rehfeld's blanket assertion that Locke's argument in the *Second Treatise* "does not depend on scriptural authority" is in all fairness to Rehfeld a commonly held assumption among Lockean scholars, but it is hardly the inviolable truth that Rehfeld presents it as. As I have shown earlier, Locke's presentation of his theory on natural law, as well as many other concepts critical to his *Two Treatises*, is drawn from the Hebrew Bible. Whether or not the Hebrew Bible is Locke's authoritative source, in the sense that had it not existed he would have arrived at his theory anyway, can be debated. What is eminently clear, though, is that he chooses to present his theory within the structure of Biblical authority, the Jephthah affair included.

As for his specific argumentation, Rehfeld makes the following points:

---

[237] Ibid, p. 61.

[238] Rehfeld repeats this on the next page, when after itemizing the alleged problems the Jephthah story poses for Locke he queries: "What could explain Locke's odd use of the bible in the *Second Treatise*?" The more accurate question would be: What could explain Locke's odd use of the Jephthah story?

1) The Jephthah story establishes him as an absolute and arbitrary ruler.
2) The Jephthah story is premised on a denial of his opponent's right to press a claim of intergenerational justice.
3) The Jephthah story involves God's active intervention in the affairs of mankind to deliver Jephthah's victory.
4) Most "striking," the appeal to heaven obliges Jephthah to sacrifice his daughter, which is a complete contradiction of the central claim throughout the *Two Treatises* that parental power *never* extends to the life of a child. (*Second Treatise*, section 170.)[239]

Rehfeld concludes:

In sum, against the content and structure of the argument in the Two Treatises, the choice of the Jephthah story seems truly bizarre, especially given the absence for most other points made in the "Second Treatise?"[240]

Rehfeld seems to overlook the fact that what Locke finds in the Jephthah story he is very specific about, *the appeal to heaven in the absence (or corruption) of an earthly authority*, and that account is clearly presented in the story. Hence Rehfeld's contention that, "If Locke sought to differentiate 'God as ultimate Judge' from 'God as active intervener in the lives of men', Jephthah is a counter-illustration,"[241] appears mistaken. It is the *appeal* under state-of-nature circumstances that interests Locke, not the eventuality or non-eventuality of divine intervention, and thus the Jephthah affair is compellingly illustrative. It is not that there are no other aspects to the story of Jephthah, but rather this is what must be known, Locke believes, because it is the most relevant point with sweeping long-term connotations. What Locke's thoughts are on every other aspect of the Jephthah account can only be left to conjecture; what is clear, though, is that Locke does not reference the entire Jephthah affair. The question then, assuming that intellectual consistency requires that every element of a resource be fully congruent with the presented argumentation in all its manifestations, is whether the Jephthah story in its entirety "*undermines* Locke's key ideas concerning the scope of paternal authority, intergenerational justice, and the expectation of divine deliverance from human action,"[242] as Rehfeld contends. I would argue otherwise.

Jephthah's recognition of God's practical role in securing victory does not mean that he depends on and anticipates "God's active intervention in

[239] Ibid, pp. 76–78.   [240] Ibid, p. 79.   [241] Ibid, p. 72.   [242] Ibid, p. 61.

the affairs of man." Jephthah means only that he recognizes that ultimate victory is in the hands of God.[243] Jephthah does not wait for divine intervention; rather, he goes to war against the Ammonites. If he had intended divine intervention as Rehfeld suggests, he would have refrained from any practical action of his own. Locke's "waiting to the end of days for judgment" is clearly not meant to suggest that mankind is to be passive, but that, because mankind knows that it will be judged by the heavenly court when the time comes, it will choose and pursue its actions judiciously and it will not "take up arms" on a whim. It is quite possible that the Israelites won only because of God's intervention as Rehfeld argues,[244] but God could also have chosen not to intervene and the fact that he does may have been the result of Jephthah not relying exclusively on him to achieve victory. This elementary point is made by Fania Oz-Salzberger:

What did Locke learn from the Hebrew Bible? First, that men left the state of nature and established civil society out of necessity. Locke's state of nature is occasionally conflictual, demanding temporal leadership and justice. *Appealing to divine intervention may prove insufficient* in such pre-political quarrels: Otherwise, why would the children of Israel and the Ammonites take up arms after the judge Jephthah had explicitly called upon God to judge between the two?[245]

(Emphasis added.)

Rejecting Oz-Salzberger's interpretation, Rehfeld curiously goes on to say that, "The sacrifice of Jephthah's daughter is ... a direct result of an appeal to heaven."[246] But why? Is Rehfeld suggesting that he would have had God intervene in order to prevent an Israelite victory so that Jephthah's daughter would have been spared from her father's impetuous promise? It is Jephthah, whom Scripture has already indicated was not the paragon of virtue (he attracted only "idlers" or men "of low character"), who had made the foolish vow to bring as "a burnt offering," in the event of a victory over Ammon, from "whatever comes out of the doors of my house to meet me."[247] Locke believed in a God who champions free will (Chapter 6), in a freedom of choice that allows for knaves not only to pledge the absurd but to perform the immoral as well. Locke's rejection of

---

[243] The Hebrew Bible is replete with examples of Israelite leaders who before engaging in battle or similar crucibles verbalized their recognition of ultimate human dependency resting on divine will. See, for example, Genesis 28:20 and Numbers 10:9.

[244] Ibid, pp. 70–72.

[245] Fania Oz-Salzberger, "The Jewish Roots of Western Freedom," *Azure* 13 (2002), p. 106.

[246] Rehfeld, "Jephthah," p. 77.   [247] Judges 11:30–31.

the notion that parents have absolute control over their children's lives would have been "undermined" if the Hebrew Bible had celebrated Jephthah's sacrifice. It, however, does not.[248] It is perhaps for the same reason that Filmer himself, in his advocacy of such absolute parental authority, does not use the story of Jephthah's daughter as proof of his own position.[249]

It is also difficult to accept some of Rehfeld's other arguments. Jephthah in no way "denied the Ammonites the Right of their Ancestors,"[250] and did not deny his opponent's right to press a claim of intergenerational justice. On the contrary, Jephthah could have made that argument and saved himself the very long legalistic-historical dissertation he offers the Ammonites as a rebuttal to their territorial claims, but does not.[251] It is not that the Ammonites have no right to make a claim because so

---

[248] As I have shown in my discussion on "Reason and Revelation" in Chapter 2 Scripture is very harsh on the issue of child sacrifice and Locke found this unconditional prohibition most significant for understanding the limitations of human reason. Locke quotes the Scripture in which the Canaanite ritual, reasoned as reasonable by the Israelites (could this have been in the back of Jephthah's mind?), is condemned. "The land was polluted with blood; therefore was the wrath of the Lord kindled against his people, insomuch that he abhorred his own inheritance." And so concludes Locke: "The killing of their children, though it were fashionable, was charged on them as innocent blood and so had in the account of God the guilt of murder, as the offering them to idols had the guilt of idolatry." I, 58, p. 201.

[249] It is worth noting that considerable rabbinical commentary exists, led by the medieval commenter R' David Kimchi (Radak), that rejects literary explication of the sacrificial episode in the Jephthah account. Radak's commentary, assuming that it is utterly impossible to accept the text literally, posits that rather than an actual "burnt offering" Jephthah physically confined his daughter and prevented her from entering into wedlock. The story is told, though, in such a way as to teach the dangers of impetuous behavior and speech. In his commentary on the Book of Judges, Don Isaac Abravanel takes the same position, adding that, in his opinion, the story of Jephthah's daughter and her reclusive chastity was actually the source that inspired monastic vows of chastity in Christianity.

Another commentary (*Midrash Bereishit Raba*, 60, *Midrash Tanhuma, Parashat Behukotai*) does not reject the literal explication of the scriptural verses and instead points to a different, equally important moral lesson. In this commentary we are taught that Jephthah could have absolved himself of his pledge by simply asking the high priest for an exemption. Being the military cum political leader, Jephthah thought it unbecoming for him to go to the high priest Pinchas and demanded that the latter come to him. Pinchas, being the religious leader of the people, thought it beneath his dignity to travel to Jephthah. Both placed their haughtiness before the life of a young woman, teaching what the horrific results of senseless vanity can be, especially in the hands of someone with absolute power.

[250] Rehfeld, "Jephthah," p. 74.   [251] Judges 11:15-28.

much time has elapsed; rather it is the content of their claim that Jephthah asserts is untenable. Jephthah's arguments against the Ammonite claims would actually have been no less valid had they been made to immediate allegations following the initial conquest of those lands, although no such claims were made for three hundred years. Jephthah's counterclaims in short are that the Ammonites refused pacific passage for the Israelites, tried to starve them, and then initiated a war against them. The conquest was the result of a defensive war in which Israel fought for its survival, and to top it off, the land in question did not originally belong to the Ammonites.[252] The time-lapse argument is the last one Jephthah uses, and it intends to establish that an intergenerational claim must be made consistently throughout the entire time in question, and must not merely be an opportunistic groping for easy land.[253]

[252] This is precisely how Grotius understood Jephthah's argument. "But this is certain, if we only respect the Law of Nations, what we take from our Enemies, cannot be claimed by those from whom our Enemies before had taken them by Right of War; because the law of Nations had first made our Enemies Proprietors of them by an outward Right, and then us. By which Right, among others, Jephtha defends himself against the *Ammonites*, (Judges xi. 23, 24, 27.) because the Land in Dispute was taken from the *Ammonites*; as also another Part of the Land from the *Moabites*, by the *Amorites*, by the Right of War; and from them by the same Right, by the *Hebrews*." Grotius, *The Rights of War and Peace*, book III, chap. VI, VII, p. 1325.

[253] Grotius in fact claims that the time-lapse claim is central to Jephthah's argument. Not that the passing of time legitimizes an injustice but that the absence of a consistent claim over time weakens the claim, a point it need not be assumed Locke disagreed with. "But if we should admit this to be true," the legitimacy of territorial claims even though they are generally assumed to have been waved, "a very great Inconvenience would follow; the Disputes about Kingdoms, and their Boundaries, would never be at an End: Which, as it directly tends to create Uneasiness, Troubles, and Wars amongst Men, so is it contrary to the common Sense of Nations. For the Holy Scriptures, when the King of the *Ammonites* demanded of *Jephthah*, the Lands that lay between the *Arnon* and *Jabbok*, and from the Desarts of *Arabia*, as far as the River *Jordan*, he pleaded three hundred Years Possession; and asked why he and his Ancestors had so long neglected to lay claim to them." Ibid, book II, chap. IV, I–II, pp. 484–485. Grotius uses the Jephthah affair to establish the legitimacy of war even when there is not a direct command by God to declare war. God has conveyed to mankind the rules of legitimate war, though, which can be comprehended through the discerning power of reason. "And further, God himself prescribed to his People certain general and established Rules of making War, *Deut*. xx. 10, 15. thereby plainly shewing, that War might sometimes be just, even without a special Command from God ... And since he does not declare the just Reasons of making War, he thereby supposes that they may be easily discovered by the Light of Nature. Such was the Cause of the War made by *Jephtha* against the *Ammonites*, in defense of their Borders, *Judges* xi." Ibid, chap. II, II, p. 186.

Lastly, it is hard to understand exactly where Rehfeld believes the Biblical text indicates the support of absolutism and arbitrariness with regard to Jephthah's rule. On the contrary, Jephthah has been chosen to lead the people in battle against an existential enemy, a charge he initially undertakes by attempting to diffuse the situation through diplomacy and negotiation. This point is actually acknowledged by Rehfeld later in his paper with regard to the one quote Locke brings from Jephthah, which Rehfeld admits poses no problem for Locke. This is in chapter VII, "Of Political or Civil Society," in which Locke references Jephthah to establish that, "the chief business of their Judges, and first Kings seems to have been to be Captains in War, and Leaders of their Armies."[254]

Sequentially, the first quote Locke offers from Jephthah appears in the *First Treatise*. Locke's intention is to show that God had not appointed leaders of Israel by hereditary authority or with the power of the original grant to non-hereditary successors.

If ... it be said God always chose the person of the successor, and so, transferring the fatherly authority to him, excluded his issue from succeeding to it, that is manifestly not so in the story of Jephthah, where he articled with the people, and they made him judge over them, as is plain (Judg. Xi).[255]

Here too, Rehfeld argues, Locke's use of Jephthah casts a giant shadow over his true agenda regarding Biblical citation, and here too, Rehfeld, I believe, is misreading Locke's intent. Rehfeld writes:

Locke rightly notes that the people articled with Jephthah, but he ignores the fact that they did not set the decision criteria, nor did they choose him in the first place. If anything, the Jephthah story supports Filmer's contention against Locke, that the people of Israel did not choose their own leaders, albeit with officer's taking God's place as the initial selection agents.[256]

Why Rehfeld asserts that Locke ignores this is hard to understand. One would find it difficult to identify even one ruler in the Book of Judges who rises without God's authority and is chosen by the people and not by God, other, that is, than Jephthah, and this is precisely Locke's point. Regarding the first judge, Ohtniel ben Knaz, the verse clearly states that, "the Lord raised a champion for the Israelites to deliver them."[257] Exactly the same is repeated for his successor, Ehud ben Gera.[258] Ehud's successor was Shamgar ben Anat, about whom the Scripture is silent regarding his

---

[254] II, 109. p. 358.   [255] I, 163, p. 278.   [256] Rehfeld, "Jephthah," p. 69.
[257] Judges 3:9   [258] Judges 3:15

ascent to power. But it should be remembered that the Book of Judges has already begun with a blanket introduction regarding the judges of Israel: all were "raised up by the Lord."[259] Shamgar is followed by Barak, who is appointed by "the Lord, God of Israel" through the prophetess Deborah.[260] They are followed by Gideon, to whom God himself appears because Gideon had not found God's angelic emissary convincing enough.[261] Rehfeld may have a point regarding Gideon's successor Abimelech, who is appointed by the people of Schechem only, but he proves to be a murderous thug whose short rule is severely limited geographically and whose tenure ends with a curse on his Schechemite sponsors.

Jephthah comes next. As we have just seen, all the judges recorded in the Book of Judges are in fact "raised up by God." Jephthah, though, precisely as Locke records, is not only "raised up by God" (not specifically, but naturally included in the blanket Biblical statement regarding all the judges recorded earlier) but is mainly approached by the "elders of Gilead" to be "the commander over all the inhabitants of Gilead." This is how the verses read:

Sometime later, the Ammonites went to war against Israel. And when the Ammonites attacked Israel, the elders of Gilead went to bring Jephthah back from the Tob country. They said to Jephthah, "Come be our chief, so that we can fight the Ammonites." Jephthah replied to the elders of Gilead, "You are the very people who rejected me and drove me out of my father's house. How can you come to me now when you are in trouble?" The elders of Gilead said to Jephthah, "Honestly, we have now turned back to you. If you come with us and fight the Ammonites, you shall be our commander over all the inhabitants of Gilead." Jephthah said to the elders of Gilead, "[Very well,] if you bring me back to fight the Ammonites and the LORD delivers them to me; I am to be your commander." And the elders of Gilead answered Jephthah, "The LORD Himself shall be witness between us: we will do just as you have said." Jephthah went with the elders of Gilead, and the people made him their commander and chief. And Jephthah repeated all these terms before the LORD at Mizpah.[262]

God clearly does not overtly authorize Jephthah's rule. The people do, and it is Jephthah who makes his rule over all the people conditional on his victory, not the people. Jephthah's subsequent plea to God to secure him a victory is not a demand for God's consent to rule, just as it is not a surrender of his own responsibility to fight, as we saw earlier. We are told that Jephthah had gone with the elders to receive his

[259] Judges 2:6–23.   [260] Judges 4:6.   [261] Judges 6:11–18.   [262] Judges 11:4–11.

appointment from the people; yet with regard to God we are told that Jephthah "repeated all these terms before the LORD." He needs an immediate response from the people in order to act, but God's response is to come later and only as a reaction to his own actions. By making his continued leadership contingent on military victory, Jephthah states the obvious; if he loses the battle he will hardly be fit to lead the people, and the people will lack interest for him to be their leader. He does not intend to rope God into intervening in the battle in order to secure his continued leadership as Rehfeld would have us believe. The simple fact is that there is no similar account telling of the assumption of leadership in Judges or elsewhere in the Bible in which the pursuit of leadership is initiated and consummated by the people in such stark terminology.[263] And where that takes place there is absolutely no suggestion of hereditary rule, precisely as Locke argues.

In conclusion, Locke is anything but cavalier about his legitimization of rebellion. His theory is radical in the sense that he attributes to individuals the right of rebellion, but cautious in the sense that it is only an appeal to the strictures of heaven that can justify it. The individual's right to rebel against "a long train of abuses" is an extension of the individual's executive political power in the state of nature, which as we discussed earlier (Chapter 2) is an idea Locke formed with a view toward the Hebrew Bible. He was preceded by Milton and Sidney, both of whom were likely influences on him, and who both resourced the Hebrew Bible directly in order to legitimate their position of the individual's right to rebel. As for the "appeal to heaven" so that the laws of nature may be retrieved, Locke draws openly and repeatedly from the account of Jephthah's politics as told in the Book of Judges because of its lessons regarding the formation of the legitimate political state and its dissolution, and that is most significantly how he chose to conclude his work. The evidence then appears rather compelling that Locke's theory on legitimate dissolution of government through revolution, the central theme of his *Second Treatise*, would have been impossible without direct as well as mediated Hebraic influences

---

[263] Compare Judges 8:22–23, where the men of Israel request of Gideon "Rule over us – you, your son, and your grandson as well." Gideon's response leaves no room for doubt about his attitude on hereditary rule. "But Gideon replied, 'I will not rule over you myself, nor shall my son rule over you; the LORD alone shall rule over you.'" Coming off the Gideon experience, the most the elders of Gilead were willing to request of Jephthah was uni-generational rule.

6

The Fall and the Extent of Human Depravity

This chapter is different in its methodology of analysis than the previous ones. With regard to Locke's theories on natural law, equality, property, and rebellion, the primary focus of my analysis was on the direct use he made of the Hebrew Bible. This was complemented by the places where it appears highly probable that Locke was influenced by the Hebrew Bible and later Hebraic sources through the mediation of other texts, and yet other places where only a thematic similarity exists between Hebraic and Lockean texts.

Conversely, this chapter concerns itself primarily with what is absent from Lockean political theory: *the Fall* and *original sin*. It is my contention that this is not an oversight on Locke's part. On the contrary; where for Augustine's New Testamentism original sin explained the unfortunate institutional necessities of human existence – government, private property, and stratified society (including slavery) – for Locke the scriptural focus for proper social order was on the Hebraic reading of creation, for which original sin had little practical consequence. Locke, I think it will become clear, did not accept, and indeed could not have accepted, the traditional Augustinian understanding of the Fall, which classifies death as punishment, points to a constant state of sin, and denies a full human capacity for free will or at the very least severely limits it, and at the same time advance a theory of natural law that would lead to just rebellion against tyrannical government. Because the right to *consent* to moral government is by definition also the right to *dissent* from amoral government, original sin could not be understood to preclude the ability to discern the nature of proper conduct and choose it.

This chapter intends to show that by defining mankind's post-lapsarian state in terms of human responsibility rather than depravity, Locke kept with the classical Hebraic reading of the Biblical text, which attributes only the forfeiture of immortality following Adam and Eve's sin and leaves human free will intact. This is in keeping with the "minimalist creed" of Christianity that Locke came to espouse.

LOCKE'S RELIGIOUS LIFE AND PURSUIT OF SYNCRETIC THEOLOGY

Locke grew up in a strict religious environment. He described his mother as a "very pious woman," and his father's notebook contained short and detailed thoughts regarding correct orthodox religious practice. The mainstream population of the community he lived in (Belluton) rejected Catholicism, and in keeping with the predominant influence of Calvin on British Protestantism the religious direction of his childhood was of Calvinistic-Puritan nature. His family kept the Sabbath day holy and invested much in sermonizing and in the intensive study of the Bible.[1]

But this was not just any Bible study, for the Puritans saw themselves acting out the Biblical role similar to that of the ancient Hebrews; to study the Bible for the young Locke meant to live it, specifically the Old Testament. Puritan identification with the Biblical chosen people was not just theoretical. In Biblical translation and scriptural exegesis the Puritans advanced the use of Hebrew, and favored the Old Testament for functional emulation because they understood it to be the most authentic part of Scripture. Eliane Glaser, who has documented the special role the Old Testament played in the Puritan creed, calls it an "extraordinary phenomenon" because "The Old Testament embodied for them the original and direct access to God enjoyed by the Israelites, a relationship which Puritans were keen to emulate."[2]

In a historical article from the year 1890, John Dow already pointed to the deep Hebrew and Puritan connection:

In the Puritan, as in the Hebrew, we find a people animated by an intense spirituality filled with the same consciousness of the ever present guidance of a Divine hand, irresistibly swift to behold the finger of God in everything, from the pride of kings to the sparrow's fall. Like the Hebrews the Puritans felt themselves to be a peculiar people, bound together by a Divine strength, favored of God as

---

[1] Woolhouse, *John Locke: A Biography*, p. 9.
[2] Eliane Glaser, *Judaism without Jews: Philosemitism and Christian Polemic in Early Modern England* (New York: Palgrave Macmillan, 2007), pp. 34, 39.

none others were and possessing the only true spiritual light ... they had their Moses ... their Red sea, Their Desert, their Promised land.[3]

And in referring to the special attitude of Puritanism toward the Old Testament, Dow wrote of the direct and semi-exclusivist focus on it:

Though ultra Christians in some aspects of their creed, they found in the Scriptures of the Old Testament rather than the New the fundamentals of their religious thought and conduct. The Books of the Judges and the kings furnished them a more potent incentive in their political walk and conversation than the milder records of the Evangelists. Moses and the Prophets spoke to them in the very voice of God ... So the Bible, and chiefly the Old Testament became their one book. It was their sole literature, their intellectual and spiritual food, their guide, philosopher and friend, their justiciary warrant and their high court of appeal. They conversed, disputed, preached in its very language. Their thought was moulded to its form. Its songs of triumph celebrated their victories, and their grief found utterance in its threnodies of lamentation.[4]

Such was the nature of Locke's exposure to Scripture during his most formative years.

Even after leaving home and its Puritan surroundings, Locke's early education in Westminster School was also saturated with religious activity. At school, the day began shortly after five in the morning with Latin prayers, and Sunday activities included prayers, religious service, and memorization of the catechism.[5]

In his *First Tract of Government*, written at Oxford shortly after the Restoration, Locke expressed what was at the time a politically correct viewpoint regarding the relations between religion and state. He argued that the English people would benefit from the practices of the reestablished Church of England imposed by Charles II. Support for the official Anglican religion was typical of Locke's mainstream attitude at the time, celebrating the assumed stability the Restoration was to bring along with its religious outlook and social mores.[6] But despite his early Puritan education and his subsequent public support for the Anglican Church, it seems that ever since his years at Oxford Locke started slowly pulling away from any strict religious practice.[7]

In 1668, he became acquainted with the leader of the Cambridge Platonists, Benjamin Whichcote, who was surrounded by a company of

---

[3] John G. Dow, "Hebrew and Puritan," *The Jewish Quarterly Review* 3, 1 (1890), p. 53.
[4] Ibid, p. 69.   [5] Woolhouse, *John Locke: A Biography*, pp. 12–13.   [6] Ibid, p. 40.
[7] Samuel C. Pearson Jr., "The Religion of John Locke and the Character of His Thought," *The Journal of Religion* 58, 3 (1978), p. 245.

younger Cambridge graduates such as John Tillotson (later the Archbishop of Canterbury), Simon Patrick (served as Bishop of Ely and wrote
extensively on the poetic books of the Old Testament), and Edward
Fowler. Fowler followed his close friend Henry More, another leader of
the Platonist group, as Bishop of Gloucester when More resigned the post
in favor of Fowler. More's writings had a particularly profound influence
on Locke as he followed More's lead on limiting requisite Christian
dogma and in enlisting rationalism as an arbiter of true revelation (to be
discussed presently).[8]

All the Platonists believed in the importance of good personal behavior
rather than mechanical religious ritual, supported religious tolerance,
and placed a strong emphasis upon reason. And while they held a liberal
and moderately rationalistic approach toward Church authority, they
stayed firmly within the confines of the Church of England. Their critics
named them Latitudinarians, and Locke, who at one time almost certainly
became a member of Whichcote's congregation at St. Lawrence Jewry,
held more than a hundred Latitudinarian books in his library. A number
of important scholars consider Locke himself to have been a Latitudinarian, and what is certain is that he was defending Latitudinarianism
early on.[9] In an article on toleration in his *Commonplace Book* written
in 1667, Locke wrote the following with regard to the dangers of
attempting to establish religious uniformity:

To consider how it comes to pass that the Christian religion has made more
factions, wars, and disturbances in civil societies than any other, and whether
Toleration and Latitudinism would not prevent those evils ... The making the
terms of church communion as large as may be, i.e. that you articles in speculative
opinions be few and large, and ceremonies in worship few and easy, which is
Latitudinism.[10]

In his *Essay on Toleration* Locke, though, went much farther than any
Latitudinarian was willing to go in encouraging toleration for noncon-
formist religious practices outside of the Church. The Latitudinarians also

[8] Lichtenstein, *Henry More*, pp. 25–29. Henry More was also referred to as a
Latitudinarian. See Spellman, *John Locke*, pp. 18–19. Gerald R. Cragg, *From
Puritanism to the Age of Reason* (Cambridge: Cambridge University Press, 1966), p. 60.
For more about Locke and More, see Rogers, *Locke's Enlightenment*, pp. 133–142.
[9] John Marshall, "John Locke and Latitudinarianism," in *Philosophy, Science and Religion
in England 1640–1700*, Ashcraft, Kroll and Zagorin (eds.) (Cambridge: Cambridge
University Press, 1992), p. 253. Henning Graff Reventlow also included Locke in his
study of the Latitudinarians. Reventlow, *The Authority of the Bible*, pp. 223–285.
[10] King, *Life and Letters of John Locke*, p. 156.

rejected resistance to all forms of government in total, something Locke obviously came to champion in the *Two Treatises*.[11]

Another important figure who played a probable role in Locke's acquaintance with the religious world of the Cambridge Platonists was Ralph Cudworth (1617–1688), a leader of the group along with Henry More, Regius Professor of Hebrew at Cambridge, and frequent correspondent of John Selden on scholarly subjects that had to do with Jewish learning. He was an advocate of social tolerance and human freedom, opposed both atheism and religious fatalism, and was a leading opponent of Thomas Hobbes, whom he regarded as a spokesman for materialistic atheism. In 1655, early in his career, Cudworth was appointed by Cromwell to decide whether Jews should be allowed to resettle in England and met at least twice with the influential Dutch rabbi and diplomat Manasseh Ben Israel (1604–1657), who was negotiating with the Cromwell government on this subject.[12] It seems that Locke did not meet Cudworth in person, but he was at one stage in love with his daughter, Damaris,

---

[11] Marshall, *Resistance, Religion and Responsibility*, pp. 59, 284.
[12] Popkin, "The Image of Judaism in Seventeenth Century Europe," p. 105. L. Finkelstein, *The Jews: Their History, Culture, and Religion* (Westport, CT: Greenwood Press, 1960), pp. 253–256. See also Cecil Roth, *A History of the Jews in England* (Oxford: Clarendon Press, 1949), pp. 149–172.
  Locke's own physical exposure to Jews was not extensive to say the least. During his diplomatic posting at Cleves in 1665, he wrote that he admired how "Jews, Anabaptists and Quakers coexisted peaceably." Ten years later, while touring France he recorded in his journal a meeting with the Jews of Avignon. "Here the Jews have a quarter to themselves where they have a synagogue. The Place where they inhibit is the nastiest & most stinking that I ever was yet in, & they all clad like beggars, though we were told some of them were rich. They were (!) yellow hats for distinction, as at Orange, where are about 12 familys of them." Lough (ed.), *Locke's Travels in France*, p. 12. And see Nabil I. Matar, "John Locke and the Jews," *The Journal of Ecclesiastical History* 44, 1 (Jan. 1993), pp. 45–62. Another interesting clue regarding a possible connection between Locke and Jewish affairs can be found in the friendship between Locke and Robert Boyle during the 1660s. It was during that time that Boyle took a keen interest in the Sabbatai Zevi affair, and it is possible that during their conversations of common intellectual interests Boyle shared his thoughts about this timely and theologically vigorous issue with his good friend. See Richard H. Popkin, "Jewish Messianism and Christian Millenarianism," in *Culture and Politics from Puritanism to the Enlightenment*, P. Zagorin (ed.) (Berkeley, CA: University of California Press, 1980), p. 80. Elsewhere, Popkin notes that John Evelyn, one of the important English historians of the Sabbatai Zevi affair, was also a member of London's Royal Society. Popkin, "Three English Tellings of the Sabbatai Zevi Story," p. 44. It is quite probable then that the paths of Evelyn and Locke crossed, as Locke was made member at the society in 1668 and Evelyn's book on Sabbatai Zevi was published the following year.
  It appears, though, that Locke did not attribute the same longevity of purpose to the Jewish people as he did to the Hebrew Bible. While there are traces of Philo-Semitism in

a well-educated woman for the times, with whom he had long conversations and extended correspondence before he left for Holland in 1683. It
is highly probable that religious issues were discussed during their discourses and that adumbrations of Cudworth's world views were on their
agenda. Locke was a permanent guest in Damaris's (later, Lady Masham)
home throughout the last years of his life, and it was she who read to him
verses from the Book of Psalms during the hours before his death.[13]

Locke's own membership in the Church of England did not compromise the constant augmentation of his toleration and acceptance of religious
diversity. In a private letter from 1680 he wrote that while it is true that he
was part of the official Church, what was required for peace and stability
in England was "unity in true religion ... rather than a unity with the
established Church ... unity does not require conformity with the Church
of England it is a matter of Christians being in peace and in Charity." This
is a notion he personalized when describing his own nondenominational
identity.

[I] read the word of God without prepossession or bias, and come to it with a
resolution to take my sense from it, and not with a design to bring it to the sense of
my system. How much that had made men wind and twist and pull the text in all
the several sects of Christians, I need not tell you. I desire to take my religion from
the scriptures, and then whether it suits or suits not any other denomination, I am
not much concerned; for I think at the last day it will not be inquired whether
I were of the church of England, or the church of Geneva, but whether I sought
and embraced the truth in the love of it.[14]

Locke argued in effect that each individual had the right to choose his
or her own preferred way to salvation and that there could be no charge
of iniquity against a person who chose to depart from the established
Church as opposed to one who remained a follower.[15]

Locke's works, it appears that at least toward the end of his life he strongly advocated
Jewish conversion to Christianity. This was not to be forced conversion; he never
abandoned his opposition to the exclusion of Jews in England, and he continued to
champion their being tolerated as a distinct entity and their naturalization into English
society. But he seems to have developed a strong evangelical streak in his later years,
which led him to a conversionary attitude toward the Jews. See Matar, "John Locke and
the Jews." Adam Sutcliffe, *Judaism and Enlightenment* (Cambridge: Cambridge
University Press, 2003), pp. 218–220.

[13] Milton, "Locke, John (1632–1704)." And see Matar, "John Locke and the Jews,"
pp. 90–106.

[14] Locke, "A Letter from Mr. Locke to Mr. Samuel Bold," *Works of John Locke*, vol. 9, p. 4.

[15] See "A letter to Edward Stillingfleet," in Woolhouse, *Locke: A Biography*, pp. 167, 169.

From Latitudinarianism, Locke was drawn to what philosopher and Locke biographer Maurice Cranston calls "its logical conclusion," Socinianism.[16] The Socinians were an anti-Trinitarian sect that followed the teachings of the sixteenth-century Italian theologians Lelio Sozzini and his nephew Fausto, who advocated a very limited Christology. They did not reject revelation, as they did the doctrine of original sin, but they insisted on the free use of reason over revelation.[17] Locke certainly had a large number of Socinian books in his library, and his private notes on the Trinity and the deity of Christ suggest that he indeed rejected both doctrines.[18] Accusations of Locke's Socinianism intensified following the publication of Anglican clergyman John Edward's *Some Thoughts Concerning the Several Causes and Occasions of Atheism*. Whether formally Socinian or not, Marshall makes the important point that Locke's limiting of requisite religious dogma while winnowing out speculative opinions was a result of his desire to strengthen belief in God, not weaken it. In relation to Locke's rejection specifically of the Trinity and the Fall, Marshall writes: "Concerned throughout his life to prove that God existed, the arguments to convince atheists to be religious were always very important to Locke; no mere rhetorical worry was being voiced in opposing such explanations and formulations of doctrine."[19]

During his exile in Holland, Locke met the Remonstrants, who were primarily followers of Jacobus Arminius but chose nonetheless not to call themselves Arminians. These theorists already had a dramatic influence on the seventeenth-century Dutch Republic; their thinking found in the writings of Hugo Grotius is but one example. Locke grew close to their religious beliefs, which were similar in many respects, particularly in their

[16] Cranston, *John Locke: A Biography*, p. 126.

[17] See D. Hedley, "Persons of Substance and the Cambridge Connection: Some Roots and Ramifications of the Trinitarian Controversy in Seventeenth Century England," in *Socinianism and Arminianism*, M. Muslow and J. Rohls (eds.) (Boston, MA: Brill Leiden, 2005), p. 232. For more about the "Socinian tradition" and its connection with the Great Tew Circle, see Roper, *Catholics, Anglicans and Puritans*, pp. 186–192.

[18] Milton, "Locke, John (1632–1704)." For more about Locke and Socinianism, see Dewey D. Wallace, Jr., "Socinianism, Justification by Faith, and the Sources of John Locke's The Reasonableness of Christianity," *Journal of the History of Ideas* 45, 1 (1984), pp. 49–66. Nicholas Jolley, "Leibniz on Locke and Socinianism," *Journal of the History of Ideas* 39, 1 (1978), pp. 223–250. Hedley, "Persons of Substance and the Cambridge Connection," p. 232. Winthrop Hudson, "John Locke – Preparing the Way for the Revolution," *Journal of Presbyterian History* 42 (1964), pp. 19–38.

[19] Marshall, *Resistance, Religion and Responsibility*, p. 64. See also pp. 138–154, for a discussion of the intellectual process whereby Locke's anti-Trinitarianism, opposition to original sin, and Socinianism developed.

more tolerant religious attitudes, to those of the Latitudinarians and Socinians.[20] In 1687, Locke lived in the home of Benjamin Furly, a liberal Quaker who influenced Locke's unconsummated plans to establish the Society of Pacific Christians, an organization that was to be open to all who received the truth that was revealed in the Scriptures, while its members were to acknowledge the duty of mutual tolerance among Christians.[21] It was probably through Furly that Locke met F. M. Van Helmont, who endeavored to foster tolerance among Christian sects by reviving the Hebrew language, which he called "the divine language of creation."[22]

Locke's religious identity then was firm but eclectic; he was educated Puritan but defended Anglicanism; he was openly Latitudinarian, passively Socinian, and close to Remonstrantism. These varied religious beliefs helped to shape his thoughts concerning the structure of society; the relationship between government, religion, and the individual; the importance of the presence of religion in the public arena; and, most importantly, his ever-growing advocacy of religious and social tolerance.[23]

Preceding the *Two Treatises* was the publication of a composition that Locke had written in collaboration with his good friend Remonstrant theologian Philip van Limborch, during his stay in the United Provinces. Entitled *Epistola de Tolerantia*, it was published in its Latin original in Amsterdam in April 1690 and reached London bookstores a few months later.[24] It was translated into English by William Popple, under the title

[20] Parker, *The Biblical Politics of John Locke*, p. 25. It is important to note that Jonathan Israel has argued that the Remonstrants were not as tolerant in practice as they were in theory. Jonathan Israel, "The Intellectual Debate about Toleration in the Dutch Republic," in *The Emergence of Tolerance in the Dutch Republic*, C. Berkvens-Stevelinck, J. Israel, and G. H. M. Posthumous Meyjes (eds.) (Leiden: Brill, 1997), pp. 3–36.

[21] Pearson, "The Religion of John Locke," p. 247.

[22] In his letters to Locke, Furly kept him abreast of Van Helmont's activities and whereabouts. See Woolhouse, *Locke: A Biography*, pp. 250, 330, and Van Helmont, *Alphabet of Nature*, pp. xii–xiii.

[23] Cranston, *John Locke: A Biography*, pp. 182, 210. See also Sanford Kessler, "John Locke's Legacy of Religious Freedom," *Polity* 17, 3 (1985), pp. 484–503.

[24] Limborch was in fact the grandnephew of Episcopius, a follower of Arminius, who founded the Remonstrants in opposition to the prevailing Dutch Calvinism at the time. See Aaron, *John Locke*, p. 20. Aaron provides us with the best possible exposé of Locke's feelings for Limborch and his movement, by offering a translation of a letter Locke sent to him a few days before he departed Holland for his homeland. "In going away, I almost feel as if I were leaving my own country and my own kinsfolk; for everything that belongs to kinship, goodwill, love, kindness – everything that binds men together with ties

A Letter Concerning Toleration, and available to the public later that year. Popple, who had published his translation without Locke's endorsement, did nevertheless respect Locke's insistence on anonymity, as with regard to the *Two Treatises*.[25]

The subject of *toleration* had become paramount in Locke's conversations with Limborch particularly following James's ascent to the throne in 1685, the same year Louis XIV revoked the Edict of Nantes (1598) that had granted French Protestants some degree of toleration. Locke feared that English Protestants would soon be subject to persecution similar to that of their French coreligionists, which even included conversion by torture.[26] Locke now went further with his advocacy of civil toleration than he did in his *Essay Concerning Toleration* that he had written some twenty years earlier (1667). If in the *ECT* he narrowed the religious concerns a magistrate could justifiably contend with to a bare minimum, in the *Epistola* he basically argued that religion was of no civil concern at all. A government, posited Locke, is charged only with ensuring that civil interests, such as "life, liberty, health ... money, land, and houses," are guaranteed to the public, not religious concernments. Because the concern of religion is salvation, and salvation requires intent, a government, which cannot conceivably know the thoughts of humans, can also not be responsible for their salvation. Even if the magistrate can coerce outward adherence, the inner conviction that God demands remains beyond his reach. For this reason Locke followed Milton's anti-Erastianism, and by doing so his intention was to strengthen the Christian faith, not weaken it, as it was Christ himself who argued who insisted on a separation of the realms.

For the commonwealth of the Jews, different in that from all others, was an absolute theocracy; nor was there, or could there be any difference between that commonwealth and the Church ... But there is no such thing under the Gospel as a

---

stronger than ties of blood – I have found in you in abundance. I leave behind my friends whom I can never forget and shall never cease to wish for an opportunity of coming back to enjoy once more the genuine fellowship of men who have been such friends that, while far away from all my own connections, while suffering in every other way, I have never felt sick at heart. As for you, best, dearest, and most worthy of men, when I think of your learning, your wisdom, your kindness and candour and gentleness, I seem to have found in your friendship alone enough to make me always rejoice that I was forced to pass so many years amongst you." Ibid, p.24.

[25] Woolhouse, *Locke: A Biography*, pp. 270, 274. Popple, Woolhouse suggests, probably belonged to the "Dry Club," a discussion group that Locke had founded upon his return to England. Ibid.

[26] Ibid, pp. 230–231.

Christian commonwealth ... [Christ] indeed taught men how, by faith and good works, they can obtain life; but He instituted no commonwealth.[27]

Locke did exclude two groups from his brand of toleration: Catholics and atheists, the former because they owed allegiance to an earthly power other than their own government, and the latter because what binds human society together are "promises, covenants, and oaths" that are kept only by those fearful of God. Locke was equally insistent on interdenominational toleration as well.[28]

But there were those at the time who thought that the toleration Locke was advocating would have a deleterious effect on the "true" religion. In an anonymously published pamphlet entitled *The Argument of the "Letter Concerning Toleration" Briefly Considered and Answered* written by an Anglican clergyman by the name of Jonas Proast, Locke's negation of *force* as a legitimate medium of coercion was condemned. Proast believed that it was the duty of the civil sovereign to apply force in order to ensure religious compliance, and Locke's contention that religiosity was not a "civil concernment" was incorrect and dangerous. In a response longer than Proast's critique itself, entitled *A Second Letter Concerning Toleration*, Locke responded that nothing was more dangerous than that which Proast was advocating because there was no guarantee that the civil sovereign would himself be Protestant, in which case the undue power of coercion could fall, for example, into the hands of "Popery." Locke again pressed his argument that the concern of the sovereign was outward compliance, while religion demanded a conviction of the heart and mind, things which could not be coerced.[29] Proast was not quieted, though, and countered with *A Third Letter Concerning Toleration*, again publishing it anonymously. Some months later Locke fired back with the *Third Letter for Toleration to the Author of the Third Letter Concerning Toleration*, in which he reiterated many of his earlier arguments against the religious enforcement on the part of the sovereign, but he also included a discussion on miracles, a negation of "original sin"

[27] From Locke, *A Letter Concerning Toleration*, p. 43. See Chapter 3, *ft.* 110 and Chapter 5, *ft.* 222.
[28] Locke, "A Letter Concerning Toleration," in *The Works of John Locke* (London: Thomas Tegg, 1823). See especially pp. 9, 10, 28. Locke, I believe, was implicitly much more inclusive of atheists and Catholics (and innatists) in the *Second Treatise* than he was in the LCT, a subject I discussed in Chapter 3.
[29] Ibid, vol. 6, pp. 73–77, 126. Woolhouse, *Locke: A Biography*, pp. 308–312.

as requisite for salvation, and an argument against the notion that Anglicanism was exclusively the true religion.[30]

While they both engendered a public buzz over their contents and
whom the author might be, the anonymity of the *Treatises* and the
Epistola prevented any notoriety. That was not the case with *An Essay
Concerning Human Understanding*, which Locke prepared for publication during this same period. It was a compendium of ideas primarily
regarding the origins of knowledge that Locke had compiled in more than
twenty years of conversation with friends on the subject, and in contrast
to the other two works, here Locke did not hide his identity. One of these
key interlocutors was Thomas Herbert, later the Earl of Pembroke
(1683), who Locke also treated for illness and remained a lifelong friend,
to whom Locke dedicated the work.[31]

Stylistically, the *Essay*'s format is similar to that of the *Two Treatises*.
First Locke puts forth that which in his opinion necessitates negation, and
then presents the notions he deems correct.[32] Locke divided the *Essay* into
four books. In the first he argues against the doctrine of innate knowledge
(such as in the philosophy of Rene Descartes, even though he does not
mention him by name), offering instead that the primeval human mind is
tabula rasa, a clean slate that attains knowledge through experience;
Book II looks into the origins of ideas, their nature and purpose; Book
III explores the connection between words and ideas; and Book IV delves
into the essence of knowledge itself. Because it was written piecemeal over
what was a long period of time, "what has been the diversion of some of
my idle and heavy hours," it necessitated major editing, which Locke
chose not to bother with. He admitted his work was bulky and repeti-
tious, but he remained uninclined to make the requisite changes.

[I]t grew insensibly to the bulk it now appears in. I will not deny, but possibly it
might be reduced to a narrower compass than it is; and that some parts of it might
be contracted: the way it has been writ in, by catches, and many long intervals of
interruption, being apt to cause some repetitions. But to confess the truth, I am
now too lazy, or too busy, to make it shorter.[33]

---

[30] Locke, "A Third Letter Concerning Toleration," in *The Works of John Locke*, A New
Edition, vol. 6, pp. 141–546.

[31] Woolhouse, *Locke: A Biography*, pp. 126, 277.

[32] This consistency of style provides further evidence that Locke similarly intended the *Two
Treatises* to be read as one interdependent text.

[33] Locke, "The Epistle to the Reader," in *An Essay Concerning Human Understanding*,
pp. 7–9.

The cumbersomeness of the text, though, did not prevent its popularity as it was owned by more English people than the work of any other philosopher, at least from the time of its publication until Locke's death.[34] It was a time in which epistemology engendered great interest, because the intense examination of nature brought on by such figures as Bayle, Descartes, Hobbes, Spinoza, and Leibniz led naturally to critical investigation into the origin and limits of human knowledge.[35] It was a hit at Oxford, where many copies were sold even though it was initially subject to an official ban, and even the library at Christ Church ultimately requested an official copy from the author.[36] Following its second printing (some four years after the first in May, 1694) Oxford tutors already recommended the *Essay* to their pupils.[37]

One of the tutors, John Wynne of Jesus College, petitioned Locke for permission to create an abridged version so that the main ideas would be sufficiently available to young students. After Locke scrupulously checked Wynn's background and determined that he was fit for the task, he granted consent. The result was a compendium entitled *An Abridgement of Mr. Locke's Essay Concerning Human Understanding*, the printing of which coincided with the printing of the third edition of the *Essay*.[38] It was not that the *Essay* escaped criticism; there was plenty of it, and it was sometimes harsh, but that may have enhanced its popularity as Locke reedited three times, making for a total of four publications in his lifetime.[39]

---

[34] Rosalie L. Colie, "John Locke and the Publication of the Private," *Philological Quarterly* 45 (1966), p. 24.

[35] See Ernst Cassirer, *The Philosophy of the Enlightenment* (Princeton, NJ: Princeton University Press, 1951), p. 99.

[36] Woolhouse, *Locke: A Biography*, p. 279.

[37] Ibid, p. 345. At Trinity College, Dublin, it became mandatory reading in 1700. Locke, "Introduction," *An Essay Concerning Human Understanding*, p. xxii.

[38] Ibid, pp. 345–346.

[39] Neal Wood, whose thesis argues for a political reading of the *Essay*, emphasizes that Locke did not intend the *Essay* as mere theory to be engaged in exclusively through esoteric analysis, but intended it rather to assist the masses with their daily lives. "Students of the *Essay* tend to forget that Locke wrote to help men act more effectively in their practical affairs, and not solely for the sake of analyzing technical philosophical problems ... the *Essay* aimed at utility ... Locke's intention was very matter-of-fact and pragmatic; he wished to show his readers how they could act more rationally in society, in religion and politics." Wood, *The Politics of Locke's Philosophy*, pp. 44–45. The popularity of the *Essay* may serve to indicate that Locke at least partially achieved his goal.

James Tyrrell, an old-time friend of Locke from his days at Christ Church and with whom Locke had left a trunk full of his belongings as well as some of his writings before departing for Holland, was the first to suggest that the *Essay* had more enemies than friends.[40] Claiming that he was just a mouthpiece for acquaintances at Oxford but probably voicing his own criticisms, Tyrrell asserted that Locke denied a law of nature and by discounting revelation established very uncertain grounds for morality. Even Isaac Newton initially picked up on this idea and alleged that in his denial of innate ideas Locke was "[striking] at the root of morality."[41] Although Locke thought both criticisms unfair and rooted in misunderstanding, they served to encourage him to make some changes for the sake of clarification in the second edition.[42] In anticipation of the second printing Locke solicited the advice of William Molyneux, a Dublin scholar who had written on astronomy and optics while serving in the Irish Parliament. In what undoubtedly endeared him greatly to Locke, he wrote of the *Essay* that, "the incomparable Mr. Locke ... has rectified more received mistakes, and delivered more profound truths ... than are to be met with in all the volumes of the ancients."[43] For his part, Molyneux could not find anything that in his mind could be excised from the *Essay*, that had been a specific query of Locke's, but he did, on the contrary, suggest that Locke actually expand the work to include *A Treatise of Morals*, as Locke had hinted that morals are "demonstrable" and could be achieved through a "mathematical method."[44] Locke promised to try and get to it at his leisure, but never felt pressed enough to find the time.[45]

---

[40] The friendship between the two began to sour when Tyrrell tried to secure a pardon for Locke from Charles without Locke's consent. When Tyrrell now tactlessly pressured Locke over the authorship of the *Treatises* and *Epistola* Locke was drawn even farther apart from his old friend. See Woolhouse, *Locke: A Biography*, pp. 21–22, 163, 258–260.

[41] Locke, *The Correspondence of John Locke*, p. 1659.

[42] Woolhouse, *Locke: A Biography*, pp. 289–290.

[43] Locke, *The Works of John Locke*, vol. 9, p. 289. Locke, *The Correspondence of John Locke*, p. 1515.

[44] Ibid, p. 1530.

[45] Woolhouse, *Locke: A Biography*, p. 314. Molyneux also recommended that Locke expand on his discussion of human liberty, a suggestion that Locke did follow up on. Another major piece of editing Locke made in the second edition had to do with the chapter "On Power," in which he changed what he saw as determining human will from *belief* to *feeling*. Locke also added a whole new chapter entitled "Of Identity and Diversity." See Ibid, pp. 320, 327–328, 329–331.

There were more critics of the *Essay* who perceived it as too iconoclastic and threatening of accepted theological norms. In a work entitled *Cursory Reflections upon a Book Called An Essay Concerning Human Understanding*, John Norris enlisted the French rationalist philosopher Nicolas Malebranche (1638–1715) in order to challenge Locke.[46] Malebranche would not sanction the notion that knowledge could be the result of sensory perception, for that would equal a diminishing of God's power; rather material things were shown to humans by God himself. In a thousand-word essay entitled "Answer to Mr. Norris," Locke retorted that, on the contrary, to suggest that God did not have the ability to enable the attainment of human knowledge through the granting of the ability of perception to the human mind (through a divine soul) was to limit the power of God.[47]

German mathematician and philosopher Gottfried Wilhelm Von Leibniz (1646–1716), with whom Locke corresponded, was another critic of Locke's attack on innatism, as ideas, so he believed, came from the soul. Locke, though, did not hold Leibniz's philosophical acumen in high enough esteem to bother writing a thorough response, much to the consternation of Leibniz.[48]

But the most persistent and unyielding critic of the *Essay* was Dr. Edward Stillingfleet, the Bishop of Worcester. Following the appearance of the third edition, Stillingfleet published an attack on the *Essay* entitled *A Discourse in Vindication of the Doctrine of the Trinity.*[49] Despite the fact that Locke attributed Stillingfleet's criticisms to his own garbled understanding of what he had actually written, Locke did not tire of answering the bishop's unstinting written attacks because of his senior stature in the Church and the broad inclination to accept everything he

---

[46] Ibid, p. 323.   [47] Ibid, pp. 316–318, 323–325.

[48] Leibniz's poor English might also have had something to do with his faulty understanding of what Locke actually meant. Ibid, pp. 367–368.

[49] This was not the first time that Locke and Stillingfleet contended over the questions of religious dogma, conformity, and toleration. When in 1680 Stillingfleet published two works, *Mischief of Separation* and *Unreasonableness of Separation*, both harshly criticizing the separatism of the nonconformists with the Church of England, Locke countered with a lengthy point-by-point refutation entitled *Critical Notes upon Edward Stillingfleet's Mischief and Unreasonableness of Separation*. Contrary to Stillingfleet, Locke insisted that "edification" was dependent on individual choice and pursuit and could not be forced top-down by the Church. Locke agreed with Stillingfleet's contention that the Church of England was the best bulwark against "popery" but contested that that would better be accomplished by lessoning standards of conformity, not by increasing them. For a full discussion of this controversy, see Marshall, *Resistance, Religion and Responsibility*, pp. 95–112.

said at face value.[50] Stillingfleet attacked Locke on many fronts, claiming, for example, as other critics of Locke had done before him that the denial of innatism was one step from atheism, but he was forceful in accusing Locke of anti-Trinitarianism, or Unitarianism, or, once again, Socinianism.[51]

The Socinians, it must be remembered, were considered a heretical sect, and for Locke to have been considered a member would have relegated his writings to a very small and proscribed grouping. It was perhaps also for this reason that Locke refused to let Stillingfleet's broadsides go unanswered. Stillingfleet's accusations were persistent and forceful, and it does not appear that Locke's incessant responses did much to mitigate them, because Locke was equally persistent in his unwillingness to come out and state unequivocally that he believed in the Trinity.[52] In his ongoing debate with Stillingfleet, Locke was to come as close as he possibly could to outward denial of the Trinity without actually saying so in so many words.

Your lordship herein lay upon me what I cannot do, without owning to know what I am sure I do not know: for how the doctrine of the Trinity has been always received in the christian church, I confess myself ignorant. I have not had time to examine the history of it, and to read those controversies that have been writ about it: and to own a doctrine as received by others, when I do not know how these others received it, is perhaps a short way to orthodoxy, that may satisfy some men: but he that takes this way to give satisfaction, in my opinion makes a little bold with truth; and it may be questioned whether such a profession be pleasing to that God, who requires truth in the inward parts, however acceptable it may in man be to his diocesan.[53]

In his *A Letter to the Bishop of Worcester* Locke distanced himself from John Toland, a Unitarian, who had written a book entitled *Christianity Not Mysterious* in which he had negated ideas of revelation that were "above reason" and with whom Locke had been lumped together by Stillingfleet. Locke insisted that his *Essay* in no way entered into questions assumed by the bishop and that he certainly did not

---

[50] Woolhouse, *Locke: A Biography*, pp. 370–371, 388.

[51] The Unitarians denied the Trinity, and the Socinians were a Unitarian sect. Marshall is of the opinion that Locke wrote the *Essay* before he was exposed to Socinian tracts. Marshall, *Resistance, Religion and Responsibility*, p. 348. See also Marshall for a brief analysis of the "Unitarian Controversy" that engulfed theological dialogue in England from 1687 through 1700. Ibid, pp. 389–398.

[52] Stillingfleet submitted that had Locke done so, it would have ended the controversy between them. See Woolhouse, *Locke: A Biography*, p. 403.

[53] Locke, "Mr. Locke's Reply to the Right Reverend the Lord Bishop of Worcester's Answer to His Second Letter," p. 144.

reject revelation. Stillingfleet responded with a *Reply* and Locke came back at him with an *Answer* that included a response as well to a clergyman named Thomas Burnett, who had also written a pamphlet critical of the *Essay*, entitled *Remarks upon an Essay Concerning Human Understanding.*

In 1698, the persistent Stillingfleet accused Locke of not answering his previously leveled criticism that Locke was supportive of irreligion in a pamphlet with the long title: *The Bishop of Worcester's Answer to Mr. Locke's Second Letter; wherein His Notion of Ideas Is Prov'd to Be Inconsistent with Itself, and with the Articles of the Christian Faith.* A few months later, Locke's rejoinder followed: *Mr. Locke's Reply to the Right Reverend the Lord Bishop of Worcester's Answer to His Second Letter.*

With the printing of the fourth edition of the *Essay* (dated 1700) Locke had tired of all the controversy, but the theoretical contest had for the most part already been determined in his favor. Locke's Remonstrant friend from his time in Amsterdam, for example, Jean Le Clerc, credited the *Essay*'s vindication to the reserve Locke showed during the course of the debate. "Never was a controversy, managed with so much skill on one side, and on the other part with so much misrepresentation, confusion, and ignorance, alike discreditable to the cause and the advocate."[54] Locke was flooded with correspondence regarding the *Essay* until his death, but did not respond to many of the letters.[55]

In another major work written during this period, *Some Thoughts Concerning Education* (1693), Locke presented his ideas regarding the proper education of children. Most of the book was based on letters he had written during his five-year exile to Edward Clarke, who sought his advice regarding the education of his own children. Locke had known Clarke ever since he joined the household of the Earl of Shaftesbury as

---

[54] King, *Life and Letters of John Locke*, pp. 179–220, esp. pp. 181, 195. Locke himself expressed his disdain for controversy in his exchange with Stillingfleet. "My lord, I so little love controversy, that I never began a dispute with any body; nor shall ever continue it, where others begin with me, any longer than the appearance of truth, which first made me write, obliges me not to quit it." Locke, "Mr Locke's Reply to the Right Reverend the Lord Bishop of Worcester's Answer to His Second Letter, p. 92.

[55] One letter he did find the time to answer was that of French jurist Jean Barbeyrac (1674–1744). Woolhouse, *Locke: A Biography*, p. 427. Barbeyrac had fled France following the revocation of the Edict of Nantes, and taught law and history in Germany and Switzerland. He is known primarily for his preface and notes to his translation of the work of Samuel Pufendorf, *De Jure Naturae et Gentium*.

Clarke served as a trustee of the Shaftesbury estate.[56] Locke, of course, had no children of his own, but his studies regarding the origins of knowledge had forced him to ponder the proper method of conditioning children to pursue knowledge and moral behavior. He also garnered practical experience when he was charged with the education of Shaftesbury's grandson, in tutoring students at Oxford, traveling in France with Caleb Banks, and in the household of Benjamin Furly of Rotterdam, where he stayed occasionally during his time in the United Provinces.[57] Locke's instructions cover general health-related issues such as diet and sleeping habits, the benefits of restraint, the encouragement of curiosity, and how reading is to be taught, virtue followed, and excellence pursued. What is of greatest importance for our interests here, though, is his focus on teaching. Locke's work on education is much less controversial than the *Treatises*, the *Essay*, or the *Letter*, but it is crucial to emphasize that Locke's pedagogy is all but irrelevant for a human nature that is singularly defined by sinfulness, Christologically ascribed to the ubiquitous and permanence of humankind's primordial descent into depravity. But more on that in a moment.

In August 1695 Locke published, once again anonymously, *The Reasonableness of Christianity*, in which he presented his theological rendering of Christianity and his understanding of its historical role. His primary motivation for writing *The Reasonableness* following the *Two Treatises*, the *Letter Concerning Toleration*, and the *Essay Concerning Human Understanding* was to present a Christian theology that was consistent with his other doctrines.[58] The importance of Locke's insistence on doctrinal compatibility cannot be overstated. In what should have caused the Straussian school a thorough reassessment of their attribution of radical secularism to Locke, it is clear that Locke wrote *The Reasonableness of Christianity* to insist on his Christian religiosity and its compatibility with his political thinking. But no less critical is the understanding that he accomplished the harmony he sought through a vital reductionist or softer approach to Christian dogma. This broadening of the tent centered on his restriction of the mandatory articles of Christian faith to two basic tenets: belief in Jesus Christ as the *Messiah* and *repentance* (or *obedience*), and contrarily, negating the "imputationist" reading of Christianity and the dogma that extended from it.

---

[56] Woolhouse, *Locke: A Biography*, p. 195.   [57] Ibid, pp. 204, 249.
[58] See Harris, *The Mind of John Locke*, p. 303.

Because the criticisms that had been leveled at his writings were primarily of a theological nature, questioning his religious loyalties and charging that his ideas on toleration and knowledge were cast in heresy, Locke's rendering of Christian dogma did not serve to calm the storm. For his individualistic, perhaps even iconoclastic exposition of religious concepts such as the Fall, the meaning of death, divine law, and the Messiah, Locke was again harshly criticized. His most strident critic was Anglican clergyman John Edwards, who excoriated Locke over the "minimalist creed" he had created,[59] and (like Stillingfleet over the *Essay*) charged him with being a Socinian. He claimed that Locke omitted ineluctable dogma, imperative for being a true Christian, such as the Trinity and the doctrine of original sin.

Locke also circumscribed the divine nature and the satisfaction of Jesus Christ by refusing to attribute essential divinity to Christ, and instead only asserted his superiority over angels. And as if that was not sufficient to prove Locke's heresy, he also ignored New Testament epistles, asserting that they were not requisite interpreters of Christian faith.[60] Edwards's initial broadside, entitled *Some Thoughts Concerning the Several Causes and Occasions of Atheism*, was published just a month after Locke published the *Reasonableness*, and Locke responded shortly thereafter with a brief tract called *Vindication of the Reasonableness of Christianity*. Locke's *Vindication*, though, did not serve to mitigate any of the charges Edwards had leveled against him; on the contrary. Because Locke clung to anonymity on the one hand and on the other claimed in his retort to never have read any Socinian books, Edwards charged that Locke was part of a Socinian plot, which advanced Socinian ideas while claiming to be ignorant of them. To this end Edwards published three works over the following year and a half, entitled *Socinianism Unmasked*, *The Socinian Creed*, and *The Causes of Atheism*.

A clergyman by the name of Samuel Bold came to Locke's defense, initially in a sermon entitled *A Discourse of the True Knowledge of Christ Jesus* and then in a longer printed tract. Bold agreed with Locke's

---

[59] Victor Nuovo writes that John Edwards appears to be the first to use the expression *minimalist creed* in his critique of the *Reasonableness*. Nuovo (ed.), *John Locke: Writings on Religion*, p. li.

[60] Ibid. Locke explained later that other parts of the New Testament, such as Paul's Epistles, were written for those already of the Christian faith, and hence contained more than the absolute dictates of Christianity, whereas he was coming just to present the most basic dogma. Locke, *A Second Vindication of the Reasonableness of Christianity*, in *The Works of John Locke*, vol. 7, p. 188.

distinction between what must be believed to be a Christian (minimalist creed) and what is then incumbent on a Christian to believe (the teachings of the Gospels), a dichotomy that Edwards does not seem to have been able to accept. Locke was grateful to Bold, as is clear from his dedication of his next work to him, but he nonetheless responded to Edwards's persistent accusations of Socinianism with a much longer defense of the *Reasonableness* simply called *A Second Vindication of the Reasonableness of Christianity*, which was published at the beginning of 1697.

As in the case of the *Essay* and the *Epistola*, dogmatic religious criticism of the *Reasonableness* subsided, probably due in no small measure to Locke's refusal to allow Proast, Stillingfleet, and Edwards to get in the last word.[61] But the theological tempest he created by breaking with rigid religious dogma in his *Reasonableness of Christianity* as well as the *Essay*,[62] not the least of which was his obviation of the centrality of original sin, did not provide him with the quiet he was looking for during his final years. It also undoubtedly helped provide the impetus to keep his two political treatises, devoid of New Testamentism, anonymous.

ORIGINAL SIN AND THE CRITICAL INFLUENCE OF AUGUSTINE

Locke makes no reference to the concept of original sin in the *Second Treatise* and only scant secondary mention of it in the *First*. This begs our attention because human nature is a primary determinant of how humankind is to be governed, and the prevailing Christian-based seventeenth-century understanding of human nature was predicated on the notion of humankind's natural fallen state of depravity. The lack of any substantive Lockean discourse on the Fall in the *Two Treatises* is particularly, but not exclusively, problematic for the Cambridge School, which interprets Locke's politics entirely in Christological terms, and the Fall was simply not a concept that would have been easily avoided in Locke's England. It

---

[61] Woolhouse, *Locke: A Biography*, pp. 376–384.

[62] Isabel Rivers points to the "freethinkers" of the time and the support they drew from these two works of Locke, a potential outcome that concerned him but that he did not intend. Anthony Collins, who spent a great deal of time with Locke before his death and of whom Locke was particularly fond, was a leader of this group together with Anthony Ashley Cooper, third Earl of Shaftesbury. Locke saw his *Reasonableness* as a defense of the importance of revelation contrary to the freethinkers who denied revelation. See Isabel Rivers, *Reason, Grace, and Sentiment* (Cambridge: Cambridge University Press, 2000), pp. 13–20. See also pp. 89–92, where Rivers documents the harsh criticism these two leveled at Locke following his death.

was as political as it was theological, and because it was political it was ubiquitous; human depravity was inescapable and had to be governed accordingly.[63]

The classic Christian concept of original sin asserts that in eating the forbidden fruit from the Tree of Knowledge, Adam and Eve, and all of humankind following them via "imputation" (meaning embodied in Adam's person), suffered an eternal loss, leading to the existence of an innate human depravity that only the grace of God can counterbalance.[64] This primordial sin changed forever the situation of mankind and brought ineluctable negative powers into being. The idea of the Fall includes an interrelated set of concepts regarding human existence, the most dominant among them being the concept of death as a curse upon mankind, the belief that all humans are in a constant state of sin, and the belief that all human actions are predestined. The theory of the Fall stemming from Adam's original sin was first expressed by Paul both in Corinthians and in

---

[63] William Poole writes that, "In early-modern England, you could not escape the Fall. It was political: if man was fallen and wayward, how should he be governed? Was the original state of Adam as, supposedly, head and ruler of his family, holding, 'by right of Fatherhood, Royal Authority over [his] children', intrinsic justification for a patriarchalist monarchy? Was 'the desire of Liberty ... the First Cause of the Fall of *Adam* '? Or, asked Republicans of Patriarchalists, was Adam, created in the image of God, originally free, and in possession of political liberty, and does this apply to his progeny too?" Poole, *Milton and the Idea of the Fall*, p. 9. And K. I. Parker writes: "In seventeenth-century England, the official church position held two opposing views of human nature: on the one hand, humans were the pinnacles of creation, made in God's image and granted dominion over the earth and its inhabitant; on the other, humans, were intractable in their evil, deliberately transgressing the commandment in the Garden of Eden and thereby condemning themselves to eternal damnation. Humans were corrupt through and through and could not, by their own means, achieve or even strive for perfection." Parker, *The Biblical Politics of John Locke*, p. 50.

[64] Imputation theology is generally of a tripartite nature: the imputation of Adam's sin to his posterity, the imputation of the sins of his people to the Redeemer, and the imputation of the righteousness of Christ to his people. See Benjamin B. Warfield, *The New Schaff-Herzog Encyclopedia of Religious Knowledge*, Samuel Macauley Jackson, D.D., LL.D. (ed.) (New York: Funk and Wagnalls Company, 1909), pp. 465–467. Poole, *Milton and the Idea of the Fall*, pp. 9–20.

Michael Heyd is of the opinion that beginning with the sixteenth century the concept of "imputation" underwent a fundamental metamorphosis. Whereas it was traditionally understood as the "genetic" or "organic" transfer of Adam's sin to all humans, from the late sixteenth century onward that notion fell out of favor and instead a more "voluntarist" concept of imputation was born. This meant that sin was transferred from Adam to all posterity due exclusively to God's will. It was this new and popular understanding of imputation as well that Locke was rejecting. Prof. Heyd was kind enough to share this insight with me in the context of his review of my PhD dissertation.

Romans. Paul submitted that the essential purpose of Christ's first coming
was to solve the problems of sin and death that arose due to the Fall.

So you see, just as death came into the world through a man, Adam, now the
resurrection from the dead has begun through another man, Christ. Everyone dies
because all of us are related to Adam, the first man. But all who are related to
Christ, the other man, will be given new life.[65]

Wherefore, as by one man sin entered into the world, and death by sin; and so
death passed upon all men, for that all have sinned.[66]

The greatest proponent of Pauline original sin was Augustine, the
reborn ascetic whose writings served to link the thinking of antiquity
with that of the Middle Ages, and who solidified church thinking on the
Fall and the extent of human depravity. Augustine was actually responding to Pelagius, who had earlier interpreted the Pauline passage differently, more in keeping with the plain reading of the original text. Pelagius
(354–420 AD) was a British (assumed to have been born in the British
Isles, perhaps Ireland) monk who in early fifth-century Rome advanced
the idea that original sin did not taint human nature, which had been
defined by God in the Book of Genesis (1:31) as "very good," that human
actions were not direct consequences of the sin, and that all humans had a
complete, independent free will and full personal responsibility in choosing good or bad.[67] As a result, he was forced to reject any notions of a
permanent human decline that deprived man of these traits and abilities.
As for Romans 5:12, Pelagius insisted that the text applied to Adam's
posterity only as an example or pattern. For Pelagius, the suggestion that
original sin and accompanying guilt were hereditarily transmitted was
merely a doctrinal fiction.

Augustine came to counter Pelagius's ideas.[68] In order to explain how
Adam and Eve could have chosen evil if God had created them "good"
and "like him," he concluded that they were actually evil to begin with. In
City of God, he writes: "the evil act was committed only by those who
were already evil ... in secret they began to be evil, and this enabled them
to fall into open disobedience."[69] All men, Augustine argued, existed

[65] Corinthians 15:21–22.   [66] Romans 5:12.
[67] Ozment, *The Age of Reform*, p. 29. And see Brinley Roderick Rees, *Pelagius: A Reluctant
Heretic* (Woodbridge, Suffolk: Boydell Press, 1991).
[68] Augustine did not limit his arguments with the Pelagians to the academic realm. As with
other schismatics such as the Donatists, Augustine engaged the full authority of political
power to denigrate and defeat those whom he saw as threatening the integrity of Church
dogma. See Deane, *The Political and Social Ideas of St. Augustine*, pp. 172–220.
[69] Quoted in Poole, *Milton and the Idea of the Fall*, p. 27.

potentially in Adam and thus participated in his guilt of disobedience and his claim of independence from God. This state meant that the only way human beings, who are in this constant state of sin, can respond to the will of God is by his divine and irresistible grace.[70] But not everyone enjoys divine grace, according to Augustine, and furthermore they cannot achieve it through moral living. Bertrand Russell describes Augustinian thinking on predestination as follows:

[I]n God's free grace certain people, among those who have been baptized, are chosen to go to heaven, these are the elect. They do not go to heaven because they are good, we are all totally depraved, except in so far as God's grace, which is only bestowed on the elect, enables us to be otherwise. No reason can be given why some are saved and the rest dammed, this is due to god's unmotived choice.[71]

In this great theological debate over the heart of mainstream Christianity, Augustine was clearly the victor, with Pelagius playing an occasional role as hero to iconoclastic thinkers. Augustine became for medieval theology what Plato and Aristotle were to philosophy,[72] and this made the fact of Adam and Eve's disobedience ubiquitous, all-encompassing, and irremediable.[73] W. M. Spellman compellingly explains the centrality of Augustine's teachings on grace and predestination to all of Christianity:

Augustine, despite what many today see as his exaggerated position on the question of man's essential nature, stands second only to Scripture as an authority in the Western Christian Churches, Catholic and Protestant alike ... For Augustine the only plausible explanation for this state of affairs seemed to rest in the Pauline interpretation of the Fall pushed to its furthest limits. This meant an acceptance of the idea that all men existed potentially in Adam and thus participated in his disobedience – his defiance of God and claim to independence – and his consequent guilt. Augustine drew from this the severest conclusion: human nature had been so corrupted by the Fall that man could not even will the good. There was absolutely no quarter given to human merit in this system, no opportunity for the sinner to work his way towards salvation with the help of God's grace. All grace was prevenient, salvation was the free gift of God who arbitrarily

---

[70] Ibid, pp. 22–23.
[71] Bertrand Russell, *History of Western Philosophy* (London: George Allen & Unwin, 1961), p. 362. Voltaire wrote about Augustine and the Fall: "Let us admit that Saint Augustine was the first to authorize this strange idea. Worthy of the fiery and romantic head of a debauched and repentant African." Quoted in Poole, *Milton and the Idea of the Fall*, p. 21.
[72] See Ozment, *The Age of Reform*, pp. 22, 26. Gordon Leff writes: "The positions that St. Augustine adopted in response to Pelagianism became the basis of the Catholic doctrine on grace, free will, and merit thenceforth." Gordon Leff, *Medieval Thought: St. Augustine to Ockham*, (Baltimore, MD: Penguin, 1958), p. 38.
[73] See Green, *Renaissance and Reformation*, p. 16.

chose some of the guilty to participate in the glories of eternal life. Again the Bishop of Hippo's personal experience played a crucial role in his interpretation of Paul. His own willfully sinful youth convinced him that he had been saved in spite of himself, by an infusion of grace working inexorably to redeem him from sin.[74]

The effects of this great Fall do therefore constrict mankind's actions to insignificant and denuded decision-making and keep mankind from any possibilities of free choice because freedom remains forever held hostage by sin. To be more precise, freedom to choose between one form of sin over another sustained the Fall, but not freedom in the sense of choosing between good and bad. What was lost is permanent, and is transmitted from generation to generation. Read from the theological to the political the ramifications of depraved humanity were clear: *city of man* government was itself an aberration, an inherently flawed construct relevant only for an inescapably flawed humanity, as both punishment and cure for the sinful fallen. As such, neither the state nor the heads of state could ever be condemned as illegitimate no matter how un-Godlike they may be. Herbert A. Deane has extensively demonstrated this line of thinking in Augustine's vast works, and it is worth quoting him at length.

Since the fraternity and concord natural to human society have been shattered by the egoism of sinful men, and the natural law regulating human relations has been all but effaced from the human heart, how is society – which is essential to man's existence – to be maintained? God's grace which brings regeneration and ransom from the captivity to sin cannot serve as the basis for social organization since, as we have seen, it liberates only a small minority of the mass of sinners. Since most men – whether they are heathen or nominal Christians – are unredeemed and will

[74] Spellman, *John Locke and the Problem of Depravity*, pp. 15–16.

Peter White has extensively documented just how central the debate over predestination was to the soul of the Church of England during the century beginning at the end of the rule of Henry XIII leading up until the outbreak of the Civil War. Calvinist orthodoxy held a doctrine of predestination that was double and absolute; the saints – or elect – were predestined to salvation and the reprobate to damnation, with good works playing no role at all. Arminianism on the other hand, while not totally rejecting the doctrine of predestination, for the most part believed it to be single, meaning that there were indeed those elected by birth for salvation, and at the same time advanced the significance of proper behavior for personal salvation. Predestination was at the heart of Elizabethan Church settlement, the Cambridge controversies of the 1590s, the Millenary Petition of 1603 and the resultant Hampton Court Conference, the theological battles between the Remonstrants and the Contra-Remonstrants regarding the Church of England, the Synod of Dort of 1619, and the York House Conference of 1626. White concludes with the assertion that by the time the Civil War erupted a via media had been found with regard to predestination, despite, or perhaps because of, Charles I's greater toleration and acceptance of Arminianism. See at length Peter O. G. White, *Predestination, Policy and Polemic*.

be so until the end of the world, new means must be provided to introduce a measure of order, stability, and peace in the midst of the strife and conflict that mark earthly life. Even to disobedient, prideful man god has been most merciful; He has established new institutions, adapted to the new conditions of sinful existence, in order to keep a check on human greed and violence and to prevent society from collapsing into complete anarchy and chaos. These institutions such as private property and the entire legal and political order, are divinely ordained as both punishments *and* remedies for the sinful condition of man. Although they provide an element of order, stability, and peace in social life that would be completely absent without them, the earthly peace and order that they make possible are no longer natural and spontaneous, but must be maintained by coercion and repression.[75]

The state and its instruments of coercion and punishment are, in Augustine's view, divinely ordained institutions designed as remedies as well as punishments for the sinful condition of fallen man. God uses the evil desires of fallen man as means for the establishment of earthy peace and order and for the just punishment of his vices. The state is thus a gift of God to man, despite the inadequacies and imperfections that necessarily mark the peace and justice that it can maintain among the unredeemed. The authority of the ruler over his subjects is therefore derived from God. The king or prince is established by God, no matter how wicked or unjust he may be, and Augustine allows no scope for any limitations of his power by his subjects or for any disobedience or resistance to his commands.[76]

Although the narrative depicted in the Hebrew Bible itself says nothing of this, referring only to the forfeiture of immortality, Christianity, however, particularly under the decisive influence of Augustine, turned this reading of the Fall into a cardinal tenet of Christian faith. This pervasiveness of original sin theology actually deepened following the Reformation as the reformers turned to the New Testament and Augustine in order to explain the nature of post-lapsarian man. And as W. M. Spellman makes abundantly clear it was only to these sources they could turn as nothing of the same vein could be found in the story of Eden itself as told in the Old Testament.

Like their Catholic opponents at the Council of Trent, the sixteenth-century Protestant reformers had quite naturally turned to St Paul and St. Augustine for Biblical support in interpreting the story of man's expulsion from the Garden and its consequences. After all, there was precious little evidence to be found in the Old Testament to buttress their view. For in that ancient book the inherent sinfulness of man is not specifically or consistently identified as the result of Adam's

[75] Deane, *The Political and Social Ideas of St. Augustine*, pp. 95–96.
[76] Ibid, p. 143. See pp. 116–153 for extensive quotes from Augustine and Deane's commentary.

transgression. More importantly, there is nothing in the Genesis narrative to suggest that the first sin automatically infected all of Adam's posterity with an internal natural corruption capable of being transmitted by physiological heredity. The narrative recounts Adam and Eve's expulsion from Paradise, the denial of access to the tree of life or immortality, and man's exposure to the physical ills of this life, but not a word is to be found about inborn sinfulness of moral infirmity inherited from our first parents.[77]

To be sure, arguments existed with regard to the proper interpretation of the Fall, with some claiming that it was a one-time "catastrophe" and others insisting that it inaugurated a process of "continual" human decline that would always persist. One side of the debate saw the Fall as all-encompassing, crippling humankind's abilities in every realm from the physical to the moral. The other, Pelagian side argued for a more limited interpretation, suggesting that it was only humanity's moral rectitude that was depreciated. Martin Luther, who Quentin Skinner describes as being "obsessed by the idea of man's complete unworthiness" and whose thinking was "ultra-Augustinian,"[78] was a proponent of the former, and it was this line of thought that ultimately carried the greatest influence.

---

[77] Spellman, *John Locke and the Problem of Depravity*, p. 9. Significantly, even Thomas Aquinas, who moderated many Augustinian ideas, adhered closely to Augustine's analysis of the transmission of sin through Adam in his *Summa Theologica*. Steven Ozment emphasizes the importance of Aquinas to the solidification of Augustinian thought on this matter. "St. Thomas crystallized medieval Catholic thinking on the issue of man's nature in a vast synthesis of knowledge and belief completed in the late thirteenth century. His *Summa Theologica* adhered closely to Augustine's analysis of the transmission of sin through Adam. 'According to Catholic Faith,' he said, 'we are bound to hold that the first sin of the first man is transmitted to his descendants, by way of origin.'" Ozment, *The Age of Reform*, pp. 31–32. See also Philip S. Watson, "Introduction," in *Luther and Erasmus: Free Will and Salvation*, E. Gordon Rupp and Philip S. Watson (eds.) (Philadelphia, PA: Westminster Press, 1969), pp. 23–24. Where Aquinas differed, though, with Augustine was on the issue of government, which he believed, following Aristotle, has a status independent of original sin. On this Gordon Leff writes: "the difference between St. Thomas's outlook and St. Augustine's is the difference between a settled society and social upheaval. Where St. Augustine cast desperately around to explain evil, St. Thomas could return to the classificatory method of Aristotle: he made the State part of the eternal order of reason where St. Augustine had seen it as punishment for an erring will." Leff, *Medieval Thought*, p. 251.

[78] Skinner, *The Foundations of Modern Political Thought*, pp. 3–4.

THE REFORMATION AND THE CENTRALITY OF THE FALL

Because they were free from the Pelagianizing influences that emanated from Rome, Protestant reformers took the Augustinian interpretation of original sin even further than their Catholic predecessors. Mainstream Catholics saw in Christ's saving grace, infused through the sacraments, the tools that enable mankind to engage in righteous works, thereby giving the process of human salvation a solid ethical component. Conversely, Martin Luther stretched to the limits the Pauline concept of salvation exclusively by faith (*sola gracia*), rendering meritorious works utterly irrelevant to the drama of salvation. Good deeds are to be performed only "as natural concomitants of Christian temperament, the fruits of a true faith,"[79] not out of any hope for reward. While attacking the sacramental and hierarchical system of the Catholic Church, the Reformed Churches joined with Luther in using the Augustinian notion of predestination to restore the uninhibited majesty of God, thereby tearing away at the fabric of the hierarchical Church and destroying the entire edifice of institutional Christianity.[80]

Fallen man for Luther spelled the termination of the primordial image of God in mankind and hence he found Augustine's recalibration of "in God's image" to mean the Trinity as unhelpful.[81] Free will belonged to the lost image of God and could not be retrieved. Jaroslav Pelikan finds this clearly stated in Luther's words:

In his later exposition, as in the earlier sermons, he (Luther) emphasized that Adam's state as one who was created in the divine image was no longer even intelligible to fallen man, who had no experience of it; much less was it correct to say that the image was still present, for "it was lost through sin in paradise." Luther's "understanding of the image of God is this: that Adam had it in his being and that he not only knew God and believed that he was good, but that he also lived a life that was wholly godly; that is, he was without the fear of death or of any other danger, and was content with God's favor." All of that was lost and would be fully restored only after Judgement Day. In its place had come death and the fear of blasphemy, hatred toward God, and lust: "These and similar evils are

---

[79] Spellman, *John Locke and the Problem of Depravity*, p. 23.

[80] Luther advanced the doctrine of *double predestination* – "the contention that some men must already be predestined to be saved while others are predestined to be damned." Skinner, *The Foundations of Modern Political Thought*, p. 6.

[81] See Augustine, *On the Trinity*, chap. 10, and *On the City of God*, chap. 11. And see Calvin, *Institutes of the Christian Religion*, book I, chap. XV, 4. "For there is no solidity in Augustine's speculation, that the soul is a mirror of the Trinity, inasmuch as it comprehends within itself, intellect, will, and memory."

the image of the devil, who stamped them on us." (Luther, *Lectures on Genesis*, 1:26 [WA 42:47–48])[82]

A generation after Luther, Jean Calvin understood original sin as necessitating a kind of stoic complacency in life with the unavoidable: all humans are in a constant state of sin; God does not will all humans to be saved; Christ died not for all humans to be saved but only for the elect; God moves the wills and inclinations of humans in the direction he wills; and there is no human free will that allows choice between good and evil. Calvin's ultimate dictum was "thy will be done."[83]

Calvin went further than Luther in defining where Catholic doctrine went wrong. By suggesting human cooperation with God's grace, the Church had essentially separated mind from body and declared that the whole of mankind had not fallen with Adam. This, argued Calvin, is false. The whole of mankind was infected by Adam's Fall, the mind as well as the body.

Calvin's theology had a dramatic influence upon Reformation thinkers in seventeenth-century England, both Anglican and Puritan.[84] While differences existed between the denominations, the totality of the Fall

[82] Jaroslav Pelikan, *The Christian Tradition: A History of the Development of Doctrine*, vol. 4 (Chicago, IL: University of Chicago Press, 1984), p. 142. Pelikan goes on to quote Matthias Flacius, a follower of Luther, who derived from his teacher the imperative to define original sin as "the image of the devil, contrary to the image of God." Because "the rational soul and especially its noblest substantial powers, namely, the intellect, and the will, which previously had been so brilliantly fashioned that they were the true image of God ... have now, by the deception of sin, been so completely inverted that they are the true and living image of Satan," original sin had become the "substance" of human nature, and, as "Scripture and Luther affirm," was not simply an "accident" that adhered to mankind but did not change its essential nature. Ibid, p. 143.

[83] Chadwick, *The Reformation*, pp. 93–95. Alister McGrath makes the observation that Calvin's doctrine of predestination was not a theological innovation but followed rather the strict Augustinian line of leading medieval theologians such as Gregory of Rimini who championed a doctrine of absolute double predestination. McGrath, *Reformation Thought*, p. 139.

William James Bouwsma detects what he calls "optimistic overtones" in Calvin's conception of the role of nature in original sin that are "hardly consistent with the doctrine of original sin" and compares some of Calvin's more extreme quotes indicating a total elimination of "God's image" in mankind following the Fall with other more moderate ones. See, William James Bouwsma, *John Calvin* (Oxford: Oxford University Press, 1988), pp. 80, 81, 142, 143. I refer the reader back to Chapter 5 where the tensions in Calvin's writings with regard to absolute submission to government as opposed to the right of rebellion were discussed.

[84] Ibid, pp. 176–178. Cragg, *From Puritanism to the Age of Reason*, p. 3. The renowned Puritan preacher William Whately described the thorough corruption of humanity in extreme but not out-of-the-ordinary terms:

was not one of the topics leading to these differences.[85] On the whole, most predominant religious Christian sects, including scholastic reactionaries and early Reformers, tenaciously clung to an Augustinian theology. William Poole succinctly explains the reason for the prevalence of this Christological dogmatism:

Indeed, original sin is a very difficult concept for any Christian to dismantle, as a proper demolition job leaves Christ with not all that much to do, and many, seeing that danger, turned back. As was affirmed in the academic disputation for 1624 in Cambridge University, "the incarnation of Christ presupposes the Fall of man into sin."[86]

And J.P. Sommerville writes,

There was, indeed, little difference between Protestant and Catholic views on the necessity of government. It is true that Protestants deduced the need for coercion from the sinfulness of man's fallen nature ... Catholics, however, likewise dated coercive authority from the Fall.[87]

"A man in the state of corrupt nature, is nothing else but a filthy dunghill of all abominable vices: he is a stinking rotten carrion, become altogether unprofitable and good for nothing his heart is the diuels store-house, an heape of odious lusts: his tongue is a fountaine of cursing and bitternesse, and rotten communication: his hand is a mischievous instrument of filthinesse, deceit, and violence: his eyes great throwfares of lust, pride, and vanity: his feet are swift engines, mouing strongly to reuenge, wantonesse and lucre: his ligfe is a long chaine of sinful actions, euery later linke being more wicked than the former: yea it is but (as it were) one continued web of wickednesse, spun out, and made up by the hands of the diuell and the flesh, an euill spinner, and a worse weauer." Quoted in Parker, *The Biblical Politics of John Locke*, p. 50. Whately (1583–1639) was a clergyman who earned a widespread reputation as a persuasive preacher and "was renowned for his eloquence and scriptural learning that espoused the Calvinist belief in predestination and regarded preaching as the chief and principal instrument to guide the elect into the necessary state of godliness." Jacqueline Eales, "Whately, William (1583–1639)," *Oxford Dictionary of National Biography* (Oxford: Oxford University Press, 2004, www.oxforddnb.com/view/article/29178).

[85] W. M. Spellman describes the effect of Calvin's influence. "The impact of Calvin's thought upon Reformation figures in England should not be underestimated ... Both the incipient Puritan party and their Anglican opponents shared common ground on a broad range of fundamental issues. Differences there were, and they should by no means be ignored. But these had more to do with the institutional and ceremonial side of religion than with such core problems as the nature of man, predestination, the conversion experience, and the role of Providence." Spellman, *John Locke and the Problem of Depravity*, p. 26.

[86] Poole, *Milton and the Idea of the Fall*, p. 5.

[87] Sommerville, *Royalists and Patriots*, p. 19. Sommerville shows that, despite their theological adversity, Catholics and Calvinists were overall very close in their theoretical justification of absolutism, which focused on mankind's fallen nature. Ibid, pp. 18–22.

Poole explains that the "incarnation of Christ" must "presuppose the Fall of man into sin," because of "Boethius' well-known formulation, '[if] there be a God, from whence proceed so many euils? And if there be no God, from whence commeth any good?'"[88] Evils then proceed from fallen mankind, and good from the love engendered through Christ's incarnation. This dogmatic necessity allows for an understanding of the ubiquitousness, persistence, and stridency of original sin in Christian theology. Poole emphasizes that:

Although within academic theology there was a good deal of strife in the late sixteenth and early seventeenth centuries about whether God had formulated his absolute decrees of predestination before the creation or after the Fall ... no one, at least in the academe, disagreed about the basic importance of the event itself. As the ninth of the Thirty-Nine Articles of 1571 ran: "Original sin standeth not in the following of Adam, as the Pelagians do vainly talk, but it is the fault and corruption of the nature of every man, that naturally is engendered of the offspring of Adam, whereby man is very far gone from original righteousness, and is of his own nature enclined to evil, so that the flesh lusteth always contrary to the spirit, and therefore in every person born into this world, it deserveth God's wrath and damnation."[89]

The cardinal importance of original sin dogma to Christian theology is poignantly demonstrated by the case of the Calvinist heretic Isaac La Peyrere. La Peyrere hypothesized that the Bible had told only of Jewish creation, while humans had actually existed long before Adam. But as a result of his need to remain theologically loyal to the concept of the Fall, he created the incredible notion of *retroimputation*, which in effect predated original sin to the ancient pre-Adamite races.[90]

While ideas like those of La Peyrere attracted but a few adherents, the mainline Pauline-Augustinian-Lutheran-Calvinist exegesis of the Fall rose to near unanimous acceptance. But critics in the spirit of Pelagius and Arminius there were, and they were becoming more vocal as Locke began to formulate his own ideas on the best body political to address human nature.

[88] Poole, *Milton and the Idea of the Fall*, p. 14.
[89] Ibid, p. 34. Deborah Kuller Shuger refers to the depravity of fallen mankind as "a Reformation commonplace." Deborah Kuller Shuger, *Habits of Thought in the English Renaissance*, p. 183.
[90] Poole, *Milton and the Idea of the Fall*, pp. 4–5.

ORIGINAL SIN CHALLENGED

The revolutionary decades of the seventeenth century left few dogmas untouched, and radical voices began to challenge the traditional Augustinian interpretation of Genesis 2–3. Some obvious voices were those of the political radicals such as the Ranters, Diggers, Seekers, and Quakers, but opposition to original sin doctrine also emanated from socially conservative and even High Church quarters.[91] These two groups created parallel interpretations of the Fall that led to strikingly similar theologies despite the fact that one side represented what was the political left of the times, and the other, the political right. The premier exponent of the first group was Robert Everard, a Leveller, Agitator, and Baptist, who served as a captain in the parliamentary army and wrote *The Creation and Fall of Adam Reviewed*.[92] The radical Everard rhetorically questioned an imputationist reading of the Fall by asking, "why might it not be said, When Adam believed, I believed; when Adam repented, I repented?"[93]

The second group was best represented by Jeremy Taylor, academic and future bishop, who also happened to be confidant and premier spokesman for Charles I.[94] Despite his royalist credentials and subsequent persecution under Cromwell, Taylor did not tow a rigid Anglican line. In his *Discourse of the Liberty of Prophesying* (1647), he argued on textual grounds that the notion of absolute scriptural authority must be rejected and that an ethical rather than a theological approach must be taken to Christianity. While he began his critique on original sin in this work, his real broadside against the Fall came almost a decade later with the publishing of *Unum necessarium* (1655) at the time when Locke was still a student at Oxford. Taylor, a protégé of William Laud, the Anglican Archbishop, and supporter of divine rights of kings, whose attack on original sin "was the most intelligent and eloquent of the period,"[95]

---

[91] See Glenn Burgess and Mathew Festenstien (eds.), *English Radicalism, 1550–1850* (Cambridge: Cambridge University Press, 2007).

[92] About Everard see George Southcombe, "Everard, Robert (fl. 1647–1664)," *Oxford Dictionary of National Biography* (Oxford: Oxford University Press, 2004, www.oxforddnb.com/view/article/9000).

[93] Poole, *Milton and the Idea of the Fall*, p. 57.

[94] About Taylor see John Spurr, "Taylor, Jeremy (bap. 1613, d. 1667)," *Oxford Dictionary of National Biography* (Oxford: Oxford University Press, 2004, www.oxforddnb.com/view/article/27041).

[95] Laud himself wrote regarding Calvinistic predestination that, "it makes God, the God of all mercy, to be the most fierce and unreasonable tyrant in the world." Cragg, *From Puritanism to the Age of Reason*, p. 15, ft. 2.

antagonized most of his fellow Anglicans but found support from his interlocutors among the Cambridge Platonists. Henry More, for example, a prominent Cambridge Platonist and rejecter of original sin, informed Taylor in a letter that the Presbyterians were calling him "a Sosinian, that yo denied Originall sinne, that you were an Arminian, and so a hereticke in graine."[96] It should be recalled that several decades later Locke was derogatorily labeled a Socinian as well, when in his *Reasonableness*, he restricted Christianity's mandatory tenets to a minimalist creed predicated on repentance and free choice. In his rejection of a freedom-depriving understanding of the Fall, Taylor too focused on the human ability to repent by choice:

I sin like a Gentleman, not like a Thief; I suffer infirmities, but doe not doe like a Devil; and though I sin, yet I repent speedily, and when I sin again, I repent again, and my spiritual state is like my natural, day and night succeed each other like a never failing revolution.[97]

In their pursuit of a rational theology, the Cambridge Platonists did not entirely reject concepts that were composed in large measure not of reason but of mystery, but they did deprecate doctrines that were wholly obscure and unintelligible, and the notion of predestination, which directly followed from original sin, belonged to the latter. And they utterly rejected it. This iconoclastic attitude of the Cambridge Platonists on the subject of predestination is best described by G. R. Cragg:

But there was one of the dogmas of Calvinism which they directly and unequivocally attacked. Predestination, they claimed, was neither intellectually nor morally defensible. More bluntly called it "the black doctrine of absolute reprobation", and Whichote declared that "it is not worth the name of religion to charge our consciences with that, which we have not reconciled to the reason and judgment of our minds, to the frame and temper of our souls."[98]

---

[96] Poole, *Milton and the Idea of the Fall*, p. 45. For more about More and free will, see Lichtenstein, *Henry More*, pp. 40–45. The author dubs More a "vigorous Freewillist." Poole, *Milton and the Idea of the Fall*, p. 40.

[97] Ibid, p. 54. Taylor, *Unum necessarium*, sg. B3v.

[98] Cragg, *From Puritan to the Age of Reason*, p. 40. Steven Ozment delineates four classical examples of the seventeenth-century debate over the Fall: Erasmus's literary combat against Luther's harsh predestination; the debate between Remonstrants and Calvinists in Holland regarding humanity's ability to set its own destination in this world; Archbishop Laud's denial of Calvinistic predestination; and the rise of the Cambridge Platonists who challenged English Calvinism with their belief in the priority of moral human ideas and responsibilities over God's divine will. See Ozment, *The Age of Reform*, p. 29. D. P. Walker, *The Decline of Hell: Seventeenth-Century Discussions of Eternal Torment* (Chicago, IL: The University of Chicago Press, 1964) pp. 13, 55–56.

The Reformation reignited the Augustine–Pelagius debate over the Fall, which, with minor exceptions, had not been center stage for hundreds of years. As with so many other issues of critical import for the future of England and Western civilization, the debate raged on, both in theoretical and practical realms, just as John Locke was developing his own attitudes regarding the political and social changes that the Reformation provoked. In the debate, many of the groups that led the opposition to the traditional doctrine of original sin were groups with whom Locke was to some degree closely affiliated, such as the Latitudinarians, the Socinians, members of the Great Tew Circle, and the Cambridge Platonists. To varying degrees, they all rejected the totality of original sin with its predestined fallen human and promoted instead a theology of personal responsibility based on the free will of human choice.[99]

Locke agreed and made what is perhaps his greatest contribution to the history of ideas by extending this conception of the human condition from the theological to the political realm.

THE HEBRAIC APPROACH TO THE FALL

Hebraic thought totally rejects the Pauline–Augustinian exegesis of the Fall, denies that there is a constant state of sin, and negates the existence of predestination. At no time, and by no sect nor denomination, has the concept of free will been negated or even limited by Hebraic thought. Even though they are obligated to choose the good, humans are considered always free to choose between good and evil. This concept can be found clearly in the Bible with God's declaration, "I call heaven and earth to witness against you this day: I have put before you life and death, blessing and curse. Choose life – if you and your offspring would live."[100] The post-Biblical Hebraic approach regarding the Fall is also extremely clear, and in fact, some of the statements regarding this issue grew polemically as a reaction to Pauline thinking.

The concept of free will echoes strongly in the Apocryphal texts of the Second Temple era. Writing in the second century BCE, Ben Sira found no

---

In Amsterdam, in 1639, while the debate between Calvinists and Remonstrants regarding the issues of free will and predestination was at its apogee, Menasseh Ben Israel published his *De Termino Vitae* arguing against Calvinistic fatalism and supporting free will. M. Dorman, *Menasseh Ben-Israel* (B'nai B'rak: Hakibutz Hameuchad Publishing House, 1989), pp. 52–53 [Hebrew].

[99] Walker, *The Decline of Hell*, pp. 8–9.   [100] Deuteronomy 30:19.

place for any kind of predestination. On the contrary, he wrote: "It was he, from the first when he created humankind, who made them subject to their own free choice."[101] The same idea rises from the *Syriac Apocalypse of Baruch*: "Although Adam sinned first ... yet each of them who has been born from him has prepared for himself the coming torment and each of them has chosen further for himself the coming glory."[102] This means plainly that human fate is not immune from the influences of personal human endeavor.

The Jewish sages of the first centuries AD also did not believe that death was a kind of punishment. It was actually suggested that human mortality is to be regarded as a good thing because it made free choice as well as reward and punishment relevant issues: "In the copy of R. Meir's Torah was found written: it was very (*me'od*) good: and behold, death (*maweth*) was good."[103] A Talmudic source suggesting that the four Biblical figures that died because of the "serpents machinations" (Benjamin the son of Jacob, Amram the father of Moses, Jesse the father of David, and Caleb the son of David) is most probably an anti-Pauline polemic intending to argue that original sin is by no means critical to the human-divine realm of reward and punishment and that this type of death affected only minor historical figures, not their fathers and sons who were well-known standard-bearers of the Jewish nation.[104]

The statement of the Talmudic sage Rabbi Akiva (50–135 AD) regarding free will, "Everything is foreseen yet free will is granted,"[105] is apparently also a direct response to Paul's ideas.[106] They echoed more

---

[101] Patrick W. Skehan (ed.), *The Wisdom of Ben Sira* (New York: Doubleday, The Anchor Bible, 1987), 15, 15–16, p. 267.

[102] *Syriac Apocalypse of Baruch* (54, 14–19). Skehan, *The Wisdom of Ben Sira*, p. 541.

[103] *Midrash Rabbah, Genesis, Bereshith*, chapter IX.

[104] Babylonian Talmud, *Tractate Shabbath*, 55b. And see E. E. Urbach, *The Sages: Their Concepts and Beliefs* (Jerusalem: Magness Press, The Hebrew University, 1971), p. 376.

[105] *Mishnah, Avot*, 3:15.

[106] It has been argued by David Flusser that Paul's beliefs regarding a constant state of sin or predestination were polemical and that he had a habit of taking Jewish sources and twisting their original meanings. The Second Temple Jewish sages believed that after the Israelites received the Torah on Mount Sinai, the filth that was attached to them was removed: "When the serpent came unto Eve he infused filthy lust into her ... when Israel stood at Sinai that lust was eliminated" (*Abodah Zarah*, 22b). But Paul argued the complete opposite, suggesting that sin and death were inherited by all humans before the giving of the Torah and that the Torah was given only for the purpose of defining what was bad, thereby increasing the crimes of humans, for they now hold complete responsibility for their actions and have no chance of avoiding the sin. Paul's explanation was used to show how crucial the coming of Jesus was for all mankind and how he was the only one who could save humans from this state. David Flusser,

than one thousand years later in the famous words of Maimonides that stand in powerful contrast to Augustinianism.

Free will is granted to all men. If one desires to turn himself to the path of good and be righteous, the choice is his. Should he desire to turn to the path of evil and be wicked, the choice is his. This is the intent of the Torah's statement (Genesis 3:22): "Behold, man has become unique as ourselves, knowing good and evil ..." A person should not entertain the thesis held by the fools among the gentiles and the majority of the undeveloped among Israel that, at the time of man's creation, God decrees whether he will be righteous or wicked. This is untrue ... This principle is a fundamental concept and a pillar on which rest the totality of the Torah and Mitzvot ... Any one of the deeds of men which a person desires to do, he may ... this is known without any doubt: that man's actions are his own hands and God does not lead him in a particular direction or decree that he do anything.[107]

In his *Guide*[108] Maimonides posits that the reason philosophers have been baffled by the prima facie contradiction between "Everything is foreseen yet free will is granted" is because they have mistakenly assessed the nature of divine knowledge through the lenses of human knowledge, the latter being finite, the former infinite. In a paragraph that appears to echo Maimonides, Locke admitted that his limited capacity for understanding prevented him from reconciling God's omnipotence and omniscience with human freedom; yet he categorically refused to deny the totality of either.

For I own freely to you the weakness of my understanding, that though it be unquestionable that there is omnipotence and omniscience in God our maker, and I cannot have a clearer perception of any thing than that I am free, yet I cannot make freedom in man consistent with omnipotence and omniscience in God, though I am as fully perswaded of both as of any truths I most firmly assent to.[109]

In summation, the Biblical story of the forbidden fruit refers in the Hebraic reading only to the forfeiture of immortality after Adam and Eve's sin. As far as classical Hebraic thought is concerned there is nothing in the Fall's account that classifies death as punishment, points to a constant state of sin, or suggests predestination. On the contrary, human

"Motifs from the Section of Creation in their Substantial Christian Form," *Mahaniem* 84 (1963), pp. 138–144 [Hebrew].

[107] Maimonides, *Mishneh Torah, Hilchot Teshuvah, The Laws of Repentance*, New Corrected Edition (New York: Feldheim Publishers, 1981), chapter 5.

[108] Maimonides, *Guide for the Perplexed*, part 3, chapter 20. See also "Shemoneh Perakim," chapter 8.

[109] Locke, *The Correspondence of John Locke*, pp. 625–626.

free will and the full significance of human actions are definitively elemental to the way Hebraic theology understands human ability and accountability.

LOCKE DOESN'T TAKE THE FALL

In the opening chapters of the *First Treatise*, Locke went about proving that the divine creation of Adam did not grant him absolute monarchical rule over all humankind, and that the dominion he was granted was in no way private or exclusive with regard to his fellow humans. In chapter V of the *First Treatise*, entitled "Of *Adam* 's Title to Sovereignty by the Subjection of *Eve*," Locke continues his strand of thought and Biblical exegesis in order to show that Adam's dominion did not include the subjection of Eve, and that on the contrary, Eve was included by God in the dominion that the human species received over all the creations of lesser intellect. As I have already shown, Locke consistently challenges Robert Filmer's interpretation of Scripture in defense of governmental absolutism, not his use of Scripture.

The next place of Scripture we find our *Author* Builds his Monarchy of *Adam* on, is 3. *Gen.* 16. And *thy desire shall be to thy Husband, and he shall rule over thee. Here we have* (says he) *the Original Grant of Government*, from whence he concludes, in the following part of the Page O. 244 [283]. *That the Supream Power is settled in the Fatherhood, and limited to one kind of Government, that is to Monarchy.*[110]

Eve is chastised by God for her dubious role in encouraging Adam to eat and for eating herself from the Tree of Knowledge. But she is not alone, as Adam is reprimanded at the same time for his heedlessness. It utterly negates reason, Locke contends, that Adam should be anointed by God as absolute monarch over his wife at the very moment when they are both being punished for the same iniquity.

The Words are the Curse of God upon the Woman, for having been the first and forwardest in the Disobedience, and if we will consider the occasion of what God says here to our first Parents, that he was Denouncing Judgment, and declaring his Wrath against them both, for their Disobedience, we cannot suppose that this was the time, wherein God was granting *Adam* Prerogatives and Priviledges, investing his with Dignity and Authority, Elevating him to Dominion and Monarchy: For though as a helper in the Temptation, as well as a Partner in the Transgression,

---

[110] I, 44, p. 189.

Eve was laid below him, and so he accidentally a Superiority over her, for her greater Punishment, yet he too had his share in the fall, as well as the sin, and was laid lower, as may be seen in the following Verses, and 'twould be hard to imagine, that God, in the same Breath, should make him Universal *Monarch* over all Mankind, and a day labourer for his Life; turn him out of *Paradise, to till the Ground, ver.* 23. and at the same time, advance him to a Throne, and all the Priviledges and Ease of Absolute Power.[111]

It might appear from the text that Adam received a lesser punishment than Eve due to her greater culpability, yet this does not diminish the objective severity with which Adam himself is divinely dealt. Locke argues that Filmer does not understand the Biblical text nor does he quote it in its entirety. The verses following the one quoted by Filmer prove that Adam's status at this post-lapsarian admonition was anything but monarchical. It is a *spade* not a *scepter*, Locke points out, that God places in Adam's hand.

This was not a time, when *Adam* could expect any Favours, and grant of Priviledges, from his offended Maker. If this be *the Original Grant of Government*, as our *Author* tells us, and *Adam* was now made Monarch, whatever Sir *Robert* would have him, 'tis plain, God made him but a very poor Monarch, such as one, as our *Author* himself would have counted to no great Priviledge to be. God sets him to work for his living, and seems rather to give him a Spade into his hand, to subdue the Earth, than a Scepter to Rule over its Inhabitants. *In the Sweat of the Face thou shalt eat thy Bread*, says God to him, *ver.* 19.[112]

Like a good litigator anticipating his or her nemesis's counterattack, Locke raises a potential rejoinder to his argument, and then, with logical progression, dismisses it entirely.

It will perhaps be answered again, in Favour of our *Author*, that these words are not spoke Personally to *Adam*, but in him, as their Representative, to all Mankind, this being a Curse upon Mankind, *because of the fall*.[113] (Italics added.)

A possible explanation, which Locke then forcefully rejects.

God, I believe, speaks differently from Men, because he speaks with more Truth, more Certainty: but when he vouchsafes to speak to Men, I do not think, he speaks differently from them, in crossing the Rules of language in use amongst them. This would not be to condescend to their Capacities, when he humbles himself to speak to them, but to lose his design in speaking, what thus spoken, they could not understand. And yet thus must we think of God, if the Interpretations of Scripture, necessary to maintain our *Author*'s Doctrine, must be

[111] I, 44, p. 190.   [112] I, 45, p. 190.   [113] I, 45, pp. 190–191.

received for good. For by the ordinary Rules of Language, it will be very hard to understand, what God says; If what he speaks here, in the Singular Number to *Adam*, must be understood to be spoken to all Mankind, and what he says in the Plural Number, 1 *Gen.* 26. and 28. must be understood of *Adam* alone, exclusive of all others, and what he says to *Noah* and his Sons Joyntly, must be understood to be meant to *Noah* alone, *Gen.* 9.[114]

Biblical exegesis must be consistent for it to be legitimate, Locke teaches; otherwise a mockery is made of the text. Here, once again, the reader is exposed to Locke's zealous insistence on textual integrity when reading the Bible. Part of that integrity is the need to pay close attention to what the text actually says, and not what one wills it to say. Not only is it wholly implausible for monarchical sovereignty to be granted to Adam at the very moment of his divine admonishment, the text too does not press any imperative of female subjugation.

But there is here no more Law to oblige a Woman to such Subjection, if the Circumstances either of her Condition or Contract with her Husband should exempt her from it, then there is, that she should bring forth her Children in Sorrow and Pain, if there could be found a Remedy for it, which is also a part of the same Curse upon her: for the whole Verse runs thus, *Unto the Woman he said, I will greatly multiply thy sorrow and thy conception; in sorrow thou shalt bring forth Children, and thy desire shall be to thy Husband, and he shall rule over thee.* 'Twould, I think, have been a hard matter for any Body, but our *Author.* to have found out a Grant of *Monarchical Government* to *Adam* in these Words, which were neither spoke to, nor of him: neither will any one, I suppose, by these Words, think the weaker Sex, as by a Law so subjected to the Curse contained in them, that 'tis their duty not to endeavor to avoid it.[115]

Adam's punishment is given to Adam, and Eve's punishment to Eve. Adam is not told directly of Eve's post-lapsarian handicaps, and nowhere does the text suggest that these handicaps cannot be overcome. What then is the Hebrew Bible teaching with regard to the conjugal human condition following the first sin? Locke goes on to explain.

God, in this text, gives not, that I see, any Authority to *Adam* over *Eve*, or to Men over their Wives, but only foretells what should be the Womans Lot, how by his Providence he would order it so, that she should be subject to her husband, as we see that generally the Laws of Mankind and customs of Nations have ordered it so; and there is, I grant, a Foundation in Nature for it.[116]

The pains of childbirth became a fact of life, but not an unavoidable curse. Just as a woman is not required to endure the pains of childbirth if

---

[114] I, 46, p. 191.   [115] I, 47, pp. 191–192.   [116] I, 47, p. 192.

they can be avoided, so too a woman need not be subservient to her husband beyond the "customs of nations," which, as we shall see in a moment, is confined to the realm of conjugal power, and does not include political power. To prove that this is the proper reading of the Biblical text, Locke offers another text with a comparable structure.

Thus when God says of *Jacob* and *Esau*, That the *Elder* should serve the *Younger*, 25 *Gen.* 23. no body supposes that God hereby made *Jacob Esau* 's Sovereign, but foretold what should *de facto* come to pass.[117]

The Bible then is telling us not what must "come to pass," says Locke, but what would most likely materialize in the natural course of events. Any other reading of the text leads once again to the absurd.

But if these words here spoke to *Eve* must needs be understood as a Law to bind her and all other Women to Subjection, it can be no other Subjection than what every Wife owes her Husband, and then if this be the *Original Grant of Government* and the *Foundation of Monarchical Power*, there will be as many Monarchs as there are Husbands. If therefore these words give any Power to *Adam*, it can be only a Conjugal Power, not Political, the Power that every Husband hath to order the things of private Concernment in his Family, as Proprietor of the Goods and Land there, and to have his Will take place before that of his wife in all things of their common Concernment; but not a Political Power of Life and Death over her, much less over any body else.[118]

In bringing this chapter to an end, Locke makes one more common-sensical appeal for the plain reading of the Biblical text as it relates to post-lapsarian humanity.

And here I leave my Reader to consider, whether my bare saying, without offering any Reasons to evince it, that this Text gives not *Adam* that *Absolute Monarchical Power*, our *Author* supposes, be not as sufficient to destroy that Power, as his bare Assertion is to Establish it, since the text mentions neither Prince nor People, speaks nothing of *Absolute* or *Monarchical Power*, but the Subjection of *Eve* to *Adam*, a Wife to her Husband.[119]

[117] I, 48, p. 192.
[118] I, 48, p. 192. Following this line of argumentation in which Locke extends Filmer's thinking to its logical yet absurd conclusion, he will later point out that if Filmer were right about children, or rather the eldest child, inheriting supreme powers from the father, then had Adam died before Eve, Cain or Seth would have "Inherited *Adam's Fatherhood*, Sovereign Power over *Eve* his Mother." I, 99, p. 231.
[119] I, 49, p. 193

LOCKE, THE FALL, AND *THE REASONABLENESS OF CHRISTIANITY*

In *The Reasonableness of Christianity*, Locke presents what appears by any theological standard to be a "minimalist creed,"[120] restricting the mandatory articles of Christian faith to two basic tenets: belief in Jesus Christ as the Messiah and repentance. Belief in original sin as we have already seen is poignantly not one of them. Locke first acknowledges the imputationist interpretation of Adam's death and then proceeds to repudiate it in no uncertain terms.

For some will have it to be a state of Guilt, [the punishment of Death imposed on Adam after he ate from the tree of knowledge] wherein not only he, but all his Posterity was so involved, that every one descended of him deserved endless torment in Hell-fire.[121]

The first reason Locke gives to prove how dubious an interpretation this is belongs to the realm of hermeneutics. Scripture must be understood in accord with the plain meaning of its words; hence when Scripture uses the term *death* to define the post-lapsarian human status it must mean just that, mortality, and not a "life of misery."

But it seems a strange way of understanding a Law, which requires the plainest and directest words, that by *Death* should be meant Eternal Life in Misery. Could any one be supposed by a Law, that says, For Felony you shall die, not that he should lose his Life, but be kept alive in perpetual exquisite Torments? And would any one think himself fairly dealt with, that was so used?[122]

K. I. Parker persuasively shows how Locke's insistence that Scripture is to be interpreted in a literal manner definitive of the express meaning of the words is actually a key point of contention that Locke has with

---

[120] As already stated (*ft.* 59), John Edwards appears to be the first to use the expression *minimalist creed* in his critique of the *Reasonableness*. Edwards was one of Locke's fiercest critics, an accuser of the latter's apparent Socinianism, and a main reason for Locke's decision to write a rejoinder to his critics, *A Vindication of the Reasonableness of Christianity*. Victor Nuovo presents Edwards' claims against Locke: "To support his charge, Edwards observed that the author of the *Reasonableness* advocated a minimalist creed, reducing the Christian faith to a single article and assuring his readers that Christians need believe no more than this; that he denied the doctrine of original sin; that he failed to assert Jesus Christ's divine nature; that he willfully ignored Biblical evidence of the Trinity; that he denied the satisfaction of Christ; that he willfully ignored the New Testament epistles in going about to show what the Christian faith is; that he was a mob-pleaser, who fashioned a version of Christianity within the limits of vulgar understanding." Nuovo, *John Locke: Writings on Religion*, p. li.

[121] Locke, *The Reasonableness of Christianity*, p. 92.   [122] Ibid.

Filmer's allegorical reading.[123] But Parker neglects to mention the source Locke himself gives to justify his position. In a footnote at the conclusion of the previously quoted paragraph, Locke divulges that the source for his hermeneutical principle is Maimonides.

The reason of this plain and Idiotical stile Maimonides gives, *More Nevochim*, part I, chap. 33: For this reason the law speaks according to the language of the sons of men, because it is the most commodious and easie way of initiating and teaching Children, women and the common people, who have not ability to apprehend things according to the very nature and essence of them, etc.[124]

Similarly, Locke wrote elsewhere that the Scriptures were designed:

for the instruction of the illiterate bulk of mankind ... [and hence] must be understood in the plain direct meanings of the words ... without such learned, artificial, and forced senses of them, as are sought out and put upon them, in most of the systems of divinity.[125]

---

[123] Parker writes: "In the *Two Treatises*, the hermeneutical principle that Locke uses against Filmer's position is to pay attention to the 'plain express words of Scripture' (I, 32), 'the direct and plain meaning of the Words' (I, 36), or 'an ordinary understanding' (I, 80) of the passage. If God speaks to humans through their reason and senses (I, 86), then humans should be able to understand God's words using 'the ordinary Rules of Language' (II, 46) and common sense ... For Locke, 'ill-grounded' or 'improbable' interpretations cannot stand up to the plain or literal meaning of the words (I, 36). Locke insists on a rational interpretation of scripture in conformity with the whole of scripture, and a reading that is, above all, based upon the express meaning of the words. Locke's principles for reading scripture in the *Two Treatises* are founded on a very literal, empirical, and commonsensical interpretation of the meaning of the words." Parker, *The Biblical Politics of John Locke*, p. 46. Elsewhere Locke wrote: "It is beyond doubt that the interpretation of the Holy Bible derives much from learning, much from reason, and, lastly, much from the Holy Spirit illuminating the minds of men, but the most certain interpreter of Scripture is Scripture itself, and it alone is infallible." Nuovo, *John Locke: Writings on Religion*, "Infallibility," p. 72.

[124] Maimonides in turn based his hermeneutical position on the Talmudic rule, "the Torah speaks the language of man," which appears many times in the Babylonian Talmud. See, for example, *Berachot*, 31b, and *Nedarim*, 3a. In Hebrew the axiom is called *dibrah torah klashon bnei adam*. A similar Talmudic adage, "scripture does not escape its simple literal meaning," which means that allegorical explanations cannot negate literal ones, appears in *Yevamot*, 11b. For an in-depth discussion of the Maimonidean understanding of this concept, see A. Nuriel, "Dibrah Torah Kilshon Beni Adam in Guide to the Perplexed," in *Revealed and Hidden in Medieval Jewish Philosophy* (Jerusalem: Magnes Press 2000), pp. 93–99 [Hebrew].

[125] Locke, *The Correspondence of John Locke*, p. 1901. Locke appears to have adapted his own literary style to that of how he understood scriptural hermeneutics. In his "Letter to the Right Reverend Edward, Lord Bishop of Worcester" Locke writes that he "did not publish (my) Essay for such great masters of knowledge as your lordship; but fitted it to men of my own size, to whom repetitions might be sometimes useful." Locke, *Works of*

And again, as we saw earlier, although in this instance without giving direct credit to Maimonides, in the *First Treatise* itself the Maimonidean rule of hermeneutics is applied by Locke in order to counter Filmer's reading of Genesis I:26 and 28 as the granting of dominion exclusively to Adam despite its plural tense: "and what is said to *Noah* and his Sons Joyntly, must be understood to be meant to Noah alone."

God, I believe, speaks differently from Men, because he speaks with more Truth, more Certainty: but when he vouchsafes to speak to Men, I do not think, he speaks differently from them, in crossing the Rules of language in use amongst them. This would not be to condescend to their Capacities, when he humbles himself to speak to them, but to lose his design in speaking, what thus spoken, they could not understand.[126]

After arguing that the scriptural term *death* in the post-lapsarian world refers to human mortality exclusively and not to a life of misery, Locke goes on to argue against imputationist theology by pointing out that nowhere does the New Testament attribute innate depravity to Adam's posterity.

If by *Death* threatned (sic) to Adam were meant the Corruption of Humane Nature in his Posterity, 'tis strange that the New Testament should not any where take notice of it, and tell us, that Corruption seized on all because of *Adam*'s Transgression, as well as it tells us so of *Death*. But as I remember every ones sin is charged upon himself only.[127]

The last sentence is an apparent reference to the verse in Deuteronomy (24:16), which reads that, "The fathers shall not be put to death for the children, neither shall the children be put to death for the fathers; every man shall be put to death for his own sin." Similarly, Locke writes elsewhere:

John Locke, vol. 3 (1696), http://oll.libertyfund.org/index.php?option=com_staticxt& staticfile=show.php%3Ftitle, p. 7.

[126] I, 46, p. 191. Locke is hardly alone in his assertion that when God "vouchsafes to speak to Men, I do not think, he speaks differently from them." Christopher Hill records that preeminent figures of Locke's time as diverse as Calvin, Galileo, Kepler, and Newton agreed that, "the Bible speaks the language of every man." See Hill, *English Bible*, p. 22. Hill does not mention whether or not the other thinkers he cites quoted Maimonides as well. What is certain, though, is that Locke did.

[127] Locke, *The Reasonableness of Christianity*, p. 93. K. I. Parker is also of the opinion that, following *The Reasonableness*, the *Paraphrase and Notes* also reject the idea that Paul believed the sin of Adam to be "imputed" to others. See Parker, *The Biblical Politics of John Locke*, p. 35.

This was the punishment of that 1st sin to Adam & Eve. viz death & the consequence but not punishment of it to all their posterity for they never having had any hopes or expectation given them of immortalitie, to be borne mortal as man was first made cannot be called a punishment.[128]

The same basic idea is evident in a note to his paraphrase of Romans 5:12. "[A] mortal father, infected now with death, [was] able to produce noe better than a mortal race."[129] This last quote is of particular import because it shows that even in a composition intended exclusively for Christians, Locke's position regarding the limited significance of the Fall remained consistent.

Having established that belief in original sin is decidedly not an elemental Christian tenet, Locke goes on to define what is.

These two, Faith and Repentance; *i.e.* believing Jesus to be the *Messiah*, and good Life; are the indispensable Conditions of the New Covenant to be performed by all those, who would obtain Eternal Life.[130]

Simple belief, though, denuded of moral living is decidedly not what Locke has in mind. In a consistent attack on antinomian notions associated with the guiding lights of the Reformation, he repeatedly makes the point that what matters is obedience to God's moral laws. Heaven is not accommodated, nor the world to come attained, by plain and abstract belief, for that, contends Locke, would actually encourage iniquity.

For Life, Eternal Life being the Reward of Justice or Righteousness only, appointed by the Righteous God (who is of purer Eyes than to behold Iniquity) to those only who had no taint or infection of Sin upon them, it is impossible that he should Justifie those who had no regard to Justice at all, whatever they believed. This would have been to encourage Iniquity, contrary to the Purity of

---

[128] Nuovo, *John Locke: Writings on Religion*, "Homo ante et post lapsum," p. 231.

[129] John Locke, *A Paraphrase and Notes on the Epistles of St. Paul to the Galatians, 1 and 2 Corinthians, Romans, Ephesians*, Arthur W. Wainwright (ed.) (Oxford: Oxford University Press, 1987), ii, p. 524.

[130] Locke, *The Reasonableness of Christianity*, p. 169. Locke goes on to attribute this honed-down theology to St. Paul himself. "This was the Sum and Substance of the Gospel which St. *Paul* Preached; and was all that he knew necessary to Salvation; viz. Repentance, and believing Jesus to be the Messiah." Ibid, 183. Significantly, though, Nuovo makes the important observation that Locke does not attribute essential divinity to Christ; he asserts rather his superiority over angels. See Nuovo, *John Locke: Writings on Religion*, p. lvi.

Prof. Michael Heyd has shared with me the important observation that even Locke's classification of the belief in *Jesus as Messiah* as requisite Christian dogma was a significant departure from heretofore traditionally held Christian codes of belief that held *Jesus as the son of God* to be the most basic tenet of faith.

his Nature; and to have condemned that Eternal Law of Right, which is Holy, Just, and Good; Of which no one Precept or Rule is abrogated or repealed; nor indeed can be; whilst God is an Holy, Just, and Righteous God, and Man a Rational Creature.[131]

And 'tis no where promised, That those who persist in wilful (sic) Disobedience to his Laws, shall be received into the eternal bliss of his Kingdom, how much soever they believe in him.[132]

It was Christ himself, argues Locke, who rejected the notion that belief in the eternity of his ministry obviates the need for righteous living.

Thus we see, by the Preaching of our Saviour and his Apostles, that he required of those who believed him to be the Messiah, and received him for their Lord and Deliverer, that they should live by his Laws: And that (through in consideration of their becoming his Subjects, by Faith in him, whereby they believed and took him to be the *Messiah*, their former Sins should be forgiven) Yet he would own none to be his, nor receive them as true denizens of the New *Jerusalem*, into the inheritance of Eternal Life; but leave them to the Condemnation of the Unrighteous; who renounced not their former Miscarriages, and lived in a sincere Obedience to his Commands. What he expects from his Followers, he has sufficiently declared as a Legislator. And that they may not be deceived, by mistaking the Doctrine of Faith, Grace, Free-Grace, and the Pardon and Forgiveness of Sins and Salvation by him, (which was the End of his Coming) He more than once declared to them; For what omissions and miscarriages he shall Judge and Condemn to Death, even those who have owned him, and done Miracles in his Name; when he comes at last to render to every one according to what he hath Done in the Flesh; Sitting upon his Great and Glorious Tribunal, at the end of the world.[133]

And, in what appears suggestive of a resounding refutation of Luther, "None are Sentenced or Punished for Unbelief; but only for their Misdeeds."[134]

Locke's motivation for writing *The Reasonableness* following the *Two Treatises* and the *Essay Concerning Human Understanding* was intended, as Ian Harris argues, to present a Christian theology that was consistent with his other doctrines. This centered on his negating the imputationist reading of Christian dogma.

Consistency obliged Locke to write about Christianity in a way which agreed with his other doctrines. Those doctrines disregarded Adam's being mankind's representative and accordingly The *Reasonableness of Christianity* took Adam's representative capacity as a target. If reasonableness did not build on imputation, what had it to say about original sin? The major losses incurred by mankind at the Fall

[131] Locke, *The Reasonableness of Christianity*, p. 174.   [132] Ibid, p. 182.
[133] Ibid, pp. 184–185.   [134] Ibid, p. 185.

were said to be immortality and the Garden of Eden. This was original sin only in the narrow sense that it directs us to a sin committed in the original position of mankind. Adam suffered the loss of immortality and Eden as punishment for his action. The rest of mankind suffered them as consequence of their descent from him. The consequence displayed original sin in terms of a loss of immortality and Eden rather than a propensity towards evil on mankind's part.[135]

In the *Second Treatise*, Locke makes no mention of Adam's Fall and his banishment from Eden. A careful reading of his two references to this primordial human calamity in the *First Treatise* shows that they are mere reflections of Robert Filmer's thinking, not his own.[136] Parker points out that Locke's "one explicit reference to the Fall in the *Essays* indicates that it 'does not particularly concern philosophers.'"[137] Even in his *Two Tracts*, where defense of absolutism was predicated on a far more pessimistic view of human nature than he was to develop later in his life, the Fall was not a rudimentary part of his thinking.[138]

In contrast to Locke, Filmer's philosophy justifying the freedom deprivation of monarchical absolutism is predicated in no small measure on the pre-/post-lapsarian conceptualization of mankind, as demonstrated in his opening salvo against the notion of human freedom. Filmer immediately attributes the fall of mankind to its pursuit of unjustified liberty:

The divines, also, of the Reformed Churches have entertained it, and the common people everywhere tenderly embrace it as being most plausible to flesh and blood, for that it prodigally distributes a portion of liberty to the meanest of the multitude, who magnify liberty as if the height of human felicity were only to be found

---

[135] Harris, *The Mind of John Locke*, p. 303.   [136] I, 16, 45, pp. 169–170, 190–219.

[137] Parker, *The Biblical Politics of John Locke*, p. 52.

[138] Parker states that: "In the *Tracts*, Locke is fully convinced that human nature is corrupt, but he does not go so far as to attribute the origin of this corruption to the Fall. He certainly discusses the pervasiveness of sin and, sounding almost Augustinian at times, writes that, 'ever since man first threw himself into the pollution of sin, he sullies whatever he takes into his hand, and he that at first could make the best and perfectest nature degenerate cannot fail now to make other things so too.' At other times, however, he seems somewhat less harsh about the state of humanity, arguing that, 'we cannot doubt there can be anything so good or innocent which the frail nature or improved corruption of man may not make use of to harm himself or his neighbour.'" Ibid, p. 52. And Philip Abrams writes: "Nevertheless, the fact that Locke also writes of humanity's 'frail nature' and 'improved corruption' indicates that he may have been leaning toward the idea that humans can improve their lot here on earth and are not condemned to the necessity of sinning continually." Abrams, "Introduction," in *Two Tracts*, p. 36.

in it, never remembering that the *desire of liberty was the first cause of the fall of Adam.*[139]

It is at the very least implicit that Locke does not associate the natural state of man with the pre-lapsarian age and does not structure man's state of war in a post-lapsarian framework as do so many of his contemporaries. The question, then, is: What is it about original sin, so basic a concept in Christian theology and so readily associated with state of nature philosophy that disturbs Locke to the extent that he chooses to exclude the notion of fallen man's ineluctable human depravity from his political philosophy?[140]

It is first worth looking at Lockean scholarship on this issue. Jeremy Waldron states matter-of-factly that "Locke was not a believer in original sin."[141] Victor Nuovo writes that, "Locke takes his place alongside the representatives of this tender-hearted tradition by restricting the consequences of Adam's sin to mere mortality, by rejecting the Augustinian doctrine of original sin which leaves mankind utterly dependent upon grace..."[142] Peter A. Schouls agrees that "The opening pages of *The Reasonableness of Christianity* leave no doubt," that, "Locke *explicitly* rejects the dominant forms of the doctrine of original sin."[143] Neal Wood writes that Locke "had little use for sectarian disputes about dogma and rejected the concept of original sin and perhaps the doctrine of the Trinity."[144] And Kim Ian Parker writes: "Admittedly, Locke's understanding of the Fall was far from orthodox."[145]

Parker quotes Locke himself, showing that for all intents and purposes he rejected original sin theology:

---

[139] Robert Filmer, *Patriarcha and Other Writings*, J. P. Somerville (ed.) (Cambridge: Cambridge University Press, 1991), chapter 1, paragraph 1.

[140] Spellman calls the original sin issue "the central issue in the drama of the Christian faith since its inception." Spellman, *John Locke and the Problem of Depravity*, p. 8.

[141] Waldron, *God, Locke, and Equality*, p. 71.

[142] Nuovo, "Introduction," in *John Locke: Writings on Religion*, p. xix.

[143] Schouls suggests instead that Locke believed in what he calls "original neutrality," which means that everything is dependent not on natural human depravity (a result of the Fall) but on the (good or bad) nature of the education of the individual. For Schouls's full discussion of "original neutrality" see Schouls, *Reasoned Freedom*, pp. 193–203.

[144] Wood, *The Politics of Locke's Philosophy*, p. 28. But then, ignoring *The Reasonableness of Christianity* claims that Locke limited Christian basic precepts to "the First Commandment and the Golden Rule: obey God and love thy neighbor." Ibid. Wood overlooks *The Reasonableness of Christianity*, where Locke plainly states that the basic precepts are Jesus as Messiah and repentance.

[145] Parker, *The Biblical Politics of John Locke*, p. 66.

In fact, in the substantial though seldom read *Third Letter*, Locke questions and comes very close to explicit rejection of original sin. He writes, "The doctrine of original sin is that which is professed and must be owned by the members of the church of England, as is evident from the xxxix Articles, and several passages in the liturgy: and yet I ask you, whether this be 'so obvious and exposed to all that diligently and sincerely seek the truth,' that one who is in the communion of the church of England, sincerely seeking the truth, may not raise to himself such difficulties concerning the doctrine of original sin as may puzzle him, though he be a man of study; and whether he may not push his inquiries so far, as to be staggered in his opinion? (*Works*, 6:411)" ... Thus, for Locke, the Fall did not mean that humans were totally depraved, but only that they had lost their chance for immortality and had consequently succumbed to the short-sighted vision that came with a finite lifespan. Humans were, in an ultimate sense, responsible for their own actions.[146]

---

[146] Ibid, p. 59. In an article Parker penned together with another Locke scholar, Greg Forster, a very different attitude toward Locke on original sin is articulated. "Understanding Locke's affirmation of sinfulness is crucial to grasping the fundamental problem of the Two Treatises, which depicts the institution of government as driven primarily by the need to cope with humanity's natural predisposition to sin." And: "Locke's political theory in the Two Treatises relies crucially on the orthodox view that moral corruption is universally present in human nature, such that the Two Treatises cannot be understood apart from that view."

I have argued in this chapter and essentially throughout this book that in fact the complete opposite is true. Whether or not Locke was fully Pelagian is less important than the recognition that on the issue of original sin he was, contrary to these authors, as optimistic as Pelagius was and fully endorsed the idea that humans could choose good over evil. But my thesis aside, I find it to be bordering on the unfathomable that two distinguished scholars of Locke could reach such a conclusion. The authors repeat this idea again and again but in my opinion offer nothing convincing to back up their claim; in fact most of the "proof" texts they offer show just the opposite. They seem to confuse human frailty and the possibility of moral failure, which Locke and no one else for that matter would deny, with a predisposition for sin, of which Locke says absolutely nothing, and everything he does say suggests a firm rejection of it. They themselves admit that nowhere in the *Two Treatises* does Locke speak of sin, yet, with a page out of Leo Strauss's play book, they don't hesitate to turn natural sinfulness into the cornerstone of Locke's political thinking. These scholars argue that Locke did reject the origin of sin, that being from Adam, but did not reject the Pauline–Augustinian bottom line of ubiquitous and inescapable sin. But this defies logic: Why would Locke cure the problem of depravity with a political theory of consent, including its right of rebellion with its "appeal to heaven," which by definition attributes the primacy of reason, not depravity, to the human condition? Certainly the theorists such as Filmer who predicated their defense of governmental absolutism on the belief that the depravity of human sinfulness could only be controlled through the deprivation of freedom by authoritarian government were far more consistent in their reasoning than was Locke according to Forster and Parker in this article. See Greg Forster and Kim Ian Parker, "'Men Being Partial to Themselves': Human Selfishness in Locke's Two Treatises," *Politics and Religion* 1 (2008), pp. 169–199.

Similarly, Joshua Mitchell writes that the attribution of "spiritual corruption, of sin," to Adam's Fall "was not" something Locke "was prepared to accept." Rather he attributed loss of eternal life alone.[147] And: "While Locke does speak of 'the baseness of human nature' (*ST*, VII, #92, p. 327) his presumption is that human nature becomes base when humans 'quit their reason, which places [them] almost equal to Angels.' (*FT*. V, #58, p. 182). Human corruption is accidental, while industriousness and rationality are essential."[148]

But others differ. Richard Cox, for example, curiously rejects this premise and assumes that Locke's entire theory regarding the state of nature follows Christian theology regarding the Fall:

[M]an was originally in a state of innocence but, through Sin, suffered a Fall; that his Fall made government necessary; and that all government is by ordinance of God, for in the words of St. Paul: "let every soul be subject unto the higher powers. For there is no power but God: the powers that be are ordained by God. (Romans xiii).[149]

The fact that Cox provides no evidence for this assertion is particularly strange because of the fact that he is a leading proponent of the opinion that Locke was not at all a religious Christian and that his religious jargon was of duplicitous intent.

The Straussian Cox is not alone in assuming a natural Lockean Christological orbit regarding the Fall; John Dunn, on the other end of the Locke scholarship spectrum, assumes the very same thing. While acknowledging that Locke's position on original sin is "muddled" and that it "changed" over time, he nevertheless takes for granted the centrality of the Fall to Locke's thinking on the state of nature.[150]

If we wish to understand the theoretical basis of the morphology of social development which Locke propounds, it is essential to grasp the role played in it by the Fall. For the sin of Adam not only originated human mortality, it also originated that lesser punitive feature of the human condition, labour, and the socio-moral category derived from labour in conditions of scarcity, private property.[151]

And again:

Human beings are only potentially and intermittently rational, because although their will is determined by what they perceive to be best in the sense of most

---

[147] Mitchell, *Not by Reason Alone*, p. 88.   [148] Ibid, p. 204, *ft.* 65.
[149] Cox, *Locke on War and Peace*, p. 52.
[150] Dunn, *The Political Thought of John Locke*, p. 23, *ft.* 1.   [151] Ibid, p. 115.

hedonically fulfilling, their rational apprehension and their skill at hedonic calculation are clouded by the corrupt passions released by the Fall.[152]

Both Cox and Dunn ignore the simple fact that nowhere in the *Second Treatise* does Locke make any reference at all to the Fall and that his two references to it in the *First Treatise* appear only in the context of his polemic with Filmer. There is no reason then for these scholars to assume that Locke himself believes in original sin theology or at least takes it for granted when developing his theories on government.

Thomas Pangle, though a follower of Strauss, points out that there is ample evidence demonstrating Locke's rejection of traditional original sin doctrine, at least in the context of his political theory:

[I]f his account is examined with any close scrutiny, it becomes clear that in it "the Children of Adam, or Noah" are described as being uncorrupted by original sin: as partaking of the "unforeseeing Innocence of the first Ages," the "Innocence and Sincerity of that poor but virtuous Age," before vices "had corrupted Mens minds" (TT II 36–37, 94, 110, 111). After all, we watched Locke already establish, in the First Treatise, the irrelevance of Adam and Eve's transgression, or fall, to the guilt or innocence of their offspring.[153]

Like Pangle, Michael Zuckert also acknowledges that Locke does not speak of a Fall and that he in fact "breaks with ... Christian political thought" with regard to it, but then strangely goes on to convey the opposite position.[154] Actually, Locke's break with traditional Christian thinking on this issue appears to be so stark that it is hard to appreciate why anyone would suggest otherwise.

It is precisely the Fall that is so pivotal to the Christian defense of the divine rights absolutism theory that Locke comes to challenge. Advocates of divine rights absolutism such as Robert Filmer argued that because of humankind's "rebellion" against God in Eden, "God withdrew from the direct relationship with humanity that had predated the Fall," and instead "made earthly authorities who were to be the recipients of the obedience that originally went directly to him."[155] This thinking is the exact opposite of Locke's advocacy of "just rebellions" that follow appeals to heaven

---

[152] Ibid, p. 194.   [153] Pangle, *The Spirit of Modern Republicanism*, p. 165.

[154] Zuckert, *Natural Rights and the New Republicanism*, pp. 84, 212. In Zuckert's later work, *Launching Liberalism*, he surprisingly counts the Fall as one of "three fundamentals of the Biblical view" that Locke presents in the *First Treatise* (p. 143). But as if to admit he was mistaken or at least on weak ground, he proceeds to discuss only the other two, creation and donation, and ignore the Fall as if it were not there, which indeed it is not.

[155] Zuckert, *Natural Rights and the New Republicanism*, p. 41.

and God's moral law against absolutist cum tyrannical governments that are never and can never be divinely ordained. Could Locke possibly have advanced his groundbreaking notion of "individual executive power" had he believed in the primacy of human depravity? Is it the irremediably fallen and those mired in inescapable sin who can appeal to heaven?

With his "appeal to heaven" Locke is knocking down the great wall that Augustine erected separating the *City of God* and the *City of Man*. Humans, from their material habitat, reach into the domicile of the divine for moral guidance in what is specifically the *political* realm, and the latter expects this of them as well. If God can be "appealed to" then he has decidedly not "withdrawn from the direct relationship with humanity" and at least that aspect of the "inter-city" relationship that predated the Fall continues to exist in its full potency in the post-lapsarian age as well.

Nowhere does Locke mention the well-known Paulian passage from Romans either. It is precisely this Christian dogma so embraced by Filmer and other champions of absolutism that Locke defies. For Locke, contrary to Pauline–Augustinian doctrine, it is not the Fall and mankind's sinning toward God that makes government necessary; it is rather *mankind's sinning toward mankind* as depicted in Cain's murder of Abel, which he discusses openly and uses authoritatively, that makes the emergence from the state of nature to an organized political society so imperative. It should be remembered (discussed at length in Chapter 2) that Cain is held responsible by God for Abel's murder because he should have known through his own autonomous cognitive reasoning that murder is wrong. This is a linchpin idea that Locke uses to structure his natural law theory. It is a particularly non-Augustinian reading of Genesis, which draws one's attention to the fact that it is only in relation to the world's first homicide that the term "sin" is used, not in relation to the Fall.[156] Natural law issues begin with interhuman affairs, not with the realm of the human versus the divine, and that Locke believes he has on Biblical authority.

Furthermore, even after sin does make its appearance, it is avoidable, it can be overcome. Just prior to Cain's act of homicide, when he is crestfallen over his shunned sacrifice, he is told by God, "If thou doest well, shalt thou not be accepted? And if thou doest not well, sin crouches at the door, and to thee shall be his desire." In Chapter 1 we saw how Filmer interpreted this as the divine gift of primogeniture; Cain would rule over Abel as would every firstborn for posterity rule over his brethren. Locke,

[156] Novak, *Natural Law in Judaism*, p. 32. And also see Adler, *The Biblical View of Man*, p. 10.

on the other hand, believes that the verse is not referring to Abel at all, but it is rather to sin and the evil inclination that the text is referring when it says, "thou shalt Rule over him."

> God tells *Cain*, Gen. 4. That however sin might set upon him, he ought or might be Master of it: For the most Learned Interpreters understand the words of sin, and not of *Abel*, and give so strong Reasons for it, that nothing can convincingly be inferr'd from so doubtful a text, to our *Author*'s purpose.[157]

The significance here to Locke's Biblically derived understanding of human nature cannot be overstated: post-lapsarian humans have not lost the ability to discern good from evil, are responsible for their actions when they choose evil, and by properly developing their character, by "ruling over" it, sin can be avoided; a constant state of sin is decidedly not the ineluctable defining characteristic of the human condition.

The issue of procreation is another powerful example of Locke's rejection of central tenets of Augustinian Christianity. Augustine sees procreation through the Fall, hence at best, a necessary evil. For Augustine, Adam and Eve had been in a state of concupiscence when they fell, and as universal parents have transmitted that state of incontinent sexuality to all of humankind, propagation of the species is therefore sinful by nature.[158] But for Locke the opposite is true. As discussed in Chapter 4, Locke sees "the great design of God" put forward in human sexuality.[159] Not only is mankind charged to "subdue the earth and have dominion over creatures," mankind is also given the directive to "increase and multiply." To Locke, this is the "great and primary Blessing of God Almighty: Be fruitful and multiply, and replenish the earth."[160] Concupiscence facilitates the divine commandment, for "God in his infinite Wisdom has put strong desires of Copulation into the Constitution of Men," in order to achieve the continuance of the species.[161]

It is important then to put Locke's thinking on original sin in the proper context. While his thinking on the subject was essentially unorthodox, it was not entirely heretical, or at least not any more heretical than the tradition running from Pelagius until the seventeenth-century thinkers discussed earlier. It was a tradition that was pre-Augustinian and pre-Pauline, and that for all intents and purposes was in effect focused on the plain and simple textual understanding of the Hebraic account of Eden.

---

[157] I, 118, p. 245.   [158] Deane, *The Political and Social Ideas of St. Augustine*, p. 56.
[159] I, 21, p. 174; 41, p. 188.   [160] I, 33, p. 182.
[161] I, 54, p. 197. See also Harris, *The Mind of John Locke*, pp. 297–298.

Locke's repudiation of absolute and arbitrary government is commensurate with his plain Hebraic reading of the Genesis text. Mortal mankind with inherent weaknesses needs to emerge from a state of nature into a civil state of government, but mankind has not lost the capacity to architect its own emergence or manage its proper maintenance. Fallen mankind, on the other hand, in its inherent depravity, obsessive sinning, and futile pursuit of what is just, has lost the ability to act as arbiter of a moral destiny, and hence, necessarily, requires that it be governed absolutely. Locke could simply not have developed his political theory on consensual government along with the right to rebel against nonconsensual government had he accepted mainstream Christian original sin theory.[162]

---

[162] Spellman concurs that Locke's analysis of the Fall remains within a general pre-Paulian or at the very least pre-Augustinian understanding of the Fall. The Fall is understood not as: "the complete depravity of humankind, the necessity of sinning, and the futility of moral endeavor, but rather the many natural infirmities consequent to mortality – the unruliness of the passions, the impairment of reason, the shortness and inconsistency of judgment, the preoccupation with sensual satisfaction." Spellman, *John Locke and the Problem of Depravity*, p. 102.

Locke's rejection of natural human depravity also had dramatic ramifications for his understanding of the malleability of the human mind and became the fulcrum of his theory on education. Spellman explains the practical historical significance of Locke's thinking on child-rearing and pedagogy. "[P]rior to Locke's work the theory and practice of child-rearing had generally emphasized control over the youngster's inherently evil nature, stressing the importance of obedience, restraint, authority, and even fear; by the end of the eighteenth century, however, the emphasis had, under Locke's influence, shifted: child-rearing was now viewed as a pursuit of rational behaviour on the part of the child, with the family as educative agency, and the parent as gentle preceptor, affectionate counsellor, and sympathetic guide. And whereas in the world of Locke's youth individual failings – moral obliquity, deliberate sinfulness, acts of willful inhumanity – would all normally have been ascribed to the inborn depravity of the perpetrator, a century later these same actions would usually be considered a result of circumstances external to the child, of parental dereliction of duty rather than of childhood degeneracy. In other words, by the beginning of the nineteenth century, if no sooner, the ultimate responsibility for the sinful behaviour of a child was no longer regarded as lying with the sinner, but rather with those charged with bringing the child into the exercise of benevolent reason. This change in attitude was without much question an intellectual metamorphosis of fundamental import, at bottom nothing less than an absolute repudiation of original sin." Ibid, p. 203.

Elsewhere, Spellman writes: "Each individual must be responsible for his own eternal fate; the child is born without inborn knowledge and the morally responsible 'person' is the product of external influences. The myth of the Fall, so central to the faith, and to absolutist political theory, yet so debilitating in its implications for the transformation of both individual and society, received its sharpest criticism in 1695 from a man who claimed a solid and lifelong attachment to the Christian story." Spellman, *John Locke*, p. 77.

See also Harris, *The Mind of John Locke*, p. 299.

One cannot be certain whether Locke rejects the traditional Christian reading of the Fall because of his belief in mankind's ability to choose between good and evil, or if his belief in human free will forces him to read the Biblical account of original sin Hebraically, in a manner restricted to the issue of mortality. What is clear, though, is that both ideas are indispensable to Locke's thinking, and are in keeping with the Hebrew Bible's teachings on both subjects.

Conclusion

England's revolution of 1688 was certainly "glorious" for John Locke, for it was only following the assent of William and Mary to the throne and his subsequent return from political exile in the Dutch Republic at the age of fifty-seven that he published the works that made him great. The quick succession in which his major writings were rolled out for publication serves to bolster the historical evidence that Locke prepared his core theories throughout his earlier life of academic study, travel, scientific investigation, governmental service, and political activism. However, his decision to make his theories public did not banish his natural inclination toward caution and reserve as he still chose to keep his own authorship concealed, the *Essay Concerning Human Understanding* the only exception.

What fate the *Two Treatises of Government* might have met had they not been published anonymously can only be left to historical conjecture, but in an ironical way it may have contributed to the longevity of the composition's relevance as it was exclusively the writing that was judged and not the writer. Further conjecture would consider whether or not that was exactly what Locke had in mind when he chose anonymity, for he offered no explanation of his own.

He also chose not to explain why he used copious references to the Old Testament in his major political work while almost entirely ignoring the New Testament. This has led to more than mere speculation over Locke's intentions, but, as I have argued throughout this book, it is in actuality the root and branch, albeit unacknowledged as such, of much of the scholarly debate over the true conceptual orientation of the *Second Treatise*. What I have tried to show is that the absenting of New Testamentism was a conscious choice of a political Hebraist, of a philosopher who saw political theory authoritatively expressed in the Old Testament, which he understood as a text that could stand on its own merits.

Locke did not come out in his *Two Treatises* and state unequivocally that he intended to anchor much of his political thought on the Hebrew Bible, but he came pretty close, much closer in fact than to suggest a duplicitous cover for his radical secularism, as Leo Strauss insists, or indicate a Christological scaffolding for his political theory, as John Dunn argues. Numerous quotations from the Hebrew Bible are clearly there, while a comparable number of quotations from New Testament sources (as well as Greek and Roman) are clearly not. And the issue here is not just one of quantity (although significant quantity can itself be indicative of qualitative intent), as the quotations are used as proof-texts and the ideas Locke expresses are also in keeping with basic Hebraic concepts, while ideas widely regarded as basic to Christianity, such as the Fall and original sin, are saliently absent.

Many Protestants of the time related to the Old Testament as a document that, unlike the New Testament, did not deal just with personal spiritual salvation, but also with issues of polity, government, and political power that could not be ignored by those religiously inclined. This was an attitude that reached its peak with the theology of Locke's upbringing, seventeenth-century Puritanism, and my own conjecture is that here lies an important key to "unlocking" Locke's Hebraism.

The early English Puritans present an interesting paradox. On the one hand, Puritanism defined the human experience as stolid and gloomy. Like the early Christian subjects of Roman dominion, the Puritans who stood under the direct influence of Calvin viewed the world as a bad place, hostile to God and filled with sexually indulgent people fighting for power and striving only for monetary wealth.[1] As a result, the Puritans tried to conduct humble and modest lives filled with austerity and restraint. This was their way of turning a cold shoulder to the frivolities of the temporal world. But, on the other hand, historians have shown that the Puritans were filled with a deep commitment to hard earthly bound work as well. In their famous research, for example, Max Weber followed by R. H. Tawney demonstrated the critical influence that the Puritans had on the development of Western capitalism in creating strong and vibrant economies through their work ethic.[2]

---

[1] See Reventlow, *The Authority of the Bible*, pp. 95–96.
[2] Max Weber, *The Protestant Ethic and the Spirit of Capitalism* (New York: Scribners, 1958). R. H. Tawney, *Religion and the Rise of Capitalism* (New Brunswick, NJ: Transaction Publishers, 1998).

The paradox therefore is this: How could such an ascetic and insular community that did not believe in the importance of this world make such a great historical contribution to one of the world's most powerful economic and social developments? Weber for one explained that Puritan activism was a theological maneuver intended to overcome Calvinistic predestination. The extreme Protestants believed that if they would succeed in this material life, their success would be a here-and-now proof that God is on their side – any success meant that God was with you. On the other hand, any failure was tragic because it meant that one's actions were undesired by God. This understanding of the world led to a lifelong effort of hard work and self-control – money was earned not for the sake of spending it but rather for the sake of accumulation alone. It was a religious logic rather than a material one.[3]

For our purposes the explanation offered by Harold Fisch is more compelling. Fisch also deciphers the austere and yet industrious Puritan way of life by using theological tools, but he posits that it was the direct exposure of the Puritans to the Hebrew Bible, which bridged the gap between their otherworldliness and their practical and earthly human effort, that made the difference. By bypassing the New Testament and reading themselves into the Old, the Puritans were filled with a new and different approach toward matters of corporeality. In the model of the ancient Hebrews, the Puritans found a down-to-earth paradigm for national life, a way to mesh the divine and the temporal. In the Hebrew Bible, the Messiah was not a figure standing between unredeemed mankind and an unfathomable holy heaven, but a flesh-and-blood person, someone like King David who was a leader of a nation, and dealt practically with wars, politics, economics, and social challenges. The story of the Hebrews showed the Puritans a way to seek holiness without decrying the present, how to remain inside human history and reshape it, rather than attempt to ignore and escape it. The direct reading of the

---

[3] Weber, *The Protestant Ethic and the Spirit of Capitalism.* Interestingly, Erich Fromm interpreted the Calvinistic-Puritan paradox through the eyes of a modern psychologist: "This mechanism can be easily observed in attacks of anxiety panic in individuals. A man who expects to receive within a few hours the doctor's diagnosis of his illness-which may be fatal quite naturally is in a state of anxiety. Usually he will not sit down quietly and wait. Most frequently his anxiety, if it does not paralyze him, will drive him to some sort of more or less frantic activity. He may pace up and down the floor, start asking questions and talk to everybody he can get hold of, clean up his desk, write letters. He may continue his usual kind of work but with added activity and more feverishly. Whatever form his effort assumes it is prompted by anxiety and tends to overcome the feeling of powerlessness by frantic activity." Fromm, *Escape from Freedom*, p. 111.

Hebrew Bible infused the Puritans with both a personal and communal dedication to develop the material world, to work hard and accomplish, and to value an individual's natural talents and the contribution he or she can make in the corporeal realm. It was a new and unique approach for many Christian believers, and it was to have a lasting impact.[4]

It was into this Puritan world that Locke was born and educated, and it was following this primordial Puritan influence that Locke found in Old Testamentism a source for spiritual and practical inspiration, a road map out of the restrictive and outsider attitude toward political life. Locke saw in the Hebrew Bible the inspiration, power, motivation, and methodology to promote a powerful alternative to the freedom-depriving notions of government, structured by centuries of church-state relations that were still popular in his time.[5]

But even in this regard Locke's originality is already poignant. Locke in fact followed the anti-Erastian Puritan John Milton but not to the exclusion of the Erastian thinking of Selden and Harrington. It will be remembered that the Erastians sought to ensure societal toleration by maintaining a total fusion between ecclesiastical and civic jurisdiction. To accomplish this unity, mandatory religiosity had to be relegated to a bare minimum. The anti-Erastian Milton feared that, on the contrary,

---

[4] Fisch, *Jerusalem and Albion*, pp. 46–63. While not directly relating to Puritanism or to Locke, the twentieth-century Jewish philosopher Franz Rosenzweig succinctly described this intellectual process: "Wherever the demands of Christian communal life were not satisfied by the all too primitive model community described in the Acts of the Apostles and in the Epistles, or by the critical attitude toward the world pronounced in the Gospels (critical in both the social and moral aspects), it was, and still is, natural to revert to the Old Testament, to law born prophecy. The Christian church, the Christian state, Christian economics, and Christian society could not and cannot be established upon the New Testament, which sees the world only in crisis, only face to face with Judgment. In contrast to the New Testament, the Jewish Bible, sprung from the richness of the life of a whole people, of a whole national literature, offered a solid ground for building the world, and for building the world, in that its faith in creation was both living and profound – even within the sphere of prophetic criticism and polemics." Franz Rosenzweig, "The Significance of the Bible in World History," in *Jewish Perspectives on Christianity*, Fritz A. Rothschild (ed.) (New York: Crossroad, 1990), p. 230.

[5] Fisch did not identify Locke as a Hebraic thinker, arguing instead that he based human knowledge purely on reason, reaching the "Humanistic approach of the Hebrew Bible without the Bible itself." Fisch, *Jerusalem and Albion*, pp. 183–186. But while discussing Locke and making this clear observation, Fisch does not quote from the *Two Treatises*. Indeed it would have been difficult, if not impossible, for Fisch to reconcile such a statement with the plain text of the *Two Treatises* as we have seen. This appears to be a serious oversight in Fisch's otherwise important work about the relationship between Albion and Jerusalem.

such fusion would lead to intemperance, and hence insisted that they be separated, with the civic authority bearing no responsibility for ecclesiastical issues. For Milton then, there was less of a need to reduce the scope of what was religiously obligating, because it wasn't the business of government anyway. Interestingly, both sides claimed precedent and legitimacy in the divinely ordained governmental structure of Biblical Israel, and Locke drew from both. Like Milton (and unlike the views he had initially expressed in his *Two Tracts*) Locke insisted that individual religious affiliation and/or belief was not in the purview of governmental authority, but conversely, like the Erastians, he asserted that toleration could not be guaranteed unless that which was held religiously binding would be reduced to a minimum.[6]

In quantitatively minimizing his Christology (in *The Reasonableness of Christianity*), Locke was able to advocate theories of government that were not wholly commensurate with certain elements of Christian dogma; however, he was not willing to abandon the need for Biblical authority for his ideas. His modus operandi for accomplishing this, his use then of the Old Testament, means that the equation is not just a quantitative one, but a qualitative one as well, and that is clearly evident from the way he makes his case. Locke, though, was not the first Christian philosopher to initiate such an approach as he was preceded by John Selden, and it is fair to assume that it was Selden whom he was following. On the need to read Hebraic sources directly, absent of Christological gloss, Selden was very specific.[7]

Locke does not do this elsewhere in his writing. Not in the *Essay* nor in his works on tolerance or education, and certainly not in *The Reasonableness*. This makes Locke a classical *political Hebraist*, rather than an academic or juridical Hebraist.

---

[6] See Chapter 3, *ft.* 113.

[7] While quoting Selden, Steven Grosby says it well: Selden does state in the Prolegomena to his first work on Jewish law, *De Successionibus in Bona Defuncti* (1631), on the inheritance of personal property, that if one relies on the writings of the Church Fathers, one will never understand Jewish law as set out in the Bible. He further tells us in a letter written sixteen years later to Francis Tayler that similar to the telescope used by Galileo to discover the moons of Jupiter, without the tool of rabbinical doctrine, "whence the whole of Christianity arose, we are often deceived in our judgments of sacred matters, deceiving others by guesswork and propagating monstrous offspring of whatever ingenuity." Steven Grosby, "What to Read in Prison? John Selden in the Tower of London," lecture (April 2013, draft March 26, 2013), p. 7. Grosby is quoting from G. J. Toomer's two-volume *John Selden: A Life in Scholarship* (Oxford: Oxford University Press, 2009), pp. 450, 846.

Locke was coming to reject a theory of absolute and arbitrary government that in large measure found its theological basis in the traditional Christian reading of original sin that argued that mankind's natural depravity, endemic to its being a result of Adam's Fall, necessitates a magistrate who enjoys divine status. To deny absolutism and define the magistrate's source of authority in the people meant to define mankind's post-lapsarian state in terms of responsibility rather than depravity. The Biblical story of the forbidden fruit refers in the Hebraic reading only to the forfeiture of immortality after Adam and Eve's sin; there is nothing in the Fall's account that classifies death as punishment, points to a constant state of sin, or suggests predestination. On the contrary, human free will and the full significance of human actions are definitively elemental to the way Hebraic theology understands human ability and accountability.

Locke was searching for a theory that would define and defend just rebellion in order to preserve the freedoms that the revolution had ushered in, and ensure that there would not be a slide back to arbitrary and absolute monarchical rule. To justifiably rebel against human authority, that authority would have to violate a law that it did not have the power to abrogate, a law that came from a higher authority, God himself, to whom even government, harnessed with the task of keeping public order, was beholden. A rebellion against the suspended law is an "appeal to heaven" paradigmatically portrayed for Locke in the Biblical account of Jephthah's response to the territorial claims of the Ammonites against the Israelites and his subsequent war against them. God's law is natural law, inviolable principles of justice that are known to humankind through the use of human reason and through revelation in the Hebrew Bible as well.

While Locke agreed with most natural law theorists that the laws of nature could be identified through reason it was with the greatest Hebraist of the age, John Selden, that he seems to be fully in tandem, that without divine positive law, revelation, as a source of natural law, there would be nothing to obligate compliance, as reason alone is insufficient to do so. Locke established, based on the Biblical story of Cain and Abel, that reason was a divine gift planted within mankind, in essence a form of revelation, and conversely that many of the laws of nature that were positively commanded by God could also be understood through the use of human reason. Cain was to know himself that murder was an abrogation of God's law through the use of his own reason and was hence held responsible despite the lack of any prior divine warning. As a result, Locke refers to the later divine positive prohibition against shedding blood as the "great law of nature." Natural law then for Locke does not replace divine law, as it is also divine; nor does divine law obviate the need for reason, because together they define the essence of humans created "in the image of God." To prove the limitations of human reason Locke deploys the Books of Exodus and Psalms.

Belief in a rational and relevant God, creator of heaven and earth, is essential for his theory of natural law, and once there is belief in such a God it is unreasonable to assume that he created mankind without a plan, without rules intended to pattern life, without a natural law. He refused to countenance a natural law theory independent of theology as Hobbes did and Grotius conceived possible. Although we cannot know if he consulted Maimonidean texts directly, his way to achieving the knowledge of God is strikingly similar to the Maimonidean depiction, which is in turn based on the Talmud and Midrash. The same can also be said regarding his approach to the limited theological significance of miracles. While Locke did not quote Maimonides directly on these issues as he did Maimonides' *Guide* with regard to the proper hermeneutical approach to the Biblical text, the similarity of thought and style is poignant.

It is also from Cain and Abel that Locke derives the "strange doctrine" of ubiquitous executive retributive power of the individual, because Cain is troubled that *anyone* could avenge Abel's murder. God does not deny that this is the case but instead offers a promise of protection against that which would otherwise be justified. This Biblically rooted notion is fundamental for Locke because this individual political power is never eliminated entirely even with the advent of legitimate government. Instead, the doctrine is held in abeyance, always poised to reassert itself should government become corrupted and illegitimate. In which case it is not only the public as a whole unit but the individual him- or herself who has the right to "appeal to heaven" and oppose it. Most advocates of rebellion, such as the author of the *Vindiciae*, who also gleaned from the Biblical text, did not go so far as to support the right of the individual to rebel. Locke, though, chose to follow Milton, whose reading of the Hebrew Bible led him to the conclusion that the right of rebellion was not a right limited to the masses. Locke probably chose such a reading because he had already constructed the doctrine of individual executive power based on his direct rendering of the Biblical text coupled with his minimized Christology.

The limits that Locke places on individual executive power, his insistence on penal proportionality, are found in the Books of Leviticus and

Deuteronomy, and if he did not draw on them directly they appear to have been mediated to him through the writings of Grotius, who is specific in his use of them, and who, scholarship widely assumes, influenced Locke on these subjects. Locke's example of executive individual power and its limitations, that of how a thief is to be contended with, also appears to closely follow the legal parameters established by the Book of Exodus.

Locke's state of nature is one in which all are equal, having been created by "one Omnipotent, and, infinitely wise Maker." Because it is God's design, as the Biblical account of creation teaches, to deny human equality is to deny divine authority to which all mankind and laws are beholden. This is an equality that preceded the advent of Christianity making men and women one, not as brothers and sisters of Christ, but as children of Adam. This Biblical structuring of equality also explains Locke's intolerance of atheists as well as those who claim an innate conception of the divine. The former destroy the basis of equality; the latter in their obviation of reason prevent an understanding of his will.

Biblical creation is also the reason humans are obligated to preserve themselves, as they never entirely leave the ultimate proprietorship of their creator. It is through the Biblical Golden Rule that Locke then deduces a Biblical augmentation of the rule of self-preservation to include the obligation to preserve society and all fellow humans. If one is obligated to love the other like oneself, and one is obligated to preserve oneself, ergo one is obligated to preserve others as well. God's eternal connection to the humans he labored in also guarantees human freedom as humans are not at liberty to self-deny their own freedom by agreeing to enslave themselves, and by extension people cannot willingly subject themselves to governmental tyranny. That, in pointed contradistinction to such thinkers as Suarez, Grotius, and Hobbes. It is to the Book of Exodus that Locke turns to find the parameters of proscribed slavery spelled out.

Locke's seminal focus on labor as the source of property acquisition also has deep roots in Biblical thought. Just as God maintains title to the humans he created he never abandons title to his other creations that humans labor in to create their own property. Hence human acquisition is not unlimited. Because God maintains ultimate title in everything he created, human labor can determine exclusive possession with regard to other humans but not with regard to God. And the limit God puts on human acquisition is an extension of the obligation, Biblically based, to preserve humans, i.e., charity. The rights to basic sustenance from the excess property of the self-sufficient that Locke puts in the hands of the poor appears to closely follow the Biblical directives of (primarily agricultural) charity as well as the Maimonidean codification of those laws. The same is true for Locke's insistence that the highest form of charity is providing work for the needy so that they too can imitate an industrious God and enjoy the fruits of their own labor.

In conclusion, it is perhaps important to restate the obvious: this book does not argue that the Hebrew Bible was Locke's *only* source for his political theory, nor does it suggest that he was always and exclusively in tandem with Hebraic attitudes. Locke undoubtedly drew from many sources, and despite the differing emphases, modern scholarship, which I have tried to thoroughly resource throughout, has shown the depth and breadth of his knowledge and resourcing. But while this is uncontestable and has enjoyed exhaustive research, Locke's near exclusive use of the Hebrew Bible in his *Two Treatises* has not been appreciated. The intention of this book then was to contribute an initial offering toward the filling of that academic vacuum, and decidedly not an attempt at claiming theoretical exclusivity. I pray that I have met that goal.

One cannot say for certain if Locke has been deprived of posthumously enjoying the fruits of his own labor by having his political Hebraism ignored for so long. But I think it is Hebraism itself that has not gotten the attention it deserves, not just Locke's, and it is perhaps just now coming of age. Once it finds its proper place under the academic sun, its proper application, such as, I believe, in the case of Locke's *Two Treatises*, will undoubtedly gain exposure, then currency, and ultimately, acceptance. When that happens, I am quite certain that general agreement will follow, that there is more that is alive than is dead in John Locke's political theory.

Bibliography

A. PUBLISHED WORKS BY JOHN LOCKE

The Correspondence of John Locke, 8 vols. Edited by E. S. de Beer. Oxford: Clarendon Press, 1976–1989.

An Essay Concerning Human Understanding. Edited by Roger Woolhouse. London: Penguin Books, 2004.

Essays on the Law of Nature. Edited by W. von Leyden. Oxford: Oxford University Press, 1954.

The First Treatise of Government. Translated by Shunamit Lifshitz. Tel Aviv: Resling Publishing, 2008 [Hebrew].

John Locke: Writings on Religion. Edited by Victor Nuovo. Oxford: Oxford University Press, 2002.

A Letter Concerning Toleration. Edited by James Tully. Indianapolis, IN: Hackett Publishing, 1983.

The Life and Letters of John Locke: With Extracts from His Journals and Commonplace Books. Edited by Peter King. London: H. Colburn & R. Bentley, 1830.

Locke: Political Essays. Edited by Mark Goldie. Cambridge: Cambridge University Press, 1997, 2006.

Luther's Works. Edited by Jaroslav Pelikan. St. Louis, MO: Concordia Publishing House, 1956.

Edited by Robert C. Schultz and Helmut T. Lehman. Philadelphia, PA: Fortress Press, 1967.

A Paraphrase and Notes on the Epistles of St. Paul to the Galatians, 1 and 2 Corinthians, Romans, Ephesians. Edited by Arthur W. Wainwright. Oxford: Oxford University Press, 1987.

The Second Treatise of Government. Translated by Joseph Ur. Jerusalem: The Magness Press, 1973 [Hebrew].

The Selected Political Writings of John Locke. Edited by Paul E. Sigmund. London: Norton & Co., 2005.

"Some Thoughts Concerning Education." In *The Clarendon Edition of the Works of John Locke*. Edited by John W. Yolton and Jean S. Yolton. Oxford: Oxford University Press, 1989.

Two Treatises of Government. Edited by Peter Laslett. Cambridge: Cambridge University Press, 1964, reprinted in 1996.

Edited by T. I. Cook. New York: Hafner Classics, 1947.

Edited by Philip Abrams. Cambridge: Cambridge University Press, 1967.

The Works of John Locke, A New Edition, corrected, 10 vols. London: Thomas Tegg, 1823.

The Works of John Locke in Nine Volumes, 12th Edition. London: Rivington, 1824.

B. SECONDARY SOURCES ON LOCKE

John Locke Bibliography, A Comprehensive Listing of Publications by and about John Locke. www.libraries.psu.edu/tas/locke.

Aaron, Richard I. *John Locke*. Oxford: Clarendon Press, 1937, 1955, 1971.

Aarsleff, Hans. "Locke's Influence." In *The Cambridge Companion to Locke*. Edited by Vere Chappell. Cambridge: Cambridge University Press, 1994, pp. 252–289.

"Some Observations on Recent Locke Scholarship." In *John Locke: Problems and Perspectives, A Collection of New Essays*. Edited by John Yolton. Cambridge: Cambridge University Press, 1969, pp. 262–272.

Alexander, Samuel. *Locke*. New York: Dodge Publishing Company, 1908, reprinted in 1993 by Thoemmes Press.

Arniel, Barbra. *John Locke and America*. Oxford: Clarendon Press, 1996.

Ashcraft, Richard. *Locke's Two Treatises of Government*. London: Unwin Hyman, 1987.

The Revolutionary Politics of John Locke. Cambridge: Cambridge University Press, 1987.

Revolutionary Politics & Locke's Two Treatises of Government. Princeton, NJ: Princeton University Press, 1986.

Axtell, J. L. "Locke, Newton and the Two Cultures." In *John Locke: Problems and Perspectives*. Edited by J. W. Yolton. Cambridge: Cambridge University Press, 1969, pp. 165–182.

Calvert, Brian. "Locke on Punishment and the Death Penalty." *Philosophy Journal of the Royal Institute of Philosophy* 68, 264 (1993), pp. 211–229.

Chappell, Vere. Editor, *The Cambridge Companion to Locke*. Cambridge: Cambridge University Press, 1994.

Coby, Patrick. "The Law of Nature in Locke's Second Treatise: Is Locke a Hobbesian?" In *Political Theory*. Edited by Joseph Losco and Leonard Williams. New York: St. Martin's Press, 1992, pp. 301–303.

Cox, Richard. *Locke on War and Peace*. Oxford: Clarendon, 1960.

Cranston, M. *John Locke: A Biography*. Oxford: Longmans, Green and Co. 1985.

De Beer, Esmond S. "Locke and English Liberalism: The Second Treatise of Government in Its Contemporary Setting." In *John Locke: Problems and Perspectives*. Edited by J. W. Yolton. Cambridge: Cambridge University Press, 1969, pp. 33–44.

Dunn, John. "What Is Living and What Is Dead in the Political Theory of John Locke." In John Dunn, *Interpreting Political Responsibility, Essays: 1981–1989*. Princeton, NJ: Princeton University Press, 1990, pp. 9–25.

   The Political Thought of John Locke. Cambridge: Cambridge University Press, 1969.

Dworetz, Steven M. *The Unvarnished Doctrine: Locke, Liberalism and the American Revolution*. Durham, NC: Duke University Press, 1990.

Farr, James, and Roberts, Clayton. "John Locke on the Glorious Revolution: A Rediscovered Document." *The Historical Journal* 28 (1985, published by Cambridge University Press), p. 386.

Forster, Greg. *John Locke's Politics of Moral Consensus*. Cambridge: Cambridge University Press, 2005.

   "A Glorious Revolution: Restoring Locke's Relevance." *Political Theory* 32, 5 (2004), pp. 706–713.

Forster, Greg, and Parker, Kim Ian. "'Men Being Partial to Themselves': Human Selfishness in Locke's Two Treatises." *Politics and Religion* 1 (2008), pp. 169–199.

Foster, David. "The Bible and Natural Freedom in John Locke's Political Thought." In *Piety and Humanity: Essays on Religion and Early Modern Political Philosophy*. Edited by Douglas Kries. New York: Rowman & Littlefield, 1997, pp. 181–211.

Fox Bourne, H. R. *The Life of John Locke*. New York: Harper and Brothers Publishers, 1876.

Franklin, Julian H. *John Locke and the Theory of Sovereignty: Mixed Monarchy and the Right of Resistance in the Political Thought of the English Revolution*. Cambridge: Cambridge University Press, 1978.

Goldie, Mark. Editor, *The Reception of Locke's Politics: From the 1690s to the 1830s*, vol. 1. London: Pickering & Chatto, 1999.

Gough, J. W. *John Locke's Political Philosophy*. Oxford: Clarendon Press, 1950.

Grant, Ruth. *John Locke's Liberalism*. Chicago, IL: The University of Chicago Press, 1991.

Gross, G. "Notes for Reading the Bible with John Locke." *Jewish Political Studies Review* 9, 3–4 (1997), pp. 5–18.

Harpham, E. J. Editor, *John Locke's Two Treatises: New Interpretations*. Lawrence, KS: University Press of Kansas, 1992.

Harris, Ian. *The Mind of John Locke: A Study of Political Theory in Its Intellectual Setting*. Cambridge: Cambridge University Press, 1994.

Harrison, John, and Laslett, Peter. Editors, *The Library of John Locke*, 2nd Edition. Oxford: Clarendon Press, 1971.

Hudson, Winthrop. "John Locke – Preparing the Way for the Revolution." *Journal of Presbyterian History* 42 (1964), pp. 19–38.

Hundert, E. J. "The Making of *Homo Faber*: John Locke between Ideology and History." *Journal of the History of Ideas* 33 (1972), pp. 3–22.

Huyler, Jerome. *Locke in America*. Lawrence, KS: University Press of Kansas, 1995.

Jolley, Nicholas. "Leibniz on Locke and Socinianism." *Journal of the History of Ideas* 39, 1 (1978), pp. 223–250.

Kessler, Sanford. "John Locke's Legacy of Religious Freedom." *Polity* 17, 3 (1985), pp. 484–503.

Kramer, Matthew H. *Locke and the Origins of Private Property*. Cambridge: Cambridge University Press, 1997.

Laslett, Peter. "The English Revolution and Locke's Two Treatises of Government." *Cambridge Historical Journal* 12, 1 (1956), pp. 43–55.

Leiter, Yechiel J. M. "The Political Hebraism of John Locke's First Treatise of Government," a Master's thesis. Supervised by Prof. Fania Oz-Salzberger, and submitted to the University of Haifa. November 2007.

Lord King. *The Life of John Locke, with Extracts from His Correspondence, Journals, and Common Place Books*, 2 vols. London: H. Colburn & R. Bentley, 1830.

Lough, J. Editor, *Locke's Travels in France 1675–1679*. Cambridge: Cambridge University Press, 1953.

Manke, George T. "A Research Note and Query on the Dating of Locke's Two Treatises." *Political Theory* 9, 4 (1981), pp. 547–550.

Marshall, John. *John Locke, Toleration and Early Enlightenment Culture*. Cambridge: Cambridge University Press, 2006.

　　"Locke, Socinianism, 'Socinianism', and Unitarianism," In *English Philosophy in the Age of Locke*. Edited by M. A Stewart. Oxford: Clarendon Press, 2000, pp. 111–182.

　　Resistance, Religion and Responsibility. Cambridge: Cambridge University Press, 1994.

　　"John Locke and Latitudinarianism." In *Philosophy, Science and Religion in England 1640–1700*. Edited by Richard Ashcraft, Richard Kroll, and Perez Zagorin, Cambridge: Cambridge University Press, 1992, pp. 253–274.

Matar, Nabil I. "John Locke and the Jews." *The Journal of Ecclesiastical History* 44, 1 (Jan. 1993), pp. 45–62.

Metha, U. S. *The Anxiety of Freedom: Imagination and Individuality in Locke's Political Thought*. Ithaca, NY: Cornell University Press, 1992.

Milton, J. R. "Locke and Gassendi: A Reappraisal." In *English Philosophy in the Age of Locke*. Edited by M. A. Stewart. Oxford: Clarendon Press, 2000, pp. 87–109.

　　Editor, *Locke's Moral, Political and Legal Philosophy*. Dartmouth: Ashgate, 1999.

　　"Dating Locke's Second Treatise." *History of Political Thought* 16 (1995), pp. 356–390.

　　"Locke in Oxford." In *Locke's Philosophy: Content and Context*. Edited by G. A. J. Rogers. Oxford: Clarendon Press, 1994, pp. 29–48.

Milton, Philip. "John Locke and the Rye House Plot." *The Historical Journal* 43, 3 (2000), pp. 647–668.

Myers, Peter C. *Our Only Star and Compass: Locke and the Struggle for Political Rationality*. New York: Lanham, Rowman & Littlefield, 1998.

Ohmori, Yuhtaro. "'The Artillery of Mr. Locke': The Use of Locke's 'Second Treatise' in Pre-Revolutionary America, 1764–1776." Ann Arbor, MI: UMI Dissertation Services, 1988.

Oz-Salzberger, Fania. "The Political Thought of John Locke and the Significance of Political Hebraism." *Hebraic Political Studies* 1, 5 (2006), pp. 568–592.

Parker, Kim Ian *The Biblical Politics of John Locke.* Waterloo, ON: Wilfrid Laurier University Press, 2004.

Paul, Ellen Frankel, Miller, Jr., Fred D., and Paul, Jeffrey. Editors, *Natural Rights Liberalism from Locke to Nozick.* Cambridge: Cambridge University Press, 2005.

Pearson, Jr., Samuel C. "The Religion of John Locke and the Character of His Thought." *The Journal of Religion* 58, 3 (1978), pp. 244–262.

Polin, Raymond. "John Locke's Conception of Freedom." In *Problems and Perspectives.* Edited by John Yolton. Cambridge: Cambridge University Press, 1969.

Rahe, Paul Anthony. *Republics, Ancient and Modern.* Chapel Hill, NC: The University of North Carolina Press, 1992.

Rayner, Jeremy. "*An Approach to Political Philosophy: Locke in Contexts* by James Tully." *Canadian Journal of Political Science* 27, 4 (1994), pp. 850–851.

Rehfeld, Andrew. "Jephthah, the Hebrew Bible, and John Locke's 'Second Treatise of Government'." *Hebraic Political Studies* 3, 1 (2008), pp. 60–93.

Rogers, G. A. J. *Locke's Enlightenment: Aspects of Its Origin and Impact of His Philosophy.* Zurich: Goerg Olms Verlag, 1998.

Romanell, Patrick. *John Locke and Medicine.* New York: Prometheus Books, 1984.

Rowen, Herbert H. "A Second Thought on Locke's First Treatise." *Journal of the History of Ideas* 17, 1 (1956), pp. 130–132.

Schochet, Gordon J. "John Locke and Religious Toleration." In *The Revolution of 1688–1689: Changing Perspectives.* Edited by Lois G. Schwoerer. Cambridge: Cambridge University Press, 1992.

Schouls, Peter A. *Reasoned Freedom: John Locke and Enlightenment.* Ithaca, NY: Cornell University Press, 1992.

Sherlock, Richard. "The Theology of Toleration: A Reading of Locke's The Reasonableness of Christianity." *Jewish Political Studies Review* 9, 3–4 (1997), pp. 19–31.

Simmons, A. J. *The Lockean Theory of Rights.* Princeton, NJ: Princeton University Press, 1994.

Snyder, David C. "Locke on Natural Law and Property Rights." In *Locke and Law.* Edited by Thom Brooks. Hampshire: Ashgate, 2007, p. 12.

"Faith and Reason in Locke's Essay." *Journal of the History of Ideas* 47, 2 (1986), pp. 197–223.

Spellman, W. M. *John Locke.* New York: Macmillan Press, 1997.

John Locke and the Problem of Depravity. Oxford: Clarendon Press, 1988.

"The Christian Estimate of Man in Locke's Essay." *The Journal of Religion* 67, 4 (1987), pp. 474–492.

Sreenivasan, Gopal. *The Limits of Lockean Rights in Property.* Oxford: Oxford University Press, 1995.

Stoner, James R. "Was Leo Strauss Wrong about John Locke?" *The Review of Politics* 66, 4 (2004), pp. 553–563.

Tarlton, Charles D. "The Rulers Now on Earth: Locke's Two Treatises and the Revolution of 1688." *The Historical Journal* 28, 2 (1985), pp. 279–298.

  "A Rope of Sand: Interpreting Locke's First Treatise of Government." *The Historical Journal* 21, 1 (1978), pp. 43–73.

Thompson, Martyn P. "The Reception of Locke's *Two Treatises of Government* 1690–1705." *Political Studies* 24 (1976), pp. 184–191.

Tully, James. *An Approach to Political Philosophy: Locke in Contexts.* Cambridge: Cambridge University Press, 1993.

  "Placing the Two Treatises." In *Ideas in Context: Political Discourse in Early Modern Britain.* Edited by N. Phillipson and Q. Skinner. Cambridge: Cambridge University Press, 1993, pp. 253–280.

  "Locke." in *The Cambridge History of Political Thought, 1450–1700.* Edited by J. H. Burns. Cambridge: Cambridge University Press, 1991, p. 620.

  A Discourse on Property: John Locke and His Adversaries. Cambridge: Cambridge University Press, 1980.

Vogt, Philip. "Locke, Eden and Two States of Nature: The Fortunate Fall Revisited." *Journal of the History of Philosophy* 35, 4 (1997), pp. 523–544.

Waldron, Jeremy. *God, Locke, and Equality: Christian Foundations in Locke's Political Thought.* Cambridge: Cambridge University Press, 2002.

Wallace, Jr., Dewey D. "Socinianism, Justification by Faith, and the Sources of John Locke's The Reasonableness of Christianity." *Journal of the History of Ideas* 45, 1 (1984), pp. 49–66.

Windstrup, George. "Locke on Suicide." *Political Theory* 8, 2 (1980), pp. 169–182.

Wolterstorff, Nicholas. *John Locke and the Ethics of Belief.* Cambridge: Cambridge University Press, 1996.

Wood, Neal. *The Politics of Locke's Philosophy.* Los Angeles, CA: University of California Press, 1983.

Woolhouse, Roger. *Locke: A Biography.* Cambridge: Cambridge University Press, 2007.

  Editor, "Lady Masham's Account of Locke." *Locke Studies* 3 (2003), pp. 190–191.

Yolton, John. *A Locke Dictionary.* Oxford: Blackwell, 1993.

  Locke and French Materialism. Oxford: Clarendon Press, 1991.

  John Locke: Problems and Perspectives: A Collection of New Essays. Cambridge: Cambridge University Press, 1969.

  John Locke, and the Way of Ideas. Oxford: Clarendon Press, 1968.

  "Locke on the Law of Nature." *The Philosophical Review* 67, 4 (1958), pp. 477–498.

Zuckert, Michael P. "Natural Rights and Imperial Constitutionalism: The American Revolution and the Development of the American Amalgam." In *Natural Rights Liberalism from Locke to Nozick.* Edited by Ellen Frankel Paul, Fred D. Miller, Jr., and Jeffrey Paul. Cambridge: Cambridge University Press, 2005.

Launching Liberalism: On Lockean Political Philosophy. Lawrence, KS: University Press of Kansas, 2002.

Natural Rights and the New Republicanism. Princeton, NJ: Princeton University Press, 1998.

C. PRIMARY SOURCES BY AUTHORS OTHER THAN LOCKE

Aquinas, Thomas. *Summa Theologica*, Complete English Edition in five volumes, vol. 2 Westminster, MD: Benziger Bros., 1981.

Aristotle. "The Household and the City." In *Politics*. Oxford: Oxford University Press, 1995, book I, chapters 4–7, pp. 13–20.

The Art of Rhetoric. Edited by John Henry Freese. Cambridge, MA: Harvard University Press, 1967.

Augustine, St. *City of God*. Edited by Vernon J. Bourke. New York: Image Books, 1958.

Bible. *The Bible: Authorized King James Version.* Edited by Robert Carroll and Stephen Prickett. Oxford: Oxford World Classics, 2008.

Tanach. Jerusalem: Koren Publishers, 2000.

New Testament in Modern English. Edited by J. B. Phillips. New York: Touchstone, 1996.

Miqraot Gedolot, 15 vols. Jerusalem: Biblia Rabbinica, 1978.

Pentateuch and Haftorahs, 2nd Edition. Edited by J. H. Hertz. London: Socino Press, 1972.

Cicero. *De Legibus.* Edited by Clinton Walker Keyes. Cambridge, MA: Harvard University Press, 2000.

Republic. Edited by Clinton Walker Keyes. Cambridge, MA: Harvard University Press, 2000.

Cunaeus, Petrus. *The Hebrew Republic.* Jerusalem: Shalem Press, 2006.

De Tocqueville, Alexis. *Democracy in America.* With an introduction by Alan Ryan. New York: Knopf, 1972, 1994.

Filmer, Robert. *Patriarcha and Other Writings.* Edited by J. P. Somerville. Cambridge: Cambridge University Press, 1991.

Grotius, Hugo. *The Rights of War and Peace.* Edited and with an introduction by Richard Tuck. Indianapolis, IN: Liberty Fund, 2005.

Harrington, James. *The Political Works of James Harrington.* Edited by J. G. A. Pocock. Cambridge: Cambridge University Press, 1977.

Hobbes, Thomas. *Leviathan.* Edited by Richard Tuck. Cambridge: Cambridge University Press, 1991.

The Elements of Law, Natural and Politic. Edited by Ferdinand Tonnies. London: Frank Cass and Company Limited, 1969.

Behemoth. New York: Burt Franklin, 1963.

Hooker, Richard. *Of the Laws of Ecclesiastical Polity,* Cambridge Texts in the History of Political Thought. Edited by Arthur Stephen McGrade. Cambridge: Cambridge University Press, 1989.

John of Salisbury. *Politicraticus.* Edited and translated by Cary J. Nederman. Cambridge: Cambridge University Press, 1990.

Luther, Martin. *Luther's Works*, 55 vols. Edited by J. Pelikan (vols. 1–30) and H. Lehmann (vols. 31–55). Philadelphia, PA: Concordia Press, 1958–1967.

Machiavelli, Niccolo. *The Prince*. With related documents, translated, edited, and with an introduction by William J. Connell. Boston, MA: Bedford St. Martin's, 2005.

Maimonides. *Mishneh Torah, Hilchot Avodat Cochavim, Laws of Idol Worship*, New Corrected Edition. New York: Feldheim Publishers, 1981.

Mishneh Torah, Hilchot Kinyan, Book of Acquisition, The Laws of Slaves, New Corrected Edition. New York: Feldheim Publishers, 1981.

Mishneh Torah, Hilchot Matnot Aniyim, The Laws Concerning Gifts to the Poor, New Corrected Edition. New York: Feldheim Publishers, 1981.

Mishneh Torah, Hilchot Rotziach, The Laws of a Murderer, New Corrected Edition. New York: Feldheim Publishers, 1981.

Mishneh Torah, Hilchot Sicherut, The Laws of Rent, New Corrected Edition. New York: Feldheim Publishers, 1981.

Mishneh Torah, Hilchot Teshuvah, The Laws of Repentance, New Corrected Edition. New York: Feldheim Publishers, 1981.

Mishneh Torah, Hilchot Yesodai Hatorah, The Book of Knowledge, New Corrected Edition. New York: Feldheim Publishers, 1981.

The Guide to the Perplexed. Translated by Shlomo Pines. Chicago, IL: The University of Chicago Press, 1963.

The Guide for the Perplexed. Translated by M. Friedlander. New York: Dover, 1956.

Milton, John. *A Defence of the People of England*. EEBO Editions, ProQuest, 2011.

Political Writings. Edited by Martin Dzelzainis. Cambridge: Cambridge University Press, 1991.

"A Treatise of Civil Power." In *The Complete Prose of John Milton*, Revised Edition, vol. VII, 1659–1660. New Haven, CT: Yale University Press, 1980, pp. 238–272.

The Complete Prose Works of John Milton, 8 vols. Edited by Don M. Wolfe. New Haven, CT: Yale University Press, 1953–1982.

More, Thomas. *Utopia and Other Essential Writings of Thomas More*. Edited by James J. Greene and John P. Dolan. New York: New American Library, 1984.

Pascal, Blaise. *Pensees*. Translated into Hebrew with an introduction and notes by Joseph Ur. Jerusalem: Magnes Press, The Hebrew University, 1976 [Hebrew].

Pensees. Translated by A. J. Krailsheimer. London: Penguin, 1966.

Pufendorf, Samuel. *De jure naturae et gentium*. Edited by Gottfried Mascovius. Translated by Michael J. Seidler. Lausanne and Geneva: Marcus-Michael Bousquet, 1744.

Selden, John. *Table Talk*. Edited by Sir Fredrick Pollock. London: Quaritch, 1927.

Sidney, Algernon. *Discourses Concerning Government*. Edited by Thomas G. West. Indianapolis, IN: Liberty Classics, 1990.

Court Maxims. Edited by Hans Blom, Eco Haitsma Mulier, and Ronald Janse. Cambridge: Cambridge University Press, 1996.

Talmud, Babylonian (BT), 45 vols. Translation and commentary in modern Hebrew. Edited by Adin Steinsaltz. Jerusalem: Institute for Talmudic Publications, 1976–2010.

Vindiciae, Contra Tyrannos. Edited by George Garnett. Cambridge: Cambridge University Press, 1994.

D. SECONDARY SOURCES

Adams, J. L. "The Law of Nature in Greco-Roman Thought." *Journal of Religion* 25 (1945), pp. 97–118.

Adler, Leo. *The Biblical View of Man.* Jerusalem: Urim Publications, 2007.

Alford, Fred. *Narrative, Nature, and the Natural Law.* New York: Palgrave Macmillan, 2010.

Allen, R. T. *Beyond Liberalism.* New Brunswick, NJ: Transaction, 1998.

Anthony, Levi. *Renaissance and Reformation: The Intellectual Genesis.* New Haven, CT: Yale University Press, 2002.

Armstrong, Karen. *A History of God.* New York: Ballantine, 1993.

Asch, Ronald. *The Thirty Years War: The Holy Roman Empire and Europe, 1618–1648.* New York: St. Martin, 1997.

Ashley, M. *The Greatness of Oliver Cromwell.* New York: Collier, 1962.

Aylmer, G. E. *The Levellers in the English Revolution.* London: Thames and Hudson, 1975.

Backman, Clifford. *The Worlds of Medieval Europe.* New York: Oxford University Press, 2003.

Bailyn, Bernard. *The Origins of American Politics.* New York: Vintage Books, 1968.

Barker, Arthur E. *Milton and the Puritan Dilemma, 1641–1660.* Toronto: University of Toronto Press, 1964.

Milton and the Puritan Dilemma 1641–1660. Toronto: University of Toronto Press, 1942, 1955.

Barlow, Frank. *Thomas Becket.* Berkeley, CA: University of California Press, 1990.

Bartolucci, Guido. "Carlo Sigonio and the 'Respublica Hebraeorum': A Re-Evaluation." *Hebraic Political Studies* 3, 1 (Winter 2008), pp. 19–59.

"The Influence of Carlo Sigonio's 'De Republica Hebraeorum' on Hugo Grotius' 'De Republica Emendanda'." *Hebraic Political Studies* 2, 2 (Spring 2007), pp. 193–210.

Bayle, Pierre. "Hobbes." In *Political Writings*, Cambridge Texts in the History of Political Thought. Edited by Sally L. Jenkins. Cambridge: Cambridge University Press, 2000, p. 89.

Becher, Matthias. *Charlemagne.* New Haven, CT: Yale University Press, 2003.

Becker, Carl. *The Declaration of Independence: A Study in the History of Political Ideas.* New York: Harcourt, 1922.

Ben Zimra, Eliyahu. "Considerations of Punishment in Jewish Criminal Law as Reflected in Responsa Literature." *Annual of the Institute for Research in Jewish Law* VIII (1981) [Hebrew].

Benedict, Philip. *Christ's Churches Purely Reformed.* New Haven, CT: Yale University Press, 2002.

Berkovits, Eliezer. "Law and Morality in Jewish Tradition," In *Essential Essays on Judaism.* Edited by David Hazony. Jerusalem: The Shalem Center, 2002.

Berkowitz, Abraham. "John Selden and the Biblical Origins of the Modern International Political System." *Jewish Political Studies Review* 6, 1–2 (1993), pp. 27–47.

Berlin, Isaiah. *Liberty.* Edited by Henry Hardy. Oxford: Oxford University Press, 1995.

"Two Concepts of Liberty (1958)." In *Four Essays on Liberty.* Oxford: Oxford University Press, 1982.

Berman, Joshua. *Created Equal.* Oxford: Oxford University Press, 2008.

Bernard, George W. *The Kings Reformation: Henry VIII and the Remaking of the English Church.* New Haven, CT: Yale University Press, 2005.

Bertram, Cornelius Bonaventure. *De politia judaica tam civili quam ecclesiastica.* Geneva: 1574.

Bevir, Mark. "The Role of Contexts in Understanding Explanation." *Human Studies* 23, 4 (2000), pp. 395–411.

Bodian, Miriam. "The Biblical 'Jewish Republic' and the Dutch 'New Israel' in Seventeenth Century Dutch Thought." *Hebraic Political Studies* 1,2 (2006), pp. 186–202.

Bordet, Josef. "Late Scholasticism." In *The Oxford International Encyclopedia of Legal History.* New York: Oxford University Press, 2009.

Bossy, John. *Christianity in the West: 1400–1700.* Oxford: Oxford University Press, 1985.

Bouwsma, William James. *John Calvin.* Oxford: Oxford University Press, 1988.

Bowen, C. Drinker. *Francis Bacon: The Temper of a Man.* Boston, MA: Little Brown and Company, 1963.

Bowle, John. *Western Political Thought: An Historical Introduction from the Origins to Rousseau.* New York: University Paperbacks, 1961.

Brailsford, H. N. *The Levellers and the English Revolution.* Edited by Christopher Hill. London: The Crescent Press, 1961.

Brown, Harvey Owen. "Martin Luther: A Natural Law Theorist?." In *The Medieval Tradition of Natural Law.* Edited by Harold J. Johnson. Kalamazoo, MI: Medieval Institute, 1987.

Buchan, J. *Cromwell.* London: Hodder & Stoughton, 1971.

Budziszewski, J. *Written on the Heart: The Case for Natural Law.* Downers Grove, IL: Inter Varsity Press, 1997.

Burgess, Glenn, and Festenstien, Mathew. Editors, *English Radicalism, 1550–1850.* Cambridge: Cambridge University Press, 2007.

Burnett, Bishop Gilbert. *History of His Own Time.* Abridged by Thomas Stackhouse. Introduction by David Allen. London: Everyman's Library, 1979.

Butterfield, Herbert. *Historical Development of the Principle of Toleration in British Life.* London: The Epworth Press, 1957.

Callow, John. *King in Exile, James II: Warrior, King, and Saint, 1989–1701.* Gloucestershire: Sutton Publishing Ltd., 2004.

The Making of King James II. Gloucestershire: Sutton Publishing Ltd., 2000.

Carey, Daniel. *Locke, Shaftesbury, and Hutcheson: Contesting Diversity in the Enlightenment and Beyond.* Cambridge: Cambridge University Press, 2009.

Carr, Craig L. Editor, *The Political Writings of Samuel Pufendorf.* Oxford: Oxford University Press, 1994.

Cassirer, Ernst. *King in Exile, James II: Warrior, King, and Saint, 1989–1701.* Gloucestershire: Sutton, 2004.

   The Philosophy of the Enlightenment. Princeton, NJ: Princeton University Press, 1951.

Chadwick, Henry. *The Early Church.* London: Penguin Books, 1993.

Chadwick, Owen. *The Reformation: The Pelican History of the Church.* London: Penguin Books, 1966.

Chakravarty, Prasanta. *Like Parchment in the Fire: Literature and Radicalism in the English Civil War.* London: Routledge, 2006.

Colbourn, Trevor. *The Lamp of Experience: Whig History and the Intellectual Origins of the American Revolution.* Indianapolis, IN: Liberty Fund, 1998.

Colie, Rosalie L. "John Locke and the Publication of the Private." *Philological Quarterly* 45 (1966), p. 24.

Colish, Marcia L. *The Stoic Tradition from Antiquity to the Early Middle Ages,* vol. 2. Leiden: Brill, 1985.

Cooke, Paul D. *Hobbes and Christianity: Reassessing the Bible in Leviathan.* Lanham, MD: Rowman & Littlefield, 1996.

Coudert, Allison P. *The Impact of the Kabbalah in the Seventeenth Century: The Life and Thought of Francis Mercury Van Helmont, 1614–1698.* Leiden: Brill, 1998.

Cragg, Gerald R. *From Puritanism to the Age of Reason.* Cambridge: Cambridge University Press, 1966.

   Puritanism in the Period of the Great Persecution 1660–1688. Cambridge: Cambridge University Press, 1957.

Curtis, Michael. Editor, *The Great Political Theories: From Plato and Aristotle to Locke and Montesquieu.* New York: Avon Books Division, 1961.

Deane, Herbert A. *The Political and Social Ideas of St. Augustine.* New York: Columbia University Press, 1963.

DeLapp, Nevada Levi. *The Reformed David(s) and the Question of the Resistance to Tyranny: Reading the Bible in the 16th and 17th Centuries.* London: Bloomsbury, 2014.

Del Grosso, Anna Maria Lazzarino. "The Respublica Hebraeorum as a Scientific Political Model in Jean Bodin's 'Methodus'." *Hebraic Political Studies* 1, 5 (Fall 2006), pp. 549–556.

D'Entreves, A. P. *Natural Law: An Introduction to Legal Philosophy,* 2nd Edition. London: Hutchison, 1970.

Dewhurst, Kenneth. *John Locke, 1632–1704: Physician and Philosopher, a Medical Biography.* London: The Wellcome Historical Medical Library, 1963.

Donnelly, M. L. "'The Great Difference of Time': The Great Tew Circle and the Emergence of the Neoclassical Mode." In *Literary Circles and Cultural Communities in Renaissance England.* Edited by Claude J.

Summers and Ted-Larry Pebworth. Columbia, MO and London: University of Missouri, 2001.

Dorman, M. *Menasseh Ben-Israel*. B'nai B'rak: Hakibutz Hameuchad Publishing House, 1989, pp. 52–84 [Hebrew].

Dow, John G. "Hebrew and Puritan." *The Jewish Quarterly Review* 3, 1 (1890).

Dumouchel, Paul. "The Political Problem of Religion: Hobbes' Reading of the Bible." In *English Philosophy in the Age of Locke*. Edited by M. A. Stewart. Oxford: Clarendon Press, 2000, pp. 1–27.

Dyson, R. W. "Introduction." In *Cambridge Texts in the History of Political Thought: Aquinas, Political Writings*. Edited and translated by R. W. Dyson. Cambridge: Cambridge University Press, 2002.

The Pilgrim City: Social and Political Ideas in the Writings of St. Augustine of Hippo. Suffolk: Boydell Press, 2001.

Elazar, Daniel J. *Covenant & Commonwealth: The Covenant Tradition in Politics*, vol. II. New Brunswick, NJ: Transaction Publishers, 1996.

Covenant Tradition and Politics, four volumes. New Brunswick, NJ: Transaction Publishers, 1996.

Covenant & Polity in Biblical Israel: Biblical Foundations and Jewish Expressions, vol. I. New Brunswick, NJ: Transaction Publishers, 1991.

"Althusius and Federalism as Grand Design." www.jcpa.org/dje/articles2/althus-fed.htm.

Elton, Geoffrey. *The English*. Oxford: Basil Blackwell, 1994.

Estes, James Martin. *Peace, Order and the Glory of God: Secular Authority and the Church in the Thought of Luther and Melanchton 1518–1559*. Leiden: Brill, 2005.

Eyffinger, Arthur. "How Wondrously Moses Goes Along with the House of Orange! Hugo Grotius' 'De Republica Emendanda' in the Context of the Dutch Revolt." In *Political Hebraism: Judaic Sources in Early Modern Political Thought*. Edited by Gordon Schochet, Fania Oz-Salzberger, and Meirav Jones. Jerusalem: Shalem Press, 2008, pp. 107–147.

"Introduction." In *Petrus Cunaeus: The Hebrew Republic*. Jerusalem: Shalem Press, 2006, pp. ix–xx.

Faulkner, Robert K. "Reason and Revelation in Hooker's Ethics." *The American Political Science Review* 59, 3 (1965), pp. 680–690.

Febvre, Lucien. *The Problem of Unbelief in the Sixteenth Century: The Religion of Rabelais*. Translated by Beatrice Gottlieb. Cambridge, MA: Harvard University Press, 1982.

Finkelstein, L. *The Jews: Their History, Culture, and Religion*. Westport, CT: Greenwood Press, 1960.

Finnis, John. *Aquinas: Moral, Political, and Legal Theory*. Oxford: Oxford University Press, 1998.

Fisch, Harold. *The Biblical Presence in Shakespeare, Milton and Blake*. Oxford: Clarendon Press, 2000.

Jerusalem and Albion. Tel Aviv: Bar Ilan University Press, 1964.

Fletcher, Harris Francis. *The Use of the Bible in Milton's Prose*. New York: Haskell House Publishers, 1970.

Milton's Rabbinical Readings. Urbana, IL: University of Illinois Press, 1930.

Flusser, David. "Motifs from the Section of Creation in their Substantial Christian Form." *Mahaniem* 84 (1963) [Hebrew].

Foley, Michael. *American Credo: The Place of Ideas in US Politics*. Oxford: Oxford University Press, 2007.

Fromm, Erich. *The Dogma of Christ*. New York: Routledge, 1963, 2004.
Escape from Freedom. New York: Avon Books, 1971.

Fryde, Natalie. *Why Magna Carta?: Angevin England Revisited*. Munster: Lit Verlag, 2002.

Fulbrook, Mary. *Piety and Politics*. Cambridge: Cambridge University Press, 1983.

Gardiner, S. R. *The First Two Stuarts and the Puritan Revolution, 1603–1660*. New York: C. Scribner's Sons, 1970.

Garnett, George. Editor, *Vindiciae, Contra Tyrannos*. Cambridge: Cambridge University Press, 1994.

Glaser, Eliane. *Judaism without Jews: Philosemitism and Christian Polemic in Early Modern England*. New York: Palgrave Macmillian, 2007.

Gooch, G. P. *English Democratic Ideas in the Seventeenth Century*, 2nd Edition. With supplementary notes and appendices by H. J. Laski. Cambridge: Cambridge University Press, 1954.

Green, V. H. H. *Renaissance and Reformation*. London: Edward Arnold, 1970.

Grosby, Steven. "Reading the Talmud in the Tower of London." Library of Law and Liberty, July 31, 2013, www.libertylawsite.org/2013/07/31/reading-the-talmud-in-the-tower-of-london/.

Haakonssen, Knud. *Natural Law and Moral Philosophy: From Grotius to the Scottish Enlightenment*. Cambridge: Cambridge University Press, 1996.

Haivry, Ofir. *John Selden and the Western Political Tradition*. Cambridge: Cambridge University Press, 2017.

Haller, William, and Davies, Godfrey. Editors and introduction, *The Levellers Tracts 1647–1653*. New York: Columbia University Press, 1944.

Hammond, Gerald. *The Making of the English Bible*. New York: Philosophical Library, 1983.

Hargreaves-Mawdsley, W. N. *Oxford in the Age of John Locke*. Norman, OK: University of Oklahoma Press, 1973.

Harrison, Roy. *Hobbes, Locke and Confusion's Masterpiece: An Examination of Seventeenth-Century Political Philosophy*. Cambridge: Cambridge University Press, 2003.

Hartz, Louis. *The Liberal Tradition in America: An Interpretation of American Political Thought Since the Revolution*. New York: Harcourt, 1955.

Harvey, Warren Zev. "The Israelite Kingdom of God in Hobbes." *Hebraic Political Studies* 1, 3 (2006), pp. 310–327.

Haskins, Charles Homer. *The Renaissance of the 12th Century*. Cleveland and New York: World Publishing Co., 1927.

Hazony, Yoram. *The Philosophy of the Hebrew Scriptures*. Cambridge: Cambridge University Press, 2012.
"Does the Bible Have a Political Teaching?" *Hebraic Political Studies* 1, 2 (2006), pp. 137–161.

"The Jewish Source of the Western Disobedience Tradition." In *Disobedience and Democracy*. Edited by Y. Weinstein. Jerusalem: Shalem Press, 1999, pp. 13–36 [Hebrew].

Healey, Robert M. "The Jew in Seventeenth-Century Protestant Thought." *Church History* 46, 1 (1977).

Hedley, D. "Persons of Substance and the Cambridge Connection: Some Roots and Ramifications of the Trinitarian Controversy in Seventeenth Century England." In *Socinianism and Arminianism*. Edited by M. Muslow and J. Rohls. Boston, MA: Brill Leiden, 2005.

Heschel, Abraham Joshua. *Man Is Not Alone*. New York: Farrar, Straus and Giroux, 1976.

Heyd, Michael. "The 'Jewish Quaker': Christian Perceptions of Sabbatai Zevi as an Enthusiast." In *Hebraica Veritas? Christian Hebraists and the Study of Judaism in Early Modern Europe*. Edited by Allison P. Coudert and Jeffrey S. Shoulson. Philadelphia: University of Pennsylvania Press, 2004, pp. 234–265.

Be Sober and Reasonable: The Critique of Enthusiasm in the Seventeenth and Early Eighteenth Centuries. Leiden: Brill Academic Publishers, 1995.

"Charisma and Establishment: The Crises of the Reformation and Its Influence on the Church-State Relationship." In *Priesthood and Monarchy: Studies in the Historical Relationships of Religion and State*. Edited by Isaiah Gafni and Gabriel Motzkin. Jerusalem: The Zalman Shazar Center For Jewish History, 1987, pp. 149–163 [Hebrew].

Hill, Christopher. *Intellectual Origins of the English Revolution Revisited*. Oxford: Clarendon, 1997.

The English Bible and the Seventeenth-Century Revolution. London: Penguin Books, 1994.

The Century of Revolution, 1603–1714. London: Van Nostrand Reinhold Co, Ltd., 1991.

A Nation of Change and Novelty. London: Routledge, 1990.

Milton and the English Revolution. New York: Viking, 1977.

The World Turned Upside Down: Radical Ideas during the English Revolution. New York: The Viking Press, 1972.

Puritanism & Revolution. New York: Schocken, 1964.

Holt, J. C. *Magna Carta*. Cambridge: Cambridge University Press, 1992.

Hopfl, Harro. Editor, *Luther and Calvin on Secular Authority*. Cambridge: Cambridge University Press, 1991.

Hoppit, Julian. *A Land of Liberty? England 1689–1727*. Oxford: Oxford University Press, 2000.

Housley, Norman. *The Avignon Papacy and the Crusades, 1305–1378*. Oxford: Clarendon Press, 1986.

Houston, Alan Craig. *Algernon Sidney and the Republican Heritage in England and America*. Princeton, NJ: Princeton University Press, 1991.

Howarth, Patrick. *Attila, King of the Huns: The Man and the Myth*. London: Constable, 1994.

Hudson, Anne. *The Premature Reformation: Wycliffite Texts and Lollard History*. Oxford: Oxford University Press, 1988.

Husik, Isaac. "The Law of Nature, Hugo Grotius and the Bible." *HUCA* 2 (1925), pp. 381–417.

Hutton, Sarah. *Anne Conway: A Woman Philosopher.* Cambridge: Cambridge University Press, 2004.

Imbonati, Carlo Giuseppe. *Bibliotheca Latino-Hebraica.* Rome: 1694.

Israel, Jonathan. *Enlightenment Contested: Philosophy, Modernity, and the Emancipation of Man 1670–1752.* Oxford: Oxford University Press, 2006.

Radical Enlightenment: Philosophy and the Making of Modernity 1650–1750. Oxford: Oxford University Press, 2002.

"The Intellectual Debate about Toleration in the Dutch Republic." In *The Emergence of Tolerance in the Dutch Republic.* Edited by C. Berkvens-Stevelinck, J. Israel, and G. H. M. Posthumous Meyjes. Leiden: Brill, 1997, pp. 3–36.

The Dutch Republic: Its Rise, Greatness and Fall, 1477–1806. Oxford: Clarendon Press, 1995.

Editor with Ole Peter Grell, *From Persecution to Toleration: The Glorious Revolution and Religion in England.* Oxford: Clarendon Press, 1991.

Editor, *The Anglo-Dutch Moment: Essays on the Glorious Revolution and Its World Impact.* Cambridge: Cambridge University Press, 1991.

Jacob, Margaret C. *Scientific Culture and the Making of the Industrial West.* Oxford: Oxford University Press, 1997.

Janz, Denis R. "Late Medieval Theology." In *The Cambridge Companion to Reformation Theology.* Edited by David Bagchi and David C. Steinmetz. Cambridge: Cambridge University Press, 2004, pp. 5–14.

Jones, Meirav. "Philo Judaeus and Hugo Grotius's Modern Natural Law." *Journal of the History of Ideas* 74, 3 (2013), pp. 339–359.

Katchen, Aaron L. *Christian Hebraists and Dutch Rabbis.* Cambridge, MA: Harvard University Press, 1984.

Katz, David S. *Philo-Semitism and the Readmission of the Jews to England 1603–1655.* Oxford: Clarendon Press, 1982.

Kejr, Jiri. *The Hussite Revolution.* Prague: Orbis Press Agency, 1988.

Kent, Susan Kingsley. "Gender Rules: Law and Politics." In *A Companion to Gender History.* Edited by Teresa A. Meade and Merry E. Wiesner-Hanks. Malden, MA: Blackwell Publishing, 2006, pp. 86–109.

Killeen, Kevin, Smith, Helen, and Willie, Rachel. Editors, *The Oxford Handbook of: The Bible in Early Modern England, c. 1530–1700.* Oxford: Oxford University Press, 2015.

Kissinger, Henry. *Diplomacy.* New York: Simon & Schuster, 1994.

Klausner, Yosef. *From Jesus to Paul.* Tel Aviv: Mada, 1951 [Hebrew].

Knowles, David. *Archbishop Thomas Becket: A Character Study.* Oxford: Oxford University Press, 1970.

Koester, Helmut. "Nomos Phuseos: The Concept of Natural Law in Greek Thought." In *Religions in Antiquity: Essays in Memory of Erwin Ramsdell Goodenough.* Edited by Jacob Neusner. Leiden: Brill, 1968, pp. 521–541.

Koziol, Geoffrey. "Lord's Law and Natural Law." In *The Medieval Tradition of Natural Law.* Edited by Harold J. Johnson. Kalamazoo, MI: Western Michigan University, 1987.

Kramnick, I. "Children's Literature and Bourgeois Ideology: Observations on Culture and Industrial Capitalism in the Later Eighteenth Century." In *Culture and Politics from Puritanism to the Enlightenment*. Edited by P. Zagorin. Berkeley, CA: University of California Press, 1980, pp. 203–240.

Kraynak, Robert P. "John Locke: From Absolutism to Toleration." *The American Political Science Review* 74, 1 (1985), pp. 53–69.

Kusukawa, Sachiko. "Melanchthon." In *The Cambridge Companion to Reformation Theology*. Edited by David Bagchi and David C. Steinmetz. Cambridge: Cambridge University Press, 2004, p. 57.

Lachs, Phyllis S. "Hugo Grotius' Use of Jewish Sources in On the Law of War and Peace." *Renaissance Quarterly* 30, 2 (Summer 1977), pp. 181–200.

Laski, H. J. Editor, *A Defence of Liberty against Tyrants*. London: Cambridge University Press, 1924.

Laslett, Peter. "Sir Robert Filmer: The Man Versus the Whig Myth," *William and Mary Quarterly* 3, 5 (1948), pp. 523–546.

Leff, Gordon. *Medieval Thought: St. Augustine to Ockham*. Baltimore, MD: Penguin, 1958.

Lichtenstein, Aharon. *Henry More: The Rational Theology of a Cambridge Platonist*. Cambridge, MA: Harvard University Press, 1962.

Lieu, Samuel N. C. Editor, *The Emperor Julian: Panegyric and Polemic*. Liverpool: Liverpool University Press, 1986.

Lilburne, John. *Come Out of Her My People*. London: 1639.

Lock, Peter. *The Routledge Companion to the Crusades*. London: Routledge, 2006.

Lorberbaum, Menachem. "Making Space for Leviathan: On Hobbes' Political Theory." *Hebraic Political Studies* 2, 1 (Winter 2007), p. 80.
 "Spinoza's Theological-Political Problem." *Hebraic Political Studies* 1, 2 (2006), pp. 203–223.

Luria, Yehoshua. *The Leveller Movement*. Tel Aviv: Poalim, 1978 [Hebrew].

Lynch, Christopher. "Machiavelli on Reading the Bible Judiciously." *Hebraic Political Studies* 1, 2 (2006), pp. 162–185.

Mackintosh, James. *Vindiciae Gallicae and Other Writings on the French Revolution*. Edited by Donald Winch. Indianapolis, IN: Liberty Fund, 2006.

Macpherson, C. B. *Political Theory of Possessive Individualism*. Oxford: Clarendon Press, 1962.

Manent, Pierre. "The Truth, Perhaps." In *Modern Liberty and Its Discontents*. Edited and translated by Daniel J. Mahoney and Paul Senton. Lanham, MD: Rowman & Littlefield, 1998, pp. 33–44.

Manuel, Frank. *The Broken Staff*. Cambridge, MA: Harvard University Press, 1992.

Marcus, Robert A. *History and Society in the Theology of St. Augustine*. Cambridge: Cambridge University Press, 1988.

Marshall, John S. *Hooker and the Anglican Tradition*. London: Adam & Charles Black, 1963.

Martin, Julian. *Francis Bacon: The State and the Reform of Natural Philosophy*. Cambridge: Cambridge University Press, 2007.

Martinich, A. P. "The Bible and Protestantism in *Leviathan*." In *The Cambridge Companion to Hobbes's Leviathan*. Edited by Patricia Springborg. Cambridge: Cambridge University Press, 2007, pp. 375–391.

Mason, Roger A., and Smith, Martin S. "Introduction." In *A Dialogue on the Law of Kingship among the Scots*, A Critical Edition and Translation of George Buchanan's *De Iure Regni apud Scotos Dialogus*. London: Ashgate, 2004, p. xv.

Mayshar, Yoram. *In His Image: The Idea of Equality from Ezra to Nietzsche.* Jerusalem: Carmel, 2007 [Hebrew].

McGrath, Alister E. *In the Beginning: The Story of the King James Bible and How It Changed a Nation, a Language, a Culture.* London: Doubleday, 2001.

  Reformation Thought: An Introduction, 3rd Edition. Oxford: Blackwell Publishers, Ltd., 1988, 1993, 1999.

Mckeon, Michael. "Sabbatai Sevi in England." *AJS Review* 2 (1977), pp. 131–169.

Melanchthon, Phillipp. "Common Topics in Theology." In *Melanchthon on Christian Doctrine*. Edited and translated by Clyde L. Manschreck. New York: Oxford University Press, 1965, p. 333.

Miller, J. *Popery and Politics in England 1660–1668.* Cambridge: Cambridge University Press, 1973.

Mitchell, Joshua. *Not by Reason Alone: Religion, History and Identity in Early Modern Political Thought.* Chicago, IL: Chicago University Press, 1993.

Mittleman, Alan. "Some Thoughts on the Covenantal Politics of Johannes Althusius." In *Political Hebraism: Judaic Sources in Early Modern Political Thought*. Edited by Gordon Schochet, Fania Oz-Salzberger, and Meirav Jones. Jerusalem: Shalem Press, 2008, pp. 72–89.

Moots, Glenn. *Politics Reformed: The Anglo-American Legacy of Covenant Theology.* Columbia, MO: University of Missouri Press, 2010.

Morrill, John. *The Nature of the English Revolution.* New York: Longman Publishing, 1993.

Mullet, Michael. *James II and English Politics 1678–1688.* London: Routledge, 1993.

Myers, William. *Milton and Free Will: An Essay in Criticism and Philosophy.* London: Croom Helm, 1987.

Nederman, Cary J. "The Liberty of the Church and the Road to Runnymede: John of Salisbury and the Intellectual Foundations of the Magna Carta." In *PS. Political Science and Politics*. New York: Cambridge University Press, 2010, pp. 457–461. Published online by CUP, June 30, 2010.

Nelson, Eric. *The Hebrew Republic: Jewish Sources and the Transformation of European Political Thought.* Cambridge, MA: Harvard University Press, 2010.

Neuman, Kalman. *The Literature of the Respublica Judaica: Descriptions of the Ancient Israelite Polity in the Antiquarian Writing for the Sixteenth and Seventeenth Centuries.* PhD thesis., Hebrew University, 2002.

Novak, David. "Maimonides and Aquinas on Natural Law." In *St. Thomas Aquinas and the Natural Law Tradition: Contemporary Perspectives*. Edited by John Goyette, Mark S. Latkovic, and Richard S. Myers. Washington, D.C.: The Catholic University of America Press, 2004, pp. 43–65.

  Natural Law in Judaism. Cambridge: Cambridge University Press, 1998.

Novak, Michael. *This Hemisphere of Liberty: A Philosophy of the Americas.* Washington, D.C.: American Enterprise Institute, 1992.

Nozick, Robert. *Anarchy, State, and Utopia.* New York: Basic Books, 1974.

Nuriel, A. "Dibrah Torah Kilshon Beni Adam in Guide to the Perplexed." In *Revealed and Hidden in Medieval Jewish Philosophy.* Jerusalem: Magnes Press, 2000, pp. 93–99 [Hebrew].

Odhal, Charles M. *Constantine and the Christian Empire.* London: Routledge, 2004.

Ohlmeyer, Jane. *Civil War and Restoration in the Three Stuart Kingdoms, 1609–1689.* Cambridge: Cambridge University Press, 1993.

Oswald, Martin. *From Popular Sovereignty to the Sovereignty of Law: Law, Society, and Politics in Fifth-Century Athens.* Berkeley, CA: University of California Press, 1986.

Ozment, Steven. *The Age of Reform: An Intellectual and Religious History of Late Medieval and Reformation Europe.* New Haven, CT and London: Yale University Press, 1980.

Oz-Salzberger, Fania. "The Jewish Roots of Western Freedom." *Azure* 13 (2002), pp. 88–132.

Translating the Enlightenment: Scottish Civic Discourse in Eighteenth Century Germany. Oxford: Clarendon Press, 2002.

Pangle, Thomas L. *The Spirit of Modern Republicanism.* Chicago, IL: University of Chicago Press, 1988.

Paolucci, Henry. Editor, *The Political Writings of St. Augustine*, Chicago, IL: Gateway, 1962.

Parker, Kim Ian "A King Like Other Nations." In *The Oxford Handbook of: The Bible in Early Modern England, c. 1530–1700.* Oxford: Oxford University Press, 2015, pp. 384–397.

Parker, T. M. *Christianity and the State in Light of History.* London: Adam and Charles Black, 1955.

Pavlac, Brian. "Emperor Henry VI (1191–1197) and the Papacy: Similarities with Innocent III's Temporal Policies." In *Pope Innocent III (1160–1216): To Root Up and to Plant.* Edited by John C. Moore. Durham, NC: Ashgate Publishing Co., 1999, pp. 255–269.

Pelikan, Jaroslav. *The Christian Tradition: A History of the Development of Doctrine*, vol. 4 Chicago, IL: University of Chicago Press, 1984.

Pocock, J. G. A. *The Machiavellian Moment.* Princeton, NJ: Princeton University Press, 2003.

"The Significance of 1688: Some Reflections on Whig History." In *The Revolutions of 1688.* Edited by Robert Beddard. Oxford: Clarendon Press, 1991.

"Time, History, and Eschatology in the Thought of Thomas Hobbes." In *Politics, Language and Time: Essays on Political Thought and History.* New York: Antheneum, 1971, pp. 148–201.

Poole, William. *Milton and the Idea of the Fall.* Cambridge: Cambridge University Press, 2005.

Popkin, Richard H. "The Image of Judaism in Seventeenth Century Europe." In *Religion, Reason and Nature in Early Modern Europe.* Edited by R. Crocker. Dordrecht: Kluwer Academic Publishers, 2001.

"Three English Tellings of the Sabbatai Zevi Story." In *Jewish History*. Edited by Lloyd P. Gartner and Kenneth R. Stow. Haifa: Haifa University Press, 1994, pp. 43–54.

"Jewish Messianism and Christian Millenarianism." In *Culture and Politics from Puritanism to the Enlightenment*. Edited by P. Zagorin, Berkeley, CA: University of California Press, 1980, pp. 67–90.

Porterfield, Amanda. *The Protestant Experience in America*. London: Greenwood Publishing, 2006.

Rawls, John. *Political Liberalism*. New York: Columbia University Press, 1993.

A Theory of Justice. Cambridge, MA: Harvard University Press, 1971.

Reedy, G. *The Bible and Reason: Anglicans and Scripture in the Late Seventeenth Century England*. Philadelphia, PA: University of Philadelphia Press, 1985.

Rees, Brinley Roderick. *Pelagius: A Reluctant Heretic*. Woodbridge, Suffolk: Boydell Press, 1991.

Remer, Gary. "After Machiavelli and Hobbes: James Harrington's Commonwealth of Israel." *Hebraic Political Studies* 1, 4 (2006), pp. 440–461.

Renouard, Yves. *The Avignon Papacy 1305–1403*. Translated by Denis Bethell. London: Faber and Faber, 1970.

Reventlow, Ernst Graf. *The Authority of the Bible and the Rise of the Modern World*. London: SCM Press, 1984.

Rivers, Isabel. *Reason, Grace, and Sentiment*. Cambridge: Cambridge University Press, 2000.

Robbins, Caroline. *The Eighteenth-Century Commonwealthman: Studies in the Transmission, Development and Circumstance of English Liberal Thought, From the Restoration of Charles II Until the War with the Thirteen Colonies*. Indianapolis, IN: Liberty Fund, 2004.

Rommen, Heinrich A. *The Natural Law: A Study in Legal and Social History and Philosophy*. Translated by Thomas R. Hanley, OSB, PhD. Indianapolis, IN: Liberty Fund, 1998.

Rogers, G. A. J. "Innate Ideas and the Infinite: The Case of Locke and Descartes." *The Locke Newsletter* 27 (1996). www.luc.edu/philosophy/LockeStudies/art icles/rogers-infinity.htm.

Roper, Hugo Trevor. *Catholics, Anglicans and Puritans: Seventeenth Century Essays*. London: Secker & Warburg, 1987.

Rosenblatt, Jason P. "Rabbinic Ideas in the Political Thought of John Selden." In *Political Hebraism: Judaic Sources in Early Modern Political Thought*. Edited by Gordon Schochet, Fania Oz-Salzberger, and Meirav Jones. Jerusalem: Shalem Press, 2008, pp. 191–206.

Renaissance England's Chief Rabbi: John Selden. Oxford: Oxford University Press, 2006.

Torah and Law in Paradise Lost. Princeton, NJ: Princeton University Press, 1994.

Rosenzweig, Franz. "The Significance of the Bible in World History." In *Jewish Perspectives on Christianity*. Edited by Fritz A. Rothschild. New York: Crossroad, 1990, pp. 137–149.

Roth, Cecil. *A History of the Jews in England*. Oxford: Clarendon Press, 1949.

Russell, Bertrand. *History of Western Philosophy*. London: George Allen & Unwin, 1961.

Ryan, Alan. *Property and Political Theory*. Oxford: Basil Blackwell, 1984.

Ryan, Todd. *Pierre Bayle's Cartesian Metaphysics*. London: Routledge, 2009.

Samuelson, Norbert M. Editor, *Reason and Revelation as Authority in Judaism*. Philadelphia, PA: Congregation Rodeph Shalom, 1981.

Sayers, Jane E. *Innocent III: Leader of Europe, 1198–1216*. London: Longman, 1994.

Schikard, William. *Mishpat Ha-Melek, Jus Regium Habraeorum, e Tenebris Rabbinicus erustum & luci donatum*. Leipzig: 1674.

Schochet, Gordon J. *Patriarchalism in Political Thought: The Authoritarian Family and Political Speculation and Attitudes Especially in Seventeenth-Century England*, Oxford: Basil Blackwell, 1975.

"Sir Robert Filmer: Some New Biographical Discoveries." *The Library* 5, 26 (1971), pp.135–160.

Schulman, Alex. "The Twilight of Probability: Locke, Bayle, and the Toleration of Atheism." http://harvard.academia.edu/AlexSchulman/Papers/.

Scott, Jonathan. *Algernon Sidney and the Reformation Crisis 1677–1683*. Cambridge: Cambridge University Press, 1991.

Algernon Sidney and the English Republic 1623–1677. Cambridge: Cambridge University Press, 1988.

Seliger, Martin. *The Liberal Politics of John Locke*. Westport, CT: Praeger Publishing, 1969.

Sewell, Arthur. *A Study in Milton's Christian Doctrine*. Hamden, CT: Archon Books, 1967.

Shanley, Brian. *The Thomist Tradition*. Boston, MA: Kluwer Academic Publishers, 2002.

Shapiro, B. J. *Probability and Certainty in Seventeenth Century England*. Princeton, NJ: Princeton University Press, 1983.

Shoulson, Jeffery S. *Milton and the Rabbis, Hebraism, Hellenism & Christianity*. New York: Columbia University Press, 2001.

Shuger, Deborah Kuller. *Habits of Thought in the English Renaissance*. Los Angeles, CA: University of California Press, 1990.

Simpson, Gary M. "Toward a Lutheran 'Delight in the Law of the Lord': Church and State in the Context of Civil Society." In *Church & State: Lutheran Perspectives*. Edited by John R. Stumme and Robert W. Tuttle. Minneapolis, MN: Fortress Press, 2003.

Sims, James H., and Ryken, Leland. Editors, *Milton and Scriptural Tradition: The Bible into Poetry*. Columbia, MO: University of Missouri Press, 1984.

Skehan, Patrick W. Editor, *The Wisdom of Ben Sira*. New York: Doubleday, The Anchor Bible, 1987.

Skinner, Quentin. *Hobbes and Republican Liberty*. Cambridge: Cambridge University Press, 2008.

"Classical Liberty and the Coming of the English Revolution." In *Republicanism: A Shared European Heritage, II, The Values of Republicanism in early Modern Europe*. Edited by Martin Van Gelderen and Quentin Skinner. Cambridge: Cambridge University Press, 2002, pp. 9–28.

Liberty before Liberalism. Cambridge: Cambridge University Press, 1998.

Reason and Rhetoric in the Philosophy of Hobbes. Cambridge: Cambridge University Press, 1996.

The Foundations of Modern Political Thought, vol. II. Cambridge: Cambridge University Press, 1978.

Smith, Steven B. *Reading Leo Strauss.* Chicago, IL: The University of Chicago Press, 2006.

Sommerville, J. P. *Royalists and Patriots: Politics and Ideology in England, 1603–1640*, 2nd Edition. London: Addison Wesley Publishing Company, 1999.

"Absolutism and Royalism." In *The Cambridge History of Political Thought 1450–1700.* Edited by J. H. Burns. Cambridge: Cambridge University Press, 1991, pp. 343–373.

"Introduction." In *Filmer, Patriarcha and Other Writings.* Edited by J. P. Somerville. Cambridge: Cambridge University Press, 1991.

"John Selden, the Law of Nature, and the Origins of Government." *The Historical Journal* 27, 2 (1984), pp. 437–447.

Southern, R. W. *Western Society and the Church in the Middle Ages.* New York: Penguin Books, 1970.

The Making of the Middle Ages. New Haven, CT: Yale University Press, 1961.

Stanwood, Paul G. "Community and Social Order in the Great Tew Circle." In *Literary Circles and Cultural Communities in Renaissance England.* Edited by Claude J. Summers and Ted-Larry Pebworth. Columbia, MO: University of Missouri Press, 2000, pp. 173–186.

Stone, Lawrence. "The Results of the English Revolutions of the Seventeenth Century." In *Three British Revolutions: 1641, 1688, 1776.* Edited by J. G. A. Pocock. Princeton, NJ: Princeton University Press, 1980, pp. 46–50.

Strauss, Leo. *Natural Right and History.* Chicago, IL: University of Chicago Press, 1968.

The Political Philosophy of Hobbes: Its Basis and Genesis. Translated by Elsa Sinclair. Chicago, IL: University of Chicago Press, 1957.

Persecution and the Art of Writing. Glencoe, IL: The Free Press, 1952.

Sutcliffe, Adam. *Judaism and Enlightenment.* Cambridge: Cambridge University Press, 2003.

Swanson, R. N. *The Twelfth Century Renaissance.* Manchester and New York: Manchester University Press, 1999.

Sykes, Norman. "The Religion of the Protestants." In *The Cambridge History of the Bible: The West from the Reformation to the Present Day.* Edited by S. L. Greenslade. Cambridge: Cambridge University Press, 1963, pp. 175–198.

Talmudical Encyclopedia. Jerusalem: Yad Harav Herzog, 1998 [Hebrew].

Tawney, R. H. *Religion and the Rise of Capitalism.* New Brunswick, NJ: Transaction Publishers, 1998.

Taylor, Quentin. "John of Salisbury, the Politicraticus, and Political Thought." *Humanitas* XIX, 1&2 (2006), pp. 133–153.

Thompson, W. D. J. Cargill. *Studies in the Reformation: Luther to Hooker.* Edited by C. W. Dugmore. London: Athlone Press, 1980.

Thornton, Helen. *State of Nature or Eden? Thomas Hobbes and His Contemporaries on the Natural Condition of Human Beings.* Rochester, NY: Rochester University Press, 2005.

Tierney, Brian. *The Idea of Natural Rights: Studies on Natural Rights, Natural Law, and Church Law 1150–1625.* Grand Rapids, MI: William B. Eerdmans Publishing Company, 1997.

The Crisis of Church and State 1050–1300. Englewood Cliffs, NJ: Prentice-Hall, Inc., 1964.

Toomer, G. J. *John Selden: A Life in Scholarship.* Oxford: Oxford University Press, 2009.

Eastern Wisdom and Learning: The Study of Arabic in Seventeenth Century England. Oxford: Oxford University Press, 1996.

Tracy, James D. *The Low Countries in the Sixteenth Century: Erasmus, Religion and Politics, Trade and Finance.* Aldershot: Ashgate, 2005.

Emperor Charles V, Impresario of War. Cambridge: Cambridge University Press, 2002.

Trevelyan, George Macuuly. *The English Revolution 1688–1689.* London: Thornton Butterworth, 1938.

Tuck, Richard. "Hobbes." In *Great Political Thinkers.* Oxford: Oxford University Press, 1992, pp. 190–221.

"Grotius and Selden." In *The Cambridge History of Political Thought, 1450–1700.* Edited by J. H. Burns. Cambridge: Cambridge University Press, 1991, pp. 499–529.

Natural Rights Theories: Their Origin and Development. Cambridge: Cambridge University Press, 1979.

Tyerman, Christopher. *Gods War: A New History of the Crusades.* Cambridge, MA: Harvard University Press, 2006.

Urbach, E. E. *The Sages: Their Concepts and Beliefs.* Jerusalem: Magness Press, The Hebrew University, 1971.

Urry, William. *Thomas Becket: His Last Days.* Edited and with an introduction by Peter A. Rowe. Gloucestershire: Sutton Publishing Ltd., 1999.

Van Gelderen, Martin. *The Political Thought of the Dutch Revolt 1555–1590.* Cambridge: Cambridge University Press, 1992.

Van Helmont, F. M. "Introduction." In *The Alphabet of Nature.* Translated with an introduction and annotations by Allison P. Coudert and Taylor Case. Leiden and Boston, MA: Brill Publishing, 2007, p. xii.

Vaughan, Frederick. *The Tradition of Political Hedonism.* New York: Fordham University Press, 1982.

Voegelin, Eric. *History of Political Ideas*, vol. V. Edited and with introduction by James L. Wiser. London: University of Missouri Press, 1998.

Waldron, Jeremy. "Welfare and the Images of Charity," *The Philosophical Quarterly* 36, 145 (1986), pp. 463–482.

"Enough and as Good Left for Others." *The Philosophical Quarterly* 29, 117 (1979), pp. 319–328.

Walker, D. P. *The Decline of Hell: Seventeenth-Century Discussions of Eternal Torment*. Chicago, IL: The University of Chicago Press, 1964.

Wallace, Ronald Stewart. *Calvin, Geneva and the Reformation: A Study of Calvin as Social Reformer, Churchman Pastor and Theologian*. Edinburgh: Scottish Academic Press, 1988.

Walzer, Michael. *The Revolution of the Saints: A Study in the Origins of Radical Politics*. New York: Atheneum, 1968.

Warfield, Benjamin B. *The New Schaff-Herzog Encyclopedia of Religious Knowledge*. Edited by Samuel Macauley Jackson, D.D., LL.D. New York: Funk and Wagnalls Company, 1909.

Watson, Philip S. "Introduction." In *Luther and Erasmus: Free Will and Salvation*. Edited by E. Gordon Rupp and Philip S. Watson. Philadelphia, PA: Westminster Press, 1969, pp. 23–24.

Weber, Max. *The Protestant Ethic and the Spirit of Capitalism*. New York: Scribners, 1958.

Westfall, R. S. *Science and Religion in Seventeenth Century England*. New Haven, CT: Yale University Press, 1958.

White, Peter O. G. *Predestination, Policy and Polemic*. Cambridge: Cambridge University Press, 1992.

Wienfeld, Moshe. *Justice and Righteousness in Israel and the Nations: Equality and Freedom in Ancient Israel in Light of Social Justice in the Ancient Near East*. Jerusalem: The Magnes Press, The Hebrew University of Jerusalem, 1985 [Hebrew].

Wilcher, Robert. *The Writing of Royalism 1628–1660*. Cambridge: Cambridge University Press, 2001.

Wilensky, M. "The Royalist Position Concerning the Readmission of Jews in England." *The Jewish Quarterly Review* 41, 4 (1951), pp. 397–409.

Willey, B. *The Seventeenth Century Background*. New York: Doubleday, 1934.

Williams, Stephen. *Theodosius: The Empire at Bay*. New Haven, CT: Yale University Press, 1994.

Wills, Gary. *Inventing America: Jefferson's Declaration of Independence*. New York: Vintage Books, 1978.

Wilson, A. N. *The Life of John Milton*. Oxford: Oxford University Press, 1983.

Wilson, Peter H. *The Holy Roman Empire, 1495–1806*. London: Macmillan Press, 1999.

Wiltshire, Susan Ford. *Greece, Rome, and the Bill of Rights*. Norman, OK and London: University of Oklahoma Press, 1992.

Wolfe, Don M. *Milton in the Puritan Revolution*. London: Cohen & West, 1963.

Wolin, S. S. *Politics and Vision*, Princeton, NJ: Princeton University Press, 2004.

Wolterstorff, Nicholas. "Can Belief in God Be Rational If It Has No Foundations." In *Faith and Rationality: Reason and Belief in God*. Edited by Alvin Plantinga and Nicholas Wolterstorff. Notre Dame, IN: Notre Dame Press, 1983, pp. 135–186.

Wood, Gordon S. *Creation of the American Republic: 1776–1787*. New York: W.W. Norton and Company, 1972.

Wood, Neal. *Cicero's Social and Political Thought.* Berkeley, CA: University of California Press, 1988.

The Politics of Locke's Philosophy: A Social Study of "An Essay Concerning Human Understanding." Berkeley, CA: University of California Press, 1983.

Yovel, Yirmiyahu. *Spinoza and Other Heretics: The Marrano of Reason.* Princeton, NJ: Princeton University Press, 1989.

Zagorin, Perez. *A History of Political Thought in the English Revolution.* London: Routledge Kegan Paul, 1954.

Zepper, Wilhelm. *Legum Mosicarum forensium explanation.* Herborn: 1604.

Zuckert, Catherine, and Zuckert, Michael. *The Truth about Leo Strauss.* Chicago, IL: University of Chicago Press, 2006.

E. *OXFORD DICTIONARY OF NATIONAL BIOGRAPHY* ARTICLES

Burgess, Glenn. "Filmer, Sir Robert (1588?–1653)." *Oxford Dictionary of National Biography.* Oxford: Oxford University Press, 2004 [www.oxforddnb.com/view/article/9424].

Campbell, Gordon. "Milton, John (1608–1674)." *Oxford Dictionary of National Biography.* Oxford: Oxford University Press, 2004 [www.oxforddnb.com/view/article/18800].

Christianson, Paul. "Selden, John (1584–1654)." *Oxford Dictionary of National Biography.* Oxford: Oxford University Press, 2004 [www.oxforddnb.com/view/article/25052].

De Queher, Hugh. "Bernard, Edward (1638–1697)." *Oxford Dictionary of National Biography.* Oxford: Oxford University Press, 2004 [www.oxforddnb.com/view/article/2240].

Eales, Jacqueline. "Whately, William (1583–1639)." *Oxford Dictionary of National Biography.* Oxford: Oxford University Press, 2004 [www.oxforddnb.com/view/article/29178].

Hamilton, Alastair. "Bedwell, William (1563–1632)." *Oxford Dictionary of National Biography.* Oxford: Oxford University Press, 2004 [www.oxforddnb.com/view/article/1942].

Harris, Tim. "Cooper, Anthony Ashley, First Earl of Shaftesbury (1621–1683)." *Oxford Dictionary of National Biography.* Oxford: Oxford University Press, 2004 [www.Oxforddnb.com/view/article/6208].

Hopfl, H. M. "Harrington, James (1611–1677)." *Oxford Dictionary of National Biography.* Oxford: Oxford University Press, 2004 [www.oxforddnb.com/view/article/12375].

Katz, David S. "Abendana, Issac (died 1699)." *Oxford Dictionary of National Biography.* Oxford: Oxford University Press, 2004 [www.oxforddnb.com/view/article/37091].

Malcolm, Noel. "Hobbes, Thomas (1588–1679)." *Oxford Dictionary of National Biography.* Oxford: Oxford University Press, 2004 [www.oxforddnb.com/view/article/13400].

Marshall, P. J. "Hyde, Thomas (1636–1703)." *Oxford Dictionary of National Biography*. Oxford: Oxford University Press, 2004 [www.oxforddnb.com/view/article/14336].

Milton, J. R. "Locke, John (1632–1704)." *Oxford Dictionary of National Biography*. Oxford: Oxford University Press, 2004 [www.oxforddnb.com/veiw/article/16885].

Newton, Key E. "Lightfoot, John (1602–1675)." *Oxford Dictionary of National Biography*. Oxford: Oxford University Press, 2004 [www.oxforddnb.com/view/article/16648].

Scott, Jonathan. "Sidney, Algernon (1623–1683)." *Oxford Dictionary of National Biography*. Oxford: Oxford University Press, 2004 [www.oxforddnb.com/view/article/25519].

Southcombe, George. "Everard, Robert (*fl.* 1647–1664)." *Oxford Dictionary of National Biography*. Oxford: Oxford University Press, 2004 [www.oxforddnb.com/view/article/9000].

Spurr, John. "Taylor, Jeremy (bap. 1613, d. 1667)." *Oxford Dictionary of National Biography*. Oxford: Oxford University Press, 2004 [www.oxforddnb.com/view/article/27041].

Toomer, G. J. "Castell, Edmund (1606–1686)." *Oxford Dictionary of National Biography*. Oxford: Oxford University Press, 2004 [www.oxforddnb.com/view/article/4865].

"Pocoke, Edward (1604–1691)." *Oxford Dictionary of National Biography*. Oxford: Oxford University Press, 2004 [www.oxforddnb.com/view/article/22430].

"Pocoke, Edward (1648–1726)." *Oxford Dictionary of National Biography*. Oxford: Oxford University Press, 2004 [www.oxforddnb.com/view/article/22431].

Index